Practical TCP/IP

Designing, using, and troubleshooting TCP/IP networks on
Linux and Windows

About this reprinted edition

This edition of *Practical TCP/IP* is a reprint of the 2003 First Edition, without any changes to the text. We had planned to produce a revised and updated Second Edition, and indeed the author, Niall Mansfield, did update about 90% of the material. However he was unfortunately unable to complete the revisions (because his day-job got in the way).

We decided to reprint this original version anyway, because the book is widely used as a course textbook in colleges and universities around the world. While the versions of the operating systems and software tools have changed since the book was first published, the book's approach to networking (and to troubleshooting in particular) remains as valid now as when it was first written.

Ethereal project changed name to Wireshark

In May 2006, Gerald Combs changed the name of his free and open-source packet analyzer project from Ethereal to Wireshark, because of trademark issues. Ethereal and the "E" logo are registered trademarks of Ethereal, Inc., and the website **ethereal.com** still exists. However, throughout the book, for **ethereal** read **wireshark** with the associated website:

www.wireshark.org

Practical TCP/IP

Designing, using, and troubleshooting TCP/IP networks on
Linux and Windows

Niall Mansfield

UIT

CAMBRIDGE, ENGLAND

Published by
UIT Cambridge Ltd.
PO Box 145
Cambridge
CB4 1GQ
England

Tel: +44 1223 302 041
Web: www.uit.co.uk

ISBN 9781906860363

10 9 8 7 6 5 4 3 2 1

Contents at a glance

Contents

4   IP addressing and netmasks in detail 85

5   Routing in detail – controlling how and where packets pass in and out of your networks 113

6   Routing in practice 149

7   The DNS – names instead of IP addresses 181

8   The DNS (2) – how the servers work 205

Part 4 Connecting to the Internet, and Internet security 595

Preface

This book is based on practical experience with TCP/IP networks and has evolved from our in-house and public training course materials. For several years our company has concentrated on installing firewalls and e-mail systems, and in that time we've found that there's a small kernel of knowledge that you need to get your network up and running quickly, and to make it run efficiently. We've noticed that many IT professionals in charge of their organization's computing understand their applications and high-level systems fully (in the old days they were called "data-processing specialists") but have a lot of trouble with the basic underlying networks. Another reason for writing this book is for training our own consultancy and services staff. For a relatively inexperienced engineer, going on-site to install a customer's network or firewall can be daunting: you're working under time pressure, on an unfamiliar network, and so many things can go wrong. You can never foresee all possible problems, so the best way to prepare people is to give them a problem-solving "methodology" – an understanding of how to analyze problems, and break them down into manageable bits – and a good set of tools that let you see exactly what's happening. We've found this is a great way to build up people's skills and confidence. (Our customers have been pleased with it too.)

The book distills out the essentials you need in practice. There are hundreds of large books and manufacturers' manuals about TCP/IP, but it's hard to find what you really need. There is so much information that newcomers are swamped with detail they don't need, and explanations they can't understand because they don't have the context to relate them to.

By contrast, this book:

- tells you *how* to build your network
- starts with a simple two-machine network and goes on to a full network connected to the Internet with a firewall and internal routers, and DNS and e-mail servers
- explains the software tools you need to diagnose problems and to understand how your network is operating
- explains *why* you would want to do things, as well as *how* to do them
- includes practical troubleshooting and diagnostic techniques that you can apply just about everywhere, so you can solve problems in your own network and in systems configured by others
- assumes things will go wrong rather than work first time. We explain error messages and other symptoms, and then how to get over problems. We've found this is great for the confidence of our own engineers out on-site because they know they'll be able to fix any errors they make, and we hope it will help you too. (Just a typo in an IP address can cause a system to fail, and as we network people live in a veritable sea of IP and Ethernet numbers, it's easy to make mistakes, especially when you're working on someone else's network. So we have to show you how to identify and fix these errors.)

- ties together the various networking components so you view a network as a whole, not just disjointed pieces. As we cover Linux® and Windows® operating systems, and how they relate, the book is relevant to just about everybody

- can be used as the basis for a course of self-study or a taught training course.

You end up with a working network, you understand what is happening at a detailed level, and you gain the ability to diagnose and fix problems, and to identify bugs in the software you're using.

We cover networking from the bottom up, in small chunks. We have found that when you're learning, if you break things down into small pieces and examine one in isolation without the complication of other factors, it's much easier to understand. Then you can go and tie all the pieces together when you understand them. Consequently, some of our topic sections are brief (but non-trivial).

Intended audience

- technical staff, technical managers, or technical sales
- consultancy and services staff installing or managing customer networks
- people using TCP/IP networks every day …
- who are managing and building networks, or …
- who are responsible for an organization's applications and systems as a whole
- people building TCP/IP networks at home
- anyone connecting to the Internet
- students at any level studying computer networks

Background

This book was inspired by Richard Stevens' *TCP/IP Illustrated* Volume 1. Stevens gives a wonderful explanation of how the TCP/IP protocols operate, and to some extent how they evolved. To get a theoretical understanding of TCP/IP, we've found no better book. But Stevens is primarily explanatory, not practical. His approach is to explain TCP/IP by showing you the packets on the wire. We also look at the packets, but:

- we use it as a diagnostic technique
- we expect you to do it as well, not just look at our pictures.

Our book differs in other ways too. As well as explaining how the protocols work in practice, we cover:

- how to set up test networks so you can experiment with the protocols
- techniques for exploring what's happening
- debugging tools and techniques
- a different balance between the various topics. For example, Stevens devotes about a page to how routing works; we do three chapters. He devotes long chapters to TCP internals such as sliding windows, slow start, etc. which we don't even mention. Our guiding

principle has been "do we need to know this in our day-to-day work?" If not, we either omit it or relegate it to the Notes sections or an appendix if it gives an interesting insight into what we're doing. However, the core knowledge we give you will always allow you to go forward and explore these other, more exotic areas if you need to.

We don't assume you are as familiar or experienced with networking as Stevens does, nor do we assume programming (or significant experience with binary arithmetic). With our book, you learn by doing as well as reading.

What this book isn't

The book does not attempt to describe the theoretical foundation of networking; the books by Stevens and Comer and many others already do this superbly and we strongly recommend them. We don't cover world-wide enterprise-scale Microsoft networks, Internet backbone router configuration, OSPF, BGP, or ATM and other ISP-level topics: 99% of the population never needs that stuff. Nor do we cover the nitty-gritty system administration of individual server packages (e.g. "how to configure **sendmail** or **Exchange**") because there are so many of them and there are lots of books dedicated to them. Instead, we concentrate on the network aspects of the system.

The operating systems that we cover

We use Linux® and Windows-NT® in equal depth, and occasionally mention Windows-95/98 and Windows-2000 ("Win-2K" and Windows XP). When we say Windows-NT we generally mean Windows NT Server, especially when dealing with routing. At a user and general networking level, Windows NT Workstation contains most of the same tools, and you configure it the same way as NT Server.

The examples in the text are based on Debian Linux, but only because that's what we've been using in-house for years. Everything we cover applies to other versions of Linux as well, although there may be the usual slight differences in where a particular command or file is located. We've deliberately isolated the Linux system-specific configuration details into a single appendix (Appendix 6), and a Red-Hat equivalent of this is available on our Web site.

We don't use any GUI-based Linux tools, because:

- in real life, you'll often have to work with servers and routers that don't have any GUI and frequently may not even have a screen
- using the command-line keeps you very close to the guts of the thing, so you really understand what's happening
- the command-line tools are available with minor differences on other versions of UNIX. The GUI-based tools aren't.

Once you understand the command-line tools, using the particular GUI tool on your platform will be child's play.

We sort of assume that you have both Linux *and* Win-NT available, if only because we often take the line of least resistance and use whatever is easiest initially.

If you have any choice, use Windows-NT or XP or 2000 instead of Windows-9x (95 or 98 or ME) because NT is a real operating system and is much more reliable than Win-9x, especially for networking. Fortunately Windows-9x systems are on the way out, gradually being replaced by the more recent operating systems.

In the body of the book we've deliberately covered only the Windows NT 4.0 variant of Windows. NT is the foundation for Win-2K and XP. Although we don't cover Win-2K and XP explicitly, everything we describe here works almost identically on those systems (apart from Active Directory, which is new in Win-2K). Win-2K and XP are now being rolled out, but very few sites have switched over completely and most still have a large number of older systems, and Win-2K and XP support the NT style of networking for compatibility.

At the general networking level (Parts 1, 2 and 4 of the book), everything we say for NT applies to Windows-2000 and XP – with minor differences in command locations, etc. For completeness we have included appendices on our Web site giving the Windows-2000 and XP equivalents of all the NT commands and configuration steps that we use throughout the book.

Other books

Instead of having a huge bibliography at the end of the book, we have a "Notes and Further Reading" section at the end of each chapter, so that the references and URLs are close to the topic that they relate to.

Good books are expensive, so we recommend only a few here, listed in order of relevance to what we cover:

- Richard Stevens' *TCP/IP Illustrated* Volume 1 (1994, Addison-Wesley) is sublime, and essential – it's the bible of networking, and we refer to it in the text just as "Stevens". (Only Volume 1 is relevant; we never refer to Volumes 2 or 3)

- the Microsoft Resource Kits for NT and its other operating systems are the best source that we've found for information and implementation detail on Microsoft Windows Networking (they also come with some very useful tools)

- Stevens' *UNIX Network Programming* (1998, Prentice Hall) is also superb, although it's aimed at programmers (but even if you don't want to program, as long as you can read C code it gives wonderful insights into how and why things work the way they do)

- Radia Perlman's *Interconnections* (1992, Addison-Wesley) is good for a different view on networking and an understanding of its fundamentals that you won't find anywhere else; we refer to it as "Perlman".

- Doug Comer's *Internetworking with TCP/IP* Volume 1, (1990, Prentice Hall) gives a good view of how all the protocols hang together. Volume 2, *Design, Implementation and Internals*, is great for seeing how the code is put together to implement a real system, but you need to understand a lot already about TCP/IP before you read it

- Charlie Kaufman, Radia Perlman, and Mike Speciner's *Network Security: Private Communication in a Public World* (2002, Prentice Hall PTR) gives in-depth coverage on cryptography, virtual private networking (VPN) and related topics which have become very important with the rise of the Internet.

In addition to the few books above, we refer to "RFCs" a lot. These are the Internet standards documents. They're free, they're from the horse's mouth, and many (well, at least some) are very readable. We also give references to a lot of other material on the Web. We know this will cause some problems because links are invariably changed or removed, so we usually give the full title of the article as well as the URL. That way you can at least search the Web and may well find the article at another location. (This is one of the down-sides of the Web but short of blindly ignoring other people's copyright, there's not a lot we can do about it. Sorry.)

For Linux-related documentation, see:

❏ **http://www.tldp.org** *The Linux Documentation Project* (formerly at **www.linuxdoc.org**)

which has many "HOWTO" documents, each of which tells you how to configure a specific aspect of the system, e.g. adding a modem, using LDAP, which Ethernet PCMCIA cards work under Linux, installing Linux on a laptop, etc. In particular, the Network Administrator's Guide is very useful:

❏ **http://www.tldp.org/LDP/nag2/index.html**

For general Linux and UNIX system administration, consider the book:

• Evi Nemeth and others *UNIX System Administration Handbook* (2001, Prentice Hall PTR).

For Windows-specific problems the Microsoft on-line Knowledgebase is invaluable:

❏ **http://support.microsoft.com** This contains thousands of "articles" describing particular problems and their fixes. Each article has a unique reference number, e.g. **Q117662**. For brevity we refer to articles like this as, for example, **MS-KB-Q117662**.

General tip: if you have a problem with any of your systems and the relevant documentation doesn't seem to help, use the Web. We've found that the Google search engine (**http://www.google.com**) is wonderful: type in a few keywords describing the problem and you often get an article describing the cause and solution to the problem. (When addressing a Windows problem, for example, it's often quicker to use Google instead of trying the Microsoft site first – because of Google's wider coverage and the way it ranks matching articles.)

Tip: Google lets you restrict a search to a specific site. For example, if you don't like the search engine on **www.example.com**, you could use Google instead and restrict the search by including site:example.com in the list of search terms.

Equipment

Even though we build some fairly large test networks in the examples later in the book, the equipment you'll need is *not* expensive:

UTP wiring hubs: small ones (e.g. 4-port, which are ideal) cost as little as US$25

PCs: the PCs we use don't need to be powerful – you can use retired PCs or laptops for building your test networks. (We run an RAS dial-in server for Windows-NT on an ancient 486 laptop with 24Mb of memory and it works fine for test purposes – although anything graphical such as a Web browser runs like a dog.) Linux runs well in tiny PCs too. For Windows or Linux, disable services you don't need. It improves performance and it's good security practice too

Routers: for all our test networks we'll use ordinary PCs, running Linux or Windows-NT – whichever you prefer – as routers. This cuts down the cost, teaches you what a router really is, and means you don't have to learn the command-language and configuration options specific to purpose-built router boxes

Software: the diagnostic tools we use are either free software or come with the operating system. The only exceptions are tools taken from Microsoft® Resource Kits for Windows-NT (and Windows-9x if you are using that). The Resource Kits are not expensive, considering the amount of software and the number of pages they contain, and almost any site seriously using Windows systems will benefit from having a copy. However, you can live without them if you have to

Network types: for our LANs we use Ethernet throughout. You can get excellent Ethernet network cards for desktop PCs at about 20% of the cost of others that offer nothing extra. The most expensive items you might need are PCMCIA Ethernet cards for laptops. For dial-up connections you will need a modem or two. We give some buying tips in Chapter 26.

A PC can be configured as "multi-boot," i.e. you can load several operating systems on the PC, and at boot time choose which one you want to run. This lets you manage with fewer PCs than you would need if each could only ever run a single operating system. For details of multi-boot configuration, see Web Appendix 1.

Notation

The symbols we use in our diagrams are very similar to Stevens', with a few extra added (see below):

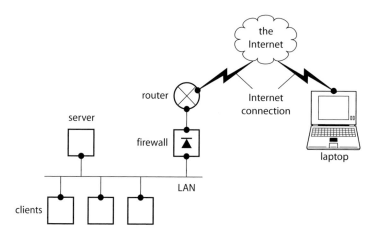

- rectangles are machines – servers, desktops or PCs
- the horizontal line is your Ethernet
- servers are usually shown above the line, end-users' desktop machines below
- a circular blob on a box is a network interface or NIC
- laptops are shown pictorially, to emphasize they are different – typically they are not permanently connected to the LAN (local area network) and are often connected via a dial-up link
- we show routers as a circle with a diagonal cross in it (which is an abstraction of the conventional 3-D "cake" representation with four arrows on it)

- a zigzag line (bolt of lightning) is an Internet connection of any type (we don't use any special notation for dial-up)
- a diode symbol in a box is a firewall (after Cheswick and Bellovin's usage)
- in Linux command-line examples the command-prompt is usually '*hostname%*' or '*hostname#*', e.g.

```
alice% ping 192.0.2.29
```

- *a.b.c.d or w.x.y.z* denotes an IP address or netmask in "dotted-decimal" notation, like 192.0.2.123
- we refer to Linux online manual pages (*manpages*) using the conventional notation, e.g. **ifconfig**(8) means the manpage for the **ifconfig** program, which is in section 8 of the manual (system administration commands)
- in URL references, the notation "*>textstring*" means click on that link, e.g. ">**RFC Pages**" means click on the **RFC Pages** link in the specified page. In menus, etc. ">" means select the indicated option or menu, as in "**File>Save As**".

Our notation was deliberately designed to be easily drawn by hand. Appendix 9 shows a real working diagram from one of our installations.

Machine names

We use the names Alice, Bob, Carol, and Dave – which are widely used in security scenarios in the literature. We've added Rupert, Richard, Robert, and other names beginning with "R" as the names of routers, to distinguish them from normal host machines on the network.

Because there are only a few of these names we have to re-use them for different machines as needed. The names are always consistent within a module (two-page opening) but Alice, for example, refers to different machines in different chapters – you can't assume that "Alice" always means "IP address 192.0.2.29."

Structure of the book, navigation and layout

We've given a lot of thought to what Aaron Copland calls *la grande ligne* ("the long line") when he discusses a piece of music – "there must be a sense of flow – a sense of continuity from first ... to last." We've endeavored to show the underlying architecture of TCP/IP, how it hangs together as a consistent and elegant system, how the different parts relate, and how simple ideas and simple building blocks combine to build incredibly powerful and useful systems.

The book consists of four parts, which are intended to be read in order, at least on first reading. Each part covers a major topic area:

Part 1: the basic infrastructure – IP, routing, DNS

Part 2: TCP and UDP and applications, including e-mail and Web

Part 3: Microsoft Windows Networking and how it fits in with TCP/IP

Part 4: connecting to the Internet, dial-up connections, and security issues.

The parts are progressively more general. Part 1 is very detailed, because basic TCP/IP networking is the same on any machine. Part 2 deals with applications, and because different implementations are configured and operate differently (e.g. a Microsoft Exchange mail server on NT compared with **sendmail** on Linux), this is more general, as we concentrate on the underlying network operation. Part 3 deals with Microsoft Windows Networking. Part 4 covers how you connect a site to the Internet and install firewalls and other security systems; this is the most general part because of the huge variety in firewall systems and even in Internet connection types, but as always, we emphasize the underlying principles that apply to them all.

The detailed structure of the book is:

- four parts (described above)
- a part contains a number of chapters. Each chapter has:
  - a one-page introduction at the beginning
  - a summary at the end, which also includes a "Notes and Further Reading" section, giving references to other books, or RFCs, or discussion of some interesting topics that don't fit into the mainstream of the book
- a chapter is made up of "modules." Each module consists of a single two-page opening in order that diagrams or tables and the text that refers to them are always visible together. A module is as self-contained as possible, and we sometimes repeat a small amount of material (often diagrams or tables) so you don't have to flick back and forth through the book.

To avoid clutter and keep up the momentum as you read the book, topics that are interesting but not essential are left until the "Notes" sections at the end of each Chapter. Longer discussions, or reference material, or points that are likely to be of interest to only a few people, we've put in the appendices. Specifically, we have relegated details on Linux configuration files to an appendix, even though they are relevant throughout; the reason is that there are many variants of Linux and each has its own specific configuration methods. Rather than clutter the body of the text with "do this if you are using Debian Linux, or that if you have

Red Hat, or ..." we've gathered it all together in Appendix 6 as a single version-specific section. Because there are so many appendices, only the essential ones are included in the printed book; the others are available on our Web site, and we call them "Web appendices." (Another advantage of keeping the appendices on the Web site is that we update them regularly with relevant new material.)

The appendices are in the order in which they are first referenced in the body of the book.

Acknowledgments

We'd like to thank all those who have reviewed drafts of some or all of the book, who were very generous with their time and expertise, and whose comments have geratly improved the content of the book: Arthur Chance here in Cambridge, Elwyn Davies of Nortel's router research group, Phil Hazel (author of the Exim mail server) at the University of Cambridge, Radia Perlman at Sun's Boston Center for Networking, Jim Reid at Nominum, Jim Warwick at the Analysys consultancy, and finally our friend Terry O'Gorman at AIB in Dublin for his help and advice on configuration since the genesis of this book, and his stimulating discussions on countless technical issues. Of course, all errors and omissions that remain are our own.

Thanks are also due to David Slight of Microsoft, to Tom Serio and Travis Davison of Safenet Inc. for permission to use the screenshots from SafeNet's SoftRemote VPN software package and for providing a test copy of the software, and to those on the net who answered specific queries: David Hinds regarding advanced PCMCIA configurations, and Guy Harris regarding Ethereal.

We must also thank our colleagues who work with us in the First Networking Group here at UIT: Martin Turner, Walter Patterson, Stuart Charlesworth, Arthur Finn, Frances Heaney, Carol Edson, and especially Sheila Stickley who has tolerated the troglodyte behavior of people who write books. And finally Dennis, for valuable if extreme criticism on an early draft of our manuscript, and our two office cats, Boodil and Arfie, for their company in the wee small hours.

Copyrights etc

Copyright notice for RFCs

Acknowledgment for Appendix 5 – **tcpdump** man page in full

Acknowledgment for Appendix 11 – **nslookup** man page in full

Acknowledgment for Appendix 12 – host man page summary
© RIPE NCC. Original author Eric Wassenaar.

Part 1

How and why packets move on the network

In this part of the book we cover the basic infrastructure of TCP/IP networking:

- TCP/IP traffic is made up of separate packets – it's not a continuous stream
- how two machines on the same local wire exchange packets, i.e. how a small LAN can operate
- routers join two otherwise separate networks and forward packets from one network to the other as required. This lets you build TCP/IP networks of any size (e.g. the Internet)
- details of IP addressing
- the Domain Name System (DNS) and how it lets you refer to machines by name instead of IP address
- the tools you need to configure your systems and diagnose problems on your network

0   A quick introduction to TCP/IP

Introduction

This is a practical book. We'll get you working hands-on as soon as possible, but first this chapter introduces some basic concepts about TCP/IP that you will need just about everywhere. By covering these now we'll speed things up later.

0.1 To debug and understand your network, trace the packets

TCP/IP networking consists entirely of packets and the best way to debug your network is to trace the packets. This gives you definitive information, straight from the horse's mouth. Don't try to guess what's happening – look at it instead so you *know* what it's doing. (Don't guess it – *sniff* it!)

TCP/IP is surprisingly easy to understand. Much of the internal code is of course complex, but learning what you need in order to use TCP/IP networks in your day-to-day work is straightforward. There are three factors that help:

1. TCP/IP traffic consists of discrete packets. When my machine communicates with yours, the data are broken into separate packets that are sent individually. Data are *not* sent as a single continuous stream.

2. All your network traffic has to leave your computer, by definition, and travel over the wire. You can use a *packet sniffer* to look at this traffic and see what's *really* happening.

3. TCP/IP consists of many simple building blocks. Because they're simple and separate, you can break down any network problem into small pieces, which aids understanding, and allows you to diagnose each separate piece on its own. Because they can be combined, they support enormously powerful systems, such as the Internet. We've found troubleshooting a system and understanding it properly go hand in hand. To solve a problem, you need to understand it, and working through a problem leads you to new insights.

In a way, TCP/IP is like the game of chess. Learning the rules of chess and the valid moves for the pieces is easy. However, to play chess well, you have to combine the moves into an effective strategy. Similarly, the individual components of TCP/IP are simple and easy to understand, but they can be combined to make very powerful and complex networks and systems.

The sniffer we use is **tcpdump**. It's good, easy to use, and free, and it's available for Windows and Linux.

Let's look at an example. We'll use the **ping** program, which sends a special packet from your machine to another – Bob, say. If Bob is alive, it sends back a reply, letting you know that he's up and running. Figure 0.1 shows one of our machines, Alice, **ping**ing another, Bob, on the same local network. (On Windows option "**-n 1**" means send only one query packet, instead of four separate packets at one-second intervals, which is the default on the Windows version of **ping**.)

Figure 0.1 Alice **ping**ing Bob on the same local network

Figure 0.2 is the **tcpdump** trace of this interaction with **tcpdump**, running on a third machine, Carol. Don't worry about the detail here – we'll cover every aspect of all this later on. For now, just notice that the trace illustrates the factors above – that we can see easily all the network traffic, and that what the user thinks of as a single TCP/IP networking activity really consists of several small pieces.

```
carol# tcpdump -n -t
arp who-has 192.0.2.19 tell 192.0.2.7
arp reply 192.0.2.19 is-at 0:0:c0:8b:c3:c5
192.0.2.7.2205 > 192.0.2.19.53:  1+ A? bob.uit.co.uk. (32)
192.0.2.19.53 > 192.0.2.7.2205:  1 1/2/2 A 192.0.2.5 (131)
arp who-has 192.0.2.5 tell 192.0.2.7
arp reply 192.0.2.5 is-at 8:0:20:c:e4:e1
192.0.2.7 > 192.0.2.5: icmp: echo request
192.0.2.5 > 192.0.2.7: icmp: echo reply
```

Figure 0.2 The **tcpdump** trace of Alice **ping**ing Bob

This looks agonizingly detailed just to **ping** a machine to see whether it's alive, and indeed it is, in a way. But on the plus side, most of the same steps apply even if we're dealing with a much more complex activity such as browsing to a Web page, and that lets us use **ping** as a simple but powerful diagnostic tool. And, because the individual steps in the conversation are well defined and separate, if anything goes wrong we can zero in on the cause, which will be *specific to that step* and quickly fix the network.

The essence of our approach to building and maintaining networks is: don't try to guess what's happening – look at it on the wire instead, so you *know* what's happening. Sniffers are an essential tool. Don't think using one is a badge of ignorance – the opposite is true: you'll find it's the network gurus who use them all the time.

Working without a sniffer is like trying to diagnose what's wrong with a car engine just by sitting in the back seat: you simply do not have all the information you need. Without a sniffer, what does a failed **ping** command tell you? Alice could be wrongly configured, or maybe Bob's network card is broken, or the network cabling itself could have a problem; the symptoms are the same if you are using **ping** on its own. But when you combine it with the sniffer, **ping** is transformed into a high-resolution, low-granularity diagnostic tool – it lets you see every little bit if you want to. **tcpdump** lets you quickly rule out possible causes and concentrate on the areas where the problem really lies. We'll show you many examples of this throughout the book. Using **tcpdump** is easy and it will soon become second nature to you.

0.2 Networks can be easier than stand-alone machines

On a network all communication to and from your machine passes a single point – the network card (or network interface card, or NIC) . Therefore that's the place to look to see what's happening. Run **tcpdump** and it looks at all the traffic entering or leaving on that NIC, giving you a great view of the network activity (Figure 0.3).

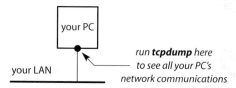

Figure 0.3 tcpdump looks at all the traffic entering or leaving on the NIC

Network traffic for different applications is often addressed to different machines. For example, your machine connects to **www.microsoft.com** to browse a Web page, but it connects to a different machine, **mailserv.example.com** say, to collect your e-mail. That makes it easy to specify the traffic from the particular application or to the particular machine that you're really interested in, and **tcpdump** has special options to let you filter out only what you specify (Figure 0.4). We'll have countless **tcpdump** examples throughout the book but Figure 0.5 illustrates a simple case – look at traffic to and from host 192.0.2.29 only. Again, don't worry about the detail for now – just note that every line shown is either sent from or received by the specified machine. (We truncated very long lines in the output to fit the page.)

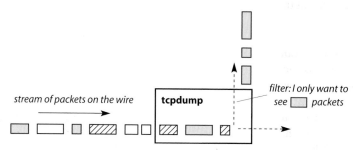

Figure 0.4 The filter option in **tcpdump**

Analyzing an application's network traffic can be much easier than trying to find out what the application is doing in memory and on disk when it runs on a stand-alone machine. Here's a real example. We use a customer database in-house, and it runs slowly. When it ran stand-alone on a dedicated machine, we didn't know what was happening. We then ran it using shared disk drives over the network, and looked at the network traffic using **tcpdump**. It showed that creating a new empty record involved between 100 and 300 writes to disk, each of about 145 bytes. We concluded that for the amount of data we had, this particular product wasn't suitable and did not scale up to the size we needed. By contrast, getting the same infor-

```
alice# tcpdump -n -t host 192.0.2.29
tcpdump: listening on eth0
192.0.2.17 > 192.0.2.29: icmp: echo request
arp who-has 192.0.2.17 (ff:ff:ff:ff:ff:ff) tell 192.0.2.29
arp reply 192.0.2.17 is-at 0:d0:b7:b6:3d:f6
192.0.2.29 > 192.0.2.17: icmp: echo reply (DF)
arp who-has 192.0.2.1 (ff:ff:ff:ff:ff:ff) tell 192.0.2.29
arp reply 192.0.2.1 is-at 0:50:73:38:ce:26
192.0.2.5.2581 > 192.0.2.29.25: S 1639808000:1639808000(0) win 4096 <mss 1460>
arp who-has 192.0.2.5 (ff:ff:ff:ff:ff:ff) tell 192.0.2.29
arp reply 192.0.2.5 is-at 8:0:20:c:e4:e1
192.0.2.29.25 > 192.0.2.5.2581: S 4267645970:4267645970(0) ack 1639808001 win 8760 <mss 1460> (DF)
192.0.2.5.2581 > 192.0.2.29.25: . ack 1 win 4096
192.0.2.29.25 > 192.0.2.5.2581: P 1:131(130) ack 1 win 8760 (DF)
192.0.2.5.2581 > 192.0.2.29.25: P 1:22(21) ack 131 win 4096
...
192.0.2.29.58561 > 64.4.49.199.25: S 4268669970:4268669970(0) win 8760 <mss 1460> (DF)
64.4.49.199.25 > 192.0.2.29.58561: S 1574539292:1574539292(0) ack 4268669971 win 64240 <mss 1460> (DF)
192.0.2.29.58561 > 64.4.49.199.25: . ack 1 win 8760 (DF)
64.4.49.199.25 > 192.0.2.29.58561: P 1:101(100) ack 1 win 64240 (DF)
192.0.2.29.58561 > 64.4.49.199.25: P 1:22(21) ack 101 win 8760 (DF)
64.4.49.199.25 > 192.0.2.29.58561: . ack 22 win 64240 (DF)
64.4.49.199.25 > 192.0.2.29.58561: P 101:156(55) ack 22 win 64240 (DF)
192.0.2.29.58561 > 64.4.49.199.25: . ack 156 win 8760 (DF)
192.0.2.29.58561 > 64.4.49.199.25: P 22:63(41) ack 156 win 8760 (DF)
64.4.49.199.25 > 192.0.2.29.58561: P 156:199(43) ack 63 win 64240 (DF)
192.0.2.29.58561 > 64.4.49.199.25: P 63:94(31) ack 199 win 8760 (DF)
64.4.49.199.25 > 192.0.2.29.58561: P 199:242(43) ack 94 win 64240 (DF)
192.0.2.29.58561 > 64.4.49.199.25: P 94:100(6) ack 242 win 8760 (DF)
64.4.49.199.25 > 192.0.2.29.58561: P 242:288(46) ack 100 win 64240 (DF)
192.0.2.29.58561 > 64.4.49.199.25: P 100:801(701) ack 288 win 8760 (DF)
arp who-has 192.0.2.29 tell 192.0.2.19
arp reply 192.0.2.29 is-at 8:0:20:a:74:aa
...
64.4.17.63.4992 > 192.0.2.29.25: S 2686685848:2686685848(0) win 16384 <mss 1460,nop,nop,sackOK>
192.0.2.29.25 > 64.4.17.63.4992: S 4275517970:4275517970(0) ack 2686685849 win 8760 <mss 1460> (DF)
64.4.17.63.4992 > 192.0.2.29.25: . ack 1 win 8760
192.0.2.29.25 > 64.4.17.63.4992: P 1:131(130) ack 1 win 8760 (DF)
192.0.2.29.25 > 64.4.17.63.4992: P 1:131(130) ack 1 win 8760 (DF)
64.4.17.63.4992 > 192.0.2.29.25: P 1:19(18) ack 131 win 17390
64.4.17.63.4992 > 192.0.2.29.25: . ack 131 win 17390
192.0.2.29.25 > 64.4.17.63.4992: P 131:215(84) ack 19 win 8760 (DF)
...
```

Figure 0.5 Looking at traffic to and from 192.0.2.29

mation on a stand-alone machine is much more difficult. We don't have the source-code for the application, so we can't add any debugging or tracing code. We're not database experts, so we can't trace the disk activity and relate it to whatever processes the application has started and how they interact with the operating system. But looking at the network traffic using **tcpdump** is child's play.

This is like trying to understand how people carry out a complex mental computation. If one person does it on their own (a "stand-alone" computer), all you get is the answer; if it's wrong, you don't know why. If several people work on it together (a "network" of people), they talk to each other and ask each other questions. You can overhear what they are saying, so you can understand much more of the process involved in finding the answer.

We use **tcpdump** on our own network every day. We use it for many different purposes, not just network diagnostics, e.g. if the flickering lights on some of our network equipment show an abnormal, sustained level of network traffic coming from our Internet connection, it's much quicker to run **tcpdump** to see what's happening than to check through all the different logs on all the different servers. If it still looks weird, we can focus in on the offending application (or user!).

In the next module, we see how the modular, building-block nature of TCP/IP helps you understand and troubleshoot your network.

0.3 TCP/IP consists of separate building blocks

TCP/IP networking is the technical foundation of the Internet and most modern LANs. It provides mechanisms for communication between computers and for moving information around. TCP/IP is a set of standards for how these mechanisms work, so that software and hardware from different vendors can "inter-operate."

TCP (transmission control protocol) and *IP (internet protocol)* are the two most important protocols used on the Internet. A *protocol* is a set of rules (standards) specifying how computers should communicate in different contexts and how the various components of the software and hardware should interact. We also frequently use "protocol" to mean the implementation of a standard, not just the standard itself, e.g. "my laptop is using the SMTP protocol to connect to our mail server." The term "TCP/IP" refers to the whole suite of related protocols, not just these two.

Note that the first word in "internet protocol" does *not* have a capital letter. The protocol was developed to allow communication throughout a collection of interconnected networks, called an "inter-network" or "internet." Networks are connected by "routers". (A very simple internet – of two networks – is shown in Figure 0.6.) The Internet with a capital "I" came about as the number of inter-connected networks grew in the 1970s and 1980s.

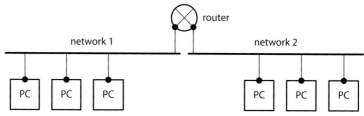

Figure 0.6 A very simple internet of two networks interconnected by a router

Layers in the TCP/IP stack

TCP/IP consists of many different protocols. You might think this would complicate things, but in fact it makes it much easier to diagnose problems on your network.

Each protocol deals with one particular aspect of networking and is separate from the rest. You can think of the protocols as layers in a stack:

- each layer provides facilities that can be used by the layer above
- each layer uses the facilities provided by (the protocols in) the layer below.

Figure 0.7 shows how some of the common TCP/IP protocols are related. This way of representing the layers of the network is derived from the OSI "network reference model." (For more detail see Appendix 1.) This layered organization of the protocols has many advantages:

- it's easier to understand. You're dealing with individual protocols (each of which is relatively simple on its own) and with only one protocol at each level. You *don't* have to learn all about a single, huge mish-mash called TCP/IP all in one go

- the separateness of a layer allows different or better facilities to be added in the layers above or below with minimum disruption. For example, because the IP (network) layer is separate from the lower link layer and physical hardware, it has proven relatively easy to make IP run over wireless, PPP dial-up links, Ethernet, and so on. You can use your web and e-mail applications over all these different media, or a mixture of them, because the applications layer doesn't even know which physical media are being used way down below
- you can break down a problem into smaller pieces, and test each little bit separately, as you saw in Module 0.1. TCP/IP was elegantly designed: it's understandable, and you don't have to be a rocket scientist to do this breaking-down-into-pieces stuff. Teaching you how to do it is one of the aims of this book.

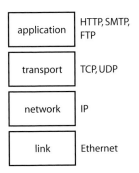

Figure 0.7 The layer model

The layer model is just a convenience for describing and understanding the network. It's not a formal standard for how things must operate, and some protocols don't fit into it very neatly.

Instead of going into a lot of abstract detail now about the functions of the layers, we'll defer the explanation of the layers until later, when it will be relevant to you in a practical way and will make a lot more sense.

RFCs ("Requests for Comments") – Internet standards documents

From 1969 onwards, as TCP/IP was being developed the researchers working on it started circulating documents giving information and requesting feedback on proposed standards. These documents were called *RFCs (Requests for Comments)*. The name is still used but nowadays the RFCs define formal Internet standards, as well as giving historical information and describing best practice.

RFCs are freely obtainable on the net. See Appendix 2 for more information on RFCs and how to obtain them.

We will frequently give you pointers to information in the RFCs – mostly for further detail about some of the topics we cover, but sometimes just for interesting background or historical information on why something works the way it does.

0.4 TCP/IP traffic is made up of packets

How we build our network and troubleshoot it is affected by the fact that TCP/IP is a *packet-switching* network:

- information to be transmitted is divided into packets, and then each packet is sent individually. For example, when I download a Web page from a remote Web server, the data aren't sent in one continuous stream. Instead I get lots of packets, which my machine re-assembles into the final Web page when all the packets have been received. Figure 0.8 shows a **tcpdump** trace of a Web page download from the server on Dave to a Web browser on Carol, illustrating that even a simple conversation consists of many packets in both directions

- each packet to a destination is independent of all the others, and can even travel over a different route to the same destination. The packets the Web server sends to the browser on my machine don't necessarily travel the same route as the packets the client sends to the server, and even packets in the same direction can take different paths. This is surprising at first sight, but later on (in Module 5.13) we'll see it's crucial to providing a resilient network that can tolerate some faults.

We'll see in Chapter 10 that individual packets can get lost or corrupted. Higher-level components of the TCP/IP system have to take account of this to ensure your data are communicated reliably across the network.

```
carol.4279 > dave.80:  S 367936000:367936000(0) win 4096 <mss 1460>
dave.80 > carol.4279:  S 538434131:538434131(0) ack 367936001 win 16060
carol.4279 > dave.80:  . ack 1 win 4096
carol.4279 > dave.80:  P 1:81(80) ack 1 win 4096
dave.80 > carol.4279:  . ack 81 win 16060 (DF)
dave.80 > carol.4279:  P 1:302(301) ack 81 win 16060 (DF)
dave.80 > carol.4279:  P 302:362(60) ack 81 win 16060 (DF)
carol.4279 > dave.80:  . ack 362 win 4096
dave.80 > carol.4279:  P 362:1822(1460) ack 81 win 16060 (DF)
dave.80 > carol.4279:  P 1822:3282(1460) ack 81 win 16060 (DF)
dave.80 > carol.4279:  FP 3282:3427(145) ack 81 win 16060 (DF)
carol.4279 > dave.80:  . ack 3428 win 1031
carol.4279 > dave.80:  . ack 3428 win 4096
carol.4279 > dave.80:  F 81:81(0) ack 3428 win 4096
dave.80 > carol.4279:  . ack 82 win 16060 (DF)
```

Figure 0.8 tcpdump trace of a Web page download from server Dave to browser on Carol

By contrast, the traditional analog telephone network was a *circuit-switching network*. When you phoned me, the call had to be "set up:" switches in the phone network created a continuous path or circuit between your phone and mine. Only when the whole circuit was ready could we start our conversation. The plus side was we had a dedicated comms link that wasn't affected by anyone else's phone traffic. The down side was first of all, call set-up took a long time (seconds, or tens of seconds), which made it unsuitable for the very short conversations that are typical of data traffic, and second, even if both of us were silent and not sending any traffic, the circuit was still tied up and its resources couldn't be used by another conversation that needed extra capacity. Telcos (telephone companies) have been using digital transmission for a long time, and now are even moving towards running all phone services over TCP/IP, so the phone network isn't circuit-switched any more.

An analogy – TCP/IP networks and the postal system

Throughout the book we'll occasionally compare TCP/IP data transmission with sending information by letters or postcards, because everyone is familiar with the postal system. This will give us a sideways view on our computer networking and will make some of the abstract concepts much more concrete and easier to understand.

A TCP/IP packet is similar to a letter or a postcard: both have the address of the sender and the address of the recipient. Sending a file over the network is like me sending you the contents of a book as a series of postcards. I'm in Cambridge (the original one, in England) and let's assume you're in Des Moines, Iowa, USA:

- to send the whole book, lots and lots of packets (postcards) are needed

- individual packets (postcards) can travel by different routes, even though they are coming from the same source, going to the same destination

- when I send a postcard (packet), I don't need to know (and in fact don't know) the route it will travel. The packet (postcard) doesn't contain any information saying which route is to be taken – just where it came from, and the address of the final destination

- the sender needs to know the destination address, but not anything about the destination network or where it is. I can send a postcard to Des Moines without knowing where Iowa is located within the USA. I might not even know where the USA is, but my postcard will still reach its destination

- postcards (packets) are sent towards their destination hop by hop, and at each stage someone (a router) decides where to send it next. For example, I put a postcard in my "out tray" and the messenger boy (me in fact, but let's pretend we have a messenger boy) collects it and puts it in the out tray for the office. The clerk at reception puts it into a public postbox. The Post Office takes it from there … to the sorting office … to the mail hub for this part of England … to Heathrow airport … to the airport in your country … to the sorting office … to your company … to your department … to your pigeon hole. We'll see in Chapter 5 how TCP/IP packets are forwarded across the network by routers, hop by hop from my PC to yours

- the reception clerk might take a diversion to do some errands, and use a different public postbox from normal. If Heathrow airport is closed because of fog, the Post Office will use a different airport instead. This ensures the system is resilient: some parts of it can break but the mail still gets through. In the same way, packets can take different routes to avoid parts of the network that are broken.

We will see each of these aspects of TCP/IP networking in later chapters. This isn't merely theoretical: these features affect how you build your network, and how you troubleshoot problems.

Summary

- all communication on a TCP/IP network is made up of individual packets
- each packet contains the IP address of the sender and the recipient
- using simple tools you can look at the packets travelling on the wire and see what your system is doing. This often makes a networked system easier to understand and debug than a stand-alone machine.

What's next?

In Chapter 2 we'll build the simplest possible network – two machines connected to a single Ethernet LAN – and we'll see how packets are sent between them. But before we do that, in Chapter 1 we install **tcpdump** so we have the tools we need for the job.

An important part of our approach is that we cover topics from the bottom up, starting simple and adding extra functions only one at a time. Our test and example networks reflect this. Here's an outline of where we're going in Part 1 of the book:

- two PCs on a single wire (Chapter 2)
- two small networks connected by a router (Chapter 3)
- a simple LAN talking to the Internet (Chapter 3)
- networks connected with multiple routers (Chapters 5 and 6)
- more than one network on the same wire (Chapter 6)
- sub-netted networks (Chapter 6). The most complex example is a network broken into sub-nets with multiple routers, talking over the Internet to another LAN elsewhere.

The final chapters in Part 1 deal with the DNS – the domain name system that lets you refer to machines by name rather than using IP numbers.

Notes and further reading

For a delightful history of how the Internet evolved, see:

❑ **Peter Salus** *Casting the Net: from ARPAnet to Internet and beyond* (1995, Addison-Wesley)

(Peter Salus also wrote *A Quarter Century of UNIX* (1994, Addison-Wesley). It's not relevant to what we're doing here but it's well worth a read.)

For a huge amount of historical material, including some fascinating maps of the early Internet – e.g. the Internet in 1969, containing just four machines – see:

❑ **http://www.archive.org/arpanet/**

Comer *Internetworking with TCP/IP* Volume 2 (2000, Prentice Hall), Chapters 1 and 2 also gives some history of the Internet and the bodies involved in developing it.

Appendices

Appendix 1: layers, the protocol stack, and network reference models
Appendix 2: RFCs and Internet standards

1

The tcpdump **packet sniffer – your eyes and ears on the network**

Introduction

You've already seen how you can use **tcpdump** in a simple way to get information about how your network is operating. This chapter describes **tcpdump** in more detail, tells you how you can display only the particular packets you are interested in, and how to tailor its display format to your particular needs.

1.1 **How** tcpdump **works**

tcpdump is a *packet sniffer* – it lets you watch the packets on your network in real-time and prints details from them in the format you specify. Because of the way Ethernet works you are able to look at other computers' traffic as well as your own. **tcpdump** is your fundamental network tool for diagnosing problems or just for understanding how your network operates. It looks at *all* the packets on the network but you can tell it to display only a particular set of packets that you're interested in.

Ethernet is a *bus* network. When one machine sends a packet to another over an Ethernet the packet is visible over the whole length of the wire (Figure 1.1).

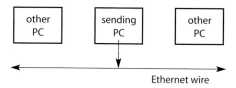

Figure 1.1 Ethernet packet visable everywhere on the wire

It is the Ethernet card (network interface card, or "NIC") in each machine that decides what to do with the packet by looking at the packet's destination address:

- if the packet is destined for this machine, the Ethernet card passes the packet up to the operating system, which passes the packet up to the appropriate application (shown at A in Figure 1.2)

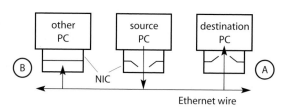

Figure 1.2 Passing the packet from source to destination

- with the Ethernet card in normal mode, if the packet wasn't addressed to this machine, the Ethernet card "discards the packet silently," i.e. it ignores it and doesn't generate any error message (B in Figure 1.2)

- however, **tcpdump** puts the Ethernet card into a special mode called *promiscuous mode*. In this mode the card passes the packet up to the operating system, no matter what the destination address of the packet is (C in Figure 1.3). Then the operating system passes it to **tcpdump**.

  Promiscuous mode is a hardware setting on the Ethernet card, so your card must support it if you're going to use **tcpdump**. (Just about every Ethernet card you get now does support it. We haven't come across one that doesn't.)

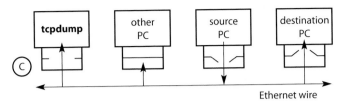

Figure 1.3 Promiscuous mode – **tcpdump** sees all traffic on the wire

By setting promiscuous mode on the Ethernet card, **tcpdump** gets to examine all the packets on the network. Then, for each packet, **tcpdump** prints the source and destination addresses, and a summary of its contents.

Types of Ethernet – coaxial cabling v. UTP hubs and switches

Figures 1.1, 1.2, and 1.3 show the Ethernet as a single cable connected to all machines via their NICs. This is exactly how old-style Thick Ethernet and Thin-net (thin Ethernet) works: you run a long coaxial cable throughout your building, and machines are connected to it using special coaxial **T**-piece connectors (Thin-net) or connection boxes called transceivers (Thick Ethernet). However, nowadays almost everybody uses *UTP (unshielded twisted pair)* cabling. With UTP you have central wiring hubs: each machine is connected to the hub with its own UTP cable, and hubs are chained together with more UTP cables.

As far as **tcpdump** is concerned, there's no difference between a network connected up using UTP hubs and the older coaxial cable network. In both, the packets are visible over the whole length of the network and therefore **tcpdump** can see everything.

However, UTP *switches* or *switched hubs* behave differently. When two machines on the same switch communicate, they are given a dedicated channel; all their traffic goes through this channel, and no other machine can see it. In configurations like this, **tcpdump** can see only traffic to/from its own machine (Figure 1.4), which is generally not what you need. There are two solutions to this: either use a hub instead of (or in conjunction with) your switch (Module 2.6) or use a "managed switch" that lets you configure the type of behavior you need for **tcpdump**. (Appendix 3 gives more information on switches and hubs in general and explains what managed switches are.)

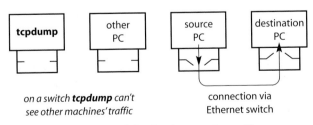

Figure 1.4 On a switch, only source and destination see the traffic

1.2 How to run tcpdump

Where to get tcpdump

See the Notes on page 24 for how to obtain and install **tcpdump**, and also the Windows version, which is called **windump**.

Running tcpdump

This module and the next give a summary of how to use **tcpdump**. Appendix 4 contains a summary of **tcpdump**'s options, and the full manpage is in Appendix 5.

1. you must be a privileged user to run **tcpdump** (because it looks at other people's network traffic). On Linux you must be user **root** (or the program must be setuid root). On Windows-NT you must be **administrator** (although not all **tcpdump** versions enforce this)

2. start the program from the command line (Command Window in Windows); it announces the name of the network interface it's listening on, followed by details of the packets (Figure 1.5). We'll explain in a moment why you use the "-n" option, but be warned: if you omit it, **tcpdump** may appear to hang for a minute or two.

   ```
   tcpdump -n
   ```

3. to terminate **tcpdump** type **ctrl-C** (or whatever the interrupt or kill character is on your system). **tcpdump** prints its usage statistics and exits.

```
Command Prompt                                                    _ □ ×
C:\> windump -n
windump: listening on \Device\Packet_E13c5741
10:44:53.339891 212.140.133.10.4141 > 212.140.133.17.139: P 75282481:75282533(52) ack 2782169524 win 8475 (DF)
10:44:53.340137 212.140.133.17.139 > 212.140.133.10.4141: P 1:40(39) ack 52 win 2920 (DF) [tos 0x10]
10:44:53.340617 212.140.133.10.4141 > 212.140.133.17.139: P 52:156(104) ack 40 win 8436 (DF)
10:44:53.341191 212.140.133.17.139 > 212.140.133.10.4141: P 40:218(178) ack 156 win 2920 (DF) [tos 0x10]
10:44:53.478196 212.140.133.10.4141 > 212.140.133.17.139: . ack 218 win 8258 (DF)
10:45:01.529369 arp who-has 212.140.133.29 tell 212.140.133.10
10:45:01.530075 arp reply 212.140.133.29 is-at 8:0:20:a:74:aa
10:45:01.530176 212.140.133.10.1928 > 193.63.88.162.80: S 37179877:37179877(0) win 8192 <mss 1460> (DF)
10:45:01.569680 212.140.133.10.1928 > 193.63.88.162.80: S 37179877:37179877(0) win 8192 <mss 1460> (DF)
...
^C
21 packets received by filter
0 packets dropped by kernel

C:\>
```

Figure 1.5 Windump session in Windows' command prompt window

The format of the output varies with the type of packet being displayed, but a typical line starts with the time of day, the "dotted decimal" four-part source IP address and destination IP address separated by a ">" symbol, and then the details for this packet. For most types of traffic, the source and destination IP addresses contain a fifth number at the end (e.g. .4141 in the source address on the first line), which is the "port number." As we'll explain in Chapter 10, different types of TCP/IP traffic are sent to different "ports" on a host. For example, to connect to a Web server, you connect to port 80 on the machine, whereas to connect to the e-mail server on the same machine, you use port 25. We'll use the port number, in conjunction with the packet contents, to determine what type of traffic (Web, e-mail, etc.) the packet contains. The inside front cover contains a list of common port numbers.

Options to display the information in different ways

Print host addresses as numbers, not names: use option "**-n**." With this option all host addresses are printed as IP numbers, as shown in the two traces below. If you omit this option, **tcpdump** attempts to print addresses as names. Depending on your configuration, it usually does this by looking up the addresses in the DNS (the Domain Name System that converts between hostnames and IP numeric addresses; see Chapter 7). If you don't have a working DNS setup, **tcpdump** will hang without printing anything for about a minute and a half, or even more, while it tries to do the lookups. Until we've covered DNS, we'll always use **-n** with **tcpdump**.

> **Warning:** omitting the "**-n**" option is the most common cause of problems with **tcpdump**. (Even though we've been using **tcpdump** for years, we still make the mistake of omitting "**-n**" when we're working on other people's systems and then get all worried that something serious is wrong.)

Don't print the time of day: use option "**-t**." This is useful, either to save space on the output, or if you're just not interested in the time details. For example,

```
alice# tcpdump -n -t
tcpdump: listening on eth0
212.140.133.38.1044 > 212.140.133.17.80: S 4089266604:4089266604(0) win 1
212.140.133.17.80 > 212.140.133.38.1044: S 69147160:69147160(0) ack 40892
212.140.133.38.1044 > 212.140.133.17.80: . ack 1 win 16060 <nop,nop,times
212.140.133.38.1044 > 212.140.133.17.80: P 1:97(96) ack 1 win 16060 <nop,
212.140.133.17.80 > 212.140.133.38.1044: . ack 97 win 16060 <nop,nop,time
```

Verbose output: option "**-v**" causes more information from the packet to be displayed. Usually you need this only for looking at DNS traffic, which we cover in Chapter 7.

Print Ethernet addresses as well as IP addresses: use option "**-e**." For example,

```
alice# tcpdump -n -t -e
tcpdump: listening on eth0
0:10:a4:98:25:43 ff:ff:ff:ff:ff:ff 0806 60: arp who-has 212.140.133.17 tell
0:d0:b7:b6:3d:f6 0:10:a4:98:25:43 0806 42: arp reply 212.140.133.17 is-at 0
0:10:a4:98:25:43 0:d0:b7:b6:3d:f6 0800 74: 212.140.133.38.1045 > 212.140.133.
0:d0:b7:b6:3d:f6 0:10:a4:98:25:43 0800 74: 212.140.133.17.80 > 212.140.133.
0:10:a4:98:25:43 0:d0:b7:b6:3d:f6 0800 66: 212.140.133.38.1045 > 212.140.13
0:10:a4:98:25:43 0:d0:b7:b6:3d:f6 0800 162: 212.140.133.38.1045 > 212.140.1
0:d0:b7:b6:3d:f6 0:10:a4:98:25:43 0800 66: 212.140.133.17.80 > 212.140.133.
0:d0:b7:b6:3d:f6 0:10:a4:98:25:43 0800 1514: 212.140.133.17.80 > 212.140.13
0:d0:b7:b6:3d:f6 0:10:a4:98:25:43 0800 1514: 212.140.133.17.80 > 212.140.13
0:10:a4:98:25:43 0:d0:b7:b6:3d:f6 0800 66: 212.140.133.38.1045 > 212.140.13
```

We'll need this option when we build our first simple network, in the next chapter.

1.3 How to select just the packets you're interested in

By default, **tcpdump** prints details of *all* the packets on the network. On a busy network this can generate a huge amount of information, making it very difficult to see what you need. You can tell **tcpdump** to select and display specific packets only. You can combine multiple selection criteria to give a very precise specification of what you want to see displayed.

In this module we cover just a few of **tcpdump**'s selection options, which will probably be all you need 80% of the time. Later on in the book, whenever you need a particular feature we'll introduce it explicitly and explain it at the time, and for reference you have the option summary and manual page in Appendices 4 and 5 in case you want to explore further in the meantime.

Selecting packets by host address

- **host** *a.b.c.d* – select only packets that have the specified IP number *a.b.c.d* as source or destination IP address, for example

  ```
  tcpdump -n host 192.168.170.5
  ```

  (You can also use the syntax "**host***name*" but that works only if you have a working DNS, which we assume you don't, yet. We cover the DNS in Chapter 7.)

- **src host** *a.b.c.d* (or just **src** *a.b.c.d*) – select only packets that are sent by host *a.b.c.d*, i.e. that have this as source IP address, for example

  ```
  tcpdump -n src 192.168.170.5
  ```

- **dst host** *a.b.c.d* (or just **dst** *a.b.c.d*) – select only packets destined for host *a.b.c.d*, i.e. that have this as destination IP address, for example

  ```
  tcpdump -n dst 192.168.170.5
  ```

Selecting packets by traffic type

Most TCP/IP traffic from a client to a server is sent to a particular "port" on the server, which uses the port number to decide which of the many services on this machine the client is requesting. We explain ports in detail in Module 10.3, but for now we'll just say that most Web servers use port 80 to accept incoming requests, and most e-mail servers use port 25.

You can tell **tcpdump** to select only a particular type of traffic by specifying a port number:

- **port** *num* – select only packets to or from port *num*, i.e. that have this as destination IP address, for example

  ```
  tcpdump -n port 80
  ```

  selects only ports to/from port 80. Most of the time that's enough to show you only Web traffic, but if you really want to be more precise you can use the **src** or **dst** prefixes in front of **port**, for example

  ```
  tcpdump -n dst port 80
  ```

Combining multiple selection criteria

You can combine multiple criteria to make your selection more precise, by using the following:

...**and** ... – select only if all the criteria match, for example

```
tcpdump -n host 192.168.170.5 and port 25
tcpdump -n src host 10.1.2.3 and dst host 10.9.8.7
```

You can use several **and**s if you want, to make even more complex selections.

...**or** ... – select if any of the criteria match, for example

```
tcpdump -n host 10.1.2.3 or dst port 25
```

not ... – reverse the meaning of the match condition, for example

```
tcpdump -n not host 10.9.8.7
```

prints everything except traffic to that host. You often use this if you are on a networked machine and you want to exclude your own traffic from the trace.

(...) – parentheses are used to group expressions, usually used with **and** and **or**, for example

```
tcpdump -n host 10.9.8.7 and "(port 80 or port 25)"
```

We've used quotes to hide the parentheses from the shell (Command prompt), which would otherwise treat them as special characters. (Try it without and see what happens.)

As a shorthand, you can omit identical "qualifier lists." The following are equivalent:

```
tcpdump -n dst port 80 or 88 or 8080
tcpdump -n dst port 80 or dst port 88 or dst port 8080
```

Tip: when you use parentheses with the logical (**and, or**) operators, it's best to put quotes around the whole expression rather than just around the special characters. It's less error-prone and it's quicker.

```
tcpdump -n "arp and ( src net 10 or 12)"     recommended
tcpdump -n arp and "(" src net 10 or 12 ")"     not recommended
```

Warning: the precedence of **not** is highest. The expression

```
    host 10.1.1.1 and not port 21 or 23 or 25
```

is probably not what you intended. It means

```
    (host 10.1.1.1 and not port 21) or (port 23) or (port 25) )
```

which shows port 23 or 25 traffic from anywhere, and all traffic from 10.1.1.1 except on port 21. You probably intended:

```
    host 10.1.1.1 and not port (21 or 23 or 25)
```

You can avoid problems like this by always using parentheses with **and** and **or**.

1.4 Common problems with tcpdump

tcpdump **prints nothing**

1. This is often caused by forgetting to specify "**-n**," especially on a test network that has no DNS. **tcpdump** hasn't stopped – it's just waiting for the DNS, and will eventually print something after a few minutes. To check whether this is the cause, re-run **tcpdump** with "**-n**" and see if you immediately get output. (Even if DNS is working correctly, it slows down **tcpdump** tracing so much that we very rarely use it so we almost always use option -n.)

2. You may have the **tcpdump** machine connected to a switch instead of a hub, so it really isn't seeing any traffic at all from other machines. To check, generate some traffic from this machine, e.g. **ping** another PC. If you see the reply and response, you know your network is OK, so you probably are connected to a switch

3. You are running "piping" **tcpdump**'s output directly into another program:

   ```
   tcpdump -n | tee /tmp/trace
   ```
   wrong

   In a pipeline like this, output is often buffered in very large chunks. To overcome this, use **tcpdump**'s "**-l**" option:

   ```
   tcpdump -l -n | tee /tmp/trace
   ```
   right

4. Your Linux kernel is a special build and doesn't have the necessary support for sniffing. (This is unlikely if your build is at all normal, but see the Notes on page 25 for more detail.)

5. You may have specified the wrong NIC using the "**-i**" option. (Some people suggest you should always explicitly specify the interface, but we never do.) You are unlikely to use multiple NICs until Chapter 3

6. Some machines can't sniff the packets they send themselves. You can overcome this problem by running a dedicated sniffer machine that isn't used for anything else, but which can see everyone else's packets.

I can't see enough of the contents of my packets

tcpdump prints only a summary of the packet's contents. You can tell **tcpdump** to be more verbose using option "**-v**." You can enter this option twice ("**-v -v**" or "**-vv**") or three times to get even more detail. Later on in the book we will use other sniffer tools that make it easy to see everything in a packet. However, most of the time they are cumbersome and slow to use compared with **tcpdump**, so we'll stick with **tcpdump** for now, especially as it's installed as standard on many machines.

packets don't contain all the necessary information

You can recognize this because the output contains a name in square brackets preceded by a pipe symbol, e.g. "**[|domain]**" or "**[|nfs]**".

    tcpdump captures only the first 68 bytes of each packet by default. Use "**-s** *num*" to increase the number of bytes captured until you don't get any more of these messages on the lines you are interested in.

my output contains lots of "SMB" and "NBT" messages

```
 (DF) (ttl 128, id 38109, len 141)
212.140.133.17.139 > 212.140.133.7.4950: P 1:103(102) ack
>>> NBT Packet
NBT Session Packet
Flags=0x0
Length=98 (0x62)

SMB PACKET: SMBtrans2 (REPLY)
SMB Command    = 0x32
```

This is supposedly a feature but it's so intrusive we'd call it a bug. **tcpdump** was extended to know about Microsoft Windows networking, which is what these messages are about. They occupy multiple lines and they can't be controlled in the usual way. However, you can exclude them by appending a "NOT" clause to your filter expression, e.g.

```
tcpdump -n "host 10.9.8.7 and not (port 137 or 138 or 139)"
```

(We'll explain these port numbers in Chapter 18.)

packets are being dropped (missed)

When **tcpdump** finishes, it prints statistics on the number of packets processed:

```
...
17:50:24.540261 192.0.2.7.4950 > 192.0.2.19.139: . 502119:5
1773 packets received by filter
12780 packets dropped by kernel
```

If packets are dropped by the kernel, there's probably too much traffic for this poor little machine to handle. You can reduce the amount of work it has to do by writing the packets to a file (see Appendix 4) and processing them later, and/or reduce the amount of data captured per packet using the "**-s** *num*" option.

New fast machines don't usually drop anything, but some of our ancient Sun workstations and old 486 laptops can't keep up with heavy traffic. Even so, they're fine for diagnosing particular network problems, because

- we can usually specify a very precise filter expression, to limit the processing the machine has to perform

- most network problems can be exercised with just a few packets, or a few dozen packets. You need to capture huge amounts of data only when you're looking for an intermittent problem caused by hardware or software bugs (rather than the misconfigurations that cause 99.9% of problems).

tcpdump: **socket: Operation not permitted**

You're not running as user **root**.

tcpdump: **parse error or problems specifying filter expressions**

Most of the time, errors are caused by forgetting to enter "**net**" or "**host**" before an IP number or name. Fortunately, **tcpdump** gives an error message, so while it's easy to make a typo, it's hard to enter a filter expression that isn't what you meant but that still is valid (except where you get mixed up using a mixture of "**and**," "**not**," and "**or**," as we still do sometimes, alas).

Summary

- **tcpdump** lets you capture and view all the packets that appear at the network interface for your machine

- because of how Ethernet works, packets for all the other machines connected to this Ethernet are also visible at your machine's interface unless you are using an Ethernet switch. If you have the necessary privileges, **tcpdump** can look at these packets too, by putting the network interface into promiscuous mode

- you can tell **tcpdump** which packets you want it to display, to focus in on the particular traffic that is of interest to you.

What's next?

In Chapter 2 we build a very small network, consisting of two machines on a single Ethernet, and explore how the packets travel between the machines. We'll use **tcpdump** extensively for that.

Notes and further reading

> **Tip:** because we often want to be able to start **tcpdump** *very* quickly if we see something suspicious on our network, we have used the Linux shell's "alias" facility to define "**t**" as a short-cut for **tcpdump**:
>
> ```
> alias t="tcpdump -n -t"
> ```
> so we can just type "**t**" to run **tcpdump**.

You can run several instances of **tcpdump** simultaneously on the same machine, each capturing a different set of packets. The separate instances do not interface with each other.

    tcpdump originated at the Lawrence Berkeley National Laboratory (**http://ee.lbl.gov/**) in Berkeley, California. **tcpdump** is now maintained by

❑ **http://www.tcpdump.org**

It runs on lots of other versions of UNIX platforms as well as Linux. It has been enhanced a lot over the years, and other versions may differ slightly in syntax from the one we describe. However, the basic operation is the same for them all.

    windump, the Windows version of **tcpdump**, comes from

❑ **http://netgroup-serv.polito.it/windump/**

which also provides the libraries (in particular the Windows version of **libpcap** called WinPcap) needed for **windump** to operate.

    tcpdump uses the **libpcap** packet capture library, which, according to the **libpcap** release notes:

provides a portable framework for low-level network monitoring. Applications include network statistics collection, security monitoring, network debugging, etc. Since almost every system vendor provides a different interface for packet capture, and since we've developed several tools that require this functionality, we've created this system-independent API to ease in porting and to alleviate the need for several system-dependent packet capture modules in each application.

…

The libpcap interface supports a filtering mechanism based on the architecture in the BSD packet filter. BPF is described in the 1993 Winter Usenix paper "The BSD Packet Filter: A New Architecture for User-level Packet Capture." A compressed postscript version is in

❏ *ftp://ftp.ee.lbl.gov/papers/bpf-usenix93.ps.Z*

libpcap is used by lots of sniffer-like tools, including **ethereal** and **ngrep** mentioned below. As a result, they all use the same syntax for selecting packets, which is convenient.

Sniffers are a security hazard. They can easily capture usernames and passwords and almost anything else that isn't encrypted. In the USA, the FBI runs a packet sniffing system called Carnivore (now renamed as the less exciting "DCS1000") to "wire-tap" traffic at ISPs. See:

❏ **http://www.fbi.gov/hq/lab/carnivore/carnivore.htm**

❏ **http://www.epic.org/privacy/carnivore/**

For lots of interesting information on sniffing and wire-tapping, see:

❏ **http://www.robertgraham.com/pubs/sniffing-faq.html**

Installation problems

We've never known a case where **windump** didn't install – although sometimes you have to check the FAQs on the **windump** site to get over some glitches. But even if you can't get **windump** working for some weird reason, all is not lost by any means: you can use either **ethereal** or Windows Network Monitor (see *Other sniffers*, below). These give you the same information but in a different format, so you can always get the information you need. We'll cover both of those sniffers later on; don't bother with them for now unless you have to.

The **libpcap** documentation says:

"In order for libpcap to be able to capture packets on a Linux system, the 'packet' protocol must be supported by your kernel. If it is not, you may get error messages such as:
modprobe: can't locate module net-pf-17
in "/var/adm/messages", or may get messages such as
socket: Address family not supported by protocol
from applications using libpcap."

The above is from the **README.linux** file of the **libpcap** distribution, also available online:

❏ **http://www.tcpdump.org/cgi-bin/cvsweb/libpcap/README.linux** and click on the most recent version number (currently 1.2) to obtain the full text of the file

However, almost all the standard Linux distributions have the necessary facilities enabled by default.

Older versions of **windump** sometimes complain with messages like:

windump: listening on \Device\Packet_E100B1
windump: Error opening adapter

We haven't seen these with recent releases, but if you do run into problems, search the Web for solutions (e.g. using Google) or look on the **windump** or **ethereal** (see below) sites for pointers. However, we do find the Linux version is more reliable, so if you have a choice of platform, go for Linux.

> **Tip:** dedicate a machine exclusively for **tcpdump** or **windump** use if you can. We use an old 486 laptop for this purpose – it cost almost nothing and we can easily move it to any part of the network where it's needed.

Other sniffers

We use several other sniffers for specific purposes later in the book:

- **ethereal** (Chapter 13): a "protocol analyzer" with a GUI that runs on both Linux and Windows. It's easy to see every detail of a packet and even the Ethernet frame data
- **ngrep** (Section 13.7): searches the data in the packets for a given string and prints matching packets as ASCII text
- **Windows Network Monitor** (Chapter 18): very similar to **ethereal** but runs only on Windows. Included as standard in Windows-NT.

Other UNIX systems have tools that are more or less similar to these, e.g. Solaris has **snoop** and ancient SunOS has **Etherfind**.

Appendices

Inside front cover: assigned TCP and UDP port numbers
Appendix 3: Ethernet UTP hubs and switches
Appendix 4: **tcpdump** command summary
Appendix 5: the full **tcpdump** manual page

2 How packets move on the local wire

Introduction

In this chapter we build the simplest possible network – two machines connected over a single piece of Ethernet. The chapter is divided into two parts:

1. the concepts involved – IP numbers and addressing, netmasks, how Ethernet works, and how TCP/IP uses an underlying Ethernet network

2. practical – we cable up a simple network, configure the TCP/IP software, and finally work through potential problems, how to diagnose them and how to fix them.

2.1 IP address and netmask – how to get a packet to your machine

In this chapter we build the simplest possible network – two PCs on a single Ethernet. This basic unit of two machines talking is fundamentally important because:

1. this is what makes up all local networks. There can be more than two machines on a LAN but all communication actually occurs between pairs of machines (Figure 2.1)

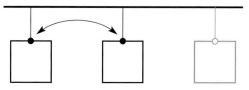

Figure 2.1 Network communication is usually between exactly two machines

2. as we mentioned in Module 0.4, when Alice communicates with Bob over the Internet, packets travel hop by hop over the network: from Alice to a router, from router to router, and finally from a router to Bob (Figure 2.2). The basic unit of connectivity is sending over a single hop – from one machine (router or host) to another on a single network, which is just the same as communication between two machines on a LAN in Figure 2.1.

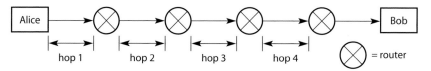

Figure 2.2 Packets travel hop by hop from router to router

Whether the communication is host-to-host, host-to-router, or router-to-router, the same mechanism is used in every case. This is what lets us extend from single-hop transmission on a simple network to an inter-network of interconnected networks where packets have to travel over many hops to reach the destination machine (which we cover in the next chapter).

In this chapter we'll explore how one PC communicates with another that's on the same Ethernet segment, and the issues involved:

- IP addresses
- netmasks – they tell my machine whether it needs to use a router to reach the destination machine
- how packets are transmitted over Ethernet
- how my PC finds your PC's Ethernet address automatically
- cabling up the test network
- configuring the TCP/IP software
- testing and troubleshooting.

IP address

In the postal system, every house and office has a unique postal address, which you use when you want to send a postcard to someone. Similarly, every machine on a TCP/IP network has a unique address – its *IP address*. When other computers send to your machine, they specify its IP address as the destination, and vice versa. IP addresses consist of four bytes, and are written as four decimal numbers separated by dots, e.g.

192.0.2.123

For obvious reasons this is called *dotted decimal notation*.

IP addresses are unique across the whole world (with exceptions for use on private networks that are not visible to anyone else, which we cover in Module 4.9). The uniqueness of addresses is guaranteed because IP numbers are allocated to sites from a single, world-wide, centrally managed pool.

To send packets to a machine using TCP/IP, you specify its IP address as the destination of the packets, and they are routed to it. For example, my workstation's IP address is 192.0.2.123; when you talk to me, you specify the destination as 192.0.2.123 in every packet you send me. That is the *only* destination addressing in the IP packet. As we mentioned in Module 0.4, the packet contains no routing information at all: routers on the network forward the packet hop by hop, until it reaches its final destination. The routers decide how to forward the packet solely on the basis of the packet's destination IP address. In other words, the routing information is held in the network itself, not in the packets.

The IP address on its own isn't enough

You might think that's all we need – a unique address for every computer on the network. If the network was a single wire spanning the globe with every computer in the world plugged into it, it would be enough. But the Internet isn't a single homogeneous network – it consists of thousands of different organizations' networks connected together. The machines on my LAN are only a small sub-set of the whole range of possible IP addresses. I can talk directly only to machines on my Ethernet segment; to communicate with machines elsewhere I have to use a router. (Similarly, I can pass postcards by hand to someone working in the same room as myself, but for people elsewhere I have to send the postcard through the mail system – our internal mail system or the public postal system.)

Now, let's say I want to send to another machine, with address 192.0.2.7. Before trying to send to this machine, my TCP/IP has to go through a decision process like this:

```
if (destination 192.0.2.7 is on my local network)
        communicate with the destination directly over the local LAN
else /* destination is remote* /
        use a router to communicate with the destination
```

The next module explains how TCP/IP uses the netmask to decide whether a machine is local or remote.

2.2 Netmask – the range of my directly connected network

When you send to other machines, a second parameter on your computer, the "netmask," tells your TCP/IP whether the destination address is on your local network, and therefore whether the packets can be sent directly, i.e. without using an intermediate router.

My machine's address is 192.0.2.123. It wants to send to 192.0.2.29. How does it decide whether 192.0.2.29 is local to the LAN and can be contacted directly? The answer is: my TCP/IP uses the *netmask* on my machine.

The combination of my IP address and my netmask specifies the range of IP addresses that my machine believes are connected directly to my LAN. I can talk to these addresses directly without using a router. (Not all the addresses in the range have to exist on the network. However, as far as my machine is concerned, the only place it will look for them is on this network. If it can't see them there, it thinks they don't exist and won't try to contact them in any other way.) Implicitly, the range also determines which machines are *not* on my LAN: all machines not in the range must be remote; I can send packets to them only by using an intermediate router.

How does the combination of (IP address, netmask) specify an IP address range? We'll cover that in a lot of detail later in Chapter 4, but for now here are simplified rules that will allow us to build our first test networks:

- the netmask consists of four bytes, written as four decimal numbers separated by dots, just like the IP address
- if the netmask is 255.255.255.0, the range consists of all the IP addresses that have the same first three bytes as the IP number of this machine. For example, the combination of my IP address = 192.0.2.7 and my netmask = 255.255.255.0 specifies the range

    192.0.2.0–192.0.2.255

    so my machine can talk directly to any machine in that range
- if the netmask is 255.255.0.0, the range consists of all the IP addresses that have the same first *two* bytes as my IP number. For example, my IP address = 192.168.45.109, my netmask = 255.255.0.0 gives the range

    192.168.0.0–192.168.255.255

Going back to our example above, when my TCP/IP wants to send to 192.0.2.29, its decision process is:

```
calculate the range specified by my IP address and my netmask
if (destination 192.0.2.29 is in this range)
        /* its on my local network */
        communicate with the destination directly over the local LAN
else
        /* destination is remote */
        use a router to communicate with the destination
        /* covered in Chapter 3 */
```

In a simple stand-alone network, all the netmasks should be the same, and all the IP addresses should be in the same range, because you want all the machines to be able to talk directly to one another. If one machine had a different netmask, it would have a different view of its network world: you could end up with Bob being part of Alice's range, but Alice outside Bob's so they won't be able to communicate (Figure 2.3), or with two ranges that don't overlap at all.

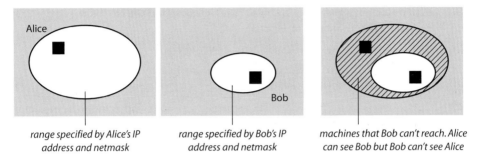

range specified by Alice's IP address and netmask   range specified by Bob's IP address and netmask   machines that Bob can't reach. Alice can see Bob but Bob can't see Alice

Figure 2.3 Different netmasks on the same LAN make some machines inaccessible

However, in a stand-alone network, the netmask isn't as important as in an inter-network. In a stand-alone network, if the netmask is such that it specifies a much bigger range of IP addresses than is actually on the network, it doesn't really matter because we're only interested in the local machines anyway. (We often find wrong netmask settings like this on sites that are just getting connected to the Internet.)

The netmask is used only when sending, because it tells my TCP/IP whether it can send to a destination directly. The netmask isn't relevant when receiving: if a packet arrives at this machine, it arrives, and that's all there is to it. It's very important to note that my netmask is stored *on my machine*; it isn't included in the packet because it's saying how my machine fits into the network around it – what are the IP numbers of the locally connected network. When a packet travels from me across other networks, the machines that forward it use *their own netmasks* to determine how to forward it. (The netmask is also referred to as the "subnet mask," for historical reasons, but we will never use that term.)

The three fundamental networking parameters

There are three fundamental TCP/IP parameters on every machine that are crucial:

1. IP address
2. netmask
3. default gateway – the address of a router to be used by default (which we cover in detail in Chapter 3).

You can't overestimate the importance of these three parameters. They govern every TCP/IP communication between this machine and any other. Whenever you have a network problem, check out these parameters first.

2.3 Ethernet networking: moving packets along the local wire

TCP/IP is a software standard – it defines what a piece of networking software in one machine must do to communicate successfully with the networking software in another. To work, TCP/IP has to use some underlying network-hardware system. Ethernet is by far the most common system nowadays for LANs so that's what we deal with in the rest of this chapter. Note that Ethernet is *not* part of TCP/IP:

- lots of network software that isn't TCP/IP uses Ethernet
- TCP/IP runs over many different types of hardware that are not Ethernet, e.g. token ring, dial-up phone lines, packet radio, etc.

TCP/IP just interacts with Ethernet (which is the network access layer) to use its capabilities to move the packets along the physical wire.

Ethernet defines the standard for electrical interface, cable types, connector configurations, etc. and how the hardware sends an Ethernet packet from one machine to another on the same wire or Ethernet *segment*. TCP/IP knows nothing about these lower-level details of cabling, Ethernet transmission, and so on – it's not its business.

Ethernet addressing

- Ethernet uses Ethernet addresses, also called *MAC* addresses (*Media Access Control* or *Medium Access Control*) or hardware addresses
- Ethernet addresses consist of six bytes, written in hexadecimal. On Linux, these are shown in uppercase, separated by colons, e.g.

    00:D0:B7:B6:3D:F6

    On Windows they are shown in lowercase, separated by dashes, e.g.

    00-d0-b7-b6-3d-f6

- Ethernet addresses are globally unique, and are allocated by the Institute of Electrical and Electronic Engineers (IEEE) in the USA. Ethernet hardware manufacturers purchase fixed-size blocks of numbers; if they need more addresses, they buy more blocks. The IEEE publishes a list of allocated blocks, so from an Ethernet address of a device, you can tell who manufactured it (or at least the Ethernet card in it). For example,

    00:50:73:38:CE:26 is a Cisco address

    08:00:20:0A:74:AA is a Sun Microsystems address

    (A tool on our Web site lets you enter an address and gives you the name of the owner of that Ethernet address block.)

Sending data over Ethernet

For my machine to send some data to yours, on the same local Ethernet, the software in my machine first constructs an Ethernet packet in memory. It:

- inserts the data to be sent in the data ("payload") area of the packet

- specifies your machine's MAC address as the Ethernet destination address
- gives my MAC address as the Ethernet source (Figure 2.4a)
- passes the packet to my machine's hardware to transmit, and the hardware does the rest.

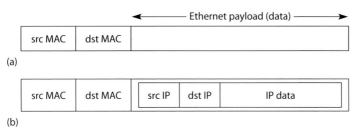

Figure 2.4 (a) Ethernet packet (b) IP packet contained as Ethernet payload

Figure 2.4 is only schematic – we've omitted other "packet header" fields and fields used for checksums, etc., and the fields are not in the order shown. We don't need that level of detail, but if you want to explore in depth, see Stevens.

Ethernet is called a "best effort" system, which means it tries to deliver the data but doesn't guarantee it, and if the packet gets lost – because of noise on the wire, or because the network is too busy, or someone pulls out a wire – it doesn't tell you. (That's one of the reasons you use TCP/IP on top of hardware networking systems like Ethernet.)

It's important to note that what Ethernet sends is an Ethernet packet, which can carry any type of data as payload (which is, of course, why you can run lots of different network systems, not just TCP/IP, on an Ethernet). To send an IP packet, the whole IP packet (which my application has constructed in memory) must be inserted into the Ethernet packet (Figure 2.4b) and the packet-type field in the Ethernet reader is set to 800 (IP). The IP packet is said to be *encapsulated* in the Ethernet packet.

Note that at this level of networking it's the MAC address, *not the IP address*, that causes the packet to be delivered to the correct machine. If I want to send to you, and put your IP address as the destination IP but use the wrong MAC destination address, the packet will go to the wrong machine and will probably be thrown away. (However, in Chapter 3 we'll see that sometimes the destination IP address and the destination MAC address are deliberately set for different machines, and routers depend on this fact to perform their magic.)

You can see the Ethernet packets on the wire using **tcpdump -n -t -e**, (**-e:** print the Ethernet details; **-n:** print addresses as numbers, not as hostnames; **-t:** don't print time on each line). Figure 2.5 shows the trace for a **ping**:

```
alice# tcpdump -n -e -t

0:d0:b7:b6:3d:f6 0:a0:c9:b4:e4:3a 0800 98: 192.0.2.17 > 192.0.2.10: icmp: echo request
0:a0:c9:b4:e4:3a 0:d0:b7:b6:3d:f6 0800 98: 192.0.2.10 > 192.0.2.17: icmp: echo reply
```

MAC address of	*MAC address of*	*Ethernet*	*Packet length*
machine	*machine*	*packet type*	*(98 bytes)*
192.0.2.10	*192.0.2.17*	*800 = IP*	

Figure 2.5 Trace for a **ping** showing Ethernet details

In the next module we see that Ethernet packets can also be broadcast, i.e. sent to every machine on this wire and not just to a single machine.

2.4 ARP – how my machine finds the Ethernet address of your machine

Alice knows Bob's IP address, but needs to find Bob's Ethernet address so she can send packets to him. TCP/IP solves this problem using *ARP*, the *Address Resolution Protocol*. Alice "broadcasts," asking who has Bob's IP address. Bob replies to mine, telling Alice his Ethernet address. Then they can communicate. Let's go through that in more detail.

Ethernet broadcasts

Normally, when one machine sends an Ethernet packet to another, the packet is processed only by the machine whose Ethernet address is in the destination field of the packet, i.e. the packet is accepted by the machine's NIC and passed up to the operating system and then to an application. Although the electrical signal is visible along the whole length of the wire, the packet flow is localized as shown in Figure 2.6. (Ethernet "switches" can affect the visibility of packets, as we'll see in Module 2.8.)

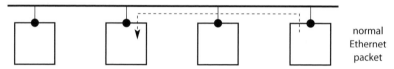

Figure 2.6 Normally, only the destination machine receives the packet

Sometimes, a machine needs to send to every machine. Ethernet supports *broadcast* packets that are received and processed by every machine on this Ethernet segment (Figure 2.7). Broadcasts are used, for example, when a machine has to ask for something but doesn't know who to ask. ("I want to use a server that offers XYZ service, is there one out there?") However, the most common use is ARP, explained below.

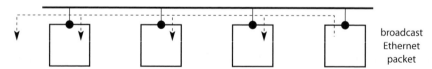

Figure 2.7 Broadcast packets are received by all machines

ARP, the Address Resolution Protocol

In the previous module, we saw that for my machine to send to yours, my machine has to know your MAC address (Ethernet address). How does it find this out? We could manually configure a table to IP-to-Ethernet address mappings and copy this to every machine; however, that would be a major maintenance headache for large sites, and wouldn't work for devices like print servers, etc. that don't have any disk storage. We need an automatic solution.

An analogy is a crowded office: Alice wants to phone Bob but doesn't know his extension. A simple solution is for Alice to shout to the whole office: "Bob: I'm on extension 29. What's your extension?" Bob hears this and calls Alice back on extension 29, saying, "Alice, I'm on extension 7." Then they can converse as much as they like without affecting other people with their shouting.

TCP/IP does something very similar, using ARP. Let's say Alice's machine is 192.0.2.7, and she wants to send to Bob's machine, 192.0.2.29. Machine .7 must find out .29's MAC address:

- Alice sends an Ethernet broadcast, containing an ARP request packet in the payload/data field. The ARP packet contains the IP address whose MAC address she needs – 192.0.2.29. **tcpdump** shows this as "arp who-has 192.0.2.29"

- all the machines on this wire receive this packet, extract the ARP packet, and look at the IP address inside it. If the address doesn't match the receiving machine's IP address, the packet is ignored, i.e. only .29 processes it further

- machine .29 replies to .7 with an ARP reply packet, containing .29's MAC address. (It does *not* broadcast the reply, because only .7 has asked for the information.) **tcpdump** shows this as "arp reply 192.0.2.29 is-at *a.b.c.d.e.f*"

- .7 now knows .29's MAC address, and can communicate freely.

When we first met ARP, it looked like magic: how can two machines exchange over a network their addresses, which they need to be able to communicate with each other over the network? It seems circular. The key of course is using the broadcast. The Ethernet broadcast address is pre-defined so all machines know what it is and can use it without having to talk to any other machine first.

Below is the **tcpdump** trace of 192.0.2.7 **ping**ing 192.0.2.29. We use options "**-e**", to show the Ethernet addresses. We also use a new feature – specifying particular protocols as part of the filter expression. In this case, we want both ARP and ICMP (**ping**) traffic.

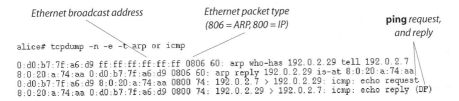

```
alice# tcpdump -n -e -t arp or icmp

0:d0:b7:7f:a6:d9 ff:ff:ff:ff:ff:ff 0806 60: arp who-has 192.0.2.29 tell 192.0.2.7
8:0:20:a:74:aa 0:d0:b7:7f:a6:d9 0806 60: arp reply 192.0.2.29 is-at 8:0:20:a:74:aa
0:d0:b7:7f:a6:d9 8:0:20:a:74:aa 0800 74: 192.0.2.7 > 192.0.2.29: icmp: echo request
8:0:20:a:74:aa 0:d0:b7:7f:a6:d9 0800 74: 192.0.2.29 > 192.0.2.7: icmp: echo reply (DF)
```

Ethernet broadcast address *Ethernet packet type (806 = ARP, 800 = IP)* **ping** *request, and reply*

Notice that there is only one ARP dialogue: .29 has sent a **ping** reply without issuing an ARP to find out .7's MAC address. .29 was able to do this because when it received the initial ARP request broadcast from .7, it extracted .7's MAC and IP addresses from the packet. It therefore didn't need to do its own ARP request afterwards – it already had all the information it needed to talk to .7.

Tip: when I'm talking to you, my machine uses ARP only when it thinks your machine is on the same wire. If you see an ARP "who-has" for a machine that you know is remote, it means your machine has an incorrect view of what the local network is: either its IP address, or more likely its netmask, is wrong.

2.5 Viewing and manipulating ARP entries

TCP/IP keeps a record of (IP address, MAC address) pairs in its *ARP cache*. It is only a cache and not a permanent store: once an entry reaches a certain age, TCP/IP deletes it. This stops the cache growing forever, and gets over the problem of how to detect whether the MAC address changes for a given IP address (e.g. if you have to replace a broken network card). On the other hand, it means the ARP dialog is repeated every so often, getting the same answer each time. (However, the load this imposes on the network is negligible.)

The **arp** command lets you view and manipulate the ARP cache (see Table 2.1).

Table 2.1

	Linux	Windows-NT
view the cache	arp arp *host* arp -a arp -a *host*	arp -a arp -a *ipnum*
show addresses as numbers instead of names	... -n ...	
delete an entry	arp -d *host*	arp -d *ipnum*
add ("set") an entry	arp -s *host macaddr*	arp -s *ipnum macaddr*

Notes:

1. on Linux, arp by default prints host addresses as names and numbers ("**arp -a**") or just names ("**arp**"). As usual this works correctly only if you have DNS configured, which we don't cover until Chapter 7. Use option "**-n**" to prevent **arp** trying to convert the IP numbers to names

2. on Linux, the "**-a**" format display (Figure 2.8a) is slightly different to the one without "**-a**". We always use "**-a**", because it works on both Linux (Figure 2.8b) and NT (Figure 2.8c)

3. on Linux, *host* can be either an IP number or a hostname; on Windows you can use only IP numbers. See your manpages for more detailed descriptions

4. we've never needed to add entries, so you're unlikely to need to use "**arp -s**"

5. On Windows-NT, by default entries are deleted from the ARP cache after two minutes if they are not used, or ten minutes if they are used; the timeout period can be edited in the Registry, although it's hard to see why you would ever want to do that. On Linux, entries are usually deleted after about five minutes. (You can check the details of your implementation by ensuring an entry for a machine is present by **ping**ing it, then running "**arp -a**" at intervals, to see when the entry vanishes.)

```
alice% arp -a -n
? (192.0.2.5) at 08:00:20:0C:E4:E1 [ether] on eth0
? (192.0.2.7) at 00:D0:B7:7F:A6:D9 [ether] on eth0
? (192.0.2.10) at 00:A0:C9:B4:E4:3A [ether] on eth0
? (192.0.2.22) at 00:02:B3:2A:49:1C [ether] on eth0
? (192.0.2.19) at 00:00:C0:8B:C3:C5 [ether] on eth0
alice%
```

(a)

```
alice% arp  -a
mars.uit.co.uk (192.0.2.5) at 08:00:20:0C:E4:E1 [ether] on eth0
techpc.uit.co.uk (192.0.2.7) at 00:D0:B7:7F:A6:D9 [ether] on eth0
scutter.uit.co.uk (192.0.2.10) at 00:A0:C9:B4:E4:3A [ether] on eth0
dennisnt.uit.co.uk (192.0.2.22) at 00:02:B3:2A:49:1C [ether] on eth0
lee.uit.co.uk (192.0.2.19) at 00:00:C0:8B:C3:C5 [ether] on eth0
mail.uit.co.uk (192.0.2.29) at 08:00:20:0A:74:AA [ether] on eth0
alice%
```

(b)

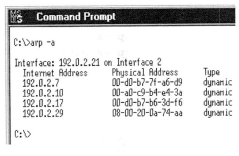

(c)

Figure 2.8 "**arp –a**" outputs

(By the way, ARP is an example of a protocol that doesn't sit neatly in the layer model. It's really at layer $2\frac{1}{2}$, linking the network or Internet or IP layer with the lower network access or link layer, as shown below.)

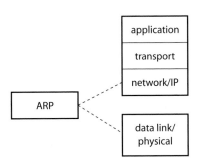

We've used **ping** several times in this this chapter and the previous one to generate some traffic, but we haven't looked at it in detail. We'll do that in the next module.

2.6 Using ping **to generate test traffic between two machines**

The **ping** program sends a special packet from my machine to yours. If your machine is connected to the network and receives the packet, it sends a reply to me saying you are alive. This is often used to check that a machine is alive, or just to generate test traffic between two machines.

ping gets its name by analogy with sonar, where a submarine sends out small pulses of sound. The pulses echo back from other submarines and make a **ping** noise on the first submarine's detector, indicating the presence of the other sub.

At its simplest, tell **ping** the IP address of the remote host you want to contact:

```
ping 192.0.2.29
```

The program sends multiple requests, and (hopefully) receives multiple replies. On Windows, the simple command "**ping** *host*" sends four requests and terminates, whereas on Linux it repeats forever (in fact until you press ctrl-C to terminate it). (There is no **ping** server on the target machine. Responding to **ping**s is built into the TCP/IP stack, because it's necessary for testing, and it's so simple and small.) Bob shows **ping**'s output on Linux; we used option "**-n**" to print addresses as numbers, and "**-c3**" to send three requests.

```
alice# ping -c3 -n 192.0.2.29
PING 192.0.2.29 (192.0.2.29): 56 data bytes
64 bytes from 192.0.2.29: icmp_seq=0 ttl=255 time=4.5 ms
64 bytes from 192.0.2.29: icmp_seq=1 ttl=255 time=0.6 ms
64 bytes from 192.0.2.29: icmp_seq=2 ttl=255 time=0.5 ms
```

We can analyze this in detail using **tcpdump**, with option "**-n**" as usual (with extra lines inserted for clarity):

```
alice# tcpdump -n arp or icmp

15:05:53.170364 arp who-has 192.0.2.29 tell 192.0.2.17
15:05:53.171368 arp reply 192.0.2.29 is-at 8:0:20:a:74:aa

15:05:53.171384 192.0.2.17 > 192.0.2.29: icmp: echo request
15:05:53.174843 192.0.2.29 > 192.0.2.17: icmp: echo reply (DF)

15:05:54.168674 192.0.2.17 > 192.0.2.29: icmp: echo request
15:05:54.169217 192.0.2.29 > 192.0.2.17: icmp: echo reply (DF)
```

> **Lines 1, 2:** the usual ARP dialog. We wouldn't see this if the target machine was on a remote network, or even if it's on the LAN but we had been talking to it recently. The ARP often causes the first **ping** response time to be slower than the rest
>
> **Lines 3, 4:** the ARP dialog is followed immediately (16 microseconds) by the first **ping** request/reply pair
>
> **Lines 5, 6:** the next **ping** request/reply pair (etc.).

You can observe several points from the outputs of the two programs:

> 1. **ping** uses ICMP (the Internet Control Message Protocol), which is part of the TCP/IP suite of protocols. We will see a few other uses of ICMP elsewhere in the book

2. **ping**'s output reports the *round-trip time* (the time from when I sent the **ping** request to when I received the reply) so I can get a feel for the performance of the intervening network

3. **ping**'s time resolution varies on different machines and different operating systems, depending on the precision of your system clock. Try **ping**ing for a variety of your machines and see what you get.

ping **command summary**

The Linux and NT versions of **ping** use confusingly different flags for the same options. The important ones are summarized in Table 2.2. (Others are listed in your systems' respective manpages (online manual pages) or Help files, but you'll probably never need them.)

	Linux	**Windows-NT**
ping **until ctrl-C terminates**	`ping` *host*	`ping -t` *host*
send *num* **requests**	`-c` *num*	`-n` *num*
print host address as name	*(default)*	`-a`
print target address as number	`-n`	*(default)*
show final summary only	`-q`	*(not applicable)*
send request of size *num* **bytes**	`-s` *num*	`-1` *num*

If ping **doesn't get a reply**

Apart from the general network problems that we cover in the troubleshooting Module 2.13, there are a couple of reasons why **ping** might not print anything:

- if the site is remote, it may be protected by a firewall that blocks **ping**s (so that Bad People can't use **ping** to find out the addresses of your internal machines in preparation for an attack on your site)

- on Linux, you can disable responding to **ping**s (see Notes on page 57 for details). We recommend you *don't* do this or you will confuse every administrator on your network (and probably yourself too when you forget what you've done)

Exercise: when you boot your NT or Linux system, see where in the boot cycle it's first prepared to respond to **ping**s it receives. Start a **ping** (which runs forever, by default) from a Linux system, or use **ping -t** from NT. If your network card or PCMCIA card has an "active" light, observe it (or the "link" light on your hub) to see when it becomes active. How does this relate to when the machine becomes **ping**able? You may find this information useful if you have boot problems on your system in the future.

Now we'll build a simple network and use the tools we've just covered.

2.7 Lab – building the simplest network possible: hubs and cabling

The simplest network we can have is two machines on a single Ethernet segment. UTP cabling is easy, flexible, and cheap. UTP hubs are easier to use than UTP switches when tracing packets.

We're now going to build the simplest possible network – two machines on a single Ethernet segment, as shown schematically in Figure 2.9. If you can, use Linux for one machine and Windows-NT for the other. It will take about five minutes to cable up the hardware (probably less than the time to find the spare hub) and another five or ten minutes to configure the software). We'll then perform experiments on it.

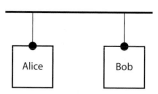

Figure 2.9 The simplest network – two machines on Ethernet

Cabling, hubs, and switches

The most commonly used cabling system nowadays is *UTP (unshielded twisted pair)*. This consists of several pairs of conductors, each pair twisted together, in a plastic outer casing, without any shielding around the pairs. By contrast, thin Ethernet ("thin-net") and thick Ethernet ("thicknet") have much thicker and more rigid coaxial, shielded cables, up to 10 or 11mm in diameter. On thin-net and thicknet, all the machines on the network attach to the single network cable. However, UTP uses a separate cable per machine, and all the cables are connected via UTP *hubs ("wiring hubs")* or UTP *switches* or a mixture of both. (We explain the difference between hubs and switches in the next module.)

We use UTP exclusively because:

- it's very flexible. You can easily run cable and sockets to where you need them, and it's very easy to build small test networks of a few PCs and hubs

- it's cheap – you can buy small UTP hubs for about US$20

- "link" indicator lights on hubs alert you to cabling problems without special diagnostic tools: if you connect a host to the hub and the link light doesn't come on, you've probably got a cable or similar problem (we say "probably" because the host and the network card must be up and running first)

- it's fast. By using the correct cable and hubs or switches, you can run 100 megabits/second Ethernet – ten times as fast as standard Ethernet but almost the same price

- it's easy to move, add, remove, or relocate computers in your network. This is very convenient when you're moving your sniffer machine to different points on the network to diagnose problems. UTP lets you keep a machine in its physical location but "cross-patch" it to connect into a different logical part of the network. If your sniffer has multiple network cards, you can, with suitable cross-patching, monitor local and remote parts of the network simultaneously from the one sniffer.

However, you can use any cabling system you like and everything we cover in this book still applies.

Using UTP, our simplest network is wired up physically as shown in Figure 2.10.

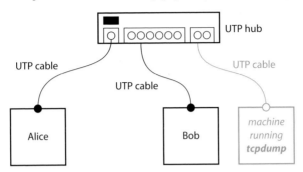

Figure 2.10 UTP cabling for a tiny network

We have shown a third machine, grayed-out in the diagram, running **tcpdump**. You can omit this if you run **tcpdump** on Alice or Bob instead. But we've found it easiest to keep **tcpdump** loaded on a dedicated laptop:

- it can be moved around at will, easily
- we know it works, whereas if you run **tcpdump** on Alice or Bob, you're using a machine to diagnose itself, which will sometimes lead you into trouble.

(We use an ancient laptop as our day-to-day portable sniffer box. It's the network administrator's equivalent of a screwdriver – although we use **tcpdump** every day and only need a screwdriver once a week.)

Troubleshooting a network begins with the cabling. As we mentioned above, make sure when you connect the PCs to the hub that the "link" lights, which indicate that the connection has been correctly made, are on.

If you haven't got a spare hub yet, you can connect Alice and Bob together directly using a *cross-over* UTP cable (Figure 2.11). Of course, with this configuration you can't add a sniffer machine at all.

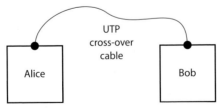

Figure 2.11 Connecting two machines using a cross-over UTP cable instead of a hub

---

Tip: we always have our desktop PC connected to a hub that's visible from where we sit. The "network activity" light on our port on the hub gives a good feel for what our machine is doing. It's a cheap but immediate diagnostic indicator. For the same reason, we try to keep other network equipment (routers, firewalls, etc.) in easy view too.

2.8 Hubs v. switches

Appendix 3 explains the background of why hubs and switches are different, but here are the practical differences. In the context below a *port* is a connection point on a switch/hub that you connect a machine's Ethernet cable into.

> **hub** – all the traffic on a port is visible on every other port and the bandwidth of the device is shared amongst all the ports (Figure 2.12). A heavy transfer from port X to Y will slow down a simultaneous transfer from A to B.

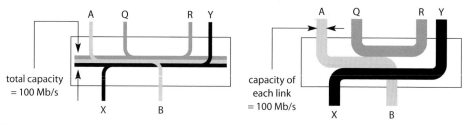

Figure 2.12 Hub   **Figure 2.13** Switch

> **switch** – traffic between two ports isn't visible on any other port. The full bandwidth of the device is available to every port (Figure 2.13). For example, if you have a 100Mb/s switch, you can transfer at 100Mb/s from port X to Y, and separately, at 100Mb/s from port A to B, and at 100Mb/s from Q to R as well. In fact, if your switch is *full-duplex*, you may even be able to transfer at 100Mb/s from B to A simultaneously with 100Mb from A to B. (When we upgraded from a 10Mb/s hub to a 100Mb/s switch, the time to update a particular file over the LAN reduced from 250 seconds to 11!)

On a switch, traffic between two ports A and B is visible only on ports A and B. On the network shown in Figure 2.14a, which uses a switch, if we run **tcpdump** on PC4, we won't see any of the PC2-to-PC5 traffic, even though our network card is in promiscuous mode, because the electrical signals just don't reach PC4.

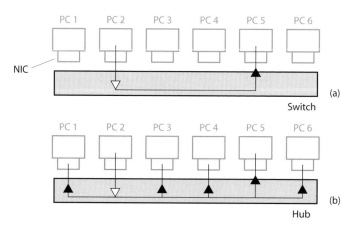

Figure 2.14 Network using a switch (a) and a hub (b)

By contrast, when we use a hub (Figure 2.14b), every port can see all the signals and **tcp-dump** works fine. Therefore ...

> **Warning:** if you use a switch instead of a hub when tracing with **tcpdump**, you will see almost nothing. For all the small test networks described in Part 1 of the book, use a hub.

Some "managed switches" (switches that use SNMP (Module 17.10) for control and monitoring, and are usually highly configurable, see Appendix 3) can be configured so that all traffic is visible on some or all ports; you can selectively enable this when you need to use **tcp-dump**. However, these are *much* more expensive than ordinary switches.

Another way round the problem is to daisy-chain a hub onto the switch port. Figure 2.15 shows the sniffer and Bob's PC connected to a daisy-chained hub, enabling us to monitor all the traffic to and from Bob's PC. You can cable this physically in two different ways:

1. **on the desktop:** remove the UTP drop cable from the back of Bob's PC and attach the cable to the hub instead. Then connect the sniffer PC and Bob's PC to the hub

2. **in the comms room:** on the switch disconnect the cable that runs to Bob's UTP wall-socket or desk. Re-connect this cable into your spare hub, and connect the hub to the switch. Connect the sniffer PC to the hub, either via another wall-socket or directly in the comms room.

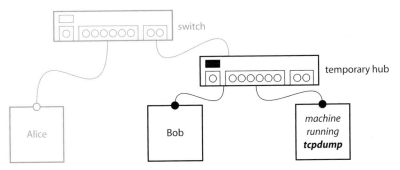

Figure 2.15 Physical cabling

Figure 2.15 correctly illustrates both methods: the only difference between them is where the hub is situated – in the comms room or on the desktop.

> **Tip:** keep a dedicated tiny 4-port hub and a few 50-cm UTP cables in your toolkit to use in situations like this. (We also keep a hub in the comms room and can centrally patch in a **tcpdump** sniffer to any point on the UTP network.)

For some problems you might need to add a hub at more than one point on your network and connect in multiple sniffer machines. If the sniffers are running Linux, you can connect to them using **telnet** (Module 10.6) or X windows (Module 17.6) and view all your traces on one screen. An alternative is to use multiple network cards on a single PC and cross-patch as above if required.

2.9 Lab – software configuration: Windows

This module tells you how to set and check the IP address and netmask on Windows systems. (We cover Windows first, because it's easier.) Module 2.11 does the same for Linux, and Module 2.12 uses these settings to build a test network.

1. start **Control Panel > Network** (Figure 2.16). Ignore the computer name and workgroup or domain; they are primarily for MS Windows Networking (Chapter 20).

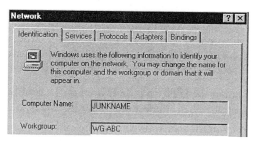

Figure 2.16 Windows TCP/IP configuration – step 1

2. click on the **Protocols** tab to give the dialog shown in Figure 2.17

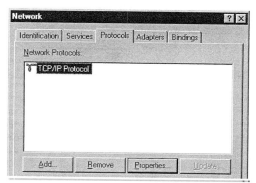

Figure 2.17 Windows TCP/IP configuration – step 2

3. double-click on **TCP/IP Protocol** or select it and press the **Properties** button to give you the TCP/IP Properties dialog (Figure 2.18)

4. enter the values as shown. Note that the dialog refers to the netmask as "Subnet mask." This terminology is historical, as we'll explain in Chapter 4. We always refer to this setting as "netmask," even if that isn't what's shown in the dialog, so that you know what it really means

5. when you've finished, press **OK** (or press **Apply** to leave the dialog open, if you expect to change the settings again soon).

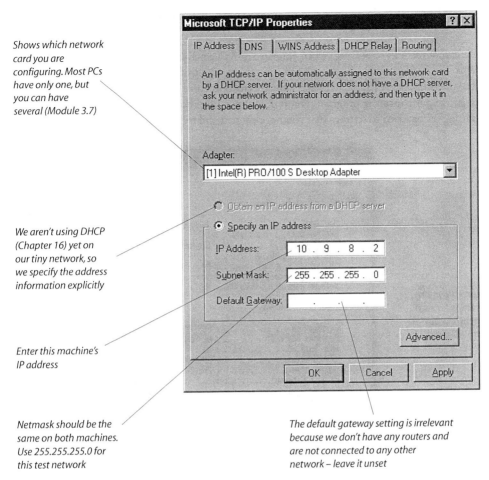

Shows which network card you are configuring. Most PCs have only one, but you can have several (Module 3.7)

We aren't using DHCP (Chapter 16) yet on our tiny network, so we specify the address information explicitly

Enter this machine's IP address

Netmask should be the same on both machines. Use 255.255.255.0 for this test network

The default gateway setting is irrelevant because we don't have any routers and are not connected to any other network – leave it unset

Figure 2.18 Windows TCP/IP configuration – step 3: TCP/IP properties

On Windows-NT, you don't have to reboot for the IP address and netmask settings to take effect, as long as your NT Service Packs are up to date. The settings are stored in the Windows Registry, so they are persistent – these are the values the system will use when you reboot.

(To save space in future, instead of saying "start **Control Panel > Network** … select … then click on …" we'll use the shorthand

Control Panel > Network > Protocols > TCP/IP > IP Address

to indicate the menus, selections or other items you need to select.)

In the next module we show you how you can verify that the settings you entered have really taken effect.

2.10 Verifying your settings – Windows

On earlier versions of NT, and when you have multiple network cards, and on Windows-9x systems, the settings don't take effect until you reboot. **Control Panel > Network** shows you only the stored values, which are not necessarily the settings currently in use. You can verify your settings using the **ipconfig** program (Figure 2.19). **ipconfig** shows the current values that TCP/IP is using (as opposed to settings that you have entered and may not have taken effect).

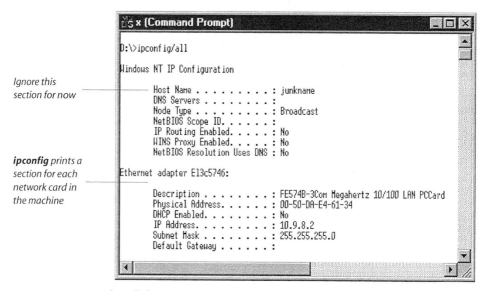

Ignore this section for now

ipconfig prints a section for each network card in the machine

```
D:\>ipconfig/all

Windows NT IP Configuration

        Host Name . . . . . . . . . : junkname
        DNS Servers . . . . . . . . :
        Node Type . . . . . . . . . : Broadcast
        NetBIOS Scope ID. . . . . . :
        IP Routing Enabled. . . . . : No
        WINS Proxy Enabled. . . . . : No
        NetBIOS Resolution Uses DNS : No

Ethernet adapter E13c5746:

        Description . . . . . . . . : FE574B-3Com Megahertz 10/100 LAN PCCard
        Physical Address. . . . . . : 00-50-DA-E4-61-34
        DHCP Enabled. . . . . . . . : No
        IP Address. . . . . . . . . : 10.9.8.2
        Subnet Mask . . . . . . . . : 255.255.255.0
        Default Gateway . . . . . . :
```

Figure 2.19 ipconfig/all shows TCP/IP settings currently in force

Windows-9x provides a similar tool called **winipcfg**, which has a graphical interface. The Windows-NT 4.0 Resource Kit contains an NT-specific version of this called **wntipcfg** (Figure 2.20). If you press on **More Info**, the display changes: the top part shows the machine-wide configuration, and the bottom part shows the settings for this particular network card (Figure 2.21).

	Windows-NT	**Windows-9x**
command-line (summary)	`ipconfig`	`ipconfig`
command-line (detailed)	`ipconfig /all`	`ipconfig /all`
command-line – help	`ipconfig /?`	`ipconfig /?`
GUI	`wntipcfg`	`winipcfg`

> **Tip:** in your Windows "Start" button, create shortcuts for **Control Panel > Network**, and for **Control Panel** itself, because you'll be using these so much.

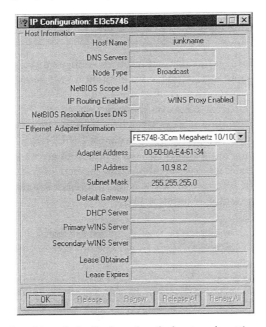

Figure 2.20 wntipcfg displays summary of network settings

Figure 2.21 wntipcfg > More Info displays detailed network settings

2.11 Lab – software configuration: Linux

On Linux you use the **ifconfig** command to **config**ure your network interface, or display the current settings. (It's called **ifconfig** and not **ipconfig** as on NT because it configures the interface and is not specific to TCP/IP – you would use it to set Novell and Appletalk parameters for your interface if you were running those networks. However, we'll use it only for TCP/IP.)

Displaying the current settings

show all interfaces in use	`ifconfig`
show details for interface *ifc* only	`ifconfig` *ifc*
show all interfaces including those that are "down"	`ifconfig -a`

(An interface that is "down" is one that has not been configured yet, or that has been explicitly disabled. You can ignore this for now – we mention it only because it explains why there is an "`-a`" option.)

ifconfig has slightly different syntax on different versions of UNIX, e.g. on some Solaris versions, **ifconfig** with no arguments prints a help message, so we've got into the habit of using only the last two variants, as they work on almost any UNIX.

Below is a typical listing for "`ifconfig -a.`" The output gives a separate section for each interface. The first Ethernet interface is called **eth0**, the next (if you have more than one) is **eth1**, then **eth2**, … The interface **lo** below is the "loopback interface" – a special name a machine uses for talking to itself (Module 4.11).

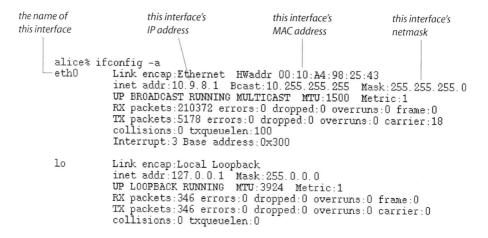

Setting your network parameters

You use "`ifconfig` *ifc*" followed by specific arguments to configure your TCP/IP settings for *ifc*. Settings take effect immediately. Like many UNIX commands, **ifconfig** is the strong silent type, and doesn't print any confirmation. It's a good idea to issue a plain "`ifconfig -a`" immediately after to check that the command did what you expected.

set the IP address	*a.b.c.d*
set the netmask	netmask *w.x.y.z*

Other options you'll need occasionally are:

disable this interface	down
re-enable this interface	up

(There are many other options but you'll probably never need them.)
   Let's look at some examples:

```
ifconfig eth0 10.9.8.1 netmask 255.255.255.0
```

   set the IP address and netmask explicitly

```
ifconfig eth0 10.9.8.1
```

   set the address of interface eth0 to 10.9.8.1. The netmask is set to the default for this IP address. As we'll see in Chapter 4, the idea of a default netmask is historical and until you become very familiar with netmasks, we recommend you always set the netmask explicitly

```
ifconfig eth1 down
```

   disable the second Ethernet interface

```
ifconfig eth1 up 192.168.168.2
```

   re-enable the second Ethernet interface and set its IP address at the same time (this type of command is common when you are building test networks)

Warning: if you make a typo when entering the IP address the first time and then correct it without specifying the netmask, the results may not be what you want or expect, for example

```
ifconfig eth0 10.9.8.111 netmask 255.255.255.0
ifconfig eth0 10.9.8.1
```

sets the IP address to 10.9.8.1 as expected, but the netmask is now 255.0.0.0, because it defaulted.

Preserving network settings across a reboot

Unlike Windows, the network parameters you define in Linux with **ifconfig** are lost when you reboot the system. To set your TCP/IP parameters permanently, you must enter them in a configuration file that the system uses at startup time. Because the location and detailed format of the config files vary with different Linux distributions, we've isolated all this Linux-version-specific information in Appendix 6.

2.12 Lab – building the simplest network possible: implement and test

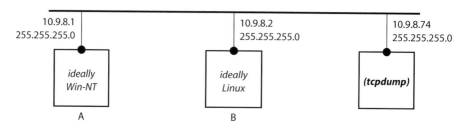

Figure 2.22 IP addresses and netmasks for simple test network

Figure 2.22 shows the network we want to build, with the IP addresses we'll allocate. We're going to configure it and then experiment with it: we'll change settings one by one, to force errors and observe the system's behavior.

If you are already running **tcpdump** on A or B, you can omit the separate **tcpdump** machine. If you include a sniffer machine in the network, it doesn't need any particular IP address because it's only sniffing the network in promiscuous mode and doesn't have to send anything or receive anything in the normal way. As long as its TCP/IP is up and running, it will work. However, if you set its parameters as shown, you can use it as another host on the LAN to perform tests from, which will be useful.

As we mentioned in Module 2.2, the three crucial networking parameters are IP address, netmask, and default gateway. (The default gateway is concerned with routing to other networks. We have only a single network here, so we don't need the default gateway at all in this chapter; we defer explaining it until the next chapter.)

- we have chosen IP addresses in the 10.x.x.x range because they are specially reserved for use on private networks and are not allocated to any specific site (Module 4.9). We've chosen the series 10.9.8.x as it's easy to remember
- don't use addresses 10.9.8.0 or 10.9.8.255 – they are special (Module 4.10) and using them may cause you problems
- we have chosen netmask 255.255.255.0, giving a range consisting of the 256 IP addresses that have the same first three bytes as the machine's IP address:

	IP address	Range derived from IP address combined with 255.255.255.0 netmask
A	10.9.8.1	10.9.8.0–10.9.8.255
B	10.9.8.2	10.9.8.0–10.9.8.255

which is what we want – both machines have the same view of the world

- we have shown the PCs in the diagram without any names but marked as A and B to make it easy to refer to them in the text. You don't have to set the machine name, but if it is set, it doesn't matter.

Making deliberate errors to observe the symptoms

This test network is almost trivial. Its value is that you can force different types of errors and observe the symptoms and any error messages that are produced. The network is a toy but the diagnostic techniques are real, and will give you confidence for working on your real network.

First, start "`tcpdump -n -e -t`" on your sniffer box. Then:

1. Change one system, ideally a Windows-NT machine ("A" in Figure 2.22), to have the same IP address as B (10.9.8.2).

   – what packets do you see on the network? Do you think this machine is making any attempt to see whether the address it's setting to is a duplicate?

   – do you get any error messages on the screen or in the event log?

   – what happens when you **ping** B from A?

   – what happens when you **ping** A from B?

2. Change A's IP address back to its correct value. Are the systems operating correctly now?

   – if necessary, re-boot one or both machines, with their correct IP addresses

3. Change B's IP address to 10.9.8.1 (assuming it has a different operating system to A's) and repeat (1) above.

   – if necessary, re-boot one or both machines, with their IP correct addresses, as before

4. Change A's IP address to 10.3.2.100. Now it has a different view of the world than B: it thinks the range on its network is 10.3.2.0–10.3.2.255, so A and B can't see each other.

   – what happens when you **ping** B from A?

   – what happens when you **ping** A from B?

5. Change B's IP address to 10.3.2.200. The machines ought to be working correctly again.

6. Change A's netmask to 255.255.0.0, and its address to 10.3.66.200. The network is:

	IP address	Netmask	Range derived from IP address and netmask
A	10.3.2.100	255.255.255.0	10.3.2.0–10.3.2.255
B	10.3.66.200	255.255.0.0	10.3.0.0–10.3.255.255

   Now B can see A, but A can't see B because A's IP address/netmask combination is telling her that 10.3.66.200 is on a different network.

   – what happens when you **ping** B from A?

   – what happens when you **ping** A from B?

7. Set the IP address and netmask on A and B back to their original values.

On Windows-NT you may get "hardware error" messages from **ping** when this PC has been given the same IP address as another. This is misleading – it's not a hardware error, but it does indicate that there is some problem.

2.13 How to diagnose a problem with your network: hop by hop and step by step

This chapter has dealt with networking over a single hop, between two local machines. This is the fundamental mechanism by which *all* our network communication is achieved: communicating with a remove machine on the Internet is made up of lots of hops, with each hop consisting of a conversation between two local machines. Once you're able to diagnose a simple network, you can scale up your experience and apply it to very big networks too: you diagnose each hop in turn, almost in isolation, until you find a problem.

Checking that A and B can communicate over the local LAN

(Here we're dealing only with basic IP connectivity. We'll cover how to troubleshoot routing and application-level issues in later chapters.)

We assume that you are running **tcpdump** on a separate sniffer machine, that you know it is working, that its network card is working in promiscuous mode, and that you can see packets on the wire.

0. from one PC, **ping** the other, by IP number. If **ping** prints replies, the connection is OK. Otherwise, on each PC:

1. run "`ifconfig -a`" (Linux) or "`ipconfig/all`" (Windows) and check that the currently active TCP/IP settings are what you expected (on Windows don't use the **Control Panel > Network** in case you are not up to date on Service Packs and the machine needs to be rebooted for the settings to take effect)

2. if you have a third PC on the network (as you will in real life), **ping** it. If **ping** doesn't print any replies for it either, the chances are that your own PC is the one with the problem. You still need to go through the steps below, but you already know the probable (not "definite") location of the problem

3. check the "link" indicator light for each PC on the UTP hub. If the light is off, you have a cable problem to fix

4. **ping** 127.0.0.1, the "loopback" address of this machine (Module 4.11 covers this in detail; it's a special IP address that means "myself"). If **ping** doesn't print replies, the TCP/IP installation on this PC is broken

5. **ping** this PC's own normal (non-loopback) IP number. If **ping** doesn't print replies, either your TCP/IP is broken, or you need to reboot, or this machine's IP number is different from what you think. If **tcpdump** shows any packets on the wire for this **ping**, you have the wrong address because packets from a machine to itself never appear on the wire

6. **ping** B's address (10.9.8.2 in our example). If **tcpdump** doesn't show an ARP "who-has 10.9.8.2" on the wire, then:

    a. run "arp -a -n" (Linux) or "arp -a" (NT) and see whether this machine has an ARP cache entry for 10.9.8.2. If it has, delete it (using "arp -d 10.9.8.2")

    b. at this point we "know" we don't have an ARP entry for 10.9.8.2, but run "arp -a -n" (Linux) or "arp -a" (NT) again to make sure

c. **ping** 10.9.8.2 again. If **tcpdump** doesn't show an ARP "who-has 10.9.8.2" (NB: make sure that is the IP address shown), then this machine doesn't think 10.9.8.2 is on the same wire: either this machine's IP address is *not* 10.9.8.1, or else its netmask is wrong. Check both

d. if **tcpdump** showed an ARP "who-has", but for a different IP address, say 10.9.8.99, this machine not only thinks that 10.9.8.2 is on a different network but also that it has a router. In real life you could clear the default gateway setting for this machine, but we haven't told you how to do that yet (at least, not on Linux). However, if you go back one step and ensure the IP address and netmask are correct, then the setting for the default gateway won't matter.

Remember, you must repeat the steps for each PC to find out exactly where the problem lies (e.g. if you go through all the steps for PC A but not for B, the fault could be as simple as a broken cable on B).

Exercise: using the network you built in the previous module (Figure 2.23), try each of the following, and see what **ping** and **tcpdump** show in each case:

- disconnect A from the hub

- re-connect A and disconnect B

- re-connect B. Try to set A's IP address to 10.9.8.0. Then try the same on B if he has a different operating system (remember we said in Module 2.12 that addresses 10.9.8.0 and 10.9.8.255 are special)

- try to set A's IP address to 10.9.8.255. Then try the same on B if he has a different operating system.

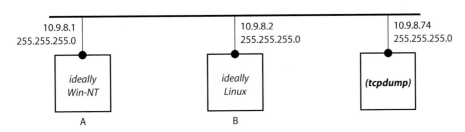

Figure 2.23 The network we built in module 2.12

Summary

- two of the three fundamental networking parameters are:
  1. the IP address is used to specify the destination machine for a packet
  2. the netmask combined with my machine's IP address specifies a range of IP addresses which my machine believes are locally connected to it. If a destination IP address is outside the range, my machine knows it can't send to it without going through a router (which we haven't covered yet)
- to send to a destination machine on the directly connected Ethernet LAN, my PC has first to find out the Ethernet address of the destination, so it can address and send the Ethernet packet correctly. It does this by using the ARP protocol. My PC broadcasts, asking which machine has the destination IP address, and that machine replies, giving its MAC address. The two machines can then communicate using IP. The **arp** command lets you view and manipulate your machine's cache of ARP entries
- on Windows use **Control Panel > Network** to configure the network settings, and **ipconfig** or **wntipcfg** to check them
- on Linux use **ifconfig** both to configure and to check the settings
- the useful **ping** program lets you check basic connectivity very easily and is an easy way to generate test traffic.

What's next?

In this chapter we restricted ourselves to networking on a single LAN – single-hop networking. The next chapter extends the capabilities of our networks. We go beyond the simple, single Ethernet segment we've used so far to wide area networking – by allowing routing. We look at how intermediate routers send the packets ("route the packets") across the many hops on the network between the source machine and the final destination. Just as importantly, we'll also see that each hop is just like the simple two-machine network we've just covered, so our diagnostic techniques will apply equally well.

Notes and further reading

We've said that the three fundamental network parameters are IP address, netmask, and default gateway router. A fourth important parameter is the address of the DNS servers that this machine should use, but as you'll see in Chapter 7, that comes into play only at a higher level. A machine can function perfectly well without using the DNS, but if the three fundamental parameters are wrong your machine will never get as far as the DNS. That's why the DNS configuration isn't as fundamentally important as the other three parameters.

We dealt only with a two-machine network in our examples in this chapter. Expanding your tiny network from two machines to many is trivial – you just connect them in exactly the way we did. Be careful that the netmasks on all machines are the same and that you don't allocate the same IP number to more than one machine.

In Module 2.12 we deliberately excluded the .0 and .255 addresses and said they are special. We'll cover that in Module 4.10.

Ethernet and other network access layer systems

The term "frame" is used as a specific term for a *hardware packet*, i.e. a packet handled by Ethernet (or other hardware) in contrast to the packet that IP passes down to the Ethernet hardware for transmission, which is called an *IP datagram*. However, we use the term "packet" for both as the distinction isn't important to us.

Our diagram of an Ethernet packet in Module 2.3 was over-simplified. There are many other header fields in the Ethernet packet, and fields used for checksums. We don't need that level of detail, but if you want to explore in depth, see Stevens, Chapter 2.

Many low-level networking standards are defined by the IEEE (**http://www.ieee.org**), including:

802.2	defines the link layer common to 802.3, 802.5 and many other standards
802.3	"Ethernet" (but see below)
802.5	token ring
802.11	wireless LANs (WLANs)
802.11b	11-Mb/s WLANs
802.11a	54-Mb/s WLANs
802.15	wireless personal area networks (WPANs), e.g. how your cell phone and PDA and page might inter-communicate
802.16	broadband wireless

IEEE 802.3 is loosely referred to as Ethernet but in fact differs slightly from "true" Ethernet, which was defined by Digital, Intel and Xerox (and is sometimes called *DIX* as a result). There's a small difference in the internal packet layout, although the two systems can co-exist on the same wire and can usually inter-operate also. We only ever had to worry about the difference once – on an AIX machine – so we won't discuss it further. If you want more information, see

❏ **RFC-894 April 1984** *A Standard for the Transmission of IP Datagrams over Ethernet Networks*

❏ **RFC-1042 February 1988** *A Standard for the Transmission of IP Datagrams over IEEE 802 Networks*

and for a comparison see Stevens, section 2.2 and Perlman, section 2.10.

The IEEE also allocates Ethernet MAC addresses. You can query or view the list of allocated blocks of addresses at, respectively:

❏ **http://standards.ieee.org/regauth/oui/index.shtml**

❏ **http://standards.ieee.org/regauth/oui/oui.txt**

In the main text we've implicitly assumed that the MAC address is hard-wired into the network interface card. While this is true, many cards allow the operating system to change the MAC address; fortunately, Windows and Linux systems don't do this.

IP using carrier pigeons

It has often been said that TCP/IP will run over wet string.

❏ **RFC-1149 1 April 1990** *IP Datagrams on Avian Carriers*

describes how TCP/IP can use carrier pigeons as transmission hardware. The Bergen Linux user group implemented this "standard" and a description of its work, with photographs and timings for **ping**s, is at:

❏ **http://www.blug.linux.no/rfc1149/**

❏ **http://www.blug.linux.no/rfc1149/pinglogg.txt**

ARP

We've described ARP only in the context of an Ethernet but it's not limited to that – it works with token ring and other network types as well. ARP lets us use IP addresses exclusively and forget about MAC address, at a cost of a tiny amount of broadcasting. Perlman (Chapter 11) covers different ways of handling this issue. Or, you *could* design a network system that didn't need ARP, by broadcasting every packet. This would work, but performance would be dreadful.

However, broadcasting has it uses. As we'll see in Chapter 16, DHCP traffic between client and server *does* use broadcasts extensively; since a machine uses DHCP only at boot time, it imposes no significant load. Some other special-purpose networking applications use broadcasts exclusively: one example we've seen is a "find-my-device" application for a hardware firewall appliance. If we receive a firewall back from a customer without knowing what the IP address is, we can run this program. It broadcasts a special packet using a proprietary protocol. The firewall hears this and broadcasts a reply. This communication works no matter what the IP address and netmask setting are on our PC or on the appliance – perfect for a diagnostic tool, and negligible performance impact as only two packets are exchanged in total.

As an interesting aside on how **tcpdump** can give you insights into your network, if you run it as "**tcpdump -n -e arp**" for a few days, you can process the output (e.g. with a Perl script) and automatically construct a list of (IP number, MAC address) mappings. We keep a recent copy of this list on the wall above our desk.

ARP has a variant called "proxy ARP," where one device sends the ARP reply on behalf of another. This is useful in firewalling (Chapter 24) and dial-up networking (Chapter 26) where we'll explain it further. For RARP ("reverse ARP"), formerly used for automatically assigning an IP address to a diskless workstation, see the Notes in Chapter 16.

For more on ARP, see Stevens, Chapter 4.

ping

You can recognize **ping** packets sent from Windows systems because they contain the string **abc … uvw** repeated as often as necessary to pad out to the full length of the packet. Normally you can't see this – you have to use **tcpdump**'s "**-X**" option (uppercase X, dump contents in decimal).

ping is useful for tracking down cabling problems, e.g. a loose connector or flaky cable:

- continuously **ping** a machine that shows up the problem – so that some or all of the **ping**s are not replied to

- then wiggle or check or replace each connector or piece of cable on the suspect run

- when the **ping** output suddenly changes to show successful responses, you know you've found the fault (or one of the faults).

For this to work, you have to be able to notice what **ping** is outputting, so you may need an accomplice to watch the screen while you play with your cables. To get over this, the BSD UNIX version of **ping** has an -a (audible) option that beeps every time a response is received, so you can hear what's happening even if you're crawling in a cable duct under the floor. To disable replying to incoming **ping**s, use the command:

```
echo 1 > /proc/sys/net/ipv4/icmp_echo_ignore_broadcasts
```

"**ping**" doesn't stand for Packet Internet Groper, in spite of what manual pages say. For the real origins of **ping**, see:

❏ **http://ftp.arl.mil/~mike/ping.html** *The Story of the PING Program* written by the late Mike Muuss, the man who invented **ping**.

There is a lovely children's book called *The Story about Ping*, by Marjorie Flack, about a duck called Ping who lived on the beautiful Yangtze river. For two amusing reviews of this (written by computer folk) see the reference above, or:

❏ **http://www.kohala.com/start/papers.others/ping.amazon.html**

(Just in case the URL changes, search for "Using deft allegory, the authors have provided an insightful and intuitive" for one review, and "Melissa Rondeau from Braintree" for the other.)

ifconfig

The Linux help message for the command says it accepts flags "**-i**" and "**-v**" but if you look at the source code you see they don't do anything. It also says you can use the "CIDR" notation for netmasks, which we cover in Module 4.5, so that these two commands ought to be equivalent:

```
ifconfig eth0 10.9.8.1 netmask 255.255.255.0
ifconfig eth0 10.9.8.1/24
```

but in fact the second one doesn't work properly on many versions of Linux so we never use it.

The "if" in **ifconfig** stands for "interface." In casual conversation this is often used as synonymous with "network card" (NIC), but that's not strictly true. In fact you can define multiple "interfaces" on one NIC, as well as having multiple NICs. This facility is called IP aliasing in Linux. Web Appendix 8 explains how this can be used to assign different functions – e.g. web server, mail server – to different IP addresses on a single machine to simplify expansion and load sharing as your network grows. It was also used widely to provide multiple instances of a Web server on a single machine before the HTTP/1.1 **Host:** header was invented (Module 14.6). Windows-NT (but not Windows-9x) provides the same IP aliasing facility, on the **Advanced** button in the **TCP/IP Properties** (Module 6.3).

Hardware problems and software bugs

Perhaps the most frustrating problem to meet is where you've configured everything correctly but the system still doesn't work properly, because of problems in the hardware or operating system. These *do* happen, alas:

- on a laptop bought from a nasty UK discount supplier, the PCMCIA hardware system has a bug. If you boot the system in Windows-9x, and then reboot in Linux or Windows-NT, the PCMCIA card becomes invisible. You have to power-cycle the machine. We lost a day and a half on this one

  ❏ **http://bugzilla.redhat.com/bugzilla/show_bug.cgi?id=212**

- Alice was sending packets and other machines were responding, but Alice never processed them. (You could see the packets with **tcpdump**, but Alice just ignored them. The only packets coming from Alice were for actions that she initiated – all ARP requests in fact.) The solution (only an hour lost!) was the network card hadn't been inserted correctly. It was only half-inserted, at an angle – the receive pins on the card weren't making contact with the socket on the motherboard, but the transmit pins were

- on a Windows-NT laptop we saw the same symptoms. This time it was solved by re-installing the latest version of the PCMCIA card drivers

- again on a Windows-NT laptop, where we had two PCMCIA cards, one of them didn't work, but without any explanation or error message. In this case we had to change the hardware IRQ setting for one of the cards, because it was clashing with some other device.

The best ways we've found to minimize time wasted on this type of problem are:

- if you're doing something new (new to you, that is), use hardware and software that are as common as possible. When you know what you're doing, you can try out odd-ball network cards, weird OEM PCs, etc.

- buy hardware from suppliers who give good support and don't leave you holding for hours on "press 1 for new problem, press …" voicemail systems. We use a local supplier and the support we get more than makes up for the few percent extra we pay

- if you need Windows, use Windows 2000 or XP or NT if you can afford to. Otherwise, use Windows-98 or whatever it's called now. If you're still using Windows-95 it's your own fault.

Appendices

Appendix 3: Ethernet hubs and switches
Appendix 6: making network settings permanent – Debian Linux

3

Basic routing – how packets move from this network to another network connected to it

Introduction

In Chapter 2 you built the simplest possible network – two or more PCs on the same Ethernet segment. Now we're going to build the simplest routed network – two PCs, each on its own LAN, connected via an intermediate router. We use a Linux or Windows-NT box with two network cards as the router, so that you can easily reproduce our test network, and do hands-on routing configuration. While routing has a complex task to perform, it breaks down into a few simple steps.

3.1 The fundamental IP routing decision

So far we have explained how to build only a simple network, where all the machines are connected directly and packets travel over a single hop. (By "connected directly" or "connected locally" we mean the machines are on the same Ethernet segment – on the same wire – so they can exchange data using Ethernet transmission.) That's fine for a stand-alone LAN but for large networks we need a lot more. We will want to use multiple segments – because we're adding many machines and have to meet certain network performance criteria, or because the network is extending over an increasingly large area, or we want to connect to other existing networks.

In this chapter we'll set up the simple inter-network shown in Figure 3.1. We'll explain how communication between Alice and Bob is made up of a series of individual hops, one after the other. Multiple hops allows us to build much bigger networks (e.g. the small inter-network shown in Figure 3.2, or of course the Internet itself). However, the fact that each hop is still between two directly connected machines allows us to diagnose each link separately, using all the same techniques that we use on a simple, single-hop network.

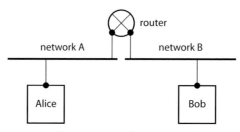

Figure 3.1 A simple inter-network consisting of two networks

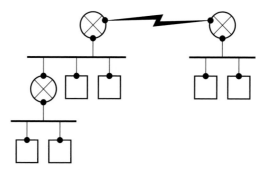

Figure 3.2 A large inter-network consisting of three networks

Send directly or via a router?

When Alice is sending to Bob, how does she make the fundamental decision of whether she can do it all herself (i.e. send to Bob on the local Ethernet) or has to rely on the services of a router? Alice's TCP/IP executes the following:

```
if (I, Alice, am directly connected to Bob)
        send the packet on the local wire (using ARP if necessary)
else
        pass the packet on to a router on the local wire, that
        knows how to forward the packet on towards its final
        destination
```

Two questions arise out of this. First, how does Alice decide what is or isn't directly connected? Second, how do you tell a router to forward a packet?

Which machines are connected directly to this one?

The combination of Alice's netmask and IP address specifies the range of addresses that Alice is connected to directly. We explain this in detail in the next chapter but for now let's just consider a simple example. My netmask is 255.255.255.0: this specifies a set of IP addresses with the same first three bytes. If my IP address is 192.0.2.7, the range is

192.0.2.0 . . . 192.0.2.255

which is a range of 256 addresses. (Note that it is the *combination* of the netmask and IP address that determines the range exactly. Using the netmask on its own says only how big the range will be, but not the actual IP addresses it contains.)

We can therefore re-write the routing decision above, made on Alice's machine, as:

```
calculate my range from my IP address and my netmask
if (Bob's IP address is in my range)
        send the packet on the local wire (using ARP if necessary)
else
        pass the packet on to a router …
```

It's important to remember that the netmask is *not* included in the packet. Alice's machine uses the netmask on her machine, and Bob uses the netmask on his machine. If machines Alice and Bob are on the same network, they usually ought to have the same netmask; if they are different, this will almost certainly cause problems.

Forwarding a packet via a router

If the destination machine isn't connected directly the packet must be sent via a router. The netmask doesn't tell Alice which router to use; some other mechanism is needed for that (Chapter 5), which can be as simple as a manually configured table. However, most LAN machines can make do with a single "default gateway" router; we cover that, and define what a router really is, in Module 3.3.

But first, in the next module we explain how we use a router to forward the packet once we have decided that the machine we are sending to isn't connected directly.

3.2 Telling a router to forward a packet

If Alice isn't connected directly to Bob, she has to pass the packet to a router and ask it to forward the packet towards Bob (Figure 3.3). (We say "towards Bob" because Alice doesn't know where Bob is, except that he is on the far side of the router. She doesn't know whether the router is connected directly to Bob, or whether it will have to pass the packet on to another router, etc.)

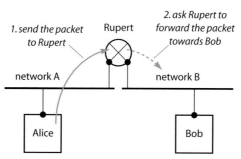

Figure 3.3 Forwarding a packet via a router

Forwarding a packet via a router is very simple. The router, Rupert, is connected directly to Alice, so she can send an Ethernet packet to him by specifying his Ethernet address as the destination, as we explained in Module 2.3.

At the IP level, however, the packet's final destination is Bob, not Rupert. Therefore, Alice sets the IP destination address (as opposed to the Ethernet destination) to Bob's IP. The result is a packet with addressing that looks like that in Figure 3.4.

	src	dst
MAC	Alice's Ethernet address	Rupert's Ethernet address
IP	Alice's IP address	Bob's IP address

Figure 3.4 Alice to Bob, via router

	src	dst
MAC	Alice's Ethernet address	Bob's Ethernet address
IP	Alice's IP address	Bob's IP address

Figure 3.5 Alice to Bob, directly connected

Several points are worth emphasizing:

- source addresses: the Ethernet and IP both relate to Alice as before (Module 2.3)
- destination addresses: the Ethernet is Rupert's, but the IP address is Bob's. The Ethernet destination in the packet deals with this hop only, whereas the IP destination is the ultimate destination of the packet
- when a router receives a packet with an IP address that isn't one of its own, this is an implicit request to forward the packet towards the packet's destination. That's how IP routing works: there's no magic "this is a special routing request" mechanism or protocol

- a machine can only forward packets to routers that are connected to it directly, because sending to a router and sending to a directly connected host uses exactly the same mechanism – transmission over Ethernet. Therefore:
  - if there are no routers on Alice's network (or if she doesn't know about them), she can't send to any machines outside her network
  - in Figure 3.5, Alice (A) can't forward packets to router Y because it's not directly connected. A can forward only to router X, which in turn may (or may not, depending on its configuration) decide to forward via router Y
  - a router also can pass packets only to hosts or routers that are on a network directly connected to it; therefore, for a router to be useful, it must be connected to more than one network (that's no surprise, because that's almost the definition of what a router is)
- packets travel across the network in hops:
  - each hop is on an Ethernet (or other networking hardware) segment
  - each hop is source-host-to-router, or router-to-router, or router-to-destination-host

  It is because TCP/IP communication is hop-to-hop that we can diagnose it so easily using **tcpdump**. We can check out each hop in turn until we find the one causing the problem.

Let's compare the packet we showed above with the packet that would have been used if Bob was connected directly to Alice (Figure 3.5). The only difference is the destination Ethernet address (which we've highlighted in black type). The payload in each case (which we haven't shown) is the IP data.

It took us about two years to realize that this is how IP routing works, and how simple it really is. If you understand the two packet diagrams above, you've learned a lot. In Figure 3.6 you can see how the Ethernet addresses in the packet change from hop to hop. On router-to-router hops (e.g. X-to-Y) neither of the Ethernet addresses is Alice's or Bob's. By contrast, the IP source destination addresses remain unaltered throughout. (**X'** and **X"** denote machine X's left and right NICs, respectively.)

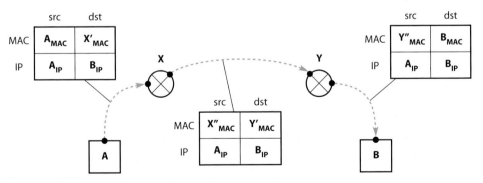

Figure 3.6 Ethernet addresses change from hop to hop

3.3 The third crucial networking parameter: default gateway router

A router is a general-purpose computer or specially built box with two or more network interfaces that forwards packets from one network to another. A router always has multiple interfaces or network cards, because its function is to exchange packets between two or more networks. For a typical small LAN connected to the Internet, one of the router interfaces is Ethernet, and the other is whatever network hardware the leased line or ISDN or ADSL Internet connection uses (Figure 3.7).

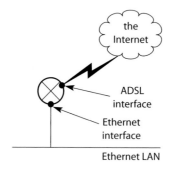

Figure 3.7 Router's ADSL interface connects to the Internet, Ethernet to the LAN

A router doesn't have to be a special-purpose box like a Cisco or a Lucent or whatever – any box that routes is a router. We'll use an NT or Linux box as a router, so we can see exactly what's happening.

The previous module explained how Alice can forward a packet towards Bob using a router, but not how Alice finds out about routers that are on her network, and how she chooses which one to use. How that is done in general can be very complex (see Chapter 5), but there is a much simpler mechanism – the "default gateway" router – that is adequate for most machines on a LAN. That's what we'll cover in the rest of this chapter.

A machine's *default gateway* is a router that this machine uses to forward packets if it does not know how else to send them. If Alice wants to send to Bob, TCP/IP on her machine executes the following:

```
if (Bob is directly connected to me)
        send the packet on the local wire (using ARP if necessary)
else /* assuming this is a typical LAN machine with only a
        default gateway route */
        use my default gateway to forward the packet on
        towards its final destination
```

This is typical of how a LAN PC is configured: it knows about its own LAN and the default gateway only. (When it comes to sending a packet to a remote destination, the LAN PC says "I don't know how to send the packet myself, but I know a man who does, so I'll pass it over to him.")

If a machine doesn't have a default gateway, the machine can only send to machines that are connected directly on the LAN. For any other addresses, it can't process the packet and gives an error such as "network is unreachable" (Linux) or "destination host unreachable" (NT).

From the network administrator's point of view, the great benefit of the default gateway router is that it keeps the TCP/IP configuration of most LAN machines very simple – they don't have to know about the detailed layout of your internal network or the Internet. All of the complexity can be isolated in your main Internet router and the LAN machines use it as their default gateway. So all your machines (on a simple LAN, or all the machines on one Ethernet segment in a more complex LAN) have the same default gateway, and if you're using DHCP (Chapter 16) you can even have machines automatically configure themselves by retrieving their default gateway setting from a central server.

Figure 3.8 shows a network that is typical of a small or medium-sized organization:

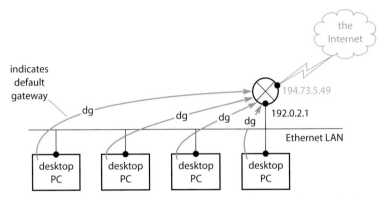

Figure 3.8 Typical network configuration for a small/medium-sized organization

- there is only a single Ethernet segment, and no internal routers
- there is a single router that is the gateway to the Internet
- the router is owned and managed by the ISP; you don't have to configure it
- your ISP allocates a range of IP addresses for you to use on your LAN. The ISP configures the near-side address of the router with an address from the allocated range. For this it typically uses the lowest or highest non-special IP address in the range, e.g. *a.b.c.*1 or *a.b.c.*254 in a 256-address range
- the netmask you use on your LAN machines is the one the ISP allocated to you.

Configuring your LAN machines for this network is very simple. For each machine:

1. set its IP address to an unused IP address from the allocated range
2. configure the netmask to the netmask your ISP gave you
3. set the default gateway to be near-side address of the Internet router.

For each machine, you are configuring the three fundamental networking parameters – IP address, netmask and default gateway. That's all you have to do. (Here we are concerned only with the routing aspects; in Chapter 23 we tell you in detail how to set up this type of network, including the security features that you *will* need but aren't shown in Figure 3.8.) So now you understand what's involved in basic LAN-to-Internet connectivity – progress indeed!

3.4 Setting your default gateway – Windows-NT

1. select **Control Panel** > **Network** > **Protocols** > **TCP/IP** > **Properties**, to give you the **TCP/IP Properties** window
2. enter the IP address of your default gateway in the dialog (Figure 3.9)
3. click on **Apply** or **OK**. The **Apply** button grays out after you press it (or if there are no changes to be applied.)

Specify an IP address
IP Address: 192 . 0 . 2 . 35
Subnet Mask: 255 . 255 . 255 . 0
Default Gateway: 192 . 0 . 2 . 1
Advanced...
OK
Cancel
Apply

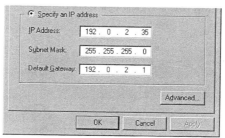

Figure 3.9 Specifying 192.0.2.1 as your default gateway

The settings take effect immediately and are permanent – they persist across reboots. You can check the current setting in two ways:

1. using **ipconfig/all** as we mentioned in Module 2.10 (Figure 3.10)

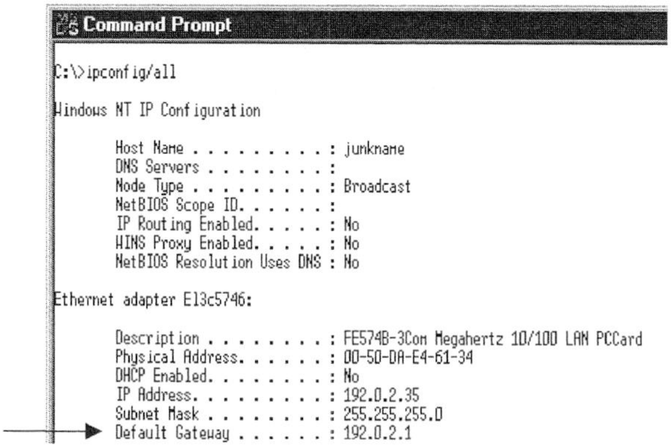

Command Prompt
C:\>ipconfig/all
Windows NT IP Configuration
Host Name . . . . : junkname
DNS Servers . . . . :
Node Type . . . . : Broadcast
NetBIOS Scope ID. . . . . . :
IP Routing Enabled. . . . . : No
WINS Proxy Enabled. . . . . : No
NetBIOS Resolution Uses DNS : No
Ethernet adapter E13c5746:
Description . . . . : FE574B-3Com Megahertz 10/100 LAN PCCard
Physical Address. . . . . . : 00-50-DA-E4-61-34
DHCP Enabled. . . . . : No
IP Address. . . . . : 192.0.2.35
Subnet Mask . . . . : 255.255.255.0
Default Gateway . . . . . . : 192.0.2.1

Figure 3.10 Using **ipconfig/all** to verify your default gateway setting

2. at the Command Prompt, run the command

```
route print
```

This gives a lot of information (Figure 3.11). For now, the only line you're interested in is the one that has the **Network Destination** set to 0.0.0.0 – that means your default gateway. On this line the **Gateway** field ought to be the value you set in the **Control Panel** > **Network**

We've shown the **route** command as well as **ipconfig** because we'll use route to set and display the default gateway on Linux in the next Module and it's nice to be able to use the same command on both systems. (We cover **route** in a lot more detail in Chapter 5.)

```
  Command Prompt

C:\>route print
=================================================================
Interface List
0x1 ......................... MS TCP Loopback interface
0x2 ...00 50 da e4 61 34 ...... FE574B-3Com Megahertz 10/100 LAN PCCard
0x3 ...00 00 00 00 00 00 ...... NdisWan Adapter
0x4 ...00 00 00 00 00 00 ...... NdisWan Adapter
=================================================================

Active Routes:
Network Destination        Netmask          Gateway       Interface  Metric
        0.0.0.0          0.0.0.0        192.0.2.1      192.0.2.35      1
      127.0.0.0        255.0.0.0        127.0.0.1      127.0.0.1       1
      192.0.2.0    255.255.255.0        192.0.2.35     192.0.2.35      1
     192.0.2.35  255.255.255.255        127.0.0.1      127.0.0.1       1
    192.0.2.255  255.255.255.255        192.0.2.35     192.0.2.35      1
      224.0.0.0        224.0.0.0        192.0.2.35     192.0.2.35      1
255.255.255.255  255.255.255.255        192.0.2.35     192.0.2.35      1
```

Figure 3.11 Using **route print** to verify your default gateway setting

The **ipconfig** and **Control Panel > Network** outputs make it look as though the default gateway is specific to an interface. It's not – it applies to the machine as a whole. It really belongs in the routing parameters, not the interface parameters, and the **route** listing makes this much more obvious. (We touch on this again in Module 5.9.)

Common errors

Your default gateway does not belong to one of the configured interfaces (from **TCP/IP Properties > Advanced > Add...** window)

The IP address you specified as the default gateway isn't in the address range directly connected to this machine, as specified by this machine's IP address and netmask. For example, if this is 192.0.2.35 netmask 255.255.255.0 the gateway address must be in the range

192.0.2.1–192.0.2.254

(which excludes .0 and .255 because they're special).

However, while this message and explanation is listed in the NT 4.0 Resource Kit docs, we've never seen it displayed, and in fact **Control Panel > Network** applet lets you *enter* impossible values for the default gateway address without complaint, although it doesn't *set* it – if you then run **ipconfig/all** or **Control Panel > Network** you will see that there is no default gateway set: the default gateway is shown as blank (and **route print** has no entry for destination 0.0.0.0).

Tip: whenever you change your TCP/IP parameters, run an **ipconfig/all** to double-check that the changes made are what you actually intended.

3.5 Setting your default gateway – Linux

Windows treats setting your default gateway as a special case and provides an easy way to do it via the **Control Panel > Network** applet, which you saw in the previous module. What you didn't see (and which we'll cover in detail in Chapter 5) is that on Windows you use the **route** program to set other, non-default routes. (A *route* is an entry telling TCP/IP that a particular range of IP addresses can be reached by a specific router.) Linux uses the **route** program for displaying and setting the default gateway as well as any other routes.

To display the current default gateway setting:
Enter the command

```
route -n
```

> **Warning:** if you omit the "-n" option, **route** will try to convert the numeric addresses in its listing to hostnames, using the DNS (which we haven't yet configured, and don't cover until Chapter 7).

If nobody has ever defined a default gateway for this machine (and people usually do specify one when Linux is being installed), you will get a listing with a heading line and one data line:

```
alice% route -n
Kernel IP routing table
Destination     Gateway        Genmask         Flags Metric Ref    Use Iface
192.0.2.0       0.0.0.0        255.255.255.0   U     0      0        0 eth0
```

If there is a default gateway already set, it's shown as Destination 0.0.0.0 just like on Windows:

```
alice% route -n
Kernel IP routing table
Destination     Gateway        Genmask         Flags Metric Ref    Use Iface
192.0.2.0       0.0.0.0        255.255.255.0   U     0      0        0 eth0
0.0.0.0         192.0.2.1      0.0.0.0         UG    0      0        0 eth0
```

The **route** command directly interrogates the operating system's internal routing tables, so whatever it prints is what is currently being used. (The values are not stored in a file, or in a registry like on Windows, so there is no way a difference can arise between the settings displayed and the settings currently in use.)

To display help for the route command:

full help message	`route -?`
	`route -h`
	`route --help`
help for IP-related commands only	`route -h -A inet`
	`route -h --inet`

To set the default gateway:
Use the **route add** command. For example, to set the default gateway to 192.0.2.1, enter:

```
route add default gw 192.0.2.1
```

As with so many UNIX commands, this is of the strong silent type, and unless you made some error in typing it in, it prints nothing and just returns you to the command prompt. If you want to check that it has done what you expected (always a good idea with **route** commands, even when you've had years of experience), run "`route -n`" to print the new settings.

The various parts of this command are:

add   we're adding a new route, not just displaying the settings, or deleting an existing route

default we're defining the default gateway. In fact **default** is just a shorthand for "`-net 0.0.0.0`" so you could instead have entered the command as

```
route add -net 0.0.0.0 gw 192.0.2.1
```

(We'll explain the "`-net`" in Chapter 5. Don't worry about it for now.)

gw   this keyword indicates that the following argument is the IP address of the router. The **route** command uses keywords like this to introduce values because, as you can see if you print the help message, you can set lots of different values for routes. Note that the words "**default gw**," which occur together in the command are *not* the phrase "default gateway," even though it looks that way. This will be even clearer in Chapter 5 where you'll see commands like

```
route add -net 10.5.0.0 netmask 255.255.0.0 gw 192.168.13.28
```

Common errors

network is unreachable

The router you've specified as the default gateway isn't in the range of IP addresses specified by this machine's IP address and netmask. For example, if your IP address is 192.0.2.34 with netmask 255.255.255.0 and you enter the command

```
route add default gw 1.2.3.4
```

you'll get the "network is unreachable" error.

SIOCADDRT: Operation not supported by device

You get this error if you omit the **gw** keyword before the IP address, as in

```
route add default 192.0.2.29
```

This is very easy to do if you're used to other UNIX systems where the syntax of the **route** command is slightly different.

Making your settings permanent

Just like the **ifconfig** settings that we covered in Module 2.11, your Linux default gateway setting defined with **route add** is lost when you reboot the system, so you must store them in a configuration file. See Appendix 6.

3.6 Lab – building the simplest possible inter-network (1)

The simplest network we can build that still includes a router consists of two separate Ethernet networks with a single router connecting them. We use a PC running either Linux or Windows-NT as the router. There are three steps:

1. cable the network
2. configure Rupert to act as a router
3. set the network parameters as shown in Figure 3.12.

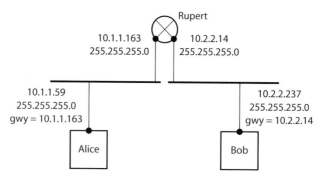

Figure 3.12 Network parameters for simple inter-network

1. Cabling up your test network

The best way to cable up is to use two hubs, one for the network on the left, containing Alice and one side of the router, and a second for the right-hand network containing Bob and the other side of the router. This makes it easy to move your sniffer machine from one side to the other as necessary. (If you have the right equipment, you could use two network cards in your sniffer, and connect one to the left network and the other to the right; then you could run two separate copies of **tcpdump** on the same machine, and monitor both networks simultaneously.)

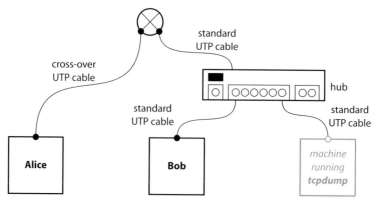

Figure 3.13 Cabling with only one hub and a cross-over cable

Alternatively, if you have only one hub, you can cable up as shown in Figure 3.13, and connect one machine directly to the router using a cross-over UTP cable (Appendix 7) instead of a hub. The disadvantage of using a cross-over cable is that you can't patch in your sniffer easily – it can only link exactly two devices and no more.

2. Configuring a machine to act as a router

To configure Windows-NT to act as a router

1. in **Control Panel** > **Network** > **Protocols** > **TCP/IP** > **Properties**, select the **Routing** tab, giving you the window shown in Figure 3.14.
2. tick the **Enable IP Forwarding** check-box, and click on **OK** or **Apply**
3. that's all you have to do, except reboot for this setting to take effect.

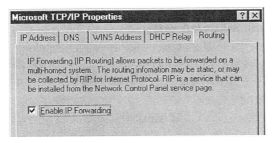

Figure 3.14 Enabling a Windows PC to act as a router

Note: Windows-9x machines can have multiple network cards, but Windows-9x doesn't support routing – because it's a desktop operating system, not a server. You can see in the Windows-9x TCP/IP Properties window that there's no **Routing** tab.

   Note: when you have multiple network cards in an NT machine, you have to reboot for any TCP/IP parameter changes – even on the first interface – to take effect.

To configure Linux to act as a router

Whether or not to forward packets is a parameter in the TCP/IP part of the operating system kernel. Linux gives you an easy way to view and set these internal system variables: you access them via specific "files" in the **/proc** pseudo-file system. To enable IP forwarding and so configure this machine to act as a router, **enter the command:**

```
echo 1 > /proc/sys/net/ipv4/ip_forward
```

If you want to disable it for any reason (and it's good security practice not to have it enabled unless you need it), enter the command:

```
echo 0 > /proc/sys/net/ipv4/ip_forward
```

To view the current status, enter

```
cat /proc/sys/net/ipv4/ip_forward
```

which prints 1 for enabled, or 0 for disabled.

   To make your settings permanent, see Appendix 6.

3.7 Lab – building the simplest possible inter-network (2)

3. Setting the network parameters

1. configuring Alice and Bob is straightforward – we've explained how to set the IP address and netmask, and the default gateway. Alice's default gateway is 10.1.1.163 – the left side of Rupert – so any packets Alice wants to send outside her network, e.g. to Bob, are passed to 10.1.1.163 for forwarding. Similarly, Bob's default gateway is 10.2.2.14

2. Rupert has two network cards. This is a new feature: we explain below how to configure them

3. Rupert has no default gateway set, and doesn't need one, because he is directly connected to all the networks in our tiny inter-network, and can therefore send packets to any machine he needs to.

Configuring multiple network cards

Linux: "`ifconfig -a`" will show you whether you have multiple interfaces, and what their names are. To set parameters for a particular interface, use that interface's name in the command (as you have done already, although you always used **eth0**). For example, to set the parameters for Rupert:

```
ifconfig eth0 10.1.1.163 netmask 255.255.255.0 up
ifconfig eth1 10.2.2.14  netmask 255.255.255.0 up
```

We use the keyword "**up**" in the commands to make sure the interfaces are active, not just present.

To make the parameters permanent, you have to store them in the appropriate configuration file: see Appendix 6.

Windows: configuring multiple network cards is even more straightforward – in the **Control Panel > Network > Protocols > TCP/IP Properties** window, select the interface you want to set from the pull-down selection list (Figure 3.15).

Figure 3.15 Selecting an interface

When you are using multiple network cards on NT, you have to reboot for the changes to take effect. As usual, use **ipconfig** to check the settings in effect after you've made the changes and rebooted.

> **Tip:** in real life, where possible we keep the last byte of all the IP addresses on a router the same, just to make it easy to remember. For example, we would normally have given Rupert the addresses 10.1.1.**163** and 10.2.2.**163**. However, here we haven't done that, to emphasize that the interfaces are completely unrelated and can have completely different IP numbers.

In Module 6.3 we'll see how to configure multiple IP addresses on a single network card, which is necessary surprisingly often.

Testing your network

The quickest test to verify that all is working correctly is to **ping** each machine from the others. As usual, use the machine's IP numbers for the machines – don't expect names to work yet. Use the table below to record the results:

	to Alice	to Bob	to Rupert
from Alice			
from Bob			
from Rupert			

If you have problems:

- if you see Alice ARP for Bob (or vice versa), she thinks he is locally connected, which he isn't, so you have a mis-configuration, either in Alice's IP address or in her netmask
- if Alice talking to Rupert fails, or vice versa, you have a basic problem in that hop's configuration. Use the troubleshooting list in Module 2.13. The same applies if the problem is on Bob's network
- work through the remaining modules in this chapter and they may help you isolate the cause
- if not, there's a full troubleshooting guide in Modules 5.14 and 5.15, but it relies on material that we haven't covered yet. If at all possible, keep your network in its non-working state until you have covered the topics and have time to diagnose what the problem really is. It's instructive to work out why you had difficulty diagnosing the problem in the first place. (We often find that it's because we had some fairly significant misunderstanding about how some part of the system works.)

Now that your network is working, it's worthwhile exploring the network some more. Go back and un-configure Rupert so it no longer acts as a router, and reboot if it's an NT machine. Then repeat all the **ping** tests above, note which fail, and record any error messages.

Everything except Alice to Bob and Bob to Alice should work fine, which is what you'd expect. But the Alice/Bob **ping**s will fail, because this communication relies on the intervening router. Even though Rupert has two interfaces, he hasn't been told explicitly that he should forward packets between his interfaces. With the **ping** from Bob to Alice, for example, the packet that Rupert receives has destination IP = Alice; Rupert sees that this isn't for him, so he discards it. However, once Rupert is re-configured to act as a router, he recognizes that this packet is to be forwarded, and as he knows the location of Alice's network (10.1.1.*), he forwards it on to Alice.

3.8 Lab – tracing packets across a router using tcpdump

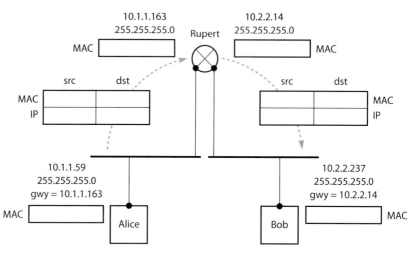

Figure 3.16 Tracing packets across a router

Now that Rupert has been configured to act as a router, you should be able to **ping** from Alice to Bob and vice versa:

1. connect your sniffer to the left-hand network

2. run **tcpdump -n -t -e** ("-e" to show the Ethernet addresses as well as the IP addresses)

3. on each of the three machines, use **ipconfig** or **ifconfig** to display the Ethernet addresses of each interface. Note them on Figure 3.16

4. on Alice, clear out any entry she might have in her ARP cache for Rupert, so you can see everything that occurs, right from the beginning:

   ```
   arp -d 10.1.1.163                                          on Alice
   ```
   and clear out the ARP caches on Rupert and Bob too:
   ```
   arp -d 10.1.1.59                                          on Rupert
   arp -d 10.2.2.237                                         on Rupert
   arp -d 10.2.2.14                                             on Bob
   ```

5. we're going to **ping** Bob from Alice. Before going any further, fill in the blank boxes in Figure 3.16 with the values you expect will appear in the **ping** request packet that is sent from Alice to Bob. This packet takes two hops, the first from Alice to Rupert, the second from Rupert to Bob, and there's a different set of addresses for each

6. ping from Alice to 10.2.2.237 (Bob):
   - this generates an initial ARP "who has 10.1.1.163" because Alice knows that she can reach 10.2.2.237 only via Rupert's address
   - check the details of the ARP request and reply, and verify that the MAC address returned in the ARP reply is what you expect

7. on each of the three machines, run "`arp -a -n`" (Linux) or "`arp -a`" (Windows) to see how each machine has learned of its neighbors' MAC addresses

8. check the MAC addresses in the ICMP request and reply packets. See how the IP address and MAC address relate to different machines, as we explained in Module 3.2.

9. move your sniffer to the right-hand network (this is where using two hubs makes life easy). Repeat steps 2–7. Alternatively, if your sniffer box has two network cards, you can trace both networks simultaneously. Figure 3.17 shows this, using two instances of **windump**, to illustrate how you specify a specific interface for the trace to be collected on. Configurations like this are ideal when you're dealing with internal routers or firewalls that have Ethernet interfaces on both sides. (You can't use it on your main Internet router because the "outside" interface usually isn't Ethernet.)

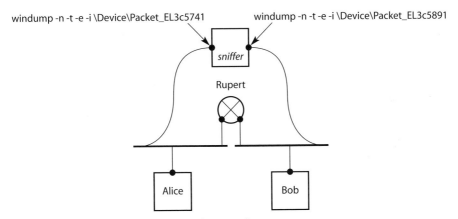

windump -n -t -e -i \Device\Packet_EL3c5741   windump -n -t -e -i \Device\Packet_EL3c5891

Figure 3.17 Tracing two networks simultaneously

10. now, from each of the three machines (Alice, Bob and Rupert) **ping** an address that is non-existent and is outside the range specified by any of your IP-address/ netmask combinations, e.g. "**ping 10.7.7.7**". What does **tcpdump** show in each case? You have enough information to understand what happens, but in any case we explain it in detail in Module 3.11.

> **Warning:** when using a sniffer with multiple interfaces, as in Figure 3.17, make sure that IP forwarding is disabled. Otherwise it could act as a router. While it is unlikely that any other machines would know about its existence, they could conceivably use it as a router, which would cause you great confusion, and if you were using it on a live network it could create a security hole, e.g. bypassing the firewall protecting your internal network from the Internet (Chapter 24).

3.9 **The** traceroute **program**

Once your network is working correctly, you can use **traceroute**, which is another valuable diagnostic tool. It traces the route actually taken by packets between this machine and the specified destination (as opposed to the route that you think the packets take). **traceroute** does this by sending out a series of packets and analyzing what's returned.

To understand how **traceroute** works, we have to introduce the concept of the *time to live (TTL)* of an IP packet. When an IP packet is sent by a machine, it travels hop by hop from router to router, to its destination. If any of the routers is misbehaving or is mis-configured, the packet could get into a *routing loop*, where it travels round and round in circles through the same set of routers. If TCP/IP had no mechanism to handle this, then the packet would loop forever. As more traffic arrived, the network would eventually be doing nothing except passing forlorn packets and would become useless. This is where the TTL comes in:

- when a host sends a packet, it sets the TTL in the packet to a "large" value, often 32 or 64 or 128 depending on the implementation
- each time the packet is forwarded by a router, the TTL is reduced by 1
- when a router receives a packet with a TTL of 1, it decrements the TTL as usual, so the TTL is now 0 – it has no time to live, so the router drops the packet and sends an ICMP "time exceeded" message packet back to the original sending host
- when a host (not a router) receives a packet with a TTL of 1, it processes it as normal. A host should never receive a packet with TTL=0 because the previous router ought to have dropped it.

In other words, the TTL is a "maximum hop count" and when that number of hops is exceeded, the packet is dropped. And even though TTL stands for *time* to live, it doesn't really have anything to do with normal clock time.

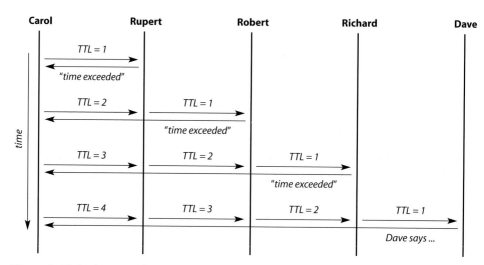

Figure 3.18 Packets sent from **traceroute** on Carol

traceroute uses this property to find out which path the packets travel, as follows. For simplicity we'll assume that we're running **traceroute** on Carol (Figure 3.18), to find the route to Dave, who is several hops away, with routers Rupert, Robert and Richard on the path in between.

1a. Carol sends a packet to the destination (Dave's IP address) and with the TTL set to 1

1b. Rupert receives the packet, decrements the TTL, which is now 0, so he discards the packet and sends an ICMP "time exceeded" back to Carol

1c. Carol receives this ICMP message, and therefore knows that Rupert is one hop away. **traceroute** prints this, with the total time in milliseconds since the packet was sent. Carol repeats steps 1a and 1b twice, to get a feel for the average round-trip time

2a. Carol now sends a packet to Dave, with the TTL set to 2

2b. Rupert receives the packet and decrements the TTL, which is now 1, so he forwards the packet towards its destination (Dave)

2c. Robert receives the packet with TTL=1, decrements it giving TTL=0, so Robert drops the packet this time, and sends an ICMP "time exceeded" back to Carol

…

Carol repeats this process until eventually, a packet with a TTL of 1 arrives at Dave, and Dave sends back a suitable message, usually that he doesn't know what to do with the packet, but definitely *not* a "time exceeded" message

99. Carol receives the message from Dave and knows that the packet has reached its final destination. Carol repeats this last step twice, prints the timing information, and terminates.

One of the many clever things about **traceroute** is that to obtain its information it doesn't need any server application on the destination machine or any of the intermediate routers. **traceroute**'s operation uses the very basic routing and ICMP features of TCP/IP.

Details of traceroute's packets

(The details below depend on material that we don't cover until Chapter 15. You can skip this section on first reading – **traceroute**'s details are rarely important in practice; we include this section here only for completeness.)

- Windows' **tracert** sends ICMP Echo Requests packets, just like **ping** but with the TTL set as described above

- **traceroute** on Linux and UNIX sends UDP packets. As we'll see later, sending UDP packets is efficient and uses few resources. The packets are sent to a high port number, usually 33435. This minimizes the probability that there is a server listening on that port on the final destination machine. For once we *don't* want a server application to receive the packet; in fact we want the final destination to generate an ICMP error message ("I don't know what to do with this packet") in order to recognize that we have reached the end of the line. The port number is incremented by one on each successive probe.

3.10 **Using** traceroute

traceroute is available for Linux and Windows. (As with **ifconfig/ipconfig**, the Windows version is named just differently enough to confuse: it's called **tracert**.)

Here are the most commonly used arguments. There's more detail in Chapter 5.

	Linux	Windows-NT
print help message	`traceroute`	`tracert`
show addresses as IP numbers	`traceroute -n` *host*	`tracert -d` *host*
show addresses as names	`traceroute` *host*	`tracert` *host*
trace all hops in parallel	`traceroute -n -P` *host*	
move to next hop as soon as one reply is received	`traceroute -n -U` *host*	

- on Windows, the option "**-d**" means "don't resolve," which is the same as "print addresses as numeric"
- on Linux, the "**-U**" and "**-P**" options can speed up your trace dramatically, although the output won't be so neat.

> **Warning:** if you forget the "**-n**" or the "**-d**," **traceroute** will pause for a long time before printing because it's trying to convert the IP numbers to names, which it can't do until we have configured DNS (Chapter 7).

```
alice%  traceroute -n -v 65.208.228.222
traceroute to 65.208.228.222 (65.208.228.222), 30 hops max, 40 byte packets
  1  192.0.2.29       47 ms      *       1 ms
  2  192.0.2.1         3 ms      3 ms    3 ms
  3  194.73.5.1       23 ms     24 ms   22 ms
  4  194.74.16.225    28 ms     26 ms   28 ms
  5  194.72.9.153     37 ms     30 ms   30 ms
  6  195.99.120.201   26 ms     33 ms   37 ms
  7  194.74.16.67     25 ms     33 ms   30 ms
  8  194.74.16.254   115 ms    107 ms  126 ms
  9  157.130.4.9     105 ms    110 ms  109 ms
 10  152.63.20.6     118 ms    122 ms  106 ms
 11  152.63.27.149   113 ms    112 ms  131 ms
 12  152.63.19.29    112 ms    119 ms  115 ms
 13  152.63.0.137    114 ms    115 ms  114 ms
 14  152.63.146.62   137 ms    141 ms  139 ms
 15  152.63.88.242   167 ms    143 ms  142 ms
 16  152.63.90.97    147 ms    147 ms  165 ms
 17  157.130.173.246 779 ms    848 ms  747 ms
 18  65.208.228.222  162 ms    162 ms  207 ms
alice%
```

Figure 3.19 Typical Linux **traceroute** output

Figure 3.19 shows a typical Linux **traceroute** output (edited for clarity) and Figure 3.20 shows the same trace from an NT machine. Note that the routes taken are not identical: lines 7–8 and 10–16 differ. This often happens. See Module 5.13 for the explanation (or can you guess why it might be?).

Figure 3.20
Typical NT
traceroute
output

```
Command Prompt

C:\> tracert -d 65.208.228.222

Tracing route to 65.208.228.222 over a maximum of 30 hops

  1    60 ms     *       40 ms  192.0.2.29
  2   <10 ms   <10 ms   <10 ms  192.0.2.1
  3    30 ms    30 ms    20 ms  194.73.5.1
  4    30 ms    40 ms    40 ms  194.74.16.225
  5    30 ms    30 ms    30 ms  194.72.9.153
  6    30 ms    40 ms    50 ms  195.99.120.201
  7    40 ms    30 ms    40 ms  194.74.16.99
  8   120 ms   120 ms   130 ms  194.74.16.250
  9   120 ms   130 ms   130 ms  157.130.4.9
 10   121 ms   120 ms   120 ms  152.63.20.2
 11   120 ms   131 ms   120 ms  152.63.28.17
 12   120 ms   140 ms   131 ms  152.63.19.33
 13   120 ms   120 ms   140 ms  152.63.0.169
 14   150 ms   160 ms   150 ms  152.63.0.42
 15   150 ms   170 ms   150 ms  152.63.88.246
 16   161 ms   150 ms   150 ms  152.63.90.109
 17   161 ms   180 ms   170 ms  157.130.173.246
 18   170 ms   191 ms   190 ms  65.208.228.222

Trace complete.
```

Testing your small inter-network with traceroute

On each machine on the test network you have just built, run the following commands to trace the route from this machine to all the others:

Linux	Windows-NT
traceroute -n 10.1.1.59	tracert -d 10.1.1.59
traceroute -n 10.1.1.163	tracert -d 10.1.1.163
traceroute -n 10.2.2.14	tracert -d 10.2.2.14
traceroute -n 10.2.2.237	tracert -d 10.2.2.237

Figure 3.21 shows the output of the traces from Alice to herself, to Rupert's left-side interface, to his right-side interface, and finally to Bob.

Figure 3.21
Trace output

```
Tracing route to 10.1.1.59 over a maximum of 30 hops

  1   <10 ms   <10 ms    10 ms  10.1.1.59
...
Tracing route to 10.1.1.163 over a maximum of 30 hops

  1   <10 ms   <10 ms   <10 ms  10.1.1.163
...
Tracing route to 10.2.2.14 over a maximum of 30 hops

  1   <10 ms   <10 ms   <10 ms  10.2.2.14
...
Tracing route to 10.2.2.237 over a maximum of 30 hops

  1   <10 ms   <10 ms   <10 ms  10.1.1.163
  2    10 ms    10 ms    10 ms  10.2.2.237
```

3.11 Error reporting from a LAN PC

Figure 3.22 shows a typical LAN PC, configured to know about its default gateway and no other routers.

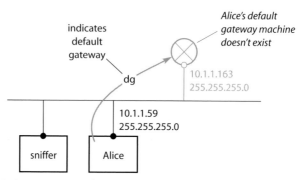

Figure 3.22 Typical LAN PC is configured to use a single router

As far as its IP layer is concerned, a host on the LAN can successfully send a packet to any destination because the default gateway is a catch-all used to forward packets for all non-local destinations. The host will never say of itself "I don't know how to route to that destination" because for every possible destination it has a suitable route – the default gateway. Let's see what effect this has in a couple of different circumstances.

Routing is OK, but the default gateway cannot contact the destination host

This may be because the default gateway is down, or the default gateway doesn't exist (e.g. the address was specified incorrectly) or the destination host is down. In this case the IP layer generates no error message. You can explore this yourself:

1. set up a PC (Alice) connected via a hub or a cross-over UTP cable to a sniffer machine running **tcpdump** (Figure 3.22). As usual it doesn't matter what the IP settings are on the sniffer

2. configure Alice with, say, IP address = 10.1.1.59, netmask = 255.255.255.0, default gateway 10.1.1.163, and reboot if necessary. We now have a machine that has a theoretical route to everywhere but in practice can't reach beyond itself (because it's default gateway machine doesn't exist)

3. **ping** 1.2.3.4

4. if your machine is running Linux, ping will sit forever ARPing for 10.1.1.163, and will not report any errors

5. if your machine is running NT, it will report "request timed out", but other than that won't tell you what's wrong

But note that we said "as far as its IP layer is concerned" up above. Higher-level protocols – such as TCP, UDP, or application-level protocols such as HTTP, all of which we discuss in Part 2 of the book – are likely to notice that there is a problem and report the error. In the example above it was the Windows **ping** *application* that noticed it didn't get any responses and reported it

6. from the command line run "`telnet 1.2.3.4`"

7. After a long wait (800 seconds on Linux) Linux says "telnet: Unable to connect to remote host: No route to host." (This is a misleading message because it has nothing to do with routing as such: it just means it can't contact the destination.) NT says "Connect failed!".

So while the IP layer isn't reporting any error, the application layer is. The low-level routing components on your machine just didn't notice anything wrong at all. (The human equivalent is the infuriating "more than my job's worth" messenger boy: "I was told I should put all letters for Bloggs Corp. into that letter-box. It's not my fault that someone set fire to the letter-box and flames were coming out of it when I dropped the letters in.")

The default gateway has no valid route to the destination

1. connect the same machine to a router

2. configure the router's IP address =10.1.1.163, netmask =255.255.255.0, no default gateway

3. **ping** 1.2.3.4

4. Linux **ping** reports "Network is unreachable;" Windows **ping** reports "Destination host unreachable"

5. **telnet** 1.2.3.4

   The default gateway can't send because it doesn't know of any appropriate route, so it reports this immediately using ICMP, which we see with **tcpdump**

   ```
   10.1.1.163 > 10.1.1.59: icmp: host 1.2.3.4 unreachable
   ```

   and the application *immediately* gives the following error and terminates:

   ```
   telnet 1.2.3.4 Unable to connect to remote host: No route to host
   ```

When a router reports an "ICMP host unreachable" error, it's final: it can't reach it now and with its current configuration it never will be able to in the future; so there's no point waiting, and the connection can be terminated immediately. On the other hand, when the routing tables indicate there is a route to the destination but packets are just not getting through, this could be caused by temporary network problems or slowness on the Internet, so applications wait for a considerable period before timing out with an error.

Exercise: telnet to a non-existent host that ought to be on the directly connected LAN, and see how long it takes to report an error, e.g.
```
telnet 10.1.1.123
```
What happens with
```
ping 10.1.1.123
```
What does **tcpdump** show if you **traceroute** to a non-existent host?

Summary

- when TCP/IP has to send a packet to another machine, it decides using its netmask whether it can send the packet directly to its destination on the local wire:
  - if it can, it sends the packet directly, using ARP if necessary
  - otherwise it sends the packet to a "router" that is also connected locally, to be forwarded on towards its final destination
- to have a router forward a packet onwards towards its destination, the sender sets the destination Ethernet address to the Ethernet address of the router, but sets the destination IP address to the IP address of the final destination. As long as the router is configured correctly to act as a router, it will forward the packet onwards towards its final destination
- to simplify the configuration of machines on the LAN, TCP/IP supports a default gateway router. If the destination IP address isn't on the directly connected LAN, this machine will send the packet to the default router to be forwarded. (This assumes that no other, more specific route to the destination has been configured explicitly on this machine. We cover such specific routes in Chapter 5)
- we have now introduced the three fundamental parameters of networking: (1) IP address, (2) netmask, (3) default gateway. Almost every networking problem you encounter will be due to an error in configuring these
- the **traceroute** program is a useful diagnostic tool, and lets you trace the route from your machine to any destination IP address.

What's next?

We've covered what routing is, in concept. Before we go on to more advanced routing – configuring multiple interfaces, and specifying routes in addition to or instead of your default gateway – we have to cover netmasks in much more detail, because they are so closely intertwined with routing and router configuration. The next chapter deals with netmasks and IP addresses in depth, and Chapter 5 then covers advanced routing.

Notes and further reading

We have covered only basic troubleshooting here. We'll go into it in much more detail in Chapter 5, when we have the necessary tools to explore routing in depth. For now, here are a couple of useful articles on routing problems with NT:

❑ **MS-KB-Q151795** *Err Msg: The Route Addition Failed: 87*

As the article says helpfully, "this message alerts you that you have an addressing problem" (as if you didn't know already). Another more general article is:

❑ **MS-KB-Q102908** *How to Troubleshoot TCP/IP Connectivity with Windows NT*

And always remember, if your machine ARPs for an address, it thinks it's a local connection. That's crucial and a great debugging tool: if your machine ARPs for an address that you know is remote, you have a problem in one of your three fundamental parameters.

Many operating systems, including Win-NT and Linux (but not Win-9x), let you define multiple *interfaces* on a single NIC. Each interface then has its own IP address and netmask, and a machine configured like this can act as a router between different logical networks running on the same Ethernet segment ("on a single wire"). We'll make use of this when building a test network in Module 6.3 where we explain it, but we mention it here because while we often use "interface" and "NIC" synonymously, we really shouldn't.

For a tool to check whether two addresses are on the same network see:

❑ **http://www.uit.co.uk/resources**

The Linux **ping--help** message says you can set the TTL on the packet using the "**-t**" flag, but on some versions this has no effect, as you can see using **tcpdump -n -t -v** (option -v :verbose, to show the TTL details).

The ARP cache is likely to contain out-of-date MAC addresses if you change the IP address of a machine, or if you leave the IP address unchanged but replace the network card. In normal running of a network this is rarely an issue, but if you're building a test network in a hurry or have to change IP addresses, e.g. when you first connect a LAN to the Internet, it can cause confusion. The best way to avoid these problems is to explicitly delete ARP entries in cases like this.

Custom-built router boxes often have a "management address" or a "stack address" which is separate from the IP addresses of the interfaces used for routing. The management address is typically used to access the box when you are configuring it manually, or automatically using SNMP (Module 17.10), or when this box is communicating with others, using dynamic or automatic routing protocols (Module 5.11).

traceroute

For more about **traceroute**, see Stevens, Chapter 7.

Folks at Bell Labs used a modified version of **traceroute** to map various aspects of the Internet, and color posters of some of the beautiful maps produced are available for purchase. For details of the project see:

❑ **http://www.cs.bell-labs.com/who/ches/map/**

Appendices

Appendix 6: making network settings permanent – Debian Linux
Appendix 7: UTP wiring

4

IP addressing and netmasks in detail

Introduction

So far we've covered how packets move from your machine to another one that's either on the same wire or on an adjacent wire with a router in between. The next step is to see how packets "find their way" across the whole Internet. However, before we can do that we need to explain IP addresses and netmasks in detail – because TCP/IP's routing uses them everywhere to make its routing decisions.

    In this chapter you'll see that a netmask in combination with an IP address specifies a range of IP addresses, and you'll see how TCP/IP uses these ranges. This is in preparation for the detailed exploration of routing in Chapter 5, where we consider complex networks with multiple segments and multiple routers. Because much of this netmask material is explanatory rather than practical, we include pointers to a number of tools on our Web site. You can use these now to explore netmasks and IP addresses, and later for the netmask calculations you'll want when designing a network or checking out your current routing configuration. If you find this chapter difficult at first, don't worry: netmasks are the hardest thing to understand in TCP/IP. All they do is specify ranges of IP addresses but they do it in a non-obvious way.

4.1 How TCP/IP identifies networks

The Internet is an inter-network – a set of individual networks inter-connected to each other with routers (Figure 4.1). TCP/IP has to route packets across this collection of networks, from the source machine to the destination.

A router is connected to more than one network. It forwards packets that arrive from one of its networks, passing them on to a router or the final destination host on one of its other networks. When a router receives a packet headed for destination **dest**, the TCP/IP code in the router goes through a decision process like this:

```
if (dest is in the IP address range for my interface-1)
     send the packet to dest directly on interface-1,
     using ARP if necessary
else if (dest is in the IP address range for my interface-2)
     send the packet to dest directly on interface-2,
     using ARP if necessary
...
/* reach here only if not local to any of my interfaces */
else if (dest is in the IP address range for remote network-A)
     forward the packet towards dest via router-1
else if (dest is in the IP address range for remote network-B)
     forward the packet towards dest via router-2
...
else
     forward the packet towards dest via my default gateway router
```

At each step in this process, TCP/IP is comparing an IP address (**dest**) with an address range for some network. We've already mentioned that TCP/IP uses the combination of a netmask and an IP address to specify a range of addresses, and that's what's used in making routing decisions. The rest of this chapter explains in detail how these range specifications work, and how TCP/IP decides whether an address is in a range.

Why netmasks and not ...?

TCP/IP could have used some form of explicit range specification, like

> **network-A = 192.0.2.0 up to and including 192.0.2.255**

or a list, like

> **network-A = 192.0.2.0, 192.0.2.1, ... 192.0.2.255**

Specifications like these either take up lots of memory, or processing them requires a lot of computation, or both. In the early days of the Internet, memory and hardware were slow and expensive, so the decision mechanism had to be very efficient, especially as TCP/IP repeats the whole routing decision process *for every packet sent*. Even now with fast, cheap hardware, the demand for very high-speed networks means routing decisions still have to be very efficient, because on a busy network there are thousands or millions of packets to be forwarded every second. Therefore some other range specifier mechanism is needed.

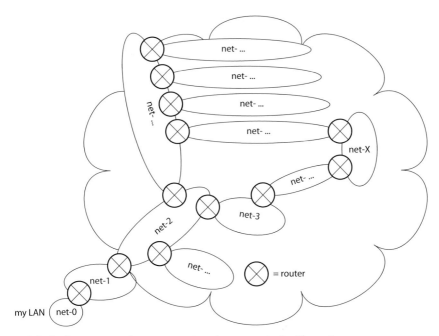

Figure 4.1 An inter-network – many networks connected with routers

As well as being fast, the mechanism must be able to cope with the size of networks that we want to work with, from huge (100,000+ machines) or tiny (a few machines, or even a single machine). And it must work efficiently with either size of network. As we'll see, netmasks meet these requirements very well.

(There is a third reason for using netmasks – compatibility with the "address class" mechanism that was used in the early days of routing and the Internet, before netmasks were invented. As we'll see in Module 4.3, netmasks can very easily replicate the address class mechanism. This allowed the old and the new technologies to co-exist on the same networks while equipment and software were gradually upgraded.)

Ranges of addresses are used in many different contexts, not just in routing. For example, they are used in firewall and other security configurations to specify sets of source and destination machines when defining which actions are allowed or prohibited. It's because they are used in different ways that we refer to them in this book as "netmasks" rather than "sub-net masks." For the same reason, in this chapter we often refer to "networks or ranges of IP addresses." This emphasizes that in many contexts what we are referring to need not be a single physical network in the sense of "my LAN" or "an Ethernet segment." Rather, it is just a range of addresses to be handled in some particular way. Often we will have no idea at all of the internal arrangement of that "network." In fact, a single range will sometimes include many different physical networks belonging to different organizations, especially in routing tables on ISP or Internet backbone routers.

(Other people frequently use the word "network" in documentation and device configuration programs to mean either a real network or an address range: you can only tell what is intended from the context.)

In summary, netmasks are a general but efficient way to specify small or large ranges of IP addresses.

4.2 The historical IP address classes

TCP/IP routing views any IP address as two parts – a *network part* and a *host part*:

- the network part of the address identifies the network the machine is connected to
- the rest of the address – the host part – identifies the particular machine on that network.

Routing on your machine uses the network part to decide whether the destination machine is on the same network as your own. If the network part of the destination address is the same as the network part of your own address, then the two machines are locally connected; otherwise they're not.

Historically, TCP/IP used *address classes* to decide how to extract the host and network parts. Addresses are divided into five classes, A, B, C, D, and E.

- D is used for multicasting (see Module 4.11)
- E is reserved and not yet used
- A, B, and C, which are all we are concerned with here, are used for normal addresses.

The class an IP address belongs to is determined by its top few bits, as shown in Figure 4.2. Just by looking at these bits TCP/IP can tell immediately from an address which class it belongs to, so class-based routing decisions can be processed quickly in the routing code.

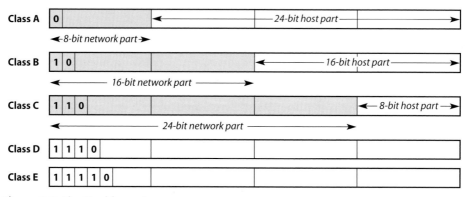

Figure 4.2 The IP address classes

Because a specific number of bytes or bits is used for network/host parts in each class, it follows automatically how many networks of each type there are, and how big each of them is (Table 4.1).

Table 4.1 Network types and sizes

	Address range	Network part	Number networks	Host part	No. hosts per network
A	0.0.0.0–127.255.255.255	1 + 7 bits	128	24 bits	16,777,216
B	128.0.0.0–191.255.255.255	2 +14 bits	16,384	16 bits	65,536
C	192.0.0.0–223.255.255.255	3 + 21 bits	2,097,152	8 bits	256

Even though a class-A address has an 8-bit network part, one of the bits is always 0. Therefore there are only 7 variable bits in the network part, which is why there are only 128 class-A networks, not 256 as you might first expect from an 8-bit network part. Similarly, class-B and class-C addresses have 2 and 3 bits respectively taken up with identifying the class type.

Table 4.1 shows there are only a few class-A networks, but each one can have a huge number of machines on it. At the other end of the scale, there are lots of class-C networks, but relatively few machines on each.

A single IP address can identify an IP address range or network, because the class is uniquely determined by that address, which in turn determines the address range. For example, 192.0.2.29 is a class-C address, so it's a range of 256 addresses:

192.0.2.0–192.0.2.255

(By convention, the lowest address in the range is used as the network address – 192.0.2.0 in this example.) Now it becomes easy to specify network addresses to be used in the routing decision code described above, e.g.

```
if (dest is part of class-C network 192.0.2.0)
    send the packet to dest directly on interface-1,
    using ARP if necessary
...
else if (dest is part of class-C network 192.168.168.0)
...
```

In practice the number of hosts per network is less than shown in the table because certain addresses are reserved. For example, in the class-C range, addresses 192.0.2.0 and 192.0.2.255 are reserved for use as broadcast addresses (see Module 4.10) so there are only $(256 - 2) = 254$ IP addresses available for use as real host addresses.

The classes reflect a view of the world-wide IP network as lots of individual networks (each a class A, B or C) owned by different organizations and connected in some way. This system worked well in the early days of the Internet, when it was used by a relatively small number of research and academic institutions. However, as the Internet expanded, the coarse division into huge, medium, and small networks proved too inflexible, and a new mechanism was introduced to give more flexibility, as described in the next module.

4.3 From address classes to netmasks

Two problems arose from the coarse division of networks into huge, medium, and small classes:

1. an organization with a large number of machines might need to divide its internal network into smaller sub-networks, for several reasons:
   - a single Ethernet segment could not accommodate hundreds of thousands of machines
   - the organization might be spread over several cities or countries
   - certain departments might need special security

   The organization will use internal routers of its own to sub-divide its network. How can these sub-networks be specified in routing tables? The addresses class mechanism is no help here. The organization has been allocated, for example, a single class-B range, so all the internal IP addresses are part of a single range. They really need to sub-divide a single class-B range

2. as the Internet has expanded, there is great demand for IP addresses and there aren't enough class A, B and Cs to go around. We'd like to be able to allocate chunks of addresses that closely match an organization's needs, e.g. "a sixteenth of a class B," or "two class cs," or whatever.

The first problem (which reared its head) was solved by introducing the concept of *sub-netting*. You divide up your single, large network into *sub-nets*. You specify each sub-net using a *sub-net mask* in combination with an IP address. For example, if your main company network is 10.0.0.0 (class A, giving a range of 10.0.0.0–10.255.255.255), you might sub-divide it as follows:

	Network address	Sub-net mask	Resulting address range
P	10.1.1.0	255.255.255.0	10.1.1.0–10.1.1.255
Q	10.1.2.0	255.255.255.0	10.1.2.0–10.1.2.255
R	10.201.0.0	255.255.0.0	10.201.0.0–10.201.255.255
S	10.202.77.0	255.255.255.0	10.202.77.0–10.202.77.255
T	10.202.0.0	255.255.0.0	10.202.0.0–10.202.255.255

This gives the network layout shown in Figure 4.3. (The area shown in gray consists of all the 10.x.x.x IP addresses that are not included in any of the specific sub-nets. As we'll see in Modules 6.8–6.12, when you sub-net your network you will often end up with sections of the total range – like the gray area in Figure 4.3 – which you don't use and which don't contain any machines.)

The second problem – how to divide a "class-full" range into smaller pieces – is much more recent, but the technical solution is the same. Instead of using just the IP address when routing (by deriving the network identifier from the address using the address class), routing is done using the IP address and netmask. Therefore, instead of a fixed division of the Internet into class A, B and C networks (huge, medium, small), we can divide the address space into chunks of whatever size is appropriate. For example, you can allocate a sixteenth of

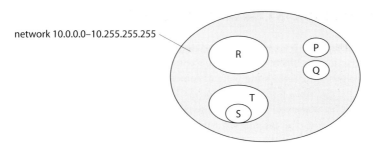

network 10.0.0.0–10.255.255.255

Figure 4.3 Network layout

a class B to an organization that is large but doesn't need the 65,536 IP addresses that a full class B offers. This is called *Classless Inter-Domain Routing (CIDR)*. It's almost universal now – it's used on the Internet backbone, and on all Windows and Linux systems. The old class-based system continues only in some historical protocols and throughout this book we deal exclusively with CIDR.

Conveniently (and it's not a coincidence – this compatibility was designed into the system) you can exactly duplicate the old class A, B, C behavior by considering each class as specifying a default netmask:

Class	Default netmask
A	255.0.0.0
B	255.255.0.0
C	255.255.255.0

In many contexts both Windows-NT and Linux will assume these default netmasks when you enter an address and don't specify an explicit netmask. Just think of classes as a convenient notation and nothing more.

4.4 How netmasks specify ranges of IP addresses

A netmask combined with an IP address specifies a range of IP addresses of a particular size, by selectively extracting the bits of the IP address corresponding to the network part of the address.

A "mask" exposes the interesting parts of something, while covering up the parts you're not interested in. For example, a semiconductor mask hides parts of a silicon wafer that are not to be exposed to light; when you are decorating, masking tape hides woodwork you want to protect, leaving exposed the pieces you want to paint; the Lone Ranger's mask hides most of his face leaving only his eyes visible.

A netmask is a type of mask. In fact it's a *bit mask* where the 1-bits in the mask indicate the pieces we are interested in, and the 0-bits are the pieces we ignore. (Bit masking is very common in programming. See Web Appendix 2.) The 1-bits in the netmask indicate the part of the IP address that makes up the network part, and the 0-bits indicate the host part. (Or, the netmask hides the host part of an IP address, leaving only the network part of the address visible.) This lets you specify a range of addresses, as follows:

> given an IP address and a particular netmask, calculate the network part. All the IP addresses that have the same network part (calculated with that netmask) form a set or range of addresses.

Now let's look at some examples to explain how you use netmasks in practice. Up to now we've used only two netmasks, 255.255.255.0 and 255.255.0.0, which are in fact the default netmasks for class C and class B addresses, so we'll start with those.

1. Using mask 255.255.255.0

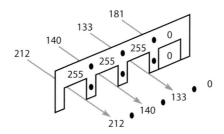

The zero byte hides the uninteresting parts, and the three 255 bytes expose the parts we want (because a byte containing 255 has all eight bits set to 1, and none set to 0). In effect, the mask 255.255.255.0 means "ignore the last byte of the IP address; the network part consists of the first three bytes only". For example:

    address = 212.140.133.181
    netmask = 255.255.255.0

gives us a network part of 212.140.133.0 (we just fill in zeros in the parts that we masked off). The range consists of all the IP addresses that have this network part, i.e. all the IP addresses that have 212.140.133 as the first three bytes. This is the range:

212.140.133.0–212.140.133.255 inclusive

containing 256 addresses, as one byte (8 bits) can take on values from 0 to 255.

2. Using mask 255.255.0.0

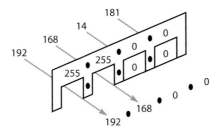

Let's calculate the range specified by

address = 192.168.14.181
netmask = 255.255.0.0

Again, the zero bytes hide the uninteresting parts, giving a network part of 192.168.0.0. The range consists of all IP addresses that have this network part, i.e. a range of 65,536 addresses

192.168.0.0–192.168.255.255 inclusive.

Repeating the calculation with the same netmask but a different address:

address = 192.168.233.91

we get the same network part as before – 192.168.0.0 (because the last two bytes are masked off). So this address is in the same range as 192.168.14.181:

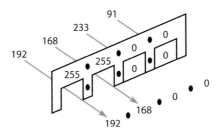

The default netmasks for the A, B, and C classes are easy to use because you can work out what ranges are specified very simply, just by looking at the first one, two or three bytes, respectively. For other netmasks, covered in the following modules, we'll have to use simple binary arithmetic to calculate the ranges.

4.5 Specifying different sizes of network range

The netmasks we've used so far give us particular sizes of networks (or address ranges):

Netmask	Number of IP addresses in range
255.255.255.0	256
255.255.0.0	65,536
255.0.0.0	16,777,216

The netmasks above are the defaults for the A, B, and C address classes that were invented when the Internet was very small. Nowadays, the Internet is used so widely that IP address space is very scarce. Everyone can't have even a full class-C, and organizations have to make do with much smaller networks, often a partial class-C with just 4, 8, or 16 addresses in the range. Our range specification mechanism must be able to handle these very small ranges. If we want to specify one of these smaller networks, or an intermediate-sized network with 1,800 or 10,000 machines, how do we do that using a netmask?

The solution is to use not one whole byte for the host part (mask 255.255.255.0) or two whole bytes (mask 255.255.0.0) but something like 3/4 byte, or 1 7/8 of a byte. From the examples in earlier modules, you'll have seen that the number of addresses in the range is determined by the number of bits in the host part of the address. It follows that the network size is always a power of two: a 1-bit host part gives two addresses (2^1), 2 bits gives $2^2=4$ addresses, 3 bits gives $2^3=8$ addresses and so on. For example, netmask 255.255.0.0 has a two-byte (16-bit) host part, which gives a range size of $2^{16}= 65,536$ addresses. To accommodate the range size we want, we work out how many bits we need in the host part, which in turn automatically determines the netmask. For example:

> We want a network with 25 machines – a range containing 25 addresses. A 4-bit host part gives 16 addresses (which isn't enough) and a host part of 5 bits gives $2^5=32$ addresses, which is OK. This implies a network part with (32 – 5) = 27 bits. Therefore the netmask consists of 27 1-bits on the left, followed by 5 0-bits on the right (Figure 4.4(a)). Converting that to decimal (using the decimal/binary conversion table inside the back cover) gives us the netmask shown in Figure 4.4(b).

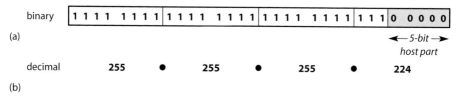

Figure 4.4 Netmask 255.255.255.224 has a 5 bit host part

You use this mask just like the others we saw, except that now you have to mask individual bits instead of whole bytes. This requires a little binary arithmetic instead of just replacing a byte with a zero, but that's not a big deal.

Let's look at an example, using this new netmask and the same IP address we used before, 212.140.133.181. Considering the last byte only (because the others are all 255 so they work exactly as before) masking gives us 10100000 binary = 160 decimal as shown below. Therefore the complete network part is 212.140.133.160. We chose the host part to have 5 bits = 32 addresses, so our range is

212.140.133.160–212.140.133.191

which is what we wanted – a range to accommodate at least 25 machines.

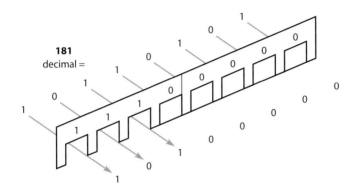

Finally, let's look at the whole calculation again, just laid out differently:

IP address	212	•	140	•	133	•	181
netmask	255	•	255	•	255	•	224

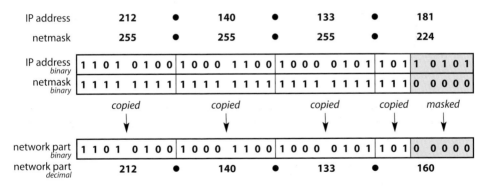

IP address *binary*	1 1 0 1 0 1 0 0	1 0 0 0 1 1 0 0	1 0 0 0 0 1 0 1	1 0 1 1	1 0 1 0 1
netmask *binary*	1 1 1 1 1 1 1 1	1 1 1 1 1 1 1 1	1 1 1 1 1 1 1 1	1 1 1	0 0 0 0 0
	copied	copied	copied	copied	masked
network part *binary*	1 1 0 1 0 1 0 0	1 0 0 0 1 1 0 0	1 0 0 0 0 1 0 1	1 0 1 0	0 0 0 0
network part *decimal*	212	•	140	•	133	•	160

4.6 Table of netmasks

Netmask in decimal	No. of 1 - bits in mask	No. addresses in net	Netmask in hex	Netmask in binary			
255.255.255.255	/32	1	ff.ff.ff.ff	11111111	. 11111111	. 11111111	. 11111111
255.255.255.254	/31	2	ff.ff.ff.fe	11111111	. 11111111	. 11111111	. 11111110
255.255.255.252	/30	4	ff.ff.ff.fc	11111111	. 11111111	. 11111111	. 11111100
255.255.255.248	/29	8	ff.ff.ff.f8	11111111	. 11111111	. 11111111	. 11111000
255.255.255.240	/28	16	ff.ff.ff.f0	11111111	. 11111111	. 11111111	. 11110000
255.255.255.224	/27	32	ff.ff.ff.e0	11111111	. 11111111	. 11111111	. 11100000
255.255.255.192	/26	64	ff.ff.ff.c0	11111111	. 11111111	. 11111111	. 11000000
255.255.255.128	/25	128	ff.ff.ff.80	11111111	. 11111111	. 11111111	. 10000000
255.255.255.0	**/24**	**256**	**ff.ff.ff.0**	**11111111**	**. 11111111**	**. 11111111**	**. 00000000**
255.255.254.0	/23	512	ff.ff.fe.0	11111111	. 11111111	. 11111110	. 00000000
255.255.252.0	/22	1024	ff.ff.fc.0	11111111	. 11111111	. 11111100	. 00000000
255.255.248.0	/21	2048	ff.ff.f8.0	11111111	. 11111111	. 11111000	. 00000000
255.255.240.0	/20	4096	ff.ff.f0.0	11111111	. 11111111	. 11110000	. 00000000
255.255.224.0	/19	8192	ff.ff.e0.0	11111111	. 11111111	. 11100000	. 00000000
255.255.192.0	/18	16384	ff.ff.c0.0	11111111	. 11111111	. 11000000	. 00000000
255.255.128.0	/17	32768	ff.ff.80.0	11111111	. 11111111	. 10000000	. 00000000
255.255.0.0	**/16**	**65536**	**ff.ff.0.0**	**11111111**	**. 11111111**	**. 00000000**	**. 00000000**
255.254.0.0	/15	131072	ff.fe.0.0	11111111	. 11111110	. 00000000	. 00000000
255.252.0.0	/14	262144	ff.fc.0.0	11111111	. 11111100	. 00000000	. 00000000
255.248.0.0	/13	524288	ff.f8.0.0	11111111	. 11111000	. 00000000	. 00000000
255.240.0.0	/12	1048576	ff.f0.0.0	11111111	. 11110000	. 00000000	. 00000000
255.224.0.0	/11	2097152	ff.e0.0.0	11111111	. 11100000	. 00000000	. 00000000
255.192.0.0	/10	4194304	ff.c0.0.0	11111111	. 11000000	. 00000000	. 00000000
255.128.0.0	/9	8388608	ff.80.0.0	11111111	. 10000000	. 00000000	. 00000000
255.0.0.0	**/8**	**16777216**	**ff.0.0.0**	**11111111**	**. 00000000**	**. 00000000**	**. 00000000**
254.0.0.0	/7	33554432	fe.0.0.0	11111110	. 00000000	. 00000000	. 00000000
252.0.0.0	/6	67108864	fc.0.0.0	11111100	. 00000000	. 00000000	. 00000000
248.0.0.0	/5	134217728	f8.0.0.0	11111000	. 00000000	. 00000000	. 00000000
240.0.0.0	/4	268435456	f0.0.0.0	11110000	. 00000000	. 00000000	. 00000000
224.0.0.0	/3	536870912	e0.0.0.0	11100000	. 00000000	. 00000000	. 00000000
192.0.0.0	/2	1073741824	c0.0.0.0	11000000	. 00000000	. 00000000	. 00000000
128.0.0.0	/1	2147483648	80.0.0.0	10000000	. 00000000	. 00000000	. 00000000
0.0.0.0	/0	4294967296	0.0.0.0	00000000	. 00000000	. 00000000	. 00000000

Notes

1. you don't have to remember these netmasks – just look them up as you need them!
2. The table rows in **bold** are the default netmasks for class A, B and C networks (Module 4.3)
3. these are *all the possible* netmasks (33 of them) and these are the only possible sizes of address range. All the 1-bits are together on the left and all the 0-bits are on the right. If there are any zero bits in amongst the 1-bits, it's not a valid netmask
4. ranges are often written as an IP address followed by a "/" and the number of 1-bits in the netmask, i.e. the number of bits in the network part. For example:

    192.0.2.181 / 24

This is shorthand for "use a 24-bit netmask", i.e. the netmask opposite the "/24" shown in the table; therefore the specification above means
"IP address = 192.0.2.181, netmask = 255.255.255.0"

This is often referred to as the "CIDR notation" for netmasks or IP address ranges

5. "/32" specifies a single IP address. For example, 192.0.2.7 / 32 means this single machine – a range of length 1. You will never use this when configuring the IP address and sub-net mask of a machine on the LAN, but you *will* see it in routing tables and the like

6. "/0" or mask 0.0.0.0 specifies the whole Internet – every possible IP address – because it gives the same network part of 0.0.0.0 when combined with any IP address whatever. Again, you will see this in practice in routing tables, on Linux and NT, in the next chapter. (In some contexts "0.0.0.0" may be written as the word default instead, to emphasize that it means "every address")

7. the 0-bits in the mask correspond to the host part of the address, which determines the network size. You can see graphically from the table that the network size gets bigger as you go down the table

8. it's very important to note that the netmask on its own doesn't specify the network. The netmask determines the size of the range, and the IP address positions it – saying where in the whole universe of IP addresses the range lies. It's only the *combination of netmask and the particular IP address* that specifies the range uniquely. The table below shows four different ranges all of which have the same netmask (255.255.255.192):

Address range	Range of last byte
192.0.2.0–192.0.2.63	0–63
192.0.2.64–192.0.2.127	64–127
192.0.2.128–192.0.2.191	128–191
192.0.2.192–192.0.2.255	192–255

As you become more experienced in using netmasks you'll get used to the start and end numbers of the common ranges.

Tip: to work out how many addresses are in a range, subtract the last byte of the netmask from 256. For example, for netmask 255.255.255.224: (256 – 224) = 32-address network/range size. (This works only where the first three bytes are all 255. For other netmasks look up the size in the table.)

4.7 Examples of the use of netmasks

The most common use of a netmask is to tell a machine which network it's connected to. Machines with multiple interfaces have multiple netmasks, one per interface, to specify which network *each* interface is connected to.

PC on a LAN

The classical use of netmask, which we've already touched on, is where your PC has a single NIC and a single IP address, and it knows about a single router – its default gateway. Figure 4.5 shows its view of the Internet.

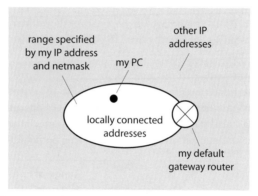

Figure 4.5 View of the Internet from a typical PC

On your PC the combination of IP address and netmask says in effect "this range of IP addresses can be reached directly via this interface." This has three consequences:

1. if a machine is in that range but can't be ARPed, then it doesn't exist (or is broken, or otherwise unreachable). We won't try elsewhere
2. if it's not in that range, we can't reach it directly and therefore we must send it to our default gateway for forwarding. If the default gateway doesn't know where to forward it, we can't reach the destination
3. if we don't even have a default gateway, the only addresses we can communicate with are the locally connected ones in the specified range. This is the case on a stand-alone LAN.

PC or router with multiple NICs

In previous Chapters we usually spoke of *the* netmask of a machine, but that was an over-simplification. A machine can have multiple NICs (and a router to be useful *must* have more than one). Such a machine has multiple netmasks. Each NIC has its own IP address, usually in different networks so that the machine can route from one network to another, as shown in Figure 4.6. Each NIC also has its own netmask, to specify the range of machines that can be accessed directly *via this NIC*. In Figure 4.6 my PC is connected to three different networks on its different NICs; it needs three different range specifications in its TCP/IP configuration, i.e. three different pairs of IP address and netmask.

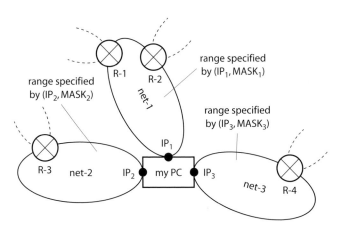

Figure 4.6 My PC acting as a router, connecting three networks

You can see how this ties in with the routing code in the PC with multiple NICs that we outlined in Module 4.1:

```
if (dest is in the IP address range for my interface-1)
        send the packet to dest directly on interface-1,
        using ARP if necessary
else if (dest is in the IP address range for my interface-2)
        send the packet to dest directly on interface-2,
        using ARP if necessary
...
/* reach here only if not local to any of my interfaces */
else if (dest is in the IP address range for remote network-A)
        forward the packet towards dest via router R-1
else if (dest is in the IP address range for remote network-B)
        forward the packet towards dest via router R-2
...
else
        forward the packet towards dest via my default gateway
router
```

Each "`if ( ... )`" decision involves comparing an IP address, **dest**, with a range specified by this NIC's own IP address and netmask.

4.8 Netmask calculations

Internally, TCP/IP uses binary AND to decide which route a packet should use, or to decide which range an address falls in.

Is that address on this network?

For this calculation, TCP/IP uses binary **AND** (also called *bitwise AND* because it works on individual bits in the numbers). To bitwise **AND** two numbers, write both numbers in binary, one under the other. If a particular bit is 1 in both numbers, the answer is 1, otherwise it's 0. This is how netmasks mask off the unwanted bits. You can think of it as "switching off" all the bits that correspond to 0s in the mask.)

You have a network or range specified by an IP address and netmask, I_1, M. To decide whether a second address, I_2, is on the same network, TCP/IP performs the calculation below:

if (I_1 **AND** M is equal to I_2 **AND** M)

   I_1 and I_2 are on same network (or are in the same specified range)

else

   they are not in the same range

A more long-winded but equivalent calculation that emphasizes the concept of the network part of an IP address is:

let network-part-1 = I_1 **AND** M

let network-part-2 = I_2 **AND** M

if (network-part-1 is equal to network-part-2)

   I_1 and I_2 are on same network (in the same specified range)

else

   they are not in the same range

These calculations are very fast because the AND operation is built into the hardware.

To calculate the range of IP addresses specified by an address and a netmask

1. calculate the network part of the address, either as shown diagrammatically in Modules 4.4 and 4.5, or using bitwise AND as above. In the resulting network part, all the host part bits are 0, giving you the lower bound of the range

2. in the network part, change all the host bits from 0 to 1. This gives you the upper bound of the range.

Examples: The first two examples are equivalent to those in Modules 4.4 and 4.5.

1. What is the range specified by 212.140.133.181/24 (i.e. with netmask 255.255.255.0)?

   a. This netmask masks off the last byte, so the network part is 212.140.133.0. This is the lower bound.

   b. Changing all the bits from 0 to 1 in the host part (the last 8 bits, i.e. the last byte) gives 212.140.133.255. This is the upper bound.

   c. The range is 212.140.133.0–212.140.133.255

2. What is the range specified by 212.140.133.181/27 (i.e. with netmask 255.255.255.224)?

   a. This netmask has five 0-bits on the right, so it will affect only the last 5 bits of the address, which are in the last byte.

   b. The last byte is decimal .181 = binary 10110101. Masking off the last 5 bits gives binary 10110000, which from the table on the inside back cover is decimal 160. Therefore the network part is 212.140.133.160. This is the lower bound.

   b. Changing all the host bits (the last 5 bits) from 0 to 1 gives binary 10111111, which our table shows is decimal 191. Therefore the upper bound is 212.140.133.191.

   c. The range is 212.140.133.160–212.140.133.191

3. What is the range specified by 212.140.133.181 /21 (i.e. with netmask 255.255.248.0)?

   a. The netmask has 11 0-bits, so it affects the last two bytes. The last byte of the netmask is 0, so the last byte of the network part is 0. We now have to handle the second-last byte: decimal 133 = binary 10000101. The three extra netmask bits mask off the last 3 bits of this, giving binary 10000000 = decimal 128. The whole network part is therefore 212.140.128.0. This is the lower bound.

   b. Changing all the host bits (the last 11 bits) from 0 to 1 gives 212.140.135.255. This is the upper bound.

   c. The range is 212.140.132.0–212.140.135.255, which is 2048 addresses, or the equivalent of eight class-C ranges.

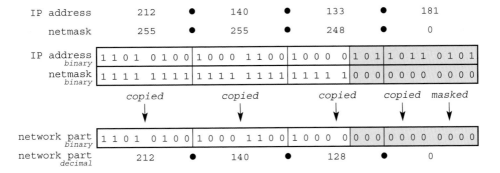

Tools to perform these calculations are available on our Web site (see Notes).

4.9 Special IP numbers (1) – private addresses

Three special sets of private or non-routable address ranges have been allocated for use on networks that are not connected to the Internet, or at least that are not directly visible. There are also special addresses for use in documentation, and for small self-configured networks.

Private/non-routable IP numbers

Three ranges of IP addresses have been allocated for use in networks that are not visible on the Internet:

10.0.0.0–10.255.255.255	1 × class-A network/range
172.16.0.0–172.31.255.255	16 × class-B networks/ranges
192.168.0.0–192.168.255.255	256 × class-C networks/ranges

These addresses are called *private* or *non-routable* addresses. They are not allocated to one site or organization – anyone may use them. However, because there is no particular site for them to go to, packets cannot be routed to these destinations. So what good are they? Why do we need them?

Private addresses are needed to save IP address space. The range of IP numbers is running out because the Internet is growing so rapidly. If some numbers can be re-used repeatedly, it will take longer before we run out of IP addresses completely.

Examples of where you can use private addresses are:

- your internal network is connected to the Internet using a firewall or other box that performs "network address translation" or "NAT" (Chapter 23). You use private addresses internally, but when packets are sent out to the Internet the NAT device translates them so they appear to the outside world as though they had all come from a single public (real) address of yours – often the public address of the outside of your firewall. This lets you run very large internal networks with just a handful of the scarce, public IP addresses (Figure 4.7).
- test networks, which are isolated both from the Internet and your real internal LAN
- private networks, e.g.
  - networks of normal workstations and servers that just don't need Internet access, or must remain very secure (e.g. in defence or financial institutions)
  - networks of instruments or machine tools in a factory or laboratory
- private addresses are often used as the initial factory settings on routers, networked printers, etc.

IP numbers for use in documentation

A special range of IP numbers has been allocated for use in documentation, example code, etc., which should never be used in real life:

192.0.2.0–192.0.2.255	1 × class-C network/range

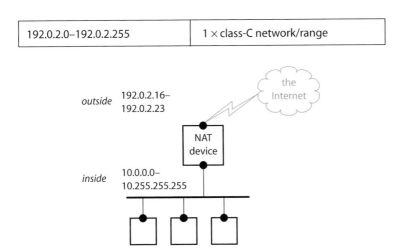

Figure 4.7 Private 10.x.x.x addresses used with network address translation

The idea behind this is that 10 or 15 years ago, most TCP/IP networks were not connected to the Internet. People often used addresses listed in the examples in manufacturers' manuals when setting up their networks. The world was full of private networks using Sun Microsystems' addresses. When these sites finally connected to the Internet, they had to renumber all their machines.

IP numbers for small self-configured networks

DHCP (Chapter 16) is a dynamic host configuration system that lets client machines obtain all their IP configuration settings at boot time from a central DHCP server. The big advantages is central administration of IP numbers and clients don't have to be individually configured.

However, if a client machine boots and can't find a DHCP server, what does it do? It could just fail to boot, but another option is for it to use a number from a specially allocated range:

169.254.0.0–169.254.255.255	1 × class-B network/range

so that it can start and work on the local network at least. This is especially useful for home machines or small organizations where there is no trained network administrator. Some versions of Windows (including Win-9x) make use of this (see Notes).

4.10 Special IP numbers (2) – IP broadcast addresses

We saw in Module 2.4 that a machine can send to every other machine on its Ethernet segment using the Ethernet broadcast address. TCP/IP also has broadcast addresses, used when it wants to send to all the TCP/IP machines on the local network. This is conceptually similar to the Ethernet broadcast, but it's separate because TCP/IP can run on many different types of network hardware, not just Ethernet, and must have a broadcast mechanism that is independent of the underlying hardware.

IP broadcasts are typically used for "I want service ABC; is there anyone out there who can provide it for me?" Examples of this are:

1. DHCP (Chapter 16) used by a PC when booting to get its TCP/IP settings from a central server

2. Microsoft Windows Networking (Chapter 18), to contact domain controllers, WINS servers and other services.

There are two broadcast addresses:

1. *limited broadcast address* 255.255.255.255. This is the same on every network. It's transmitted only on the local wire and never forwarded by a router. Used in case (1) above

2. *network broadcast address* (also called the *network-directed broadcast address*): this is formed by taking the network address (i.e. the network part of any one of the host addresses) and then setting all the host-bits to 1. In other words, it's the upper limit of the address range.

    This broadcast can be forwarded by a router. For example, assuming your organization is using the 192.0.2.x addresses internally, the net-directed broadcast is 192.0.2.255. If your internal network consists of several sub-nets within this range, e.g. 192.0.2.32/27, 192.0.2.64/27, 192.0.2.192/26, etc., each on a separate segment (wire), the net-directed broadcast ought to be forwarded to each segment, and all of your machines, on any wire, will see it.

    Depending on your netmask, Linux may not set the network broadcast address correctly. See the Warning in the Notes at the end of this chapter.

What is the difference between the broadcasts? In practice we've never had to worry about this difference at all, because in every case the packet is sent to all the machines on the local wire and that's usually all that concerns you. The difference between the network broadcast address and limited broadcast addresses is that the limited broadcast never goes beyond the local wire, whereas the other may be forwarded by routers, as shown in Figure 4.8. However, forwarding of broadcasts by routers isn't consistent; many routers *don't* forward the network broadcasts so in practice there's no difference at all between the two.

Early versions of UNIX from the University of California at Berkeley used a broadcast address with all zeroes in the host part instead of all ones, e.g. 192.0.2.0. Linux and many Berkeley-derived systems still view this as a broadcast and respond to it.

The network broadcast addresses have an important consequence: in any network or sub-net you lose the top address in the range to the all-1s broadcast address, and the bottom one for the all-0s (old, incorrect) broadcast. If you have n addresses in your network range, you have only ($n - 2$) legal addresses for hosts. (Consequently, you can't have a real network with netmask /32 or /31: these have only one and two addresses in their ranges, so they don't contain any legal host addresses.)

Exercise: First, read the warning below! Then, on your test network, **ping** your network's broadcast address. For example, on our network we entered

```
ping 192.0.2.255
```

You get multiple replies for each packet sent, because *each host* on the local wire correctly receives the **ping** request and replies to it. Now **ping** the limited broadcast address, and the address of your network. For example, on our network we entered

```
ping 255.255.255.255
ping 192.0.2.0
```

When you run this on NT, it says these destinations are invalid; NT doesn't respond to **pings** on the broadcast addresses. When you run it on Linux, you get the same result as for 192.0.2.255. The first Linux result is what you'd expect – 255.255.255.255 ought to go to each of the local machines; the second is because Linux responds to the old, incorrect all-0s broadcast address.

Warning: if you **ping** broadcast addresses on a real, large network, a lot of packets are generated. If some machines are mis-configured, you could get a *broadcast storm* where the network is flooded with broadcast packets, with some packets generating further broadcasts, etc. (Some denial-of-service attacks depend on this type of behavior. They **ping** a network broadcast address but spoof the **ping** packet's source address to be the address of the target they are attacking. The target gets swamped with useless packets.)

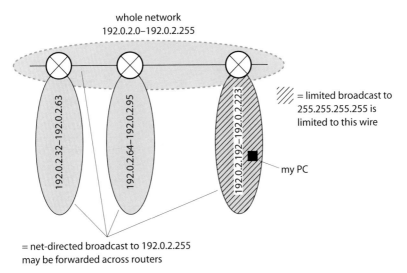

Figure 4.8 Limited and net-directed broadcast addresses

4.11 Special IP numbers (3) – multicast, network, and loopback addresses

There are a few more sets of special IP numbers.

Multicast addresses 224.0.0.0 – 239.255.255.255

Multicasting is like broadcasting in that a single packet goes to multiple destinations. Unlike broadcast packets, the multicast packets are only delivered to hosts that are members of a *multicast group* to minimize the load on both the sending host (which doesn't have to generate a packet per destination) and other machines that are not participating in the group. Applications that benefit from multicasting are one-to-many or many-to-many, e.g. audio and video "broadcasting" or conferencing, stocks and shares information services, and collaborative applications such as shared whiteboards, etc. Although these are becoming popular, multicast applications are not yet deployed widely, so we won't mention multicasting any further in this book (except in the Notes). Multicasting uses the class-D addresses, i.e in the range 224.0.0.0–239.255.255.255.

Network address

The address of a network itself, as opposed to any of its hosts, is the network part of any of its host addresses. (The network parts of all the hosts are the same, by definition, so there is only one address for the network.) In the network part, all the host bits are zero, which distinguishes the network from any host on it. This is another reason why no machine can have a host part of zero in its IP address, and that in any network, one address is "lost", for use as the network address. The table below shows the network address for the networks we looked at in Module 4.6.

Network range	Network address	First host no.
192.0.2.0–192.0.2.63	192.0.2.0	192.0.2.1
192.0.2.64–192.0.2.127	192.0.2.64	192.0.2.65
192.0.2.128–192.0.2.191	192.0.2.128	192.0.2.129
192.0.2.192–192.0.2.255	192.0.2.192	192.0.2.193

The "I don't know my address yet" address 0.0.0.0

Consider a machine that uses some network service such as DHCP (Chapter 16) to obtain its address at boot-time from a central server. When it starts up it doesn't know its own IP address, but it still has to use the network to talk to the server. In cases like this a machine uses 0.0.0.0 as its source address. (You will never need to use this address yourself.)

Loopback address 127.0.0.1

A TCP/IP computer uses the special address 127.0.0.1 as its "loopback" address – a special address for itself. No matter how many ordinary IP addresses a machine has, or even if it has none, it can always send to itself using this address. This is useful for testing, or for using a network service that happens to be on the local machine; you never have to perform a lookup to find your own address.

You will see the loopback address in routing tables on Windows systems, and on some UNIX variants. (Many Linux versions don't show the loopback address in the routing tables but do process loopback packets correctly.)

On many systems, it's not just 127.0.0.1 that works in this way, but any 127.x.x.x address. You can check out what your system does using **ping**.

Exercise: start **tcpdump** on your computer

```
tcpdump -n -t arp or icmp
```

Then

```
ping 127.0.0.1
```

This should always work for 127.0.0.1. However, you will normally see nothing in **tcpdump**. What's happening is that TCP/IP knows that packet is for this machine and doesn't send it out on the wire, but instead sends it on the loopback interface (which is called **lo** on Linux). **tcpdump** by default listens on the Ethernet interface (typically eth0) so it doesn't see the packets on **lo**. However, if you run **tcpdump** with option "**-i lo**" or "**-i any**" you will see the looped-back packets.

Now

```
ping 127.4.5.6
```

This works on Linux and Windows-NT, but it may not work on some other systems, depending on their implementation.

Summary

- the 4-byte (32-bit) IP address is divided into two parts, one to specify the network that this IP address belongs to, and a second to identify this particular host within that network. It is the netmask that determines which bits in the IP address are the network part
- combining the netmask with an IP address specifies a range of IP addresses of a particular size, and that's the really important concept to take from this chapter
- TCP/IP uses address ranges extensively, especially to indicate which machines your PC can send to on the local wire, and which machines it has to forward to via a router
- the historical IP address classes A, B, and C have 1-, 2-, and 3-byte default netmasks, for huge, large and medium networks
- that level of structure was adequate in the early years of the Internet's development. However, now that IP addresses are scarce, there's a need to specify smaller ranges, and ranges of intermediate size, which you can do using netmasks of different sizes, not just 8, 16, or 24 bits
- we showed examples of how ranges are used – on a PC with a single network interface and one with multiple interfaces – and how to calculate ranges, and whether a destination IP address is part of a given network
- some address ranges are reserved for special purposes: private addresses for networks that are not visible on the Internet; the address of a network; loopback addresses so a machine can talk to itself easily, and IP broadcast addresses that allow a machine to talk to all the machines that are part of its network, or just those on the local wire.

What's next?

In the next chapter we use netmasks and address ranges in configuring routing for your network – to divide it into subnets for administrative or performance reasons, or to add a test network, or to connect to the Internet. You will be pleased to know that while it's important to understand what netmasks are and how to interpret them, in day-to-day networking you rarely have to do any detailed netmask calculations.

Notes and further reading

We've set up netmask calculation tools on our website **www.uit.co.uk**, which you can use now to explore netmasks and get a gut-feel for how they work. You may also find them useful later on if you have to configure a network or sub-nets, or want to check out what a set of routing tables means. There are several different tools:

1. you enter an IP address, and an optional netmask (or use the default for the IP address class). The calculator shows the range specified by that combination of IP address and netmask. You can also enter extra IP addresses or extra netmasks to see how changing one or the other affects the resulting range

2. you first enter an IP address and a netmask to specify a network or range, and then a second IP address. The calculator tells you whether the two IP addresses are on the same network.

Netmasks

Sub-netting and netmasks were introduced in:

❑ **RFC-917 October 1994** *Internet Subnets*

❑ **RFC-940 April 1985** *Toward an Internet Standard Scheme for Subnetting*

Before that, the terms "netmask" and "sub-net mask" weren't used in RFCs; TCP/IP used the class of an IP address to decide which byte(s) represented the network part. For practical purposes, now that networks of every size are so common, you can regard the IP address classes merely as a naming convention, and a way to specify a default netmask. For example, both Windows-NT and Linux will use the default netmask if you don't specify one explicitly when configuring an interface. Classes are also often used to indicate that a network is of a particular size. For example, "they have a class C" means they have a 256-address range allocated to them. Sometimes this is used imprecisely, e.g. "10.2.3.4/24 is a class C network." (It's not, it's a class-C sized sub-net of a class-A network.)

You may see some other types of masks in some proprietary router configurations. The principle is the same – masking out areas of interest – but unless you have equipment that uses them, you can forget about them completely. In four years of network configuring we've never had to use them.

Some TCP/IP implementations also support *non-contiguous sub-net masks*, where all the 1-bits in the mask are not together, i.e. not contiguous. This means that the network part of the IP address consists of several separate chunks of bits, and the netmask will be different to anything we've seen, e.g. 255.0.127.0. Almost nobody uses these now – they were a nightmare to use – and we mention them only in case you read about them elsewhere, or enter one by mistake on Windows-NT, which does indeed support them.

CIDR – Classless Inter-Domain Routing

This was initially proposed in

❑ **RFC-1367 October 1992** *Schedule for IP Address Space Management Guidelines*

❑ **RFC-1481 July 1993** *IAB Recommendation for an Intermediate Strategy to Address the Issue of Scaling*

and later it was agreed as a standard in:

❑ **RFC-1517 September 1993** *Applicability Statement for the Implementation of Classless Inter-Domain Routing (CIDR)*

❑ **RFC-1518 September 1993** *An Architecture for IP Address Allocation with CIDR*

❑ **RFC-1519 September 1993** *Classless Inter-Domain Routing (CIDR): an Address Assignment and Aggregation Strategy*

The introduction to RFC-1519 is very readable, describing how rapidly the use of IP addresses is growing, the problems of running out of IP addresses, and how CIDR helps. (We'll also see in Module 23.2 how network address translation (NAT) lets you connect a very large LAN to the Internet using only a handful of IP addresses. That has gone a long way to eke out the limited set of IP addresses that are available.)

Special addresses

The standard private addresses for use on test networks, VPNs, etc. are defined in

❑ **RFC-1918 February 1996** *Address Allocation for Private Internets*

(10.0.0.0 was the address of the old ARPANET, which was the precursor of the Internet as we know it.)

Packets addressed to private addresses ought to be blocked by your Internet router as they leave your site. However, if your ISP hasn't set things up correctly, they may travel some distance before being dropped. You can see this by doing a **traceroute**, e.g. "traceroute 10.4.5.6." Packets with addresses that ought never to appear on this network, but that have arrived here because of bad routing entries (e.g. 10.*.*.* packets travelling over the Internet backbone) are often called "Martians."

Private addresses were first suggested in:

❑ **RFC-1597 March 1994** *Address Allocation for Private Internets*

which gives other examples of where you might want non-routable, private addresses: information displays at an airport, or cash registers in a retail chain, adding that these would probably never need Internet connectivity. Opinions are changing: a big benefit of *IP version 6* (or IPng – IP Next Generation – Web Appendix 4) is that its huge address space allows *every* TCP/IP device to have a unique IP address and so be Internet accessible if required. You could use your TCP/IP mobile phone to tell your TCP/IP microwave oven to start cooking, and to turn on your TCP/IP central heating boiler as you travel home from work. With this world view, you can easily imagine that an airline would update its information display in Singapore from its HQ in Dublin, or a retailer in Arkansas might update its cash registers in London stores with details of global special deals. Having every device potentially Internet-connected may be desirable, at least in principle. (On the other hand, this level of accessibility poses horrific security problems.)

The 192.0.2.* addresses used in documentation ought not to be routed either, but as this usage isn't an official standard, they may be. See:

❑ **http://www.isi.edu/~bmanning/dsua.html**

(or if that isn't available, search for "draft-manning-dsua" using Google or similar.

IP numbers for small self-configured networks should never be routed. See

❑ **MS-KB-Q220874** *Automatic Windows 98/Me TCP/IP Addressing Without a DHCP Server*

which describes "Automatic Private IP Addressing" (APIPA).

In Module 4.10 we said there are two different broadcast addresses, but Stevens Chapter 12 explains that there are in fact four: limited broadcast address, network-directed broadcast address, sub-net-directed broadcast address, and all-sub-nets-directed broadcast address. These distinctions don't matter any more, partly because nobody implements them, and partly because the distinction between "network-directed" and "sub-net-directed" only made sense in the pre-CIDR days. Then, as now, an IP address had a network part and a host part. But the host part could be divided further into a sub-net-ID part and a host-ID part. The idea was that your "network" described the view of your site from the Internet, e.g. "we have a class-B network". Then, within your site, you used sub-netting to arrange you internal routing, using the sub-net part. However, with CIDR, we can have network parts of any number of bits (not just 8, 16, or 24) and so we no longer distinguish between network part and sub-net part. (And consequently, throughout the book we use "subnet-directed" and "network-directed" broadcast synonymously to refer to the broadcast address derived from the netmask on this machine.) We explain in more detail how "old" sub-netting was done in the Notes to Chapter 6.

Warning: on many versions of Linux, the subnet-directed broadcast address is set incorrectly if your netmask is not the default for your IP address's "class". Instead, when you configure your IP address, the broadcast address defaults to the broadcast address for the address class. For example, if your IP address is 10.1.2.3, netmask 255.255.255.0, the broadcast address ought to be 10.1.2.255, but it defaults to 10.255.255.255, because 10.1.2.3 is a class-A address.

To correct this you must define the broadcast address explicity using **ifconfig**. You can do it when defining the IP address, as in:

```
ifconfig eth0 10.1.2.3 netmask 255.255.255.0 broadcast 10.1.2.255
```

or you can do it separately afterwards:

```
ifconfig eth0 broadcast 10.1.2.255
```

Windows-NT sets the broadcast address correctly, based on the actual IP address and not the address class.

Multicasting

Stevens Chapters 12 and 13, and Perlman Chapter 15 cover multicasting. See also

❑ http://www.internet2.edu/html/multicast.html/

❑ http://www.abilene.iu.edu/advanced.html

although the latter URL may change so you'll have to rummage around the site to find the multicast information.

Appendices

Web Appendix 2: more about bitmasks
Web Appendix 3: more netmask examples
Web Appendix 4: IP version 6
Inside back cover: decimal/binary, and hex conversion table

5 Routing in detail – controlling how and where packets pass in and out of your networks

Introduction

Now you are familiar with the three fundamental network parameters – IP address, netmask, and default gateway router. This chapter tells you how to apply these practically to your own network in two ways. First, you'll interpret the routing tables on your existing network, to understand and debug how the packets are moving in and out of your network. You will see that ranges specified using netmasks are used all over the place. Secondly, you'll learn to add/modify/delete routes in order to divide your network into sub-nets for testing, or for performance, security, or other reasons.

5.1 Routing tables direct the movement of packets on your networks

This module briefly repeats several topics we've touched on already, bringing them together as an introduction to the more advanced routing we cover in this chapter.

The Internet is an inter-network of many separate networks. These networks are connected to one another by routers. When I communicate with you, packets from my PC travel hop by hop across all the intervening networks, on to your network and finally on to your PC (Figure 5.1). At each hop a router forwards the packet towards its destination. However, the packets themselves contain only the destination IP address and *no routing information whatsoever*. When a packet arrives at a router, the router decides where to send the packet next; a router forwards the packet one more hop towards its final destination; it decides where to forward it using its *routing tables* – a set of rules that tells it the next-hop router to forward to for a particular destination.

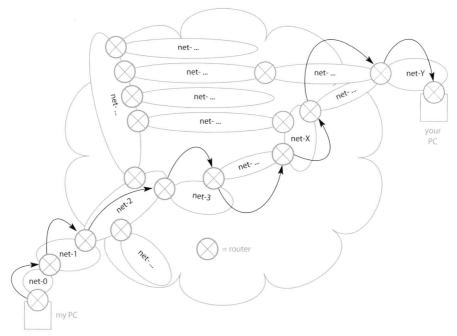

Figure 5.1 Travelling hop by hop across networks

We have already seen the code a router uses to make its decisions (Figure 5.2). Obvious questions are:

- how do the routers find out what routes there are to various destinations?
- how are all the routers configured? Does someone have to configure them manually?
- how does a machine (host or router) find out what routers are on its network?

If the Internet was organized in a rigid, hierarchical tree structure, it might be possible to derive answers to some of these questions automatically. However, the Internet is not owned or run by a single organization, and sites aren't connected to it in a hierarchical way. In fact, the connections form an untidy web or mesh as shown in Figure 5.1, so the routing system must be able to cope with this.

```
…
/* reach here only if not local to any of my interfaces */
else if (dest is in the IP address range for remote network-A)
        forward the packet towards dest via router-1
else if (dest is in the IP address range for remote network-B)
        forward the packet towards dest via router-2
…
```

Figure 5.2 Code a router uses to make decisions

Up to now we have implicitly assumed that a router is configured manually – that a network administrator tells this router about the various destinations and how to find them. This is the case for the internal networks in almost every small and medium-sized organization, and this chapter is devoted to configuring routing tables manually. For larger networks, and on the backbone of the Internet, something more sophisticated is needed, and in the Notes we look briefly at automatic routing protocols. These let routers find out from one another how to send to various destinations, and to inform one another when a connection breaks so that packets can be sent along a different path. This adaptive behavior is crucial for making the Internet resilient, allowing it to work even when individual components have failed.

But for now we'll consider only how routers are configured manually with their routing tables, which define both routes to other systems and, implicitly, which routers this machine can rely on to forward packets to other networks. Figure 5.3 shows a routing table from a Linux PC on a LAN, with three network cards. Ignore the detail for now – we'll explain it soon. Just notice that each entry consists of an IP address and netmask: as usual the combination specifies a range of IP addresses, and means "if I receive a packet with a destination address that belongs in this range, I will forward it to the gateway (router) specified." In other words, an entry is a *route* to a destination. Routing table entries are often referred to simply as "routes."

```
alice% route -n
Kernel IP routing table
Destination      Gateway        Genmask           Flags Metric Ref  Use Iface
192.0.2.0        0.0.0.0        255.255.255.128   U     0      0      0 eth0
192.168.168.0    0.0.0.0        255.255.255.0     U     0      0      0 eth1
10.0.0.0         0.0.0.0        255.0.0.0         U     0      0      0 eth2
0.0.0.0          192.0.2.29     0.0.0.0           UG    0      0      0 eth0
```

Figure 5.3 Routing table from a Linux PC on a LAN

That's what routing tables are all about. You already know all the concepts involved. The hardest part to learn is how ranges are specified using netmasks, which you are an expert in by now! What complicates things is that the command syntax and output/GUI formats for setting and displaying routes are not very clear (i.e. it's their fault, not yours, but the burden still falls on you). In the rest of this chapter we go on to look in detail at Linux and Windows routing tables and how to view them (and make sense of them), how to modify them, and how to troubleshoot them. (In the next chapter we apply all these techniques in practice, using them to set up test networks, and to divide a network into sub-nets.)

5.2 Routing table details – Linux

We start with Linux because it displays routing tables more simply than Windows. (Windows does the same thing but its display is more complicated.)

To display the routing table on this machine, use either of the commands:

```
route -n
netstat -r -n
```

which do exactly the same thing. (As usual, "**-n**" says to display IP addresses of networks and machines as numerics, not names.) **netstat** performs many network status functions; option "**-r**" selects the routing details display. Figure 5.4 shows the output for a typical LAN PC with one network interface. ("Genmask" means netmask. We don't know why it's called this – maybe to avoid calling it a sub-net mask, which would be even more confusing.)

```
alice% route -n
Kernel IP routing table
Destination   Gateway      Genmask           Flags Metric Ref   Use Iface
192.0.2.0     0.0.0.0      255.255.255.128   U     0      0       0 eth0
0.0.0.0       192.0.2.29   0.0.0.0           UG    0      0       0 eth0
```

Figure 5.4 routes output for a typical LAN PC with one network interface

> **Warning:** If you omit the "**-n**" by mistake, the information will be printed with names instead of numbers for gateways (see Figure 5.5) as long as your DNS is working correctly. But be warned: if your DNS (see Chapter 7) isn't configured, **route** will still try the lookup, and will wait for about a minute and a half before giving up and printing the details numerically. Because this format is harder to interpret we won't use it, even when the DNS is working.

```
alice% route
Kernel IP routing table
Destination   Gateway         Genmask           Flags Metric Ref   Use Iface
localnet      *               255.255.255.128   U     0      0       0 eth0
default       gate.uit.co.uk  0.0.0.0           UG    0      0       0 eth0
```

Figure 5.5 route's output if you omit "**-n**"

Here's what the output means. When this machine receives a packet destined for IP address **pktdest**, TCP/IP executes the following for each line in the table:

```
if (pktdest is in the range specified by (Destination, Genmask))
        use this route
else
        move on to next line and try again
if no line matches pktdest, we can't send the packet so report
an error.
```

Then, if it has selected a route to use, it executes:

```
if (Gateway is 0.0.0.0)
/* means "we don't need a router; dest is directly connected " */
          send packet directly to pktdest, using ARP if necessary,
          via interface Iface
else
          send the packet to router Gateway for forwarding, via
          interface Iface
```

The comparison "if (Gateway is 0.0.0.0)" is confusing. It is merely Linux's way of saying "this network is directly connected." It is a notation only. The by-name listing in Figure 5.5 shows it as a "*", which is much clearer. Don't be misled into thinking the 0.0.0.0 has a special technical meaning you can't understand.

In Module 5.3 we'll explain in detail how these routing table entries are created (although you already used them implicitly back in Chapter 3).

You can use the clever tool on our Web site to interpret Linux **route -n** or **netstat -r -n** command output, and print it in an operating-system-independent format.

Routes are ordered in the table from most specific down to least specific, and are selected in the same order, which is necessary if the default gateway route is to apply only when no other route is found.

Linux routing table flags

Each entry in the Linux routing table listing can have zero or more one-letter "flags," giving more information about the type of route it is.

Flag	If present	If absent
U	interface is Up, route is active	interface is down, making route inactive (but never shown: route is removed when interface goes down)
H	this route is for a single Host	this route is for a range of addresses (i.e. for a "network")
G	destination is reachable via this Gateway (router)	destination is connected directly; send packets directly on **Iface**, using ARP if necessary

The **H** flag is historical, and is compatible with other versions of UNIX. You don't need it on Linux because the **Genmask** field tells you whether the address range contains only one address (a host) or many addresses (a "network").

5.3 Linux routing tables (1) – adding routes

The **route** command displays the current contents of the routing tables, as you've seen. You also use it to add or delete routes. It interacts directly with the kernel's tables, so changes you enter take effect immediately.

Using the **route** command is confusing and error-prone because of the number of options available and really horrible error messages, not because what you're doing is complicated. (It's just as bad on Windows too.) The **route**(8) manpage describes the command in detail, but doesn't show clearly which arguments apply to which sub-command (**add**, **del**, etc.) so we've spelled them out in the table below. When you're getting used to **route**, the best advice is to follow the command syntax from the table; you'll make fewer errors that way.

The "help" listing ("**route -help -A inet**") says you have to use "/" notation for net-masks; the manpage says you have to use full netmask notation. In fact you can use either, e.g. instead of "**netmask 255.255.255.0**", append "**/8**" to the *destaddr* without any spaces on either side of the "/". You can also use the keyword **delete** (compatible with the Windows **route** command) instead of **del**.

Adding routes

add a route to a "network" (range of addresses)

      `route add -net`   *destaddr* `netmask` *a.b.c.d*   `gw` *routeraddr*

The route will be displayed with the **U** and **G** flags. This is the type of route you will want to create most of the time.

add a default gateway

      `route add`   `default`   `gw` *routeraddr*

add a route to a single host

      `route add -host`   *destaddr*   `gw` *routeraddr*

The route will be displayed with the **U**, **G**, and **H** flags.

Examples

To make the examples more concrete, assume we're adding routes on the PC shown in the little network in Figure 5.6. (The link to the Internet is dotted because the private 10.x.x.x addresses shown are not routable over the Internet.) To follow the examples on your own PC, it doesn't need to be connected to a network at all, and you certainly don't have to add the routers.

For the **route** commands to work, just ensure that your IP address is 10.1.1.11, netmask 255.255.255.0. "**route -n**" should then display output similar to Figure 5.7.

> **Tip:** after you enter each command, do a "**route -n**" to check the command has done what you expected.

Tip: when adding or deleting, always specify "`-net`" or "`-host`" explicitly (except when it's the default gateway route). Don't rely on whatever the default happens to be.

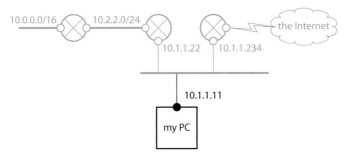

Figure 5.6 Adding routes

```
Kernel IP routing table
Destination     Gateway        Genmask         Flags Metric Ref    Use Iface
10.1.1.0        0.0.0.0        255.255.255.0   U     0      0        0 eth0
```

Figure 5.7 "`route -n`" output

In some of the examples we have used unusual spacing to highlight differences between similar lines.

1. Create a default route:

   ```
   route add default gw 10.1.1.254
   ```

2. Create a route saying that we can get to the range of addresses specified by 10.2.2.0/24 (i.e. 10.2.2.0, netmask 255.255.255.0) by using the router 10.1.1.22. Use either of:

   ```
   route add -net  10.2.2.0 netmask 255.255.255.0  gw 10.1.1.22
   route add -net  10.2.2.0/24                      gw 10.1.1.22
   ```

3. Create a route to the range 10.0.0.0 netmask 255.255.0.0 via the same router. Use either of:

   ```
   route add -net  10.0.0.0/16                      gw 10.1.1.22
   route add -net  10.0.0.0 netmask 255.255.0.0     gw 10.1.1.22
   ```

It's easy to make mistakes with the **route** command, and hard to correct them because the error messages are weird. There's a summary of common errors in the next module. In addition, the tools on our Web site make it easier to construct the correct commands, and Web Appendix 5 lists **route** command error messages and how to avoid them.

Making your settings permanent

Changes made with the **route** command don't persist across reboots – to make a change permanent you have to enter it in a startup configuration file. The file to use depends on your version of Linux: see Appendix 6.

5.4 Linux routing tables (2) – deleting routes; common problems

Deleting existing routes

delete a route to a "network"

```
route delete -net    destaddr netmask a.b.c.d
route delete -net    destaddr/maskbits
```

delete a route to a single host

```
route delete -host   destaddr                      gw  routeraddr
```

delete the route that uses a specific gateway to a "network"

```
route delete -net    destaddr/maskbits            gw  routeraddr
route delete -net    destaddr netmask a.b.c.d     gw  routeraddr
```

delete a default gateway

```
route delete         default
```

delete a specific default gateway

```
route delete         default                        gw  routeraddr
```

Examples

For these examples we're using the same scenario as in the previous module so we have repeated the network diagram here.

1. Delete the route we created in step 2. Use any of:
```
route delete -net 10.2.2.0 netmask 255.255.255.0
route delete -net 10.2.2.0/24
route delete -net 10.2.2.0 netmask 255.255.255.0 gw 10.1.1.22
route delete -net 10.2.2.0/24                    gw 10.1.1.22
```

2. Delete the route we created in step 3, just for the sake of it. Use any of:
```
route delete -net 10.0.0.0 netmask 255.255.0.0
route delete -net 10.0.0.0/16
route delete -net 10.0.0.0 netmask 255.255.0.0   gw 10.1.1.22
route delete -net 10.0.0.0/16                    gw 10.1.1.22
```

3. Finally, delete the default gateway. Use either of:
```
route delete default
route delete default                             gw 10.1.1.254
```

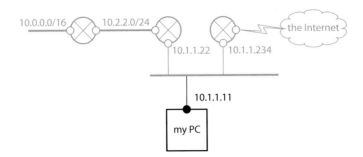

Common problems with adding and deleting routes

Web Appendix 5 gives a list of error messages and their causes. This section looks at it the other way round and lists the most common mistakes that cause errors.

- omitting the **gw** keyword when adding a route:

  ```
  route add default                    1.2.3.4              wrong
  route add default                    gw 1.2.3.4           OK
  ```

- omitting the **-net** option or the netmask when adding a network route, so you might end up creating a route to a single host instead:

  ```
  route add 10.2.2.0               gw 10.1.1.22         wrong
  route add -net 10.2.2.0          gw 10.1.1.22         wrong
  route add -net 10.2.2.0/24       gw 10.1.1.22         OK
  ```

- specifying a network using one of the host addresses in its range instead of the network address:

  ```
  route add -net 10.2.2.47/24      gw 10.1.1.22         wrong
  route add -net 10.2.2.0/24       gw 10.1.1.22         OK
  ```

5.5 Routing table details – Windows

The Windows routing display is harder to understand than Linux's, although the routing works in exactly the same way.

To print routing information, open a Command ("DOS") Prompt window, and use the **route** command, but with a slightly different syntax (of course) to Linux:

```
route print
```

(Option "**-n**" is neither permitted nor necessary – route details are always printed numerically.) Instead of **route print**, you can use **netstat -r -n**. While this gives you extra information you don't need (about active connections) and the "**-n**" option only affects the extra information you're not interested in, it does mean you can use the same command on both Linux and Windows. Figure 5.8 shows the routing tables for a typical LAN PC (192.168.20.22) with one network card and one router (its default gateway).

Figure 5.8

Routing tables for a typical LAN PC

```
  Command Prompt

C:\> route print
=================================================================
Interface List
0x1 ........................... MS TCP Loopback interface
0x2 ...00 02 b3 2a 49 1c ...... Intel(R) PRO Adapter
0x3 ...00 00 00 00 00 00 ...... NdisWan Adapter
=================================================================
Active Routes:
  Network Address          Netmask  Gateway Address       Interface  Metric
        0.0.0.0          0.0.0.0   192.168.20.254   192.168.20.22       1
      127.0.0.0          255.0.0.0        127.0.0.1        127.0.0.1       1
   192.168.20.0    255.255.255.0   192.168.20.22   192.168.20.22       1
  192.168.20.22  255.255.255.255        127.0.0.1        127.0.0.1       1
 192.168.20.255  255.255.255.255   192.168.20.22   192.168.20.22       1
      224.0.0.0          224.0.0.0   192.168.20.22   192.168.20.22       1
255.255.255.255  255.255.255.255   192.168.20.22   192.168.20.22       1
```

Unlike Linux, Windows doesn't show any flags in the routing table listings and routes are ordered numerically in the table. The routing, however, is just like Linux, with the most specific route that applies to a destination address used in preference to less specific routes. As we said in Module 5.2, this is necessary if the default gateway route is to apply only when no other route is found.

  Interface List: you'd think this was to make interpreting the **Interface** field easier, but it's useless, so forget it (if you don't have up-to-date NT Service Packs this may not even be displayed)

  Network Address: this is what Linux called **Destination** (other NT versions may call it "Network Destination")

  Netmask: this combined with the **Network Address** specifies the address range this route applies to. If this is 255.255.255.255, the address range contains only a single address (and would have an **H** flag on Linux)

  Interface: this means the same as Linux's **Iface**. But to work out which physical NIC is used you have to run **ipconfig/all** and see which NIC has the address shown in the **Interface** field

Gateway Address (or **Gateway**): if this is different from the **Interface** field, this route is using the router specified in the **Gateway Address** field (and would have a **G** flag on Linux). Otherwise (i.e. the same as the **Interface** field) this is a route for something that's connected directly, not forwarded via a router. If the gateway is 127.0.0.1, the route refers to one of my own addresses – talking to myself. The interface will also be 127.0.0.1

Metric: you can ignore this (see Notes).

It's easier to understand the listing reading it line by line, and from bottom to top:

```
255.255.255.255   255.255.255.255   192.168.20.22   192.168.20.22   1
```

the limited broadcast address (Module 4.10) reachable on the local wire via our single (real) interface, IP address 192.168.20.22

```
224.0.0.0         224.0.0.0         192.168.20.22   192.168.20.22   1
```

multicast addresses (Module 4.11). Forget about this entry.

```
192.168.20.255    255.255.255.255   192.168.20.22   192.168.20.22   1
```

broadcast address for our specific network, again reachable directly on our single real interface, 192.168.20.22. (NT derives this from the historical address class of the IP address. If your network isn't an exact class A, B, or C, the Network Destination shown here will not be what you expected. For example, for 192.168.20.150 netmask 255.255.255.224 you'd expect a broadcast address of 192.168.20.191 but you get 192.168.20.255. On the other hand, when NT actually broadcasts, it uses the correct broadcast address, 192.168.20.191

```
192.168.20.22     255.255.255.255   127.0.0.1       127.0.0.1       1
```

my own IP address. I can contact this by sending packets to 127.0.0.1, which is my loopback address, i.e. this is talking to myself

```
192.168.20.0      255.255.255.0     192.168.20.22   192.168.20.22   1
```

The range of 256 addresses making up the network on my wire. I can contact these directly, using ARP if necessary, sending out on my single interface 192.168.20.22

```
127.0.0.0         255.0.0.0         127.0.0.1       127.0.0.1       1
```

My loopback address, talking to myself again

```
0.0.0.0           0.0.0.0           192.168.20.254  192.168.20.22   1
```

As we saw with Linux, this range includes all possible IP addresses, so this line represents my default gateway router, with address 192.168.20.254, reached via my 192.168.20.22 interface.

In the next module we explain how to create and delete routes on Windows.

5.6 Windows routing tables (1) – displaying and adding routes

Appendix 8 contains our manual page for the Windows **route** command. This module and the next show the command formats in more detail.

Displaying existing routes

print all routes

```
route print
```

print a specific route

```
route print       mask a.b.c.d                    routeraddr
```

print matching routes

```
route print       *                               routeraddr
route print       destaddr
route print       wildcard
route print       destaddr                         *
route print       wildcard                         wildcard
```

print persistent routes as well as currently active routes

```
route -p print
```

You can use wildcards in *destination*: * matches any string of characters, and ? matches any one character.

Adding routes

add a route to a "network" (range of addresses)

```
route add         destaddr mask a.b.c.d            routeraddr
```

add a default gateway

```
route add         0.0.0.0 mask 0.0.0.0    routeraddr
```

add a route to a single host

```
route add         destaddr                         routeraddr
```

Examples

We'll use the same example network as we did for Linux in Module 5.3. Again, to follow the examples on your own PC, it doesn't need to be connected to a network at all. For the **route** commands to work, just ensure that your IP address is 10.1.1.11, netmask 255.255.255.0.

> **Tip:** after you enter each command, do a "**route print**" to check the command has done what you expected.

In some of the examples we have used unusual spacing to highlight differences between similar lines.

1. Print all routes to any 10.2.x.x network

    ```
    route print 10.2.*
    ```

2. Print any route using 10.1.1.22 as a gateway

    ```
    route print * 10.1.1.22
    ```

3. Print only routes to 10.2.x.x networks using 10.1.1.22 as a gateway

    ```
    route print 10.2.* 10.1.1.22
    ```

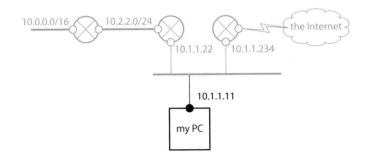

4. Create a default route:

    ```
    route add 0.0.0.0 mask 0.0.0.0 10.1.1.254
    ```

5. Create a route saying that we can get to the range of addresses specified by 10.2.2.0/24 (i.e. 10.2.2.0, netmask 255.255.255.0) by using the router 10.1.1.22:

    ```
    route add 10.2.2.0 mask 255.255.255.0 10.1.1.22
    ```

6. Create a route to the range 10.0.0.0 netmask 255.0.0.0 via the same router:

    ```
    route add 10.0.0.0 mask 255.255.0.0 10.1.1.22
    ```

As with Linux, using the **route** command is error-prone because of its syntax; however, the Windows error messages, explained below, are even worse than Linux's. The tools on our Web site make it easier to construct the correct commands.

Note that when you have multiple NICs in your machine, **Control Panel > Network** settings aren't actioned immediately – you have to reboot.

Making your settings permanent

By default, routes **added** with the **route** command do not persist across reboots. If you use the "**-p**" option in the command when you create the route, it is considered a *persistent* route and will remain in effect after rebooting. Anything you do to a persistent route also persists, so you don't have to use "**-p**" with **change** or **delete**.

5.7 Windows routing tables (2) – deleting routes; common problems

Deleting routes

delete all routes to this destination (single host or network)

```
route delete  destaddr
```

```
route delete  destaddr                    routeraddr
```

delete all routes that use a specific gateway (to hosts or networks)

```
route delete  *                    routeraddr
```

delete a route to a "network"

```
route delete  destaddr mask a.b.c.d
```

delete the route that uses a specific gateway to a "network"

```
route delete  destaddr mask a.b.c.d    routeraddr
```

delete a default gateway

```
route delete  0.0.0.0
```

delete a specific default gateway

```
route delete  0.0.0.0
```

```
route delete  0.0.0.0                    routeraddr
```

(This is just a special case of the first command shown in this section.)

delete all "gateway" routes

```
route -f
```

This deletes your default gateway if you have one, and also the route to any directly connected network that you will probably never need. (If you do this by mistake, you can re-instate the normal entries by going into **Control Panel > Network** and changing a setting (e.g. your IP address) to itself and pressing **OK** or **Apply**.)

Modifying an existing route

Windows-NT lets you modify existing routes using the "`route change`" command. We never use this because it's so hard to remember its syntax – we just delete the wrong route and add the correct one instead. These examples respectively change the default gateway to a new value, and change the netmask on a specific route:

```
route change    0.0.0.0    mask    0.0.0.0              10.1.1.22
route change    10.2.2.0   mask    255.255.255.128      10.1.1.22
```

Examples

For these examples we're using the same scenario as in the previous Module (Figure 5.6).

1. Delete the route we created in step 2. Use either of:

```
route delete   10.2.2.0     mask     255.255.255.0
route delete   10.2.2.0     mask     255.255.255.0 10.1.1.22
```

2. Delete the route we created in step 3, just for the sake of it. Use either of:

```
route delete   10.0.0.0     mask     255.255.0.0
route delete   10.0.0.0     mask     255.255.0.0 10.1.1.22
```

3. Finally, delete the default gateway. Use any of:

```
route delete   0.0.0.0
route delete   0.0.0.0      mask     0.0.0.0
route delete   0.0.0.0      mask     0.0.0.0   10.1.1.254
```

Common problems

Web Appendix 5 lists common error messages when entering routes. Here we note a few common mistakes:

- forgetting to specify a netmask defines a host route, which is almost certainly not what you wanted, and it's hard to diagnose because the output format is complicated. For example,

```
route add  0.0.0.0     10.1.1.254                      probably wrong
route add  0.0.0.0     mask 0.0.0.0   10.1.1.254           probably OK
```

- just as we saw for Linux in Module 5.4, when you specify a network route you must use the network address, not just any one of the host addresses in its range:

```
route add  10.2.2.47   mask   255.255.0.0   10.1.1.22        wrong
route add  10.2.0.0    mask   255.255.0.0   10.1.1.22           OK
```

- if you enter an impossible gateway address (via **Control Panel > Network**) it won't show at all in **route print**, but it may interfere with the route command's operation, so that even commands with the correct syntax don't work, with misleading messages like "no such route." The solution is to remove the silly default gateway via **Control Panel > Network** and reboot. (You can try this out easily. For example, your PC has address 10.5.5.77, netmask 255.255.255.0. In **Control Panel > Network** set the default gateway to 192.168.1.2 or some other address not on your directly connected network.)

5.8 Creating routes for directly connected networks and default gateways

We were able to delay our detailed discussion of routing until this chapter for two reasons:

1. TCP/IP automatically creates or modifies the routing table when you configure or alter the IP address and netmask of your machine's network interface. The route configuration you needed to talk to directly connected local machines was done transparently for you

2. a typical LAN PC needs only one router – its default gateway. Both Linux and Windows let you specify the permanent setting for the default gateway without using the route **command**.

As a result, we've been able to manage perfectly well without having to create or modify routes by hand. In this module we look at automatically created routes and default gateways in a little more detail (but only so you can understand how your routing tables were created – you won't have to do any extra work!).

Linux

If you start Linux with no network interfaces enabled, it has an empty routing table, except perhaps for the loopback interface (reasonably enough, because without any real interface, the machine can't send any packets except to itself).

When you configure an interface and bring it up (**ifconfig up**), the routes necessary for this interface – how to contact the directly connected network – are added automatically.

When you bring down an interface (**ifconfig down**), the routes for this interface, and any routes to gateways reached via this interface, are removed automatically.

Exercise:

```
ifconfig eth0 down                              to ensure we start with nothing
route -n                                        view initial routing tables (empty)
ifconfig eth0 10.1.1.11 netmask 255.255.255.0 up    configure this
                                                              interface
route -n                                        view changes
ifconfig eth0 netmask 255.0.0.0                 change the netmask
route -n                              view changes – Genmask changed on local network
ifconfig eth0 down                              disable this interface
route -n                                        view changes – routes removed
```

Your output ought to be similar to that shown below.

```
alice# ifconfig eth0 down
alice# route -n
Kernel IP routing table
Destination     Gateway     Genmask         Flags Metric Ref Use Iface

alice# ifconfig eth0 10.1.1.11 netmask 255.255.255.0 up

alice# route -n
Kernel IP routing table
Destination     Gateway     Genmask         Flags Metric Ref Use Iface
10.1.1.0        0.0.0.0     255.255.255.0   U     0      0   0 eth0

alice# ifconfig eth0 10.1.1.11 netmask 255.0.0.0

alice# route -n
Kernel IP routing table
Destination     Gateway     Genmask         Flags Metric Ref Use Iface
10.0.0.0        0.0.0.0     255.0.0.0       U     0      0   0 eth0

alice# ifconfig eth0 down

alice# route -n
Kernel IP routing table
Destination     Gateway     Genmask         Flags Metric Ref Use Iface
```

Windows

Windows also creates automatically all the routes you need when you add a particular interface, and deletes them when you remove the interface. Figure 5.9(a) shows the routing tables for a machine with its network card disabled. Figure 5.9(b) shows the same machine rebooted after the card has been re-enabled. (If you are using more than one interface (IP address) per network card, or multiple network cards, you'll have to reboot for the changes to take effect.)

Figure 5.9
Routing tables
for a machine
(a) with network
card disabled;
(b) with card
re-enabled

(a)

Command Prompt

```
C:\>route print
Active Routes:
  Network Address          Netmask   Gateway Address      Interface Metric
      127.0.0.0          255.0.0.0        127.0.0.1       127.0.0.1      1
  255.255.255.255  255.255.255.255  255.255.255.255         0.0.0.0      1
```

(b)

Command Prompt

```
C:\>route print
Active Routes:
  Network Address          Netmask   Gateway Address      Interface Metric
        0.0.0.0            0.0.0.0       192.0.2.29      192.0.2.35      1
      127.0.0.0          255.0.0.0        127.0.0.1       127.0.0.1      1
      192.0.2.0    255.255.255.128       192.0.2.35      192.0.2.35      1
     192.0.2.35  255.255.255.255        127.0.0.1       127.0.0.1      1
    192.0.2.255  255.255.255.255       192.0.2.35      192.0.2.35      1
      224.0.0.0          224.0.0.0       192.0.2.35      192.0.2.35      1
  255.255.255.255  255.255.255.255       192.0.2.35      192.0.2.35      1
```

If you start NT with no network cards (or if TCP/IP isn't bound to any adapter using the **Control Panel > Network > Bindings > All Protocols** dialog), the routing table will show only a single entry, for the loopback interface, 127.0.0.1.

5.9 Multiple default gateways

Using multiple default gateways is confusing in two respects – what it means, and what it does. A common misapprehension is that if you have two Internet connections, as in Figure 5.10, you should configure two default gateways on your PC, one for each connection, and that traffic that comes in from connection A will be replied to using gateway A, with traffic from connection B replied to on connection B. That's all wrong. It's perfectly possible that traffic can enter via connection A and its response leave by connection B.

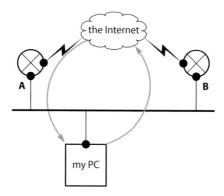

Figure 5.10 Incoming and outgoing packets can take different paths

You can see why that's wrong by remembering what routing information is in a packet: nothing apart from the source and destination IP addresses. Let's say a packet enters the LAN via connection A, for Alice. Once Alice's TCP/IP receives it, she doesn't know or care how it entered the network. When she replies to it, she will use her routing tables, which also don't know that this packet is a reply to something that came in earlier, let alone try to remember which connection that earlier something might have come in on!

What multiple default gateways are intended for is described in RFC-1122: if a host's default gateway goes down, the host should select another from its list of default gateways. (How it chooses isn't specified – it could just take the next in the list, or it might decide on the basis of performance statistics it had accumulated.) For example, you might have the router of your permanent leased line or ADSL connection defined as your first default gateway, to be used all the time as long it's working. You could also define a second default gateway, an ISDN router, say, to be used only when your main connection has failed.

Both Linux and NT implement multiple default gateways to some extent.

Linux

You can easily define multiple default gateways by issuing multiple **route add** commands with the different routes. However, only some Linux versions do anything with the extra gateways, and you'll have to try it to see if it works on your system. The easiest way to do this is to add your real gateway address as the default; then add a non-existent one, which, as it's the most recently added, will be used first, as you'll see if you do "route -n"; run "**tcpdump -e -n**" to check which router is being used (by seeing which MAC address your PC sends the packets to).

```
route add default gw 192.0.2.99          non-existent gateway
route add default gw 192.0.2.1                   real gateway
```

(One of our Linux systems ARPs for the non-existent gateway for 5–10 minutes, and then switches to the second gateway successfully, whereas another different version of Linux tries the non-existent gateway seemingly forever.)

Windows

The Windows **Control Panel > Network** applet makes it look as though the default gateway is specific to an interface; it isn't – it's a routing table entry and not an interface parameter. The NT Resource Kit recommends you specify default gateways on one network card only to avoid confusion.

You can set multiple default gateways on a single interface using the **Advanced** button in the **Control Panel > Network > TCP/IP Properties** window. Windows uses "dead gateway detection" (see Notes) to decide when to switch from one to another. This is activated only by certain protocols (TCP) so testing it out with **ping**, etc. is difficult.

Because very few sites have multiple Internet connections we don't discuss this topic further, other than in the Notes at the end of the chapter.

5.10 ICMP redirects affect routing tables and simplify LAN configuration

So far we've created all our routes manually, either directly using the **route** command, or indirectly by configuring the network interface or setting the default gateway parameter in a configuration file. In this module we explain how a mechanism called *ICMP redirects* can create routes automatically and simplify configuring the routing tables on your LAN machines. We'll use an example network (Figure 5.11) similar to that used in Module 5.3.

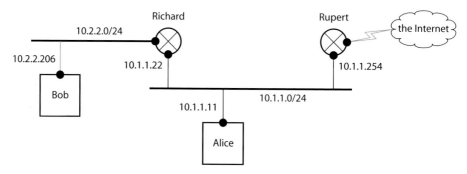

Figure 5.11 Example network for ICMP redirects

We're going to configure Alice's routing tables. The routes for the directly connected LAN (10.1.1.0/24) are added automatically by **ifconfig** or the Windows equivalent. Then we explicitly add the default gateway route to Rupert (10.1.1.254) who connects our LAN to the Internet.

But what about the 10.2.2.0 network which is behind Richard? We could manually configure Alice – and every other LAN PC – to know about this network. But that would be a lot of work, and if we change the 10.2.2.0 network layout, or Richard's IP address, or add another network elsewhere, we'd have to change the routing information on every LAN PC. (So that's a bad idea.)

Fortunately, we don't have to do that. The ICMP redirect mechanism lets us configure one router manually, and have it automatically pass routing information to the LAN PCs as and when they need it. This is how we do it:

- configure Rupert with the details of the internal LAN routes ("forward packets to 10.2.2.0/24 using Richard = 10.1.1.22, etc."). Initially only Rupert knows the full story. We've chosen to configure Rupert with the complete routing information because he's the default gateway for all the PCs on our LAN

- the rest happens automatically, as described below.

Let's work through an example (Figure 5.12). Alice wants to send to Bob (10.2.2.206). Alice has the very simple routing tables we've come to expect of typical LAN machines: her tables say "if dest is on 10.1.1.11/24, I'll send it directly, using ARP if necessary; otherwise I'll use my default gateway (Rupert)." Bob isn't on Alice's locally connected network, so:

1. Alice sends the packet to her default gateway, Rupert (10.1.1.254)
2. Rupert *does know* how to reach the 10.2.2.0 network, so Rupert forwards the packet to Richard …
3. … and Richard forwards it to Bob, as we've seen before.

Now, here comes the clever bit:

2b. as well as forwarding the packet to Richard, Rupert sends a special message – an ICMP redirect – back to Alice, saying, "Hey Alice, you gave me a packet to send to Bob. I gave it to Richard to pass on to him, but next time it would be quicker if you just gave it to Richard yourself, instead of passing it to me first." When Alice receives this ICMP redirect she uses the information in it to automatically add a dynamic route to her tables, equivalent to:

```
route add -host 10.2.2.206 10.1.1.22      generated by ICMP redirect
```

4. the next time Alice has a packet for Bob, her TCP/IP knows to route it straight to Richard (4a) who forwards to Bob as usual (4b).

Alice is automatically learning routes to machines she wants to communicate with in the network behind Richard. Of course, if we had any other networks internally, she would learn about them too. The same applies to all our LAN machines; by relying on ICMP redirects, we have simple initial network configuration and efficient routing too.

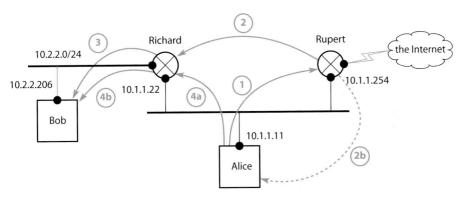

Figure 5.12 How ICMP redirects operate

The benefit of all this is that while you can configure any LAN machine – not just a router – to know about multiple routers and not just its default gateway, because of ICMP redirects you often don't have to bother. The configuration of the typical LAN PCs is as simple as can be – they only need to know their own IP address, netmask, and default gateway.

5.11 ICMP redirects implementations; automatic routing protocols

Linux route command and routing table flags

The Linux manpage documents two flag types (in addition to the **U**, **G**, and **H** entries we saw in Module 5.2) that indicate whether the entry was created:

a. normally (manually, or via **ifconfig** or the default gateway setting), or

b. automatically by some component of the system itself.

The flags are shown in Table 5.1. However, most current versions of Linux *don't* include the routes created by ICMP redirects in the default listing. The manpage is describing what happens on other versions of UNIX. To see these extra entries on Linux you have to use the command

```
route -n -C
```

which displays the *routing table cache*. (But this doesn't display the D flag either.)

Flag	If present	If absent
D	**D**ynamic: this entry was created automatically from an ICMP redirect or by a routing daemon (see below)	normal (manually configured) entry
M	**M**odified by an ICMP redirect or a routing daemon	normal (manually configured) entry

Table 5.1 Two Linux manpage flags

ICMP redirect notes

There are a few more features relating to ICMP redirects that you may need to know:

1. the RFCs say that routers may legitimately choose to ignore redirects. If Alice is configured as a router, what we described in the previous module may not work

2. Windows-NT doesn't show ICMP-created routes in its routing tables. There's no convenient way to display them

3. after ten minutes Windows-NT removes ICMP-created routes, so if this machine is still sending to that destination, the ICMP redirect procedure will be repeated every ten minutes

4. when a Linux host (Alice) receives an ICMP redirect to use a router (Rupert), if Alice doesn't have Rupert already in her ARP cache she won't successfully create the route until she receives the same ICMP redirect a second time. (This doesn't make much difference to the efficiency of the network, but it does clutter the **tcpdump** traces when you're trying to see what's happening.)

Automatic routing protocols – RIP, OSPF, BGP

(Strictly this doesn't belong here, but it explains what a routing daemon is and how you could get **M**- or **D**-flagged entries in your routing tables.)

All the routing decisions we've considered so far have been like this:

```
if (dest is in range-A)
          send packet via router-1
else if (dest is in range-B)
          send packet via router-2
...
```

A system that uses rules like this and nothing else can't have any resilience. The same action is decided on every time because the rules are completely deterministic. How then do we get resilience on the Internet?

The answer is that resilience is not provided at the IP routing level, but through higher, application-level mechanisms instead. The basic routing operates exactly as we've described, using the routing tables we've seen. However, application programs called *routing daemons* run on the routers and detect when network links go down or come up again, and communicate this information to the corresponding programs on other routers. These programs then modify the routing tables. By separating this adaptive, resilient functionality from the second-to-second packet forwarding, the basic routing can be performed very quickly, which is crucial for high-speed networks.

Using our postal analogy again, the Internet is like messenger boys running to and fro between offices with postcards to be delivered (Figure 5.13). There's a Big Boss (routing daemon) sitting in each office. When he hears from returning messenger boys that they're getting delayed because High Street is closed, he does two things:

1. he tells all his boys not to go via High Street, but to use Main Street instead (changes the routing tables on his own router)

2. he sends messages to neighboring offices that they should avoid High Street too.

Of course, he sends the messages using the boys, but he can give them special instructions. (In this analogy we have to assume that the boys are moronic and never themselves learn not to go down a closed street, which is of course completely unlike any real postal service.)

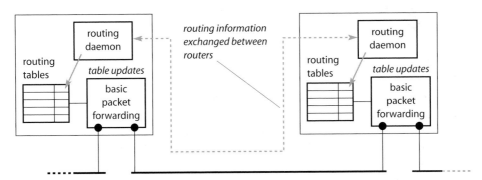

Figure 5.13 Routing daemons

Common routing protocols in use are *BGP (Border Gateway Protocol)* used on the Internet backbone, *OSPF (Open Shortest Path First)*, and *RIP (Routing Information Protocol)*, which is old and less flexible than BGP, and has fallen out of favor.

This type of routing is very different from what is needed on a typical internal network, so we discuss it no further (except in the Notes).

5.12 Lab – test network to demonstrate ICMP redirects

The best way to see ICMP redirects working would be to construct on your real LAN the network we had in Module 5.10. However, that requires several test machines and we haven't really told you how to configure a network like this yet. The next best way is to use the network in Figure 5.14 but with the IP addresses changed to match your real LAN; the only extra machine you need is a test machine to use as Richard. (You can build a test network with just two machines – Alice and Richard – to see ICMP redirects generated, but you need the bigger networks to see the routing change as a result of the redirects.)

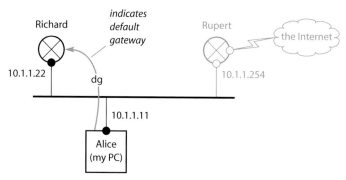

Figure 5.14 Small test network to exercise ICMP redirects

We're going to configure Alice to use Richard as her default gateway. Then, when Alice sends to an address on the Internet, say 128.9.0.107, the packet goes to Richard, who forwards it to Rupert … Richard will send an ICMP redirect to Alice, saying "use Rupert in future for this address." (The example is artificial. It's causing at least one ICMP redirect and a double hop on the first packet to every external address. We did it this way only because it doesn't need many machines or a lot of configuration to set up.)

1. ensure Richard is configured to act as a router (Module 3.6)

2. run "**tcpdump -n -t -e**" on any machine connected to this LAN wire

    ("-e" shows the Ethernet addresses, which we need in order to see which router is being used when a packet is forwarded)

3. Alice:

    IP address: 10.1.1.11

    Netmask: 255.255.255.0

    Default gateway: 10.1.1.22 (i.e. Richard)

4. Richard

    IP address: 10.1.1.22

    Netmask: 255.255.255.0

    Default gateway: 10.1.1.254 (i.e. Rupert)

5. From Alice, "`ping -c1 128.9.0.107`" (Linux), "`ping -n 1 128.9.0.107`" (Windows). Alice sends this using Richard as router

6   Richard forwards the packet to Rupert (and **tcpdump** can't see beyond Rupert, so that's the end of this packet as far as **tcpdump** is concerned)

7. Richard sends an ICMP redirect to Alice, saying "use Rupert (10.1.1.254) in future when trying to reach 128.9.0.107"

8. from Alice, again "`ping -c1 128.9.0.107`" (Linux), "`ping -n 1 128.9.0.107`" (Windows). This time Alice sends the packet via Rupert, without troubling Richard at all

9. on Alice, "`route -n`" (Linux), "`route print`" (Windows) shows the current routing tables. The ICMP-created entry isn't shown

10. if Alice is running Linux, "`route -nC`" shows the current routing table cache, which does show ICMP-created entries.

The relevant lines extracted from the **tcpdump** trace are:

```
00:d0:b7:b6:3d:f6 00:50:da:e4:61:34 ip 98: 10.1.1.11 > 128.9.0.107: icmp: echo request
00:50:da:e4:61:34 00:d0:b7:b6:3d:f6 ip 70: 10.1.1.22 > 10.1.1.11: icmp: redirect 128.9.0.107 to host 10.1.1.254
00:50:da:e4:61:34 00:00:c0:1a:aa:6e ip 98: 10.1.1.11 > 128.9.0.107: icmp: echo request

00:d0:b7:b6:3d:f6 00:00:c0:1a:aa:6e ip 98: 10.1.1.11 > 128.9.0.107: icmp: echo request
```

The output of **route -nC** in which you can see the temporary route for destination 128.0.89.107 reachable via gateway 10.1.1.254 is:

```
. . .
10.1.1.22    10.1.1.255    10.1.1.255    ibl    0    0    0 lo
10.1.1.11    128.9.0.107   10.1.1.254           0    0    2 eth0
. . .
```

Using names instead of numeric MAC addresses

Working with MAC addresses is awkward because they're so long. On Linux we can store MAC-address-to-name mappings in the file **/etc/ethers** and then have **tcpdump** print the addresses as names instead of numbers. Our **/etc/ethers** file for the test network looks like:

```
00:D0:B7:B6:3D:F6        ALICE
00:50:DA:E4:61:34        RICHARD
00:00:C0:1A:AA:6E        RUPERT
```

(By convention, names for MAC addresses are entered in uppercase, so as not to confuse them with IP hostnames.) Now if we run "`tcpdump -f -t -e`" ("`-f`": show "foreign" addresses as numeric – prevents name lookups for external IP addresses) we get the much more readable trace:

```
ALICE RICHARD ip 98: 10.1.1.11 > 128.9.0.107: icmp: echo request
RICHARD ALICE ip 70: 10.1.1.22 > 10.1.1.11: icmp: redirect 128.9.0.107 to host 10.1.1.254
RICHARD RUPERT ip 98: 10.1.1.11 > 128.9.0.107: icmp: echo request

ALICE RUPERT ip 98: 10.1.1.11 > 128.9.0.107: icmp: echo request
```

5.13 **More about** traceroute

You need to be aware of a few points when interpreting **traceroute** output.

1. the path that **traceroute** prints isn't cast in stone – it can vary from day to day, or in exceptional circumstances even from packet to packet. Figure 5.15 shows two **traceroutes** we ran within a few seconds of one another, giving very different paths.

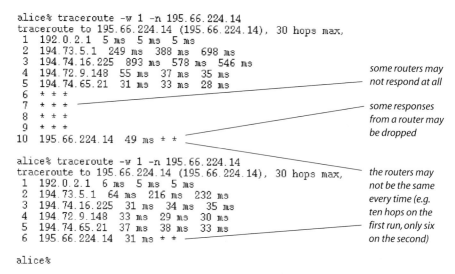

```
alice% traceroute -w 1 -n 195.66.224.14
traceroute to 195.66.224.14 (195.66.224.14), 30 hops max,
 1   192.0.2.1   5 ms   5 ms   5 ms
 2   194.73.5.1   249 ms   388 ms   698 ms
 3   194.74.16.225   893 ms   578 ms   546 ms
 4   194.72.9.148   55 ms   37 ms   35 ms
 5   194.74.65.21   31 ms   33 ms   28 ms
 6   * * *
 7   * * *
 8   * * *
 9   * * *
10   195.66.224.14   49 ms * *

alice% traceroute -w 1 -n 195.66.224.14
traceroute to 195.66.224.14 (195.66.224.14), 30 hops max,
 1   192.0.2.1   6 ms   5 ms   5 ms
 2   194.73.5.1   64 ms   216 ms   232 ms
 3   194.74.16.225   31 ms   34 ms   35 ms
 4   194.72.9.148   33 ms   29 ms   30 ms
 5   194.74.65.21   37 ms   38 ms   33 ms
 6   195.66.224.14   31 ms * *

alice%
```

some routers may not respond at all

some responses from a router may be dropped

the routers may not be the same every time (e.g. ten hops on the first run, only six on the second)

Figure 5.15 Two **traceroute**s with very different paths

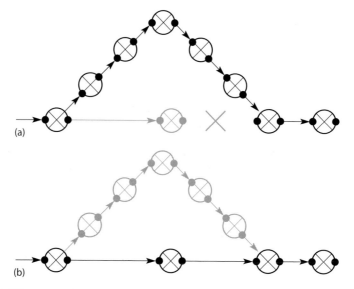

(a)

(b)

Figure 5.16 Why successive **traceroute** outputs can differ

The output in Figure 5.15 is explained if the path the packets are taking is the long way round a broken link, as shown in Figure 5.16(a). Then when the link recovers (or when the routers find out that the link is up again), packets are routed along the "normal" path, in Figure 5.16(b).

2. **traceroute** prints a "*" when it hasn't received a response to one of its probes. By default it issues three probes per hop. If one response is shown as a "*", probably the probe or the response got lost. If all responses show as "*" (like hops 7, 8 and 9 in Figure 5.15) then this router is down, or doesn't respond to **traceroutes**, or it has a fairly common TCP/IP bug (see Notes)

3. **traceroute** shows the IP address of only one side (the first side it meets) of a router the packets pass through. Figure 5.17 shows our Internet router.

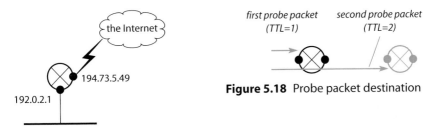

Figure 5.18 Probe packet destination

Figure 5.17 Our Internet router's IP address

192.0.2.1 is one of our addresses, and 194.73.5.49 belongs to our ISP. If we **traceroute** out to a distant site, the trace looks like:

   alice# traceroute -n 195.66.224.14

   traceroute to 195.66.224.14 (195.66.224.14), 30 hops max, ...

   1 192.0.2.1 6 ms * 6 ms

   ...

whereas, if someone **traceroute**s in to our router, what they get is:

   elsewhere# traceroute -n 192.0.2.1

   ...

   18 194.74.16.226 168.378 ms 169.851 ms 176.364 ms

   19 194.73.5.49 193.520 ms * 194.14 ms   *(trace completed)*

This behavior is reasonable because only the first-met side of a router is ever a destination of a probe packet. The other side of the router can be reached from the first-met side without any extra network hops (Figure 5.18).

4. For the same reason as in (3), if we **traceroute** from the LAN to the external address of our router, we get

   alice# traceroute -n 194.73.5.49

   traceroute to 194.73.5.49 (194.73.5.49), 30 hops max, 40 byte packets

   1 192.0.2.1 6 ms * 6 ms   *(trace completed)*

showing only the inside address of the router. Confusing but correct!

5.14 Troubleshooting (1) – netmasks and addresses

For some of the problems below we suggest you try it yourself, and give instructions on how you can reproduce the problem. When working through problems like this, we've often found the following tips useful:

- as always, run **tcpdump** on the wire so you can see exactly what's happening
- remember that if you see Alice ARP for Bob, she thinks he's connected directly to her LAN
- draw a diagram of your network, and write in the values of the IP addresses, netmasks, routes, and default gateways that you *think* are there. Then check them off one by one against the real values. (Appendix 9 shows a real working diagram from one of our installations. Our notation was deliberately designed to be easily drawn by hand.)

In this module we are concentrating on troubleshooting routing tables you've already entered. For problems creating routes, see Web Appendix 5.

Netmasks

1. **Symptom:** Alice ARPs for addresses that are not on this LAN instead of using her default gateway (or other router if she's been told about it)

   Cause: Alice's sub-net mask is too broad – it's saying that her range of directly connected IP addresses is much bigger than it really is

   Try it, Linux: IP address = 192.168.160.11, netmask 128.0.0.0, no default gateway. This says that half of all the IP addresses in the world are connected directly to you!

   Windows-NT: NT won't let you enter 128.0.0.0 as a netmask. Instead use IP address = 212.3.4.5, netmask 255.0.0.0, no default gateway. Your directly connected LAN is all the 212.*.*.* addresses, which includes a large part of Europe!

   Now **ping** 198.41.0.4 and **ping** 18.181.0.31 and see what happens

2. **Symptom:** on the LAN, a machine ARPs for another on the same LAN but gets no ARP reply or other response

   Cause: (trivial) you typed the wrong IP address, and the machine you're trying to reach doesn't exist

   Cause: my sub-net mask isn't the same as yours – you can *receive* my packets but can't *send* to me, so no communication is possible. We saw this in Module 2.2 and repeat the diagram here (Figure 5.19).

   Try it:
   - Alice: IP address = 10.1.1.22 netmask 255.255.255.0, no default gateway
   - Bob: IP address = 10.1.1.11 netmask 255.255.255.248, no default gateway
   - **ping** Alice from Bob and vice versa

   Alice ARPs for Bob but gets no reply. Bob doesn't even ARP because his configuration tells him Alice isn't connected locally and he has no routers. Now change your sub-net mask to each of 255.0.0.0, 0.0.0.0, 255.255.255.252 and 255.255.255.255 to see what happens

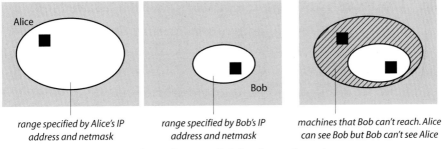

range specified by Alice's IP
address and netmask

range specified by Bob's IP
address and netmask

machines that Bob can't reach. Alice
can see Bob but Bob can't see Alice

Figure 5.19 Different netmasks – Alice sees Bob but he can't see her

3. **Symptom:** on the LAN, a machine can communicate successfully with some machines but not others, whereas all the others can communicate amongst themselves

   Cause: a wrong netmask on the machine that can't see the others (this is the same as (2) above, but the symptoms are different because of what the IP numbers happen to be)

   Try it:
   - Alice and Bob as above
   - Carol: IP address = 10.1.1.6 netmask 255.255.255.0, no default gateway
   - Dave: IP address = 10.1.1.233 netmask 255.255.255.0, no default gateway

   Alice, Carol, and Dave work correctly. Bob can see Carol, but not Alice or Dave because his netmask is wrong (Figure 5.20).

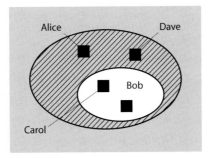

Figure 5.20 Wrong netmask on Bob – he can only see Carol

4. **Symptom:** over the Internet, you are trying to communicate with a remote machine. Someone at that site (using **tcpdump** or an equivalent) tells you your packets are coming in, but you are not getting any replies

   Cause: (one of many possibles) the remote machine has no default gateway set. This happens surprisingly often, especially when you are setting up a new service (e.g. we saw it when an SQL server was being made available to customers over the net) or when an existing machine is being accessed in a new way (e.g. a big server was accessible to everyone locally, but users at a remote branch – who had just been connected using a virtual private network over the Internet – couldn't see it). Machines that are accessed only from the LAN don't need default gateways, especially servers that don't have users surfing the net from them.

5.15 Troubleshooting (2) – routing

The approach to take when you are troubleshooting routing is:

- treat the packet's path as a series of individual hops
- draw a diagram of the network
- verify each hop:
  - treat each hop as a single machine-to-machine link, as we did in Chapter 2. Run **tcpdump** of course
  - remember the three fundamental networking parameters – IP address, netmask, and default gateway
  - check this machine's routing tables to see whether it has been configured to use any other router
  - annotate your diagram as you check each hop
- at the source machine, and at every intermediate router, see which next-hop router is being used, by looking at the destination MAC address in the Ethernet frame, just as we did in Module 3.8. At each point, if the packet is being forwarded to somewhere you didn't expect, check out the routing tables on this machine. The tools on our Web site may help you decide why a packet is being routed in a particular way.

A mistake we often made in the beginning (and continue to make, sigh …) is, for example, to assume that we "know" hops 1 and 2 are configured correctly and spend ages trying to find out what's wrong on hop 3, only to find out that the problem is back in hop 1. Moral: trace it step by step, from start to finish.

Here are a couple of common problems and their causes.

1. **Symptom:** you can see (**ping**) the near-side interface of a router, and the far-side interface, but nothing beyond it

   Cause: (trivial) the link onwards from that router is dead

   Cause: you haven't configured the box to act as a router. You can see the far-side interface because it doesn't involve packet forwarding, even though that IP address belongs to the far-side network

   Try it: the network diagram is shown in Figure 5.21.

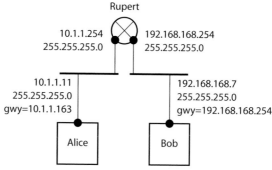

Figure 5.21 Test network to explore routing problems

Alice: IP address = 10.1.1.11, netmask =255.255.255.0,

   default gateway = 10.1.1.254

Bob: IP address = 192.168.168.7, netmask = 255.255.255.0,

   default gateway =192.168.168.254

Rupert: needs two network cards; ensure he's initially *not* configured to act as a router.

   IP address-1= 10.1.1.254 netmask-1 = 255.255.255.0

   IP address-2= 192.168.168.254 netmask-2 = 255.255.255.0

   No default gateway.

Connect Alice to network-card-1 and Bob to network-card-2 (using hubs or cross-over cables).

From Alice:

   ping 10.1.1.254 – should be OK

   ping 192.168.168.254 – should be OK

   ping 192.168.168.7 – should fail

Now reconfigure Rupert to act as a router, and try again. Alice can **ping** Bob.

2. **Symptom:** you get the error message "no route to host" when you run **telnet** or **ftp**, etc. on Linux

   Cause: (trivial) the IP address you're connecting to doesn't exist. The error message is very misleading: it has nothing to do with routing and really means your machine can't ARP the destination

   Try it:

```
ftp 10.1.1.188
```

   where 10.1.1.188 is an IP address that doesn't exist on your LAN. On Linux this gives:

```
ftp: connect: No route to host
```

   and running

```
telnet 10.1.1.188
```

   from Linux gives

```
telnet: Unable to connect to remote host: No route to host
```

Summary

- a router's routing tables determine how it forwards a packet that it receives for another destination. The packet itself contains no routing information – just the final IP destination
- route entries consists of:
  - a range of IP addresses, specified by a netmask and an IP address
  - the IP address of a router (gateway)

  If the packet's IP destination address is in the specified range, the router will forward it to the specified router
- route entries are applied in order, from the most specific to the least specific, so that the default gateway router acts as a catch-all only for destinations that don't have a specific route entry configured for them
- the **route** command is used to display or create routing table entries on both Windows and Linux, although the syntax in each case is different. You can also use the **netstat -r** command to display the routing tables. Much of the complexity in routing is not because what you are doing is intrinsically difficult, but because the syntax and error messages of the **route** command are horrible
- ICMP redirects let you configure most machines on your LAN very simply – usually with a single, default gateway route. If the default gateway forwards a packet for a destination to another, "better" router on the directly connected network, it also automatically informs the sending machine of this. In this way the sender learns of other routes automatically, without any need for manual configuration
- always remember the three fundamental networking parameters when troubleshooting.

What's next?

In Chapter 6 we put our routing knowledge into practice, dividing our network into smaller subnets, embedding test networks in our live LAN, and running multiple networks on the same wire.

We've deliberately deferred DNS and machine names until the end of Part 1 because network debugging is best done using raw IP numbers. DNS imposes an extra layer, which can cause problems and generates extra traffic. In any case, all routing is done at the IP level so DNS isn't involved.

Notes and further reading

Throughout the book we use general-purpose Linux and NT machines as routers – for simplicity and for reasons of expense. Custom-built router devices include a lot of functionality in addition to basic routing. For example, they often support "packet filtering" – the ability to block packets to/from specified sets of addresses/ports, which can be used to provide firewall security (Chapter 24).

Both Linux and Windows show in their routing tables a route *metric*, which we have so far ignored. Most of the time it doesn't matter and we don't need it. The idea is that the metric measures in some way "how good" the specified route is – perhaps how fast or how expensive. The smaller the value, the better the route. This can be used to specify a priority of one route over another – the "better" router is preferred. The only time we will see this used is in Module 26.10 when we look at dial-up network connections.

Linux route command

The format of **route** commands and **route's** output differs on the various flavors of UNIX, and it can be very confusing. If you have to work with lots of different systems it's worthwhile writing your own "wrapper" script that takes the same arguments on each platform but internally uses the platform-specific command syntax.

On older versions of UNIX, **netstat -r** didn't show any netmask. To find out what the routes really meant, you had to use **ifconfig** to list the netmask for the relevant network interface. This was a hangover from the A/B/C address classes, where you could safely tell the netmask from the address.

Let's take a concrete example and work through the specific values printed in Figure 5.4. You'll recall from Module 4.6 that netmask 0.0.0.0 combined with any IP address represents a range containing all possible IP addresses; in this case Linux is combining netmask 0.0.0.0 with destination 0.0.0.0 to indicate the range containing all addresses. In other words, this is the default gateway route.

The routing decision boils down to this:

```
if (dest is in the range 192.0.2.0 - 192.0.2.127)
        /* i.e. dest is directly connected */
        send packet directly to dest via interface eth0, using ARP if
        necessary
else if (dest is in the range 0.0.0.0 - 255.255.255.255)
/* this will always match because this range matches every possible address */
        forward the packet to 192.0.2.29 (our default gateway)
        via interface eth0
```

This routing table is completely representative of a typical LAN PC: it has only one interface and knows about only one router (its default gateway) that handles everything except traffic for the local wire.

Windows route command

If you insert details of your sub-nets into your **networks** file (Chapter 8, Notes) Linux's **route** command (but not Windows') shows items in the "network address" as names instead of numbers. We don't know anybody who uses this; we find it better to work with the raw numeric output. While this is harder to interpret, it has less scope for error – if you don't have a number-to-name mapping, it can't be incorrect!

You could argue that Windows' more complex **route** listing is better than Linux's because it shows more of the internal operation of routing, including even loopback and both broadcast addresses. However, we've always found it cluttered and confusing – you really have to work hard to decipher what's happening. There's a clever tool on our Web site to convert Windows routing tables to an operating-system-independent format.

Multiple default gateways

Section 3.3.1 of

❏ **RFC-1122 October 1989** *Requirements for Internet Hosts – Communication Layers*

deals with multiple gateways – how a "dead" gateway should be detected and a new one selected instead.

The Linux commands we have covered here don't handle multiple default gateways. However, the more sophisticated, the IProute2 package, does. It also lets you selectively enable "equal cost multipath" routing if your kernel supports it, to load-share traffic, e.g. over more than one Internet connection. In fact, IProute2 can route packets on almost any criteria, such as *source* address (not just destination address), type of traffic, etc. and can control the amount of bandwidth used by any subset of the traffic. For most networks this level of complexity isn't necessary.

❏ **http://www.linuxdoc.org/HOWTO/Adv-Routing-HOWTO.html** *Linux Advanced Routing HowTo*

❏ **http://lartc.org/** *Linux Advanced Routing & Traffic Control*

Windows-NT uses an algorithm similar to the "triggered reselection" described in:

❏ **RFC-816 July 1982** *Fault Isolation and Recovery*

NT uses "Dead Gateway Detection": "*With this feature enabled, TCP will ask IP to change to a backup gateway if it retransmits a segment several times without receiving a response. Backup gateways may be defined in the Advanced section of the TCP/IP configuration dialog in the Network Control Panel.*" Note that it's only the higher-level TCP protocol, used by e-mail, HTTP, etc., that does this; traffic such as **ping**, DNS, and others that don't use TCP don't trigger this behaviour. (We explain what TCP is in Chapter 10.) For details, see:

❏ **MS-KB-Q171564** *TCP/IP Dead Gateway Detection Algorithm Updated for Windows NT*
❏ **MS-KB-Q120642** *TCP/IP and NBT Configuration Parameters for Windows*

However,

❏ **Windows-NT 4.0 Resource Kit,** page 555 recommends you define only one default gateway

ICMP redirects

❏ **RFC-1122 October 1989** *Requirements for Internet Hosts – Communication Layers*

says that

1. only routers, not hosts, should send redirects
2. a router should ignore redirects if it is automatically exchanging routing information with other routers, e.g. using a dynamic routing protocol (Module 5.11).

❏ **RFC-1812 June 1995** *Requirements for IP Version 4 Routers*

adds:

3. routers should no longer generate redirects for networks, only for hosts. (In other words, if there's a **D** flag on the routing table entry, there will be an **H** flag too.) This change came about because of the change from address classes to CIDR (Module 4.3); routers can no longer assume what netmask to use by looking at the IP address alone

4. routers can choose whether to ignore redirects, if they are not exchanging routing information with other routers

NT uses redirects, and discards ICMP-created routes after ten minutes:

❏ **MS-KB-Q195686** *Explanation of ICMP Redirect Behavior*

Dynamic routing protocols

See Stevens, Chapter 10, and Perlman, Chapters 12–14.

traceroute **problems**

traceroute can give reliable information only if all the machines from sender to destination operate correctly. However, many TCP/IP implementations have bugs, especially in handling packets with TTL of 1 or 0, and generating ICMP messages/packets. Here are some common problems:

- router doesn't decrement the TTL on a packet it forwards. This router won't show up in the **traceroute** output
- router forwards a packet with TTL = 0. Again, this router won't show in the output
- this machine generates an ICMP packet with the same TTL as the original packet. As the original packet had TTL = 1, the ICMP packet will only travel one hop back towards us before it gets dropped (because *its* TTL is decremented by the first router it passes through). If this machine is a router intermediate on the way to the final destination, we just get a **traceroute** output line containing three "*"s

  However, if this machine is the final destination, we get a weird result: the **traceroute** output contains about twice as many lines as it ought to, with half of them consisting of three "*"s. The easiest way to explain this is to consider an example. From Alice we **traceroute** to Bob, with routers Rupert and Richard in between. Now let's see how the probes go:

  TTL = 1: reaches Rupert, who correctly returns an ICMP timeout, giving a normal **traceroute** output line

  TTL = 2: reaches Richard, who also replies with a correct ICMP packet

  TTL = 3: reaches Bob, by which time the TTL = 1. Bob is the final destination of the **traceroute** probe, so he doesn't generate an ICMP timeout, but:

    – he does generate an ICMP "destination unreachable" because there's no application listening and able to handle the incoming packet. As explained in Module 3.9, this is correct behavior and it's how **traceroute** recognizes that the probe has reached the final destination machine.

    – Bob sends this ICMP packet back to Alice, with TTL = 1

    – the ICMP packet reaches Richard, who decrements its TTL; the TTL is now zero, so Richard drops it silently (you don't generate ICMP packets in response to problems with other ICMP packets, to avoid flooding the network with error messages about error messages)

- this probe generates another "* * *" output

TTL = 4: this behaves like TTL = 3, but gets as far as Rupert, who drops it silently. Again we get a "* * *" output

TTL = 5: the TTL is 3 when the packet reaches Bob, who replies with an ICMP packet with TTL = 3. This *does* reach Alice finally, so we get the last output line, giving the response times for Bob

Out of a total of five lines, we have two containing three "*"s; the trace is almost twice as long as it ought to be.

traceroute prints a "!" after a response that had a TTL = 0 or 1, so if you see three "!"s in the last line of the output, it's almost certain that the destination machine is behaving as described above

- as we explained in Module 3.9, Windows' **tracert** sends ICMP Echo Request packets as probes whereas Linux's **traceroute** sends UDP packets. If the probes have to pass through a firewall to the final destination, they may be blocked, so your trace will be incomplete. As firewalls may have different configuration settings for different types of traffic, for some destinations you may find that a Windows **tracert** works fine but the Linux **traceroute** is incomplete, or vice versa.

Troubleshooting

In Module 5.15 we suggested tracing packets hop by hop. If you're not on your own site you probably won't be able to install tools like **tcpdump** or **windump** on other people's machines. If the machines are running Windows, Microsoft's Network Monitor (Chapter 18) is a useful alternative.

Terminology: "host," "router," "machine"

We use the following common convention when talking about routing. "Host" means a computer that is not acting as a router, e.g. a desktop workstation or a server. "Router" means a computer that is acting as a router and forwards packets between networks. (It may be acting as a server or a desktop PC too, although that's unlikely – and we're only concerned with its routing function.) When we say "machine" we mean either a host or a router – typically when discussing something that applies to any TCP/IP computer, no matter what its role is in the network.

Tools

Our Web site contains several tools for interpreting route table listings, taking account of all the flags etc.:

❏ **http://www.uit.co.uk/resources**

Appendices

6　Routing in practice

Introduction

This chapter explains why you might want to divide your internal network into sub-nets, and how to do it. Reasons for sub-netting include physical limitations on individual network size, performance considerations, geographical separation of parts of your organization's network, ease of administration, and security (e.g. isolating confidential machines from the rest of your network), and for testing. Sub-netting is essential for medium- to large-sized networks.

6.1 Hosts using multiple routers

Up to now all our hosts have only used the services of a single router, and that was usually their default gateway. In the next two modules we're going to configure a more complex network that is representative of medium-sized installations (Figure 6.1). It uses multiple Ethernet segments and individual PCs are configured to use multiple routers.

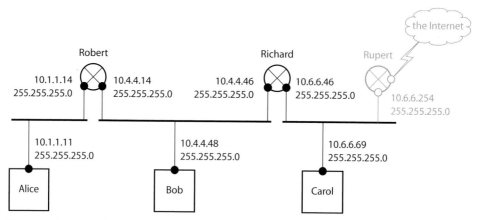

Figure 6.1 Network typical of medium-sized installations

We've shown the network as being connected to the Internet; this is only possible using the private (non-routable) IP addresses we've shown in the diagram if the main Internet router (Rupert) performs network address translation (NAT, Module 23.2). NAT is very common for larger sites nowadays, but if you're not going to use NAT, change the IP addresses in the diagram to the real numbers you're using on your network.

We'll configure the network in two ways, first "by hand," and second, taking advantage of ICMP to cut down on the configuration details we have to enter. From this exercise you'll see how to plan your router configuration, and how routes cascade from the deepest part of the internal network towards the main Internet router. Configuring a network like this (whether in real-life or as an exercise) is painstaking work: there's lots of detail and if you're not careful it's very easy to get an IP number wrong so the whole thing doesn't work.

To build this network you don't need an Internet connection and you don't need the Rupert machine, because almost all the configuration work is on the internal routers. However, we've shown Rupert because networks like this are not symmetrical – the location of the Internet gateway is very significant.

Note:

- we've used the private address range 10.x.x.x
- by using "whole class C" (256-address) ranges for the different sub-networks, the netmasks are very simple. You don't have to do any binary arithmetic to calculate what the ranges are – you can tell at a glance which network an IP address belongs to.

Instead of writing down a table of the configuration for each machine, we show it directly on the diagram (which is how we do it in real life).

In the next module we use this notation (Figure 6.2):

- on a machine, a route is shown as

      R(10.6.6.0, 255.255.255.0 -> 10.4.4.46=Richard)

  which means a route to the network/range 10.6.6.0, netmask 255.255.255.0 uses 10.4.4.46 (the router Richard) as gateway

- a large curved arrow, usually marked **dg**, points from a machine to its default gateway router.

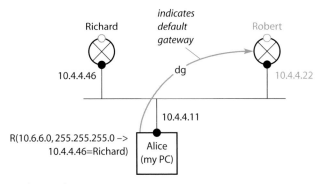

Figure 6.2 Network notation

Tip: when we use diagrams like this on-site for building a real network, we often make a photocopy of it. Then, as we configure a parameter, we scratch it off using a fluorescent highlighter, so it's easy to see what we have and haven't done.

Configuring a machine to use multiple routers

Use the **route add** command to create a route to the routers, just as we did in the previous chapter. For example, if Bob is a Linux box, to tell it to use Robert and Richard to get to the adjacent networks (but nothing else) you might use:

```
route add -net 10.1.1.0 netmask 255.255.255.0 gw 10.4.4.14
route add -net 10.6.6.0 netmask 255.255.255.0 gw 10.4.4.46
```

whereas on Windows it would be:

```
route add 10.1.1.0 mask 255.255.255.0 10.4.4.14
route add 10.6.6.0 mask 255.255.255.0 10.4.4.46
```

6.2 Lab – building a network with multiple routers

Method 1 – manual configuration

Figure 6.3 shows what we need to do.

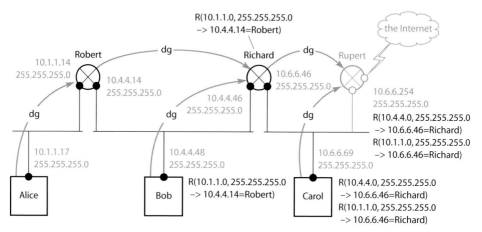

Figure 6.3 Manual configuration

To double-check we've got it right, let's see how Alice, Bob, and Carol reach the three internal networks and the external Internet:

	10.1.1.0	10.4.4.0	10.6.6.0	Internet
Alice	connected directly	> Robert	> Robert > Richard	> Robert > Richard > Rupert
Bob	> Robert	connected directly	> Richard	> Richard > Rupert
Carol	> Richard > Robert	> Richard	connected directly	> Rupert

Let's look at one row of the table in more detail, Bob for example.

10.1.1.0   Bob has an explicit route, telling him to forward via Robert. Robert's left hand interface is connected directly to this range, so Robert can forward the packets on the local wire

10.4.4.0   Bob is connected directly to this range so he can access it on the local wire

10.6.6.0   Bob has no special route for this, so he forwards via his default gateway, Richard. Richard's right-hand interface is connected directly to this range so Richard forwards on the local wire

Internet   Bob has no special route for this, so he forwards via his default gateway, Richard. Richard's doesn't have any special route either, so Richard forwards to Rupert, who sends it on to the Internet.

Method 2 – using ICMP redirects

Now, more realistically, let's use the flexibility ICMP redirects give us. This allows us to configure special routes only on the routers; host machines only need their single default gateway; ICMP redirects will take care of the rest (Figure 6.4).

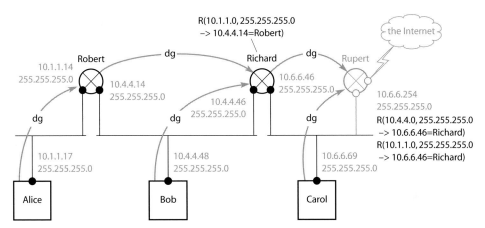

Figure 6.4 Using ICMP redirects to simplify host machine configuration

(Even without ICMP redirects we could omit the specific routes on Alice, Bob, and Carol and the network would still work. However, every packet travelling to a network on its left would generate twice as much traffic because it would go to its default gateway first and then back to the router on its left.)

6.3 Lab – multiple networks on the same local wire

We built the simplest possible routed network back in Chapter 3. Sometimes you want to build a test network like that, but your "router" machine has only one network card. Or you want to test something but don't have enough spare machines to dedicate to it. Often, running multiple networks on the same wire is what you need (Figure 6.5). All the machines are cabled into a single hub. Rupert has two different sets of IP address and netmask on the one network card. Routing works just as before, except all the packets will travel over the one wire. Windows-NT and Linux both support multiple addresses on one network card (but Windows-9x doesn't).

Even though all the machines are on the same wire, Rupert is still performing a routing function, and must be configured to act as a router. Otherwise, Alice and Bob won't be able to communicate.

Figure 6.5
Running
multiple
networks on
the same wire

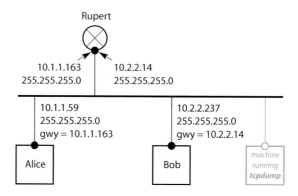

Configuring multiple IP addresses on a single network card – NT

This is very easy. Use **Control Panel > Network > TCP/IP Properties > Advanced** (Figure 6.6(a)) > **Advanced IP Addressing** (Figure 6.6(b)) > **Add.** Enter the second IP address and its netmask (Figure 6.7(a)). Click on **Add** to apply it. **Advanced IP Addressing** now shows the two addresses and netmasks (Figure 6.7(b)).

Once you're using more than one IP address on a NIC, you have to reboot for NT to apply them. As before, use **ipconfig** (Figure 6.8) or **ipconfig/all** to verify your settings and to confirm that you do have two sets of addresses.

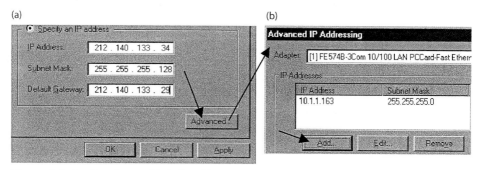

Figure 6.6 Configuring multiple IP addresses

(a)   (b)

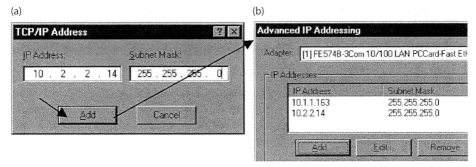

Figure 6.7 Entering the second IP address

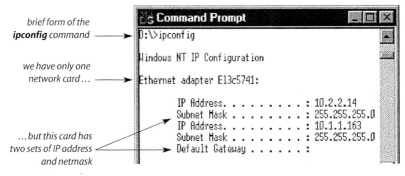

brief form of the
ipconfig *command* ⟶

we have only one
network card... ⟶

...but this card has
two sets of IP address
and netmask

Figure 6.8 Use **ipconfig** to verify settings

Your NT network settings are persistent – as usual, check by running **ipconfig**. Now do a "**route print**" to see how adding the extra interface automatically created the necessary routes for you. Figure 6.9 shows two new routes have been added.

```
Command Prompt
Active Routes:
Network Destination      Netmask        Gateway     Interface  Metric
         10.1.1.0    255.255.255.0    10.1.1.163   10.1.1.163    1
       10.1.1.163  255.255.255.255     127.0.0.1    127.0.0.1    1
         10.2.2.0    255.255.255.0    10.2.2.14    10.1.1.163    1
       10.2.2.14  255.255.255.255     127.0.0.1    127.0.0.1    1
  10.255.255.255  255.255.255.255    10.1.1.163   10.1.1.163    1
       127.0.0.0        255.0.0.0     127.0.0.1    127.0.0.1    1
       224.0.0.0        224.0.0.0    10.1.1.163   10.1.1.163    1
  255.255.255.255  255.255.255.255   10.1.1.163   10.1.1.163    1
```

Figure 6.9 Two new routes have been added by adding the 10.2.2.14 address

> **Tip:** in Module 3.7 we recommended that where possible in real life we keep the last byte of all the IP addresses on a router the same, just to make it easy to remember. For example, we would normally have given Rupert the addresses 10.1.1.**163** and 10.2.2.**163**. We didn't do that here to emphasize that the addresses can of course be completely different.

In the next module we perform the same configuration, but for Linux, and then look at how this modified test network behaves.

6.4 Lab – multiple networks on the same local wire – Linux

Configuring multiple IP addresses on a single network card – Linux

In networking, the terms "network card" and "interface" are often used interchangeably, but there is a difference, and it's important here. The network card (or network interface card, or NIC) is the physical hardware in the machine. The interface is the software entity used to interact with the hardware. Each network card can have multiple interfaces defined for it, as we saw for NT in the previous module, and Linux supports this too, calling it *IP aliasing* (see Notes). On Linux, the **ifconfig** program operates on the interface, *not* on the network card.

The names of extra interfaces on a network card are created by appending "**:1**," "**:2**," etc. to the base name, giving interfaces called "**eth0:1**," "**eth0:2**," etc. You use these names as usual. There is no special "create interface" command: setting the parameters for a new interface on an existing network card implicitly creates the interface.

For our test network, entering the command

```
ifconfig eth0:1 10.2.2.14 netmask 255.255.255.0
```

creates and configures the interface. You can confirm this with "`ifconfig -a`":

To delete an interface, again there is no explicit command – just disable it using **ifconfig**'s **down** option, e.g.

```
ifconfig eth0:1 down
```

> **Warning:** on some versions of Linux, using, for example,
>
> ```
> ifconfig eth0:1 down
> ```
>
> to disable an extra interface behaves incorrectly: it brings down *all* the interfaces on this network card instead of just this one.

Making your settings permanent

As usual, changes made with **ifconfig** and **route** don't persist across reboot. To make your changes permanent they have to be entered in a startup configuration or script file. See Appendix 6 for details.

Behavior of your test network

This section repeats our exploration of the network from Module 3.8, but the packet flow is different because there is only one Ethernet segment involved.

a. on your sniffer machine: "`tcpdump -n -e -t`"

b. on Alice:

```
arp -d 10.1.1.163
```
to clear out any entry that might be in the ARP cache, in preparation for what follows

c. from Alice, **ping** 10.2.2.237 (Bob).

The packet flow is as follows:

1,2. the **ping** generates an ARP "who-has 10.1.1.163" for Rupert, and Rupert replies

3. Alice now knows Rupert's MAC address and sends the **ping** request to Rupert to forward

4. Rupert sends an ICMP redirect to Alice, because Rupert knows Bob (10.2.2.237) is on the same wire and thinks Alice might be able to contact Bob directly (which she can't, in fact)

5,6. Rupert ARPs for Bob and Bob replies

7. Rupert now knows Bob's MAC address and forwards the **ping** request

8. Bob replies to the **ping**, sending the reply via Rupert

9. Rupert sends an ICMP redirect to Bob, because Rupert thinks Bob might be able to contact Alice (10.1.1.59) directly (which he can't)

10. At long last the **ping** reply is sent to Alice, who prints the result.

The **tcpdump** trace of this exchange on our test network is shown below. (We used **tcp-dump**'s "-**f**" option to show foreign addresses as numbers but display Ethernet addresses as names, as we have them listed in our **/etc/ethers** file (Module 5.12) and inserted line numbers for reference.)

```
bob% tcpdump -n -t -e -f

1.   ALICE (BCAST)   0806 60: arp who-has 10.1.1.163 tell 10.1.1.59
2.   RUPERT ALICE    0806 60: arp reply 10.1.1.163 is-at RUPERT
3.   ALICE RUPERT    0800 74: 10.1.1.59 > 10.2.2.237: icmp: echo request
4.   RUPERT ALICE    0800 122: 10.1.1.163 > 10.1.1.59: icmp:
     redirect 10.2.2.237 to host 10.2.2.237 [tos 0xc0]
5.   RUPERT (BCAST)  0806 60: arp who-has 10.2.2.237 tell 10.2.2.14
6.   BOB RUPERT      0806 42: arp reply 10.2.2.237 is-at BOB
7.   RUPERT BOB      0800 74: 10.1.1.59 > 10.2.2.237: icmp: echo request
8.   BOB RUPERT      0800 74: 10.2.2.237 > 10.1.1.59: icmp: echo reply
9.   RUPERT BOB      0800 122: 10.2.2.14 > 10.2.2.237: icmp:
     redirect 10.1.1.59 to host 10.1.1.59 [tos 0xc0]
10.  RUPERT ALICE    0800 74: 10.2.2.237 > 10.1.1.59: icmp: echo reply
```

There are a couple of interesting points:

1. Alice sends the **ping** packet via *Rupert*. Even though Bob is connected to the same wire as Alice, she doesn't know this and doesn't know any route to him, so she has to route via Rupert.

    Check the MAC addresses in your packet from Alice to Rupert, and that they are what you expect

2. run "**arp -a -n**" (Linux) "**arp -a**" (Windows) on Alice and Bob. They have ARP entries for each other, because they saw them on the local wire. However, they can't do anything with them, because their simple routing tables – containing only their own local net and a default gateway – don't allow them to send directly. This is an absolute limitation of IP: even if two machines are on the same physical wire, if their networks (address ranges specified by IP address and netmask) don't include the other machine's IP address, they can't communicate. We explore this in more detail in the next module.

6.5 How to embed a test network in your live LAN

As we mentioned in the previous module, IP imposes an absolute limitation on whether two machines on the same wire can communicate in the "direct-connected, using ARP if necessary" way. Their directly connected address ranges, specified by their IP address and netmask, must overlap and each range must contain the other machine's IP address; otherwise they can't communicate without using a router.

Sometimes this is frustrating. For example, you buy a new network printer (or ISDN router, or ...). Its factory-default IP address is 192.168.1.1 and you want to configure it using a Web browser; you can't connect to it because your PC's LAN is 10.0.0.0, netmask 255.0.0.0. So you have to reconfigure your own PC's TCP/IP settings, but that takes time, you may have to reboot if you have multiple NICs, and changing your TCP/IP settings causes connections to other servers to drop. We have two different solutions for this.

A. Allocate extra addresses to testing machines

The simple solution is to allocate extra IP addresses to each of your test or configuration group's PCs. These addresses should be in the commonly required ranges, so they can access all the usual kit you have to work with. In Figure 6.10, our normal network is 192.0.2.0/24; on test machines we add extra addresses in the private/non-routable network ranges 192.168.0.0 and 172.16.0.0.

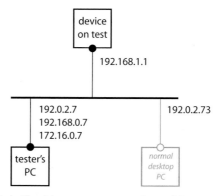

Figure 6.10 Using multiple IP addresses on a tester's machine to access test networks

B. Use an internal router as default gateway in a test department

Figure 6.11 shows a more flexible arrangement, where test-department machines use an internal router, Ralph, as their default gateway. (Ralph's default gateway is Rupert – the "real" default gateway for our LAN, which is used directly by all non-test machines.)

The benefits of this layout are:

- only one machine (Ralph) needs to be configured with the test addresses, but all the tester machines can still access all the resources they need

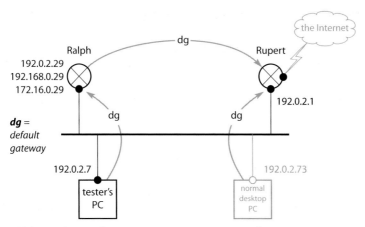

Figure 6.11 Using an internal router to access a test network

- if Ralph is a Linux box, you can dynamically add extra interfaces without rebooting. For example, if we temporarily want to add a test net of 10.0.0.0/8, on Ralph we can add an interface using **ifconfig** and immediately all our tester machines can access the new test network (on the local wire)

  ```
  ifconfig etho:3 10.0.0.0 netmask 255.0.0.0 up
  ```

- it's easy to insert a test network for dial-up access, or for firewall or VPN testing (we'll show how in the chapters devoted to these topics)

- we can add a test Internet connection – say to test a new ISDN router – and just by changing the default gateway on Ralph to use that instead of Rupert, all our test machines can be used to check out the new Internet link. (The example LAN shown in the figure uses real (public) IP addresses. These could only work through the test ISDN router if that performed network address translation (NAT, Module 23.2) for two reasons:

  a. the ISP providing the ISDN might reject packets coming from source addresses that belong to another ISP (the one providing our leased line, called ISP-1, say)

  b. packets responding to our outgoing traffic would still come back in via ISP-1 as usual, because we're using addresses allocated to us by ISP-1.

Warning: some devices (e.g. firewall appliances, or routers) don't use pure IP connectivity for their initial configuration. They perform special tricks (e.g. communicating using only broadcasts) to make the initial configuration of the box easier. These funny protocols can't be routed properly. Because of this we combine both the above approaches on one or two tester machines. See the Notes for a network diagram showing how to do this.

6.6 Dividing your network into sub-nets – motivation

We mentioned in Module 4.3 that TCP/IP was extended from the old A/B/C address classes to support *sub-nets*. There are many reasons why you might want to sub-divide a single network:

1. performance reasons: to limit the number of broadcasts on a given segment, or to limit traffic, e.g. between this file server and its clients (Figure 6.12). However, with UTP switches, this is not as significant as in the days of Thick Ethernet and ThinNet. (In the early days of switches, when they were very expensive, you would often use a switch only on the backbone – to speed up traffic between the segments, as this often involved heavy server-to-server traffic – but still use hubs on the individual sub-networks because they were cheaper.)

2. physical limitations on the cable length in a single network segment (although again this is not so significant with UTP cabling, hubs/switches.)

3. to accommodate different physical networking technologies (e.g. Ethernet, point-to-point for remote small offices, Token Ring). A mixture of different network hardware is especially common when companies merge

4. you have several branches. Each office's own LAN forms a separate sub-net and the only traffic that leaves a branch sub-net is traffic intended for a different branch. The network diagram will be identical to that in Figure 6.12, but the backbone will be linking separate geographical branches instead of departments within the same building

5. flexibility in configuring your internal network layout, by hiding the structure of your internal network from the rest of the world. For example, if your external address range is a single class B, external routers need only a single routing table entry for your entire site. Internally, you can divide the network however you want, and change the internal layout of routers and network segments without having to inform the external world. (Without sub-netting, you might have dozens of class-C addresses, say, all of which have to be known to external routers, giving larger routing tables and reducing your internal flexibility.)

6. to divide your network to match your geographical and administrative organization. This is similar to sub-netting by branch but you may have several levels of hierarchy. For example, you might organize your sub-networks as follows:

   - human resources department
   - operations department
       - operations, sub-net for sales
       - operations, sub-net for technical
   - finance department

   with responsibility and administration for each sub-net delegated locally. Your organizational units can hide internal changes from the company network as a whole, in just the same way as changes on your overall site are insulated from the Internet. Delegation in this way has proven to work very well on the Internet, for administration of DNS, e-mail, etc.

7. security considerations. For example, to avoid **tcpdump** snooping of passwords, etc. on sensitive machines, or to allow sensitive departments (human resources, finance, confidential R&D) to be firewalled off from the rest of the internal network.

How sub-netting works

Sub-netting works by dividing a single range of IP addresses into multiple ranges (Figure 6.12). To implement it you:

1. allocate one of these smaller ranges to the main network
2. allocate one range to each of the sub-networks connected by routers to your main network
3. configure the routers with the necessary details of which range is reached via which router.

You will not be surprised to learn that all the ranges involved are specified using combinations of an IP address with a netmask. (This is what netmasks were invented for, and why they are often called *sub-net masks*.) The final result is you have different sub-net masks in different parts of your network, e.g. from outside your mask appears to be 255.255.255.0, but you might have 255.255.255.192 and 255.255.255.240 on different internal sub-nets.

In the next two modules we work through a simple sub-netting example, and after that go through a more complex and more realistic example.

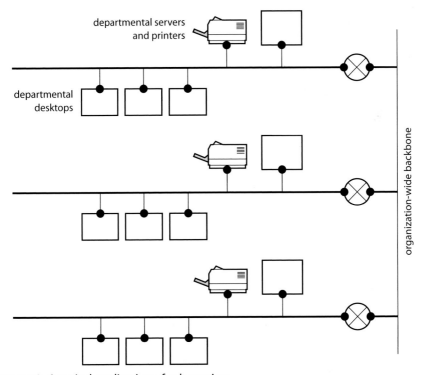

Figure 6.12 A typical application of sub-netting

6.7 Lab – creating simple sub-nets (1) – the wrong way

We'll start with a simple example to highlight a few points that we found surprising (or confusing) when we first used sub-netting. Let's say we have half a class C network, 192.0.2.0, netmask 255.255.255.128 (range = 192.0.2.0–192.0.2.127), and we want to make a sub-net that's isolated from the main network, for tech support and testing. This test network needs to accommodate only a small number of machines, nine at most, say. It's shown schematically in Figure 6.13.

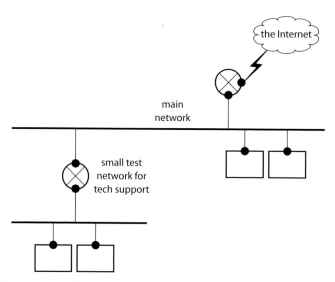

Figure 6.13 We want to add a small test network to our main network

The wrong way to do it

The test network has to accommodate nine machines, so a range containing 16 addresses will be plenty big enough. Let's choose the range 192.0.2.64–192.0.2.79, which has netmask 255.255.255.240. We might think this layout would work:

Alice (like all machines on the test sub-net) uses Robert as her default gateway (Figure 6.14). Rupert is configured to know the range of the test sub-net, and that it is reached via router Robert. Alice can reach the Internet – packets are forwarded to Robert, and then to Rupert, and then onwards, which is correct. Incoming packets for Alice reach Rupert; Rupert knows that Alice's address is in the test sub-net range, so he forwards to Robert, who forwards to Alice. That's all hunky dory.

If Alice wants to send to Bob, she sees that his IP address, 192.0.2.4, is outside her directly connected range, so she forwards via Robert. That's fine, but a problem arises when Bob tries to reply to Alice. Her address is 192.0.2.44, which as far as Bob is concerned is directly connected to his wire, because he is configured with IP = 192.0.2.4, netmask = 255.255.255.128, giving a range of 128 addresses. So now Bob ARPs for Alice, but never gets a reply because she can't see the ARPs because she's on a different wire. Alice's packets reach Bob, but he can never reach her, so that's our first surprise: this network design doesn't work properly.

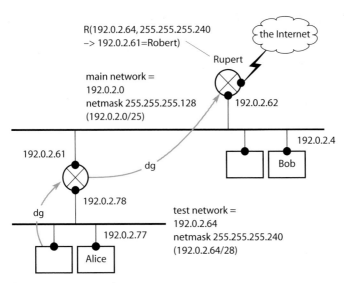

Figure 6.14 The wrong way to subnet

What's happening is that we're trying to specify the main network as "the range .0–.255 except for .64–.79" but you can't specify this using a single netmask, and therefore it can't work correctly.

There are three ways to get over this problem:

1. you can manually configure explicit routes on every PC on the main LAN to says that network 192.0.2.64/28 is accessible via Robert. As this is a more specific route than the default route to Rupert, it will work correctly

2. in certain circumstances, if the numbers are right, you could use DHCP (Chapter 16) to automatically configure the explicit routes in (1) above. However, at present, DHCP can only disseminate "class-ful" routes, i.e. it doesn't include a netmask with the network address, so the usefulness of this is limited. (A proposal to modify DHCP to handle CIDR routes, i.e. with netmasks, is currently working its way through the Internet standards process.)

3. sub-net the network the correct way, as described in the next module.

6.8 Lab – creating simple sub-nets (2) – the right way

To sub-net our network properly, we'll need to use several different sizes of network range. The size of network ranges and where they start are not arbitrary. They are constrained because they are all specified with an address/netmask combination:

- the size of a range is always a power of two, and the common sizes for medium networks are 8, 16, 32, 64, 128, and 256 addresses
- the start of a range is always a multiple of 128, 64, 32, 16, 8, or 4, depending on the netmask used, as shown in Figure 6.15. For example, 192.0.**2.0**, 192.0.2.**64**, 192.0.2.**128**, 192.0.2.**192** for netmask 255.255.255.192 (i.e. /26).
- you can't have, say, a range of 17 addresses – it's not one of the available sizes. If you want to accommodate 17 machines, choose the next power-of-two size up from 17, which is 32. (When you start sub-netting, you will see that this rounding up wastes some of your IP address space, but there's nothing you can do about it.)
- you also can't have a range of 64 machines starting at **.120**. The size is OK but the range has to start on **.0**, **.64**, **.128**, or **.192**. Figure 6.15 shows all the valid combinations of range size and start/end address, for ranges containing 1, 2, 4, 8, … 128, 256

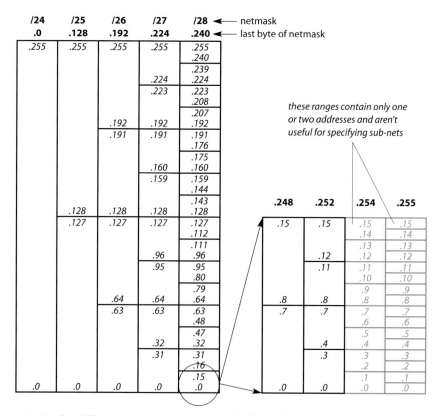

Figure 6.15 The different network ranges specified by different netmasks

addresses; it shows only the last byte of the address; the first three bytes can have any value that falls in the A, B or C classes

- here's a different perspective on sub-netting. By using netmasks you can divide a given IP address range into halves or quarters, or eighths, etc. (a bit like dividing a slab of chocolate or toffee) and a sub-net must consist of only one of these pieces.

The right way to do it

Let's put into practice what we learned above. Bob and the other PCs on Bob's wire must be configured to know that Alice and her friends are not on his local wire: his directly connected range must not include Alice's range. Therefore, instead of allocating our whole 128-address range to the main network, we must allocate a smaller range, which must be 64, 32, 16, 8, or 4. Therefore, the biggest range we can have on the main network is 64 addresses, either **.0–.63** or **.64–.127**. In other words, the main network can be at most half the size of our full range. That's the second surprise.

A direct consequence is that if you want to sub-net your address range, you have to make sure that on your main network you use addresses in at most one half of the range, i.e. all your addresses must be in **.0–.63** or they must all be in **.64–.127**. If they're not, you won't be able to sub-net unless you change the IP numbers of some machines so they do all fall within the correct range.

To correct the network in the previous module, you only need to change the netmasks on the main network machines, from 255.255.255.128 to 255.255.255.192, giving a 64-address range, **.0–.63**. All the main-network machines are conveniently within the **.0–.63** range, so the configuration will work as soon as you change the netmask on Bob, the near-side (internal interface) of Rupert, and the main-network side of Robert.

> **Exercise:** implement the example above on your own network. If you can't sub-net your real network because it has used IP numbers throughout your whole range and not just half of it, use the private addresses 10.*.*.* on the test sub-net instead. These machines won't be able to route to the external Internet, but at least you will have an isolated test network to play with that will cause minimal interference with your live network.

As we mentioned in the previous module, each sub-net must consist of a single range, specified by an IP address and a single netmask. You can't, for instance, join an eight-address range and a 16-address range to make a 24-address sub-net. Because this can't be specified with a single netmask, and a normal machine with a single interface has only a single netmask, you would have no way to tell a machine that this is the range of addresses connected directly on its local wire. The result would be that this machine couldn't ARP all the machines on its local wire and some of the local machines would be unreachable.

The final surprise is that we can make the main network range very small, say eight addresses, from .0 to .7, and use the rest for sub-nets. That means that we could have the following arrangement: main network = **.0–.7**, sub-net-1 = **.64–.127**, with all the other little ranges **.8–.15**, **.16–.31**, **32–.63** still available for use by other sub-nets later. This is the complete opposite of where we started. We thought we could have a main network containing most of the addresses and a tiny little test sub-net, but that's impossible. You *can* have a tiny main network and many bigger sub-nets.

6.9 Lab – complex sub-nets (1) – planning

As an example of how to plan and implement a whole sub-netted internal network for a whole organization, we're going to sub-net the hypothetical small company that we mentioned in Module 6.6, using the IP address range 192.0.2.0/24. We'll take it step by step.

1. **make a list of the separate networks you require**
   - main network, not part of any sub-net ("HQ machines")
   - human resources department ("HR")
   - operations department ("Ops")
     - operations, sub-net for sales ("Sales")
     - operations, sub-net for technical ("Tech")
   - finance department ("Fin")

2. **draw a diagram of the networks (Figure 6.16)**

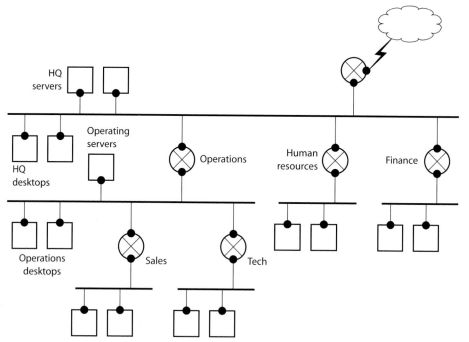

Figure 6.16 Networks

3. **specify the maximum number of hosts for each network**

   Enter the details as shown in Table 6.1. For each sub-net:
   - enter only the number of hosts on that network's own wire; don't include hosts in its child sub-nets if it has any, and don't include any routers, because we do that explicitly in a moment

- even if a network has child sub-nets, the parent network may contain machines that are not in any child network, i.e. that are on its own wire. We've labeled these as "**-self**" to emphasize they are connected locally to the router above (e.g. **HQ-self** for the HQ servers and desktops on the main network, and **Ops-self** for the Operations servers and desktops shown in Figure 6.16). If there are no hosts on the wire, enter zero in the table. (You can't omit this wire completely from your calculations because it has routers connected to it.)

- allow for reasonable future expansion in the numbers you specify. (We've chosen 14, 15 and 8 as example numbers because they're going to raise interesting issues in a moment.)

4. **add in "lost IP numbers" and routers**

    every range loses its lowest and highest IP numbers for use as broadcast addresses (Module 4.10), so add two (shown shaded) to each row.

    Each sub-net is connected to at least one router. The number of IP addresses for router connections is the number of children this sub-net has, plus one for connecting to the parent network. (The HQ network's parent is the Internet.)

Table 6.1 Host details

Network	No. hosts	Lost addresses	Routers children	Routers parents	Total addresses	Range size
HQ-self	10	+2	+3	+1	=16	⇨ 16
HR	8	+2	+0	+1	=11	⇨ 16
Ops-self	6	+2	+3	+1	=11	⇨ 16
Sales	50	+2	+0	+1	=53	⇨ 64
Tech	15	+2	+0	+1	=18	⇨ 32
Fin	14	+2	+0	+1	=17	⇨ 32

5. **calculate the range sizes needed**

    round up from the total number of addresses to the nearest valid range size (8, 16, 32, etc.). (We've used the symbol ⇨ to indicate rounding up.) At first glance it looked as though the HR and Ops-self subnets could use eight-address ranges, and Fin, Tech and HQ-self could use three 16-address ranges, but that's not true – because of the two lost IP numbers and the routers. Notice that the HQ-self network is completely full: we can't even add a sniffer temporarily, or a printer. (In real life that would be a Bad Idea and we'd use a larger range, but we'll live with it in this example.)

    Note that these ranges are only for the machines on each wire. We now have to work out what size a network has to be to accommodate its child sub-nets as well. We cover that in the next module.

6.10 Lab – complex sub-nets (2a) – calculate ranges

6. **amalgamate parent and child network sizes and recalculate ranges**

   We start at the deepest level of sub-net and work upwards. But before completing this step, what does it mean and why are we doing it? Consider only the Ops network and its sub-nets, Sales and Tech (Figure 6.17); forget about the HR and Fin sub-nets for now:

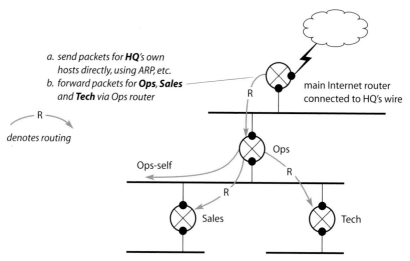

a. *send packets for* **HQ'**s *own*
   hosts directly, using ARP, etc.
b. *forward packets for* **Ops, Sales**
   and **Tech** *via Ops router*

denotes routing

main Internet router
connected to HQ's wire

Ops

Ops-self

Sales

Tech

Figure 6.17 How packets are routed to Internal subnets

We can divide traffic coming from the Internet to the main Internet router into two types:

a. packets for locally connected hosts on HQ's own wire. The router forwards these directly, using ARP if necessary

b. packets for Ops, for Sales, or for Tech. All of these must be forwarded to the Ops router, which takes care of the rest.

That last sentence is crucial: we have to configure the main Internet router to perform this forwarding. We can do that in two ways:

i. **the Bad Way:** configure a separate route for each of the three subnets, Ops, Sales, and Tech.

   This works, but it complicates our configuration and defeats one of the main purposes of sub-netting – keeping configuration details as local as possible and hiding them from higher levels in the sub-net tree (item 5 in Module 6.6). If we change the size of the Tech network, or add another little sub-net below Ops, not only do we have to reconfigure the Ops router (which is reasonable) but we also have to modify the configuration of the HQ router. Having low-level alterations ripple up and require changes at higher levels in this way is a Bad Thing

ii. **the Good Way:** we amalgamate the Ops, Sales, and Tech sub-nets into a single range, and configure that single range on the HQ router.

Sales has 64 addresses, Tech has 32 and Ops-self has 16, making 112 in all. The next range size up from this is 128, so out of our total space we allocate a 128-address range to Ops. Later on, out of those 128 addresses we will allocate further sub-ranges of 64 and 32 for Sales and Tech respectively.

Now we can configure the HQ router with a single entry: "route any packets for Ops or any of its sub-nets to the Ops router." The HQ router doesn't know and doesn't care what the Ops router does in the privacy of its own network: all the HQ router needs to know is "there are 128 addresses behind the Ops router" (Figure 6.18). We can change the size of the Sales or the Tech networks, or add a new Marketing sub-net below Ops, etc. without having to tell any other router about it. We've reduced the number of route entries needed *and* made our network more flexible and easier to manage.

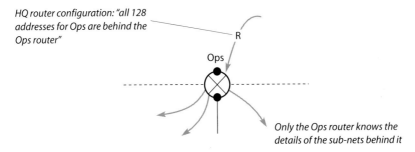

Figure 6.18 128 addresses behind the Ops router

We complete the calculations in the next module

6.11 Lab – complex sub-nets (2b) – calculate ranges (contd.)

For ease of reference we have repeated the table of the sub-nets and their sizes from step-4 in Module 6.9.

Network	No. hosts	Lost addresses	Routers children	Routers parents	Total addresses	Range size
HQ-self	10	+2	+3	+1	=16	⇨ 16
HR	8	+2	+0	+1	=11	⇨ 16
Ops-self	6	+2	+3	+1	=11	⇨ 16
Sales	50	+2	+0	+1	=53	⇨ 64
Tech	15	+2	+0	+1	=18	⇨ 32
Fin	14	+2	+0	+1	=17	⇨ 32

Now let's return to the calculation:

- Sales and Tech are children of the Ops sub-net, so the total number of IP addresses behind the Ops router is:

Sales	64	
Tech	32	
Ops-self	16	
behind-Ops	112	⇨ 128

There are no more sub-nets at this third level down, so we go up a level.

- Fin, HR, and Operations are children of the HQ network, so the total number of IP addresses behind the HQ router (the main Internet router) is:

HR	16	
Ops-total	128	as calculated above
Fin	32	
HQ-self	16	
behind-HQ	192	⇨ 256

You can do the same thing diagrammatically (Figure 6.19), which we find easier, because it graphically mirrors the structure of your networks.

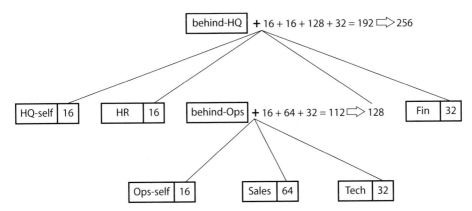

Figure 6.19 Calculating ranges

In the next module we allocate the IP numbers.

6.12 Complex sub-nets (3) – assign IP numbers

7. **assign IP numbers**

   Again we can do this diagrammatically

   a. starting at the top, at each level arrange the children in descending order of size (Figure 6.20)

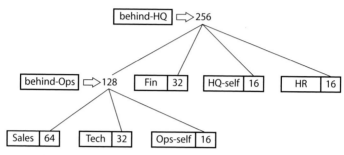

Figure 6.20 Assigning IP numbers to the subnets

   b. remove the detailed calculations because all we need are the totals. We've shown the overall HQ and Ops networks as **behind-HQ** and **behind-Ops** to emphasize that these are the amalgamated sizes and not the ranges for the machines on the Ops and HQ wires themselves

   c. now starting at the top of the tree allocate the range sizes indicated from the overall range for the network. We finish one level before going on to the next to make it easier to see what's happening.

   Top level:

   behind-HQ: 256 addresses = 192.0.2.0 netmask 255.255.255.0. This is the range that we started out with that was allocated to us by our ISP.

   Mid-level:

   Allocate these ranges from the parent network (HQ in this instance). It's like breaking a slab of chocolate into correct-sized pieces. Figure 6.21 shows the division process and the final result.

   behind-Ops: 128 addresses = 192.0.2.0–192.0.2.127 netmask 255.255.255.128

   Fin: 32 addresses = 192.0.2.128–192.0.2.159 netmask 255.255.224

   HQ-self: 16 addresses = 192.0.2.160–192.0.2.175 netmask 255.255.255.240

   HR: 16 addresses = 192.0.2.176–192.0.2.191 netmask 255.255.255.240

Bottom level:

Allocate these ranges from the parent network (Ops in this instance).

   Sales: 64 addresses = 192.0.2.0 netmask 255.255.255.192

   Tech: 32 addresses = 192.0.2.64 netmask 255.255.255.224

   Ops-self: 16 addresses = 192.0.2.96 netmask 255.255.255.240

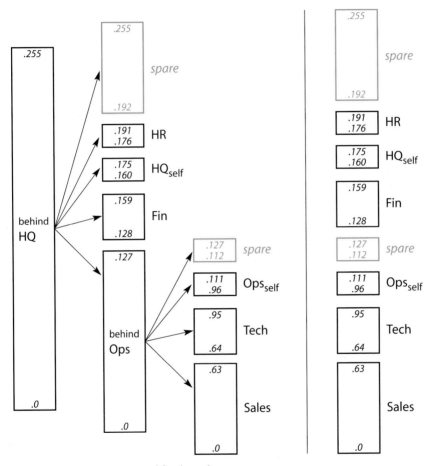

Figure 6.21 Division process and final result

That completes the sub-net design. In the next module we show how to implement it.

6.13 Complex sub-nets (4) – implementation

Finally we come to implementing the sub-net scheme we have designed. Figure 6.22 shows the full network diagram. We've included part of the sub-net allocation diagram from Module 6.12 for reference. The only items missing from the figure are:

1. the default gateway for a router is the router above it, i.e.
   - default gateway for Sales and Tech is Ops
   - default gateway for Ops, HR, and Fin is HQ's router
   - (your ISP configures your HQ router or tells you what its default gateway is – the router upstream on your ISP connection)

2. the default gateway for a host on a sub-net is the router above it, i.e. the router connecting this sub-net to its parent

3. the IP address for a host in a sub-net must obviously be chosen from that sub-net's range. The netmask for the host is the same as the netmask specifying the sub-net's range. For example, a host on the HR sub-net might be:

IP number:	192.0.2.179
netmask:	255.255.255.240

   and a host on the Tech sub-net might be

IP number:	192.0.2.85
netmask:	255.255.255.224

4. we have a couple of ranges left over as spares:
   - on the Ops network, we have a range of 16 addresses that we can use for another small sub-net later on, or to expand the Ops-self network that occupies the numbers directly below it
   - on the HQ network we have a 64-address range that we can use for extra sub-nets later on. In this instance we *couldn't* combine it with the HR range (.176– .191) below because the maximum size of range that can start on .176 is 16, as shown in Figure 6.15.

We've used a few conventions in the diagram:

- we've numbered the routers with the highest IP numbers in their ranges. This is common practice on many sites.

  For example, the HQ network range is 192.0.2.160–192.0.2.175. The broadcast address is .175, so we've used .174, .173, .172, and.171 for the routers

- to reduce the clutter a little, we've shown the network ranges with a gray background. To familiarize you with the different range notations, we show each network range in three different but equivalent ways:

  a. as IP number and netmask, e.g. 192.0.2.64, netmask 255.255.255.224

  b. CIDR notation of IP number and number of bits in the netmask, e.g. 192.0.2.64/27

  c. bottom and top IP numbers of the range, e.g. 192.0.2.64–192.0.2.95.

If you do implement a network like this, the first sanity check to carry out when you've designed it is that all interfaces on the same wire are in the same range and have the same netmask.

Figure 6.22 The full network diagram

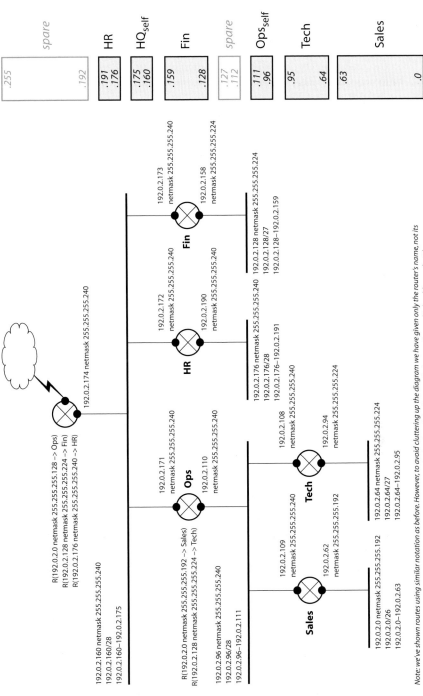

spare

.255
.192

HR
.191
.176

HQ_{self}
.175
.160

Fin
.159
.128

spare
.127
.112

Ops_{self}
.111
.96

Tech
.95
.64

Sales
.63
.0

R(192.0.2.0 netmask 255.255.255.128 –> Ops)
R(192.0.2.128 netmask 255.255.255.224 –> Fin)
R(192.0.2.176 netmask 255.255.255.240 –> HR)

192.0.2.174 netmask 255.255.255.240

192.0.2.160 netmask 255.255.255.240
192.0.2.160/28
192.0.2.160–192.0.2.175

192.0.2.173
netmask 255.255.255.240
192.0.2.158
netmask 255.255.255.224

Fin

192.0.2.172
netmask 255.255.255.240
192.0.2.190
netmask 255.255.255.240

HR

192.0.2.128 netmask 255.255.255.224
192.0.2.128/27
192.0.2.128–192.0.2.159

192.0.2.176 netmask 255.255.255.240
192.0.2.176/28
192.0.2.176–192.0.2.191

192.0.2.171
netmask 255.255.255.240
192.0.2.110
netmask 255.255.255.240

Ops

192.0.2.108
netmask 255.255.255.240
192.0.2.94
netmask 255.255.255.224

Tech

R(192.0.2.0 netmask 255.255.255.192 –> Sales)
R(192.0.2.128 netmask 255.255.255.224 –> Tech)

192.0.2.96 netmask 255.255.255.240
192.0.2.96/28
192.0.2.96–192.0.2.111

192.0.2.109
netmask 255.255.255.240
192.0.2.62
netmask 255.255.255.192

Sales

192.0.2.0 netmask 255.255.255.192
192.0.2.0/26
192.0.2.0–192.0.2.63

192.0.2.64 netmask 255.255.255.224
192.0.2.64/27
192.0.2.64–192.0.2.95

Note: we've shown routes using similar notation as before. However, to avoid cluttering up the diagram we have given only the router's name, not its IP address, as in R(192.0.2.0 netmask 255.255.255.128 –> Ops) in the first line of the diagram. Each router has multiple addresses, but the address to use is of course the one of the interface on the same network as this machine, i.e. the nearest interface. For example in the first line of the diagram –> Ops refers to 192.0.2.171 and not 192.0.2.110

6.14 Routing to connect remote sites

You can connect two separate sites using a private telco leased line, or even a dial-up or ISDN connection (Figure 6.23). The routing is very straightforward:

1. on the left-hand network, tell the main Internet router to forward traffic for the right-hand network 10.2.0.0/16 to router Ralph

2. on the right-hand network, tell the main Internet router to forward traffic for the left-hand network 10.1.0.0/16 to router Robert

3. configure Ralph and Rupert appropriately. Most of the work is in getting the telco line and equipment working, and configuring the proprietary aspects of the routers, which we won't cover

4. each LAN machine is configured to use its respective network's main Internet router as its default gateway

5. ICMP redirects take care of the rest.

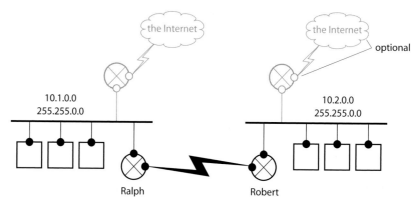

Figure 6.23 Connecting two sites using a private link

Notes

- we've used the private address range 10.x.x.x, which implies that the main routers to the Internet are performing network address translation (see Module 23.2). Each site could equally well be using its own set of public IP numbers allocated to it by the respective ISP.

- we've numbered the networks sequentially:

  10.1.x.x, 10.2.x.x, ...

  so you can tell at a glance which network an IP address belongs to

- on each side we've allocated a whole "class B" range, allowing 65,534 hosts on each side. While this is probably much bigger than is necessary, it makes it easy to sub-net one or both of the networks later on. We would then extend the numbering convention so that it remains easy to identify where an IP address belongs. For example, we might sub-net the right network as:

  10.2.1.x, 10.2.2.x, 10.2.3.x, ...

- by using whole "class B and class C" ranges, the netmasks are very simple and we don't need binary arithmetic to work out what the ranges are

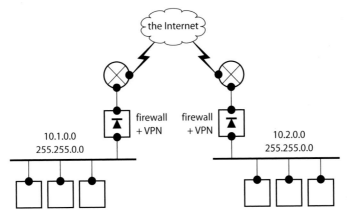

Figure 6.24 Connecting two sites using VPN

Nowadays, many organizations use VPN; VPN (virtual private networking, Chapter 26) instead of a private telco line for this type of connectivity, as shown in Figure 6.24. The reason for this is cost: if the offices are in different countries or far apart, a private telco line will be very expensive. Table 6.2 compares the costs of the two approaches assuming that you have an Internet connection at only one of the sites initially. (If you have a connection at both sites, the VPN option becomes very much cheaper.)

Table 6.2 Comparing costs

Private telco line	VPN over Internet
• cost of telco line	• cost of Internet connection for second site. ADSL connections are very cheap (relatively). Using ADSL for your second site can often make the VPN option very attractive
• cost of two internal routers	• cost of second firewall • cost of VPN software
• administration of internal routers	• administration of VPN

If you own the Internet routers at both sites you may be able to reduce the cost of the private telco option by having your routers handle both your leased line to the Internet and the private line to the other office. Whether your router can handle this already or can be upgraded, e.g. by adding an extra card, depends on the model and manufacturer.

   If you have several sites, e.g. HQ plus three branches, you either have to have three private lines at every site, connecting to each of the other branches, or else have to arrange routing so that, for example, traffic from branch to branch goes via the HQ office, in a hub-and-spoke configuration. (The same applies to VPN, but with VPN there's no extra cost for setting up connections to extra sites.)

Summary

- you configure a machine to use more than one router by creating routes using the **route** command

- you can configure each machine on your LAN manually, but it's usually much easier to configure only your routers with a detailed knowledge of the topology of your network; your hosts can learn about extra routes using ICMP redirects generated by the routers

- you can run more than one network on the same wire. If machines on separate networks are to inter-communicate, they must use a router, even though they are on the same wire. You can easily configure a router to handle this situation by assigning more than one IP address to one of its interfaces; both NT and Linux support this

- there are many reasons why you might want to sub-net your network – performance, geographical distribution, ease of administration, security, etc.

- to sub-net, you have to divide your internal IP address space into chunks (ranges of IP addresses), with one chunk per sub-net. Because ranges are, as always, specified using a combination of an IP address and a netmask, there are constraints on what size of range you can use. If you do sub-net your network, plan out in advance what range sizes you need for particular sub-nets, and draw up a full network diagram before you start implementing.

What's next?

We have finished our treatment of routing. What we have covered up to now allows IP communication between any two machines on an inter-network. You have, therefore, all the mechanisms needed to build networks of any size, from tiny to huge.

In the next three chapters we cover the DNS – the Domain Name System. This allows us to refer to machines by name rather than IP number. While strictly this is a level above the fundamental networking mechanisms we have covered up to now, in practice it is part of the basic infrastructure that allows us to build and manage our networks conveniently.

Notes and further reading

For building test networks and for implementing routed networks at customer sites, we've found it handy to use a laptop with two PCMCIA network cards as a test router. For general information we include the contents of our on-site toolbox in Appendix 10.

Multiple networks on the same wire

IP aliasing (multiple IP addresses on a single network card) is supported in Linux 2.2 and earlier, assuming it has been enabled in your build of the kernel, which it usually is in out-of-the-box configurations. Very recent Linux versions (2.4+) may take a different approach but even then it's usually a compile-time option that you can enable.

The **ifconfig** problem with multiple interfaces mentioned in Module 6.4 is present in Debian Linux 2.2.17, whereas Debian 2.2.12 works OK.

For more about IP alias support, see

❑ **http://www.linuxdoc.org/HOWTO/mini/IP-Alias/** *Setting up IP Aliasing on A Linux Machine Mini-HOWTO*

Using multiple addresses and an internal router together

In Module 6.5 we mentioned that in some special circumstances it's useful to have extra IP addresses on a tester's PC, to access internal test networks. You can combine this approach with using an internal router, as shown in the figure below. The tester's PC uses its extra addresses to access non-standard devices directly, and uses the internal router for easy access to any extra test networks that may be added temporarily.

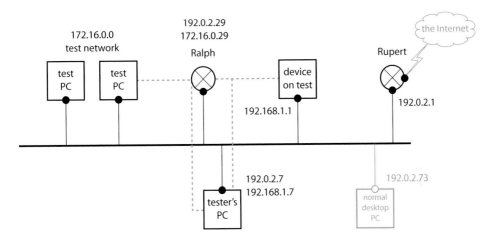

Sub-netting

For readable background on how and why sub-netting came about, see:

❏ **RFC-917 October 1984** *Internet Subnets*

For information on using DHCP with CIDR (i.e. not class-ful) routes, see:

❏ **http://www.ietf.org/internet-drafts/draft-ietf-dhc-csr-06.txt** (Expires April-2002) IETF draft on DHCP and CIDR sub-nets

An interesting consequence of how ranges work is that if two networks overlap at all, they are either identical or one is completely contained in the other. It's impossible to have two ranges as below:

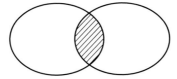

Sub-net mask as opposed to netmask

We mention this not because it's useful nowadays, but out of historical interest and also in case you're reading older documents and get confused with "network IDs" and "sub-net IDs."

Before CIDR was invented, sub-netting was "different" and quite separate from basic inter-networking technology. Every site on the Internet had a class A, B, or C set of addresses and the address classes were used for routing between sites over the Internet backbone. Sub-netting was used within your site to divide up your class A, B, or C range and this is what the "sub-net mask" was invented for. It worked as follows. For simplicity, let's assume your Internet site has been allocated the class B range of addresses, 192.0.2.0–192.0.2.255:

- Figure 4.2 in Section 4.2 shows this network has a 21-bit network part preceded by the bits **110** making a **24**-bit *network ID* in all. This was used for routing on the Internet backbone. The network ID in this example is 192.0.2.

- the sub-net mask is applied to an IP address to divide the host part into two, the *sub-net ID* and the *host ID*, so the IP address is broken into a total of three pieces: network ID, sub-net ID, and host ID. The sub-net ID consists of the upper bits of the host part that overlap the sub-net mask and is used to distinguish between various sub-nets within the main address range (see below).

All you're doing is stealing a few bits from the host part to use as the sub-net ID, and the bits that are left over you call the host ID (which can never be bigger than the host part).

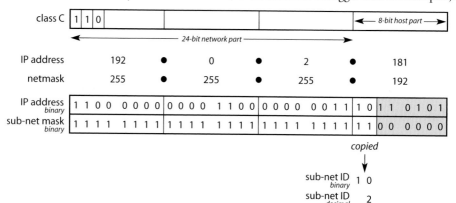

For example, if our sub-net mask is 255.255.255.192 (26 bits, like the /26 we're used to) that gives us the top 2 bits of the host part for the sub-net ID. A 2-bit number can take on the values 0–3, so we can have four sub-nets, each with its own sub-net ID as follows:

Sub-net range	Sub-net ID
192.0.2.0–63	0
192.0.2.64–127	1
192.0.2.128–191	2
192.0.2.192–255	3

and internal routing uses this sub-net ID.

However, with the advent of CIDR the distinction between network ID and sub-net ID isn't useful: the network ID and sub-net ID just merge, and become what we've called the "network part" of the address. (Perlman, Module 9.5 refers to the network part as the "link number").

For more information on these old sub-net masks see Stevens, Modules 3.4 and 3.5. Unfortunately, Stevens is now out of date in this area and mentions CIDR only very briefly.

Appendices

Appendix 6: making network settings permanent – Debian Linux
Appendix 10: our on-site toolkit

7 The DNS – names instead of IP addresses

Introduction

So far, all communication between machines has used IP addresses. While this is fine for machines, people prefer to use easily remembered names. In this chapter we cover the DNS (Domain Name System) from the perspective of a client machine using it to look up names and IP numbers of machines on the Internet (i.e. machines outside your own site) and how to use two programs, **nslookup** and **host**, to get a more detailed understanding of DNS internals and to help diagnose problems. This is the tip of the DNS iceberg, and is usually all you need to think about. In the second half of the chapter we start to look at the huge submerged bit of the iceberg – the mechanics of the DNS and what information DNS servers store.

Chapter 8 continues with DNS mechanisms in detail, covering names in the DNS servers and how they are organized on the Internet, and how you can use DNS internally (rather than over the Internet) to look up names of the machines on your own LAN.

Chapter 9 explains how to troubleshoot DNS problems. Throughout the chapters on the DNS, we deliberately distinguish between an address specified as an "IP number" and an address specified as a "hostname;" in the context of the DNS the distinction between the two is important, as we'll soon see.

7.1 DNS – the domain name system

The *Domain Name System (DNS)* lets you refer to machines by name instead of IP number. DNS converts machine names to IP numbers and vice versa.

So far, in all our examples and **tcpdump** traces, we've referred to hosts by their IP number, never by name. All the internals of TCP/IP – ARP, **ping**, routing, Web browsing, e-mail, etc. – work with numerical IP addresses. This is inconvenient for users, because numerical addresses are hard to remember and bear no relation to the organization they belong to (compare **www.ibm.com** with 129.42.18.99). To overcome this difficulty, TCP/IP applications use the DNS.

The DNS is a client/server facility that translates names to IP addresses so that humans can use easily-remembered names, while still allowing TCP/IP internally to use numeric IP addresses as usual. Once we have DNS working, we'll be able to use hostnames with **ping**, **traceroute**, **tcpdump**, our Web browser, e-mail programs, etc. (but we can still use numeric addresses instead whenever we want, e.g. for troubleshooting).

Let's look at a simple example using **tcpdump**. From Alice on our LAN, we **ping** an external machine, **www.debian.org**. We use option "**-c1**" to send only a single **ping** packet to keep the output short. Below is **ping**'s output (edited to save space):

```
alice% ping -c1 www.debian.org
PING www.debian.org (198.186.203.20): 56 data bytes
64 bytes from 198.186.203.20: icmp_seq=0 ttl=237 time=223.7 ms
```

The **tcpdump** trace of this is shown below. (Option **-s200**: capture 200 bytes, because DNS packets are often longer than **tcpdump**'s default 68-byte capture size; **-n**: print addresses as numerics, so that **tcpdump** itself doesn't use the DNS to translate the IP numbers in its output, which would only complicate things.) Lines 3 and 4 show the **ping** packets we expected: the **ping** request is sent to the remote site and the **ping** reply comes back. What's new and interesting is the first two lines:

```
alice# tcpdump -n -s200 -t

192.0.2.34.1039 > 194.72.6.51.53: 18829+ A? www.debian.org. (32)
194.72.6.51.53 > 192.0.2.34.1039: 18829 1/9/4 A 198.186.203.20 (314) (DF)
192.0.2.34 > 198.186.203.20: icmp: echo request
198.186.203.20 > 192.0.2.34: icmp: echo reply
```

1. the **ping** program realized that the specified address **www.debian.org** was not an IP number, and therefore sent a query to a DNS server at 194.72.6.51 to translate **www.debian.org** to an IP number. (We'll explain how **ping** knows which DNS server to send to in Module 7.3.)

2. the DNS server translated the name to the IP number 198.186.203.20 and sent this information back to the **ping** program on Alice. (We'll see in the next chapter that the server may have automatically contacted other servers in turn to get the information it needed.)

(The .53 in the addresses the "port number" of the DNS server. We mentioned port numbers very briefly in Module 1.2, and explain them in detail in Chapters 10 and 15.)

Then, and only then, could Alice send the **ping** request to 198.186.203.20. The packet flow is shown schematically in Figure 7.1.

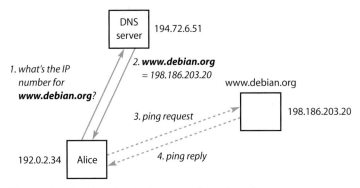

Figure 7.1 The packet flow involved when you **ping** a host by name

This small example illustrates several important features of the DNS:

- the end-user can specify a host address as a name
- the application sends the name to a DNS server, asking for the corresponding IP number. The end-user doesn't have to request this, or even know that it's happening
- the DNS server sends back the numeric IP address
- the application then uses the numeric address just as if the user had specified it explicitly in the first place.

In effect, the DNS is just an extra step inserted at the beginning of the transaction. It's separate from everything else, and once the name has been translated to an IP number the involvement of the DNS is over. From that point on, everything within TCP/IP works in terms of IP numbers. Packet routing, etc. *always* uses IP numbers and *never* uses names, whether or not you used the DNS to translate the name in the first place.

Conceptually, a DNS server holds a table of names and their corresponding numbers. Table 7.1 shows a schematic representation of the DNS entries for **debian.org**. When the server receives a request containing a name, it looks up the name in the table, and returns the corresponding IP address, or an error if it wasn't found. That's the key concept of DNS – the rest is detail. (Unfortunately there is a lot of detail, and it's often confusing because of the way many DNS systems have been programmed.)

Table 7.1 DNS entries for **debian.org**

Name	IP address
auric.debian.org	206.246.226.45
klecker.debian.org	198.186.203.20
saens.debian.org	216.66.54.50
www.debian.org	198.186.203.20

It's important to remember that DNS is *only* about translating between names and numbers. It has nothing to do with routing or the geographical location of the machines in question. Nor have DNS domains anything whatever to do with Microsoft Windows domains (Chapter 18).

The next few modules explain how to configure your LAN machines to use DNS.

7.2 The DNS client – how an application "resolves" a name

As we said in the previous module, the DNS is a client/server system.

- the DNS server(s) are somewhere on the network:
    - you can run your own DNS servers. You can locate them on your LAN or on an external part of your network outside your firewall to allow them to be accessed from other sites on the Internet
    - you can use your ISP's DNS servers. In this case, the servers are remote from your site, somewhere on the Internet.

    We'll explore the location of DNS servers in more detail in the next module. However, it's worth noting here that it doesn't make any difference to the client where the server is – the client just sends queries to the server and receives replies from it. To the client, the server is just an IP number to which it sends DNS queries

- the DNS client isn't a separate program but is a piece of code built into every TCP/IP application that uses hostnames instead of IP numbers, and is usually contained in the application as a library or set of subroutines.

Translating a hostname into an IP number is called *resolving* the hostname or address. Because of this, the DNS client code is called *the resolver*. In some documentation it often sounds as though the resolver is a separate component of the system, perhaps a separate application, like a server on the local machine. Don't be confused: it isn't separate – the resolver is just the DNS client code within the application (Figure 7.2).

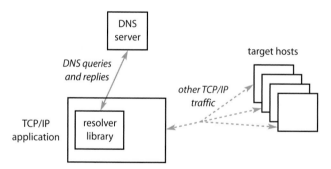

Figure 7.2 The resolver library is part of the application

Configuring a client PC to use the DNS

When you configure a PC to use the DNS to resolve names:

- there is one essential setting: the IP number(s) of the DNS server(s) this client should send its DNS queries to. We cover this in the next module.
- there are two more settings that are not essential as far as the DNS is concerned, but that make life easier:

    a. the name of the domain that this host belongs to (e.g. **example.com** or **uit.co.uk**)

    b. the name of this host. (In Windows, this is part of the DNS settings; on Linux it isn't.)

It's very surprising at first sight that these settings aren't essential, but it emphasizes some significant features of the DNS:

    – only DNS servers and not clients maintain the databases of hostnames and IP addresses. If you ask a server to translate a name to an IP number, the reply it gives you is completely unrelated to the name or domain you configured your PC with

    – looking at it from another perspective, what you're configuring is *how* the client PC uses the DNS. The contents of the DNS database are held entirely separately, on the DNS server, and how your client is configured can't affect those contents. Therefore your PC's configuration doesn't affect how any other machine looks up your PC's name or IP number. Figure 7.3 illustrates an extreme example of this: your PC is configured with a wrong hostname and domain name, but other machines can still resolve the correct name and address for your machine

    – configuring this PC's domain name setting to be **example.com** doesn't "make this PC a member" of the **example.com** domain. It only determines how this PC resolves a simple name like "**alice**" as opposed to a full name like "**alice.ibm.com.**"

It is because of these features that the hostname and domain name settings aren't essential for the DNS to work correctly. However, we'll see in the next chapter – where we look at these settings in detail – that using them can be very convenient.

- there is a fourth setting – the "searchlist" or "domain suffix search order" – that is rarely used but can be convenient for sites that use many domain names, or have subdomains of their main domains. We cover this in Module 8.15.

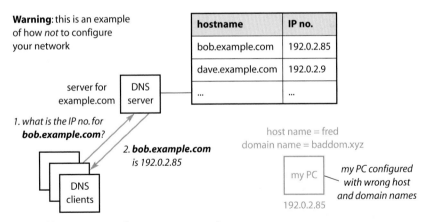

Figure 7.3 How *not* to configure your network

7.3 Configuring your PC to use DNS – DNS server addresses

The DNS server can be on your own LAN or at your ISP. In this chapter we'll deal only with a site that doesn't run its own DNS server, but relies on the DNS server(s) operated by the site's ISP to resolve names of Internet sites they wish to access (Figure 7.4). This configuration is typical of small sites, especially those using only Microsoft systems with no UNIX or Linux machines (but see the Notes for how Active Directory® in Windows-2000 affects this). In this configuration all queries sent to the DNS are for names of external machines and sites. The DNS can also be used to resolve the names and IP numbers of internal machines on your own network; for that you need to run your own internal DNS server, and we defer that until the next chapter.

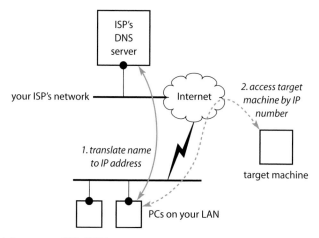

Figure 7.4 Relying on an ISP's DNS server

In this type of network, the only configuration information the resolver needs is the numeric IP address for one or more DNS servers (and that's all we cover in this module). If you don't specify at least one server, this machine won't use DNS at all. (More accurately, the resolver may try to access the server on 127.0.0.1, i.e. the local machine, but if it can't find a server there, it will try nowhere else.)

You must specify the address of servers as IP numbers and not as names. (If you specified a server by name, something would have to resolve that name before the resolver could be fully configured. As that "something" is the resolver itself, you would have an unusable, circular configuration.)

You can configure the client with the addresses of several servers, for resilience. If (and only if) the client can't contact the first server in a reasonable amount of time, it will try the next server instead. Resilience is important because *any* program that uses hostnames will hang or fail when it can't resolve the names. If you don't specify multiple DNS servers, the failure of a single DNS server run by your ISP could make your whole network almost useless. For that reason we recommend you always use more than one if you can.

A down-side of this configuration is that all your DNS queries are going out over your external Internet connection, which means they are relatively slow. On the other hand, it does save you the trouble of running your own DNS servers.

7.4 Lab – configuring Linux to use the DNS

The IP address(es) of the DNS server(s) are stored in **/etc/resolv.conf** (resolver configuration file). To use the DNS, the only line you *must* enter in this file is the IP number of one DNS server preceded by the keyword **nameserver**. You can enter more than one server (see below) and the earlier ones are used in preference to the later ones. You don't have to reboot for the settings to take effect and they persist across reboots since they are stored in a file.

```
nameserver 192.0.2.52
nameserver 192.0.2.57
nameserver 192.0.2.51
```

> **Tip:** you can enter comments in your **/etc/resolv.conf** file by putting them on a line that begins with a hash ("**#**"). Insert comments giving the *names* of the DNS servers that you've entered on the **nameserver** lines. (It's also a good idea to insert your contact details, in case someone needs to query why this configuration has been chosen.)

> **Warning:** if you specify the nameserver by hostname instead of IP number, you won't get any warning but the DNS won't operate correctly – see the exercise below.

> **Exercise:** comment out your valid **nameserver** lines (by inserting a hash at the beginning of each line). Then insert an invalid **nameserver** line, specifying the server by name instead of number. Now run "**tcpdump -n**", and then **ping** some external host (e.g. **www.tcpdump.org**). Do you see any DNS packets on the wire? Don't forget to remove the invalid line, and un-comment the correct lines, when you've finished.

Checking that it's working

Check that the DNS is working by **ping**ing a host by name, or connecting to a site by name in your Web browser (or using any other application that uses hostnames).

> **Warning:** many Internet sites block **ping**s. To be sure that DNS really is working, use **tcpdump** to see the DNS packets on the wire.

> **Exercise 1:** run **tcpdump** (with option "**-n**"). **ping** the host **www.debian.org** (or any other machine on the Web) and see the DNS packets go out and in.

Exercise 2: change your DNS configuration so that the first DNS server in the list doesn't exist. (Use something like 10.10.10.123 or some other number from a private address set that you know isn't in use on your network. Make sure it is not an address in your local segment's range or you will see only failing ARPs.) Now try the **ping** again. Do you see any pattern in the intervals between successive DNS attempts? Now try two non-existent servers, and then all non-existent servers.

7.5 Lab – configuring your Windows PC to use DNS

Now we'll do the basic DNS configuration for a PC on a typical small site connected to the Internet that relies on the DNS servers operated by the site's ISP and has no internal DNS servers.

The only settings you *must* enter are one DNS server address and the hostname; if you don't enter at least one server address your PC won't use DNS. (Windows automatically fills in the hostname. See Module 8.14 for more detail. It is Windows that insists you enter a name here; DNS doesn't care.)

Enter the IP number of the DNS server(s): **Control Panel > Network > Protocols > TCP/IP > DNS > DNS Service Search Order > Add ...** (Figure 7.5).

Figure 7.5 Entering the IP number of the DNS server

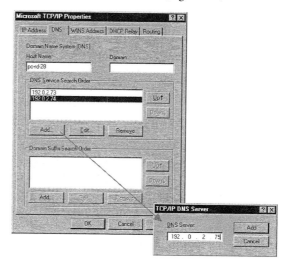

You can enter up to three servers. As with Linux, servers closer to the top of the list are used first; the **Up** and **Down** buttons let you change the order of the servers, so you can set your own preference for the order in which the servers are used. Modified settings take effect as soon as you press **OK** or **Apply**; you don't have to reboot. (**Apply** is the same as **OK** but it doesn't close the window. **Apply** is useful when you are experimenting with the settings: if you leave the **Network** window and come back to it, it will be open at the appropriate place.) As usual you can verify the changes using **ipconfig/all** (Figure 7.6) or **wntipfcg** (Figure 7.7).

Figure 7.6 Verify changes using **ipconfig/all**

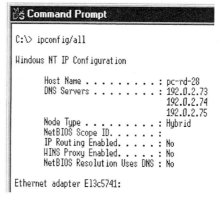

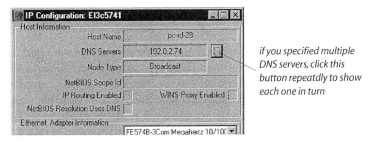

Figure 7.7 Verify changes using **wntipfcg**

The output shows clearly that the DNS settings are *not* related to an individual IP address or network interface: they apply to the machine as a whole.

While it may seem strange not to configure the domain name (and hostname) yet, it does emphasize the functions of the various settings and clarifies how DNS operates, as we explained in Module 7.2. We will configure domain name and hostname in Module 8.14.

Checking that it's working

(This section is identical to the tests we ran for Linux in the previous module.)

Check that the DNS is working by **ping**ing a host by name, or connecting to a site by name in your Web browser (or using any other application that uses hostnames).

Warning: many Internet sites block **ping**s. To be sure that DNS really is working, use **tcpdump** to see the DNS packets on the wire.

Warning: if the **Domain** field is empty, Windows-NT will *not* use the DNS to resolve a simple name (i.e. one that doesn't contain any dots, such as "**bob**"). However, that doesn't matter as we are not using DNS internally, so all the names we want to resolve do contain dots (e.g. **www.ibm.com**) and resolve correctly. (See Chapter 8 Notes.)

Exercise 1: run **tcpdump** (with option "**-n**"). **ping** the host **www.debian.org** (or any other machine on the Web) and see the DNS packets go out and in. Now **ping abcdef**. What do you see on the wire?

Exercise 2: change your DNS configuration so that the first DNS server in the list doesn't exist. (Use something like 10.10.10.123 or some other number from a private address set that you know isn't in use on your network. Make sure it is not an address in your local segment's range or you will only see failing ARPs.) Now try the **ping** again. Do you see any pattern in the intervals between successive DNS attempts? Now try two non-existent servers, and then all non-existent servers.

7.6 Lab – interrogating the DNS – nslookup and host

We said that the DNS client software isn't a separate program – it's built into every TCP/IP application. Even so, there are several special applications for checking out the operation of the DNS. These of course contain the resolver; in effect they are just a convenient front end to it. The two tools we'll use are **nslookup** and **host**. Both are command-line programs without any GUI. We prefer **host** because it's faster and easier to use; however, it's available only for Linux (but see the Notes) whereas **nslookup** is standard on Windows too, so we'll cover **nslookup** first.

> **Tip:** these commands are ideal as diagnostic tools for the DNS. When troubleshooting, we recommend you always run **tcpdump** too, to see *exactly* what's happening.

You can run **nslookup** in two ways.

1. non-interactively: enter all the details of your DNS query on the command line. **nslookup** performs the query, prints the results, and exits:

   ```
   alice% nslookup www.debian.org
   Server:   ns0.bt.net
   Address:  194.72.6.51

   Name:     www.debian.org
   Address:  198.186.203.20
   alice%
   ```

2. interactively: enter the command name on its own, without any arguments. The program runs and gives you its own prompt. You enter a query, **nslookup** prints the result, and gives you its prompt again:

   ```
   alice% nslookup
   Default Server:  ns0.bt.net
   Address:  194.72.6.51 ─────────── nslookup's
                                      interactive prompt
   >  ─────────────────
   ```

   Interactive mode is convenient if you have lots of queries to enter: you don't have to type the command name each time, and you can set various parameters that persist from one query to the next. However, we've found it's rarely necessary (especially as Linux shells and NT's Command Prompt let you recall your previous command line and edit it) so we won't deal with it any further here; see Appendix 11 if you need more information on it.

Format of nslookup and host commands

The simplest command, which we used above, is:

```
nslookup hostname
```

nslookup prints the details of the DNS server it's querying (it defaults to the one you specified in **Control Panel > Network** or **/etc/resolv.conf**) followed by the IP address corresponding to *hostname*, or an error message if it couldn't resolve the name. The command

```
nslookup ipnumber
```

is similar, but prints the name corresponding to *ipnumber*, which is the reverse of a normal lookup. (From now on, for brevity we'll use the term *hostaddr* to mean either a hostname or IP number.)

```
alice% nslookup 198.186.203.20
Name:   klecker.debian.org        (edited to save space)
Address: 198.186.203.20
```

You can interrogate a DNS server other than the default using the command:

```
alice% nslookup 198.186.203.20 res2.dns.uk.psi.net
Server:  res2.dns.uk.psi.net
Address: 154.32.107.18
                                \
Name:   klecker.debian.org    use this DNS server to
Address: 198.186.203.20       resolve the IP address
```

This is useful if you think there's a problem with your machine's configuration and you want to specify a server explicitly, or if you think your default server is misbehaving and you want to see how a different server handles the same query.

Warning: if **nslookup** can't resolve the IP number of the server being used (specified in the resolver configuration, or explicitly as an IP number on the command line), **nslookup** fails completely. This is a big problem with **nslookup**.

Irritatingly, **nslookup** has no "help" option that you can invoke from the command line. You have to go into interactive mode, and type **help** or **?**.

The **host** command is similar to **nslookup**. It doesn't have an interactive mode (but that doesn't matter) and is not available for Windows. We prefer it to **nslookup** because it's faster and its output is more informative, but its usage is very similar to **nslookup**'s.

```
. hostname                       what's the IP address for this name?

alice% host www.debian.org
www.debian.org        A      198.186.203.20

: ipaddr                         what's the name for this IP address?

alice% host 198.186.203.20
Name: klecker.debian.org
Address: 198.186.203.20

: hostaddr serverhostaddr        use non-default DNS server

alice% host 198.186.203.20 res3.dns.uk.psi.net
Name: klecker.debian.org              \
Address: 198.186.203.20      use this DNS server
```

You can see that **host**'s output is less verbose, and because it doesn't print the address of the DNS server that's being used or try to resolve it, it's faster than **nslookup**.

So far we've covered the tip of the iceberg: what follows is the submerged mass. In the next two modules we examine in more detail the contents of DNS queries and replies, and how you can see them in more detail using **tcpdump**. Then in Modules 7.9 and 7.10 we see how advanced options in **nslookup** and **host** let you see this detail (without using **tcpdump**) and how exactly a name is being resolved.

7.7 Other information contained in the DNS

Before we start testing DNS, we need to look in more detail at the information the DNS stores. We implied in Module 7.1 that the DNS contains only a list of hostnames and their corresponding IP addresses. That was an over-simplification: in fact the DNS can contain a lot more, and this module explains the commonly used types of data.

Table 7.2 shows schematically the basic information stored in a DNS database. The left two columns are a list of hostnames with the corresponding IP addresses. Entries in the database are called *records*. The items the entries define are called *resources*, and so the entries are often called *resource records* (*RRs*). The basic "name X has IP number N" records are called *A (address)* records.

Table 7.2 Basic information stored in a DNS database

Name	IP address		IP address	Name
firstpc.example.com	10.22.33.4		10.22.33.4	firstpc.example.com
pc2.example.com	10.22.33.7		10.22.33.7	pc2.example.com
mailgate.example.com	10.22.33.89		10.22.33.89	mailgate.example.com
…			…	

The right two columns show the reverse mappings, i.e. "IP number N has name X." You'd think that this information could be derived from the A records, but DNS doesn't work that way for two reasons. First, because the usual implementation of reverse lookups requires that its information be stored in a separate database from the A records, and second, because of how reverse lookups work (Module 8.16). As a result, the reverse mappings are stored in a particular record format of their own, and they are called *PTR (pointer)* records – they point back to a domain name. Because A and PTR records are separate, it's easy for a DNS administrator to forget to update the PTR records when the corresponding A records are changed, so it's not uncommon for PTR records to be wrong, or missing. (Other reasons for problems with PTRs are that some administrators don't understand them, and others just don't bother with them.)

There is a third common type of host-specific record, the *CNAME (canonical name)* record. This says that the name you are resolving is actually an alias for another name that is the proper ("canonical") name of the resource. The table below shows a CNAME entry schematically; it says that **www.example.com** is only an alias, and that the real hostname is **pc2.example.com**:

Name	Proper name
www.example.com	pc2.example.com

When the server sends a reply for a CNAME back to the client, it says that the record you asked for is an alias but it may also send back the A record for the real resource, so that the client doesn't have to issue another request and wait for another reply. (If the server doesn't send the A record, the client has to resolve the CNAME explicitly.) **host** tells you when you're dealing with a CNAME; **nslookup** tells you the name you queried is an alias:

```
alice% host www.ncd.com
www.ncd.com        CNAME    gilligan.ncd.com
gilligan.ncd.com   A        192.43.160.247
```

```
MS x [Command Prompt]
C:\>nslookup www.ncd.com
Non-authoritative answer:
Name:    gilligan.ncd.com
Address: 192.43.160.247
Aliases: www.ncd.com
```

Records relating to the site as a whole

The DNS also contains records that describe the site as a whole
rather than an individual machine. These include:

> MX (mail exchanger) records: we cover these in detail in Chapter 11, but briefly, an MX
> record gives the name of the mail server that mail should be sent to for any e-mail address
> in this domain. For example, the MX record shown below says that e-mail for
> *anybody*@example.com should be sent to the mail server machine **mailgate.example.com**:

> NS (name server) records: these give the addresses of DNS servers that hold the definitive
> database of information for this domain. They
> are used in the delegation process described in
> the next chapter, but we won't mention these
> further (except in Web Appendix 10).

Domain	Mail server
example.com	mailgate.example.com

Querying specific record types

All our examples so far have been queries for either **A** record types, i.e. the IP address corresponding to a name, or the reverse (**PTR**) records, giving the name corresponding to an IP
number. That is the default operation of both **nslookup** and **host**. You can explicitly specify a
query type if you want:

```
nslookup -querytype=type hostaddr
nslookup -q=type hostaddr                                shorter form
```

where *type* is **MX**, **CNAME**, **NS**, or any other RR type. For example,

```
alice% nslookup -q=mx ncd.com
ncd.com        preference = 10, mail exchanger = mail.ncd.com
ncd.com        preference = 200, mail exchanger = mail.uu.net
mail.ncd.com   internet address = 138.43.168.10
mail.uu.net    internet address = 199.171.54.106
```

host's "**-t**" option is similar, and its "**-t ANY**" (which you can abbreviate as "**-a**") looks up
all record types for the specified address:

```
host -t type hostaddr
host -a hostaddr

alice% host www.ncd.com
www.ncd.com        CNAME    gilligan.ncd.com
gilligan.ncd.com   A        192.43.160.247
```

Exercise: run the commands **host -a www.ibm.com** and **host -a www.aol.com**.

7.8 Contents of DNS packets and how tcpdump shows them

tcpdump shows DNS packets in a format that's so compact it's hard to decipher. We have to master it because we use **tcpdump** a lot, both for DNS troubleshooting and understanding what the DNS is really doing in a particular circumstance. Much of what we cover in these three modules is details of the (not very clear) user interface of the various tools and how they present the data in the DNS packet. What's in the DNS itself is fairly simple so don't be put off.

The reply to a DNS query isn't as simple as "name **bob.example.com** has IP number 1.2.3.4" – it actually contains a lot more information, which is divided into four sections, some of which may be empty:

1. **question:** the query that you sent, which I am replying to. This contains the name (or IP number) being queried, and other query parameters. There is always at least one question

2. **answer:** the resource records that answer the query directly. If this section is empty, this reply does *not* contain the information that you requested (as we'll see in the next chapter, that doesn't necessarily mean there's an error)

3. **authority:** these resource records list the particular nameservers that contain the information you queried for (as we'll see in the next chapter, the server you've configured your DNS client to send queries to will usually talk to other DNS servers on the Internet to retrieve the information you asked for. Most DNS servers contain very little information of their own)

4. **additional:** these are resource records that may be useful to the DNS client if it needs to use any of the records in the earlier sections. Frequently, this section contains a list of the A records corresponding to the server names returned in section 3.

The record format of the query is identical to the response; however, there is a special flag to distinguish between query and reply packets; moreover, in a query, sections 2, 3, and 4 are empty.

tcpdump **standard (non-verbose) display**

The **tcpdump** standard (non-verbose) display of a simple DNS name lookup caused by "`ping gilligan.ncd.com`" is as follows:

```
                                              the question
alice% tcpdump -n -t                        /
192.0.2.38.1025 > 194.72.6.52.53:   553+ A? gilligan.ncd.com. (34)
194.72.6.52.53 > 192.0.2.38.1025:   553 1/2/2 A 192.43.160.247 (122)
```

For the query packet, **tcpdump** prints the question as the name (or IP number if you are doing a reverse lookup) and the type of query it is, e.g. "**A?**", "**PTR?**" or "**MX?**," with the question mark to emphasize that it is a question.

For the reply, **tcpdump** prints the number of answers, nameserver records and additional records after the question, in the format *n/n/n*. For example, above we have one answer, two authority/nameserver records, and two additional records, which **tcpdump** indicates by

"1/2/2". **tcpdump** in this mode doesn't bother showing the number of questions as it's always one. It doesn't show the question either, because you've already seen it in the query, and for compactness it doesn't show any detail for the authority or additional records sections.

tcpdump **detailed (verbose) display**

To see more of the information in the packet, run **tcpdump** with option **-vv** (very verbose) and **-s200** to capture 200 bytes (because DNS packets can be large). The verbose **tcpdump** trace of the same packets is shown below; the output is still only two (very long) lines but we have split them and laid them out to show the structure more clearly. (The **[|domain]** in the first line says that the packet was so long it wasn't all captured; that's not true in this case – it's a bug in **tcpdump**.)

the question in the query   *the question repeated in the reply*

```
alice% tcpdump -n -t -vv -s200                              one answer
192.0.2.38.1025 > 194.72.6.52.53:    [udp sum ok] 553+
    A? gilligan.ncd.com. [|domain] (ttl 63, id 186, len 62)
194.72.6.52.53 > 192.0.2.38.1025:    [udp sum ok] 553
    q: A? gilligan.ncd.com. 1/2/2 gilligan.ncd.com. A 192.43.160.247
    ns: ncd.com. NS NS.ncd.com., ncd.com. NS NS.UU.NET.
    ar: NS.ncd.com. A 192.43.160.250, NS.UU.NET. A 137.39.1.3 (122) (DF)
    (ttl 248, id 9373, len 150)
```

two nameserver records   *two additional records*

The output shows the question (**gilligan.ncd.com**) preceded by **q:** and then the answer (IP number 192.43.160.247). The **authority** section is prefixed with **ns:** and shows that domain **ncd.com** has two nameservers, **NS.ncd.com** and **NS.UU.NET**, each of which is prefixed with "**NS**" indicating a nameserver record. Finally, the **additional** section, which is prefixed with **ar:**, gives the IP addresses, i.e. **A** records, for the two nameservers it returned in the **ns:** section.

How the resolver relates the replies to the original query – the "identifier" field

For simplicity all our examples have shown a single query sent from resolver to server, and a single reply. However, a busy client machine (e.g. a mail server) may send dozens of queries per second, and replies could come back in any order. The resolver includes a unique *identifier* in the query, and the server includes the same identifier in the reply, so the client can match replies to the respective queries. For example, in the single DNS conversation shown above the identifier is **553**.

The plus sign, "+," after the identifier in the query says that this query is *recursive* – that the client wants the server to find the complete answer, even if it has to contact other servers in turn. (Normal client queries are always recursive, so you can usually ignore this. However, we'll see that the queries servers send to one another can be recursive or not, as we explain in Module 8.7.) You will often see a "*" after the identifier in a reply; we cover this in Module 8.10.

In the next two modules we look at options in the **nslookup** and **host** programs to give us more detailed output.

7.9 Lab – interrogating the DNS – nslookup **command debug options**

nslookup has an option, "**-d**" (debug), to print extra information on how it's resolving an address. We use it to find out why a query is unexpectedly failing or not doing what we expect, or, combined with **tcpdump** just to get a useful insight into the detailed working of the DNS. Bear in mind that in this module we're not covering anything new about the DNS itself – we're just showing how a particular tool displays the DNS information. (As we explain in the Notes, there are much better tools than **nslookup**, but as **nslookup** may be the only tool available on some of your machines, we are covering it in detail.)

Figure 7.8 shows an annotated example of **nslookup**, reformatted to save space. The output shows clearly:

- the four sections (questions, answers, authority/nameserver records, additional records) that we explained in Module 7.7. In a section each resource record is shown prefixed with "**->.**" (The **TTL** information against each record shows how long it will remain valid – its "time to live." This is used by the DNS when caching replies, as we explain in Module 8.10.)

- the header of the DNS packet, which contains an opcode indicating the type of query this is (this will almost always be a normal question, shown as **QUERY**), the identifier, the status ("response code," **rcode**) of the query, and how many records are in each of the four sections of the packet.

What the output shows less clearly is that there are four separate packets involved in this particular example. Remember that unlike **tcpdump**, **nslookup** isn't tracing a query initiated by someone else: it's doing the query itself and showing all the details as it does so. If you run **tcpdump** at the same time as **nslookup**, it's much easier to see the actual packet flow (Figure 7.9). As usual, run **tcpdump** with option **-n** to show addresses as numbers, to prevent it generating DNS queries of its own, which would only confuse. The packets involved are:

1. **nslookup** itself sends a query to get details about the DNS server that it's going to use (queries are shown on lines beginning with **;; res_mkquery**)

2. the reply containing details of the nameserver, introduced with **Got answer**: If we were using **tcpdump** to trace a query originated by another program such as **ping**, packets 1 and 2 would not occur at all

3. the query for what we're really interested in – **gilligan.ncd.com** in this case

4. the reply containing the answer and the other three sections of information relating to **gilligan.ncd.com**.

We've found that people often have difficulty when first interpreting **nslookup** output. One reason is that you are dealing with the "hidden part of the iceberg" – DNS contains a lot of detail, and it takes a while to get used to it. However, another reason is that the output isn't clearly presented – it's more like a debug trace printed for the benefit of the tool's developers than a detailed listing of information for the benefit of the user. Don't be put off by this – it's their fault for not making it clear, not your fault for not understanding it immediately. And as we said above, there are better tools than **nslookup** that present the information much more clearly.

```
alice% nslookup -d gilligan.ncd.com
;; res_mkquery(0, 52.6.72.194.in-addr.arpa, 1, 12)
------------
Got answer:                                                    packet 1 - get name of
  HEADER:                                                      the DNS server we're
    opcode = QUERY, id = 33005, rcode = NOERROR
    header flags: response, auth. answer, want recursion, recursion avail.
    questions = 1,  answers = 1,  authority records = 3,  additional = 3
  QUESTIONS:
    52.6.72.194.in-addr.arpa, type = PTR, class = IN
  ANSWERS:
    ->  52.6.72.194.in-addr.arpa         name = ns1.bt.net       ttl = 86400 (1D)
  AUTHORITY RECORDS:
    ->  6.72.194.in-addr.arpa    nameserver = ns0.bt.net ttl = 86400 (1D)
    ->  6.72.194.in-addr.arpa    nameserver = ns1.bt.net ttl = 86400 (1D)
    ->  6.72.194.in-addr.arpa    nameserver = ns2.bt.net ttl = 86400 (1D)
  ADDITIONAL RECORDS:
    ->  ns0.bt.net        internet address = 194.72.6.51  ttl = 86400 (1D)
    ->  ns1.bt.net        internet address = 194.72.6.52  ttl = 86400 (1D)
    ->  ns2.bt.net        internet address = 193.113.212.38   ttl = 86400 (1D)
------------
Server:  ns1.bt.net                                            packet 2 - reply giving name
Address:  194.72.6.52                                          of DNS server

;; res_mkquery(0, gilligan.ncd.com, 1, 1)                      packet 3 - query for
------------                                                   gilligan.ncd.com
Got answer:
  HEADER:
    opcode = QUERY, id = 33006, rcode = NOERROR
    header flags: response, auth. answer, want recursion, recursion avail.
    questions = 1,  answers = 1,  authority records = 2,  additional = 2
  QUESTIONS:
    gilligan.ncd.com, type = A, class = IN
  ANSWERS:
    ->  gilligan.ncd.com         internet address = 192.43.160.247  ttl = 3600 (1H)
  AUTHORITY RECORDS:
    ->  ncd.com         nameserver = ns.ncd.com          ttl = 3600 (1H)
    ->  ncd.com         nameserver = ns.UU.NET           ttl = 3600 (1H)
  ADDITIONAL RECORDS:
    ->  ns.ncd.com      internet address = 192.43.160.250 ttl = 3600 (1H)
    ->  ns.UU.NET               internet address = 137.39.1.3    ttl = 162401 (1d
------------
Name:     gilligan.ncd.com                                     packet 4 - reply giving the
Address:  192.43.160.247                                       IP number we asked for
```

Figure 7.8 Annotated example of **nslookup**'s debug output

```
alice% tcpdump -n -t -s300
192.0.2.34.1025 > 194.72.6.52.53:  33005+ PTR? 52.6.72.194.in-addr.arpa. (42)
194.72.6.52.53 > 192.0.2.34.1025:  33005* 1/3/3 PTR ns1.bt.net. (164) (DF)
192.0.2.34.1025 > 194.72.6.52.53:  33006+ A? gilligan.ncd.com. (34)
194.72.6.52.53 > 192.0.2.34.1025:  33006* 1/2/2 A 192.43.160.247 (129) (DF)
```

Figure 7.9 Actual packet flow for the query in Figure 7.8

7.10 Lab – interrogating the DNS – host **command debug options**

For a more verbose listing of any query, use **host**'s "**-v**" (verbose) option, which shows the contents of all the fields in the reply packet:

```
alice% host -v gilligan.ncd.com
Query about gilligan.ncd.com for record types A
Trying gilligan.ncd.com ...
Query done, 1 answer, authoritative status: no error
gilligan.ncd.com        3578    IN      A       192.43.160.247
Authority information:
ncd.com                 125275  IN      NS      NS.ncd.com
ncd.com                 125275  IN      NS      NS.UU.NET
Additional information:
NS.ncd.com              125275  IN      A       192.43.160.250
NS.UU.NET               14056   IN      A       137.39.1.3
```

We've found that **host -v** is the best compromise between getting all the information you need and being overburdened with clutter.

You can get an even more verbose listing with the "**-d**" (debug) option, showing which server is being queried and other details:

```
alice% host -d gilligan.ncd.com
;; res_send()
;; ->>HEADER<<- opcode: QUERY, status: NOERROR, id: 10560
;; flags: rd; Ques: 1, Ans: 0, Auth: 0, Addit: 0
;; QUESTIONS:
;;      gilligan.ncd.com, type = A, class = IN

;; Querying server (# 1) udp address = 194.72.6.52
;; got answer, 129 bytes:
;; ->>HEADER<<- opcode: QUERY, status: NOERROR, id: 10560
;; flags: qr aa rd ra; Ques: 1, Ans: 1, Auth: 2, Addit: 2
;; QUESTIONS:
;;      gilligan.ncd.com, type = A, class = IN

;; ANSWERS:
gilligan.ncd.com.       3600    IN      A       192.43.160.247

;; AUTHORITY RECORDS:
ncd.com.        3600    IN      NS      ns.ncd.com.
ncd.com.        3600    IN      NS      ns.UU.NET.

;; ADDITIONAL RECORDS:
ns.ncd.com.     3600    IN      A       192.43.160.250
ns.UU.NET.      156586  IN      A       137.39.1.3

;; Query done, 1 answer, authoritative status: no error
gilligan.ncd.com        A       192.43.160.247
```

(You can repeat this option, e.g. "**-d -d**" or "**-dd**," to get still more debug detail, but this shows only values of internal variables, which are rarely of interest. You can repeat "**-v**" in the same way too.)

We find **host**'s output is much clearer than **nslookup**'s, which is why we use **host** whenever possible. But on Windows we often have to use **nslookup** – **host** isn't standard on Windows-NT and isn't available for Win-9x.

As we mentioned in Module 7.6, the **host** command's "**-a**" option (or "**-t ANY**") looks up all record types for the specified address. An example is:

```
alice% host -a ibm.com
ibm.com              A        129.42.18.99
ibm.com              NS       INTERNET-SERVER.ZURICH.ibm.com
ibm.com              NS       NS.WATSON.ibm.com
ibm.com              NS       NS.ERS.ibm.com
ibm.com              NS       NS.ALMADEN.ibm.com
ibm.com              NS       NS.AUSTIN.ibm.com
ibm.com              MX       0 NS.WATSON.ibm.com
```

and combining options "**-a**" and "**-v**" is often a quick way to get all the information you need about a particular name:

```
alice% host -a -v ibm.com
Query about ibm.com for record types ANY
Trying ibm.com ...
Query done, 7 answers, status: no error
The following answer is not authoritative:
ibm.com              172569   IN   A    129.42.18.99
ibm.com              172569   IN   NS   INTERNET-SERVER.ZURICH.ibm.com
ibm.com              172569   IN   NS   NS.WATSON.ibm.com
ibm.com              172569   IN   NS   NS.ERS.ibm.com
ibm.com              172569   IN   NS   NS.ALMADEN.ibm.com
ibm.com              172569   IN   NS   NS.AUSTIN.ibm.com
ibm.com              375      IN   MX   0 NS.WATSON.ibm.com
Authority information:
ibm.com              172569   IN   NS   INTERNET-SERVER.ZURICH.ibm.com
ibm.com              172569   IN   NS   NS.WATSON.ibm.com
ibm.com              172569   IN   NS   NS.ERS.ibm.com
ibm.com              172569   IN   NS   NS.ALMADEN.ibm.com
ibm.com              172569   IN   NS   NS.AUSTIN.ibm.com
Additional information:
INTERNET-SERVER.ZURICH.ibm.com         140519  IN   A    195.212.119.252
NS.WATSON.ibm.com    133482   IN   A    198.81.209.2
NS.ERS.ibm.com       140519   IN   A    204.146.173.35
NS.ALMADEN.ibm.com   140519   IN   A    198.4.83.35
NS.AUSTIN.ibm.com    140519   IN   A    192.35.232.34
```

(We explain the meaning of "this answer is not authoritative" in Module 8.2.)

host has many other options, several of which are particularly useful if you are running DNS internally, as described in Module 8.13. See Appendix 12 for a summary of the **host** manpage.

Summary

- the DNS converts machine names to IP numbers and vice versa; this is called "resolving"
- TCP/IP still does all routing, etc. by numeric IP address, even when you use the DNS – names are primarily a convenience for human users
- DNS clients include code called the "resolver," which they use to resolve names and IP numbers
- you configure your resolver by giving it the IP numbers of one or more DNS servers. The resolver sends your DNS queries to one of these servers and gets the answer in reply. On Linux, the resolver configuration is in the file **/etc/resolv.conf**. On Windows, use **Control Panel > Network > TCP/IP > DNS** to configure the resolver
- you can use the **nslookup** command on Windows and Linux to interrogate the DNS. On Linux the **host** command is better and easier to use
- as well as the machine-name/IP-number mappings, the DNS contains information that relates to the site as a whole – such as the address of the e-mail server that accepts e-mail messages for this site. **nslookup** and **host** let you view this information if you need it
- the **nslookup** and **host** commands have debug options to give you more information on how a resolution has been performed.

IP address, netmask, and default gateway are the three fundamental networking parameters. The DNS resolver configuration is the fourth and last component of a machine's basic network settings.

Now that we have DNS up and running we can at last avoid using IP numbers everywhere, and instead can browse to **www.microsoft.com**, for example, by name. We can also omit the -n "show addresses as numbers" option in tools like **tcpdump** and **traceroute** and **route** when we choose, to give more readable listings. (However, when troubleshooting, it's often better to stick with IP numbers only to avoid any errors due to DNS mis-configuration, and to cut down on the network traffic you have to look at.)

What's next?

This chapter has dealt with the tip of the DNS iceberg – how a client PC uses the DNS to resolve names or IP numbers. In the next chapter we look at the rest of the iceberg: DNS servers, how they are organized on the Internet, how they inter-communicate, and how you can use your own internal DNS server to resolve names on your private LAN.

Notes and related reading

You should use someone else's DNS name server only if you have permission to do so. (Many ISPs enforce this on their systems and restrict their servers so that only their customers or other authorized users can have full access to the servers.)

nslookup has another debug option, "-d2." It gives an even longer listing than "-d" without giving any extra interesting information.

In Chapter 13 we introduce a new sniffer, **ethereal**, which shows DNS queries much more clearly, as does Window Network Monitor (Module 18.6), but we have deliberately deferred those. They use a GUI, which you may not have on your system, and you certainly won't have on all the routers, servers, and hosts that you'll have to debug later on. So rather than spend more time discussing tools instead of the guts of TCP/IP, we'll stick with **tcp-dump** for now.

In addition to the **nslookup** and **host** commands, there is a third DNS interrogation program called **dig** ("domain information groper"), which like **host** is often available on Linux but not on Windows. We prefer **host**, which is by default less verbose than **dig**, but that's a matter of personal preference.

The Internet Software Consortium (ISC):

❑ **http://www.isc.org**

maintains a version of the DNS software that is the de facto standard implementation for Linux and many other UNIX versions. Its distribution includes **host** and **nslookup** and **dig**. However, it *very strongly* recommends you to use **dig** or **host** instead of **nslookup**. **nslookup** is messy and its design is intrinsically flawed: as we saw in Module 7.5, it unnecessarily resolves the address of the nameserver it's using, and if it needs to do a reverse lookup for this and fails, it aborts. In spite of this, we have covered **nslookup** because it's the only command that's available as standard on NT and you will often have to use it, e.g. when looking at someone else's machines. However, for your own use, and if you have authority over what software is installed on your network, you can get NT and Windows-2K versions of **dig** and **host** (and DNS servers) as part of the ISC distribution of **bind**, the de facto standard nameserver. See:

❑ **http://www.isc.org/products/BIND/**

None of these standard tools is available for Windows-9x but there are other shareware/free tools, e.g.

❑ **http://www.simtel.net/pub/pd/39598.html** *resolvfg.zip, NSLookup for Windows, queries DNS servers*

❑ **http://www.samspade.org/ssw/download.html** *Sam Spade* – a single graphical tool that combines the functionality of **ping**, **dig**, **traceroute**, and other programs.

Other name resolution systems

DNS is the "Internet" way to convert between hostnames and IP addresses. However, there are many other name resolution systems, and they may be running on your system in addition to DNS, especially on Windows (Module 9.4).

Resolver

To show how simple the resolver function is as used by an application, here's a tiny Perl program to retrieve and print the IP address of a machine:

```
/* get IP address. This is returned as 4 binary bytes */
$bytes = gethostbyname("www.uit.co.uk");
/* convert the 4 binary bytes to a printable representation */
($a, $b, $c, $d) = unpack ('C4', $bytes);
/* print the result */
printf "$a.$b.$c.$d\n";
```

When you run this under Perl, it prints the correct value, 212.140.133.28.

Microsoft's Active Directory and DNS

Prior to Windows-2000, many Microsoft-only sites didn't need to use DNS. However, Windows-2000's Active Directory uses DNS extensively and you can't run Active Directory without running a DNS server too.

Appendices

Appendix 11: **nslookup** manual page summary
Appendix 12: **host** manual page summary

8 The DNS (2) – how the servers work

Introduction

So far, we have looked at the DNS only from the client (resolver) perspective – how a client can use the DNS to convert a name to an IP address or vice versa, and then only for names of remote machines, i.e. on the public Internet. Now we look at how DNS servers operate and how they interact with one another. We also see how you can use a private DNS server of your own to resolve names on your own private LAN. (You can skip this chapter on first reading if you don't want to run your own DNS server, e.g. if you don't have any public Web or e-mail or other servers, or if your ISP manages your public DNS entries for you, and you don't use DNS for names on your internal LAN, and don't run Microsoft's Active Directory).

8.1 Domains and domain names

Recall what the DNS is all about: we want to refer to machines at remote sites on the Internet by name rather than IP number, e.g. to connect to the Web site **www.tcpdump.org** or send e-mail to **fred@example.com**. (DNS is also used internally – see Module 8.13 – but ignore that for now while we concentrate on the big issue of using DNS on the Internet.)

Before domains were thought of, there was a single file called **HOSTS.TXT** that contained the names and IP numbers of every host on the Internet. This was maintained centrally by a couple of volunteers. Machine names were simple one-part names without any dots. When you gave a name to a new machine, it had to be unique across the whole Internet. To add a new machine to your site you had to coordinate with the **host's** file maintainers, who entered the changes in the **host's** file for you. Every site on the Internet had to download a fresh copy of the **host's** file periodically. The "resolver" just looked up names and IP numbers in this file. As the Internet grew, this arrangement became unmanageable and the DNS was introduced instead.

How domains are named in the DNS

DNS names are organized hierarchically in a tree structure (Figure 8.1) like the names of files and directories on disk. In Linux, the full "pathname" of a file is the basic filename, e.g.

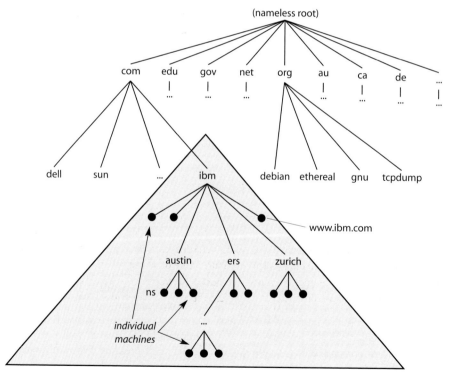

Figure 8.1 Tree structure of DNS names

readme.txt, combined with the path to the file from the root, e.g. **/usr/local/doc/readme.txt**. DNS naming works in much the same way. The basic name of a node in the DNS tree is called its *simple name*. A node's *fully qualified domain name (FQDN)*, i.e. its full name, is its simple name followed by the names of each of its parents in turn, separated by dots instead of slashes. In Figure 8.1 the FQDN of the node **ns** is **ns.austin.ibm.com**. Note that in DNS the most significant parts are on the right, whereas in a file pathname they are on the left.

A *domain* is a node in the naming tree, plus all its children, grandchildren, etc. if it has any; its domain name is the full name of the node. For example, **ibm.com** is the name of the domain consisting of the whole subtree highlighted in gray in Figure 8.1, including the **ibm** node itself, right down to the individual machines. Your DNS domain is a specific part of the name space that is dedicated to you, so you can create your own names without clashing with anyone else's.

A hierarchy or tree structure avoids names clashes if you simply insist that no two children of the same parent have the same name. For example, two different children of **.com** can't have the same name, so you're not allowed to have two separate domains called **ibm.com** and **ibm.com**. However, IBM can have a machine called **www** and you can have one called **www** too, because they are *not* children of the same parent; their full domain names are **www.ibm.com** and **www.example.com** so there's no ambiguity. (Files name work in exactly the same way: you can't have two files of the same name in the same directory. However, you *can* have the same basic filename, e.g. **readme.txt**, in many different directories, because the full pathname of the file is unique. Pathname lets you refer unambiguously to any file.)

The root of the tree has no name but is sometimes represented as a single dot, for ease of reference or to emphasize the "tree-ness" of a name. Similarly, fully qualified domain names (FQDNs) are often written with a trailing dot, e.g. **bob.example.com•** to emphasize that they are fully qualified and go all the way back to the root.

Subdomains

Just as a file directory can contain subdirectories, a domain contains *subdomains*. The root domain • contains all the subdomains **dell.com**, **.edu**, **.org**, **.uk**, etc. (and therefore contains the entire DNS tree). In turn, domain **.com** has subdomains **.com**, **ibm.com**, **sun.com**, etc. and each of these has its own subdomains too. For example, **ibm.com** contains every domain whose name ends with ".ibm.com", including **zurich.ibm.com**, which in turn contains anything that ends with ".zurich.ibm.com".

By the way, the name of an individual machine, e.g. **mail3.microsoft.com**, is a "domain name" because the name is a node in the DNS tree. The only thing in this domain is the machine itself. In practice the name of a single machine isn't usually referred to as a domain, even though we frequently *do* refer to the "domain name of a host."

That describes in an abstract way how the nodes (domains) in the DNS tree are named. Next we see how that abstract structure is implemented by real-world servers on the net.

8.2 The DNS database is distributed

The DNS is a distributed database. There is no single database or single machine that contains the list of all hosts on the Internet. Instead, when you want to resolve a name, e.g. **alice.ibm.com**, you query the DNS server at the root of the DNS tree. (There are several of these servers in fact, all containing exactly the same information, and they are called *root servers* or *root name servers*.) The root server knows only about its direct children (**.com, .edu, .uk,** etc.) so it gives you the address of another server – one that knows about the **.com** domain. Then you query that server, which knows only about its children: it points you to a server that knows about **.ibm.com**. Finally you ask that server for **alice**'s IP number, and when you receive the answer the process is finished. This happens every time you resolve a name, so you never have to download a **HOSTS.TXT** file as you did in the old days. Your DNS software retrieves the information automatically, so you always get up-to-date answers, and as soon as I add a machine **bob.example.co.uk** to my domain, you can resolve it immediately.

That explains how the DNS database is distributed, but it raises another issue: how does a root server know where to find a **.com** server, and how does a **.com** server know where the DNS servers for **ibm.com** are? (What's to stop a fraudster saying that she runs the servers for **ibm.com** and redirecting all traffic for IBM to her site?) The DNS uses the concepts of *authority* and *delegation* to handle this and to control how the database is distributed in manageable chunks.

Terminology – top-level domains

The children of the root, i.e. the domains **.com, .edu, .org, .uk,** etc., are called *top-level domains (TLDs)*, as shown in Figure 8.2. Some TLDs (**.uk, .ca, .de, .au,** …) are country specific: domains within them can be allocated only to organizations in the particular country; they are called *country code top-level domains (ccTLDs)*. The other TLDs (**.com, .org,** etc.) are called *generic top-level domains (gTLDs)* because you can obtain a name in these domains irrespective of where you are located (although in practice **.gov** and **.mil** are used only for the USA and **.edu** is only for the USA and Canada).

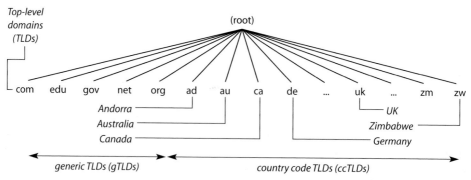

Figure 8.2 Top-level domains

Authority, delegation, and zones

The root server – the server for the root domain – *delegates authority* for the top-level domains to other organizations. It does this with special entries in the root server database. For example, the entry for **.com** says "if you want to find any names that end in **.com**, I don't have this information, but you should look on the server XYZ instead, which will tell you everything you need to know" (where XYZ is of course the address of the particular server).

The **.uk** domain is delegated to an organization called Nominet UK Ltd, which is responsible for running the server for the **.uk** domain and which manages registration of names ending in **.uk**. Similarly **.com** is delegated to Network Solutions Inc. The root servers have to know only about all the TLDs; the delegated organizations take care of the rest. The organizations in charge of the TLDs in turn delegate subdomains of their own domain, until at last a domain name is delegated to an end-user organization, e.g. **ibm.com** is delegated to IBM (Figure 8.3).

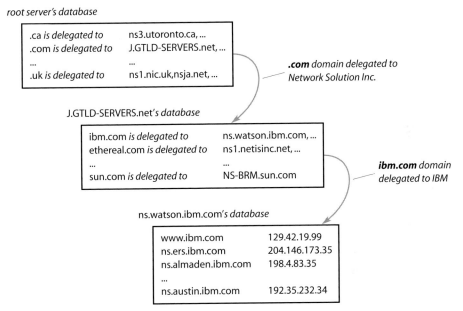

Figure 8.3 ibm.com is delegated to IBM

The organization that is delegated to typically runs multiple servers to handle queries for its part of the name space, as shown in the delegation entry in Figure 8.3 for domain **.uk**. The servers that are delegated to are said to be *authoritative* for the part of the DNS tree that they hold the database for, because they and only they hold the definitive information for that part of the tree. The part of the tree that the servers are authoritative for is called a *zone*. As we'll see in the next module, zones and domains overlap but are not at all the same thing. (You can think of a zone imprecisely as the contents of a server's DNS database, or more precisely as the part of the DNS tree the database relates to.)

The effect of delegation is that the DNS information is distributed over a huge number of servers on the Internet, each one containing some part of the information. Some of these servers are authoritative for their own zones while others don't hold any information of their own but just retrieve information from other servers, as we'll see in Module 8.11.

In the next module we look at zones and delegation in more detail.

8.3 Delegation and zones – top-level domains

As we said, a domain is a node in the DNS tree, which includes all the nodes (domains) underneath it, so a domain always runs "to the bottom of the tree." A zone on the other hand is only that portion of a tree that a particular DNS server is authoritative for. Thus zones are related to authority and delegation, whereas domains are just how nodes are named but not who owns the names.

Let's look at how this works in practice. Assume we're "Example Corp" and domain **example.com** has been delegated to us.

1. the root domain contains the whole DNS tree, because every domain in the world is a descendant of the root (Figure 8.4). However, the root zone, shown as a shaded gray triangle, consists only of the root node because the root has delegated all the TLDs to other organizations

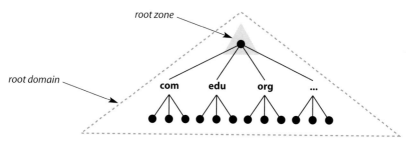

Figure 8.4 The root domain

2. the **.com** domain consists of every domain that ends in **.com** (the large, dotted, truncated triangle in Figure 8.5). However, the **.com** zone contains only the **.com**, node itself and any other **.com** domains that haven't been delegated to other organizations. The **.com** zone *doesn't* contain **example.com** or **ibm.com** data because those domain have been delegated to Example Corp and IBM respectively (Figure 8.5).

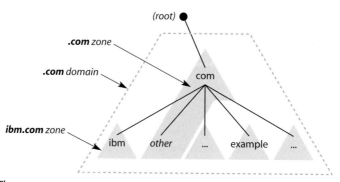

Figure 8.5 The **.com** zone

3. the **example.com** zone contains some or all of the **example.com** domain, but we can't be sure about the detail of this until we know whether our Example Corp administrators have delegated subdomains of **example.com** and set up authoritative names servers for them.

The difference between zones and domains

A zone coincides exactly with a domain when there are no delegations within that domain. This is almost always true for small and medium organizations, and most network administrators never need to get involved with delegation. However, near the top (root) of the tree particularly, zones and domains have relatively little overlap, and large organizations – especially multi-site and multi-national ones – will often delegate subdomains of their own, as we'll see in the next module, to allow parts of their DNS to be administered by the people who use those subdomains.

You can think of a zone in concrete terms as the contents of the database file on a name server. Zones relate to which name servers are authoritative for this part of the DNS tree. On the other hand, domains relate to how nodes are named, but not who's responsible for them.

However, the two terms often get jumbled in together because it is a domain that's delegated and zones follow afterwards almost as an implementation detail. For example, the RFCs say a DNS domain "defines a region of jurisdiction for name assignment and of responsibility for name-to-address translation," which involves both naming and authority.

What the RFC definition means is:

- a domain is a set of names that all share a common ending (e.g. any name that ends in **uit.co.uk** is part of our domain)

- one organization has responsibility/ownership for all the names in this domain. We can add or delete names within our own domain without having to ask someone else for permission (and we can do this safely because we know that they can never clash with anything outside our domain)

- one organization (the domain's owner) is responsible for providing name servers (DNS servers) to resolve any name in a given domain.

Looking at it another way, if you want to find out the IP address for any name in this domain, the information is stored on the DNS server(s) nominated by whoever owns or administers this domain; your DNS server must directly or indirectly obtain the information from that server. So if you "own" the domain name **example.com**, you have to provide (or ask your ISP to provide) name servers to resolve any names that end in **example.com**.

Domains and zones are concerned with *converting between* hostnames and IP numbers but they have nothing to do with who *allocates* your IP numbers to you in the first place; that's covered in Web Appendix 11, which also explains how domain names are allocated and registered.

8.4 Delegation and zones – lower-down domains

So far we've seen how top-level domains are delegated. Delegation doesn't apply only to top-level domains. You can delegate within your own domain if you wish.

Consider **example.com** again. Let's say our operations department is opening a factory in Australia. We could continue to maintain all our DNS information here in Cambridge, but that causes problems because the folks in Australia have a 12-hour time difference; if they want a change entered in the DNS because they've added a new mail server, they have to wait for us to wake up to modify the data base. A better solution might be:

- we create a new subdomain **oz.ops.example.com**
- our Australian folks set up a DNS server that contains all the information about the **oz.ops.example.com** machines. Let's say the name of this server is **bondi-srv.oz.ops.example.com**
- we insert a delegation entry in the database on our DNS server here in Cambridge that says "if you want to find any names that end in **oz.ops.example.com**, I don't have this information – query the server **bondi-srv.oz.ops.example.com** instead."

Assuming that is the only delegation, Figure 8.6 shows the zones and domains:

1. the **example.com** zone (the light gray shaded area) contains all the **example.com** data, except for **oz.ops.example.com**
2. the **oz.ops.example.com** zone and domain overlap exactly (the dark shaded area) because there are no further delegations in **oz.ops.example.com**.

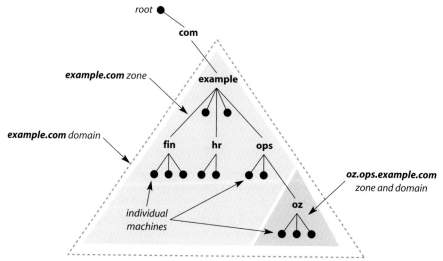

Figure 8.6 Zones and domains

When we delegate authority for the **oz.ops.example.com** domain to the other server, that server's administrators have complete control over the subdomain we delegated to them. They can delegate further if they want. For example, they could set up new domains **sydney.oz.ops.example.com** and **perth.oz.ops.example.com**, each with its own server, and delegate to them. They can do this entirely autonomously, and don't have to refer to us at all (although we would expect them to comply with our corporate naming standard if one has been laid down).

Organizations often delegate large subdomains to individual divisional or departmental control, so that day-to-day modifications of the DNS can be carried out by the people who generate the changes. The delegations typically mirror the organization's structure to a greater or lesser degree.

To summarize, domains are about where names appear in the tree. Zones are related to authority and which server holds the data for a delegated subdomain.

Notice that you can delegate at whatever level you want. We delegated **oz** even though its parent, **ops**, wasn't delegated. And we can delegate at different levels in different places: the **fin** subdomain could be delegated in its entirety, which would give us the structure in Figure 8.7, emphasizing the delegations at different levels.

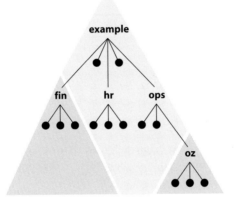

Figure 8.7 Delegations at different levels

That's the theory of delegation. In the next module we look at it in practice, and use **tcpdump** to see how delegation affects the flow of DNS packets.

8.5 Delegation – tracing the packets

Now we'll trace a DNS conversation to see how delegation works in practice, and how a server responds to a query for a subdomain that it has delegated. We'll send a query for the IP address for **www.ibm.com** (use "`ping www.ibm.com`") and follow what happens. In order to see exactly what packets are sent and received, we won't use our ISP's name servers at all: instead, we set up a simple name server on our LAN and configure the client PC's resolver to use that (Figure 8.8).

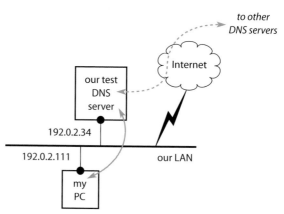

Figure 8.8 Resolver configuration

There are a few points to note:

- as we'll see in a moment from Figure 8.9, if we didn't use our own DNS server but relied on the ISP's instead, we'd miss about 80% of the conversation, because most of it is server-to-server

- the resolver configuration, as we saw in the previous chapter, is specific to a PC. We changed the configuration of my PC in Figure 8.8 to use our test DNS server but left all the other PCs alone; they continue to work just as before and don't even know we have a test DNS server on the network

- similarly, the presence of the test DNS server doesn't affect any other DNS servers we might be running, so we can use the test configuration above on our live network without worrying about breaking our live systems

- you may not want to set up a server like this just for exploring how DNS works, and it's not essential, but if you do want to, we give you some guidance on setting up a server on both Windows-NT (which is easy – see Web Appendix 7) and Linux (Web Appendix 9).

tcpdump shows the conversation (below), edited and with line numbers added. **tcpdump**'s standard output format doesn't contain enough detail for us to work out exactly what's happening, so we'll display exactly the same trace in more detail in the next module, and explain it line by line, but for now concentrate on Figure 8.9, which shows the same information diagrammatically.

```
1  192.0.2.34.1045 > 198.41.0.4.53:        34480 NS? . (17)
2  198.41.0.4.53 > 192.0.2.34.1045:        34480*- 13/0/13 NS K.ROOT-SERVERS.NET.
3  192.0.2.111.1025 > 192.0.2.34.53:       16692+ A? www.ibm.com. (29)
4  192.0.2.34.1045 > 193.0.14.129.53:      34481 A? www.ibm.com. (29)
5  193.0.14.129.53 > 192.0.2.34.1045:      34481- 0/13/13 (461) (DF)
6  192.0.2.34.1045 > 192.12.94.30.53:      34482 A? www.ibm.com. (29)
7  192.12.94.30.53 > 192.0.2.34.1045:      34482- 0/5/5 (240)
8  192.0.2.34.1045 > 204.146.173.35.53:    34483 A? www.ibm.com. (29)
9  204.146.173.35.53 > 192.0.2.34.1045:    34483* 4/5/5 A 129.42.17.99, ... (304)
10 192.0.2.34.53 > 192.0.2.111.1025:       16692* 4/5/5 A 129.42.17.99, ... (304)
```

From the diagram in Figure 8.9 you can see that the packet flows follow the delegations of the DNS domains. When our server first starts up, it gets a list of the root servers (packets 1, 2 above, arrows 1, 2 Figure 8.9). Our nameserver retains this list until it closes down, so in most traces of name resolutions you won't see this step. Some time later, the client sends the query (3) for **www.ibm.com** to our server, which queries the root for a subdomain in ".com" (4); the root server says that it has delegated ".com" (5), and gives the list of nameservers that have authority for ".com." When we query the ".com" server (6), it says that it has delegated **ibm.com** and returns IBM's nameserver details (7). Finally we query one of IBM's servers (8), and it returns the IP number of the name we queried for (9); this answer is then passed back to our client (10).

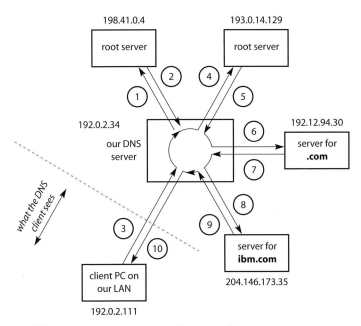

Figure 8.9 The full DNS conversation to resolve **www.ibm.com**

Notice that only two packets (3 and 10) travel to/from the client, whereas ten packets travel to/from our server. That's why we ran our own DNS server on our LAN – to see the packets going out from our server. If we relied on our ISP's DNS server instead, we would see only the two client packets and wouldn't be able to trace what was happening.

    The format of request that our server sends to external servers is the same as the client resolver sends to our server – there's no special "server-to-server" protocol.

    In the next module we look at the contents of the individual packets.

8.6 Delegation – how the packets flow

Below is a line-by-line trace of the same DNS conversation (resolving **www.ibm.com**) that we saw in the previous module (Figure 8.9). Figure 8.10 is the output from **tcpdump** run with options "**-vvv**" (very very verbose) and "**-s 500**" (capture 500 bytes of each packet) to show everything in the packets and reformatted to make the structure of the output clearer.

1. when our DNS server starts up, it sends a query to find the DNS servers for the root zone ("●"). It sends this query to a root server. If that sounds circular, it is! In fact the DNS servers are configured with a file, often called **named.root** or **db.cache**, that contains a fairly up-to-date list of root servers. Our server queries one of these servers to get the current, definitive list of root servers; after that it uses this list instead of its pre-configured one

2. reply to (1), giving a list of 13 root servers: the **13/0/13** in the **tcpdump** output means there are 13 answers to this query, 0 authority/nameserver records, and 13 additional records (as we explained in Module 7.7)

   (Remember that steps 1 and 2 occur only once – immediately after our nameserver has started – and therefore will not appear for most lookups.)

3. the client PC (192.0.2.111) sends a query for **www.ibm.com** to the local DNS server (192.0.2.34). (In real life this would happen long after packets 1 and 2.)

4. our server sends the same query to one of the root servers (193.0.14.129) that it found in line 2

5. the root server responds with 13 nameserver records for the top-level domain **.com** but 0 answer records for **www.ibm.com** and the **tcpdump** output shows **0/13/13**

6. our server sends the query for **www.ibm.com** to one of the **.com** nameservers (192.12.94.30) that it found in line 5

7. the **.com** server replies with five name server records (**0/5/5**) for domain **ibm.com** but still no answer record for our full query

8. the local DNS server repeats the query to one of the **ibm.com** servers (204.146.173.35)

9. the **ibm.com** server replies with four answers for **www.ibm.com**, the first of which is 129.42.17.99. There are also five nameserver records and five additional records (**4/5/5**)

10. our server, now that it has resolved the query for the client, sends the answer back to the client and the conversation is complete.

```
1    192.0.2.34.1045 > 198.41.0.4.53:   34480 NS? . (45)
-------------------------------------------------------------
2    198.41.0.4.53 > 192.0.2.34.1045:   34480*-
     q: NS? .                13/0/13
       . NS K.ROOT-SERVERS.NET., . NS L.ROOT-SERVERS.NET., . NS M.ROOT-SERVERS.NET.,
       . NS I.ROOT-SERVERS.NET., . NS E.ROOT-SERVERS.NET., . NS D.ROOT-SERVERS.NET.,
       . NS A.ROOT-SERVERS.NET., . NS H.ROOT-SERVERS.NET., . NS C.ROOT-SERVERS.NET.,
       . NS G.ROOT-SERVERS.NET., . NS F.ROOT-SERVERS.NET., . NS B.ROOT-SERVERS.NET.,
       . NS J.ROOT-SERVERS.NET.
     ar: K.ROOT-SERVERS.NET. A 193.0.14.129,    L.ROOT-SERVERS.NET. A 198.32.64.12,
         M.ROOT-SERVERS.NET. A 202.12.27.33,    I.ROOT-SERVERS.NET. A 192.36.148.17,
         E.ROOT-SERVERS.NET. A 192.203.230.10,  D.ROOT-SERVERS.NET. A 128.8.10.90,
         A.ROOT-SERVERS.NET. A 198.41.0.4,      H.ROOT-SERVERS.NET. A 128.63.2.53,
         C.ROOT-SERVERS.NET. A 192.33.4.12,     G.ROOT-SERVERS.NET. A 192.112.36.4,
         F.ROOT-SERVERS.NET. A 192.5.5.241,     B.ROOT-SERVERS.NET. A 128.9.0.107,
         J.ROOT-SERVERS.NET. A 198.41.0.10 (464)
-----------------------------------------------------------------------
3    192.0.2.111.1025 > 192.0.2.34.53:   16692+ A? www.ibm.com. (57)
-----------------------------------------------------------------------
4    192.0.2.34.1045 > 193.0.14.129.53:  34481 A? www.ibm.com. (57)
-----------------------------------------------------------------------
5    193.0.14.129.53 > 192.0.2.34.1045:  34481-
     q: A? www.ibm.com.  0/13/13
     ns: com. NS A.GTLD-SERVERS.NET.,   com. NS G.GTLD-SERVERS.NET.,   com. NS H.GTLD-SERVERS.NET.,
         com. NS C.GTLD-SERVERS.NET.,   com. NS I.GTLD-SERVERS.NET.,   com. NS B.GTLD-SERVERS.NET.,
         com. NS D.GTLD-SERVERS.NET.,   com. NS L.GTLD-SERVERS.NET.,   com. NS F.GTLD-SERVERS.NET.,
         com. NS J.GTLD-SERVERS.NET.,   com. NS K.GTLD-SERVERS.NET.,   com. NS E.GTLD-SERVERS.NET.,
         com. NS M.GTLD-SERVERS.NET.
     ar: A.GTLD-SERVERS.NET. A 192.5.6.30,      G.GTLD-SERVERS.NET. A 192.42.93.30,
         H.GTLD-SERVERS.NET. A 192.54.112.30,   C.GTLD-SERVERS.NET. A 192.26.92.30,
         I.GTLD-SERVERS.NET. A 192.36.144.133,  B.GTLD-SERVERS.NET. A 192.33.14.30,
         D.GTLD-SERVERS.NET. A 192.31.80.30,    L.GTLD-SERVERS.NET. A 192.41.162.30,
         F.GTLD-SERVERS.NET. A 192.35.51.30,    J.GTLD-SERVERS.NET. A 210.132.100.101,
         K.GTLD-SERVERS.NET. A 213.177.194.5,   E.GTLD-SERVERS.NET. A 192.12.94.30,
         M.GTLD-SERVERS.NET. A 202.153.114.101 (489)
-----------------------------------------------------------------------
6    192.0.2.34.1045 > 192.12.94.30.53:  34482 A? www.ibm.com. (57)
-----------------------------------------------------------------------
7    192.12.94.30.53 > 192.0.2.34.1045:  34482-
     q: A? www.ibm.com.  0/5/5
     ns: ibm.com. NS INTERNET-SERVER.ZURICH.ibm.com.,   ibm.com. NS NS.WATSON.ibm.com.,
         ibm.com. NS NS.ERS.ibm.com.,                    ibm.com. NS NS.ALMADEN.ibm.com.,
         ibm.com. NS NS.AUSTIN.ibm.com.
     ar: INTERNET-SERVER.ZURICH.ibm.com.  A 195.212.119.252,
         NS.WATSON.ibm.com.  A 198.81.209.2,      NS.ERS.ibm.com.    A 204.146.173.35,
         NS.ALMADEN.ibm.com. A 198.4.83.35,       NS.AUSTIN.ibm.com. A 192.35.232.34   (268)
-----------------------------------------------------------------------
8    192.0.2.34.1045 > 204.146.173.35.53:  34483 A? www.ibm.com. (57)
-----------------------------------------------------------------------
9    204.146.173.35.53 > 192.0.2.34.1045:  34483*
     q: A? www.ibm.com.  4/5/5
         www.ibm.com. A 129.42.17.99,    www.ibm.com. A 129.42.18.99,
         www.ibm.com. A 129.42.19.99,    www.ibm.com. A 129.42.16.99
     ns: ibm.com. NS ns.watson.ibm.com.,       ibm.com. NS ns.austin.ibm.com.,
         ibm.com. NS ns.almaden.ibm.com.,      ibm.com. NS ns.ers.ibm.com.,
         ibm.com. NS internet-server.zurich.ibm.com.
     ar: ns.watson.ibm.com.  A 198.81.209.2,    ns.austin.ibm.com. A 192.35.232.34,
         ns.almaden.ibm.com. A 198.4.83.35,     ns.ers.ibm.com.    A 204.146.173.35,
         internet-server.zurich.ibm.com. A 195.212.119.252 (332)
-----------------------------------------------------------------------
10   192.0.2.34.53 > 192.0.2.111.1025:  16692*
     q: A? www.ibm.com.  4/5/5
         www.ibm.com. A 129.42.17.99,    www.ibm.com. A 129.42.18.99,
         www.ibm.com. A 129.42.19.99,    www.ibm.com. A 129.42.16.99
     ns: ibm.com. NS ns.watson.ibm.com.,       ibm.com. NS ns.austin.ibm.com.,
         ibm.com. NS ns.almaden.ibm.com.,      ibm.com. NS ns.ers.ibm.com.,
         ibm.com. NS internet-server.zurich.ibm.com.
     ar: ns.watson.ibm.com.  A 198.81.209.2,    ns.austin.ibm.com. A 192.35.232.34,
         ns.almaden.ibm.com. A 198.4.83.35,     ns.ers.ibm.com.    A 204.146.173.35,
         internet-server.zurich.ibm.com. A 195.212.119.252 (332)
```

Figure 8.10 Output from **tcpdump** run with "**-vvv**"

8.7 Delegation – iterative and recursive queries; subdomains

For convenience we have repeated here the diagram and **tcpdump** trace from Module 8.5.

Iterative and recursive queries

In Module 8.5 we said there was no difference in format between queries sent from a client to a DNS server, and from one DNS server to another. However, Figure 8.11 suggests there is a difference. When our DNS server received the query (step 3 in the diagram) it sent off several queries (4, 6, 8) until it had resolved the question completely. However, when the other servers in the diagram received a query, they resolved only one component of the query and immediately returned the answer.

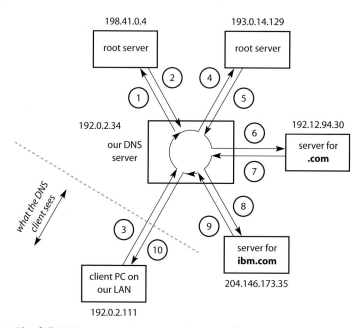

Figure 8.11 The full DNS conversation to resolve **www.ibm.com**

What's happening is that DNS allows two types of queries, which are distinguished by setting a special flag on or off in the packet.

1. *recursive*: the requestor (which could be the resolver in our client, or our DNS server when it's talking to the other servers) says "please resolve this query completely; you should carry out all the intermediate steps to process delegations, and just give me the final answer." The query (3) from the resolver in our client is recursive

2. *iterative*: the requestor expects the server to perform only the first step of the resolving. If further steps are needed, the requestor uses the information in the reply to issue the next request, etc. Queries (4 and 8) from the server are iterative.

A server may be configured to not accept recursive queries – because they involve a lot of work and it's expected that you or your ISP's server will do most of this work for your own queries.

A resolver client issues recursive queries by default (because it doesn't contain the code that a server needs to work its way down through the delegations hierarchy) and expects the server to do all the work for it. A DNS server may issue recursive or iterative requests, depending on how it's configured, as we'll see in Module 8.11 dealing with "forwarding" servers. You can force an iterative query using **host -r** or **nslookup -norecurse**.

tcpdump indicates that a query is recursive by printing "**+**" after the identifier number (e.g. line 3 from the client in Figure 8.12); if there's no "**+**" the query is iterative (e.g. lines 4, 6, 8 from our server). In the reply, a "**-**" means the server doesn't do recursion even if you ask it to (e.g. lines 2, 5, and 7); the other replies (9, 10) indicate those servers will handle recursive queries. **nslookup -v** output says whether queries and replies are recursive, and **host -d** includes "**flags: rd**" ("recursion desired") in recursive queries and replies.

```
1   192.0.2.34.1045 > 198.41.0.4.53:          34480 NS? . (17)
2   198.41.0.4.53 > 192.0.2.34.1045:          34480*- 13/0/13 NS K.ROOT-SERVERS.NET.
3   192.0.2.111.1025 > 192.0.2.34.53:         16692+ A? www.ibm.com. (29)
4   192.0.2.34.1045 > 193.0.14.129.53:        34481 A? www.ibm.com. (29)
5   193.0.14.129.53 > 192.0.2.34.1045:        34481- 0/13/13 (461) (DF)
6   192.0.2.34.1045 > 192.12.94.30.53:        34482 A? www.ibm.com. (29)
7   192.12.94.30.53 > 192.0.2.34.1045:        34482- 0/5/5 (240)
8   192.0.2.34.1045 > 204.146.173.35.53:      34483 A? www.ibm.com. (29)
9   204.146.173.35.53 > 192.0.2.34.1045:      34483* 4/5/5 A 129.42.17.99, ... (304)
10  192.0.2.34.53 > 192.0.2.111.1025:         16692+ 4/5/5 A 129.42.17.99, ... (304)
```

Figure 8.12 A recursive query

Subdomains and delegation (or no delegation)

We mentioned in Module 8.1 that a domain can contain subdomains. If you "own" a particular domain name, e.g. **example.com**, you own all subdomains too. Subdomains can be delegated, as we've seen, but they don't have to be. For example, **hr.example.com** in Figure 8.6 is a subdomain of **example.com** but isn't delegated.

You create subdomains to help you organize many aspects of your network:

- how your machines are named, e.g. **pc7.sales.example.com** is clearly a host in the sales department

- allocation of IP numbers, e.g. dedicate the range 10.5.*.* to subdomain **hr.example.com** and 10.6.*.* to **fin.example.com**

- routing, and how your network is structured, e.g. you'd allocate IP numbers to subdomain **fin** as above, and then create a sub-net for those machines, as we explained in Chapter 6. Subdomains and sub-nets work very well together (although you don't have to use one in order to use the other).

Creating a subdomain is trivial. In fact, you create hosts or other resources in the subdomain rather than creating the subdomain as such. For example, to create subdomain **fin.example.com** containing a host **pc7**, we enter the following "**A**" resource record in our DNS database:

Name	IP address
pc7.hr.example.com	10.5.1.107

That's the end of delegation and zones. Now we move on to how the DNS servers are organized on the Internet.

8.8 Types of server (1) – root, primary, secondary

A DNS server can perform different roles, depending on where it is, how it is configured, and whether other servers are configured to refer queries to it. However, the server software can be the same in each case – only the configuration differs. (In fact, one server often fulfills several different roles at the same time.) We explain the different roles below and in Modules 8.11–8.13.

Root servers

As we mentioned in Module 8.2, the root servers hold definitive information about all the top-level domains (TLDs). You saw in the traces in Module 8.5 that when your own DNS server (or your ISP's) resolves a domain name, the root server is the first server it contacts, to find out the address of the delegated-to server that holds the specific information for the name you're resolving.

There are 13 root servers worldwide, most of them in the USA. They are run on a more or less voluntary basis by a variety of government, university, and commercial organizations. They are named:

A.root-servers.net, B.root-servers.net, … M.root-servers.net

You can get a feel for the load on the root servers from statistics published by the Internet Software Consortium. It runs server F and it receives about 275 million queries/day, an average of about 3,000/second, and often running with a sustained load of 5,000 queries/second.

Authoritative servers: primary master and secondary (slave)

As we said in Module 8.2, the servers that are delegated to a zone are authoritative for that zone. To the outside world, all the authoritative servers for a zone are the same. However, as far as the administrators of the zone are concerned, there are differences, which relate to how the servers are managed internally.

A *primary master server* (or *primary* for short) for a zone is the DNS server that contains the single, definitive copy of the database for all the resources (hostnames, IP numbers, etc.) in that zone. There can be only one primary server for a zone. For resilience you obviously don't want to depend on one server to provide the information for a zone – it would be a single, world-wide point of failure for all accesses to the zone's domain. To avoid this DNS supports *secondary servers*. A secondary server:

- holds a copy of the database from the primary server
- keeps it up to date by updating it periodically, either directly from the primary, or from another secondary.

In this update process (Figure 8.13), the machine sending the information is called the *master server* and the machine retrieving the information is called the *slave server*. (Unfortunately, the term "slave server" is also used as just another word for "secondary server," and Microsoft uses it to mean something else again – see Module 8.11 – so we have to use the old-fashioned term "secondary" to refer to a secondary server to avoid ambiguity.)

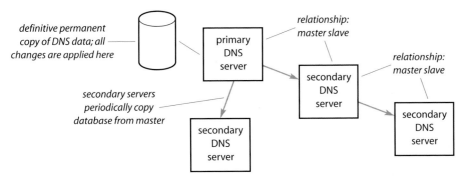

Figure 8.13 The update process

All changes to a zone's entries are made on the primary nameserver only. There are two ways for the secondary to keep its database in synch with the primary, depending on the implementation.

1. the primary pushes the changes (or the whole changed database) to the secondary whenever changes are made
2. the secondary checks with its primary at regular intervals (typically once or twice a day) to see if the database has changed. If it has changed (and only if it has) the secondary copies over the new version of the database.
This method is the most common, used by BIND – the de facto standard implementation for Linux and UNIX. The secondary requests the whole database (i.e. the data file for this zone) using a special DNS request called a *zone transfer* and the primary returns the data in reply. You can perform a zone transfer with the **host** command using option "**-l**":

```
host -l zonename            show basic info
host -l -a zonename         show everything
host -l -a -Z zonename      show everything in "official" format
```

The information is transferred to the **host** application, not to any server, so you're not in danger of interfering with any of your real systems by doing this. However, the command rarely succeeds in practice because most servers block zone transfers except from the primary/secondary servers they are related to, for security reasons.

nslookup also has a zone-transfer facility: run the program in interactive mode, and use its internal **ls** command. (Some versions also let you zone transfer non-interactively using option -q=axfr on the command-line.)

Many sites have multiple secondary servers, both for greater resilience, and for performance and load sharing. (Secondaries are not just backup servers for when the primary fails: they are referenced all the time, and share the load.)

The role of a server – primary master or secondary (slave) – is defined in the configuration files for the server software, not in the database of DNS resource records that clients can query from the server. Consequently, only a zone's administrators can tell whether a particular authoritative server is a primary or a secondary; outsiders can't tell the difference. (See Notes for details.)

The next module discusses where you locate the primary and secondary servers.

8.9 Where primary and secondary servers are located

If you don't run the primary server for your own domain, but rely on your ISP to do this for you instead, they run the primary server and secondary server(s) for you on their own machines. (They don't have to run a separate machine for each primary domain they serve. In fact, they don't even have to run multiple copies of the domain server software: a single software server can handle multiple domains simultaneously, and with most servers configuring this is very easy.)

If you do run your own primary, you ought to have at least one secondary, so that the primary server isn't a single point of failure for everyone trying to access your site. In fact, whoever allocated your domain to you and delegated authority to your server may insist on this. Depending on the size and complexity of your network, and what level of downtime you're prepared to tolerate, you should consider some or all of the following, illustrated in Figure 8.14:

- the primary and secondary server ought to be on separate hosts and on separate switches/hubs, and ideally on separate networks
- have your ISP run a secondary server for you at their site
- if you have multiple sites, run a secondary at one or all of your other sites
- ask an organization that has friendly relations with yours to run a secondary for you. And if you run a secondary for their domain, everyone's happy! This is an example of where a single server fulfills more than one different role. Your server is acting as a primary for your domain, but a secondary for the friendly organization
- there are some Web sites that offer free DNS secondarying (we haven't used them so we can't comment on the quality of service they provide).

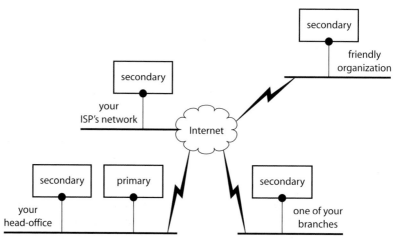

Figure 8.14 Primary and secondary server options

What you want to ensure is that you have a range of servers that are as independent of each other as possible:

- the primary and secondary on your own network rely on different hosts and different pieces of your internal network (and perhaps even on different operating systems)

- the secondary at your ISP doesn't depend on your Internet connection being up

- the secondary in one of your other branches in a different country can overcome nation-wide failures in your head office's country

- the secondary at the friendly organization who uses a different ISP makes you independent of your ISP's network and DNS infrastructure.

Why bother running such a collection of secondaries? If your Internet connection is down or your ISP is down, there are no servers to respond to any incoming traffic, so does it matter? Yes, it matters for two reasons:

1. if other sites can't even resolve your name, they may assume you've gone out of business (or are technically incompetent at least, which would be true!)

2. e-mail for your domain can be automatically sent to a backup server until your own e-mail server is back up again (Module 11.3). This fallback mechanism depends completely on the DNS, so having a secondary nameserver at another site could make all the difference between losing e-mail for as long as your systems are down, or having everything stored safely elsewhere awaiting the return of your servers.

Should you run your own primary server or have your ISP do it for you? The advantage of running it yourself is that you are in control of your own DNS entries: you can make changes quickly instead of having to wait for the ISP to do it. ISPs often have a fixed procedure for rolling out changes – e.g. they record the modifications in a file as they are requested during the day, but the changes in the file are only transferred to the live servers every 12 hours. If you're running mission-critical e-mail and you have to make an urgent DNS change, relying on your ISP could lose you up to 12 hours. (Another consideration is that some ISPs are dreadful. We asked one – a large telco – to add entries for extra servers for us: they didn't think to put in the reverse PTR entries.) The disadvantages of running your own primary are the administrative load (including the initial training so you know what you're doing), and that DNS servers have been attacked successfully, providing entry to people's LANs (see Notes).

Figure 8.14 shows the location of your primary and secondary servers with respect to the Internet – which sites they're at. You also have to decide where *within* your site the server should live. Remember, you are providing these servers so that users at other sites can resolve names for your domain, so these servers are constantly being accessed from the Internet. For security reasons they should not be on your LAN, but nonetheless protected from attackers. Because of this they are usually located on a "demilitarized zone" (DMZ, Module 24.6) behind your firewall – a half-way house between your LAN and the Internet.

The primary and secondary servers for your site's domain name are provided principally for use by users at other sites, not your own. In the rest of the chapter we look at the DNS servers used internally – either to resolve external names as before, or to resolve names of internal machines on your own network, and we'll see that in those configurations you may also have primary and secondary servers that are *internal.*

8.10 DNS servers cache query results but clients don't

There are two main reasons people provide their own DNS servers for their own users, instead of relying on the ISPs DNS servers:

1. to resolve the addresses of internal machines – we cover this in Module 8.12
2. for performance, which we cover here.

DNS servers cache the results of queries but the DNS client (the resolver) doesn't. Because of this, the location and configuration of your DNS servers can have a significant effect on your network's performance.

The purpose of caching is, as usual, to improve performance and response time and reduce the amount of processing necessary. Client's don't cache because you can get better performance and less overall traffic by caching in the server instead. That's because a group of clients using the same nameserver usually have a lot of repeat queries for the same hostnames and IP addresses. (For example, the staff in a company send and receive e-mail from a core group of customers, suppliers and partners, and there's a lot of overlap in the sets of Web sites that people in the same organization refer to.) By caching the results in the server and not in each client, the server can build up a richer and more comprehensive cache, which can be shared amongst all the clients. This reduces the (slow) wide-area traffic from the local server to the rest of the Internet at the cost of (fast) local traffic between the client and local server (Figure 8.15).

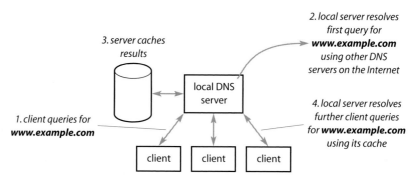

Figure 8.15 DNS results cached on server

A server used like this to provide resolution for the local clients is called a *caching server*. If it isn't a primary master or secondary slave for some zone, it's called a *caching-only server*; this configuration is very common for sites that rely on their ISP to publish their public DNS entries to the Internet, but run a caching-only server internally for performance reasons.

You can see caching working in practice using **tcpdump**. From our client, Alice, we look up a name that we haven't used recently:

```
alice% nslookup www.ibm.com
Name:    www.ibm.com
Addresses:  129.42.17.99, ...
```

(a) below shows the **tcpdump** trace of the packets, which is similar to the conversations we saw earlier in Module 8.5. Now we repeat the same query on the client (b), giving the much shorter **tcpdump** trace of (c).

```
(a)   alice.1026 > myserver.53:          36209+ A? www.ibm.com. (29)
      myserver.1028 > 128.63.2.53.53:    60572 A? www.ibm.com. (29)
      128.63.2.53.53 > myserver.1028:    60572- 0/13/13 (461) (DF)
      myserver.1028 > 192.5.6.30.53:     60573+ A? www.ibm.com. (29)
      192.5.6.30.53 > myserver.1028:     60573- 0/5/5 (240)
      myserver.1028 > 198.4.83.35.53:    60574 A? www.ibm.com. (29)
      198.4.83.35.53 > myserver.1028:    60574*- 4/5/5 A 129.42.19.99, (304)
      myserver.53 > alice.1026:          36209* 4/5/5 A 129.42.19.99, (304)

(b)              alice% nslookup www.ibm.com
                 Non-authoritative answer:
                 Name:     www.ibm.com
                 Addresses:  129.42.16.99, ...

(c)   alice.1026 > myserver.53:          17498+ A? www.ibm.com. (29)
      myserver.53 > alice.1026:          17498 4/5/5 A 129.42.16.99, (311)
```

In (b) **nslookup** now says the answer is "non-authoritative." This means it has obtained the answer from a server that is not authoritative for the zone, i.e. not a primary or secondary server for the zone. That's perfectly correct – it obtained the answer this time from our local server, which answered the query from its cache. (We used **nslookup** because **host** doesn't show whether the answer is authoritative unless you use the "**-v**" option, which often gives more information than we want.) **tcpdump** includes a "*" after the identifier in a reply to indicate that it's authoritative (lines 7, 8 of (a)).

Caching and DNS time-to-live (TTL)

DNS servers know how long to keep a resource record in the cache because each record includes a *time-to-live (TTL)* field, in seconds. Before that length of time has expired, the server considers the record valid and uses the cached value to respond to a relevant query. After the TTL has expired, the record is out of date and is removed from the cache; if a client subsequently queries for that record again, the server must itself issue a query to obtain the necessary information (which is of course cached again).

    tcpdump doesn't show the TTL, but both the **host** command with **-T** option (show TTL) and **nslookup -d** show the TTL. Below we see two successive **host** commands run with a 20-second gap in between. You can see the TTL has decreased by 20 seconds in the second output. (86,400 seconds is 24 hours exactly, by the way, and is a very common TTL value. Because this is such a round number, it's likely that the first query went all the way back to a server for **sun.com**. The second query presumably must have come from a cache as its TTL has decreased.)

```
alice% date ; host -T www.sun.com
Wed Nov 28 09:35:36 GMT 2001
www.sun.com        86400    A    192.18.97.241

alice% date ; host -T www.sun.com
Wed Nov 28 09:35:56 GMT 2001
www.sun.com        86380    A    192.18.97.241
```

In the next module we see how caching affects server performance and how you lay out your network and DNS servers to take account of this.

8.11 Types of server (2) – caching-only; forwarders

Now we consider DNS servers you provide for your own, internal users.

Caching-only servers

We explained the typical use of a caching-only server in the previous module. You might also run a caching-only server on a mail or Web server machine, in addition to any other DNS servers you might have (Figure 8.16). This reduces network traffic and overcomes the fact that the resolver (in the mail software) doesn't cache. This configuration can improve performance significantly because a mail server usually does at least one DNS lookup for every message it sends or receives from the Internet. For very large mail or Web servers, you might run the caching-only server on a nearby machine, so that the DNS cache doesn't consume most of the memory on your mail server and degrade its performance.

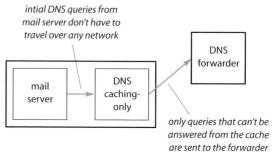

Figure 8.16 A caching-only server used on a mail server machine

Forwarders

A *forwarder* is a nameserver that other servers, usually internal ones, forward queries to, and it does all the resolving. The servers that originate the queries are called *slaves* – at least by Microsoft – if they don't perform any other DNS role. (Don't confuse this "slave" with other meanings of the word – master/slave, or secondary server – that we covered in Module 8.8.) The query sent from the slave to the forwarder is recursive, which is unusual. If the forwarder can't resolve the query, it returns an error to the slave, and the query has failed.

We cover forwarders here because you will often come across them in other documentation. In spite of what we say below, DNS experts strongly discourage the use of forwarders because they are often single points of failure in a network and in practice rarely give the expected performance benefits.

The suggested advantages of a forwarder are:

- it lets you restrict DNS traffic to only one server – the forwarder. Only the forwarder needs to be able to access the Internet: traffic to/from other servers is entirely on LAN, so they can have private NAT addresses and/or your firewall can block all traffic between them and the Internet, for security reasons (Figure 8.17)
- it builds up a rich cache of replies that improves the performance of all the slaves and cuts down on long-distance traffic. Networks with multiple sites on a private WAN may use a slave at each site to keep as much of the DNS traffic local as possible.

Each slave can be configured to use multiple forwarders, for resilience.

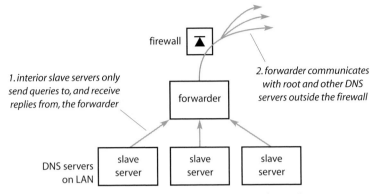

1. *interior slave servers only send queries to, and receive replies from, the forwarder*

2. *forwarder communicates with root and other DNS servers outside the firewall*

Figure 8.17 Only the forwarder communicates through the firewall

The terminology is a bit confusing. There's no special configuration to make a server a forwarder – it just needs to handle recursive queries. On the other hand, the slaves *are* specially configured: they are told to send all queries that they can't resolve to the forwarders, and to send them as recursive queries.

ISPs often provide forwarders, especially for use by small sites. A typical use (Figure 8.18) is where you run your own internal server because it's quicker for your internal clients to access a DNS server on your LAN rather than at the ISP. Your server uses the ISP's forwarder in turn to resolve external queries. This network design minimizes the configuration required for your own server, but also gives good performance: the ISP's network connections are faster than yours, and you get the benefit of their (probably large) cache. (On the other hand, if your ISP is dreadful, you might be safer not depending on their forwarder: if it fails, you've lost much of your Internet connectivity.)

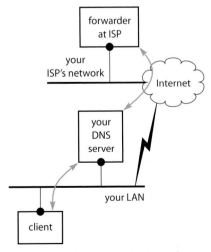

Figure 8.18 Running your own internal server and using a forwarder at your ISP

8.12 Types of server (3) – servers for internal names

In the previous chapter for simplicity we assumed you're not running your own DNS server but rely on the DNS server(s) operated by your ISP. We've already seen in the modules before this that sites often run their own servers for performance reasons. There's another, completely different reason for having your own server: to allow you to refer by name to machines on your own LAN, and not just to external Web sites and e-mail destinations. Sites that have a significant number of non-Windows machines often run DNS for this reason. DNS is also essential if you run Microsoft's Active Directory.

Figure 8.19 shows a typical configuration. All DNS traffic for resolving internal host addresses is completely local to the LAN so this configuration can be used even on sites not connected to the Internet.

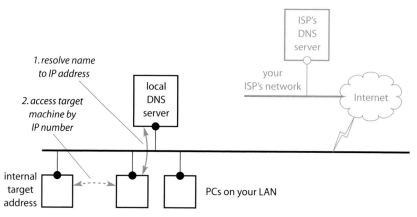

Figure 8.19 A typical Internal DNS configuration

Note that the server for your internal machines is a primary master (although probably no one outside your network can see it) and the usual considerations apply. It should therefore have one or more internal secondaries. Otherwise, losing the server would cripple your internal network because none of your internal machines would be able to access internal resources referenced by machine name.

We said that the internal server is "probably" not visible from outside. In fact some sites use the same server for one or two other purposes as well:

1. it can be your external primary master name server as well, providing DNS information about your site to external users on the Internet, in which case it must be visible from outside. However, this has disadvantages and a better option is to use "split" or "shadow" servers as described below

2. to give better DNS performance to all DNS clients on your LAN, it can act as a full caching-only server (A in Figure 8.20) or forward queries to your ISP's forwarder (B in Figure 8.20). Your server doesn't have to be accessible to outside users; your firewall can allow outgoing queries but block incoming ones.

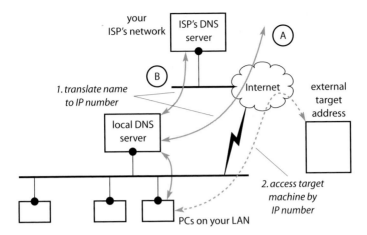

Figure 8.20 Giving better DNS performance

Split (shadow) DNS servers

If you use the same server for external addresses as well as internal, as might be shown in Figure 8.19, external users can get a lot of information about your internal network that could help someone attack your site. From a list of hostnames and IP numbers you can guess what the different machines are and what the likely structure of the network is. To avoid this, you can run *split* or *shadow* DNS servers – use different servers for inside and outside addresses with only the "public addresses" server accessible from outside. You configure your LAN clients to use the "private addresses" server, which can also act as a caching-only server resolving external addresses for our LAN clients (Figure 8.21). (Or it could use the "public addresses" server or your ISP's server as a forwarder; many different configurations are possible.)

The "public addresses" server is often located on the "demilitarized zone" of a firewall for security reasons (Module 24.6).

The next module deals with the part of a PC's DNS configuration that particularly affects how the PC resolves local (internal) names.

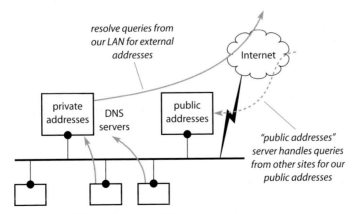

Figure 8.21 Separate public and private DNS servers

8.13 DNS for internal names – client configuration

In the next three modules we assume you have an internal server, configured with the names and numbers of your internal machines as just described, and that your LAN machine's resolvers are configured with its IP number so they use it as their server.

Now we can configure the remaining three DNS settings for a client PC: the domain name, the DNS searchlist (or "domain suffix search order" on Windows) and the hostname (Windows only). Recall from Module 7.2 that configuring DNS on this client PC is only to control how this PC uses the DNS. It does *not* alter the contents of the DNS databases or how any other host views the hostname or IP address of this machine. In that sense the client's hostname and domain name are not essential for DNS to work properly – even with junk settings for these parameters your PC could still resolve external Web sites, e-mail addresses, etc. However, these settings are necessary:

- this PC uses its combined host and domain name when identifying itself to some other machine or application (e.g. e-mail programs insert the name in outgoing messages). For this reason alone you should always set the hostname and domain name on live systems

- the domain name controls how this PC looks up names of machines on your own network. (The searchlist also affects how that works, as we explain in Module 8.15.)

The domain name and hostname are also used by this host when talking to itself (e.g. when you are troubleshooting). For example, Alice sets her PC's domain name value to **oz.ops.example.com**, so her machine believes its full name is **alice.oz.ops.example.com** and will use this as its full Internet name (its FQDN), to the extent that on Windows, if she **pings** Alice or **pings alice.oz.ops.example.com**, the packets are sent to the local machine without using the DNS at all.

What if Alice now wants to **ping** another machine, Bob? She surely can use the full name **bob.oz.ops.example.com**, but that's long to type.

> **Note:** most of this and the following modules apply only if you run a DNS server inter-nally that is configured with the names and IP numbers of some or all of your internal hosts. As we mentioned in Module 7.3, many small sites and Microsoft-only sites don't use DNS for their internal hostnames; in their case the only purpose of the domain name is to allow this machine to know its full name, by combining the specified domain name with the hostname.

It would be nice just to be able to say "**ping bob**" and that's where the domain name setting comes in. If you try to resolve a name that doesn't contain any dots at all, your resolver – depending on its version and configuration – automatically appends your PC's domain name value to the simple name, so it becomes "**bob.oz.ops.example.com.**" However, if you didn't enter any value for the domain name field, the resolver tries to resolve the simple name exactly as it is: if that doesn't succeed, the resolution fails, so plain old "**ping bob**" would fail. (As we mentioned in Module 7.4, Windows-NT now specifically avoids this behavior; see Notes for why that's a good idea.)

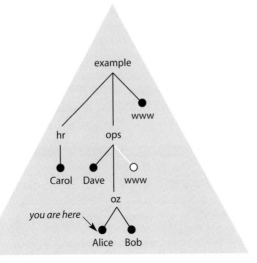

Figure 8.22 *"ping www"*: which **www** does it mean?

Alice wants to **ping** the Web server, whose FQDN is **www.example.com** (Figure 8.22). If she says **ping www**, the resolver appends her domain name setting, so it tries **www.oz.ops. example.com**, which is not what we wanted. The resolver gets over this problem by making a *searchlist* of possible domain parts to append, and tries each in turn until one succeeds. The list consists of the local domain name unaltered, then with the first part ("oz.") removed, then the first two parts removed, etc. until only two parts (".example.com") are left. By default, only the first three entries in the searchlist are used, i.e. the resolver tries each of the following in turn:

www.oz.ops.example.com www.ops.example.com www.example.com

You can watch this in a **tcpdump**; in the output, "NXDOMAIN" means "non-existent domain," i.e. can't resolve this name:

```
myclient.1026 > myserver.53:   20540+ A? www.oz.ops.example.com. (40)
myserver.53 > myclient.1026:   20540 NXDomain 0/1/0 (95)
myclient.1026 > myserver.53:   20541+ A? www.ops.example.com. (37)
myserver.53 > myclient.1026:   20541 NXDomain 0/1/0 (92)
myclient.1026 > myserver.53:   20542+ A? www.example.com. (33)
myserver.53 > myclient.1026:   20542 2/4/4 CNAME[|domain]
```

(Note that if there is a machine called **www.ops.example.com** – shown in white in Figure 8.22 – when you **ping www** you will of course get **www.ops.example.com**. To refer to **www.example.com** you would have to specify its FQDN.)

That's how the resolver handles a name without any dots. What if we now want to **ping** Carol, whose FQDN is **carol.hr.example.com?** The mechanism we've just described can't handle that, but the searchlist, which we cover in Module 8.15, is designed specifically for cases like that.

The next module shows the client configuration steps in detail.

8.14 Lab – configuring your PC to use DNS (2) – domain name (and hostname)

Windows

Configure your DNS settings using **Control Panel > Network > TCP/IP > Properties > DNS** (Figure 8.23). As we mentioned in Module 7.4, changed settings take effect as soon as you press **OK** or **Apply** – you don't have to reboot.

Figure 8.23
Configuring your
DNS settings

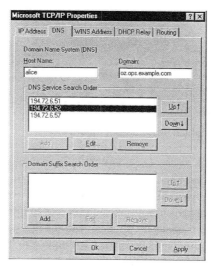

Windows automatically fills in the **hostname** field with the name that you gave your PC when you installed it, or that you modified using the **Control Panel > Network > Identification > Computer Name** dialog. We recommend you never change the value in the **hostname** field. (Having a DNS hostname different from the inherent Windows hostname could be very confusing, so leave it alone.)

In the **Domain** field enter the DNS domain name or subdomain of this machine. Do *not* enter a leading dot; if you do, you get the message "Domain name is not a valid name."

> **Warning:** this field is completely unrelated to the Windows-NT "domain" that you specify in **Control Panel > Network > Identification**, which is used only for Microsoft Windows Networking (Chapter 18). Don't confuse them.

You can modify several aspects of the domain-name and searchlist operations using Windows Registry settings (see Notes).

Linux

On Linux, the hostname isn't part of the DNS settings at all, but for consistency with the Windows coverage we cover it here:

	Command
display the current hostname	`hostname`
set name to *string*	`hostname` *string*

As usual, the settings are not persistent. To preserve the settings, see Appendix 6.

To set the domain name, edit the file */etc/resolv.conf* and insert your domain name on a line prefixed with the word **domain** as in:

```
domain oz.ops.example.com
```

As with Windows, don't enter a leading dot; if you do, when you try to look up a simple name such as alice at your own site, it will get confused, and incorrectly look for a name like alice••oz.ops.example.com (with two dots instead of one after the initial name). It will also cause problems when this machine tries to tell other machines or applications its name.

Exercise: configure your domain name on your Linux box to be •example.com, i.e. with a leading dot. What happens when you "**ping alice**"?

Exercise: start **tcpdump**. From a Windows PC, **ping** its own simple name, e.g. **alice**. Then **ping** its full name (FQDN), e.g. **alice.oz.ops.example.com**. What DNS traffic do you see on the wire?
Repeat this on a Linux machine.

Notice in the **tcpdump** output that the names in the DNS queries end in a dot, e.g. **alice.oz.ops.example.com•**, which emphasizes that they are FQDNs.

Side effects

Generating the searchlist from the domain-name setting can have unwanted side effects if your site's domain contains more than two parts (e.g. **example.co.uk** as opposed to **example.com**). Here's an example: our domain name is **uit.co.uk**; we were testing e-mail and sent dummy messages to **fred@junk**, where **junk** was a non-existent host on our network. The mail server looked first for **junk.uit.co.uk**, which failed as expected, but because of the searchlist, it also tried to resolve **junk.co.uk**, which by chance *did* exist, so they received lots of rubbish by mistake.

That's why the resolver stops searching when there are only two parts left of the domain-name setting. Consequently, for domains like **example.com** the resolver will not append **.com** on its own to a simple name (i.e. it won't try to resolve **junk.com**). But for a domain like **example.co.uk**, the resolver *does* append **.co.uk** to the simple name, which is why it tried **junk.co.uk** above. (The "stop at two parts" idea was fine in the early Internet days when most sites were in the USA and had **.com**, **.edu**, etc. domains.)

You can get over this by configuring the explicit searchlist, in the next module.

8.15 Lab – configuring your PC to use DNS (3) – the "searchlist"

This option is relatively rarely used (partly because lots of people don't know what it's for) but it is useful in a couple of circumstances, where:

1. the domain name of this host contains more than two components, like **example.co.uk** or **ops.example.com** (as opposed to a name with just two components, like **example.com**)

2. your machine communicates regularly with machines whose domain-name setting isn't the same as yours, and which isn't a parent of yours. For example, if my domain-name setting is **ops.example.com**, the normal searching derived from the domain name will let me reach my parent **example.com** machines, but it won't let me get automatically to **hr.example.com** or **partnerco.com** machines.

We'll continue with the scenario we used in Module 8.13. Alice is a PC on our LAN and her FQDN is **alice.oz.ops.example.com**.

Instead of relying on the automatic searchlist derived from Alice's domain-name setting, she can configure an explicit searchlist herself. This completely over-rides the derived list and is used instead of it – i.e. the domain-name and searchlist settings are mutually exclusive. Now when attempting to resolve a name, the resolver appends each searchlist entry in turn, until it succeeds, or else fails because there are no entries left. The resolver tries the searchlist entries exactly as they are; it doesn't remove any components as happened with the domain-name setting.

Based on the **example.com** network, and Alice's position in it (as far as naming is concerned – her location on a physical subnet is irrelevant), she might configure her searchlist to be:

> oz.ops.example.com
> hr.example.com
> example.com
> partnerco.com
> ops.example.com
> fin.example.com

Note that we have to include **example.com** and **ops.example.com** explicitly: no variants are created automatically when you're using the explicit searchlist.

The order of entries is significant but not crucial – it's a question of efficiency. Earliest entries are tried first, so if Alice refers to machines at the partner company **partnerco.com** more often than she deals with her own operations or finance departments, the order shown makes sense. If the order isn't optimal, all that happens is that more failed lookup requests are made than is strictly necessary.

This type of configuration is obviously useful for sites that use subdomains.

If your domain name has more than two components (e.g. **example.co.uk**), as discussed in the previous module it's advisable to set the searchlist. This prevents the resolver appending the final two components (**.co.uk** in this example) to simple names. For a small site, we might set the searchlist to the single entry:

> example.co.uk

Because the domain-name and searchlist settings are mutually exclusive, this prevents the resolver appending anything other than **example.co.uk** in full to simple names.

One disadvantage of the searchlist is that the optimal order of entries depends on where you are in the naming tree. The best order for Alice wouldn't be the best for, for example, **www.example.com** or **carol.hr.example.com**. If you configure your machines manually, you can take account of this, at the cost of having slightly different "standard" configurations in different parts of your network. If you configure your network automatically using DHCP (Chapter 16) you're probably better choosing one order and using it everywhere for simplicity.

Windows

Enter one or more searchlist entries in the **Domain Suffix Search Order** window. If this field isn't empty, it completely over-rides the effect of the **Domain** field on how names are resolved. Entries must not start with a dot or you'll be told "Domain name is not a valid name." As usual, you can verify that settings have taken effect using **ipconfig/all** or **wntipcfg > More info ….. ipconfig/all** shows multiple servers more clearly, but it doesn't show "other domain suffix" setting, and it shows the domain setting combined with the hostname.

Linux

In the file **/etc/resolv.conf** enter up to six searchlist entries, all on the same line, preceded by the keyword "**search**", e.g.

```
search ops.example.com example.co.uk partnerco.com
```

> **Exercise:** set your searchlist to a suitable value for your network. Then start **tcpdump**, and from your PC **ping** *badname*, where *badname* is a name you know doesn't exist on your LAN. This will force the resolver to try every entry in the searchlist, and you'll see it in operation.

> **Warning:** if you mistype the **search** keyword, the resolver won't work properly but you won't get any error message.

> **Warning:** the DNS is not the only name resolution system that may be running on Windows or on Linux – see Module 9.4.

Queries containing dots

The explicit and domain-derived searchlists are for simple names, i.e. names that don't contain any dots. If a name does contain a dot, the resolver first tries to resolve it unmodified, but if that fails, it employs the searchlist procedure. (The difference is that a name without any dots is not tried unmodified, or is only tried unmodified after all the others have failed, depending on the implementation.)

You can prevent the searchlist being used by appending a dot to the end of the name, e.g. "alice•" or "alice•hr•". (The latter could be the name of a site in Croatia; Croatia's country code is "**hr**".) The trailing dot means "this is a FQDN".

> **Exercise:** run **tcpdump** and **ping alice•**; what queries do you see?

8.16 How reverse lookups work

A *reverse lookup* is where we want to find the name that corresponds to an IP address instead of the other way round. Let's say we want to find the name that corresponds to 129.42.17.99. How do we do it? How does our DNS server find out which server on the Internet holds this information?

If we had a DNS server containing all our internal names and IP numbers, maybe we could send the query to that. It could scan down its list of hostnames until it found one with the IP address we're trying to resolve. But that could only work for one specific server. To be able to resolve *any* IP number, we'd need a DNS server somewhere that contained all the hostnames in the world, with their IP numbers. As we know, there is no such server.

To see how the DNS solves this problem, let's look again at how DNS resolves a hostname, e.g. **bob.example.com•**. Our DNS server:

1. finds a server for the root domain "•"

2. queries that, to get the server for **.com**. (As we saw, our server in fact sends the whole query for **bob.example.com**, not just for **.com**. It knows from the reply that there is no answer for the full name, but only a list of name servers in the nameserver/authority records section. So in effect this step is "querying for the **.com** name servers".)

3. queries that, to get the server for **.example.com**

4. queries that, to get the address for **bob.example.com**.

The task is broken into small steps, very general at the beginning (the root domain), more specific as it proceeds through the large **.com** domain, and then the more specific **.example.com**, until at the end it queries one server for a single IP number.

Reverse lookups use a similar technique. Our server queries for the name **99.17.42.129.in-addr.arpa**. This consists of the IP number reversed, so that the more significant or more general bytes are on the *right* instead of on the left. Then the special domain name **.in-addr.arpa**, reserved for reverse lookups, is appended. The IP number's bytes are reversed like this because in domain *names* the most significant part is written on the right, **bob.example.<u>com</u>**, whereas with a numeric IP address, the most significant part is on the left, **<u>129</u>.42.17.99**. The lookup now proceeds exactly as a normal hostname lookup, working through all the delegations. Our server goes through the following steps:

1. finds a server for the root domain "•"

2. queries that, and gets the server ("A", say) for domain **129.in-addr.arpa**

3. our server prepends the next most significant byte, **.42**, to the query and sends it to server A to get the server ("B") for the next most significant part, **42.129.in-addr.arpa**

4. our server queries B to get the server for **17.42.129.in-addr.arpa**. The list of servers for that domain is returned. In this particular case the full answer – that the name of **129.42.17.99** is **www.ibm.com** – is returned at the same time, because that server happens to have the reverse lookup database we wanted. For a different IP number, we might have had an extra step: query domain **17.42.129.in-addr.arpa**'s server to get the final answer for **99.17.42.129.in-addr.arpa**.

(In fact, in each case the full name **99.17.42.129.in-addr.arpa** is sent in the query, but we've shown which parts of it are resolved at each step.) So reverse lookups work identically to forward lookups. They just use different domain names – names that are derived from the IP number, instead of the normal hostnames. This is why the databases for forward and reverse lookups are stored separately (Module 7.6) – they really are two different domains and two separate zones. For example, our domains are **example.com** *and* **2.0.192.in-addr.arpa**.

The trace below shows the whole conversation. (As with forward lookups, you can only see all these packets when using your own DNS server and not relying on your ISP's or other server located at a remote site.) We issued the command **host 129.42.17.99** on our DNS server, so the client PC we used before (192.0.2.111) isn't involved. The output is edited to save space, with line numbers added and the time shown as seconds and tenths of seconds. (As in Module 8.6, this level of trace doesn't show enough detail to let you see exactly what's happening – you'd have to use **tcpdump**'s "-vvv" option to follow the process in detail.)

```
 1  03.3   192.0.2.34.1045 > 198.41.0.4.53:          34492 PTR? 99.17.42.129.in-addr.arpa.
 2  03.5   198.41.0.4.53 > 192.0.2.34.1045:          34492- 0/10/0 (259)
 3  03.5   192.0.2.34.1045 > 202.153.114.101.53:     34493 A? ARROWROOT.ARIN.NET.  (36)
 4  03.5   192.0.2.34.1045 > 202.153.114.101.53:     34494 A? BUCHU.ARIN.NET.  (32)
 5  03.5   192.0.2.34.1045 > 202.153.114.101.53:     34495 A? CHIA.ARIN.NET.  (31)
 6  03.5   192.0.2.34.1045 > 202.153.114.101.53:     34496 A? DILL.ARIN.NET.  (31)
 7  03.5   192.0.2.34.1045 > 202.153.114.101.53:     34497 A? EPAZOTE.ARIN.NET.  (34)
 8  03.5   192.0.2.34.1045 > 202.153.114.101.53:     34498 A? FIGWORT.ARIN.NET  (34)
 9  03.5   192.0.2.34.1045 > 202.153.114.101.53:     34499 A? GINSENG.ARIN.NET.  (34)
10  03.5   192.0.2.34.1045 > 202.153.114.101.53:     34500 A? HENNA.ARIN.NET.  (32)
11  03.5   192.0.2.34.1045 > 202.153.114.101.53:     34501 A? INDIGO.ARIN.NET.  (33)
12  03.5   192.0.2.34.1045 > 202.153.114.101.53:     34502 A? JERK.ARIN.NET.  (31)
13  03.9   202.153.114.101.53 > 192.0.2.34.1045:     34493- 1/7/7 A 198.133.199.110 (292)
14  04.0   202.153.114.101.53 > 192.0.2.34.1045:     34494- 1/7/7 A 192.100.59.110 (292)
15  04.0   202.153.114.101.53 > 192.0.2.34.1045:     34495- 0/7/7 (281)
16  04.0   192.0.2.34.1045 > 198.133.199.110.53:     34503 A? CHIA.ARIN.NET.  (31)
17  04.0   202.153.114.101.53 > 192.0.2.34.1045:     34496- 0/7/7 (281)
18  04.0   192.0.2.34.1045 > 198.133.199.110.53:     34504 A? DILL.ARIN.NET.  (31)
19  04.1   202.153.114.101.53 > 192.0.2.34.1045:     34497- 0/7/7 (284)
20  04.1   192.0.2.34.1045 > 198.133.199.110.53:     34505 A? EPAZOTE.ARIN.NET.  (34)
21  04.1   202.153.114.101.53 > 192.0.2.34.1045:     34498- 0/7/7 (284)
22  04.1   192.0.2.34.1045 > 198.133.199.110.53:     34506 A? FIGWORT.ARIN.NET.  (34)
23  04.2   202.153.114.101.53 > 192.0.2.34.1045:     34499- 0/7/7 (284)
24  04.2   192.0.2.34.1045 > 198.133.199.110.53:     34507 A? GINSENG.ARIN.NET.  (34)
25  04.2   202.153.114.101.53 > 192.0.2.34.1045:     34500- 0/7/7 (282)
26  04.2   192.0.2.34.1045 > 198.133.199.110.53:     34508 A? HENNA.ARIN.NET.  (32)
27  04.2   202.153.114.101.53 > 192.0.2.34.1045:     34501- 0/7/7 (283)
28  04.2   192.0.2.34.1045 > 198.133.199.110.53:     34509 A? INDIGO.ARIN.NET.  (33)
29  04.3   202.153.114.101.53 > 192.0.2.34.1045:     34502- 0/7/7 (281)
30  04.3   192.0.2.34.1045 > 198.133.199.110.53:     34510 A? JERK.ARIN.NET.  (31)
31  04.3   198.133.199.110.53 > 192.0.2.34.1045:     34503*- 1/10/2 A 192.5.6.32 (268)
32  04.4   198.133.199.110.53 > 192.0.2.34.1045:     34504*- 1/10/2 A 192.35.51.32 (268)
33  04.4   198.133.199.110.53 > 192.0.2.34.1045:     34505*- 1/10/2 A 192.41.162.32 (271)
34  04.4   198.133.199.110.53 > 192.0.2.34.1045:     34506*- 1/10/2 A 192.42.93.32 (271)
35  04.5   198.133.199.110.53 > 192.0.2.34.1045:     34507*- 1/10/2 A 192.33.14.32 (271)
36  04.5   198.133.199.110.53 > 192.0.2.34.1045:     34508*- 1/10/2 A 192.26.92.32 (269)
37  04.6   198.133.199.110.53 > 192.0.2.34.1045:     34509*- 1/10/2 A 192.31.80.32 (270)
38  04.6   198.133.199.110.53 > 192.0.2.34.1045:     34510*- 1/10/2 A 192.12.94.32 (268)
39  08.3   192.0.2.34.1045 > 192.33.14.32.53:        34511 PTR? 99.17.42.129.in-addr.arpa.
40  08.6   192.33.14.32.53 > 192.0.2.34.1045:        34511- 0/3/0 (112)
41  08.6   192.0.2.34.1045 > 213.177.194.5.53:       34512 A? NS.EVENTS.IHOST.COM.  (37)
42  08.6   192.0.2.34.1045 > 213.177.194.5.53:       34513 A? NS1.EVENTS.IHOST.COM.  (38)
43  08.6   192.0.2.34.1045 > 213.177.194.5.53:       34514 A? NS2.EVENTS.IHOST.COM.  (38)
44  08.6   213.177.194.5.53 > 192.0.2.34.1045:       34512- 1/5/5 A 129.42.2.5 (268)
45  08.7   213.177.194.5.53 > 192.0.2.34.1045:       34513- 1/5/5 A 129.42.4.133 (269)
46  08.7   213.177.194.5.53 > 192.0.2.34.1045:       34514- 1/5/5 A 129.42.2.3 (269)
47  18.3   192.0.2.34.1045 > 129.42.4.133.53:        34515 PTR? 99.17.42.129.in-addr.arpa.
48  18.5   129.42.4.133.53 > 192.0.2.34.1045:        34515*- 1/3/3 PTR www.ibm.com. (182)
```

However the trace does show clearly that:

- there are very many packets involved in getting the details of all the relevant servers (although if you issued another reverse lookup, there would be fewer packets because our server would have many of the replies cached)

- the whole conversation took a long time – about 15 seconds. Reverse lookups can be slow because they often involve more lookups

- reverse-lookup domains and subdomains are delegated in just the same way as normal forward lookups.

Summary

- DNS names are organized hierarchically in a tree structure. Each node in the tree is a domain name

- the DNS database is distributed. One DNS server will often call on another to obtain the information needed to resolve a query

- authority for parts of the DNS tree are delegated to various organizations. These can in turn delegate parts of their sub-tree to other organizations, and so on

- DNS servers hold databases of name and IP number details. The part of the tree they have authority for is called a zone. A zone is not the same as a domain, although they frequently coincide, especially at end-user sites

- to resolve a name the DNS often has to follow the chain of delegation through several steps, getting progressively more detailed information at each step until finally it gets the full details for the name it's trying to resolve

- DNS servers are configured in many different ways, to fulfill different roles: primary and secondary servers are authoritative for a zone, caching-only servers improve DNS performance for their clients, and forwarders just rely on other servers to do all their work for them

- you can run your own DNS server(s) to resolve the names of your internal machines on your private LAN. These servers should not normally be visible from outside your site and are usually separate from the DNS server that holds the public entries (Web and mail server addresses, etc.) for your site

- for internal name lookups especially, you can configure your client resolver with either a domain name or a searchlist, which makes it easy for you to refer to a machine by a simple name rather than having to specify its fully qualified domain name

- reverse lookups convert IP numbers to their corresponding names. The mechanisms used are exactly the same as for name lookups. However they use the root servers for the special domain name **in-addr.arpa** to access the tree of IP numbers as opposed to more common tree of names.

What's next?

Troubleshooting the DNS.

Notes and related reading

The *Oxford English Dictionary* defines "domain" as "*a district or region under rule, control, or influence, or contained within certain limits; realm; sphere of activity, influence, or dominion.*" Your DNS domain is a specific part of the name space that is dedicated to you, so you can create your own names without clashing with anyone else's.

There's a good DNS glossary at:

  ❏ **http://www.menandmice.com/ONLINE%20DOCS%20AND%20FAQ/Glossary/ index.htm**

Stevens, Chapter 14 covers the DNS although it's more a theoretical than a practical treatment. Many people recommend

  ❏ **Paul Ablitz & Cricket Liu**, *DNS and BIND* (O'Reilly, 2001)

A little history

Before the DNS was invented, using the **hosts** file involved a lot of centralized administration, and it inhibited change on the net because in practice almost every local copy of HOSTS.TXT was out of date to a greater or lesser extent. (RFC-799 in 1981 said that with 400 machines on the network, managing the **hosts** file was becoming "awkward"). When the DNS was introduced it overcame these problems. The last list of hosts published as an RFC was:

  ❏ **RFC-1166 July 1990** *Internet Numbers*

The **hosts** file still exists on both Linux and Windows. It is useful when you don't use DNS, i.e. on small or test networks, or networks not connected to the Internet. As we'll see in the next chapter, keeping values in the **hosts** file can cause confusion – they don't change when you alter the corresponding DNS records. Assuming you have a regular network connected to the Internet, don't use **hosts** unless you have to.

    As we mentioned in Chapter 5's Notes, there is a related file called **networks** although it is of debatable use. On Linux this is **/etc/networks**. On Windows-NT the files are stored in **C:\winnt\system32\drivers\etc**.

    Microsoft Windows Networking also uses a special hosts file of its own called **Lmhosts** ("LAN Manager hosts file", Chapter 19). You can store network names/numbers in the DNS although it's rarely done:

  ❏ **RFC-1101 April 1989** *DNS Encoding of Network Names and Other Types*

Domain naming

Hierarchical domains as we know them were proposed in

  ❏ **RFC-805 February 1982** *Computer Mail Meeting Notes*

A good discussion of the ideas behind the DNS is in:

  ❏ **RFC-819 August 1982** *The Domain Naming Convention for Internet User Applications*

For historical information and notes on the evolution of the DNS see:

  ❏ **RFC-830 October 1982** *A Distributed System for Internet Name Service*

  ❏ **RFC-883 November 1983** *Domain Names – Implementation And Specification*

The DNS specifications are:

  ❏ **RFC-1034 November 1987** *Domain Names – Concepts and Facilities*

  ❏ **RFC-1035 November 1987** *Domain Names – Implementation and Specification*

Top-level domain names

The full list of country codes for TLDs is at:

❏ http://www.iso.org/iso/en/prods-services/iso3166ma/02iso-3166-code-code-lists/index.html *ISO 3166 code lists* > **English country names and code elements**

In fact a few ccTLDs, including **.uk**, don't use the ISO standard country codes. See:

❏ http://www.iso.org/iso/en/prods-services/iso3166ma/04background-on-iso-3166/iso3166-1-and-ccTLDs.html *ISO 3166-1 and country coded Top-Level Domains (ccTLDs)*

For details of each of the root zones see:

❏ http://www.iana.org/cctld/cctld-whois.htm

Code **TV** stands for Tuvalu, but names in this domain have been marketed to television companies. Similarly, **MD** stands for Moldova, but might be of interest to medical doctors.

It is only a convention that many Web sites are called **www.***something*. A "Web site name" is only a DNS hostname, so it can be anything. An interesting example is **http://cr.yp.to** (which has little to do with Tonga, in spite of its **TO** country code).

Some Internet free spirits think there ought to be much greater freedom in creating top-level domains:

❏ **http://www.open-rsc.org** "If, instead of using the nameservers you use now, you use ours, then you will be able to get to sites like http://free.tibet and http://chrono.faq."

DNS servers

BIND, the Berkeley Internet Name Domain, is the DNS client and server implementation used by almost every UNIX version. It is distributed free by

❏ **http://www.isc.org** The Internet Software Consortium

The latest version at the time of writing is 9.2.0. Version 8 is also widely used; its current version is 8.3.1.

BIND now has a facility called "views" so you can in effect run two nameservers in one: one view – of your public Web, e-mail server, etc. addresses for public access from the Internet, and a second view – of your internal machine addresses – accessible only from inside your LAN. This means you don't need two separate machines to provide the split/shadow servers we mentioned in Module 8.12.

On some Linux distributions, the BIND documentation is a mixture of old and new versions. In particular, the "BOG" (Basic Operations Guide) is for version 4.x.x and is massively out of date. There is no BOG for version 9, although there is an up-to-date "ARM" (Administrator Reference Manual).

On Linux **in.named** or **named** is the nameserver process. On Windows-NT the process (for the standard NT version) is **DNS.EXE**. The Internet Software Consortium has a binary (ready-to-run) distribution of BIND for Windows-NT and 2000.

For a less conventional view of DNS implementations, and some acerbic comments on BIND, see DJ Bernstein's site:

❏ **http://cr.yp.to/djbdns.html**

❏ **http://cr.yp.to/djbdns/blurb/unbind.html**

DNS servers have had bugs that were serious security holes:

❏ **http://www.cert.org/advisories/CA-2000-03.html April 2000** *CERT® Advisory CA-2000-03 Continuing Compromises of DNS servers*

❏ **http://www.cert.org/advisories/CA-2001-02.html January 2001** *CERT® Advisory CA-2001-02 Multiple Vulnerabilities in BIND*

Root servers

For details and discussion of root servers:

❏ **http://www.wia.org/database/**

❏ **http://www.icann.org/icp/icp-3.htm July 2001** *ICP-3: A Unique, Authoritative Root for the DNS*

❏ **RFC-2870 June 2000** *Root Name Server Operational Requirements*

Primary master and secondary (slave) servers

All authoritative servers for a zone are identified by **NS** resource records in the database for the zone; you can list these for a zone with, for example,

```
host -t ns example.com
```

From outside, that's all you can find out about the servers; you can't tell which is the primary and which are the secondaries (slaves).

Internally, the primary master server is identified by a special option in its configuration file. (The configuration file is separate from the database of resource records that are sent in reply to queries received by this server.)

- BIND version 4 (which is now old) uses the statement **primary**
- BIND versions 8 and 9 use the statement **zone ... type master**

Secondary (slave) servers are identified in a similar way:

- BIND version 4 uses the statement **secondary**
- BIND versions 8 and 9 use the statement **zone ... type slave**

The role a server plays is specific to a zone, so a single instance of the server software could be a primary master for some zones, a secondary (slave) for others, and a caching-only server for still others, all at the same time.

Caching

In Module 8.10 we said that clients don't cache DNS responses. However, as we'll see in Module 19.7, when Microsoft Windows NetBIOS programs use the DNS, they *do* cache the responses.

Domain and hostname configuration

Windows-2000 imposes different constraints than NT-4 on the Windows computer name and the DNS name that you give a machine:

❏ **MS-KB-Q227410** *Computer Name and hostname Must Be the Same in Windows 2000*

In spite of what we said in Module 8.14, some people contend there is a good reason to have a different Windows hostname and DNS or WINS name:

❏ **http://www.windowsitlibrary.com/Content/386/10/5.html** *NetBIOS: Friend or Foe?*

makes a case for setting the "Computer name" to the machine's MAC address, and using the more convention descriptive name as the DNS name. (However Windows-2000 forces you to use the same name for both.)

In Module 7.4 we mentioned that NT will not attempt to use the DNS to resolve a simple name (i.e. without any dots) such as "**bob**". This is correct behavior – see:

❏ **MS-KB-Q230744** *Windows NT 4.0 SP4 DNR Client Does Not Send Unqualified DNS Queries* ("DNR" is not a typo: it stands for "domain name resolver"). Before this modification was introduced, Win-NT behaved as Win-9x still does: if both **Domain** and **Domain Suffix Search Order** are empty, when you **ping bob**, a DNS query is sent for the name **bob**. This will go all the way back to the root DNS servers (whose administrators growl and complain that about 90% of root server queries are for unqualified names like this from Windows PCs or the servers they are using). For this reason, and for the convenience of use we described in Module 8.13 – Module 8.15, you should get into the habit of always defining one of the domain-related fields. This will make the Internet a better place for everyone!

❏ **MS-KB-Q198550** *SP4 Changes DNS Name Resolution*

❏ **MS-KB-Q195611** *DNS Client Does Not Try All Servers in DNS Service List* (bug, fixed in SP5)

❏ **MS-KB-Q214467** *Windows NT 4.0 DNR Only "Devolves" Two Domain Suffixes*

Reverse lookups

The same lateral-thinking approach used for reverse lookups is also used in an entirely different context to publish lists of e-mail servers known to send spam (Module 25.4).

Miscellaneous

"Secure DNS" is under development, so that you can really know that the IP addresses the DNS gives you for a machine name is the correct one, and not a fake address served by someone who wants to hijack traffic to that machine. Secure DNS will also be used for distributing cryptographic public keys (Module 27.6).

If your site expands in the future, instead of running all your public servers (Web, FTP, SMTP e-mail, POP3 e-mail, DNS, etc.) on a single machine you might have to split the functions over several machines to handle the increased load. You can save yourself a lot of trouble by planning your IP address allocation and DNS configuration in advance. For details see:

❏ **http://www.uit.co.uk/resources** > *DNS Planning*.

A single name (e.g. **www.ibm.com**) can have multiple A records, i.e. multiple IP numbers. As we'll see in Chapter 14, many Web sites use this facility to share the load across multiple Web servers.

Almost all DNS traffic uses the UDP transport, which we cover in Chapter 15, and is sent on port 53. We'll explain UDP and TCP and ports in Chapter 10. For now, if you want to trace only DNS traffic, you can instruct **tcpdump** to do so using a command like:

```
tcpdump -n port 53
```

For zone transfers, and if you use **nslookup**'s "**-vc**" option ("virtual circuit"), the DNS uses TCP instead of UDP. However, forget about that for now as we don't explain TCP and UDP until Chapters 10 and 15; we mention it here only for completeness.

Appendices

Appendix 6: making network settings permanent – Debian Linux
Web Appendix 7: setting up a simple DNS server on Windows-NT
Web Appendix 9: setting up a simple DNS server on Linux
Web Appendix 10: sample DNS config files for a basic DNS server
Web Appendix 11: name and domain registration

9 Troubleshooting the DNS

Introduction

In this chapter we cover problems that you may encounter when resolving names or IP numbers from a DNS client

9.1   Troubleshooting – identifying a problem

> **Tip:** you can often short-circuit the step-by-step troubleshooting approach below by running **tcpdump -n** immediately you get a DNS problem. After a while you'll be able to get a good idea of what's happening just from the **tcpdump**'s output, even though it is terse.

Some DNS difficulties you have might not be due to misconfiguration or network problems at your site:

1a. the DNS can't find the IP address for a name you're trying to resolve because the name doesn't exist. If you haven't got any of the errors described below, you'll see the status **NXDomain** (non-existent domain name) in the **tcpdump** trace:

```
192.0.2.17.3566 > 192.0.2.19.53:   19588+ A? junk.example.com. (34)
192.0.2.19.53 > 192.0.2.17.3566:   19588 NXDomain* 0/1/0 (95)
```

The application that requested the name resolution will report an error too. If the name resolution is deep inside the application, the application's error message may not be clear. To make sure, run **host** or **nslookup** on the name that's causing the problem and then you'll get a clear message below. The cause could be either a typo on your part, or the name in question really doesn't exist.

```
alice% host junk.example.com
junk.example.com does not exist (Authoritative answer)
```

Note that **host** said the answer was authoritative (and **tcpdump** indicated it was authoritative by printing its "*" after NXDomain). That means that DNS really did go all the way through the delegations (for **ibm.com** in this example) and was told the name definitely doesn't exist. This ought to assure you there were no other problems along the way (but there is a known bug in this area – see the Notes). The next module shows a typical failed resolution in full detail.

1b. if DNS fails to resolve an internal name (which assumes you're running your own DNS server for internal names) then maybe you do have a problem. For example, if you're trying to resolve "**alice**" but you know Alice exists, a likely cause is that the domain-name and searchlist settings on your machine are empty. As a result DNS is trying to resolve the FQDN **alice•** instead of, for example, **alice.example.com•**

1c. or, it may be that internal machine Alice exists, but your site's DNS administrator hasn't entered the name **alice** in your DNS database. (Or your DNS server may be misconfigured in some other way.)

2. the DNS can't find the name corresponding to an IP number, i.e. a reverse lookup fails. Unfortunately this is very common; frequently it's because the DNS administrator for the site in question didn't set up the PTR records properly. There's nothing you can do about this

3. if you're using Microsoft's Internet Explorer (IE) browser, and a DNS lookup fails, IE itself caches the result. If the problem was caused by a problem with your DNS, even

when you reconfigure your DNS to overcome it, IE remembers that it couldn't resolve the name and doesn't try again. To get over this you have to exit IE and restart it. For this reason it's best not to use IE when checking out DNS problems; use **host** (or **nslookup** if you have nothing better) for troubleshooting instead. (Some versions of Netscape's browser may behave this way too.)

4. is there really a problem? As with every software problem, try it again and see if the problem is reproducible. DNS packets can get dropped, especially on a busy network. (We'll explain how this can happen and why dropped packets are not automatically detected in Chapter 15). It is possible (but unlikely) that all your packets got dropped.

    - see if the same problem happens on another machine that is configured similarly (using the same DNS servers). If it doesn't, you do have a problem with the first machine

5. occasionally you'll see a warning message that the TTL for a record is zero. This is not your fault – it's something wrong at the server for the domain you queried:

```
alice% host -T www.ryanair.ie
www.ryanair.ie       0      A       62.73.129.134
 !!! www.ryanair.ie A record has zero ttl
```

6. weird names show up in queries, e.g. **junk.ibm.com.uit.co.uk** If you've configured the domain-name setting of your PC, your resolver will try several different combinations of names when it can't resolve the name exactly as you specified it. For example, Alice's domain name is set to **uit.co.uk**. If we start **tcpdump** and then run the command "**ping junk.ibm.com**" on Alice, we get the DNS traffic shown below. As we explained in Module 8.13, this is valid but inefficient and ugly behavior.

```
192.0.2.34.1025 > 194.72.6.52.53:   10182+ A? junk.ibm.com. (30)
194.72.6.52.53 > 192.0.2.34.1025:   10182 NXDomain 0/1/0 (80) (DF)
192.0.2.34.1025 > 194.72.6.52.53:   10183+ A? junk.ibm.com.uit.co.uk.
194.72.6.52.53 > 192.0.2.34.1025:   10183 NXDomain* 0/1/0 (97) (DF)
192.0.2.34.1025 > 194.72.6.52.53:   10184+ A? junk.ibm.com.co.uk. (36)
194.72.6.52.53 > 192.0.2.34.1025:   10184 NXDomain* 0/1/0 (103) (DF)
```

7. **host** can give different values for the same query if you run it more than once. This is starting to get into weird circumstances and you probably don't have to worry about it, but what happens is that a "type=**ANY**" query can return only what's in the queried server's cache, rather than causing a full recursive query to be done. (This is documented in **host**'s manpage.)

Exercise: using **host** (or **nslookup**) run the following:

```
host -a sun.com
host -t mx sun.com
host -a sun.com
```

Module 9.3 covers more complex problems you're likely to meet. But first, in the next module we show a typical failed name resolution for a non-existent name.

9.2   Debug output for a failed name resolution

The most common problem with a DNS configuration that has been working correctly is that you try to look up a name but it can't be resolved. Below is the **tcpdump** trace of the DNS traffic for "**ping junk.ibm.com**" which will query for a name that we know doesn't exist. The names queried are just what we expect, given that our PC has its searchlist setting as **uit.co.uk**.

```
192.0.2.17.3569 > 192.0.2.19.53:   53790+ A? junk.example.com.  (34)
192.0.2.19.53 > 192.0.2.17.3569:   53790 NXDomain 0/1/0 (106)
192.0.2.17.3569 > 192.0.2.19.53:   53791+ A? junk.example.com.uit.co.uk.
192.0.2.19.53 > 192.0.2.17.3569:   53791 NXDomain* 0/1/0 (104)
```

Let's say we want to explore what's happening in more detail with this failing resolution. We run **tcpdump** and **nslookup -d** at the same time:

```
192.0.2.17.3571 > 192.0.2.19.53:   33590+ PTR? 19.133.140.212.in-addr.arpa.  (45)
192.0.2.19.53 > 192.0.2.17.3571:   33590* 1/1/1 PTR res3lx.uit.co.uk.  (126)
192.0.2.17.3571 > 192.0.2.19.53:   33591+ A? junk.example.com.  (34)
192.0.2.19.53 > 192.0.2.17.3571:   33591 NXDomain* 0/1/0 (95)
192.0.2.17.3571 > 192.0.2.19.53:   33592+ A? junk.example.com.uit.co.uk.  (44)
192.0.2.19.53 > 192.0.2.17.3571:   33592 NXDomain* 0/1/0 (104)
```

There are a few points worth noting:

- **nslookup** always queries for the name of the DNS server it's using, so we expect the reverse lookup shown at the beginning of the above traces. (As we mentioned in Module 7.5, if the reverse lookup fails, **nslookup** terminates, which is why many people prefer to use other **host** or **dig** instead.)

- after the query for **junk.ibm.com** failed because the name didn't exist, **nslookup** then tried **junk.ibm.com.uit.co.uk** as expected.

Now let's see what "**host -v**" does. Below is the **tcpdump** trace (we haven't shown **host** for lack of space because it isn't just a simple name's output):

```
192.0.2.17.3579 > 192.0.2.19.53:   20100+ A? junk.example.com.  (34)
192.0.2.19.53 > 192.0.2.17.3579:   20100 NXDomain 0/1/0 (106)
```

Because the name you're looking up isn't just a simple name, **host** queries only for the name exactly as you entered it. This is an important point: both **nslookup** and **host** refer to the resolver configuration files but do *not* use the standard resolver code. This makes testing difficult. If you really need to look at a resolution problem on this level, we recommend you:

1. run "**tcpdump -n**" as always

2a. use **ping**, not **nslookup** or **host**, to generate the lookup. **ping** uses your machine's standard resolver so it will generate the same queries that any other standard application would

2b. append a dot to the name you're querying, e.g. "**host junk.ibm.com•**" so that it's interpreted as an FQDN and some or all of the domain or explicit searchlist activity is bypassed. If the name you're querying is internal, e.g. "**alice,**" append your domain name manually yourself, and add the dot, as in "**host alice.example.com•**" Then you'll know exactly what's what.

However, for ordinary day-to-day checking of DNS names, etc., **host** is just fine.

```
alice% nslookup -d junk.example.com
;; res_nmkquery(QUERY, 19.2.0.192.in-addr.arpa, IN, PTR find the
------------
Got answer:
    HEADER:
        opcode = QUERY, id = 33590, rcode = NOERROR
        header flags: response, auth. answer, want recursion, recursion avail.
        questions = 1,  answers = 1,  authority records = 1,  additional = 1
    QUESTIONS:
        19.2.0.192.in-addr.arpa, type = PTR, class = IN
    ANSWERS:
    ->  19.2.0.192.in-addr.arpa
        name = res3lx.uit.co.uk
        ttl = 86400 (1D)
    AUTHORITY RECORDS:
    ->  2.0.192.in-addr.arpa
        nameserver = res3lx.uit.co.uk
        ttl = 86400 (1D)
    ADDITIONAL RECORDS:
    ->  res3lx.uit.co.uk
        internet address = 192.0.2.19
        ttl = 86400 (1D)
------------
Server:  res3lx.uit.co.uk
Address: 192.0.2.19

;; res_nmkquery(QUERY, junk.example.com, IN, A)
------------
Got answer:
    HEADER:
        opcode = QUERY, id = 33591, rcode = NXDOMAIN
        header flags: response, auth. answer, want recursion, recursion avail.
        questions = 1,  answers = 0,  authority records = 1,  additional = 0
    QUESTIONS:
        junk.example.com, type = A, class = IN
    AUTHORITY RECORDS:
    ->  example.com
        ttl = 21600 (6H)
        origin = dns1.icann.org
        mail addr = hostmaster.icann.org
        serial = 2002020400
        refresh = 7200 (2H)
        retry   = 3600 (1H)
        expire  = 1209600 (2W)
        minimum ttl = 21600 (6H)
------------
;; res_nmkquery(QUERY, junk.example.com.uit.co.uk., IN, A)
------------
Got answer:
    HEADER:
        opcode = QUERY, id = 33592, rcode = NXDOMAIN
        header flags: response, auth. answer, want recursion, recursion avail.
        questions = 1,  answers = 0,  authority records = 1,  additional = 0
    QUESTIONS:
        junk.example.com.uit.co.uk, type = A, class = IN
    AUTHORITY RECORDS:
    ->  uit.co.uk
        ttl = 86400 (1D)
        origin = res3lx.uit.co.uk
        mail addr = hostmaster.uit.co.uk
        serial = 167
        refresh = 10800 (3H)
        retry   = 3600 (1H)
        expire  = 604800 (1W)
        minimum ttl = 86400 (1D)
------------
*** res3lx.uit.co.uk can't find junk.example.com: Non-existent host/domain
```

find the **name** of the
DNS server we'er using

query for the name exactly
as we entered it

no A record found for
this name so answer = 0
and mode (response) =
NXDOMAIN

the first query failed,
so see if we can find
the name with our
domain name
appended to it

no A record found for
this name either

9.3   DNS problems and causes

This module concentrates on the types of DNS problems that can occur and how you can identify them.

1. DNS relies on all your underlying networking infrastructure. If your basic connectivity and routing don't work, neither will DNS. You can prove that 99% of your networking is OK by:

   a. **ping**ing any host on your LAN, by IP number

   b. **ping**ing any host on the Internet, by IP number

2. your client is wrongly configured:

   - see if the same problem occurs on another machine that is configured similarly (using the same DNS servers). If it doesn't, the problem lies somewhere on the first machine.

   - run **tcpdump** and watch the packets. If there are no DNS packets reaching the wire, your PC is almost certainly not using DNS at all. Check that you configured the resolver with at least one DNS server and that you didn't enter its address as a name instead of an IP number. See also the next module for other name resolution systems that may be interfering.

3. your client is configured to use a DNS server on your own directly connected LAN and that server is down. If the whole server machine is down **tcpdump** won't show any DNS packets unless the server has failed in the last few seconds. Instead you'll see ARP requests from the client to the server, and no ARP replies. If only the DNS server has died, **tcpdump** will show DNS queries sent to the server but no DNS replies, only ICMP error messages saying something like "ICMP udp port domain unreachable"

4. your ISP's servers are down (assuming that you are not running an internal DNS server of your own, but relying on your ISP's servers), or you're using your own DNS server that's not on the client's directly connected wire. **tcpdump** will show packets going out to the server but none coming back:

```
12:06:50.939044 192.0.2.38.1025 > 1.2.3.4.53:   6018+ A? www.ibm.com. (29)
12:07:00.939863 192.0.2.38.1025 > 1.2.3.4.53:   6018+ A? www.ibm.com. (29)
12:07:20.941742 192.0.2.38.1025 > 1.2.3.4.53:   6018+ A? www.ibm.com. (29)
```

Notice the pattern in the times of the packets. (If you configured more than one DNS server address in the resolver, you'll see several of these patterns intermingled. The precise pattern depends on your implementation, by the way.) The resolver sent queries at times 0 (not shown), 5, 10, and 20 seconds, unless it has received a reply. After sending the last query it waited a further 40 seconds; if no reply is received then it times out and gives an error to the application that asked for the resolution. Potential causes of this problem are:

- you entered the wrong IP address for the server in the resolver configuration (as we did in this example). Check the documentation from your ISP. (The problem *can't* be caused by entering the server address as a name instead of a number. If you did that, the DNS wouldn't even try to contact the server.)

- the server machine is dead. Try **ping**ing it

- you are not allowed to use this nameserver and it therefore refuses to reply
- the machine is alive but the DNS server software isn't running. You'd have to check this with your ISP. (However, most ISPs run several DNS servers. It's unlikely that all the machines are up and running but all the DNS software is down, unless you've got a really bad ISP. We've never had to report this sort of thing ourselves.)
- an easy way to check if the nameserver on is running is to

    `telnet` *hostaddr* `53`

    If you get a "Connected to *hostaddr*" message, the server is running. (We explain how this works in Chapter 10.)

5. the DNS server that contains the data for the site you requested is down or inaccessible. Your query will complete but will contain an error message like "nameserver not responding."

If you cannot resolve *any* names at all, the problem is probably at your ISP, assuming you're using their nameservers. If some names resolve but not others, the problem is probably with the DNS server for the machine (e.g. Web server) you're trying to contact; when this happens you normally just have to wait until it's fixed. (If you know the people there, it would be good citizenship to phone – e-mail won't reach them – to let them know.)

There are three simple tests to distinguish between problems (4) and (5) above:

a. use a different nameserver instead of your ISP's servers. Either change your resolver configuration, or much more simply, use the

    `nslookup` *hostaddr server_IP_number*
    `host` *hostaddr server_IP_number*

    versions of the commands (Module 7.5) to bypass the server you've configured. (You'll have to find the IP addresses of other nameservers before you can do this; also, some ISPs restrict who they allow to use their DNS servers.)

b. use a dial-up account to connect a stand-alone PC or laptop to the Internet, and see how name resolution behaves on that connection. To be most valuable, you should use a different ISP for dial-up to the one providing your main Internet connection, so that you're using different DNS servers and different paths through the Internet

c. we use this one when we're out on customer sites: if you have a secure way to connect back to your own site, logon to a Linux machine there and run the usual **host** or **nslookup** commands from there, so that you are using the DNS configuration and servers and network that are completely separate from the ones where the problem is suspected. (You might be able to do the same on a Windows system if you have the right software installed, e.g. Windows-2000 has a **telnet** server (Chapter 10) and there's one for Windows-NT 4.0 in the Resource Kit.)

6. whenever you get unusually long delays in an application, e.g. in **telnet** or **ping** or your e-mail client, it's often due to DNS problems. You can see that the system in the code displayed in point 4 above takes 75 seconds before the DNS reports a failure; your application will hang for all that time before it decides that something really is wrong and gives an error message.

In the next module we explain how other name resolution systems on your network can interfere with DNS resolution.

9.4   Interference from other name resolution systems

Both Windows and Linux can have other name resolution systems running instead of DNS or in conjunction with it. This can complicate your diagnosis, or at best be just confusing. For example, you're using **tcpdump** to look at DNS packets; you **ping alice** from your machine and Alice responds, but there are no DNS packets on the wire. This surprising effect is caused by your machine using a different resolution mechanism.

Below we outline the other name resolution systems specific to Microsoft Windows Networking and to Linux. However, the same type of consideration applies to any other name resolution you might be running, e.g. if you have Novell on your machine, it too may have its own name resolution system.

While these services may resolve names without using the DNS (causing you surprise) or resolve names to values different from those in the DNS, it's unlikely (but possible) they will actually prevent a name being resolved at all.

Windows-NT

NT can use some or all of the following (we'll cover these in detail in Chapter 19) as well as or instead of DNS:

- **hosts** file – a static list of hostnames and IP numbers used by TCP/IP programs, equivalent to the old Internet **HOSTS.TXT** file
- **Lmhosts** file – a static list of hostnames and IP numbers used by TCP/IP programs and MS Windows Networking programs. (The "LM" stands for "LAN Manager".)
- WINS ("Windows Internet Name Service"). To make life even more complicated, WINS can use the DNS to obtain some of its information
- NetBIOS name resolution using broadcasts on the local wire

If any of these are in operation, you'll have to be careful and very painstaking when sorting out a problem that you think is in the DNS. (We explain all these resolution systems in detail in Chapter 19.) However, you can quickly check that your name resolution is using DNS by running **tcpdump** and looking at the packets.

Although NetBIOS can be disabled, it's just about universal on Windows machines and Windows often uses it in preference to DNS, giving you the **ping** surprise above. Another side effect of all these systems is that it can slow things down a lot. What happens is that some of these systems are being used to attempt resolution before DNS. If they're not needed or not configured properly, Windows has to wait for them to time-out or fail to resolve a name before it uses DNS to resolve the query. Even though this may not impose a huge amount of network traffic it can be very noticeable to the user (especially if another name resolution system takes as long as DNS's 75 seconds that we mentioned in the previous module.)

Linux

Linux can use some or all of the following as well as or instead of DNS:

- the **/etc/hosts** file – a static list of hostnames and IP numbers used by TCP/IP programs
- NIS ("Network Information Service"): a system developed by Sun Microsystems for sharing a central database of usernames, passwords, hostnames, IP addresses, etc. across a network, usually a LAN
- NIS+: a more secure (and complex) version of NIS.

We don't cover these any further elsewhere because we've found they are not relevant to most sites (even some that run a lot of UNIX systems). We mention them here only because they can cause confusion if any of them are in operation on your system. If they are, you'll have to be careful when sorting out a problem that you think is in the DNS. Settings in a "name services switch" configuration file (see Appendix 6) determine which of these services to use, so it's worth checking that file on your system to find out what *might* be happening. As usual, you can easily make sure that your name resolution is using DNS by running **tcpdump** and looking at the packets.

`hosts` **file problems**

Both Windows and Linux can use the **hosts** file. (It's **/etc/hosts** on Linux, **C:\WINNT\system32\drivers\etc\HOSTS** on NT; in neither system does it have a filename extension such as **.txt**, even though it is a plain text file.) Having any values in the **hosts** file can mess you up:

- a copy of the file is stored on every machine. Keeping them in synch is a nightmare.
- systems usually try **hosts** before the DNS. If a name is found in **hosts** its value is used. If it's out of date, you end up horribly confused: the name resolves, but to the wrong value
- let's say Bob's **hosts** file contains a simple name and IP number for, for example, **alice** = 1.2.3. When a connection comes in to Bob from IP address 1.2.3.4, e.g. to use a resource on this machine, the relevant server application on Bob will often try to find out the name of the connecting machine for authorization (e.g. "only machines in domain **hr.example.com** are allowed to use the HR department's shared files"). The name resolution system on Bob will (usually, depending on the configuration) try the **hosts** file first. There it will see that 1.2.3.4 is called "**alice**." This doesn't end in **hr.example.com** so access will be denied.

In summary, don't use **hosts** *anywhere* unless you have to.

Summary

We have covered DNS problems only from a client perspective. We haven't covered problems with DNS servers, because we don't know what servers you're going to use, if any. However, the background we've given you will be of great benefit when you start using and configuring your own servers, and the symptoms of the problem as seen from the client will often give you a good pointer to what's going wrong on the server.

- the approach to take when troubleshooting DNS is first to identify the problem clearly, and then look for possible causes
- use **tcpdump** as soon as you suspect a problem. Look at the details of the queries your resolver is sending
- check the three fundamental networking parameters of your machine. Is it even successfully sending the queries to the DNS servers?
- check your machine's DNS configuration
- using **nslookup** or **host**, try the same resolution using a different nameserver
- use the debug options in **nslookup** or **host**
- is it really the DNS that's trying to resolve the name, or is another resolution system, and/or the **hosts** file, interfering? Again, **tcpdump** will let you see exactly what traffic your machine is sending.

What's next?

That completes the DNS. We have all the basic networking infrastructure we need:

- we can communicate between two or more machines on a single wire, which lets us build small LANs
- we can use routers to interconnect separate networks and so build inter-networks of any size (including the Internet)
- we can refer to machines by name, not just by IP number, which is easier for human users (and also makes application's configuration files much clearer).

This is the end of Part 1 of the book, which in many ways is the hardest because there is so much low-level detail. In Part 2 we deal with applications – what the user really wants – where we work at a higher and less detailed level.

Notes and further reading

On some very old versions of some operating systems, hostnames used for the "r-commands" (**rsh**, **rcp**, etc.; see Notes, Chapter 10) must be in **hosts** to be authorized, even if they can be resolved successfully using the DNS. However, that's now historical usage – you don't need it with NT or Linux.

In Module 9.1 we said there's a bug relating to authoritative answers. What can happen is that client Alice queries a nameserver, Dave say, for a name. Dave gets an authoritative answer, and returns it to Alice. Dave also keeps the answer in his cache. If Alice or any other client sends a query for the same name to Dave, Dave returns the cached answer, but incorrectly marks the answer as "authoritative," which it isn't – because it has been in the cache for some time, and the answer for the name may have changed on the name's authoritative servers in the meantime. In the context of Module 9.1, this means that if you get an authoritative answer saying some domain name is non-existent, it's probably true but you can't be 100% sure.

A problem on UNIX and Linux systems is that it's so easy to replace a "standard" piece of functionality with your own. Some applications (especially e-mail servers) implement their own resolver. This has two inter-related consequences:

1. **nslookup** and **hosts** may not give the same results as the application's resolver because they use their own resolver code too

2. the application's (non-standard) resolver may have bugs. For example, we once saw an e-mail server that for each message sent generated about 100 DNS queries, many of which were to the sub-net broadcast address. The application's resolver had a bug: if a "nameserver" record in **/etc/resolv.conf** was commented out, the resolver failed to find *any* of the real nameservers. It therefore broadcast its queries, hoping some nameserver would hear. The query was heard and processed by the real nameserver on the LAN, but also by several dormant test nameservers (which normally did nothing because nobody sent them any queries), which went through full resolution with queries to root servers, etc.

Part 2

End-user and system applications

Introduction

In Part 1 we discussed communications from the perspective of individual packets moving from source to destination, but we didn't use the packets to do anything useful for the user – we didn't discuss any end-user applications. In Part 2 we move "up the stack" and introduce applications including e-mail, the Web, FTP, DHCP, and many others. We cover the network protocols these programs require, and explain how to troubleshoot problems with these applications.

10

The TCP protocol; the application layer and the telnet **application**

Introduction

In coming chapters we cover applications such as e-mail (SMTP, POP) and the Web (HTTP). These maintain an ongoing session or connection between client and server, in contrast to the "send a packet when I want to" method that we saw with DNS. To explain how those connection-oriented protocols work, we first must explain TCP ("Transmission Control Protocol"). In what we covered in Part 1 – how the packets move between machines on the same wire, and how they are routed from network to network across an inter-network – we were in fact dealing only with the IP protocol. TCP on the other hand isn't concerned with the intermediate hops – it is concerned only with the two hosts at either end, and providing a reliable data channel to individual applications. TCP leaves all routing, etc. to be handled by the lower IP layer.

We explain what a TCP "connection" really is, and use the **telnet** application both as an example of a TCP application and as a general diagnostic tool for other TCP applications, in preparation for the later chapters.

10.1 Why we need TCP and transport protocols

Up to now we have dealt only with the "IP" part of "TCP/IP." As we saw throughout Part 1, IP is the protocol that moves the packets from the source machine to the destination machine, over the intervening networks via routers. That's why the IP layer of the stack is also called the internet or network layer (Figure 10.1). From here on we deal with the upper layers in the TCP/IP stack – the *transport* (or *host-to-host*) *layer* and the *application layer*, both of which perform functions that applications need but that are not provided by the raw IP (network) or link layers. In this chapter we concentrate on TCP, the Transmission Control Protocol. This is the transport layer protocol used by the World Wide Web, e-mail, FTP, and other applications that account for most of the traffic on the Internet. The other widely used transport is UDP, which we cover in Chapter 15.

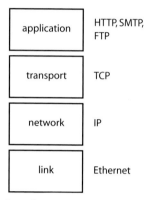

Figure 10.1 The TCP/IP protocol stack

Why do we need these higher-level transport protocols at all and not just use raw IP packets for everything? TCP gives us three major benefits over IP:

1. IP is an *unreliable* (or *best-effort*) protocol. It does its best to deliver the data but packets can get lost, e.g. if a router fails or a connection breaks, or if the underlying Ethernet network, which is also only best-effort, fails to deliver a packet. When IP drops a packet like this, the packet is lost, silently – no error message is generated anywhere. For many applications this isn't acceptable, and that's where TCP comes in. TCP is a *reliable* network protocol: it goes to great lengths to guarantee to deliver all your data, and in the order you sent it, so I know that you receive exactly what I sent. For this reason applications that need to exchange large volumes of data usually use TCP.

   We explain how TCP provides a reliable connection over unreliable IP in the next module. (By contrast, UDP is not reliable – it's only best-effort, as we'll see in Chapter 15.)

2. the IP layer routes packets only to the level of a machine. Once the packets arrive at this machine, IP doesn't have a mechanism for distinguishing packets for different applications on this machine, or for discriminating between multiple connections

within a single application. Instead, these functions are provided by the transport layer protocols, both TCP and UDP. The IP layer routes to a machine whereas the transport layer delivers to individual "connections" within an application, which TCP identifies by assigning a unique "port number" to each, as we explain in Module 10.3.

3. IP is *connectionless* – packets are transmitted individually, completely independently of one another. For many applications this isn't suitable. They view the data communication as a whole session; individual exchanges are part of an overall transaction so the application must preserve information about the ongoing state of the conversation. For example, when using a POP mail server, a "retrieve messages" command is allowed only if the user has already entered a valid username and password. Or in **ftp**, when you request a file, e.g. "**get readme.txt**," the precise file to send obviously depends on which directory you were in when you issued the command. TCP answers these needs: it is a *connection-oriented* protocol, which allows you to have a persistent session. Before communicating using TCP, the applications at either end *establish* (open) *a connection* between them. Then they exchange data over this connection, and when they finish, they *terminate* the connection. We explain connection in more detail in Module 10.3.

TCP still uses packets, of course, because it is layered on top of IP and ARP and ICMP and all the routing mechanisms we covered in Part 1. But while it uses those, they are separate layers and TCP doesn't duplicate their functionality. TCP doesn't get involved in, or know anything about, the routing: that's handled exclusively by the IP layer lower down. As shown in Figure 10.2, to the TCP layer on the source machine it appears that it's talking directly to the TCP layer on the destination. That's why the transport layer is also called the host-to-host layer and TCP and UDP are called *end-to-end* protocols. (Looking at it another way, the intermediate routers only look at the IP source and destination addresses; they don't know or care whether the information in the packets is TCP, UDP, or other traffic.)

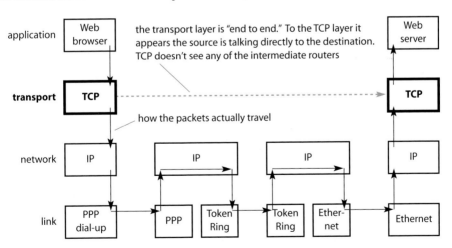

Figure 10.2 Communication between TCP layers is "end-to-end"

In the next module we see how TCP provides reliable transport over unreliable underlying layers.

10.2 How TCP provides a reliable connection over unreliable IP

In networking, a reliable connection is one that guarantees that all the data are delivered to the destination and none are lost, in the correct order, without any duplication. I receive exactly what you send me, and both of us know it.

TCP provides reliable connections, on top of the "unreliable" IP protocol. IP does its best to deliver the data, but packets can get lost, and IP does not retransmit lost packets. In fact, IP often has no way of even knowing a packet is lost. Once IP sends a packet, it's gone and IP doesn't keep track of it. IP itself does not expect, and therefore doesn't send, acknowledgments that packets have arrived.

Although "unreliable" in the formal sense, IP is pretty good. The routing protocols work well. They overcome router breakdowns, broken communications links, and lots of other glitches. But packets can get lost, e.g. if a router breaks down after it has received the packet from the previous-hop router but before it sends it on to the next. Packets can get out of order because they can take different paths through the network: a packet sent later could arrive before an earlier one if it is routed across a shorter path (Figure 10.3). And packets can be duplicated, because of hardware errors in routers or comms equipment, or because packets were re-sent because the sender thinks the original packets got lost.

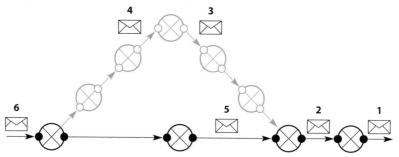

Figure 10.3 Successive packets can take different paths through the network

We'll use our postal service analogy again to explain how TCP copes with these potential problems. Let's say I want to send you the contents of a book as a series of postcards. Because postcards (packets) can arrive out of order:

- you need some way of knowing what order I sent them in
- ... and you have to be able to tell me:
  - when you have received the postcards (packets)
  - just as importantly, when you are missing some, so I can re-send them
- you must be able to detect duplicate postcards (packets).

The following shows how we can handle these and related issues:

- before I start sending, I have to tell you that I'm going to send a book, otherwise you won't know what to do with a card (packet) when it arrives – that it is part of a book. Also I might be sending you several different books or magazine articles in several different streams, or you might already be sending another book to me. We avoid mixing up the different streams of cards (TCP connections) by marking each card with a unique reference for this stream. (With TCP, the combination (N_1, P_1, N_2, P_2) of source and destination IP and port numbers is the unique reference – see Module 10.4.)

- I put sequence numbers on the cards (packets). If they arrive out of order you rearrange them into the correct order

- as you receive packets you occasionally send me an acknowledgment card (packet) telling me the last one in sequence that you received. I can see if some have got lost, and can re-send those after the last one I know you received. (You could send an acknowledgment card for every card I sent you, but that would slow things down a lot. When we set up the connection in the first place, you tell me how many cards I can send you before I should expect an acknowledgment

- your acknowledgment cards (packets) can get lost too, so if I have sent a lot of cards (packets) and haven't had any acknowledgment for a long time, I re-send the cards (packets) after the last sequence number that you did acknowledge

- neither of us has to understand the content of what I'm sending, only the system of sequence numbers and acknowledgments. Even if the information we're sending is in ancient Greek, the system works and we can both be sure that you got everything I sent, and in the correct order. (TCP just delivers "data" to the application without attaching any particular meaning to it. It's the application in the layer above that interprets the data – it adds the semantics. For example, the **telnet** application (Module 10.6) treats the data as characters to be printed on screen or to be sent to the shell, etc. whereas an FTP server application which receives "GET cat.gif" realizes this is a request to download that file to the client

- only you and I pay any attention to the sequence numbers and acknowledgment cards (packets). To everyone in the middle – messenger boy, mail clerk, etc. (routers on the Internet) – a card (packet) is just something to be forwarded to its destination. (TCP is used only on the source and destination machines. The IP layer alone is used on the intermediate routers.)

- at the end, I tell you when I've finished sending so you know that you've received everything and that there's no more to come.

The end result is that TCP is reliable, in the strict networking sense: you receive exactly what I send, and in the correct order, without duplicates.

This analogy isn't rigorous – it's only to give you a gut feel for how TCP works. TCP has lots of subtleties that we haven't included. In particular TCP supports two-way traffic over a single connection, and the acknowledgment packets can also contain data, to make the whole process as efficient as possible. (See the Notes for further information.)

In the next module we look in more detail at what a TCP connection is, and how it ties in with TCP "ports."

10.3 TCP connections and ports

A client application uses port numbers to tell the destination machine which of the many different TCP services it wants. The server for a particular application listens on a well-known port for connections from clients requesting its services. Let's go through that now in more detail.

TCP is used for application-to-application communication of data (with the IP layer below handling the donkey-work of getting the packets from one machine to the other across the network). Lots of different applications – the Web, e-mail, FTP, database systems, window systems, etc. – use TCP.

For one of Bob's applications to talk to an application on Alice, the two applications have to set up a TCP *connection* – a dedicated TCP data channel – between them. TCP connections are normally set up by using a client/server model. The server for a particular application runs all the time, waiting and *listening* for incoming connection requests from *clients*. When it detects an incoming connection for it, the server establishes a TCP connection with the requesting client. They can now use this connection to exchange data until one or both of them terminates the connection. The server receives requests over this connection, services them, and sends back responses to the client over the same connection. Because the server must always be running, listening for connections, it's usually started at system boot time.

The above explanation prompts several questions about how connections work:

1. let's say Bob wants to browse some Web pages on Alice. How does TCP in Bob's Web browser tell Alice that he wants to use her Web server, which is just one of many services Alice offers (Figure 10.4)?

2. when a TCP connection request comes in from Bob, how does Alice know which application (i.e. which server) should service it?

3. if Bob has several TCP connections to Alice, all the packets travel over the same wire and up through the same TCP/IP stack. How does Alice know which packet goes where (Figure10.5)? And why don't packets from Carol and Dave get mixed up with Bob's?

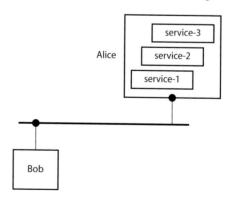

Figure 10.4 How does Bob specify which service on Alice he wants to use?

This is where TCP ports come in:

- a *port* is an address to distinguish between different TCP connections on the same machine. Whereas the IP address is a number that identifies which of many machines a packet is destined for, the TCP port is a number that identifies which connection within a specific machine the packet relates to.

- particular *port numbers* are allocated by convention to particular services:

Service	Port
telnet	23
e-mail (SMTP)	25
HTTP	80
e-mail (POP-3)	110

These are called *well-known ports*. The server for a particular service listens on the appropriate well-known port. For example, the Web server listens on port 80, and treats any incoming requests on that port as HTTP requests and processes them accordingly. (See inside front cover for a fuller list of port numbers.)

- the client specifies which *destination port* it wants to connect to when it issues a connection request to the server. By specifying a specific port number the client is saying what service is required. For example, Bob uses Alice's Web server by connecting to her TCP port 80

- the client also specifies a *source port* number in the connection request. The server will send its replies to this port on the source machine, and the client reads the replies from it.

That answers questions 1 and 2 above. You might think it answers question 3 too, and that Alice could assume that all data coming on a specific port belong to one connection. However, that's not true, for two reasons, both illustrated in Figure 10.5.

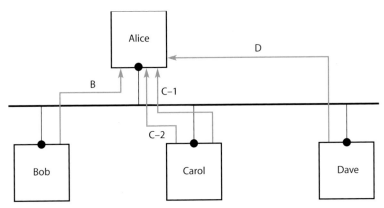

Figure 10.5 Connecting to the same port

a. many different remote machines can have connections to the same port, e.g. Web browsers on Carol and Dave are using Alice's Web server in addition to Bob

b. you could even have several connections to the same port from the same machine, or even the same application. (E.g. Carol has two Web browsers connected to Alice's Web server.) This is more common than you might think: Web browsers often use multiple connections to download multiple images from the same server simultaneously, for speed (Module 4.9) and FTP applications (Module 14.9) use two separate connections, one for data, the other for commands.

In the next module we show how TCP solves this problem.

10.4 TCP connections are identified by ports

The destination port on its own isn't enough to enable TCP to deliver packets to the correct connection on this machine and to prevent packets for different connections from getting mixed up. TCP solves this problem by identifying a connection using the source port and source IP address as well as the destination, i.e. the combination of

1. the source IP number (N_1)
2. the source port number (P_1)
3. the destination IP number (N_2)
4. the destination IP number (P_2)

specifies a connection uniquely, so all packets for this connection can be delivered to it without getting mixed up with any others.

We've just explained that items 1, 3, and 4 can be the same for several connections; so for this scheme to work, item 2, the source port number, must never be the same. TCP ensures this in a very simple way: by never allowing a *client* application to use the same port number that another application on the same machine is using. In effect, TCP on a machine has a pool of currently unused ports, and these are allocated on request to clients that are about to establish connections with remote servers. When a connection is terminated, the port number is put back in the pool again for re-use (after a certain amount of time to make sure it really, *really* is finished with.) TCP gives these pooled ports a fancy name: they are called *ephemeral* ports, because they come and go like the flowers of spring.

Figure 10.6 shows connections from Bob, Carol, and Dave to Alice's Web server. All the destination ports and IP numbers are the same, port 80 on Alice. But note that on Carol the two source ports (the P_1s) are different as they must be, because all the other parameters, N_1, N_2, and P_2, are the same. (As it happens the port numbers on Bob and Dave are different too, but either of their source port numbers could be the same as one of Carol's without causing any problems because they don't have the same source IP address as Carol.)

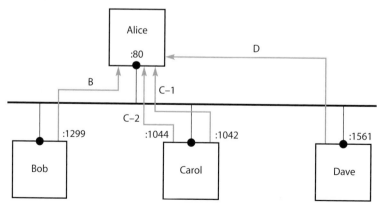

Figure 10.6 Connections to Alice's Web server

A connection is an individual, separate TCP data channel between two applications. As we said, two applications can have more than one connection between them, and we gave the example of a Web browser with multiple connections to a server. Even though the connections are from the same client, they must be kept completely separate. For example, if one is downloading an image file **a.gif** and the other is downloading a Web page **index.htm**, if the connections aren't kept separate, you'd get a jumble of data on each connection, which would be useless. Figure 10.7 illustrates schematically how the separate connections in Figure 10.6 are handled.

You can think of connections like phone conversations between two offices. You can have lots of different phone conversations between the same two offices, but if you have crossed wires and the conversations get mixed up, the system doesn't work – you can't communicate properly.

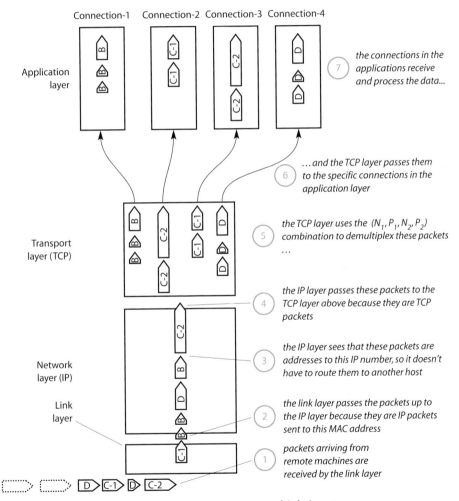

Figure 10.7 How port numbers let TCP separate out multiple inputs

In the next module we show how the **netstat** program lists the connections that are in use and how you can see which ports are used.

10.5 **Viewing connections with the** netstat **command**

We'll look at two examples of connections on a real network, using the **netstat** command. We have used **netstat** already to look at routing information, using the "**-r**" option. When run as plain "**netstat**", without "**-r**", **netstat** shows details of TCP and UDP connections on this machine. (As usual, "**-n**" displays details as numbers rather than names, but we can omit "**-n**" now when we want to, because we have a running DNS system.)

First, we'll look at a simple example of an e-mail client on Alice connecting to an SMTP mail server on Bob. Before the client starts, run **netstat** on Bob, with option "**-l**" to show "listeners", i.e. servers listening for incoming connections. (By default, without "**-l**", **netstat** doesn't show listeners, only established connections.) Below are two **netstat** listings, one without "**-n**" and one with, to display port details in both numeric and symbolic forms. The output shows that there is a listener on TCP port 25, which is for **smtp** e-mail. Ports are often shown prefixed with a colon ("**:**") to distinguish them from the numbers in the IP address. Notice that there is no foreign address for this connection, indicated as address 0.0.0.0. This is what we'd expect, because no client has connected yet; only the listening server is using this connection so far. In a sense it's only half a connection in this state. (All listings are edited to show just the parts we're interested in.)

```
bob# netstat -l
Proto Recv-Q Send-Q Local Address      Foreign Address      State
...
tcp        0      0 *:smtp             *:*                  LISTEN
bob# netstat -l -n
...
tcp        0      0 0.0.0.0:25         0.0.0.0:*            LISTEN
```

Now the e-mail client connects to the server. When the listener (Bob's mail server) detects an incoming connection for it, in this case from Alice's e-mail client program, the listener responds and the two programs establish a TCP connection that they will use for the rest of this e-mail session. Run **netstat** on Bob again (below), this time without "**-l**" because we want to see only established connections, not ones listening, waiting before a connection is established. The connection is now shown as "established" (i.e. it's up and running) and we can see the source and destination IP and port numbers.

```
bob# netstat
tcp        0      0 bob.uit.co.uk:smtp   alice.uit.co.uk:1428   ESTABLISHED
bob# netstat -n
tcp        0      0 192.0.2.19:25        192.0.2.17:1428        ESTABLISHED
```

Running **netstat** on Alice (below) gives the same information as on Bob, but with the local and foreign addresses reversed, which is correct when you think about it, because we're looking at the same connection but from the other end.

The connection is now established, so the client on Alice should be talking to a server on Bob and indeed we can see the server running on Bob by listing the processes on Bob. If there are lots of servers already running, it's hard to identify the right one, but **netstat** makes it easy.

```
alice# netstat
Proto Recv-Q Send-Q Local Address          Foreign Address       State
tcp         0      0 alice.uit.co.uk:1428  bob.uit.co.uk:smtp    ESTABLISHED

alice# netstat -n
tcp         0      0 192.0.2.17:1428       192.0.2.19:25         ESTABLISHED
```

On Bob run "**netstat -p**" – the "**-p**" means "show program information", which displays the name and process ID of the program that "owns" this connection; Alice's e-mail client is connected to process number 24266 on Bob, which is called **exim**. That looks reasonable, because **exim** is the mail server that we use on Bob:

```
tcp    0    0   192.0.2.19:25    192.0.2.17:1428   ESTABLISHED    24266/exim
```

Now we'll look at the second example – the connections from Web clients on Bob, Carol (twice), and Dave to Alice's Web server that we showed in Figure 10.6. We run **netstat** on each machine:

```
alice# netstat
Proto Recv-Q Send-Q Local Address          Foreign Address        State
tcp         0      0 alice.uit.co.uk:www   bob.uit.co.uk:1299     ESTABLISHED
tcp         0      0 alice.uit.co.uk:www   dave.uit.co.uk:1561    ESTABLISHED
tcp         0      0 alice.uit.co.uk:www   carol.uit.co.uk:1044   ESTABLISHED
tcp         0      0 alice.uit.co.uk:www   carol.uit.co.uk:1042   ESTABLISHED

bob# netstat
tcp         0      0 bob.uit.co.uk:1299    alice.uit.co.uk:www    ESTABLISHED

Carol:\>netstat
  Proto  Local Address    Foreign Address        State
  TCP    carol:1042       alice.uit.co.uk:www    ESTABLISHED
  TCP    carol:1044       alice.uit.co.uk:www    ESTABLISHED

dave# netstat
tcp         0      0 dave.1561             alice.80               ESTABLISHED
```

- on Alice, all the connections have identical local addresses (N_1) and local ports (P_1), as expected
- for each of the four connections, the combination (N_1, P_1, N_2, P_2) is unique, as required, because either the source port or source IP number differs
- **netstat** shows the ephemeral ports (which are on the machines that initiated the connections) numerically because they are not specially allocated to any one protocol – they are used as required for a initiating TCP connections to TCP servers
- Carol is a Windows machine so the **netstat** output format is different. It takes the "**-n**" option to print addresses numerically should you want that
- Dave is an ancient SunOS UNIX box whose **netstat** behaves slightly differently to Linux: it doesn't print ports as names even without "**-n**". This type of variation in command behavior is common across different UNIXes.

In the next module we introduce the **telnet** command, which we'll use in this chapter as an example of a TCP application, but which is also very handy as a diagnostic tool for troubleshooting other TCP applications, as we'll see later.

10.6 The telnet application

"Telnet" stands for "telecommunications network protocol." **telnet** is one of the oldest Internet applications. It lets you connect your "terminal" to a remote host over the network. In the old ARPANET days before graphical workstations or personal computers were invented, everyone used a terminal connected to a mainframe or minicomputer via a serial connection (Figure 10.8). A terminal has a keyboard for input, and for output a screen or a printer that can print characters only (no graphics). Before screens became common, most people used Teletypes or teleprinters or similar hardcopy terminals – like electric typewriters used for input and output to a computer. The key features of terminals are:

- they are text devices only – no graphics or mouse
- every character sent to the output part of the device is printed as a character
- they have no CPU, so they can't run programs, but they handle input and output to a program running on the minicomputer or mainframe.

For obvious reasons they were often called "dumb terminals." Usually many terminals (tens or hundreds) were connected to the minicomputer and it was called a "timesharing system" as it shared CPU time amongst all the terminal users.

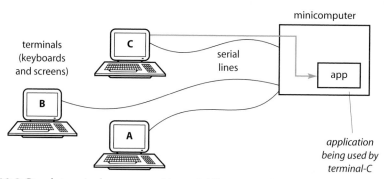

Figure 10.8 Dumb terminals connected by serial lines to a minicomputer

Before the Web became popular, **telnet** was used widely to access bulletin boards for discussion groups, and public information services – especially library and catalog systems – were available over **telnet** too. Few, if any, of these are available now.

Real terminals are very rare nowadays. They live on mainly as "terminal emulators" (like Hyperterm on Windows) – software packages that provide terminal functionality for PCs or workstations, in order to access character-only systems or applications. These are still necessary occasionally to log on to historical bulletin board systems, or to configure devices like routers and firewall boxes (Figure 10.9), although newer systems usually provide a Web interface instead, or as well.

telnet is typically used to "remote login" from your own PC to another elsewhere on the network. Remote login like this lets you use applications on the remote system (Figure 10.10). It provides a text-only connection, usually to a "command-line prompt" like a UNIX shell, or

Windows Command/DOS prompt, as though you were sitting at a terminal wired directly to a serial port on the remote machine. This was how networked computing was performed for years.

```
alice% telnet 192.0.2.41
Trying 192.0.2.41...
Connected to fwl-test.uit.co.uk.        "ns10->" is the
Escape character is '^]'.               prompt from the
NetScreen Remote Management Console     remote system

login: netscreen
password:
ns10-> set console timeout 5
ns10-> set syslog traffic
ns10-> set interface trust ip 192.0.2.41 255.255.255.128
ns10-> exit
Connection closed by foreign host.
alice%
```

Figure 10.9 Using **telnet** to configure a firewall

telnet is a client/server application. The client takes the characters you input at the keyboard, sends them to the server, and prints whatever output the server sends back. The server does more work: it passes the input characters from the client to a shell process, which interprets them as commands; then it reads the command output and sends it back to the client, to be printed on your terminal's output device. The client is conceptually very simple, although on Windows and other graphical systems, the code to print characters in a window, to manage the window's scrolling, fonts, etc. adds to the complexity of the program. However, that's not relevant to our discussion of TCP/IP; as far as networking goes, the client *is* simple.

The **telnet** server isn't a huge application like an SQL or a Web server. In fact, most UNIX boxes – even small workstations – have a **telnet** server (reflecting that much of the Internet development was done on UNIX). Windows-2000 has a **telnet** server as standard; Windows-NT does not, although there is one in the NT 4.0 Resource Kit.

We've gone into some detail on what **telnet** is and how it works, because almost everyone thinks of a PC as the standard computing device nowadays, and many people have never seen dumb terminals or know what they are.

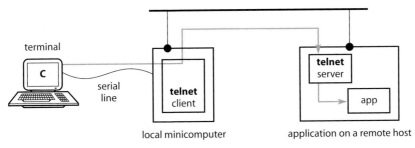

Figure 10.10 Using **telnet** to log on to a remote host

In the next module we show you how to use **telnet** and we'll use it to run a small TCP session for test purposes.

10.7 Lab – using telnet as the universal TCP client

telnet isn't used as much now as it used be – the Web has supplanted it for retrieving information and as a graphical interface for configuring applications and devices. If you have an all-Windows network, you may never have used **telnet**. However, it is very useful as a general-purpose TCP client for testing and diagnostic purposes, on Windows and Linux.

When you run the command normally:

```
telnet alice
telnet 192.0.2.5
```
specify remote host by name
specify remote host by IP number

the client defaults to using the well-known port for **telnet**, which is 23. However, you can explicitly specify a destination port number by entering it as a separate argument on the command line (separate from the destination host address and without a colon in front), so the above command is equivalent to:

```
telnet alice 23
```

We're going to connect to a Web server and see what happens:

```
telnet www.w3c.org 80
```

On Linux **telnet** prints the IP number it's about to connect to, and then says it has connected – to the Web server:

```
alice# telnet www.w3c.org 80
Trying 18.29.1.34...
Connected to www.w3.org.
Escape character is '^]'.
```

(Forget about the "escape character" stuff for now.) If you're running **telnet** from a Windows system, you'll know you're connected when the mouse pointer changes from the hour glass and the title-bar of the **telnet** window changes to show the address of the remote site instead of "(None)":

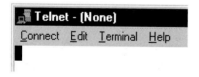   

Even though the server hasn't given you a prompt, it is waiting for input from you. (Before you go on, if you are running **telnet** from Windows, enable local echo using the menu **Terminal > Preferences > Local Echo** = yes.) Now enter the line "**GET /**" which must be in uppercase. The server responds with the home page for the site, and the connection terminates (see below).

You have just acted as a manual Web browser and retrieved a Web page! (When you connect to some other sites you may get HTML code saying something like "No Web site is configured at this address"; we'll cover that in Chapter 13.)

```
GET /
<!DOCTYPE html PUBLIC "-//W3C//DTD XHTML 1.0 Transitional//EN"
    "http://www.w3.org/TR/xhtml1/DTD/xhtml1-transitional.dtd">
<html xmlns="http://www.w3.org/1999/xhtml" xml:lang="en-US"
lang="en-US">
<head profile="http://www.w3.org/2000/08/w3c-synd/#">
<meta name="generator"
content="HTML Tidy for Mac OS, see www.w3.org" />
. . .
href="Consortium/Legal/privacy-statement#Members">Member</a> privacy
statements.</p>
</body>
</html>

Connection closed by foreign host.
alice#
```

How come we can we use **telnet** as a client like this?

- many Internet protocols work by sending text "commands" to the server, which responds with text replies. E-mail (POP and SMTP) and HTTP and several others do this. There is no fancy "encoding" of the commands sent and received: they are sent in plain ASCII, as we'll see in the next module when we use "**tcpdump -X**"

- the **telnet** client just reads the characters you enter at the keyboard, sends them to the server at the far end, printing any responses that it receives. The client does almost nothing to the transmitted data.

The protocols work this way for historical reasons amongst others. In the early Internet days different computers used different byte sizes (6, 8, or 9 bits per byte, which is why RFCs use the more specific term *octet* to mean a "byte" with 8 bits) and different word sizes (2, 4, or more bytes per word), so exchanging data in binary format was difficult. The one thing that had a fairly standard representation was text, so exchanging data in text format was often the easiest way to do things.

Using **telnet** for testing has many advantages:

- it's very quick to start up – much quicker than a bloated mega-browser or e-mail client

- if you have a problem when using a mail, Web, or other client, the problem may be caused by a bug in the client configuration problem in the client itself. By using **telnet** you bypass all that extra baggage and can see if the network connection and basic server operation are OK.

- the machine you're working on may not have a Web or mail client anyway, e.g. if you've just installed a new server machine and want to check out its networking before loading any server applications

So we'll use **telnet** a lot for testing TCP applications, rather like we used **ping** as an easy way to generate packets destined for a remote machine.

10.8 The life-cycle of a TCP connection (1)

In this module and the next we're going to look at a TCP connection from establishment to termination, using **tcpdump**. This will explain how **tcpdump** shows TCP sessions and also illustrate some of the features of how TCP works, in particular:

- how a connection is established
- how to see how many data are transferred in each packet, and how this ties in with the TCP sequence numbers
- TCP acknowledgments
- how a connection is terminated.

These modules contain a lot of detail. You'll be glad to know that apart from recognizing the establishment and termination of a connection, we've almost never had to look at packets at this level. We're including the information here just in case, and Web Appendix 13 contains some related exercises.

Below is our brief **telnet** session (edited for space): login from Alice to Bob, print the date, and exit.

```
alice% telnet bob
Trying 192.0.2.22...
Connected to bob.uit.co.uk
Escape character is '^]'.
Debian GNU/Linux 2.1 bob
bob login: rmm
Password: xxxxxx
Linux bob 2.2.12 #2 Thu Aug 26 11:46:26 PDT 1999 i586 unknown
$ date
Fri Dec  7 06:42:09 GMT 2001
$ exit
logout
Connection closed by foreign host.
alice%
```

1. Establishing the connection

Before Alice can communicate with Bob over TCP, they must establish a connection. Alice initiates this by connecting to the **telnet** well-known port on Bob. However, the packets Alice and Bob exchange to establish the connection could (as always) get lost, so TCP uses a *three-way handshake* to ensure the integrity of the connection establishment:

1. the client sends a packet to the server, with a special "flag" set – the *SYN* (*synchronize*) flag
2. the server replies to the client, sending a packet with both the SYN flag and another flag, *ACK* (*acknowledge*), set
3. the client replies with a packet with the ACK flag set.

The relevant lines from the **tcpdump** trace are shown below. This SYN, SYN/ACK, ACK sequence marks the opening of *every* TCP connection, and recognizing it will become second nature to you.

```
alice.1067 > bob.telnet: S 1259089756:1259089756(0) win 16060 <mss 1460,
bob.telnet > alice.1067: S 1429101337:1429101337(0) ack 1259089757 win 1
alice.1067 > bob.telnet: . ack 1 win 16060 <nop,nop,timestamp 60119012 (
```
    1. SYN   *2. SYN/ACK*   *3. ACK*

2a. Exchanging data

The connection is now established and data are exchanged. During this session we ran a second instance of **tcpdump**, with the option "**-X**" – uppercase 'x' – to dump packet contents as ASCII. (If your version of **tcpdump** doesn't have the -X option, see the Notes at the end of the chapter for an alternative.) Below is an extract from the trace. You can see the date string transmitted as plain text:

```
bob.telnet > alice.1067: P 635:669(34) ack 130 win 16060 <nop,nop,timestamp 601<
0x0000     4500 0056 b04f 4000 4006 0610 c000 0216     E..V.0@.@.......
0x0010     c000 022c 0017 042b 552e 5d94 4b0c 2fde     ...,...+U.].K./.
0x0020     8018 3ebc ab5e 0000 0101 080a 0395 c2b3     ..>..^..........
0x0030     0395 5b29 0d0a 4672 6920 4465 6320 2037     ..[)..Fri.Dec..7
0x0040     2030 363a 3432 3a30 3920 474d 5420 3230     .06:42:09.GMT.20
0x0050     3031 0d0a 2420                               01..$.
```

This emphasizes that **telnet** is sending the characters over the network just as they were typed. TCP doesn't transform them or perform any magic on them: it just transports them to the destination application. (This example also illustrates that **tcpdump** is a security hole – you can steal people's passwords with it.)

2b. Sequence numbers and how many data are in the packet

- we didn't tell the whole truth in Module 10.2. In fact TCP works in terms of bytes, not packets, and sequence numbers are for bytes, not packets

- the sequence numbers are very large, because large numbers of bytes can be exchanged, and because the sequence numbers don't start at zero. (The initial one from Alice is 1259089756, and from Bob 1429101337 as you can see above) To make the trace easier to read, after the first two lines of the connection establishment, **tcpdump** prints sequence numbers as "relative" rather than absolute – showing each as (*absolute number – initial number*). As well as being more compact, this makes it easier to see how many bytes are in each packet

- the **tcpdump** line for a packet shows the sequence number of the start and end data bytes contained in the packet, separated by a colon, and followed by the number of data bytes. For example, the packet below contains 66 bytes of data, whose sequence numbers run from 120 to 185 (not 186 – that will be the next byte sent).

```
bob.telnet > alice.1067: P 120:186(66) ack 125 win 16060 <no
```

The "P" shown above means "push" the data up to the application as soon as possible. This flag is set on almost every data packet; ignore it

- if the packet contains no data, but only an acknowledgment or other control information, the sequence numbers are omitted:

```
alice.1067 > bob.telnet: . ack 669 win 16060 <nop,nop,ti
```

10.9 The life-cycle of a TCP connection (2)

2c. TCP acknowledgments

- each packet containing an ACK flag also contains the sequence number of the data that it is acknowledging. This is how the two ends know which data the other has received, as described in Module 10.2

- the ACK gives the sequence number of the last byte successfully received in sequence, plus one (i.e. if packets 1, 2, 3, and 6 are received, TCP only ACKs packet 3, so that the other side knows it has to re-transmit 4 and 5) In other words, the ACK gives the sequence number of the next byte expected

- e.g. Alice sends Bob 79 bytes (sequence numbers 28–106) so Bob ACKs 107:

```
alice.1067 > bob.telnet: P 28:107(79) ack 52 win 16060 <nop
bob.telnet > alice.1067: . ack 107 win 16060 <nop,nop,times
```

- for efficiency, not every packet is ACKed, but when an ACK is sent it is cumulative – it says what was the most recent byte received in the correct order. Here Bob sends two successive packets, and Alice only ACKs the second:

```
bob.telnet > alice.1067: P 103:106(3) ack 116 win 16060 <nop
bob.telnet > alice.1067: P 106:108(2) ack 116 win 16060 <nop
alice.1067 > bob.telnet: . ack 108 win 16060 <nop,nop,timest
```

- ACKs are needed in case packets get lost or out of order. Most of the time packets arrive as they are sent, so the ACKs are overhead, which can be minimized by ACKing only every so often. Fig 10.11(a) shows how ACKing every packet in a one-sided conversation slows down the transfer, compared with the Fig 10.11(b), which shows how TCP actually does things – sending ACKs occasionally, giving much higher throughput

- again for efficiency, ACKs "piggy-back" on normal packets containing real data and don't need a packet all of their own: if data are being sent, the ACK hitches a ride on the data packet. Three packets are shown below, containing 32, 3, and 16 data bytes respectively, all of which contain ACKs too:

```
bob.telnet > alice.1067: P 55:87(32) ack 110 win 16060 <n
alice.1067 > bob.telnet: P 110:113(3) ack 87 win 16060 <n
bob.telnet > alice.1067: P 87:103(16) ack 113 win 16060 <
```

- packets containing only an ACK and no data are sent as required, as we saw at the end of the previous module. This type of packet is very common in Web transactions, which are very one-sided: the client sends requests, which are very small (the names of the Web pages to be retrieved) and the server sends back the contents of the pages, which can be very large. You will often see the server ACK the same sequence number to the client many times in a row, because the client has sent no further data in the intervening period.

3. Terminating the connection

When one end of the connection (Bob, in this case) is finished and has no more data to transmit, it sends a packet with the FIN ("*finis*") flag set, shown as "F" in **tcpdump**. Alice ACKs this. Now Alice has to tell Bob that *she* has no more data to transmit to him, so she has to send a FIN packet too. Only when Bob ACKs this is the connection closed completely:

```
bob.telnet > alice.1067: FP 673:683(10) ack 135 win 16060$
alice.1067 > bob.telnet: . ack 684 win 16060 <nop,nop,tim$
alice.1067 > bob.telnet: F 135:135(0) ack 684 win 16060 <$
bob.telnet > alice.1067: . ack 136 win 16060 <nop,nop,tim$
```

So it takes four packets to terminate the connection, but only three to establish it. The typical packet flow for a whole session, where the server terminates the connection, is shown in Figure 10.12(a), and Figure 10.12(b) shows the flow where the client terminates it.

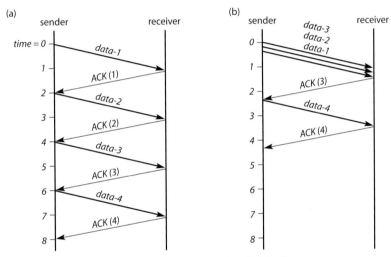

Figure 10.11 Each packet doesn't have to be ACKed individually

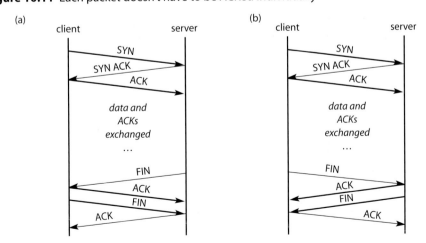

Figure 10.12 Connection establishment and termination

10.10 More about ports and servers

We said that specific well-known ports are allocated to particular services (e.g. port 80 is for HTTP Web servers), which is how clients specify the service they want and servers recognize what service the client is asking for. In more detail, what happens in normal running is:

- on the server machine, the administrator specifies in a configuration file which services are to be run

- at boot time, the system reads the configuration file(s) and starts the specified servers, so all the configured servers run as long as this machine is up and running

- when a server starts up it tells TCP that it wants to receive connections coming in on a specific port, and then waits, listening on that port, for TCP to pass connections to it as they arrive

- there are listeners only on the ports the server applications are configured for. For example, if we don't run a Web server on our machine, there will be no listener on port 80. You can list all the listeners using "`netstat -l`" as we saw in Module 10.5. If a client tries to connect to a port that isn't being listened for, you get an error message like:

```
Unable to connect to remote host: Connection refused      Linux
Connect Failed! hostname: alice                           Windows
```

When this happens, TCP on the server machine replies with a packet that has the *RST* (*RESET*) flag set. You can easily see this by connecting to a port that you know has no listening server, e.g.

```
telnet bob 12345                          deliberate error – no server on :12345
```

and then running **tcpdump**. **tcpdump** indicates resets with an "R" at the beginning of the packet contents:

```
alice.4827 > bob.12345: S 2678103771:2678103771(0) win 16060
bob.12345 > alice.4827: R 0:0(0) ack 2678103772 win 0
```

While the port the server listens on is usually its well-known port number, it doesn't have to be. As far as TCP is concerned, the well-known ports are just a convention. It makes life easier for users because they can assume the port number for a service is the well-known one, and applications can use this by default, but TCP internally doesn't care which port any service uses. This can be useful in a number of ways:

- to run multiple, different copies of the same server. For example, we might run our Web server for access by external users on the well-known HTTP port, 80, as normal (e.g. **alice:80**) but run the server for our internal intranet on the same machine on port 81 (**alice:81**) with test versions on **alice:1234** and **alice:3197**, respectively

- in a security setting, where one server performs a special security function and then passes on the data to a normal server on the same machine. For example, incoming mail is accepted by a secure mail server on the well-known SMTP port, 25. This server scans for viruses and rejects messages from spammers, and passes on clean messages to a real SMTP server on port 12063:

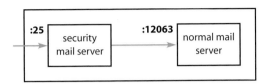

We'll explore virus scanning in more detail in Module 25.2.

What happens if you run the wrong service on a well-known port? For example, if a mail server instead of a Web server is running on port :80, what happens when you connect to it with a Web browser? The short answer is it doesn't work. The client gets whatever service the server is providing on that port. The well-known ports convention is designed to avoid this sort of problem (which only occurs when you – or a hacker – tinkers with your system). We discuss in more detail how servers are configured to use particular ports in Appendix 20.

Port names

netstat lists symbolic names for ports when you don't use the "**-n**" option. The names are not hard-coded. They are listed in the **services** file (**/etc/services** on Linux, **\WINNT\system32\drivers\etc\Services** on Windows-NT). This file is used to translate between port numbers and names. Below is an excerpt of this file from one of our Linux systems. The fields are name (e.g. **smtp**), port number (**25**), protocol (**tcp**), and optionally any aliases for this service (**mail**):

```
ftp             21/tcp
telnet          23/tcp
smtp            25/tcp      mail
domain          53/udp
domain          53/tcp
www             80/tcp
pop3            110/tcp
```

Most programs that take a port number will also accept a port name instead. For example,

```
telnet alice www
tcpdump host 192.0.2.29 and port domain
```
"www" instead of 80
"domain" instead of 53

For more information on the **services** file, see Appendix 20.

The **netstat** listings in Module 10.5 showed an SMTP server listening on port 25 on local address 0.0.0.0. What this meant was that if this host has multiple IP addresses, this server will accept incoming connection requests to port 25 on *any* of these addresses. In fact, TCP/IP gives the server programmer a choice: they can listen on any of this machine's addresses as above, or explicitly specify just one of the addresses to listen on. The latter would let you run two entirely different applications (or two separate copies of the same application) on the same port on the same machine but with different IP addresses, which is often useful in test environments.

Summary

- TCP provides reliable connections over unreliable lower layers by using sequence numbers and acknowledgments to signal which packets have been successfully received, and re-transmitting any lost data as necessary
- TCP applications use a client/server model:
  - the server listens on its well-known port for incoming connection requests from clients
  - the client uses a specific destination port number to tell the server which of the many different TCP services it wants to connect to
  - the server uses the incoming source port number to send back replies to the client
  - for each connection, the combination (N_1, P_1, N_2, P_2) is unique. This allows TCP to distinguish between multiple connections on the same machine, whether they are for the same service (e.g. World Wide Web) or not. This is what TCP uses to demultiplex the packets coming in from the IP layer and pass them up to the respective connections in the application layer. This is an important function of the transport layer, because it's not provided by the network (IP) layer lower down
- the **netstat** command displays TCP connections
- a TCP connection is established with the SYN, SYN/ACK, ACK, three-way handshake, and terminated with FIN, ACK, FIN, ACK
- **telnet** uses TCP as its transport
- because the **telnet** client does little more than read characters the user types and transmit them to the server, it can be used as a general-purpose client for many different TCP applications.

What's next?

In the next chapter we look at the other main application of the Internet – e-mail, using the SMTP and POP3 protocols.

Notes and further reading

In Part 1 we skirted round the difference between IP and TCP. We were able to do this for two reasons:

1. all packet routing, etc. is handled by IP
2. DNS usually uses UDP, not TCP. We didn't need to explain UDP either because all DNS conversations conveniently fitted into single packets (which is what UDP uses) and we could view DNS entirely as the exchange of separate packets. Most of the "big" Internet applications use TCP, so we'll defer UDP until Chapter 15.

Recent versions of **tcpdump** have an "**-x**" option to show ASCII, but not all versions you're likely to come across include this; if your version doesn't have this option, you can use the **ngrep** sniffer instead (Module 13.7) or, ideally, upgrade your **tcpdump**.

TCP

We've deliberately steered clear of most of the guts of TCP, and explained how it works using our postcards/packets analogy. This was acceptable on the basis of our "do you need to know this in your day-to-day work" guiding principle. You *don't* need to worry about the guts of TCP – it just works. What you do need is to be able to recognize when a TCP connection is being established and terminated, and what a RESET is when a connection is refused.

Surprisingly at first sight, not all applications need or use the reliability and connection-oriented features of TCP. In Chapter 15 we'll see that several important applications use the UDP transport (host-to-host) layer protocol. While this is connectionless and only best-effort ("unreliable"), it is sometimes more appropriate than TCP.

ping doesn't use UDP or TCP – it uses ICMP only. If you look at the processes running on a target machine you won't see any **ping** server; it's not needed because replying to **ping**s is built into the TCP/IP stack, which is easily done because it's so simple and small.

Other features of TCP

Stevens, Chapters 17–24 covers TCP and all its features in great detail. We'll just mention two features here.

TCP supports "congestion control" – how the client and server can avoid saturating the network and making it unusable because there is too much traffic to be handled properly. The "old" way of doing this was for the systems to send *ICMP source quench* messages to each other, in effect saying "please send more slowly." Nowadays this isn't recommended; instead, if packets are coming too quickly, some of them are just dropped silently (i.e. without generating any ICMP messages) and the two ends of the connection "learn" – by seeing they have to retransmit frequently – that they should reduce their transmission rate. It is surprising that some of today's sophisticated "bandwidth management" devices – which let you allocate, for example, 20% of your Internet connection's bandwidth to incoming Web traffic, and 30% to VPNs between your offices, operate using what seems such a crude mechanism.

The other point we'll mention is that some security systems actively generate TCP RSTs (resets). For example, if the security system detects that a user is accessing an unauthorized Web site, it sends a RST to the client on the LAN, with the IP source address faked to be that of the remote Web server, thus aborting the client's connection to the unauthorized site.

TCP itself is a large and complex protocol, but because all the complexity is isolated in networking stack, you don't see it at the application level so writing TCP applications is easy (relatively). You only have to worry about the application-specific code since the huge amounts of functionality in the TCP layer are provided free. This is an example of good software engineering.

"Sockets," ports, and connections

You will frequently come across references to "sockets" in TCP/IP documentation. The most common application programming interface (API) to TCP/IP is the *Sockets API*. This originated at Berkeley, in their 4.2BSD release of UNIX in 1983, and sockets are often referred to as "Berkeley sockets" or "BSD sockets."

A socket is one end of a TCP connection. It is specified by the host IP address and the port number. To create a connection, the server creates a socket on its own address and its well-known port, and then listens on that socket. The client creates a socket on its own address and an ephemeral port, and connects this socket to the server's well-known port. This establishes the connection; you can think of it as joining the two sockets together to make the connection, and indeed a connection is often referred to as a *socket pair* (so a socket is half a connection).

For details of sockets and programming with TCP/IP see the sublime book:

❏ **Stevens** *UNIX Network Programming* (1990, Prentice Hall, PTR)

While this is a programming text, it gives a lot of useful insights into how TCP/IP works, especially how clients and servers interact.

telnet

In the early days of the Internet, **telnet** and **ftp** (Module 17.2) made up almost all the traffic on the Internet. By the mid-1990s, this had dropped to about 40% and now it makes up 10% or less, and is still dropping rapidly. This reflects the growth in e-mail, Web and multimedia applications.

The Windows NT Server 4.0 Resource Kit contains a **telnet** server, as does Windows-2000.

telnet has a huge number of special options, which nowadays don't seem very interesting. See Stevens, Chapter 26, or the **telnet** (1) manpage on a Linux or UNIX system.

Because **telnet** normally sends to the remote system everything you type – including control characters – you need a special way to send commands to **telnet** itself. On Windows the window menus let you do this. On Linux, **telnet** has an "escape character," which is usually Ctrl-]. When you type this, **telnet** gives you its own prompt, and treats the next line you type as an instruction to **telnet**, not something to send to the remote machine. We rarely use this for anything except to quit. For more information, type Ctrl-] in a **telnet** session and enter "help".

You can start the **telnet** client manually from the command line, or in your Web browser enter the URL "`telnet://`*machinename*".

telnet-**related programs**

The program **netcat** (also known as **nc**, Module 17.4) is like a trimmed-down version of **telnet** – it doesn't have any of **telnet**'s fancy options – but in other ways it is much more flexible and is ideal for testing network services.

The **rsh**, **rcp**, and **rlogin** are functionally related to **telnet** although they don't use the **telnet** protocol. These are collectively known as the "r-commands" ("r" for remote) and originated in the Berkeley (BSD) version of UNIX, where a lot of TCP/IP was developed and networking was made practical for day-to-day use.

rsh (remote shell) and **rexec** (remote execute) let you execute a single command on a remote system. For example,

```
rsh bob date                                    what time does Bob say it is?
```

rcp (remote copy) copies a file between the locate and a remote system. For example,

```
rcp bob:/tmp/abc.txt mine.txt                         copies a file from Bob
```

rlogin (remote login) lets you logon to a remote system without having to enter your username and password.

These are very convenient because they don't ask you to enter your username and password each time. But that is of course a security hole, which was exploited in the once-famous "Morris Internet worm" that was let loose on 2 November 1988:

❏ **RFC-1135 December 1989** *The Helminthiasis of the Internet*

"Helminthiasis" means infested with disease caused by worms. The worm made extensive use of the "r" commands.

telnet **and security; SSH – secure login over the network**

telnet isn't secure. When you authenticate to the remote system, **telnet** sends the username and password as clear text – not encrypted in any way – and a hacker sniffing your traffic can steal your password and then impersonate you. Sniffing is easy (as you now know from experience!) so using **telnet** is a big security hole. SSH ("secure shell") gets over this, as explained by the SSH manpage:

> *The idea is that each user creates a public/private key pair for authentication purposes. The server knows the public key, and only the user knows the private key. The file $HOME/.ssh/authorized_keys lists the public keys that are permitted for logging in. When the user logs in, the ssh program tells the server which key pair it would like to use for authentication. The server checks if this key is permitted, and if so, sends the user (actually the ssh program running on behalf of the user) a challenge, a random number, encrypted by the user's public key. The challenge can only be decrypted using the proper private key. The user's client then decrypts the challenge using the private key, proving that he/she knows the private key but without disclosing it to the server.*

> *ssh implements the RSA authentication protocol automatically. … RSA authentication is much more secure than rhosts authentication.* [**rhosts** authentication is what the r-commands use.]

Appendices

Inside front cover: table of port numbers
Appendix 20: controlling network services
Web Appendix 13: exercises on connections and ports

11

E-mail – SMTP and POP3

Introduction

E-mail is our first real application – the one that just about everyone uses. For years this was the "killer app" that drove the demand for the Internet. We explain:

- how messages are sent and received using the SMTP and POP protocols
- how mail clients locate mail servers
- how you can send and receive messages manually using **telnet** and avoid using a custom e-mail client, for diagnostic and test purposes.

11.1 Overview of Internet e-mail

Internet e-mail systems use TCP as their transport layer and are client/server applications. On a typical LAN, Internet e-mail involves three separate steps:

1. your client sends messages using *SMTP (Simple Mail Transfer Protocol)*
2. your client receives messages from the server using *POP3 (Post Office Protocol, version 3)*
3. your server (or your ISP's server) sends and receives messages from other servers using SMTP.

That is, SMTP is used everywhere except by clients retrieving their mail from their own (or their ISP's) server. All e-mail over the Internet is sent using SMTP. Even if your mail server is Microsoft Exchange or Lotus, it uses SMTP to send to remote sites, and to receive from them (Module 12.6).

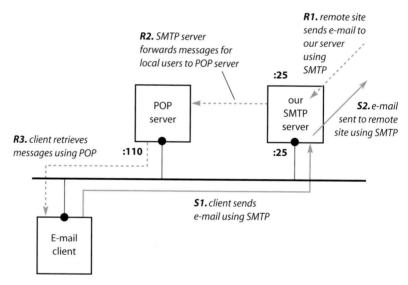

Figure 11.1 E-mail protocols

There are separate servers for each protocol. Some implementations combine the two functions into a single application for convenience, but it's easier to understand what's happening if we keep them separate. In normal configurations the servers listen on the well-known ports:

Service	Port
SMTP	25
POP3	110

Your e-mail client program (Netscape, Outlook® Express, Eudora, etc.) connects to the POP and SMTP servers by specifying their IP addresses and ports. The client configuration normally allows you to specify different IP addresses for the two server functions, so you can use POP and SMTP servers that are combined in one application, or are separate applications on the same machine or on completely separate machines.

In fact, the POP and SMTP servers need not be on your LAN at all. Small sites often don't run their own mail servers, but use their ISP's servers instead (Figure 11.2) saving the cost and administration effort of a local mail server. The disadvantages of this approach are that internal e-mail – between local users on the LAN – has to go out to the ISP's mail server and then come back in again. This slows down internal mail, increases phone costs if your Internet connection is a dial-up or ISDN link, and means your internal e-mail can't work while your Internet connection is down. In practice, very small sites tend to use their ISP's server, large sites use their own server, and intermediate-sized sites are split evenly between the two options.

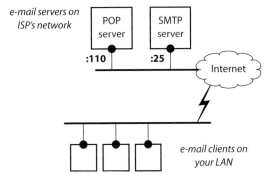

Figure 11.2 Small sites often use mail servers at their ISP

Surprisingly, in both SMTP and POP the conversations between client and server are in plain text. For example, the POP client sends the line "**RETR 7**" to retrieve message number 7 from the POP server. Because both protocols use TCP we'll be able to use **telnet**:

- to view the internal working of the protocols
- as a test client to identify and troubleshoot client and server problems.

While a full-blown e-mail client is a large and complex beast, you will see that conceptually it's very simple and doesn't use any magic communications mechanisms – just basic TCP networking, with a lot of extra non-networking functionality on top to let the user type in and display messages.

(By the way, in our network diagrams we usually stick to a convention that servers are shown above the line representing the Ethernet LAN, clients below.)

In the next module we explain how your SMTP server (or your ISP's) finds out the IP address of the server to send a message to any e-mail address on the Internet.

11.2 Locating the destination mail server – MX records

You want to e-mail **fred@example.com**. You compose the message in your mail client, which then sends it to your SMTP server (or your ISP's). What does your server do next? A reasonable guess would be "establish a TCP connection with **example.com**'s SMTP server in order to send the message." But how does your server find out the IP address of **example.com**'s SMTP server, or even if they have one? This is where the DNS *mail exchange records* (*MX records*) come in.

Your server queries the DNS for the MX record(s) of the recipient's domain name – everything after the "@" in the e-mail address. For example, our server does an MX lookup for "**example.com**" in our scenario. The DNS returns the names of the SMTP server machines for **example.com**. This list of names was entered in **example.com**'s DNS server database by **example.com**'s DNS administrators when they set up their DNS. The list usually contains one or more entries:

```
alice% host -t mx example.com
example.com     MX     10      mailgate.example.com
```

Your server then queries the DNS for the IP address of **mailgate.example.com**:

```
alice% host mailgate.example.com
mailgate.example.com    A       192.0.2.29
```

Your server now knows the address (192.0.2.29) of **example.com**'s server and can connect to it on the well-known SMTP port (25) to transmit the message. Once the message has been received by **mailgate.example.com**, it is passed on internally to user **fred**, typically by POP. Figure 11.3 shows the whole process. (In Module 11.8 we discuss how long this takes.)

If you rely on your ISP's mail servers and don't run your own SMTP server, the process is still as shown in Figure 11.3, but the "your SMTP server" box is located on your ISP's network. (And consequently, the MX records for your domain – which other people on the Internet will use when they are sending e-mail to you – will point to your ISP's mail servers.)

Alternatively, your SMTP server may be configured to send all messages to a *relay* server at your ISP. The relay server does the MX lookups and transmits the message to the destination site's SMTP server (Figure 11.4). (The relay server in this context is sometimes called a *smart host* – the e-mail equivalent of a default gateway.) This configuration is good if you have an intermittent (dial-up) or slow Internet connection: all the MX lookups and the work of delivering the message to the final destination can be done by your ISP's server, and you don't have to keep your Internet connection open while that happens.

Notice by the way how we're viewing our e-mail systems at an application-to-application level now. We're considering the interaction between the mail client at our site and the mail server at a remote location. We haven't mentioned packets or routing at all – we take it for granted that the TCP layer gives us the connection we want and that the IP and lower layers route the packets correctly across the Internet. That's the beauty of layering: we just say "connect to server 1.2.3.4 on port 25" and it happens as though by magic.

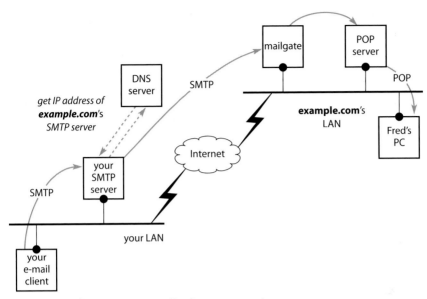

Figure 11.3 E-mailing a message to Fred at a remote site

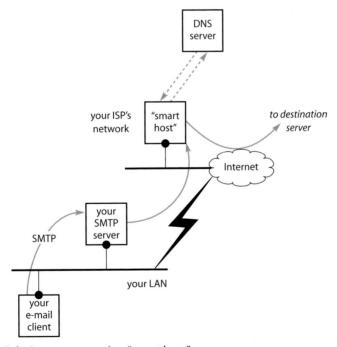

Figure 11.4 Relaying messages via a "smart host"

Now let's see how the MX facility can give us more flexibility in configuring our mail networks, and resilience to overcome temporary Internet or server failures.

11.3 MX records for resilience

We want e-mail to be as reliable as possible. Making the user re-send messages just because our Internet connection was down for a while, or because the recipient's server was being rebooted, is irritating at best and can lead to lost or forgotten messages. The DNS helps overcome this problem by letting you specify multiple SMTP servers for a domain. Here's an example: below we see that the DNS for **example.com** says that five SMTP servers know about this domain and will accept mail for its users:

```
alice% host -t mx example.com

example.com    MX    10    msrv1.example.com
example.com    MX    10    msrv2.example.com
example.com    MX    20    mailgate.uit.co.uk
example.com    MX    50    relay1.theirisp.com
example.com    MX    70    burelay.theirisp.com
```

This example illustrates two important features of how MX records are used.

1. MX preference values for multiple servers

The third column above is the *preference value*: the smaller the value, the more preferred this entry is. Thus, our server will first try to contact **msrv1.example.com**. If that isn't available it will move on to try **msrv2.example.com**, and so on. This is how you specify which are your "main" or preferred servers, and which servers are backups to be used when your main server(s) are unavailable.

If more than one address has the same preference value, your SMTP server will (or ought to) try them in random order. As soon as it successfully connects to one, it sends the message and that's that. It only tries the later servers in the list if it can't access the earlier ones. Trying the servers in random order spreads the incoming message load evenly across all the same-preference-value servers. But even if sending servers always choose the first server in the returned MX listing, there is another mechanism that gives a form of load-balancing. The DNS server involved here, i.e. for the recipient's domain, doesn't return the list of MX records in the same order every time. Instead, it round-robins them in successive DNS responses, so that each entry gets an equal number of turns at being top in the list. The result is that each successive incoming message will go to a different server. In the example above, **msrv1** and **msrv2** will each receive about the same number of messages. This is a common arrangement at large sites, for handling large messages volumes (by adding extra servers as needed) and for redundancy: if the first server tried is down, the message will be sent to the next server in the list.

You can see this round-robin effect easily by looking up the MX records for **cus.cam.ac.uk** a few times, and observing how the order of the entries changes:

```
alice% host -t mx cus.cam.ac.uk
cus.cam.ac.uk          MX       4 libra.cus.cam.ac.uk
cus.cam.ac.uk          MX       4 virgo.cus.cam.ac.uk
cus.cam.ac.uk          MX       7 ppsw.cam.ac.uk
cus.cam.ac.uk          MX      99 route-back-x.cam.ac.uk
cus.cam.ac.uk          MX       4 draco.cus.cam.ac.uk
alice% host -t mx cus.cam.ac.uk
cus.cam.ac.uk          MX       7 ppsw.cam.ac.uk
cus.cam.ac.uk          MX      99 route-back-x.cam.ac.uk
cus.cam.ac.uk          MX       4 draco.cus.cam.ac.uk
cus.cam.ac.uk          MX       4 libra.cus.cam.ac.uk
cus.cam.ac.uk          MX       4 virgo.cus.cam.ac.uk
```

2. Backup mail servers at other sites and at your ISP

The other three entries in the first list illustrate another common practice – using *backup mail servers* (sometimes called *backup relays*) at other sites who agree to provide this service for you. If **example.com**'s Internet connection is down, we won't be able to connect to any of their servers; what happens to the mail then? With the MX entries shown, the sender will first try **mailgate.uit.co.uk** and if possible send to there. If **mailgate.uit.co.uk** is also down, the sender will try the servers at **theirisp.com**.

Backup servers can be provided by other divisions of your own organization, or by friendly companies you are associated with, or by your ISP. If you have several sites worldwide, it's good practice to use servers in different countries as backups for one another. That way, you are protected even from the failure of a whole country's network. Even if you have several sites in the same country, use them as backups for each other to protect against the failure of an individual site's Internet connection or mail server.

The example above is for a large site. Many sites use a single mail server of their own, and rely on their ISP for relay backup, giving simpler MX lists:

```
ncd.com                MX      10 mail.ncd.com
ncd.com                MX     200 mail.uu.net
```

SMTP store and forward

If the message is sent to a backup server at another site, what happens to it? The e-mail system (unlike IP packet transmission) is *store and forward*. When a server accepts a message it stores it safely on disk, and then attempts to forward it to its final destination. It becomes just another message in this server's queue of messages, where it goes through the normal cycle of retries. In the first example, if a message for **example.com** was sent to **mailgate.uit.co.uk**, **mailgate.uit.co.uk** will repeatedly attempt to forward to **msrv1.example.com** and **msrv2.example.com**; as soon as they come back on stream, the connection will succeed, and any stored messages will be forwarded. We cover this in a little more detail in the next module.

11.4 MX records for intermittent connections; mail delivery problems

MX records for intermittent and dynamic connections; ETRN

For an intermittent, dial-up connection (for a single PC, or for a network without a local mail server) the MX entries for your domain will point to the SMTP servers at your ISP and you will retrieve your mail from there, probably using POP.

If you have a fixed address for your mail server but your Internet connection is intermittent, you will definitely need to include at least one permanently accessible server – probably your ISP's – in your MX entries, so that there is always an available server to accept mail for your domain. It's up to you whether you also include your own server's address. If you do and your connection is up only a few minutes a day, most servers sending to you will try your server first and fail before sending to your ISP's server, so you're causing a bit of wasted effort.

If you don't include your server in the list of MX records, to collect your mail you have to signal to the ISP's server somehow, each time your Internet connection comes up, that you're ready to accept your stored messages. You can do this by establishing an SMTP connection to the ISP server and issuing the *TURN* command: this "turns" the connection round the other way, so that their server delivers its stored messages to you. In fact TURN has a security hole allowing people to steal other sites' messages, so nowadays you should use the *ETRN* (*extended turn*) command instead if your ISP's server and your own support it. Your ISP or your mail server documentation will tell you how you ought to use this in your specific context.

If you do have an e-mail server on your LAN but your Internet connection gives you a dynamically allocated IP address rather than fixed IP addresses for your site, then you can't include your mail server's address in the MX records because you can never tell what it's IP address will be. Again, the MX records for your domain will cause messages to be delivered to your ISP's server. To retrieve your mail from your ISP you can use ETRN as above. Or, when you connect, the ISP's dial-in system software may determine your current IP address and signal to the ISP's mail server that you have now connected, so it can send the messages to your server in the normal way.

If there are problems delivering mail to the destination ...

We have to consider two special cases:

1. **the DNS gives the address of one or more destination SMTP servers, but your server can't connect to any of them**
   This occurs when your Internet connection is down, or their Internet connection is down, or their server is unavailable (perhaps because it is rebooting, or just broken). The sending server normally holds the message for some time and periodically attempts to re-send it. The number of retries and the time to wait between retries are configuration options in the server. Typically a server will try to re-send 5–10 times over four or five days. If the message still can't be sent, the sending server gives up and

sends a "bounce message" to the originator of the original message saying it can't be sent. Some small companies only publish a single MX record for their sites. However, because the DNS allows backup SMTP servers to be specified for a domain as explained in the previous module, not being able to find *any* server to send to is relatively rare unless the problem is with your own Internet connection.

2. **the DNS has no MX records for the destination domain**

   If your server gets no MX records in response to its lookup, it then does an IP address lookup (not an MX lookup) on the domain name itself, to see if it is a *host*name. If it's not a valid hostname, the server gives up and says it can't send the message.

   If it is a valid host, the sending server tries to connect to an SMTP server on the host's IP address, with the usual cycle of retries.

   This behavior is a carry-over from the pre-MX days, when e-mail was addressed to a specific machine – often the recipient's own machine – rather than just to the domain name. As we explain below, addressing messages to a specific machine within a domain can cause problems.

Some background to the concept of MX records

Originally, to send mail to someone you had to know the address of their individual machine, e.g. **fred@pc29.sales.example.com**. In a small community that was fine, but as the Internet grew, the concept of MX records evolved. By including only the site's domain name in an e-mail address, rather than the FQDN of a machine, we hide details of where a person is located within our organization. They can move to a different geographical office or change department or use a different desktop PC and their e-mail is still routed in correctly. People outside our organization are insulated from changes inside.

The MX record mechanism has other advantages: we can easily specify multiple e-mail servers for our domain, and it's possible for third-party service provides to handle e-mail for their customers, e.g. small sites rely on their ISP's mail servers and don't have to run their own.

MX records for subdomains

As we've seen, the destination server is located by querying the DNS for MX records for the part of the e-mail address following the "@," which may in fact be a subdomain of a site's primary domain, as in **fred@asia.example.com**. If the subdomain is delegated, the DNS can contain MX records for it, allowing you to have mail for your main domain sent to one set of servers, and for the subdomain to a different set. Because this configuration limits user e-mail named to specific subdomains, it's most useful where the subdomain is organizationally very separate from the parent, e.g. a separate division covering a distinct geographical region.

Now that we know how to find the destination mail server, we explain how to send a message to it in the next module.

11.5 Lab – using telnet to send an SMTP message

We're going to send a message "manually", using **telnet** as a client on Alice to connect to an SMTP server on Dave, and typing the commands in by hand. Just as we did with HTTP in Module 10.7, we're going to act as a very simple e-mail client. We'll see the server responses in our **telnet** client, and we'll also look at the TCP traffic using **tcpdump**. You can repeat this using your own SMTP server if you have one, or your ISP's server if not – or even someone else's mail server remote on the Internet. If you're not sure which server to use, either look up a site's MX records using **host** or **nslookup**, as described in Module 11.2, or use the SMTP server that you or someone else on your LAN has configured in their e-mail client. Change the user and domain names in the example appropriately.

Before beginning the **telnet** session, we started two copies of **tcpdump**, one with "**-X**" to dump the packet contents in ASCII, the other without. On both we use "**-t -N**" to suppress timestamps and to print names without their full domain suffix (e.g. **alice** instead of **alice.example.com**). We explicitly specify the hosts we're interested in, and the well-known SMTP port (25) so that only the traffic we want is displayed:

```
tcpdump -t -N -X port 25 and host dave and alice    -X to dump in ASCII
tcpdump -t -N port 25 and host dave and alice
```

In the **telnet** session below we've shown the responses from the server indented for clarity. You can see that the SMTP "conversation" between client and server consists of commands and responses in plain text.

```
alice% telnet dave smtp
      Trying 192.0.2.5...
      Connected to dave.
      Escape character is '^]'.
      220 dave ESMTP Sendmail 8.7.3/8.7.3/dave; Fri, 6 Jul 2001 13:55:36
EHLO mydom.com
      250-dave Hello alice [192.0.2.17], pleased to meet you
MAIL FROM:<vanderb@mydom.com>
      250 <vanderb@mydom.com>... Sender ok
RCPT TO:<taybay@example.com>
      250 Recipient ok
DATA
      354 Enter mail, end with "." on a line by itself
from: <vanderb@mydom.com>
to: <taybay@example.com>
subject: cat food

Are there any tins of Yum Yum in the fridge?

      Bye, v.
.
      250 NAA21635 Message accepted for delivery
QUIT
      221 dave closing connection
      Connection closed by foreign host.
alice%
```

This sends a message from user **vanderb@mydom.com** to user **taybay@example.com**. The message received, as viewed in a typical e-mail client, is shown below:

```
Date: Fri, 6 Jul 2001 13:55:36 +0100 (BST)
from: <vanderb@mydom.com>
to: <taybay@example.com>
subject: cat food

Are there any tins of Yum Yum in the fridge?

     Bye, v.
```

We'll go through each of the commands and responses in the next module. First, let's look at the **tcpdump** traces. The normal trace below (edited to show only the start and end of the session) illustrates the three-way handshake (SYN, SYN-ACK, ACK) that establishes the connection, and the FIN, ACK, FIN, ACK termination that we covered in Module 10.9.

```
alice# tcpdump -t -N port 25 and host dave and alice
alice.1618 > dave.smtp: S 2242172728:2242172728(0) win 16060 <mss 1460,
dave.smtp > alice.1618: S 1486400000:1486400000(0) ack 2242172729 win ?
alice.1618 > dave.smtp: . ack 1 win 16060 (DF) [tos 0x10]
...
alice.1618 > dave.smtp: P 183:189(6) ack 298 win 16060 (DF) [tos 0x10]
dave.smtp > alice.1618: P 298:327(29) ack 189 win 4096
dave.smtp > alice.1618: F 327:327(0) ack 189 win 4096
alice.1618 > dave.smtp: . ack 328 win 16060 (DF) [tos 0x10]
alice.1618 > dave.smtp: F 189:189(0) ack 328 win 16060 (DF) [tos 0x10]
dave.smtp > alice.1618: . ack 190 win 4096
```

Below we see one line of the **tcpdump** ASCII dump, illustrating that the characters in the mail message are transmitted within the TCP packet "as is" – there's no magic encoding or clever tricks:

```
alice.1618 > dave.smtp: P 126:171(45) ack 254 win 16060 (DF) [tos 0x10]
0x0000      4510 0055 839e 4000 4006 03c5 d48c 8511      E..U..@.@......
0x0010      d48c 8505 0652 0019 85a4 d7b6 5898 aafe      .....R...X...
0x0020      5018 3ebc 4715 0000 4172 6520 7468 6572      P.>.G...Are.ther
0x0030      6520 616e 7920 7469 6e73 206f 6620 5975      e.any.tins.of.Yu
0x0040      6d20 5975 6d20 696e 2074 6865 2066 7269      m.Yum.in.the.fri
0x0050      6467                                          dg
```

Using **telnet** as an e-mail client in this way, to send a message, can be very useful:

- it helps us understand at a fundamental level how the mail system works

- a regular mail client may not be available, e.g. when you've just started installing a network, or are working on a non-desktop machine that doesn't have any mail clients but you need to troubleshoot the e-mail system, or are on a system that you are not familiar with or when you can't use a normal mail client because you don't have the necessary logon codes

- it avoids the extra layers of configuration detail (and possible errors) that come with standard mail clients, so if you have a problem, **telnet** can help you isolate the cause: if **telnet** works and your client doesn't the problem is in the client.

In the next module we look at each of the SMTP commands we have used above.

11.6 Components of an SMTP session (1) – the envelope

SMTP was described in the now obsolete RFC-821, which has been superseded by the very recent RFC-2821. These RFCs give full details of the SMTP commands, but here we'll cover just the few we need to send a simple message. We'll use the message we sent in the previous module as an example, so we duplicate it here:

```
alice% telnet dave smtp
        Trying 192.0.2.5...
        Connected to dave.
        Escape character is '^]'.
        220 dave ESMTP Sendmail 8.7.3/8.7.3/dave; Fri, 6 Jul 2001 13:55:36
EHLO mydom.com
        250-dave Hello alice [192.0.2.17], pleased to meet you
MAIL FROM:<vanderb@mydom.com>
        250 <vanderb@mydom.com>... Sender ok
RCPT TO:<taybay@example.com>
        250 Recipient ok
DATA
        354 Enter mail, end with "." on a line by itself
from: <vanderb@mydom.com>
to: <taybay@example.com>
subject: cat food

Are there any tins of Yum Yum in the fridge?

        Bye, v.
.
        250 NAA21635 Message accepted for delivery
QUIT
        221 dave closing connection
        Connection closed by foreign host.
alice%
```

`telnet dave smtp`   *not an SMTP command*

From Alice we **telnet** to Dave, to connect to the SMTP server which we hope is listening on the well-known **smtp** port (which our **services** file maps to the numeric port number 25). An equivalent command is:

`telnet dave 25`

The server replies with its greeting, which is prefixed with the code **220**. All SMTP response codes consist of three digits, divided into four classes:

2xx: OK – all is well

3xx: server is asking you to send data

4xx: temporary error. If the sender tries again it might work correctly next time

5xx: permanent error. If the sender tries again, the same error will occur.

`EHLO mydom.com`   *incorrect but it works*
`EHLO alice.mydom.com`   *correct*

(EHLO = "Extended Hello") This identifies the client to the server.. The argument ought to be either the full name of the client machine ("**alice.mydom.com**") or the IP address in square brackets ("[192.0.2.17]") but most servers don't insist on this and usually extract the client's IP address from the TCP packets as happened here. Alice didn't give her proper machine name but Dave saw from the TCP data that her IP address was **192.0.2.17** and looked this up in the DNS. The server acknowledges the client with a line beginning with code **250**.

EHLO is an extended version of the **HELO** ("hello") command from the early RFC-821 standard for SMTP. **EHLO** was introduced in the more recent RFC-2821, which allows a range of extensions to SMTP to be supported. However, for checking out the network and the basic operation of the mail service, the old **HELO** command is adequate, even though almost obsolete.

```
MAIL FROM:<vanderb@mydom.com>
```

The client gives the e-mail address of the sender, and the server acknowledges it, prefixed with code 250. This starts the mail sending transaction proper. Note that angle brackets are used here but not in **EHLO**.

```
RCPT TO:<taybay@example.com>
```

The client gives the e-mail address of the recipient (RCPT stands for recipient) and if the server can send (or accept) the message for that receipient, it acknowledges positively with a **250** line.

You can enter multiple **RCPT TO** lines, with one recipient named on each, to send to many people at the same time. Where there's more than one recipient at the same site (same domain) this is very efficient: only one copy of the message is transmitted to the recipient server, and it then delivers multiple copies of the message, one to each recipient. However, some may be accepted and some rejected.

```
DATA
```

This introduces the start of the "mail data", i.e. the content of the message to be sent. The server acknowledges with a **354** ("intermediate" reply, i.e. "I expect more to follow but it's OK so far").

At this point the client has told the server who the client is, and the address(es) the server is to send the message to. In SMTP terminology all this information forms the *envelope*, by analogy with regular snail-mail. The envelope information is used for routing the message through the mail system, and determines where it will be delivered. But just like a paper letter, the address on the inside – on the letter itself rather than the envelope – can be different. (This is often the case when you are sending on to a third party a copy of something you received.) What follows after the **DATA** command is the equivalent of the letter itself, "inside the envelope." The server doesn't give any further acknowledgments until we've finished entering the body of the "letter" or mail message. That's what we cover in the next module.

11.7 Components of an SMTP session (2) – the message body

We're using the same example message as in Modules 11.3 and 11.4, so we duplicate it here:

```
alice% telnet dave smtp
      Trying 192.0.2.5...
      Connected to dave.
      Escape character is '^]'.
      220 dave ESMTP Sendmail 8.7.3/8.7.3/dave; Fri, 6 Jul 2001 13:55:36
EHLO mydom.com
      250-dave Hello alice [192.0.2.17], pleased to meet you
MAIL FROM:<vanderb@mydom.com>
      250 <vanderb@mydom.com>... Sender ok
RCPT TO:<taybay@example.com>
      250 Recipient ok
DATA
      354 Enter mail, end with "." on a line by itself
from: <vanderb@mydom.com>
to: <taybay@example.com>
subject: cat food

Are there any tins of Yum Yum in the fridge?

      Bye, v.
.
      250 NAA21635 Message accepted for delivery
QUIT
      221 dave closing connection
      Connection closed by foreign host.
alice%
```

from: <vanderb@mydom.com>

In this and the next two lines the client specifies the *header lines* to appear in the actual mail message the recipient will receive. The **from** header identifies the sender. As this is "inside the envelope" and not used for mail routing, it doesn't have to be just an e-mail address, so lines like

"Fred Bloggs" <fred@bloggs.com>

fred@bloggs.com (Fred Bloggs)

make sense. (The format is described in RFC-2822.)

to: <taybay@example.com>

This header specifies the recipient(s) that are *to be shown in the message headers*. They are normally the same as the **RCPT TO** recipients, but could be different for several good reasons and some bad ones. A good reason is the message is delivered (**RCPT TO**) several people, A, B, C, and D, but the **to** header lists only A and another header, **cc:**, includes B and C. What about D, you ask? D is in fact a **bcc:** (blind carbon copy) recipient: they get a copy of the message, but there's nothing in the message itself to indicate this. We'll look at bad reasons (e.g. junk mail) in Module 11.14.

```
subject: cat food
```
This is the subject header line.

blank line

The blank line indicates that we've entered all the headers we want to enter. Anything else that follows is the body of the message.

```
Are there any tins of Yum Yum in the fridge?
Bye, v.
```
These three lines are the body of this profound message.

- *contains only a period*

A period at the beginning of a line and followed by nothing else indicates that we've finished entering body lines. The server replies with a **250** code line, saying the message has been accepted. Depending on your server, it may deliver it immediately.

At this point we could start another whole transaction, repeating the commands in the previous module to send another message. (You can omit the initial **EHLO** though, if you want.) We'd have to enter all the details again even if sending to the same recipients because the first message is completely finished with.

QUIT

We want to exit. The server acknowledges with a code 221 termination message, and the TCP connection is terminated.

These commands insert basic mail headers in the message – **to:**, **from:**, and **subject:**. Other headers are inserted into the message automatically:

- real e-mail clients include headers giving the date and information about themselves, e.g. product name and version information
- any mail servers that handle the message on its way to its destination should insert a "**Received:**" header. For example, the smart host at your ISP, the recipient's own mail server ISP, and any backup relay (e.g. at the recipient's ISP) that might have been involved.

A real mail client obviously includes a lot more functionality than we've shown, to make it easy to send and receive messages, and must store and retrieve messages in a local file, etc. But in principle, those extras are just conveniences for the user – the fundamental operation of sending mail happens just as you've done it by hand.

If you're a programmer or do crosswords, you've probably asked yourself a couple of interesting questions. First, if the mail message we're sending contains a line consisting of a single period, will that cause our e-mail program to go wrong? (It obviously doesn't, but why not? See the Notes.) Second, if I want to send a binary file such as a spreadsheet or executable program, or a graphics file, how can I do it, because these could easily contain runs of characters that appear to be SMTP commands? Binary files *do* cause problems, for the reason above and because RFC-2821 says the maximum length of a text line is 1000 characters. The solution to these problems is MIME (Multipurpose Internet Mail Extension) (Module 12.1).

We examine the mail headers in more detail in the next module.

11.8 Mail headers

We've seen that a mail message is handled by several SMTP servers – usually two at least – as it travels from sender to recipient. As the message passes through each server, an extra mail header is added to the message, giving information about this mail hop – which server handled the message and when. These headers are often useful when resolving problems. (We didn't show any of these extra headers in the example in Module 11.5 because most e-mail clients hide them by default, both to avoid cluttering the screen and so as not to confuse naive end-users.)

Below we show a message we received:

```
Received: from mgate (mgate [212.140.133.29]) by dave
        (8.7.3/8.7.3/dave) with ESMTP id VAA13434 for <bex9@uit.co.uk>;
        Sun, 17 Jun 2001 21:53:29 +0100 (BST)
Received: from eagle.example.com ([192.0.2.1]) by mgate
        (Post.Office MTA v3.1.2 release (P0203-101c) ID# 0-0U10L2S100)
        with ESMTP id AAA21148 for <bex9@uit.co.uk>;
        Sun, 17 Jun 2001 21:51:05 +0100
Received: by eagle.example.com with SMTP
        from 2k_5.example.com (pc248-126.example.com [192.0.2.126])
        id VAA31012 for <bex9@uit.co.uk> (3.2.1/3.1.37);
        Sun, 17 Jun 2001 21:49:57 +0100
Received: FROM 2k_exch.example.com BY 2k_5.example.com ;
        Sun Jun 17 21:42:15 2001 +0100
Received: from DJW2KPC ([10.1.1.16]) by 2k_exch.example.com
        with Microsoft SMTPSVC(5.0.2195.2966);
        Sun, 17 Jun 2001 21:42:14 +0100
Message-ID: <002001c0f76d$fde51a80$1001010a@example.com>
From: "John K Largle" <jkl@example.com>
To: "Bill Xanathin" <bex9@uit.co.uk>
References: <1010613141718.ZM4623@techpc>
Subject: Re: r14 upgrade
Date: Sun, 17 Jun 2001 21:42:14 +0100
```

This message passed through five machines at least, and the timestamps show how long it takes the message to travel over each hop:

No.	Machine name	Forwarded message at	Hop duration
1	DJW2KPC	21:42:14	–
2	2k_exch.example.com	21:42:15	0:01
3	2k_5.example.com	21:49:57	7:42
4	eagle.example.com	21:51:05	1:08
5	mgate (at **uit.co.uk**)	21:53:29	2:24
6	dave (at **uit.co.uk**)	–	–

The hop times are unusually slow. It's not uncommon for us to send a message to someone when we're talking to them on the phone, and a few seconds later we hear the "beep beep" of their e-mail client and they say they have received our message. On the other hand, when problems occur and messages take hours or days to arrive, checking the headers and the hop times can give you a pointer to where the problem lies. We've occasionally seen messages sent to us that have sat for hours on some virus-scanning or content-filtering machine on the sender's site, only to be released late at night (see Module 25.2).

Timestamps are often not very accurate because computer clocks often drift over time. (The clock on one of our server machines had drifted about 12 minutes in 10 weeks uptime.) It's a good idea to run NTP (Network Time Protocol – Module 17.13) to keep all your clocks in synch.

Most e-mail clients show only selected mail headers, to save space on the screen and to avoid confusing users who just want to read the content of their mail messages and not the gory details of every machine the message happened to pass through. When you *do* want to see all the headers, you choose specifically to display them. Figure 11.5 shows Outlook's display of the headers (select message > **File** > **Properties** > **Internet**).

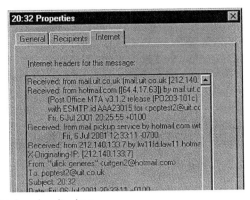

Figure 11.5 Outlook's header displays

Figure 11.6 shows Outlook Express (select message > **File** > **Properties** > **Details**).

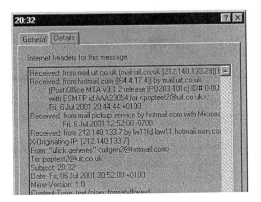

Figure 11.6 Outlook Express: select message

In Netscape, you set an option for the level of header detail to be displayed in the message windows using the menu **View** > **Headers** > **All**.

In the next module we explain how the client receives messages using POP.

11.9 POP3 clients and servers

POP3 is the "Post Office Protocol." The name comes from the idea that my messages are stored in a mailbox somewhere (the POP server) and I need a mechanism to retrieve them, which I can do from any workstation on my network, in the same way that I might collect my snail-mail from an office of my country's postal service. A significant element of the design is that all the mail messages for this site are delivered to the mailbox server (POP server) and not to individual users' machines, because:

- a server machine is more likely to be available 24 hours/day, and not switched off at night like many client machines

- a central delivery point insulates external sites from the details of which workstation I happen to be using because messages are delivered to the POP server, my individual machine.

Figure 11.7 shows the message flow for a typical site. The incoming message is received by the SMTP server, *not* the POP server, although they may be on the same machine, and one software application may include both components. But that's more a marketing or packaging issue: from a technical point of view, you need two separate components. (How the SMTP server passes the message to the POP server doesn't concern us, and isn't covered by any Internet standard – it's up to the implementers of the particular applications.)

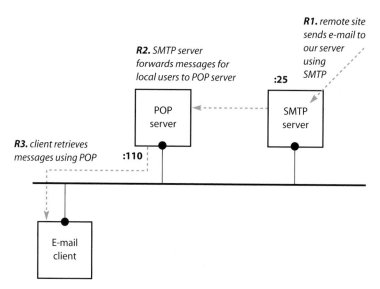

Figure 11.7 How a pop client receives a message

The POP server has three functions:

1. transfer messages, somehow, from the SMTP server (or servers) that receives the incoming e-mail for our users

2. manage the message store, inserting new messages, and extracting messages from it when users connect to this server to retrieve messages

3. handle the connections from clients and participate in the POP dialog, which we describe in the next module.

As with SMTP, the address of the POP server to use is part of the e-mail client's configuration. As the client connects to server using an IP address and the well-known POP port (:110), the POP server can be anywhere – it doesn't have to be on the local LAN. The configuration shown in Figure 11.8 is used by small sites that rely on their ISP to provide the mail servers. This is how most clients using single-user dial-up accounts collect their mail.

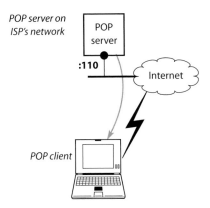

Figure 11.8 How dial-up PC's use POP

Like SMTP, POP uses TCP for its networking, and uses text commands and responses. This means we can use **telnet** as a POP client to interact with a POP server, which is what we do in the next module. We show two examples, using **telnet** from Alice to retrieve messages from our POP server on Dave. (As preparation, in advance we sent four messages to user **fred**.)

Server response lines that begin with **+OK** indicate that the last command you entered succeeded; if the command failed, the line begins with **-ERR**. For clarity, we indented the server responses and show commands in uppercase, although most servers will accept lowercase too. To save space, we've deleted a few blank lines and some of the mail headers from the received messages.

The second example gives more of a feel for how a real POP client works. It can delete messages from the server after they've been read, which is the way it's normally done. Or the client can leave them on the server, simply by not issuing the delete command. You may want this if you read your mail both with a POP client on your desktop, and with a Web mail system from outside your LAN: mail clients usually provide a configuration option like "Leave messages on server." Particularly useful in this context is the **LAST** command, which gives the number of the message that you last retrieved; clients use this to "get only new messages" when they are using the "leave messages on server" option.

That's all a mail client does really. Having a purpose-built mail client is just a convenience. It does nothing network-wise that you can't do with **telnet** (but gosh, that would be tedious!).

11.10 Lab – using telnet to retrieve messages from your POP server

```
alice% telnet dave 110
Trying 192.0.2.5... Connected to dave.
+OK Welcome to ZPOP server version 1.0 (patchlevel 51027a).
USER fred
+OK Password required for fred.
PASS XXXXX
+OK fred logged in
HELP
-ERR Unknown command: "help".
LIST
+OK 4 messages (4803 octets)
1 1193
2 1199
3 1221
4 1190
RETR 1
+OK 1193 octets
Received: from exmgate [192.0.2.29]) by dave for <fred@example.com>
From: "Mary L Lamb" <mary@mydom.com>
To: fred@example.com
Subject: Monday's jobs
Date: Sat, 07 Jul 2001 06:10:13 +0100

Feed the cat.
RETR 2
+OK 1199 octets
Received: from exmgate [192.0.2.29]) by dave for <fred@example.com>
From: "Mary L Lamb" <mary@mydom.com>
To: fred@example.com
Subject: Tuesday's jobs
Date: Sat, 07 Jul 2001 06:10:38 +0100

Buy cat food and feed the cat.
QUIT
+OK ZPOP exiting normally at Sat Jul  7 06:43:59 2001
Connection closed by foreign host.
alice%
```

connect the **telnet** client to the POP server on Dave on well-known port 110, POP. The server replies with its banner

login as user **fred** and give the password. We've shown the password as XXXXX but in real life it shows in full as clear text

POP doesn't have a **HELP** command so the server gives an error response

shown information about message in the mailbox. There are four messages, containing a total of 4803 bytes ("octets") and the size of each in bytes is given. The line containing only a period indicates end-of-list

retrieve message 1. The server confirms that this is OK, and says how long the message is in bytes. It then prints the message, and indicates end-of-message with a line containing only a period

retrieve message 2

we're finished. The server says it is exiting and the TCP connection is terminated

login as in previous example

```
alice%    telnet dave 110
Trying 192.0.2.5... Connected to dave.
+OK Welcome to ZPOP server version 1.0 (patchlevel 51027a).
USER fred
+OK Password required for fred.
PASS xxxxxx
+OK fred logged in
```

show status. The server shows the number of messages and the total size of the messages

```
STAT
+OK 4 4814
LIST
+OK 4 messages (4814 octets)
1 1193
2 1210
3 1221
4 1190
```

give the number of the last message I retrieved

```
LAST
+OK 2 is the last message seen.
```

show me the top (all the header lines) of message number 3 plus one line of the body. This is useful when a client is connecting to the POP server over a slow link. The client can check whether there are any big attachments and give the user the option of downloading the message, just by looking at the header lines

```
TOP 3 1
+OK 1221 octets
Received: from exmgate [192.0.2.29]) by dave for <fred@example.com>
From: "Mary L Lamb" <mary@mydom.com>
To: fred@example.com
Subject: Wednesday's jobs
Date: Sat, 07 Jul 2001 06:11:15 +0100

Borrow tina of tuna from Kinky Friedman.
```

Delete message number 3. When I delete a message, it's no longer included in the LISTing

```
DELE 3
+OK Message 3 has been deleted.
LIST
+OK 3 messages (3593 octets)
1 1193
2 1210
4 1190
```

however, deleted messages aren't removed until I quit. If I change my mind, I can reset the mailbox to its original state and the server shows I have the same four messages that I started with

```
RSET
+OK Maildrop has 4 messages (4814 octets)
QUIT
+OK ZPOP exiting normally at Sat Jul  7 06:44:51 2001
Connection closed by foreign host.
alice%
```

11.11 Lab – configuring your e-mail client's POP and SMTP server settings

Now that you know how things work you can configure your e-mail client. In each of the examples below we're setting the SMTP server to be **saturn** (for outgoing mail) and the POP server to be **pluto** (for incoming mail). The username is **fred**.

Netscape (version 6.2.3)

Select menu **Edit > Mail and Newsgroup Account Settings > Outgoing Server (SMTP)** (Figure 11.9(a)). Enter the name of the SMTP server; this defines the outgoing SMTP server used by all Netscape accounts on this machine. (**Use name and password** isn't required by any mail servers that we know of; you can almost always omit it.)

You now have to set up a user account. Press the **New Account** button to start the "Account Wizard". We haven't shown the Wizard step by step. Instead, Figure 11.9(b) shows how you check the information for an account once you've set it up. Select the account in the left hand pane, and click on the triangle to expand the display. Select **Server Settings** to give the dialog which lets you leave messages on the server (Module 11.9). Note: in this version of Netscape you can't change the POP server name; you have to delete the account and create it again using the new server name. (Web Appendix 37 shows the setup for other versions of Netscape.)

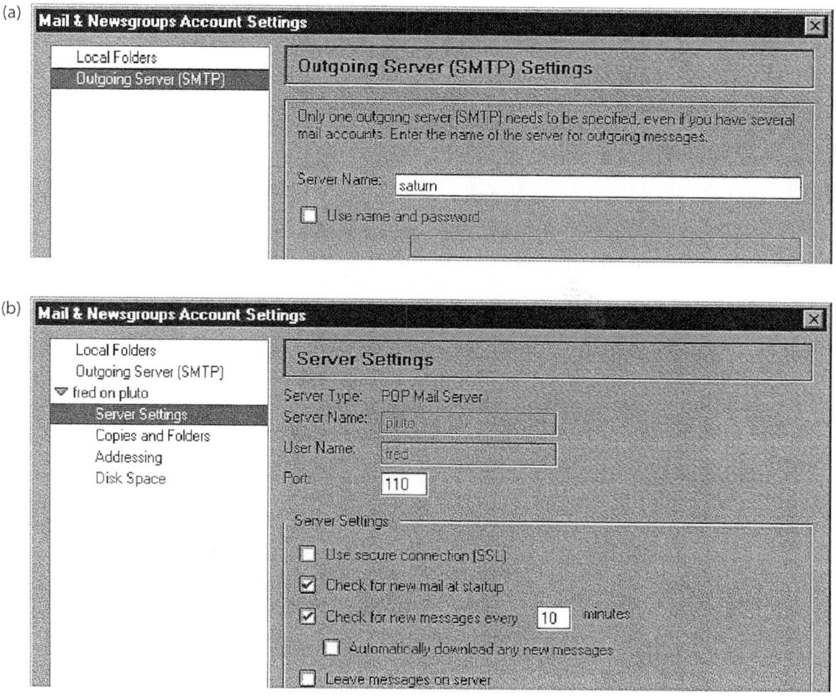

(a)
Mail & Newsgroups Account Settings

Local Folders
Outgoing Server (SMTP)

Outgoing Server (SMTP) Settings

Only one outgoing server (SMTP) needs to be specified, even if you have several mail accounts. Enter the name of the server for outgoing messages.

Server Name: saturn

☐ Use name and password

(b)
Mail & Newsgroups Account Settings

Local Folders
Outgoing Server (SMTP)
▽ fred on pluto
    Server Settings
    Copies and Folders
    Addressing
    Disk Space

Server Settings

Server Type: POP Mail Server
Server Name: pluto
User Name: fred
Port: 110

Server Settings
☐ Use secure connection (SSL)
☑ Check for new mail at startup
☑ Check for new messages every 10 minutes
    ☐ Automatically download any new messages
☐ Leave messages on server

Figure 11.9 Netscape

Outlook Express

Figure 11.10 shows Outlook Express version 5.50. Select menu **Tools** > **Accounts** > **Mail**. Enter the details for a new account using **Add**, or set details for an existing account by highlighting it and clicking on **Properties**. Enter the POP and SMTP server details in **Properties** > **Servers**. (In **Properties** > **Advanced** you can set "**Leave a copy of messages on server**" if necessary (c.f. Module 11.9).)

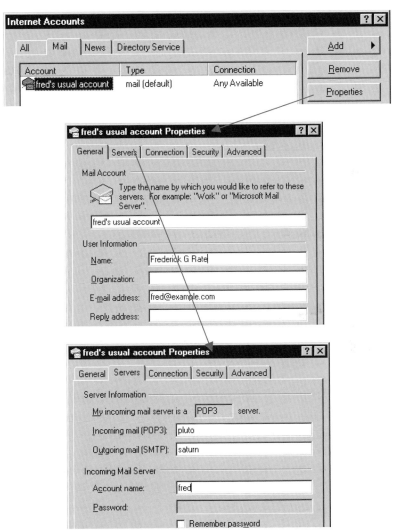

Figure 11.10 Outlook Express version 5.50

11.12 Troubleshooting (1) – you can't send to a remote site

The steps you take to troubleshoot an e-mail problem follow directly from how a message travels through the system. We've duplicated Figure 11.3 from Module 11.2 for convenience. Mail problems fall into two broad categories:

1. you (or one of your users) can't send to a user at a remote site, which we cover here

2. a user at a remote site has tried to send a message to your site but your end-user hasn't received it, which we cover in the next module.

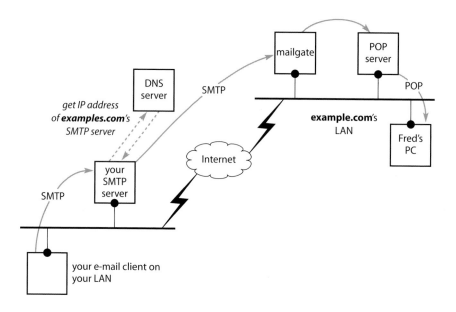

You can't send to a remote site

Let's say you can't send to **fred@example.com**. Try the following steps in turn until you find the failure point:

1. before investigating the mail system in detail, check that your Internet connection and basic network connectivity are OK

2. we're assuming you can send to other sites, and that only one specific site is causing problems. Make sure this is a valid assumption by sending a test message to a remote site

> **Tip:** we keep a Hotmail Web-based mail account specially for sending test messages to, and also a dial-up account with a different ISP from the one that provides our leased line. We can send test messages to either of these and check they have arrived.

3. if you can't send messages to any site:

- your Internet connection is down: see if you can **ping** any remote site. Or …
- your mail server isn't working properly: see if its log files say what the problem is. Check it out by sending a test message to it, as in step 6 below. Or …
- your DNS isn't working correctly. See Chapter 9

4. do an MX lookup for the remote site ("**host -t mx example.com**"). If that fails, try it again. If it fails repeatedly:
    - your DNS is misbehaving. Do an MX lookup using your ISP's server:

      ```
      host -t mx aw.com res1.yourisp.com
      ```

      If this also fails or gives no MX records, it's very likely the fault is with the destination site's DNS. If it resolves correctly, then your DNS has a problem
    - the remote site's DNS isn't set up properly (rare) or their DNS server is temporarily down (fairly common). If you're friendly with the remote site's administrator you can call them. (There's not much point trying to e-mail them, is there?)

5. if you reached here, the DNS returned at least one MX record (and IP number) for the remote site's mail server(s). Try connecting to the SMTP server with **telnet**:

   ```
   telnet serveraddress 25
   ```

   If you get no response after a reasonable wait (2 minutes, say) the remote site has a problem with their server. If the MX lookup in step 4 gave more than one MX record, try the other servers in order of MX preference value. If all fail, wait a while and try again later, or try and contact their administrator (without using e-mail)

6. send a simple test message manually with **telnet**, as described in Module 11.6, ideally to someone you know, asking them to phone you if they receive the message. Watch carefully for any error messages from the server as you type in the SMTP commands

7. logon to an external Web-based e-mail system like Hotmail or use a dial-up account, and send a simple test message, ideally to someone you know, asking them to phone you if they receive the message

8. if you reached here, the basic networking between your site and their mail server is OK, but you still can't send. In the steps above, you verified that the MX record for the remote server exists, and that you can connect to that server. The most likely cause of your problem now is that your mail client isn't configured correctly – possibly a typo entering the name or IP address of your SMTP server. Run **tcpdump** and try sending again, looking for any error messages from the client, and watching for any DNS name-resolution failures

9. check all your mail server and client logs for any error or warning messages.

Sending to a particular user failed

We find that nowadays 99% of bounce messages (notification from the destination server that it can't deliver to a particular user) are because the specified destination user doesn't exist (either we typed the name wrong, or the user has gone away so their name has been deleted from the site's server), or because a dial-up user hasn't collected their POP mail within a reasonable number of days. If the username is correct, either the remote server has a problem or it's blocking you sending to it.

11.13 Troubleshooting (2) – a remote site can't send to you

1. check your server logs. If the message wasn't received, you need to find out if you're receiving any mail at all. Your logs will tell you, but to be satisfyingly sure, logon to an external Web-based e-mail system like Hotmail, or a dial-up account, and send a short message to the end-user at your site who's having the problem, and CC: the message to yourself at your own site too

   - if you receive the Hotmail message, and especially if you are receiving mail for other sites, the problem may lie with the sender:

     - see if you can send a message to them. To avoid any complications, do it manually using **telnet** to connect to their mail server

     - ask them to send you another, short message, but before you do, run **tcpdump** to watch for any packets coming from their site. For example, if their mail server is 198.4.159.40, you could use

       ```
       tcpdump port 25 and host 198.4.159.40
       ```

       or if they have several servers use a "net" specification like

       ```
       tcpdump port 25 and net 198.4.159
       ```

       We've omitted "**-n**" because it will be easier to decipher the trace with names instead of numbers, and we've omitted "**-t**" because e-mail activity (as we saw in the mail headers in Module 11.8) can take minutes or hours, and you need to know at what time things happened.

       If you don't see any activity at all from their mail server(s), it looks even more like the problem is at their end. Ask them to send a test message to your Hotmail or other Web-mail account

   - if you don't receive the message you sent from Hotmail to your user and yourself, go to step 3 below.

2. if the logs show the message from the other site was received successfully but the user hasn't retrieved it, check your POP server – see below.

3. you're not receiving any mail. Check your SMTP server as you did in the previous module.

Checking POP message retrieval

1. make sure the user's client really is trying to retrieve messages. Run **tcpdump** to see what's happening. For example, if the user's PC is IP address 10.2.3.4, run

   ```
   tcpdump port 110 and host 10.2.3.4
   ```

2. make sure the mail client has specified the correct POP server to retrieve from. You can check this manually but will also see it in the **tcpdump** trace

3. check that other people can retrieve messages: send yourself a short test message

4. try to retrieve the message manually as we showed in Module 11.10. If you can retrieve manually, the problem probably lies in this user's client configuration, or this message

may be causing problems (e.g. some POP servers and some old clients have problems with very large messages).

Mail log files

Your mail server's log files can be very informative. For incoming messages you can confirm that the message has arrived and when. Your logs are very useful if you have to track down what happened to a message that someone says was sent to your site but has not been delivered to your end-user. Log formats and contents are particular to each type of server. Below is a representative entry, telling us the server received a message from **eagle.example.com** (IP address 192.0.2.1) at 21:51:05 on 17 June 2001, with message size 3859 byes:

```
20010617215105+0100
     :SMTP-Accept:Received
     :[192.0.2.1]
     :20010617215104.AAA21148@eagle.example.com
     :3859:1
     :<jkl@example.com>:<bex9@uit.co.uk>
```

Logs are also helpful where your users have sent messages but the intended recipient says they haven't received it. We had an irate customer who complained we had not e-mailed the promised price list. We checked our mail server log, saw the entry for the message addressed to them, and were able to tell them when the message had been sent. We could see that the message went to their ISP's mail server and not to their own; running "**host -t mx** *domain-name*" showed us they don't run their own server at all. It transpired that their ISP wasn't very good and the ISP's server was up and down like a yo-yo.

Below is a log entry that is typical of an organization that doesn't run their own mail server but relies on their ISP's servers instead:

```
20010610193744+0100
     :SMTP-Deliver
     :20010610183628.AAA26903@mars-1
     :Delivered
     :435406
     :punt-2.mail.demon.net
     :<bex9@uit.co.uk>
     :<info@blueprint.co.uk>
```

"**demon.net**" is a fairly commonly chosen ISP for dial-up connections. It's possible that this site, **example.co.uk**, has a leased-line connection and has chosen either not to run an internal mail server, or not to have mail delivered to it direcly from the Internet but only via their ISP (Module 25.4). However, on balance the likelihood is that they have a dial-up connection.

11.14 Security problems with e-mail: spoofing, spamming, relaying

SMTP's very simplicity can cause irritations and security problems. Module 11.7 showed that the sender explicitly enters their "from address" in both the envelope and the mail message headers. The protocol doesn't impose any checking on these fields, making it easy to forge a message to look like it came from someone else, or to create a message that gives as little information as possible about its sender. Bad people do this for their own nefarious purposes. It is difficult at the TCP/IP level to get over this problem because a message can legitimately be delivered from a server that isn't the sender's (e.g. the ISP's smart host that you send all your outgoing mail to, or a relay host that receives incoming messages for you). Therefore the receiving server can't just check that the IP address of the incoming TCP connection matches the sender of the message.

Forged ("spoofed") messages

```
From: george-dubya@whitehouse.gov
to: gullible@example.com
date: 10-Jul-2001
subject: come to dinner

We would like you and your cat to come to
dinner next Monday.  We'll send Airforce One
over to collect you.
```

A message as you read it in a standard e-mail client (above) gives you no information to show that it isn't what it pretends to be. However, if you look at the message headers (Module 11.8) you can see where the message really came from. If the originating machine as shown in the **Received: from** headers doesn't match the body of the message, it probably is a forgery:

```
Received: (from root@localhost) by dave
From: george-dubya@whitehouse.gov
Received: from www.whitehouse.gov (alice [192.0.2.17]) by dave
Message-Id: <200107101133.MAA12356@dave>
to: gullible@example.com
date: 10-Jul-2001
subject: come to dinner

We would like you and your cat to come to
dinner next Monday.  We'll send Airforce One
over to collect you.
```

The IP address shows this message didn't originate from where it says. No special dinner for the cat on Monday

Junk mailing houses often insert false headers in their messages to make them look like they might have come from someone you might just know, to fool you into reading them.

Spam and UCE (unsolicited commercial e-mail)

Spam is junk e-mail. There's a lot of it, because it's so cheap to send. (Junk mailing houses sell CD-ROMs with 150 million e-mail addresses for about US$100.)

Spam messages sent without forgery to users on your network are valid e-mail messages. Nothing at the protocol level can detect them because there's nothing wrong with them. There are two common ways to detect and reject them:

1. scan the content of the message for words and phrases that typically occur in spam, e.g. "get rich quick," "earn *N* dollars in just a few hours," "this is not a get rich quick scheme," "amazing beautiful girls," etc. There are many add-on packages to perform this checking

2. compare the sender's address against a database of known spammers (Module 25.4).

These checks can be performed in the mail client on the desktop or your site's SMTP server. Doing it in the server has two advantages: first, you only have to install and configure the software in one place instead of on every desktop, and second, the server can perform the check as the message is being received and reject the TCP connection before the message even comes into your site. See the Notes section for further information on anti-spam techniques and packages.

"Open relays"

Sending e-mail to millions of machines ties up an Internet connection for a long time and uses a lot of bandwidth. So spammers often try to *relay* messages using someone else's server. SMTP lets you send a single message body to multiple recipients for a message in a single SMTP transaction by entering multiple **RCPT TO:** lines (Module 11.6). The spammer might send, for example, 700 messages to your server, with 900 remote recipients specified for each; 700 messages isn't a lot for the spammer to handle, and this only involves one MX lookup (to get your mail server address.) On the other hand, your server now has to send messages to 700 × 900 = 630,000 different recipients, and it has to do all the DNS lookups for all those different sites, and handle errors and retries:

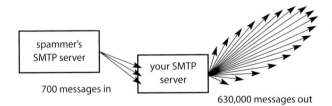

An SMTP server that allows messages to be relayed like this is called an open relay. Most SMTP servers can be configured easily to prevent it. Open relays are Bad Things: sites used as open relays spend so much time processing the spam messages that their own valid users' mail takes much longer than usual and other applications (e.g. Web servers) become so slow as to be useless. They are also Bad Things for everyone who gets spammed, so we recommend you block open relaying, and allow outgoing messages to be sent only from users inside your LAN.

Summary

- a typical e-mail client on a LAN PC uses SMTP to send e-mail messages and POP3 to receive them. SMTP and POP both run over TCP as transport
- using SMTP, your client sends the message to your e-mail server (or your ISPs) for delivery to the ultimate destination
- your server determines the IP address of the server for the final destination by looking up MX (mail exchange) records in the DNS
- a site (domain) can have multiple MX records for resilience and load sharing
- an SMTP session consists of an exchange of plain-text lines over a TCP connection, and consequently ....
- you can use **telnet** as a test and debugging tool to sending and receiving messages "manually"
- there are two parts to an SMTP session:
  - the envelope. This is the level at which SMTP servers converse and the destination address in the envelope determines which machine will receive the message
  - the body. This contains the **From:**, **To:**, **Subject:**, etc. headers that you see when you read the message in your e-mail client
- a POP session also consists of an exchange of plain-text lines over a TCP connection between your e-mail client and a POP server
- when troubleshooting, **tcpdump** can show you the DNS queries and other traffic that sending/receiving a message involves
- using **telnet** as a test client bypasses a lot of the complexity and possible configuration errors in a normal e-mail client
- open relay e-mail servers are often a source of spam.

What's next?

Chapter 12 looks at MIME, which allows you to send arbitrary data conveniently over e-mail using attachments. We also look briefly at IMAP and other mail systems.

Notes and further reading

The scenarios we described are what is typical nowadays. In the past, at sites with networks of UNIX machines, it was common for every desktop machine to:

- send its own messages using SMTP
- receive messages from other internal workstations, and from the outside world, using SMTP.

This involved running a full mail server, and often a DNS server, on every machine on the network, and each one had to have its own MX record(s) listed in the public DNS. It was dreadful: SMTP traffic had to be allowed in from the Internet to each machine, potentially causing security holes, you had to maintain dozens or hundreds of copies of the mail server, and if there was a problem you had to debug the e-mail and network configuration on the specific machine. Running a centralized mail server or two on high-performance machines with good redundancy (e.g. RAIDed disks), a good backup system, and plenty of disk space for mail messages in transit is very much easier and more reliable.

(You still can have separate MX records for an individual host if you want, e.g. for **pc29.sales.example.com**, but we haven't dealt with that because almost nobody uses that type of configuration nowadays. We have described today's common practice for MX configurations.)

MX records were introduced in:

❏ **RFC-973 January 1986** *Domain System Changes and Observations*

MX record priorities let you modify your mail system without any downtime. See Web Appendix 8.

In Module 11.4 we said that if you have an intermittent connection to the Internet, including your own (intermittently available) mail servers in your MX list causes wasted effort on the part of servers trying to send to you. There is now an Internet Draft RFC saying that you should not do this:

❏ **http://www.ietf.org/internet-drafts/draft-ietf-dnsop-dontpublish-unreachable-03.txt**
   IP Addresses that should never appear in the public DNS

Terminology

The SMTP server is sometimes called a *Message Transfer Agent* (*MTA*) and the client a *Message User Agent* (*MUA*) to emphasize that they perform very different functions. An MTA doesn't include POP functionality. The POP server is sometimes called a *mailbox server* or *message store*. When discussing how the components interact on large e-mail networks, these terms let you specify clearly which aspect of a "mail server" you are referring to. For example, the **sendmail** and **Exim** mail servers are MTAs; if you're using one of these you need another server application to provide POP services. (Instead of using POP to retrieve messages, some sites use IMAP, which is a newer and more flexible protocol; see Module 12.5.)

For a glossary, see the Internet Mail Consortium site:

❏ **http://www.imc.org/terms.html** *Terms Used In Internet Mail*

SMTP and ESMTP

SMTP and the message format were defined in:

❏ **RFC-821 August 1982** *Simple Mail Transfer Protocol*

❏ **RFC-822 August 1982** *Standard for the Format of ARPA Internet Text Messages*

These have been superseded by:

❏ **RFC-2821 April 2001** *Simple Mail Transfer Protocol*

❏ **RFC-2822 April 2001** *Internet Message Format*

"ESMTP" is "extended SMTP," which defines the EHLO command – see:

❏ **RFC-1869 November 1995** *SMTP Service Extensions*

RFC-821 defined the TURN command. The ETRN command was introduced in:

❏ **RFC-1985 August 1996** *SMTP Service Extension for Remote Message Queue Starting*

In Module 11.6 we explained the **MAIL FROM:** command. When a mail server sends a "bounce message" to say it cannot deliver a message, it uses

```
MAIL FROM:<>
```

i.e. a null sending domain name. Occasionally you will find mail servers that incorrectly won't accept such a message, because of bugs or mis-configuration.

POP3 and mail clients

The original and current standards for POP3 are, respectively:

❏ **RFC-1081 November 1988** *Post Office Protocol – Version 3*

❏ **RFC-1939 May 1996** *Post Office Protocol – Version 3*

Linux and most if not all UNIX systems have a command-line e-mail client (or several) that you can use in scripts. These are useful for sending alerts to the system administrator. We use it within a security system that detects whether any files have been changed without authorization (and also in a script which retrieves the lottery results from a Web page and e-mails them to us). These clients can also read mail messages but they don't use POP: they just extract the messages directly from the message store on this machine.

Spam and security

The **sendmail** mail server has historically been a great source of security problems. (Lots of other mail servers have security holes too, probably because they are such large and complex programs.) Module 24.6 and Chapter 25 explain how you can protect your mail server by hiding it behind your firewall, and interposing a small designed-for-security proxy mail server to send/receive messages on the Internet. Chapter 25 also explains how you can counter e-mail virus threats and block spam automatically.

One dial-up ISP (let's call them **some-isp.com**) in the UK does strange things with mail traffic. When you try to connect to any mail server, e.g. with "**telnet mailserv.example.com smtp**," the ISP hijacks the connection and connects you to their own mail server, at **some-isp.com**, instead. We assume this is so they can control people sending spam, but it can be confusing when you are troubleshooting if you haven't seen it before.

For pointers on how to combat spam, see:

❏ **http://spam.abuse.net**

❏ **http://mail-abuse.org** MAPS, the Mail Abuse Prevention System

Appendices

Web Appendix 8: future-proofing your DNS
Web Appendix 37: configuring e-mail settings on different Netscape versions

12 E-mail – MIME, IMAP; other mail systems

Introduction

This chapter explains MIME – the mechanism Internet e-mail uses to include files and arbitrary content in e-mail messages as "attachments." We also look briefly at the IMAP system, which can give you distributed, network-wide access to your e-mail messages stored centrally, and at other e-mail systems.

12.1 Sending and receiving non-text messages

RFC-2821 and the SMTP conversation impose restrictions on the format of messages that can be transmitted through e-mail systems. Several issues have to be addressed:

- how do you send files that have longer lines than the 1000-character maximum specified in RFC-2821? Even simple word-processing documents like Microsoft Notepad files use a new line only to separate paragraphs, so long paragraphs can easily exceed the maximum line length. Binary or non-text files such as GIF images or spreadsheets or data files may not contain any new lines at all

- how do you send a file that may contain some of the special sequences that occurs in the SMTP conversation, e.g. a line containing only a dot?

- how do you send files that contain non-ASCII characters?

To explain how modern mail systems handle these issues, automatically, we'll show how end-users used to handle them manually in the old days, before mail systems were extended to take account of them.

The way to send completely general data, without restriction, is to perform a simple transformation on it so that:

- lines are less than about 75 characters long (because some old mail systems garbled lines longer than 80 characters, the old punched card length!)

- lines contain only printable ASCII characters – no control characters or other funnies that could be misinterpreted

- lines don't contain a dot on its own.

The output data can be transmitted safely through any mail system – it won't be inadvertently modified or cause any problems. When it arrives at the other end, it's passed through a reverse transformation to recreate an identical copy of the original data.

In the old days, the UNIX program **uuencode** was used to transform the input. The companion program **uudecode** was used to extract the original content at the far end. (The "uu" in the program names came from "UUCP" because the programs were used widely on the UUCP network (Web Appendix 14.) For example, to **uuencode** the file **300b** (which contains 300 bytes of binary data) we use the command:

```
uuencode < 300b yourcopy.dat > tempfile.dat
```

The resulting transformed file is shown below. You include this text in your mail message, perhaps by cutting and pasting with some type of editor, and then send the message. When I receive this message, I extract the encoded part of the message (from the **begin** line to the **end** line) and run it through **uudecode**. This creates the file **yourcopy.dat**, whose content is identical to the original file **300b**.

This system allows you to send any data safely, but it's cumbersome for both sender and recipient: it requires too much manual intervention.

```
begin 644 yourcopy.dat
M(,L2J2-@_6,$S+R6U(!5(Y)78@L51`"]7>&9>2GYYL8*QGGJ&"&H@TQ%1FB%!F
M:8HA;8ADBE\(T`A30P4-S[R2U!Q--+6&!@;8U#KF#%&%DODHJJ%JP[6US,@&&%VI
M";I2$ST#[["X`.0"+4FP.,,+*N%(0])A"5`%!+'`PG4````""`"]8L(B[SQ<2+\.
M````(````$````&1I<VLQ%3>3"Y%6&%7MZ7M[MM17L4LE[BOF
M(%\\H.#$R, *>[R-CL+;#&F;;[&E#L\J!D!!e[!K "@*0KC3;bK+H@M74S7;
M*75WFWH()5F>RFYYCU@%@2) <-9CL;'MMLPB.1(TVS, (NI0W3W._=*???B1DVL[L
M?'YTI1W/UG?\/['N<[W_G_.0U?K'E7%''"H\9%Dec#"H"@`'
`
end
```

To overcome this problem, *MIME* (*Multipurpose Internet Mail Extensions*) were developed. The first RFC standard for MIME was RFC-1345, in June 1992.

The MIME standard specifies how a mail message can be formatted so that "special" pieces of it can be recognized automatically by mail client programs; these special pieces are called *attachments*. MIME also allows the sender to give extra information about the type of data the special pieces contain, so they can be automatically extracted or processed by the mail client, saving the end-user a lot of tedious manual work.

We look at an example of a MIME-encoded mail message in the next module.

12.2 E-mail attachments and MIME

Figure 12.1 shows the full content of a small MIME-encoded mail message:

- it says which pieces of the message are encoded and where these pieces start and end
- it shows how they are encoded
- and it includes some optional extra information, e.g. on the second attachment it gives the name of the file this attachment was created from ("**300b**") so the recipient's mail client can extract the data to a file of the same name.

MIME therefore goes beyond the simple aim of allowing any data whatever to be sent safely. In addition it specifies the *type* of data that are being sent, so the receiving client can process the data suitably. (In the next chapter we'll see how HTTP also uses MIME to give information about Web pages and other data downloaded from a Web server.)

You can see clearly in Figure 12.1 how everything consists of plain text, and the parts are obviously separated. Note that the end of the attachments is terminated by the same boundary delimiter as between the attachments, but with two extra hyphens added at the end.

The data in the second (binary) attachment have been transformed into a safely transmittable format using *base64 encoding*. This is conceptually very similar to using **uuencode** – in the transformed output lines are no longer than 76 characters, and all characters are printable ASCII, so there can be no control or other awkward characters. For details see Appendix 13.

From this example you can see that there are three MIME-specific headers that can be used to describe an attachment:

1. **Content-Type:** specifies the nature of the data in the attachment – text, or audio information, or binary data, etc. It can also indicate which application was used to create the data, e.g. a spreadsheet might have been created by Microsoft Excel, so the recipient of the attachment can use the correct application to handle the data received

2. **Content-Transfer-Encoding:** if encoding was necessary to allow the data in this attachment to be transported ("transferred") safely through the mail network, this header specifies how the data have been encoded

3. **Content-Description:** this gives descriptive information about what's in the attachment (for the benefit of the human user rather than to allow the mail client to process the data automatically).

There is a fourth header, **Content-Disposition**, which is used to give the mail client more information about how to display the various attachments, in particular whether they should be viewed inline as part of the mail message, or whether they ought to be considered as separate files. We cover this briefly in Module 12.4.

We look at each of these headers in detail in the following modules.

usual mail headers —————

this message uses MIME

*the separator between
the various MIME
attachments is the string
"PART-BOUNDARY=.310
....dennis"*

start of first attachment

*first attachment is ASCII,
plain text*

*end of first attachment,
start of second*

*second attachment is ——————
binary data*

*this attachment was
created from the
file "300b"*

*data are encoded
in "base64"*

*end of second attachment
(and of message)*

```
Received: from dennis (dennis.uit.co.uk [212.140.133.21]) by dave
From: trudo <trudo@uit.co.uk>
Date: Wed, 11 Jul 2001 10:27:57 +0100
To: bex11@uit.co.uk
Subject: example of binary attachment
Mime-Version: 1.0
Content-Type: multipart/mixed;
        boundary="PART-BOUNDARY=.31010711102758.ZM5527.dennis"

--
--PART-BOUNDARY=.31010711102758.ZM5527.dennis
Content-Type: text/plain; charset=us-ascii

Hi Bex,

Here's a small test file containing 300 bytes.

        Enjoy!

        Trudo von Snit

--PART-BOUNDARY=.31010711102758.ZM5527.dennis
Content-Description: Data
Content-Type: application/octet-stream ; name="300b"
Content-Transfer-Encoding: base64

IMsSqNq/WMEzLyW1IBVI5JXYgsVRAC9XeGZeSn55sYKxnqGCGogOxFRmiFBmaYohbYhk
il8IOAhTQwUNz7yS1BxNNLWGBgbY1DrmFGQkoqs1wq7W1zMgGF2pCbpSEzOD7C4AOQCL
UmwOMMKuFIv9JhCVAFBLAwQUAAAACAA9YsIi7zxcSL8OAAAAIAAAEAAAAGRpc2sxL19J
UORFTC5FWEXtWXtwU9eZ/46udGXLttC6Rs2mIF8oODyMKyNjoDbmYSxiaoxsBRsCWDG2
QAIjuVdXNukkYEYZJ5qLqZtXUzXbKXV3m3oIJVmaym5jjO1gSJcNZjsbHttswiORIOqz
MIupQ3T3O/dKfiRk2s7sH5OpR3P1nfP7Huc73/nOQ1frHllFCACo8ZEkgDAoCg==
--PART-BOUNDARY=.31010711102758.ZM5527.dennis--
```

Figure 12.1 Full content of a MIME-encoded mail message

12.3 MIME headers (1) – Content-Type

Three header fields in a MIME message or attachment specify the type of data that are included, how they can be extracted, and what they relate to.

The **Content-Type** header specifies the type of content (data) in the attachment – that it's text, or audio, or binary data, etc. Optionally, it can also indicate which application was used to create the data, e.g. a spreadsheet created by Microsoft Excel. This header can be used by the recipient's mail client to process the attachment automatically. For example, when you "open" the attachment, your client extracts the attachment and saves it to file, and then runs the correct program to open the file. This header is also informative to the human user – you can see what type of data are in the attachment and decide whether you want to open it or not.

The header consists of three parts

top-level-media type / subtype optional-parameters

with the first two separated by a slash, optionally followed by a set of parameters to give some extra information. The *top-level media type* specifies the general type of data, while the subtype specifies a specific format for that type of data. For example, "**image/gif**" tells the client program that the data are an image, and specifically that the image file is in GIF format. We explain the most common subtypes below; see the Notes for further information.

There are seven different top-level media types. The first five types specify the type of content directly:

1. **text** – textual information.

   No special software should be needed to be able to read this type of content.

   Subtypes: **/plain** = no formatting at all, no special characters

   /enriched = rich text

   /richtext = older variant of rich text – almost obsolete

   /html = Web page content

   For example, an attachment containing a Web page might have

   Content-type: text/html

2. **image** – some form of pictorial image

3. **audio** – some form of audio data

4. **video** – some form of video data

5. **application** – some other kind of data that does not fit in any of the other categories, often binary data, and particularly information to be processed by some type of application program. Subtypes are:

   /octet-stream indicates that the body contains arbitrary binary data. The recommended action for the mail client when it receives this is to offer to extract the data in the attachment and save them to a file.

   /x-*name* is an "experimental" subtype, often used when the mail client that created the attachment didn't know the correct subtype to use. You will often see this in messages from old mail clients.

/**vnd.** *name* is a vendor-specific subtype, indicating that the commercial product name should be used to process this. For example, **application/vnd.ms-excel** is how a Microsoft Excel spreadsheet is attached. (Microsoft Word documents are **application/msword** without the "**vnd.**" because this subtype was registered as a standard before the **vnd** convention existed.)

There are two further "composite" top-level media types. These are container-type items that require further processing by MIME itself to extract the sub-attachments from the container. Each sub-attachment is specified in the usual way, with its own MIME headers. These headers are most often used in the headers for the overall message, which is how MIME says there are attachments within.

6. **multipart** – data consisting of multiple entities. Subtypes are:

 /**alternative:** each of the body parts is an "alternative" version of the same information. This is used widely to send the same e-mail message in both HTML and plain text.

 /**mixed** – the body parts are independent and their order is significant. We saw an example of this in Module 12.2, to indicate that the message contained a text part and a binary part.

 /**digest** the body parts are a series of mail messages

7. **message** – a mail message within a mail message. Subtypes are:

 /**rfc822** – a full mail message included as an attachment

 /**partial** – one fragment of a larger message (which the mail client is expected to reassemble when all the fragments have been received).

You can have nested structures – attachments within attachments – using the composite content types (Appendix 14).

Optional parameters

The optional parameters give further information about this attachment and are specified as *name=value*. For example,

 charset=us-ascii specifies the character set as ASCII, which is the default, and may be omitted.

If the character set is anything else, it must be specified explicitly as a parameter in the Content-Type field, e.g.

 Content-Type: text/plain; charset=ISO-8859-1

 Content-type: text/plain; charset=Windows-1252

Other common parameters you will see frequently are "**boundary=**", which specifies the string separating the parts of the body, e.g.

 Content-Type: multipart/mixed; boundary="—— main boundary ——"

and "**name=**", giving the filename that an attachment originated from:

 Content-Type: application/msword; name="proposal.doc"

The **name** parameter is also used with the **Content-Disposition** header (Module 12.5).

12.4 MIME headers (2) – Content-Transfer-Encoding, etc.

The Content-Transfer-Encoding header

This specifies how the content was encoded to allow it to be transferred safely across the mail system and overcome the "only ASCII characters, lines less than 1000 characters long" restrictions. Encoding is the process of transforming the content into a safe format. In Module 12.1 we saw that the **uuencode** program was used for this in the old days, but MIME now specifies other standard encoding systems instead.

This header need not be present if the message didn't have to be specially encoded, e.g. if it was just plain text.

The common values are:

base64 the input data have been encoded using the **base64** encoding scheme. This can safely transfer any type of data whatever. Typically when you see **base64**, you can consider that the attachment contains binary, non-text information. (You don't need to know how **base64** encoding and decoding is carried out but we've explained it in Appendix 13 just for interest's sake.)

quoted-printable the input is mostly 7-bit printable characters. Any other character (e.g. control characters or 8-bit ones) is shown as a three-character sequence consisting of an equals sign followed by the two-digit hexadecimal value of the original byte. For example, a space (ASCII decimal 32 or hex 20) is output as "**=20**", often seen at the end of lines, and a UK currency symbol "£" (ASCII decimal 243, hex A3) is shown as "**=A3**" and an equals sign itself is "**=3D**". See inside back cover for a conversion table. (This explains why you often see **=20** if you view an e-mail message with a non-email-aware text editor.)

Other values are:

7bit: the data consist of characters with decimal values in the range 1–127, and all lines are less than 1000 characters long, so the data can be transmitted safely without any special processing. If no Content-Transfer-Encoding header is specified, **7bit** is assumed

8bit: all lines are less than 1000 characters long, but characters outside the 1–127 range are included

binary: any sequence of bytes at all.

7bit, **8bit**, and **binary** all mean that the data have *not* been encoded for transmission; they merely tell you what type of bytes the data consists of. Sending 8-bit data un-encoded is risky – it could easily get corrupted by a mail server or client along the way.

The Content-Description header

This header is completely optional. It gives purely descriptive information about the data. You often see something like

Content-Description: Card for Trudo von Snit

in an attachment giving somebody's name and contact details.

The Content-Disposition header

This fourth header type gives the mail client more information about how to display the various attachments, in particular whether they should be viewed inline as part of the mail message, or whether they ought to be considered as separate files. Admissible values are:

Content-Disposition: inline

Content-Disposition: attachment

With the **attachment** type, there is often an optional parameter specifying the filename that the attachment should be saved to by default, e.g.

Content-Disposition: attachment; filename="costs.xls"

How the different headers are used together

If the message contains any attachments at all, the headers for the overall message will contain a header like:

Content-Type: multipart/mixed; boundary=*"separating-string"*

Then each individual attachment, delimited by *separating-string* , will have its own **Content-Type** header saying what's in this attachment, and optionally **Content-Transfer-Encoding** and other headers if they are required.

Note that if the message contains what you think of as only a single binary attachment, this still applies. Your message actually consists of two attachments: a plain text attachment, and the binary attachment. The text part could be empty, but more usually it contains what you think of as the basic content of the message, e.g. "Hi Fred, here's the spreadsheet we were talking about." The example back in Module 12.2 illustrates this.

A good way to explore MIME is to send yourself messages with different mixes of attachments and types, and see what the headers contain and how the message is built up. See Web Appendix 15 for more information.

12.5 IMAP – the Internet Message Access Protocol

A big disadvantage of POP is that your POP mail client removes your messages from the POP server and stores them on the hard disk on your local PC instead, where it can read them, print them, etc. But if you then sit at a different PC in the office, or use Web-mail from home, the files on your original PC are not accessible. You can partly overcome this problem by storing the retrieved files on a shared disk on a central server instead of on your own hard disk, but it still doesn't allow you to access all your messages from outside, or from a remote office of your organization, and if you use different clients on different machines (say, Outlook Express on Windows, Netscape on Linux) they may not be able to read each other's files.

IMAP, the *Internet Message Access Protocol*, overcomes these and other problems. With IMAP, the storage, viewing, and searching of e-mail messages is provided as a client/server service over the network:

- messages are stored permanently on the IMAP server. They *never* live on the client
- to view a message, a *copy* of the content is transferred to your mail client, but the message itself remains on the server. (The client "displays pictures of the message" rather than holding the message itself.)
- because messages remain on the server, they can be accessed from any client that can connect to the server. If your network is set up appropriately, you can access your messages from any desktop machine on the local LAN, or from any remote office, or using Web-mail from the Internet, or even using your normal IMAP client on your laptop from a hotel room. (Of course, this does raise some security issues.)
- message searches can be run on the server itself, instead of having to transfer all the contents over the network to the client, for the client to search, keeping network traffic to a minimum
- clients can retrieve just specific parts of a message instead of it all, e.g. when you're dialing up from a hotel room, you can request just the headers, and then decide whether you want to view the messages in full
- the client can get a list of a message's attachments and their sizes, e.g. if someone sends you a large spreadsheet as an attachment, with some comments in a cover note, you can read the cover note without downloading the spreadsheet – a very useful facility for remote users
- e-mail is mission critical for many organizations. By keeping users' mailboxes on a central IMAP server rather than on desktop or laptop PCs, the mailboxes are more likely to be backed up regularly and properly.

Like POP, IMAP is used only for retrieving mail; IMAP mail clients still use SMTP to send messages. (Many clients – Netscape, Outlook, Eudora amongst others – now give you the choice of using POP or IMAP.)

The IMAP well-known server port is 143.

Below is a sample IMAP session, using **telnet** as the client, to the IMAP well-known port on server Bob. As with POP and SMTP examples, we have indented the server's responses for clarity. An annotated version of this session is included as Appendix 15.

```
alice# telnet bob imap
Trying 212.140.133.63..
Connected to localhost.
Escape character is '^]'.
        * OK localhost IMAP4rev1 v12.264 server ready
a1 login bex15 xxx
        a1 OK LOGIN completed
a2 SELECT /htiw/imap/mbox
        * 3 EXISTS
        * 0 RECENT
        * OK [UIDVALIDITY 995036481] UID validity status
        * OK [UIDNEXT 4] Predicted next UID
        * FLAGS (\Answered \Flagged \Deleted \Draft \Seen)
        * OK [PERMANENTFLAGS (\* \Answered \Flagged \Deleted \Draft \Seen)] Permanent flags
        a2 OK [READ-WRITE] SELECT completed
a3 SEARCH SUBJECT "elephants" FROM "snit"
        * SEARCH 2 3
        a3 OK SEARCH completed
a4 FETCH 2,3 (BODY[HEADER.FIELDS (DATE FROM TO SUBJECT)])
        * 2 FETCH (BODY[HEADER.FIELDS ("DATE" "FROM" "TO" "SUBJECT")] {142}
        From: "Trudo von Snit" trudo@von-snit.com
        Date: Fri, 13 Jul 2001 15:51:46 +0100
        To: bex15@uit.co.uk
        Subject: Mice are desktop elephants


        )
        * 3 FETCH (BODY[HEADER.FIELDS ("DATE" "FROM" "TO" "SUBJECT")] {167}
        From: "Trudo von Snit" trudo@von-snit.com
        Date: Fri, 13 Jul 2001 15:52:31 +0100
        To: bex15@uit.co.uk
        Subject: Assembler programmers hunt elephants on their knees


        )
        a4 OK FETCH completed
a5 FETCH 1 (BODYSTRUCTURE)
        * 1 FETCH
                (BODYSTRUCTURE
                        (
                                ("TEXT" "PLAIN" ("CHARSET" "us-ascii") NIL NIL "7BIT" 67 1 NIL NIL NIL)
                                ("IMAGE" "GIF" ("NAME" "dir.gif") NIL NIL "BASE64" 188 NIL NIL NIL)
                        "MIXED" ("BOUNDARY" "PART-BOUNDARY=.21010713154504.ZM5863.dennis") NIL NIL
                        )
                )
        a5 OK FETCH completed
a6 FETCH 1 (BODY[1])
        * 1 FETCH (BODY[1] {67}
        This message has one line of text and a small GIF image attached.
        )
        a6 OK FETCH completed
a7 LOGOUT
        * BYE bob.uit.co.uk IMAP4rev1 server terminating connection
        a7 OK LOGOUT completed
Connection closed by foreign host.
alice#
```

12.6 Other mail systems

Proprietary mail systems such as Microsoft Exchange and Lotus Notes or Domino use their own specific protocols to communicate between their server and clients. However, to enable them to send and receive mail from other Internet sites, they use the Internet standard protocols. They will often in addition support:

- POP and/or IMAP for message retrieval so that other, non-proprietary or other-vendor clients can still use the servers. (POP and IMAP clients send using SMTP, which is supported automatically if the server can receive from external servers using SMTP.)

- a Web interface so that people externally can use the e-mail system with just a Web browser, allowing them to access their mail from, for example, an Internet café. (Some sites we know have made a policy decision to use Web access as their sole e-mail "client," even on the internal LAN, for consistency and ease of use.)

As an example, Figure 12.2 shows a Microsoft Exchange server with many of the options it supports. To standard Internet e-mail clients (POP, IMAP, SMTP) it appears as a normal Internet server using the Internet protocols, and therefore everything we discussed so far about e-mail applies.

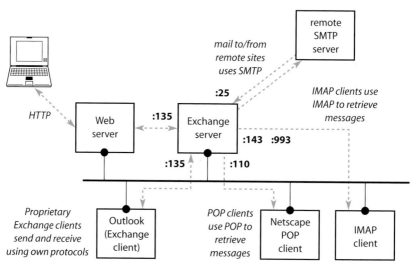

Figure 12.2 The Microsoft Exchange server uses many different ports and protocols

However, once Exchange starts communicating with its own proprietary clients, things change:

- initial connections use port 135, but then the server allocates two random ephemeral ports for further communications

- to provide e-mail access via a Web client, a special application is loaded on a Web server, and this communicates with the Exchange server in the same way – initially using port 135, and then using two ports allocated by the Exchange server.

Other components these systems can include are:

- LDAP support, for looking up or publishing lists of e-mail and user addresses (see Module 17.7)
- DNS lookups, for sending to remote Internet SMTP servers.

And of course they also include a lot of functionality unrelated to e-mail. For example, Exchange includes a scheduling sub-system, and the Lotus systems include a large database component.

Web-based e-mail systems

As we mentioned above, it can be very convenient to gives users access to their e-mail via a Web browser, for use when they are on the road, or even when on the local LAN. Figure 12.2 shows that Microsoft Exchange offers this as an option, via a separate Web server. Other e-mail systems provide it directly as part of the mail application, without having to use a separate application (although that's of relevance only to the system manager – the end-user doesn't see any difference).

X.400

X.400 is the OSI e-mail system, based on the OSI network protocols rather than TCP/IP. It was adopted by a significant number of very large companies. There are still some residual X.400 networks but Internet e-mail has almost completely supplanted it.

Summary

- the e-mail RFC standards impose restrictions on what can be sent safely using Internet e-mail. Binary files and files containing special characters have to be encoded to be sent safely

- MIME automates the process of sending arbitrary data in e-mail messages by encoding it appropriately and including the encoded data as attachments

- attachments are included in the body of the SMTP data

- attachments are recognized by e-mail clients using attachment headers that are included at the beginning of each attachment in the message

- the attachment headers specify how the data have been encoded (and therefore how to decode them) and can also specify what application is best used to display or process the attachment

- IMAP is a true client/server system for managing e-mail messages

- messages are always stored on the IMAP server, never on the client. The client merely displays information that the server sends to it. IMAP lets you selectively display only parts of messages, e.g. just the headers, or the whole message but without any attachments

- other e-mail systems may use proprietary protocols for their own special purposes, but they use SMTP for sending and receiving messages from other Internet mail servers, just like everyone else.

What's next?

In Chapter 14 we look at the World Wide Web and its HTTP – the other killer app for the Internet. But before we do that, in the next chapter we look at another packet sniffing tool, the **ethereal** protocol analyzer, which we will find useful when looking at Web traffic.

Notes and further reading

MIME

The precursor to MIME was:

❑ **RFC-934 January 1985** *Proposed standard for message encapsulation*

and some of the MIME content-type concepts were introduced in:

❑ **RFC-1049 March 1988** *A Content-Type Header Field for Internet Messages*

The first MIME RFC standard was:

❑ **RFC-1341 June 1992** *MIME (Multipurpose Internet Mail Extensions)*

The current MIME standards are:

❑ **RFC-2045 November 1996** *(MIME) Part One: Format of Internet Message Bodies*

❏ **RFC-2046 November 1996** *(MIME) Part Two: Media Types*

❏ **RFC-2047 November 1996** *(MIME) Part Three: Message Header Extensions for Non-ASCII Text*

❏ **RFC-2048 November 1996** *(MIME) Part Four: Registration Procedures*

❏ **RFC-2049 November 1996** *(MIME) Part Five: Conformance Criteria and Examples*

❏ **RFC-2183 August 1997** *Communicating Presentation Information in Internet Messages: The Content-Disposition Header Field*

The Internet Assigned Numbers Authority (IANA) acts as a central registry for defined MIME keywords. For a list of types and subtypes, see:

❏ **http://www.isi.edu/in-notes/iana/assignments/media-types/media-types**

The fact that it was possible to introduce MIME without breaking all non-MIME systems at the time is a good example of the old principle "Be conservative in what you send and liberal in what you receive." Just by ignoring the MIME-specific headers, old non-MIME mailers were able to receive MIME messages; they weren't able to display or extract the contents, but often the user could do this manually, if it was important enough. If instead the mail systems were "conservative in what they received," they would have rejected MIME messages on the grounds that they couldn't understand the headers. That would have been a Bad Thing.

IMAP

The early RFCs contain good discussions of the motivation for IMAP and are better introductions than later standards:

❏ **RFC-1176 August 1990** *Interactive Mail Access Protocol: Version 2*

The original and current standards for IMAP, Version 4 are respectively:

❏ **RFC-1730 December 1994** *Internet Message Access Protocol – Version 4*

❏ **RFC-2060 December 1996** *Internet Message Access Protocol – Version 4rev1*

The Internet Mail Consortium, at:

❏ **http://ww.imc.org**

has a list of mail-related RFCs, and more importantly a list of mail-related Internet drafts – which are indicators of possible future developments in Internet e-mail. At the time of writing, several of these drafts relate to IMAP.

Microsoft Exchange

For details of the ports Exchange uses for "Outlook Web Access," i.e. its Web-mail add-on, and for an indication of the complexity of Exchange, see:

❏ **MS-KB-Q176466** *XGEN: TCP Ports and Microsoft Exchange: In-depth Discussion*

❏ **http://www.microsoft.com/exchange/techinfo/outlook/2000/OWA2000.asp**

Appendices

Appendix 8: Windows-NT **route** command manpage
Appendix 13: base64 encoding
Appendix 14: nested MIME attachments
Appendix 15: example of an IMAP session
Web Appendix 14: the UUCP mail network
Web Appendix 15: how to look at the raw content of mail messages

13 The ethereal **protocol analyzer and** ngrep **packet sniffer**

Introduction

In this chapter we introduce two new packet sniffers:

1. **ethereal** is like **tcpdump** but gives more detailed information in a GUI

2. **ngrep** outputs text lines, like **tcpdump**, but it shows the contents of each packet as ASCII characters, and displays only packets whose contents match a specified search pattern.

13.1 **What** ethereal **is and how it compares with** tcpdump

ethereal is a protocol analyzer, like **tcpdump** but different. Like **tcpdump** it looks at all or selected packets on the wire, and prints their details; it even uses the same **libpcap** subroutine library as **tcpdump** and **ngrep** (Module 13.7) to capture the packets, so the syntax for specifying which packets to look at is the same. Where **ethereal** differs is:

- it has a graphical user interface
- it shows full details of the different fields used in each protocol
- you can drill down into a packet and see the different protocols used at different levels.

It also keeps a copy of the packets in a *capture file*, instead of just printing details of the packets as they are detected, which in turn enables the following features:

- you can browse forward or backwards through all the captured packets
- you can apply a "display filter" to the current set of packets you are operating on, so that only selected ones are displayed (e.g. "display only DNS packets"). You can change or remove the filter to display a different set at any time. The set of packets remains unaltered throughout – the filter affects only what is displayed, not what is stored or captured.

Because you're now on the way to being expert with **tcpdump** and understand how and why to sniff the wire, our coverage of **ethereal** will be fairly concise, concentrating on its essentials, leaving you to explore its more exotic features on your own. Below is a **tcpdump** trace, with a DNS response highlighted.

```
192.43.160.250.53 > 212.140.133.19.1031:  [udp sum ok] 21953* 2/2/2 www.ncd.com. CNAME gilligar
212.140.133.19.53 > 212.140.133.17.2343:  [udp sum ok] 9875* 2/2/2 www.ncd.com. CNAME gilligan.
212.140.133.17 > 192.43.160.247: icmp: echo request (ttl 64, id 4724, len 84)
```

Figure 13.1 shows the **ethereal** view of the same traffic, with the highlighted packet analyzed in detail, and it also shows the component parts of the **ethereal** window.

If **ethereal** is so powerful, why would you ever bother using **tcpdump**? Each has its own advantages and disadvantages:

- **ethereal** is ideal for browsing, if you're not sure what you're looking for, or for examining individual packets in detail (e.g. while learning about an unfamiliar protocol)
- **ethereal** understands more protocols than **tcpdump** and shows much more detail. We use it especially for Microsoft Windows Networking and for DNS
- **tcpdump** is much quicker to use. You often don't need the detail that **ethereal** gives you
- we've found **tcpdump** is more reliable and easier to install on many systems
- **tcpdump** doesn't need a graphical display. It's more likely to be installed on servers, and you can easily run it in a **telnet** session on a remote system. **ethereal** does use a graphical display, which on Linux is the X window system (Module 17.6). When used over the network, if the DNS isn't running **ethereal** may fail with errors "Capture child process died" or "_X11TransSocketINETConnect: Can't get address for *display-name*." This is no good if you're using **ethereal** to troubleshoot a DNS failure!

- **tcpdump** shows more information in its summary lines, so you can get an overview of a whole networking conversation at a glance. With **ethereal** you have to drill down into each packet in turn to get a feel for what's happening.

ethereal is free and is available for both Linux and Windows. See Appendix 16 for more details on obtaining and installing it.

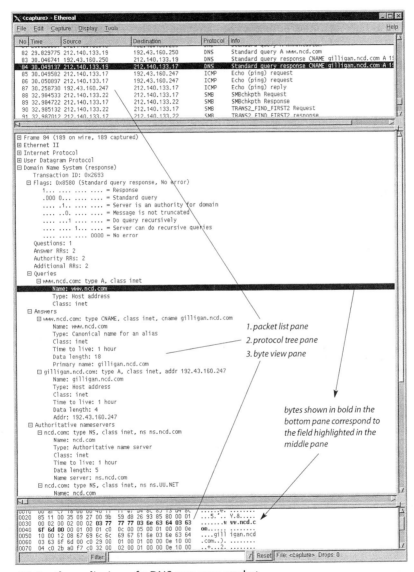

Figure 13.1 ethereal's view of a DNS response packet

In the next module we explain how to start **ethereal** and its various options.

13.2 How to start ethereal and select the packets you want

To start **ethereal**, just run it from the command line:

```
ethereal
```

Significant differences from **tcpdump** are:

- by default **ethereal** doesn't start capturing until you tell it to: either use a menu in the GUI to start capturing, or specify the **-k** option on the command line
- if you use **-k** as above, you must also specify the interface to capture on, using "**-i**". Unless you specify **-S** in addition, the packets won't be displayed until you stop capturing.

	Starting and stopping capture and print
-k	start capturing immediately (otherwise you have to explicitly select the start option from the **Capture** menu). Requires you to specify the **-i** *interface* option
-c *num*	("count") stop capturing when you've collected *num* packets. This applies only when you use the **-k** or **-Q** option
-Q	("quit") exit when you've collected the specified number of packets. Ignored if you also use the **-S** option (on some versions you have to specify **-w** with **-Q**)
-S	automatically update packet list in top window pane as packets are captured. This happens by default except when you are using either the **-k** or **-Q** option (**-S** if present overrides **-Q**)
	Specify which packets to collect, and how
-f *capturexpr*	capture only packets that match the capture-filter expression *capturexpr*. This expression is specified in exactly the same way as for **tcpdump** (but because it is a single argument you will need to enclose it in quotes if it is more than one word) `ethereal -f "host alice and port smtp"` **Warning: tcpdump** users often forget the **-f** option
-i *interface*	use *interface* instead of the default interface `ethereal -i eth1` *sniff on eth1 – Linux* `ethereal -i \Device\Packet_EL3c5741` *Windows-NT*
-s *num*	grab a snapshot of only *num* bytes instead of the whole packet

As we mentioned, **ethereal** uses the same syntax as **tcpdump** to specify which packets to select, so we don't need to cover that again. However, **ethereal** expects this spec to be entered as the single argument to its **-f** option, so if the spec contains more than one "word" you must quote it. (Quoting it is a good idea anyway in case the expression contains symbols that your command shell might misinterpret.) For example, to select HTTP packets between Alice and Bob:

```
ethereal -f "port http and host bob and alice"
tcpdump port http and host bob and alice          doesn't need quotes or -f
```

Specify how items are printed	
`-t` *format*	where *format* is one of: `r` (relative) time in seconds since first packet (default) `a` (absolute) time of day `d` (delta) time in seconds since previous packet
`-n`	print machine addresses (and ports) as numerics rather than names
Other	
`-w` *outfile*	write the packets – as they are captured and displayed – to *outfile* (instead of to a default-named capture file)
`-r` *infile*	read and display packets from *infile* instead of from the network interface. (By the way, **ethereal** can read capture files from **tcpdump** and lots of other packet sniffers.)
`-R` *readfilter*	(applies only with `-r`) when using a previously collected capture file, read in only packets matching the *readfilter* display filter. (Other packets are discarded but as the capture file is unaltered, you can display them again in another session if you need to.)
`-h`	print help message and exit. (Doesn't work on some Windows versions.)
`-v`	print version number of **ethereal** and exit
Layout and appearance of the ethereal window	
`-B` *num*	initial size of byte view (bottom, hex/ASCII dump) pane is *num* pixels. To hide the pane specify *num* = 1
`-P` *num*	initial size of packet list (top) pane is *num* pixels. To hide the pane specify *num* = 1
`-T` *num*	initial size of protocol tree (middle) pane is *num* pixels. To hide the pane specify *num* = 1
`-m` *fontname*	use *fontname* for most text
`-b` *fontname*	in the byte view pane use *fontname* for bold text to highlight the bytes corresponding to the selected line in the protocol tree pane.

These tables document **ethereal** version 0.8.0. Later versions are likely to have a few more flags. We almost always want to start capturing and displaying immediately, so we use, e.g.:

```
ethereal -S -k -i eth0 -n          mnemonic for options: "Skin"
ethereal -f "icmp or arp" -i eth0 -n -k -S   mnemonic for options: "finkS"
```

> **Warning:** just as with **tcpdump**, if you don't specify -n to suppress name resolution when capturing, **ethereal** may appear to hang for seconds or minutes while it translates IP numbers to hostnames. We always use -n when capturing. If we want to view hostnames, we enable name resolution (using menu **Display > Options > Name resolution**) when we've stopped the capture.

13.3 Lab – a typical ethereal session

1. run **ethereal** without any command-line options: the **ethereal** window appears, with three empty panes (Figure 13.2)

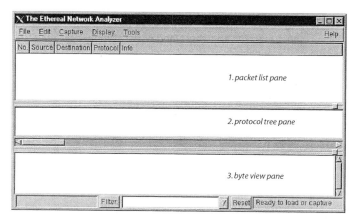

Figure 13.2 The **ethereal** window

2. select menu **Capture > Start** (or press Ctrl-k) to get the **Capture Preferences** window with its default options (Figure 13.3(a) shows Linux, Figure 13.3(b) shows NT):

3a. we always change the options to **Update list of packets in real time**, and not to **Enable name resolution**. (We could have done this by using options **-S** and **-n** on the command line.)

3b. enter the **Filter** you want, if any. This is the capture filter – which you can also enter with the **-f option** on the command line

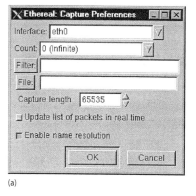

(a)

(b)

Figure 13.4
Capture window

Figure 13.3 Capture Preferences dialogs:
(a) Linux   (b) Windows

4. press OK. **ethereal** gives its **capture** window (Figure 13.4), which contains a statistics summary, and as packets are captured, they are added to the **Packet list** pane of the main window
5. click on the **Stop** button in the **capture** window when you've collected the packets you want.

Browsing the packet list

You can browse forward or backward through the packet list whether you've stopped capturing or not. (You may want to adjust the sizes of **ethereal**'s panes by dragging its resize handle (Linux, Figure 13.5a) or the bar separating the panes (Windows, Figure 13.5b).

(a)   (b)

Figure 13.5 Adjusting **ethereal**'s panes (a) Linux (b) Windows

1. click on a line in the **packet list** pane: its protocol details are shown in the middle pane, and a hex/ASCII dump of its bytes in the bottom pane
2. in the **protocol tree** pane, click on a **+** to expand the protocol tree and show the detail at this level (Figure 13.6(a)) or click on a **–** to collapse this level of the tree
3. when you click on a line in the **protocol** pane, the bytes corresponding to these fields are shown in bold in the **byte view pane** (Figure13.6(b)).

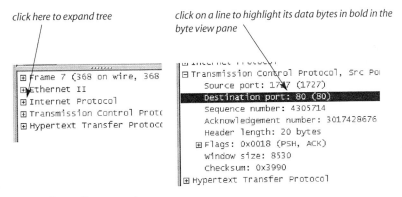

Figure 13.6 ethereal's protocol tree pane

13.4 Using display filters

ethereal's capture filters, which have the same syntax as **tcpdump**'s, say which packets to capture from the wire, and you're familiar with these already. However, **ethereal** also supports a *display filter*: this specifies which of the already captured packets are to be displayed. (Non-matching packets are not displayed, but they are retained in the packet list; you can display them later by changing or removing the display filter.)

Display filter syntax

The display filter syntax is very different to the capture filter syntax and uses its own names and notation for protocol fields. For example "`dns.count.queries`" is the number of queries in a DNS record.

There are three ways a packet can match an expression in a display filter:

a. if a protocol is present, it matches:

```
arp
nfs
```
match any ARP packet
match any Network File System packet

b. if a field is present in the packet and it's not a Boolean-valued (true/false) field, it matches irrespective of the value. Boolean fields are considered present only if the value is **true**

`dns.query`   *match only DNS queries*

c. the value of a field matches a specified value – which can be either a literal value or the value of another field:

```
ip.addr == mail.uit.co.uk
ip.addr == 212.140.133.29
ip.addr == 212.140.133.29/24
ip.dst == ip.src
!tcp.port eq 6000
```
IP addr values can be hostname …
… or dotted decimal
is the address in this class-C range?
which hosts talk to themselves?
ignore X window system packets

As you'd expect, you can combine individual filter expressions using logical operators **and, or,** etc. and group sub-expressions within parentheses:

```
tcp.dstport >= 19 and tcp.dstport < 30
(tcp.port == 25 and ip.dst == mailgate) or tcp.port == 80
```

How to enter and apply a display filter

The simplest way to enter and apply a filter is to type it directly into the **Filter:** text-entry box at the bottom of the main window (Figure 13.7), and press **Enter** on the keyboard to apply it to the packet list. This is ideal if the filter expression is short and uncomplicated, and you know the names of the fields or protocols that you want to filter on. You can apply, modify, or remove a display filter at any time.

*type your display filter expression in here and press **Enter***

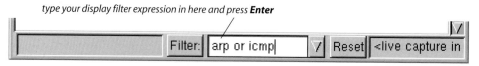

Figure 13.7 Entering and displaying a filter

Another way to enter filters, especially more complex ones, or ones that you want to save for use again later, is to use the filter dialog (Figure 13.8) that you get when you click on the **Filter:** button at the bottom of the page. (We have found this dialog confusing. For example, the **New** button works only if you have already entered a filter name and filter string below. The dialog lets you do everything it says, but in a curious way.)

Figure 13.8
Using the filter
dialog

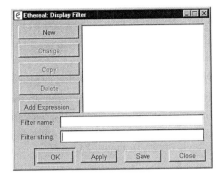

- if you enter a filter string and press **Apply** or **OK**, the filter takes immediate effect but isn't saved
- to create a new filter, enter a name and filter expression, and press **New**. Its name is added to the list of filters
- to change a filter, click on its name in the list. Its name and filter string are displayed in the text boxes. Modify them as required, and then click on the **Change** button
- new and changed filters are not by default saved for future sessions. If you want to keep your modifications for next time, press the **Save** button
- to remove all filters, click on the **Reset** button to the right of the **Filter:** text-entry box. The **packet list** pane will then show all captured packets
- the **Add Expression** button (not available in older versions) brings up a dialog (Figure 13.9) that shows all the available protocol names and field names. You can drill down into a protocol to find the field you want; when you click on it, the dialog shows what type of value you are allowed to enter
- when you highlight a field and then select any relational operator other than **is present**, the acceptable options for the value fields are displayed.

Figure 13.9 Available
protocol names and
field names

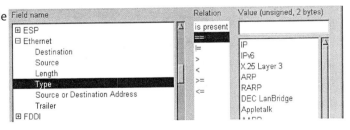

For more information on field and protocol names, see Appendix 16. (Don't be put off if you don't know what all the fields or protocols mean. You will very rarely need to work at this level of detail, and just in case, there are helpful references in the Notes.)

13.5 ethereal – **other features**

Coloring your traces

ethereal lets you set up color schemes for some or all of your packets. You define one or more filters, which are used only for coloring, using the display-filter syntax. Then you specify the foreground and/or background color to be applied to packets in the packet list pane that match the filter:

1. select menu **Display > Colorize Display**, which gives you the **Add color to protocols** dialog (Figure 13.10)
2. click on **New**, giving the **Edit color filter** dialog (Figure 13.11)
3. enter the name you want, and the filter expression, in their text boxes
4. click on the buttons to set the foreground and/or background colors. (We've found this buggy; if one button doesn't work, try the other, then go back to the first again.) The color selection dialog is shown in Figure 13.12
5. press **Save** if you want to keep these settings for next time
6. press **Apply** or **OK** for the filters to take effect.

Filters are applied from the top down to each packet. As soon as a filter matches a packet, this filter's color scheme is applied, and the colorizer moves on to the next packet in the list. This means the order of your color filters is important: the most specific should appear high up in the list, e.g. "HTTP" should occur before "TCP." (If you have them the other way round, the TCP filter will color the HTTP packets – because TCP is the transport used by HTTP – and the HTTP filter will never get the opportunity to be applied.)

Figure 13.13 shows a session where all UDP packets are highlighted (in green, but you can't see that!).

Other options

- menu **Tools > Summary** displays basic statistics for this session
- menu **Tools > Protocol Hierarchy Statistics** displays more detailed statistics, but this option is only included in recent versions of the program

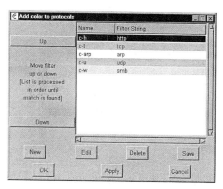

Figure 13.10 Add color dialog

Figure 13.11 Edit color filter dialog

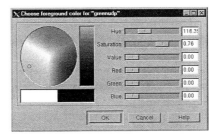

Figure 13.12 Color selection dialog

Figure 13.13 UDP packets are highlighted when the color filter is applied

- menu **Display > Options** lets you set the print format for timestamps and addresses
- menu **Edit > Preferences** lets you customize which columns to show, and how various fields are displayed
- **ethereal** and **tcpdump** have the same capture file format. We often use **ethereal** to save a capture file of a session and then use **tcpdump** to print a summary of it
- **ethereal** can read the capture files from lots of other packet sniffers too (see the **ethereal** manpage for details)
- menu **Tools > Plugins** is intended to let you add extensions to the standard, base functionality (by means of shared libraries). However, nothing generally useful is available yet.

As with **tcpdump**, you can run several instances of **ethereal** simultaneously on the same machine, each capturing a different set of packets. The separate instances do not interfere with each other.

The user interface we have described here is for **ethereal** version 0.8.x. We have used that because it is included in many Linux distributions. Newer versions have a more sophisticated interface, which simplifies many operations, such as defining display filters.

13.6 Tips and tricks

An easy way to specify display filters

If you highlight a line in the protocol tree, and then select the menu **Display > Match Selected**, ethereal constructs and applies a display filter that matches the highlighted line. The complexity of the filter expression depends on which line you click. If you click a line that's high up in the protocol tree, (e.g. the TCP top-level line "Transmission Control Protocol," the filter matches that particular packet in great detail. However, if you expand the Transmission Control Protocol, highlight the destination port line, and then **Display > Match Selected**, the filter expression will be simple, as shown at the bottom of Figure 13.14.

Figure 13.14 Simple filter expression

- if this isn't exactly what you want, you can edit expression in the text box, press **Enter** on the keyboard, and the revised filter is applied
- to exclude rather than include a particular set of packets, we often create a filter, using **Display > Match Selected**, that matches the packets we *don't* want. Then we type in the word "**not**" at the beginning of the filter to reverse the effect of the filter
- we can never remember what **ethereal**'s names for the fields are, so we often use **Display > Match Selected** to find them out.

Problems with negated expressions

Let's say you want to exclude packets coming from Alice, whose IP address is 192.0.2.5. You enter the display filter expression:

```
ip.addr != 192.0.2.5
```
                                                          probably wrong

and think this will work like the **tcpdump** capture filter expression

```
not host 192.0.2.5
```

It doesn't. It will probably have no effect at all. The reason is that both the packets:

```
1.2.3.4 > 192.0.2.5
192.0.2.5 > 1.2.3.4
```

match your filter expression, because in both there is an IP address that isn't 192.0.2.5. To get over this, you first create an expression that matches the packets you want to exclude:

```
ip.addr == 192.0.2.5
```

and then negate it by inserting the word "**not**" at the beginning:

```
not ip.addr == 192.0.2.5
```

Follow TCP stream

ethereal has a facility to show you the contents of a whole TCP session. This is especially useful for protocols like HTTP, SMTP, and POP that use plain-text commands and responses.

Instead of manually identifying and selecting all the packets that belong to a session, click on any packet in the session, and then menu **Tools > Follow TCP stream**. This does two things:

1. gives you a new window (Figure 13.15) containing a dump of the data in the session. (The radio buttons at the bottom of the window let you change the format of the dump.)
2. limits the display in the packet list to packets that are part of this session.

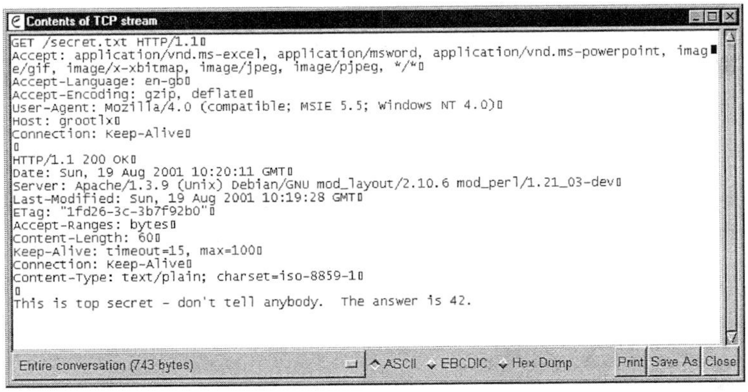

Figure 13.15 A dump of the data on the session

Saving a capture session

ethereal, unlike **tcpdump**, saves the packets on the fly to a temporary file as they are captured. The **File > Save** menu just copies them to a permanent file.

> **Warning:** the **File > Save** and **File > Save As** menu items are inactive until you stop packet collection.

ethereal can read and write capture files in many different formats. You can use this facility to convert a capture file from one format to another. For example, you can convert a file captured using Windows Network Monitor (Module 18.6) and convert it so you can view it using **tcpdump**, and vice versa.

13.7 The ngrep **packet sniffer**

ngrep is a packet sniffer that lets you search the contents of the packets for a text pattern that you specify. It's available in binary and source forms for both Windows and Linux. **ngrep** is the network equivalent of the UNIX search program, **grep**:

- like **tcpdump** its sniffs the traffic on the wire. You use exactly the same specifications as with **tcpdump** to specify which packets are to be sniffed (e.g. "host alice and port 25"). In fact, to sniff the packets **ngrep** uses the same internal subroutine library as **tcpdump**, which explains why the filter expressions are identical. A slight difference is that **ngrep** deliberately supports only the TCP, UDP, and ICMP protocols

- instead of printing all packets, **ngrep** only prints those that match a specified search pattern. (It also prints a "#" for every packet sniffed, whether it matches the search expression or not, so you can see that packets really are being processed even if none match your pattern.)

- it shows the packet's contents in ASCII instead of interpreting it as a particular protocol, e.g. as a DNS lookup response or a **ping** packet or whatever it happens to be.

For example, to sniff SMTP packets (port 25) from Carol and print only those that contain the string "ferret", use

```
ngrep ferret port 25 and host carol
```

To show the packets in a usefully different format to **tcpdump** rather than actually searching for a pattern, you can omit the search pattern completely, as in:

```
ngrep port 25 and host carol
```

When **ngrep** starts, it prints out the values of the search pattern and filter expression that it's using, preceded by **match:** and **filter:**.

Warning: ngrep lets you omit the search pattern completely, and just specify a filter expression. **ngrep** recognizes this by checking the first argument on the command line to see if it's a word that occurs in filter expressions, e.g. "host" or "port." If so, it assumes you omitted the search pattern. **tcpdump** lets you quote the expression so it can contain shell-special characters, such as '(' and ')', for example,

```
tcpdump '(host carol and alice) and port 80'
```

but if you try this with **ngrep** it gets confused. Try inserting an empty first argument (a pair of quotes with nothing in between) to overcome this, but in any case we recommend you always look at the **filter:** and **match:** values that **ngrep** prints when it starts up, to make sure it's doing what you intend.

```
alice# tcpdump -n -t port 80 and host carol and alice
212.140.133.21.3884 > 212.140.133.17.80: S 1971252:1971252(0) win 8192 <mss
212.140.133.17.80 > 212.140.133.21.3884: S 2149033967:2149033967(0) ack 1971
212.140.133.21.3884 > 212.140.133.17.80: . ack 1 win 8760 (DF)
212.140.133.21.3884 > 212.140.133.17.80: P 1:242(241) ack 1 win 8760 (DF)

alice# ngrep port 80 and host carol and alice
interface: eth0 (212.140.133.0/255.255.255.128)
filter: ip and ( port 80 and host carol and alice )
####
T 212.140.133.21:3884 -> 212.140.133.17:80 [AP]
  GET /std-inx.htm HTTP/1.1..Accept: */*..Referer: http://alice/..Accept
  -Language: en-gb..Accept-Encoding: gzip, deflate..User-Agent: Mozilla/
  4.0 (compatible; MSIE 5.5; Windows NT 4.0)..Host: alice..Connection: K
  eep-Alive..Pragma: no-cache....
```

For comparison, above are **tcpdump** and **ngrep** traces of the same traffic.

For looking at packets that contain a lot of text (which is the case for most HTTP traffic, as we'll see in the next chapter) **ngrep** is much more convenient than **tcpdump**.

Options for controlling ngrep

Function	Option	Notes
Pattern matching		
match upper- or lowercase (case insensitive)	-i	
match the search pattern only as a whole word	-w	*don't match if the pattern occurs as a sub-string of a larger word*
invert the matching	-v	*include only packets that **don't** match a search pattern*
How to display packets		
dump packet contents as hex as well as ASCII	-x	
quiet – don't print the search and filter expressions at startup	-q	*useful if you are passing **ngrep**'s output to another program*
show empty packets	-e	*by default, empty packets are discarded*
print *num* packets after every packet that matched search pattern	-A *num*	
exit after printing *num* packets	-n *num*	
Other		
listen on this interface device	-d *ifc*	*use ifc instead of default interface*
help	-h	
print **ngrep**'s version number	-V	*NB: uppercase "V"*

In the next module we look at the sophisticated search patterns that **ngrep** lets you specify.

13.8 ngrep **search patterns – regular expressions**

As with Linux's **grep**, the pattern you specify for **ngrep** can be just a simple string, as in the examples earlier. If this string occurs anywhere in the packet contents, it's considered a match and the packet is printed in full. However, the pattern can be more sophisticated: it is actually a *regular expression*, or *regex* for short. (This explains the name of the **grep** program – it stands for **G**lobal **R**egular **E**xpression **P**rint.)

Regexs are a little language for specifying searches, with sophisticated options for matching. Your match can include any or all of the following match criteria:

- wildcards
- sets of characters that you specify
- optional elements
- only if the pattern occurs at the beginning of the text, or only at the end, or both.

Web Appendix 16 gives the regex syntax in detail, but here's a summary to get you started, and to highlight the special uses of some characters so you won't be too surprised if a pattern does something that at first glance seems strange.

In regex's syntax, a few characters are special constructs and the rest are *ordinary*. The special characters are:

$$ \$ \; \wedge \; . \; * \; + \; ? \; [\;] \; (\;) \; \backslash \; | $$

- a string of ordinary characters matches that string anywhere in the text, e.g. "cat" matches "catharsis," "scatological," and "Magnificat" as well as plain old "cat"
- a dot "." matches any character, including a dot
- a "∧" at the beginning of a pattern string means "match only if the string occurs at the beginning of a line," e.g. "∧cat" matches only "cat" and "catharsis" from the five examples above
- matching is case sensitive by default. You can make it ignore case by giving the "-i" option to **ngrep**
- a "$" at the end of the pattern string means "match only if the pattern occurs at the end of a line," e.g. "cat$" matches only "cat" and "Magnificat" above. It follows that "∧cat$" matches only lines that contain "cat" exactly and nothing else
- you can hide a special character's special-ness by preceding it with a "\," e.g. if you want to search for a currency reference you could use "US\$". ("US$" without the "\"would look for the two-character string "US" at the end of a line.)
- square brackets " [" and "]" around a set of characters mean "match any of the enclosed characters," e.g. "[mcsb]at" matches "cat," "sat," "mat," "bat" if they occur anywhere in a line. You can use a dash as shorthand to specify ranges of characters, e.g. "[a-z]" means any lowercase alphabetic, "[0-7]" matches any octal digit, "[a-zA-Z0-9]" means any letter or digit, and "[Hh]" matches a lower- or uppercase H
- a character set that starts with a "∧" means "match any character *except* those enclosed," e.g. "[∧cb]at" matches "sat" and "mat" but not "bat" or "cat." You can use a dash as shorthand to specify ranges of characters as above.

- a "*" after a portion of the pattern means "zero or more occurrences of the element of the pattern that precedes the *." We haven't defined what "element" means – you'll have to look at Web Appendix 16 for that, but here are a couple of examples: "B[a-z]*" matches any word starting with uppercase B, and "[0-9]*" matches a string of zero or more digits
- a "+" after a portion of the pattern means "one or more occurrences of the element of the pattern that precedes it," e.g. "[0-9]+" matches a string of digits, but doesn't match the empty string
- a "?" after a portion of the pattern means "zero or one occurrences of the element of the pattern that precedes it," e.g. "[0-9]?" matches a single digit or the empty string.
- a "|" between two patterns means "match either of these". E.g. "cat|dog" matches "cat" or "dog".

Don't be put off by the complexity of the patterns. Most of the time you just need the ordinary characters, which include alphabetics, numerics, and spaces; these match exactly as you type them. Later on, if you need to search for wildcards, etc., you can experiment with more sophisticated patterns. Here are some examples

Look for any traffic on port 80 that contains the string "HTTP/1.1", irrespective of whether it's upper- or lowercase:

```
ngrep -i "http/1.1" port 80
```

Show any packets that contain the POP commands LIST, RETR, or DELE, ignoring case:

```
ngrep -i 'retr|list|dele'
```

Tip: if you're new to regular expressions and have a Linux system, you can experiment using **egrep**, Linux's extended **grep** program, it uses the same regexs as **ngrep**. **egrep** reads lines from input files or its standard input (your keyboard in the example below). If the input line matches the pattern you specified, it's copied to the standard output (printed on your terminal). If the line doesn't match it's not printed.

Below is an example. For clarity we've indented **egrep**'s output.

```
alice% egrep -i '^retr|list|dele'
retrieve
        retrieve
firetrap
deleted
        deleted
yodeler
        yodeler
listing
        listing
vocalist
        vocalist
```

The example shows an easy mistake to make: the "^" applies only to the **retr** part of the pattern, so **retr** is matched only at the beginning of a line, **but list** and **dele** are matched anywhere in the line. If you intended to match any of the words only at the beginning of the line, the correct command is "**egrep -i '^(retr|list|dele)'**" (See Notes for details).

Summary

- like **tcpdump**, **ethereal** sniffs packets on the wire
- unlike **tcpdump**, **ethereal** has a GUI and lets you drill down into the detailed structure of each packet
- just as with **tcpdump**, you can apply a capture filter to capture only the packets you are interested in
- you can also apply a display filter to show only some of the packets you have captured. You can change or remove the display filter at any time to show a different set of packets, or all the packets you have captured.
- you can use **ethereal** to convert capture file formats, by reading in a file in one format and saving it as another
- the **ngrep** packet sniffer is a quick way to display the contents of packets as ASCII text, and/or to select packets that match a given textual pattern. You specify patterns using regular expressions.

What's next?

In the next chapter we look at the World Wide Web and its HTTP protocol.

Notes and further reading

❏ http://www.ethereal.com

is the **ethereal** Web site. It has a tutorial, as well as all the downloads. The **ethereal** distribution includes the **editcap** (edit capture file) program, which lets you edit or convert capture files. However, an easier way to edit a capture file is to exclude packets you don't want using a display filter, and then tick the **Save only packets currently being displayed** option in the **Save as** dialog.

❏ http://www.packetfactory.net/Projects/ngrep/

is the **ngrep** Web site. **ngrep** on Windows needs **packet.dll**, but if you've installed **Windump** (the Windows version of **tcpdump**) you'll have that already.

ngrep uses the same **libpcap** library as **tcpdump** and **ethereal** to capture packets, which explains why the filter expressions are identical.

Regular expressions are used in many different programs on Linux and UNIX (and occasionally elsewhere, such as Microsoft's Operations Manager, MOM) for specifying search patterns, and search-and-replace operations. The expressions used in **ngrep** are the same as used in the Emacs programmable editor (which we used for almost all our UNIX-based work for this book). For a reference table giving the full regex syntax, which explains the use of the " (...) " construct we used in the tip in Module 13.8, see Web Appendix 16.

❏ http://www.uit.co.uk/resources>ngrep regular expressions

We'll use one more packet sniffer for specific purposes later on: the Windows Network Monitor (Module 18.6), which is particularly good for Microsoft Windows Networking traffic.

Appendices

Appendix 16: installing **ethereal**; **ethereal**'s field names
Web Appendix 16: **ngrep** regular expressions.

14 HTTP and the World Wide Web

Introduction

The World Wide Web is the application that transformed the Internet from a specialized tool for technical and research use into the universal information medium it is today. This chapter describes the Web and its Hypertext Transfer Protocol. We cover how the protocol works, the different versions of it that are in common use, and how you can use **telnet** as a diagnostic tool to troubleshoot your Web problems. (Some of the modules in the middle of this chapter are more specialized and can be skipped on first reading.).

14.1 HTTP – the Hypertext Transfer Protocol

Just about everybody knows how to use a browser to surf the Web. What we're going to explain is what happens underneath the surface, at the network level, and in some ways, people's familiarity with using the Web gets in the way of this.

Two important points to grasp, which aren't obvious at first glance, are:

1. *HTTP*, the *Hypertext Transfer Protocol,* determines *how* data are transferred, not what the type of data is, or how it's processed. HTTP can be used to transfer any type of data, not just Web pages, and any suitably written application, not just a Web browser, can use HTTP to transfer data

2. it is the Web browser (or other application) on the client machine that determines how data are processed once they have been retrieved.

To explore these points we'll look in detail at how a Web browser downloads a Web page from a server.

There are two ways you can tell your browser to download a page:

- click on a link to the page you want, from a page already open in your browser

- in your browser's **Go to:** or **Address:** text entry box explicitly enter the address of the page you want to view:

The internal mechanism is the same in each case – the browser issues a request to the server to retrieve the page specified.

How Web page addresses are specified – URLs

Web page addresses are specified using *URLs* (*Uniform Resource Locators*). The above figure shows a typical example of a URL giving the address for a Web page. This specifies four different aspects of the information we want to retrieve:

1. **http** – the protocol we want to use – *how* the information is to be retrieved
2. **www.uit.co.uk** – the machine the information resides on
3. **:80** – the port to connect to on this machine
4. **/case-studies/cs-vpn.htm** – the particular information we want from this machine.

URLs are called "uniform" because the same syntax can be used to locate different types of resource. You can have values other than **http** in the protocol field. URLs to retrieve data using **ftp** are common, e.g.

```
ftp://ftp.isi.edu/in-notes/rfc1738.txt
```

but you can have others protocols too:

- **telnet** – open a **telnet** session to the remote machine, e.g.

```
telnet://mail1.microsoft.com:25
```

connects to Microsoft's SMTP server, by starting up your **telnet** client

- **mailto** – the resource is an e-mail address we want to send a message to:

      mailto:fred@example.com

  and this starts up your e-mail client (if you have one) with the specified e-mail address filled in as the destination
- **file** – the resource is a file, usually on the local machine, e.g.

      file:///c:/winnt/system32/drivers/etc/services
- **https** – HTTP over SSL, the Secure Sockets Layer (see Module 14.18).

However, in the rest of this chapter we'll deal only with HTTP (and we'll say more about the machine, port, and name part of URLs in Module 14.10.)

How Web page addresses are specified as links within a page

Web pages are usually written in *HTML*, the *HyperText Markup Language*. This is stored as a plain text file, but it contains both text to be displayed and commands for how the displayed text is to be formatted. For example, to display the following line as a paragraph in a Web page, with underlining, bold, and italic formatting as shown:

The **fat** rat <u>sat</u> on the *cat*.

the HTML code is:

    <P>The fat rat <u>sat</u> on the cat.</P>

The HTML commands are called *tags* and are enclosed in angle brackets. You can see that tags occur in pairs, e.g. **** and ****, which are called *opening* and *closing* tags, respectively, because the closing tag (with the /) ends the effect of the corresponding opening tag.

To include a link to another page in an HTML document, "**A**" tags are used, and the URL of the desired page is included within them. ("A" stands for "anchor" – a link has two ends, a source and a destination, anchored at particular places in the text.) For example, to create a link to our Web site, to appear like this in a Web page:

Visit the <u>case studies page</u> to find out about …

include the following HTML code:

    Visit the <A HREF="http://www.uit.co.uk:80/case-studies/
    cs-vpn.htm">case studies page</A> to find out about ...

Image files are included in a page using the **IMG** tag, e.g. the following includes our company logo in a page:

    <IMG SRC="http://www.uit.co.uk:80/uit-logo.gif" >

When you click on a link in your browser window, the browser issues a request for the specified URL just as if you had typed in the URL in the **Go to:** or **Address:** text box.

That's all we'll say about the internals of HTML. In the next module we look in more detail at the functions the Web browser performs.

14.2 What a Web browser does

Figure 14.1 The "Go to" (or Address or Location) box

To understand in more detail what happens in a normal Web session, we'll look at the major functions of the Web browser (or Web client, or "user agent"):

1. processing input from the user
   - reading the URL to be retrieved that the user typed in the "Address" or "Location" or "Go to" box (Figure 14.1):
   - interpreting the mouse click on a link from one page to another to download the linked-to page
2. TCP/IP networking – connecting to the server and sending requests and receiving the requested Web pages. (Most browsers can handle several different network protocols – FTP, **telnet**, etc., not just HTTP.)
3. interpreting the HTML code in the pages it has downloaded.
   - rendering (i.e. drawing on screen) the text of the page, formatted appropriately
   - recognizing in the HTML code the link tags that refer to other pages and displaying them specially, so you can click on them to jump to the linked page
   - recognizing the **IMG** tags in the HTML code that refer to image files. For each image in the page, a graphical browser will automatically connect to the server, retrieve the image file, and display it inline in the page if it understands the image format. (However, not all browsers are graphical – see below.)
   - caching pages and images to speed things up (Module 14.16)

   Note that all this is completely independent of what network protocol was used to download the page in the first place. Pages transferred using HTTP, FTP or read from disk are all displayed and handled in the same way.
4. interpreting special content, if the browser knows how:
   - images: images are stored as separate files on the server. Each file is downloaded individually and displayed inline, using special code in the browser that interprets the file format and renders it on screen
   - audio, video, spreadsheets, word processor documents, etc.: displaying these usually involves executing other applications to process the downloaded information (in much the same way that attachments of these types are processed by e-mail clients)
   - program and script code in the downloaded pages, such as JavaScript, Java, and Active-X: for these to work, the browser must have in-built special-purpose code to interpret (execute) them.

In Module 14.8 we explain how the HTTP server uses MIME to tell the client what type of data it's sending, so the client can decide exactly what to do with the data when it receives them.

Most of the functions listed above are not at the network protocol level – they are built into the application. From a purely networking point of view, the Web browser is very simple, just as we saw with e-mail client programs. Using **telnet** as a client, you *could* download a Web page, manually look through the downloaded code for links to images, then manually download the image files, etc. You can easily perform many of the browser functions yourself, but it would be very tedious.

Browsers for character (non-graphic) screens

Many of the browser functions don't involve graphics, and there are browsers that work on character-based, non-graphic screens (i.e. the dumb terminals we looked at when discussing **telnet**, Module 10.6). Even though most people won't ever use these, it's worthwhile describing them briefly, because they clarify what the essential features of browsers are.

The most widely used dumb-terminal browser is Lynx; Figure 14.2 shows the **www.microsoft.com** home page displayed in a Lynx window. While Lynx takes some getting used to, it has advantages:

- it's very fast. Because it doesn't have to display any graphics (because it can't!) it doesn't have to download any images

- it is easier to interface to special Braille or screen-reading software for visually handicapped people, than are normal GUI browsers

- you can use it in scripts to automate Web-page retrieval (Module 14.18).

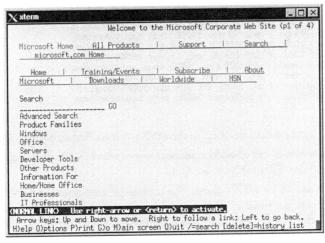

Figure 14.2 Microsoft.com home page displayed in a Lynx window

Another nice feature from our point of view is that Lynx prints a lot of information in its status line about the progress of a request – that it's connecting to the site, which version of HTTP it's using, how much data it has downloaded so far, etc.

Now we'll look at HTTP itself in some detail, using **telnet** as an HTTP client.

14.3 Lab – components of a very simple HTTP session

Like POP, SMTP, and IMAP e-mail, HTTP uses TCP as its transport, and the conversation between client and server consists of plain-text commands. This lets us use **telnet** as a simple client to interact with a Web server, by connecting to HTTP's well-known port, which is 80. We'll use the HTTP **GET** command to retrieve a page. Below is a very simple HTTP session, connecting from Bob to the Web server on Alice, and retrieving a small HTML page:

```
bob# telnet alice http
Trying 192.0.2.17...
Connected to alice.example.com.
Escape character is '^]'.
GET /htiw.htm
<HTML>
  <HEAD>
    <TITLE>Baby's first web page</TITLE>
  </HEAD>
<body>
<P>The fat cat sat on the rat.</P>
  </BODY>
</HTML>
Connection closed by foreign host.
bob#
```

Running **tcpdump**, with options "**-N**" (print only local machine addresses as names rather than numbers), "**-t**" (no timestamps), and "**-f**" (don't print the domain part of the name), we can see what's involved:

```
bob.1024 > resbox.domain:  49507+ A? alice. (33)
resbox.domain > bob.1024:  49507 1/2/2 A alice (132)
bob.1031 > alice.www: S 1691288354:1691288354(0) win 16060
alice.www > bob.1031: S 2962874098:2962874098(0) ack 169128
bob.1031 > alice.www: . ack 1 win 16060 <nop,nop,timestamp
bob.1031 > alice.www: P 1:16(15) ack 1 win 16060 <nop,nop,t
alice.www > bob.1031: . ack 16 win 16060 <nop,nop,timestamp
alice.www > bob.1031: P 1:128(127) ack 16 win 16060 <nop,no
alice.www > bob.1031: F 128:128(0) ack 16 win 16060 <nop,no
bob.1031 > alice.www: . ack 128 win 16060 <nop,nop,timestam
bob.1031 > alice.www: . ack 129 win 16060 <nop,nop,timestam
bob.1031 > alice.www: F 16:16(0) ack 129 win 16060 <nop,nop
alice.www > bob.1031: . ack 17 win 16060 <nop,nop,timestamp
```

1. Bob looks up the hostname "alice" in the DNS server on Resbox and gets Alice's IP address

2. Bob connects to Alice's IP address on port **www** (which is 80), and you see the three-way handshake (SYN, SYN-ACK, ACK)

3. Bob sends an HTTP **GET** request. This consists of a single line, containing the command and the name of the page that the client is requesting, **/htiw.htm**. The request in this case consists of 15 bytes, including the carriage-return and linefeed at the end, as line 6 of the trace shows.

   Request names are case sensitive: if you use **get** instead of **GET** the server will return an error

4. Alice replies with the little Web page above, which consists of 127 bytes

5. Alice terminates the connection, and we see the usual connection close – FIN, ACK, FIN, ACK.

Figure 14.3 shows the flow diagrammatically. The important features of the session are:

- the address the client connects to is the IP address of a machine. We could have used the command

```
telnet 192.0.2.17 80
```

  instead. So when you connect your browser to a Web address like **www.uit.co.uk**, you are specifying the address of a machine, and its IP address must be in the DNS. (This is different from an e-mail address, which is not the address of an individual machine – it's just the name of a domain, e.g. **example.com**. The DNS is searched for MX records for this name, to give the address of an actual server machine.) We'll say more about this in Module 14.10

- commands from the client are sent as plain text

- in this example the TCP connection persisted only for the duration of this command and response, and was then terminated

- once the data are downloaded, HTTP's involvement is finished. After that it's up to the browser to decide what to actually do with the data, e.g. interpret as HTML and display it on the screen or whatever. But whatever it does, it's not HTTP (at least, not until the next time it downloads something from the server). In other words, you can download HTML data using any transfer method, not just HTTP; and contrariwise, you can use HTTP to download any type of data, not just HTML. HTML and HTTP grew up together on the Web, but they're completely separate.

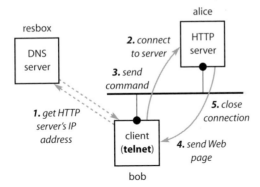

Figure 14.3 A simple HTTP session

14.4 The different versions of HTTP

For basic troubleshooting of an HTTP problem, the conversation we illustrated in the previous module is often all you need. What we were using is the very early version of HTTP – version 0.9 from 1991. The next version was HTTP/1.0 (May 1996), which formalized and enhanced the protocol. HTTP/1.1 (January 1997) developed it even further, and resolved some problems with how the HTTP/1.0 was being interpreted and implemented. (To indicate how the complexity has increased, it's interesting to compare the size of the specifications of the various versions. The spec for 0.9 is two pages long in its original format (see Notes). RFC-1945, specifying HTTP/1.0, has 60 pages, and RFC-2616, specifying HTTP/1.1, has 176 pages.)

Fortunately, the only differences that we need to consider here are:

- in HTTP/0.9 the server has no way to tell the client the type of data that are being returned. The client just receives a lump of data and has to guess what format they're in and how best to handle them – by looking at the content or the name of the page. Most transfers on the Web are pages containing HTML so in practice this system worked quite well, but for more sophisticated data types – word processor files, different image types, etc. – it is inadequate. HTTP/1.0 overcomes this problem by using exactly the same mechanism that e-mail does – MIME. In HTTP/1.0 and 1.1, the server sends the client details of the format and type of the data, before sending the actual data (Module 14.8)

- in HTTP/0.9 the server has no way to tell the client if there is a problem with the page that the client requested (e.g. if it doesn't exist). The only thing the server can do is return an HTML page containing a human-readable error message (Figure 14.4) for the end-user to interpret (Figure 14.5). HTTP/1.0 and 1.1 overcome this by sending a status response to each request (Module 14.6).

- HTTP/1.1 allows a single instance of a Web server to handle multiple site names (e.g. **www.alice.com**, **www.bob.com**, **www.carol.com**, **www.dave.com** on a single IP address. Earlier HTTP versions had to use a separate IP address for each site name (Module 14.6)

- HTTP/0.9 and 1.0 initiate a new TCP connection for every download. For example, if a page contains five GIF images, six TCP connections are used – one for the page itself and five for the images. HTTP/1.1 uses *persistent connections* to allow multiple downloads over a single TCP connection in a single session (Module 14.9).

In the next module we look at HTTP/1.0 and HTTP/1.1. We'll see how clients use headers to give more information about the data requested and servers use headers to inform the client about what data will be sent back.

```
bob% telnet alice 80
Trying 192.0.2.17...
Connected to alice.example.com.
Escape character is '^]'.
GET /badpage.htm
    <!DOCTYPE HTML PUBLIC "-//IETF//DTD HTML 2.0//EN">
    <HTML><HEAD>
    <TITLE>404 Not Found</TITLE>
    </HEAD><BODY>
    <H1>Not Found</H1>
    The requested URL /badpage.htm was not found on this server.<P>
    </BODY></HTML>
Connection closed by foreign host.
bob%
```

Figure 14.4 HTML page containing error message

Figure 14.5 HTML from figure 14.4 as viewed in browser

14.5 HTTP/1.0 and 1.1 – requests and response headers

The simple Web session in Module 14.3 used the HTTP/0.9 protocol. As we said, this doesn't provide any mechanism to allow the server to give information to the client, e.g. status information about whether the client's request succeeded, or type information about the data that the server is about to send. Figure 14.6a shows an HTTP/0.9 session diagrammatically.

HTTP/1.0 addressed both these issues by extending the request and response format and using *headers* in both. The headers used are very like e-mail headers.

For compatibility, the old HTTP/0.9 **GET** has been re-classified as a *simple request*. Newly introduced *full requests* use headers to pass the extra information needed between client and server. Simple requests are still handled, for compatibility reasons, but now full requests are distinguished by including the protocol version; if no protocol version is included, the request is assumed to be a simple request, e.g.

GET *pagename*	*simple request*
GET *pagename* HTTP/1.0	*full request – HTTP/1.0*
GET *pagename* HTTP/1.1	*full request – HTTP/1.1*

The client then sends:

1. any *request headers* it wants to send, immediately after the request, one per line
2. a blank line to indicate end-of-headers (just as we saw with e-mail in Module 11.7 where a blank line marks the end-of-headers in the message body).

When the server responds:

1. it first sends a response status line
2. then any *response headers*
3. a blank line to indicate end-of-headers
4. finally, the body of the response.

The headers are sent before the body, not after, so the client can decide in advance what to do with the data when they arrive. In this respect the response headers in particular are very like e-mail headers. Figure 14.6b shows an HTTP/1.0 session diagrammatically.

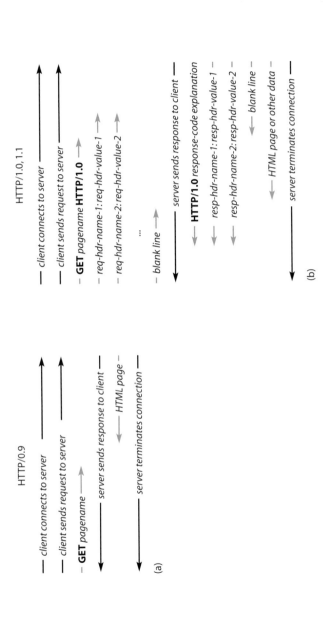

Figure 14.6 (a) HTTP/0.9 session; (b) HTTP/1.0 session

14.6 Request and response headers (contd.)

Request headers; host request header

The client uses request headers to pass additional information to the server, either about the request or about the client itself. Some of the more interesting are:

`Accept:`	the type of data the client can accept from the server, e.g. `text/html` or `video/mpeg` or `image/gif`. The content type specifications are the same as in MIME
`Accept-charset:`	the character sets the client can handle
`Authorization:`	authentication information for a protected page, e.g. username and password or some other "credentials" to allow access to the page, depending on the protection schemes implemented by the server (see Module 14.17).
`If-Modified-Since:`	the client has a copy of this page in its cache, and has a last-modified date for it. This header tells the server to send the page again only if it has been modified since this date. This cuts down on the amount of traffic the server has to send while still allowing the client to have the very latest page
`Host:`	which Web site this request relates to. This header was introduced in HTTP/1.1. It allows multiple Web sites to be hosted on a single machine with a single IP address. Previously, you had to have a separate IP address for each Web site on the machine, and a separate copy of the Web server software listening on this address.
	The value of this header is how the client tells the server which of the many "Web sites" on this IP address the client wants to retrieve data from.
	HTTP/1.1 now requires the client to include the **Host** header on every full HTTP/1.1 request it sends; if it's omitted, the server gives an error response.
	We explore the **Host:** header in more detail in the next module
`User-Agent:`	the name and version number of the browser
`Referrer:`	the URL of the page that contains the link the user clicked on to request this page, i.e. the page that pointed to the one requested. This is useful in case the user requests a non-existent page: it allows the server administrator to find the page that has an out-of-date link in it.

Status line and response headers

The first thing the server returns is a status code to tell the client whether the request succeeded. The format of the status line is the protocol version, followed by a response code, and an explanation of the code, e.g.

```
HTTP/1.0 200 OK
```

Notice that the status line isn't a header – it isn't in the usual "*tag : value*" format. Appendix 17 lists the response codes defined in HTTP/1.1 but here's a summary:

The first digit of the three-digit status code defines the class of response:

1xx: Informational – Request received, continuing process

2xx: Success – The action was successfully received, understood, and accepted

3xx: Redirection – Further action must be taken in order to complete the request

4xx: Client error – The request contains bad syntax or cannot be fulfilled

5xx: Server error – The server failed to fulfill an apparently valid request.

After the status line, the server sends its response headers to give any extra information – about the *type* of data that the server is returning as the Web page (or more precisely, as the body of the response) or about the server itself. HTTP uses MIME in almost exactly the same way as e-mail to specify content type. (This is a good example of not re-inventing the wheel when a perfectly good mechanism already exists to do what you need.) We cover the MIME headers in Module 14.8. Other headers include:

`expires:`	the date/time after which the content is considered "stale," so if it is cached, it should only be considered current before the expiry date. After that, the content should not be copied from the cache, but should be fetched again in full from the server
`last-modified:`	the date/time when the content was last updated. This is often the modification time of the file (on the Web server) containing the Web page.

In the next module we show how to use headers in a more complex HTTP session.

14.7 Lab – more advanced HTTP sessions

First, we use **ngrep** to view what is exchanged between client and server. Below we give the trace of a browser retrieving one page, **std-inx.htm** from a local Web server:

```
alice# ngrep port 80 and host carol and alice
interface: eth0 (192.0.2.0/255.255.255.128)
filter: ip and ( port 80 and host carol and alice )
####
T 192.0.2.21:3884 -> 192.0.2.17:80 [AP]
  GET /std-inx.htm HTTP/1.1..Accept: */*..Referer: http://alice/..Accept
  -Language: en-gb..Accept-Encoding: gzip, deflate..User-Agent: Mozilla/
  4.0 (compatible; MSIE 5.5; Windows NT 4.0)..Host: alice..Connection: K
  eep-Alive..Pragma: no-cache....
##
T 192.0.2.17:80 -> 192.0.2.21:3884 [AP]
  HTTP/1.0 200 OK..Date: Sun, 15 Jul 2001 08:02:57 GMT..Server: Apache/1
  .3.9 (Unix) Debian/GNU mod_layout/2.10.6 mod_perl/1.21_03-dev..Last-Mo
  dified: Mon, 17 Mar 1997 13:11:41 GMT..ETag: "1fe63-211-332d430d"..Acc
  ept-Ranges: bytes..Content-Length: 529..Connection: close..Content-Typ
  e: text/html; charset=iso-8859-1....<!DOCTYPE HTML PUBLIC "-//SQ//DTD
  HTML 2.0 + all extensions//EN" "hmpro3.dtd">..<HTML>..<HEAD>..<TITLE>S
  tandards - UIT</TITLE></HEAD>..<BODY BGCOLOR="#FFFFFF">..<H1 ALIGN="CE
  NTER">UIT STANDARDS</H1>..<CENTER>..<TABLE>..<TR>..<TD></TD>..<TD><A H
  REF="std-web.htm">UITnet web page layout</A>..<TD></TD></TR>..<TR
  >..<TD></TD>..<TD><A HREF="std-cols.htm">Colour conventions</A></TD>..
  <TD></TD></TR>..<TR>..<TD></TD>..<TD><A HREF="std-mktmaterials.htm">Ma
  rketing materials</A></TD>..<TD></TD></TR></TABLE></CENTER></BODY></HT
  ML>..
####
```

ngrep shows you all the request and response headers clearly (even though they all run together because **ngrep** shows carriage returns and linefeeds as dots to save space). You can see that the headers are giving information both about the data being transferred, and about the client and server involved in the transfer: the client is Microsoft Internet Explorer, and the server is Apache running on Debian Linux.

Now we connect to a Web server using **telnet** to run sessions by hand so we can control and observe what's happening. The trace below illustrates what often happens nowadays when you use the old HTTP/0.9 simple request format with modern servers – you get an error reported in the page returned, saying there is no such site:

```
alice% telnet www.microsoft.com 80
    Connected to www.microsoft.akadns.net.
GET /
    HTTP/1.1 404 Object Not Found
    Server: Microsoft-IIS/5.0
    Date: Thu, 19 Jul 2001 16:37:57 GMT
    Content-Type: text/html
    Content-Length: 111

    <html><head><title>Site Not Found</title></head>
    <body>No web site is configured at this address.</body></html>
    Connection closed by foreign host.
alice%
```

What's happening is that the server machine is hosting many different Web sites, all on the same IP address, and it doesn't know which one you want. To get over this, you must include a **Host:** header, specifying the Web site name you want, and to do that, you must use the full-request format:

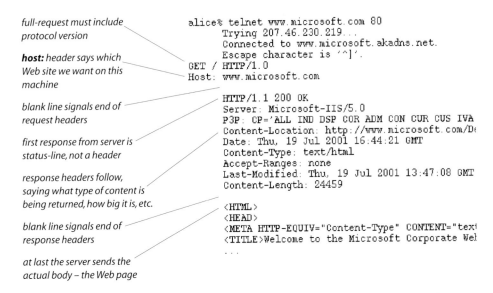

full-request must include
protocol version

host: header says which
Web site we want on this
machine

blank line signals end of
request headers

first response from server is
status-line, not a header

response headers follow,
saying what type of content is
being returned, how big it is, etc.

blank line signals end of
response headers

at last the server sends the
actual body – the Web page

```
alice% telnet www.microsoft.com 80
      Trying 207.46.230.219...
      Connected to www.microsoft.akadns.net.
      Escape character is '^]'.
GET / HTTP/1.0
Host: www.microsoft.com

HTTP/1.1 200 OK
      Server: Microsoft-IIS/5.0
      P3P: CP='ALL IND DSP COR ADM CON CUR CUS IVA
      Content-Location: http://www.microsoft.com/De
      Date: Thu, 19 Jul 2001 16:44:21 GMT
      Content-Type: text/html
      Accept-Ranges: none
      Last-Modified: Thu, 19 Jul 2001 13:47:08 GMT
      Content-Length: 24459

<HTML>
<HEAD>
<META HTTP-EQUIV="Content-Type" CONTENT="text
<TITLE>Welcome to the Microsoft Corporate Wel
...
```

You *must* include a **Host:** header with HTTP/1.1. If you omit it you get an error, although
some servers may just say "Site not found":

```
alice% telnet www.netscape.com 80
    Trying 207.200.89.193...
    Connected to home-gslb.netscape.com.
    Escape character is '^]'.                    ─── host: header missing
GET / HTTP/1.1

    HTTP/1.1 400 Bad request
    Server: Netscape-Enterprise/4.1
    Date: Thu, 19 Jul 2001 17:15:44 GMT
    Content-length: 147
    Content-type: text/html
    Connection: close

    <HTML><HEAD><TITLE>Bad request</TITLE></HEAD>
    <BODY><H1>Bad request</H1>
    Your browser sent a query this server could not understand.
    </BODY></HTML>
    Connection closed by foreign host.
alice%
```

In the next module we continue with headers, and see how the server uses MIME to specify
the type of data being returned.

14.8 How MIME fits in with HTTP

As we explained in Module 12.2, MIME, the Multipurpose Internet Mail Extensions, performs two important functions for e-mail: allowing arbitrary binary content to be sent safely over links that can only handle 7-bit characters, and specifying the type of content in the message. In HTTP, the Web client and server also use MIME, but they use it only to exchange information about the type of data they are transferring to one another. (They don't need to worry about encoding binary data as 7-bit characters, because HTTP is running over TCP, which handles 8-bit binary data faithfully – it's "8-bit safe" or "8-bit clean.") Below we show a simple session using **telnet** to retrieve a GIF image file:

```
alice% telnet dave 80
    Trying 192.0.2.5...
    Connected to dave.example.com.          we're using HTTP/1.0 so
    Escape character is '^]'.               we don't have to include a
GET /dir.gif HTTP/1.0                        Host: header

    HTTP/1.0 200 Document follows
    MIME-Version: 1.0
    Server: CERN/3.0pre6
    Date: Thursday, 12-Jul-01 06:07:31 GMT
    Content-Type: image/gif
    Content-Length: 138
    Last-Modified: Friday, 06-Dec-96 17:11:41 GMT
    X-httpd-warning: Your browser didn't send the Accept header line for this

    GIF89a^L^@^K^@\242^@^@\377^@\375^@\375\375^@^@^@\375\375^@\375^@^@^@\375^@
    ^@^@, ^@^@^@^@^L^@^K^@^B^C^W^H\272\274\367\247\251\350\340^CT\316\254\257\336
    ^_^Xz^_\331Y(\224^@^@!MACGCon ^D^C^P0^@^@^@^AWritten by GIFConverter 2.3.2 of
    Mar 6, 1993^@;
    Connection closed by foreign host.
alice%
```

This illustrates several points:

- the server says it's using MIME to describe the contents of the data it's returning
- the data are an **image**, specifically in the **gif** image format
- the data consist of 138 bytes
- browsers can use an **Accept:** header in their request to the server to tell it what type of data formats the browser is prepared to handle. We, as client, didn't send an **Accept:** header, so the server gives a warning. (We don't cover **Accept** any further; we only mentioned it here to avoid confusion in case you come across it.)
- the server transfers the data un-encoded, as raw binary data, because it's working over an 8-bit safe TCP transport. The contents of the file show as gobbledygook because that's how the binary characters in the GIF file print on our terminal.

MIME is important because it lets the browser take informed decisions about what to do with the content, relieving the user of having to specify what's to be done:

- the obvious examples are GIF and JPEG images, which are normally displayed inline as an integral part of the page

- when your browser downloads a page that is specified, say, as type **application/Zip** and you have configured your browser (or Windows Explorer if you're on Windows) to use the WinZip program to handle ZIP files, the browser can automatically prompt (Figure 14.7) and ask if you want to open the file when it's downloaded. This saves you having to save the file to disk, and then explicitly start WinZip to process the file

- if the browser doesn't recognize the content-type of the Web page, or if it doesn't have the necessary code in-built to handle it, or doesn't know what program to use to process the data, it will typically offer to save the file to disk for you.

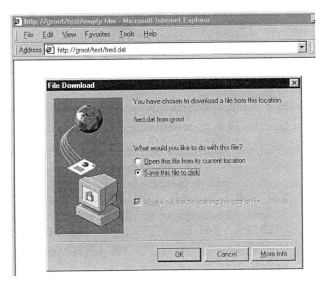

Figure 14.7 Automatic prompt

ngrep is a very easy way to see what MIME headers are being transmitted from the server in a live session. This is useful if a browser seems to be misbehaving and is doing something strange with a particular page or type of data – you can see whether the server is sending the correct information about content-type. If the server is specifying the wrong content-type, the client may be acting correctly but in response to incorrect data.

14.9 Lab – HTTP/1.1 – persistent TCP connections

use HTTP version 1.0, which doesn't support persistent connections

connection is terminated immediately data have been sent

```
alice# telnet bob 80
Escape character is '^]'.
GET /test/tinyfile.txt HTTP/1.0

HTTP/1.1 200 OK
Date: Fri, 20 Jul 2001 06:08:40 GMT
Content-Length: 70
Connection: close
Content-Type: text/plain; charset=iso-8859-1

Now yiz are in the Willingdone Museyroom.
This is a Prooshious gunn.
Connection closed by foreign host.
alice#
```

In HTTP/0.9 and 1.0, the TCP connection is:

- established by the client just before the client sends the request to the server
- terminated by the server when the server has finished sending the Web page.

One connection is used for every request: if a Web page contains 12 GIF images, then a total of 13 TCP connections are used – one for the main page, and one each for the image file transfers. TCP connections are relatively expensive in terms of performance: they need three packets (SYN, SYN-ACK, ACK) to establish, and four (FIN, ACK, FIN, ACK) to terminate, but these in turn involve many round-trips, so we'd like to minimize the number of separate connections if we can. HTTP/1.1 does this by allowing *persistent TCP connections:* the same TCP connection can be used for several requests in a row. The advantages are:

- fewer packets are sent
- fewer round-trips are required
- the client can "pipeline" requests, i.e. send several requests without waiting for a response for each. As a result, the elapsed time per request is only the time taken to transmit its packets, not the round-trip time for transmit/wait/receive-response.

*use HTTP version 1.1 (so must include a **host:** header)*

connection remains open even though all the data have been sent

```
alice# telnet bob 80
Escape character is '^]'.
GET /test/tinyfile.txt HTTP/1.1
host: bob

HTTP/1.1 200 OK
Date: Fri, 20 Jul 2001 06:17:30 GMT
Content-Length: 70
Content-Type: text/plain; charset=iso-8859-1

Now yiz are in the Willingdone Museyroom.
This is a Prooshious gunn.
```

You can see the difference very easily by running two **telnet** HTTP sessions, the first with version 1.0 and the second with 1.1. (We've removed some of the headers, etc. from the examples above to save space.) With HTTP/1.0, the termination closes immediately. However, with HTTP/1.1, the connection remains open for about 15 seconds, during which you can issue further requests.

> **Exercise:** repeat the HTTP/1.1 session, but while the connection is waiting to terminate, issue another request (or repeat the same one again). Don't forget to include the **host:** header again, and the blank line terminating the headers.

Below are the **tcpdump** traces of two HTTP sessions, side by side, lines truncated to save space. The left-hand trace is HTTP/1.0, the right-hand is HTTP/1.1. In both cases the browser has requested the same small Web page that contains several images. You can see HTTP/1.0 establishes and terminates several connections (S and F flags in the trace), whereas HTTP/1.1 uses a single session:

```
dave.1354 > bob.80:  S 1615168000:1615168000(0)        dave.1353 > bob.80:  S 1598272000:1598272000(0)
bob.80 > dave.1354:  S 1061641448:1061641448(0)        bob.80 > dave.1353:  S 923937705:923937705(0) a
dave.1354 > bob.80:  . ack 1 win 4096                  dave.1353 > bob.80:  . ack 1 win 4096
dave.1354 > bob.80:  P 1:30(29) ack 1 win 4096         dave.1353 > bob.80:  P 1:30(29) ack 1 win 4096
bob.80 > dave.1354:  . ack 30 win 16060 (DF)           bob.80 > dave.1353:  . ack 30 win 16060 (DF)
dave.1354 > bob.80:  P 30:32(2) ack 1 win 4096         dave.1353 > bob.80:  P 30:41(11) ack 1 win 4096
bob.80 > dave.1354:  P 1:1461(1460) ack 32 win         bob.80 > dave.1353:  . ack 41 win 16060 (DF)
bob.80 > dave.1354:  P 1461:2424(963) ack 32 wi        dave.1353 > bob.80:  P 41:43(2) ack 1 win 4096
bob.80 > dave.1354:  F 2424:2424(0) ack 32 win         bob.80 > dave.1353:  P 1:1461(1460) ack 43 win
dave.1354 > bob.80:  . ack 2425 win 2697               bob.80 > dave.1353:  P 1461:2405(944) ack 43 wi
bob.80 > dave.1354:  F 32:32(0) ack 2425 win 40        dave.1353 > bob.80:  . ack 2405 win 3740
bob.80 > dave.1354:  . ack 33 win 16060 (DF)           dave.1353 > bob.80:  P 43:76(33) ack 2405 win 4
dave.1355 > bob.80:  S 1617472000:1617472000(0)        bob.80 > dave.1353:  . ack 76 win 16060 (DF)
bob.80 > dave.1355:  S 1085181942:1085181942(0)        dave.1353 > bob.80:  P 76:87(11) ack 2405 win 4
dave.1355 > bob.80:  . ack 1 win 4096                  bob.80 > dave.1353:  . ack 87 win 16060 (DF)
dave.1355 > bob.80:  P 1:34(33) ack 1 win 4096         dave.1353 > bob.80:  P 87:89(2) ack 2405 win 40
bob.80 > dave.1355:  . ack 34 win 16060 (DF)           bob.80 > dave.1353:  P 2405:3865(1460) ack 89 w
dave.1355 > bob.80:  P 34:36(2) ack 1 win 4096         bob.80 > dave.1353:  P 3865:5325(1460) ack 89 w
bob.80 > dave.1355:  P 1:1461(1460) ack 36 win         dave.1353 > bob.80:  . ack 5325 win 3224
bob.80 > dave.1355:  P 1461:2921(1460) ack 36 w        bob.80 > dave.1353:  P 5325:6785(1460) ack 89 w
dave.1355 > bob.80:  . ack 2921 win 3224               bob.80 > dave.1353:  P 6785:7410(625) ack 89 wi
bob.80 > dave.1355:  P 2921:4381(1460) ack 36 w        dave.1353 > bob.80:  . ack 7410 win 3187
bob.80 > dave.1355:  FP 4381:5025(644) ack 36 w        dave.1353 > bob.80:  P 89:123(34) ack 7410 win
dave.1355 > bob.80:  . ack 5026 win 1120               bob.80 > dave.1353:  . ack 123 win 16060 (DF)
dave.1355 > bob.80:  . ack 5026 win 3168               dave.1353 > bob.80:  P 123:134(11) ack 7410 win
dave.1355 > bob.80:  F 36:36(0) ack 5026 win 40        bob.80 > dave.1353:  . ack 134 win 16060 (DF)
bob.80 > dave.1355:  . ack 37 win 16060 (DF)           dave.1353 > bob.80:  P 134:136(2) ack 7410 win
dave.1356 > bob.80:  S 1619264000:1619264000(0)        bob.80 > dave.1353:  P 7410:8870(1460) ack 136
bob.80 > dave.1356:  S 1102775340:1102775340(0)        bob.80 > dave.1353:  . 8870:10330(1460) ack 136
dave.1356 > bob.80:  . ack 1 win 4096                  dave.1353 > bob.80:  . ack 10330 win 3224
dave.1356 > bob.80:  P 1:35(34) ack 1 win 4096         bob.80 > dave.1353:  P 10330:11219(889) ack 136
bob.80 > dave.1356:  . ack 35 win 16060 (DF)           dave.1353 > bob.80:  . ack 11219 win 4096
dave.1356 > bob.80:  P 35:37(2) ack 1 win 4096         bob.80 > dave.1353:  F 11219:11219(0) ack 136 w
bob.80 > dave.1356:  P 1:1461(1460) ack 37 win         dave.1353 > bob.80:  . ack 11220 win 4096
bob.80 > dave.1356:  P 1461:2921(1460) ack 37 w        dave.1353 > bob.80:  F 136:136(0) ack 11220 win
dave.1356 > bob.80:  . ack 2921 win 3224               bob.80 > dave.1353:  . ack 137 win 16060 (DF)
bob.80 > dave.1356:  FP 2921:3829(908) ack 37 w
dave.1356 > bob.80:  . ack 3830 win 2316
dave.1356 > bob.80:  . ack 3830 win 4096
dave.1356 > bob.80:  F 37:37(0) ack 3830 win 40
bob.80 > dave.1356:  . ack 38 win 16060 (DF)
```

In traces like this you may sometimes see HTTP/1.1 using more than one connection. What's happening is not that the client is using a separate connection per request, but that it's using multiple persistent connections simultaneously, e.g. so that it can download images on one connection at the same time as retrieving the main Web page on another connection. You will see that in HTTP/1.1 the connection terminations all happen together, very close to the end of the session, when they are no longer required because everything has been retrieved. By contrast, in HTTP/1.0 the terminations happen throughout the trace, as each individual retrieval finishes. Different browsers use different numbers of simultaneous connections to a single server; the recommended number is two, in order to avoid congestion in server traffic, but some browsers use four or six.

14.10 URLs, machine names, and the DNS

In Module 14.1 we said that a URL (Uniform Resource Locator) consists of four parts:

protocol-scheme :// host-address [:port] pagename

and we'll look at some of these in a little more detail here.

Protocol scheme

This is "**HTTP**" for normal Web transfers, and "**HTTPS**" for secure Web transfers (Module 14.18). This field is not case-sensitive.

Host address component of a URL

This is the address of an individual machine – either its IP number or its name. As usual, if you specify a name, the client uses the DNS to convert the name to an IP number, and your Web client will then use the IP number to connect to the server. Of course, if the name isn't in the DNS you will get an error.

In Module 11.3 we saw that the DNS can contain multiple MX records, to support multiple e-mail servers. The DNS also allows a machine or hostname to have several different IP address entries ("A" records) meaning that several different machines share this name. You can see that **www.ibm.com** has four different addresses, and presumably, four different servers:

```
alice# host www.ibm.com
www.ibm.com            A        129.42.17.99
www.ibm.com            A        129.42.18.99
www.ibm.com            A        129.42.19.99
www.ibm.com            A        129.42.16.99
```

Just as with e-mail, this gives us a form of load balancing. Instead of returning the entries in the same order every time, the DNS server round-robins them in successive DNS responses, so that each entry gets an equal number of turns at being top in the list:

```
alice# host www.ibm.com
www.ibm.com            A        129.42.19.99
www.ibm.com            A        129.42.16.99
www.ibm.com            A        129.42.17.99
www.ibm.com            A        129.42.18.99
alice# host www.ibm.com
www.ibm.com            A        129.42.16.99
www.ibm.com            A        129.42.17.99
www.ibm.com            A        129.42.18.99
www.ibm.com            A        129.42.19.99
```

Because each successive Web connection will go to a different server, the load is shared more or less equally across the four servers. However, unlike with MX records, if the first host that's tried isn't available, you got an error: successive hosts are not tried.

Most Web server hostnames start with "**www**," but this is only a convention. As you see above, the whole name, e.g. **www.ibm.com**, is treated as just a name in the DNS, so *any* name that you enter in the DNS, and that has an IP number, can be used as the name of a Web server, e.g.

search.support.microsoft.com

cgi-bin.web.cern

ftp.gnu.org

proxy.belnet.be

ddda.ie

(Our favorite weird Web site name is **cr.yp.to**.)

The host address field is not case-sensitive, because hostnames in the DNS are not case-sensitive.

Port number

The port number defaults to HTTP's well-known port (:80) but any number can be used if the server's configuration allows it. Other common numbers are :81 and :8080 for connecting to proxy servers.

As the Web interface is used increasingly often for configuring individual applications (e.g. mail servers, database applications, etc.), it's not uncommon nowadays to have several different Web server applications running on a single machine. Each of course has to listen on its own port – otherwise the client would have no way of specifying which one is required. These "servers" are usually small, special-purpose servers dedicated to the one application, and may even be built into the application itself.

14.11 URLs and Web page names

For simple Web pages, the page name is often the path name of the file containing the HTML code for the page, on the Web server machine. The path is usually not the full path of the file on the machine, but is relative to some base "document root directory" beneath which are stored all the Web page files. For example, the URL **http://www.uit.co.uk/training/course-index.htm** refers to the page name

   /training/course-index.htm

which in fact refers to the file on our UNIX Web server machine (Figure 14.8):

   /usr/local/netscape/doc/training/course-index.htm

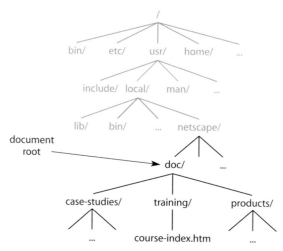

Figure 14.8 How a Web page name relates to the file name

Because the page name often refers to a real file, the page name is case-sensitive if the filename is too. In practice this means that page names are case-sensitive on UNIX servers and not on Windows-NT servers. As you usually don't know which is which, the best policy is to enter page names exactly as you were given them.

If no page name is specified, it is interpreted as "/", which is what is referred to as the *home page* of the Web site. This is why we usually use the request "**GET /**" when we're testing a Web connection using **telnet**.

The page name doesn't have to refer to a relative path name. It's entirely up to the server to interpret the page name as it wishes. Mapping page names to filenames as above is very easy on a conventional computer. However, if the Web server is the interface to a special-purpose box such as a router, or a network printer, or a firewall, there may be no conventional file system or even operating system on the box, and in these cases page names are interpreted by the server to display some internal data or to present a form for modifying the configuration.

"Dynamic" Web pages

The course-index.htm page in Figure 14.8 is a *static* page: it consists of HTML contained in a text file on disk. The contents of the file don't change, and each time you request this page you get exactly the same content.

However, it's often necessary to include dynamically generated information in a page. For example, when you search a Web site for a particular term, the list of matches depends (we hope) on what you're searching for, or, if you use a Web-based tool like our sub-net calculators from Part 1, the results displayed are generated from the network details you input earlier.

Pages like this are created by special applications or scripts that run under the control of the Web server. Typically, you enter some information via a form on a Web page. When you press "Enter" or "Submit" or "Go," the data you entered on the form are sent to the Web server, which runs the application configured to handle this form, and the Web server copies the input data to the application. The application performs its calculations or searches the pages on disk or whatever it's supposed to do, and generates an HTML page containing the results (Figure 14.9). This stream of HTML data is passed to the Web server, which serves it to the client. These applications are often called *CGI scripts* or *CGI programs* because the standard for exchanging information between server and application is the *Common Gateway Interface (CGI)*.

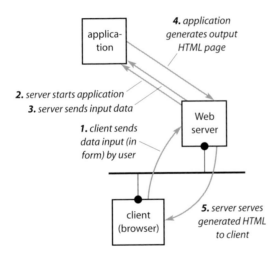

Figure 14.9 Browser retrieving a dynamic page from a server

Another type of page is where some of the page is stored as HTML on disk, but it also contains special commands that are interpreted by the Web server before it serves the page to the client. *Server-side includes* and Microsoft's *Active Server Pages* (*ASP*) and PHP work in this way. They can be used for simple tasks (e.g. to insert a "last updated" time on the page automatically), or for very complex applications interrogating and updating databases.

14.12 Web proxy servers

A "proxy" in both human and computing senses is an agent that does something on your behalf, so you don't have to do it yourself. A common example is appointing someone as your proxy to vote for you at a shareholders' meeting when you can't attend. For HTTP, a proxy server is a server that your browser connects to for some or all of its transfers; your browser sends requests to the proxy server, and then the proxy server retrieves the pages from the real servers (which are called *origin servers*). Figure 14.10 shows how a proxy server is typically installed on a LAN; all clients on the LAN connect to the proxy, and it retrieves the pages from the remote Web sites.

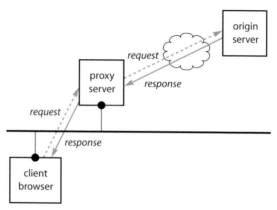

Figure 14.10 Typical proxy server configuration on a LAN

The proxy appears as a server to the client, and as a client to the origin server. Figure 14.11 shows a small network that we've used to show proxying in operation. The browser client requests the page **/images/navtop.gif** from the Web server on 192.0.2.29, via the proxy server on 192.0.2.17. (Neither server is using port 80 just to emphasize that it's not essential.) Figure 14.12 shows an **ngrep** trace for the conversations. (Because **ngrep** doesn't have the facility to print host addresses as named, we've cheated and edited the trace by hand to show names instead of numbers, to make it easier to see what each machine is doing.)

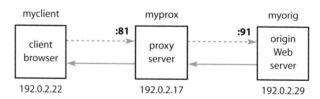

Figure 14.11 Proxying in operation

The trace shows all the headers, in both directions, and illustrates:

- the conversation from browser to proxy is almost the same as if the client was talking to a normal Web server

- however, the client sends the *full* URL to the proxy, including the protocol scheme, host address, port number and page name. The proxy needs this information to know which Web server to connect to, and on which port

- the proxy specifies only the page name when connecting to the real (origin) Web server – it specified the IP address and port number implicitly when it established the TCP connection to this server.

```
alice% ngrep port 80 or 81 or 91
interface: eth0 (192.0.2.0/255.255.255.128)          full URL
filter: ip and ( port 80 or 81 or 91 )
####
T myclient:4003 -> myprox:81 [AP]
  GET http://mail:91/images/navtop.gif HTTP/1.1..Accept: */*..Accept-Lan
  guage: en-gb..User-Agent: Mozilla/4.0 (compatible; MSIE 5.5; Windows N
  T 4.0)..Host: mail:91..Proxy-Connection: Keep-Alive..Pragma: no-cache.
    ...
#####                                              page name only
T myprox:1246 -> myorig:91 [AP]
  GET /images/navtop.gif HTTP/1.0..
##
T myprox:1246 -> myorig:91 [AP]
  Accept: */*..Accept-Language: en-gb..User-Agent: Mozilla/4.0 (compatib
  le; MSIE 5.5; Windows NT 4.0)..Host: mail:91..Proxy-Connection: Keep-A
  live..Pragma: no-cache....
##
T myorig:91 -> myprox:1246 [AP]
  HTTP/1.0 200 Document Follows..MIME-Version: 1.0..Content-Type: image/
  gif..Content-Length: 179....GIF89a ...1.........................,....
  ..@......0.R. ..M{. .mBi.h*d.D...Y4..U...}........9...L~.L....D!:..j
  .d....z,..e...$...s2...xu.....x].S.%J5..9Z. }..."0c.a..._k.7.......;
##
T myprox:81 -> myclient:4003 [AP]
  HTTP/1.0 200 Document Follows..
####
T myprox:81 -> myclient:4003 [AFP]
  MIME-Version: 1.0..Content-Type: image/gif..Content-Length: 179....GIF
  89a ....1............................,.... ..@......0.R. ..M{. .mBi.h*d.
  D...Y4..U...}........9...L~.L....D!:..j.d....z,..e...$...s2...xu......
  x].S.%J5..9Z. }..."0c.a..._k.7.......;
####exit
alice%
```

Figure 14.12 ngrep trace of Web page retrieved via proxy on network in Figure 14.11

14.13 Why use a Web proxy server?

The two main reasons for using a proxy are performance and security.

1. proxy servers can improve performance by caching the Web pages they retrieve. If another client on the LAN requests a page that the proxy server has cached, the proxy can send it to the client straight away, without having to contact the origin server again. This is very much faster because the proxy server is on the LAN, and the data are transferred over 10Mbps or 100Mbps Ethernet, instead of using the Internet connection, which is often 100 times slower. Caching can give big performance improvements because there's usually a lot of duplication in the sets of Web pages retrieved by different people in the same organization. An unusually nice side effect of this is that the more clients that use the proxy, the more pages are cached, the better the chance that any given page is already in cache and the better the average response time.

   Other benefits are that the load on the Internet connection is reduced, making it more responsive for retrievals and other traffic that have to go to the Internet, and that the overall traffic on the Internet is reduced too.

   Because the proxy caches pages, caching in the desktop clients, i.e. in the Web browsers, can be disabled, saving a lot of disk space over the network as a whole, with little performance penalty.

   Some proxy servers allow you to specify a list of Web sites or pages that your users commonly refer to. These pages are then downloaded off-peak, ready for use from the cache in the proxy next day. This may allow users to retrieve the information they need even if the Internet connection fails during the day

2. proxies are also used for security reasons. In many organizations, desktop PCs on the LAN don't have direct access to the Internet as a matter of policy: they are blocked by the firewall (Chapter 24). However, clients can access a proxy server on the LAN, which in turn retrieves Web pages for them, because it is allowed access to the Internet

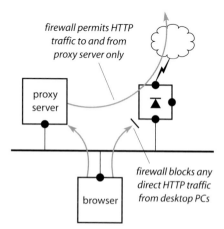

firewall permits HTTP traffic to and from proxy server only

proxy server

browser

firewall blocks any direct HTTP traffic from desktop PCs

Figure 14.13 Only the proxy server is allowed access to the Internet

(Figure 14.13). This reduces the contact between the LAN and the Internet, while still giving users the access they need. It also allows the network administrator to control and log what users download, which we discuss further in Module 25.3.

Finally, there are also special-purpose proxies to help you cut down on downloads of pages and components that you don't want, e.g. banner ads, pop-up windows, animated GIF images, and other rubbish. For example, on its Web page the "Proxomitron Universal Web Filter" explains it does the following:

- *"Stop or limit Pop-up windows*
- *Control MIDI music and other sounds*
- *Freeze animated .GIFs – load only the first frame*
- *Kill most all advertising banners*
- *Stop Web-Branding and other scripts added by web space providers*
- *Stop Pop-up alert/confirm boxes*
- *Remove slow web counters*
- *Stop web pages and ads from "auto-refreshing"*
- *Remove Dynamic HTML*
- *Prevent getting stuck in someone's frames*
- *Remove frames or tables altogether for that matter*
- *Kill or change selected Java scripts and applets*
- *Add your own scripts to pages!*
- *Remove or replace web page and/or table background images*
- *Stop Status bar scrollers*
- *Unhide URLs obscured by status line text*
- *Convert blinking text to bold*
- *Remove Layers and Style sheets."*

The next module explains how to configure your browser to use a proxy server.

14.14 Lab – configuring your browser to use a proxy server, Internet Explorer

This section assumes you are configuring a browser on a LAN connected to the Internet, rather than on a dial-up PC. We're using version 5.5 of Internet Explorer.

Select menu **Tools > Internet Options > Connections > LAN Settings** (Figure 14.14):

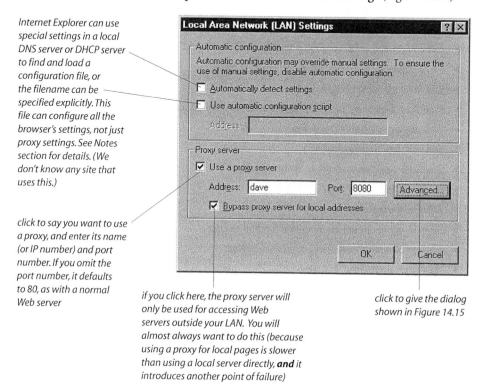

Internet Explorer can use special settings in a local DNS server or DHCP server to find and load a configuration file, or the filename can be specified explicitly. This file can configure all the browser's settings, not just proxy settings. See Notes section for details. (We don't know any site that uses this.)

click to say you want to use a proxy, and enter its name (or IP number) and port number. If you omit the port number, it defaults to 80, as with a normal Web server

*if you click here, the proxy server will only be used for accessing Web servers outside your LAN. You will almost always want to do this (because using a proxy for local pages is slower than using a local server directly, **and** it introduces another point of failure)*

click to give the dialog shown in Figure 14.15

Figure 14.14 Proxy configuration – basic

You can easily see whether a request is being sent to the proxy server or to the origin server by running **tcpdump** and watching the connection being established. Or, if you're quick enough, observe the status bar at the bottom of the browser (Figure 14.16), which shows the name of the proxy server if a proxy is being used. (To slow down the status message display, you can temporarily change the name of the proxy server in the settings dialog to a non-existent name, so the status line displays its message for several seconds, before finally giving an error message. But don't forget to set the name back to its correct value when you've finished your investigations.)

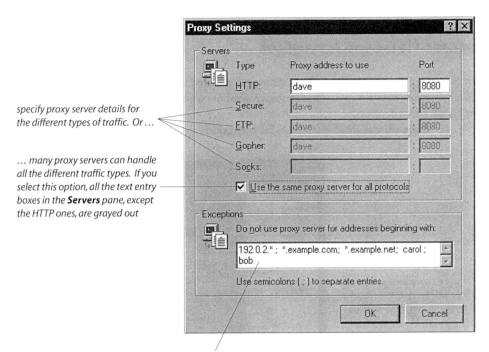

specify proxy server details for
the different types of traffic. Or ...

... many proxy servers can handle
all the different traffic types. If you
select this option, all the text entry
boxes in the **Servers** pane, except
the HTTP ones, are grayed out

don't use the proxy server when retrieving pages from these servers.
We've specified the address of our local LAN by IP number, the names of
our local intranet Web servers (**carol** and **bob**) and the Web sites for
our overseas branches, because we can reach them over our private
network without going out to the Internet

Figure 14.15 Proxy configuration – advanced

Figure 14.16 Name of the proxy server displayed in status bar

14.15 Lab – configuring your browser to use a proxy server, Netscape Navigator

In Netscape 6.2, select menu **Edit** > **Preferences** > **Advanced** > **Proxies** > **Manual proxy configuration** (Figure 14.17). (For earlier versions of Netscape see the equivalent two dialogs in Figure 14.18.)

Enter the details of the proxies for the various protocols.

Netscape can load a configuration file to configure all the browser's settings, not just proxy settings. See Notes section for details

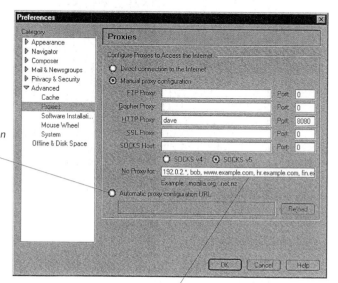

*don't use the proxy server when retrieving pages from these servers. We've specified the address of our local LAN by IP number, the names of our local intranet Web servers (**carol** and **bob**) and the Web sites for our overseas branches, because we can reach them over our private network without going out to the Internet. Unlike Internet Explorer, we can't use wildcards in the names, so we've had to enumerate all our Web servers explicitly:* **hr.example.com, fin.example.com** *, etc.*

Figure 14.17 Selecting Manual proxy configuration

(a)

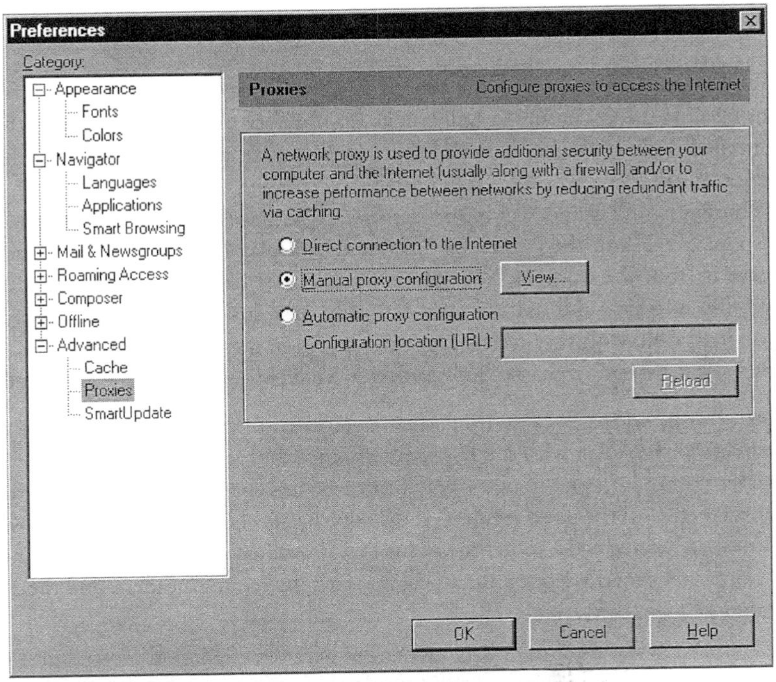

Preferences

Category:

- Appearance
  - Fonts
  - Colors
- Navigator
  - Languages
  - Applications
  - Smart Browsing
- Mail & Newsgroups
- Roaming Access
- Composer
- Offline
- Advanced
  - Cache
  - **Proxies**
  - SmartUpdate

Proxies   Configure proxies to access the Internet

A network proxy is used to provide additional security between your computer and the Internet (usually along with a firewall) and/or to increase performance between networks by reducing redundant traffic via caching.

○ Direct connection to the Internet

⦿ Manual proxy configuration   View...

○ Automatic proxy configuration

Configuration location (URL): [   ]

Reload

OK   Cancel   Help

(b)

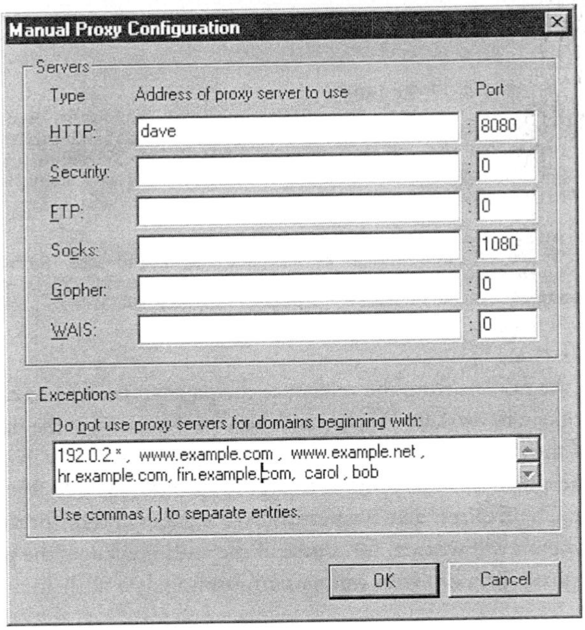

Manual Proxy Configuration

Servers

Type	Address of proxy server to use	Port
HTTP:	dave	8080
Security:		0
FTP:		0
Socks:		1080
Gopher:		0
WAIS:		0

Exceptions

Do not use proxy servers for domains beginning with:

192.0.2.* , www.example.com , www.example.net , hr.example.com, fin.example.com, carol , bob

Use commas (,) to separate entries.

OK   Cancel

Figure 14.18 Manual Proxy configuration (earlier Netscape versions)

14.16 Caching in the browser

We already mentioned caching in the context of DNS (Module 8.10) but just to remind you, it means keeping a copy locally in fast storage (in memory or on disk) so that if the information is needed again it can be displayed more quickly than retrieving it again in full from its original location.

Web browsers, like some Web proxy servers, cache pages they have retrieved. If the user requests a page that's in the cache, the browser can display it immediately, instead of having to retrieve it from the original Web server. ("Oh, I just downloaded '**logo.gif**', so I won't bother doing it again – I'll use the copy I already have instead.") Cached pages are usually stored on hard disk, with very recent pages also stored in memory for faster access.

Browsers use two principal methods to decide whether a page in cache is up to date:

1. the browser knows the date/time when it retrieved the page the first time. It sends a request to the server with the **If-Modified-Since:** header set to this date/time. The server responds in one of two ways. If the page has changed, it returns the page as normal with all the usual headers. If the page hasn't changed, it returns a 304 "Not Modified" status code, to tell the client that its cached copy is up to date. The **ngrep** trace below shows a request for a GIF file with the request headers, and the 304 response from the server.

   This reduces the amount of data exchanged between client and server, but if the network connection is slow, it still causes a noticeable delay for the user, because it involves a round-trip between client and server

```
T 192.0.2.22:1273 -> 192.0.2.17:80 [AP]
  GET /uit-xpt.gif HTTP/1.1..Accept: */*..Referer: http://grootlx..Accep
  t-Language: en-gb..Accept-Encoding: gzip, deflate..If-Modified-Since:
  Tue, 08 Jun 1999 14:30:02 GMT..If-None-Match: "1fde0-3b8-375d28ea"..Us
  er-Agent: Mozilla/4.0 (compatible; MSIE 5.5; Windows NT 4.0)..Host: gr
  ootlx..Connection: Keep-Alive....
#
T 192.0.2.17:80 -> 192.0.2.22:1273 [AP]
  HTTP/1.1 304 Not Modified..Date: Tue, 24 Jul 2001 07:29:44 GMT..Server
  : Apache/1.3.9 (Unix) Debian/GNU mod_layout/2.10.6 mod_perl/1.21_03-de
  v..Connection: Keep-Alive..Keep-Alive: timeout=15, max=98..ETag: "1fde
  0-3b8-375d28ea"....
```

2. the browser can use the headers from the version of the page in its cache to calculate whether the page is likely to be stale. The **Expires:** header, if present, is the date/time when this version of the page will become out of date. If you have a copy in your cache, and the **Expires:** date is before today, the page should be retrieved from the original server again. The **Expires:** date is specified by the page's author (or the program creating the page) when it was written. Of course, if the author changes the page on the server before the **Expires:** date, browsers will have misleading data in their caches.

   Other headers are used too. There are specific **Cache-Control:** headers that the server can use. The trace below shows such a header containing the specification **max-age=1800**, which says this can be kept in a cache and considered up to date for the next 1800 seconds = 30 minutes, which, as you can see, ties in exactly with the **Expires:** time.

```
T 156.27.8.202:80 -> 192.0.2.22:1290 [AP]
   HTTP/1.1 304 Not Modified..Server: Microsoft-IIS/4.0..Date: Tue, 24 Ju
   l 2001 08:35:40 GMT..Cache-Control: max-age=1800..Expires: Tue, 24 Jul
   2001 09:05:40 GMT..ETag: "1a7f38aa313c11:1769"..Content-Length: 0....
```

Browsers typically let you specify whether to perform the above validation checks every time a page is retrieved from the cache. To be completely up to date, you should check it every time. However, for most purposes it's adequate to check only if the last time you retrieved the page was in a different browser session.

To configure the cache operation in Internet Explorer, select menu **Tools > Internet Options > General > Temporary Internet Files > Settings** (Figure 14.19). The meanings of the options are obvious, with one exception: **Automatically** (Internet Explorer 5 and later only). Microsoft "explains" this as follows: this setting is the same as **Every time you start Internet Explorer** but with a logic algorithm to understand the habits of Web page behavior. When you return to a page you viewed previously, it checks for new content only if you last viewed this page in an earlier session of Internet Explorer or on an earlier day. Over time, if Internet Explorer determines that images on the page are changing infrequently, it checks for newer images even less frequently.

The cache settings for Netscape are so similar we haven't illustrated them.

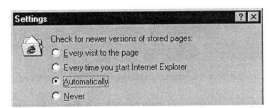

Figure 14.19 Cache Settings

	Internet Explorer	**Netscape Navigator**
check with the origin server whether the page is up to date, re-loading if necessary	*key* F5 *or click* **Refresh**	*key* Ctrl-R *or menu* **View > Reload**
force a re-load even if the cache appears up to date	*key* Ctrl-F5	*press key* Shift *with menu* **View > Reload**
re-draw the page on-screen without retrieving the page from cache or the origin server	*N/A*	*menu* **View > Refresh** (not in versions after 4.x)

The history mechanism (**Back** and **Forward** buttons in the browser) doesn't perform cache checking, deliberately. Its function is to provide a quick way to view what you were looking at previously.

14.17 Security – authentication

Web servers can "protect" specific pages or directories, so that when they are requested, the user has to authenticate in some way, e.g. enter a username and password. Internally, the server maintains a list of protected pages and how users must authenticate themselves to gain access; these details are usually specified in the server's configuration files. A typical conversation is as follows:

1. the client requests a protected page, **/ours/treasure-map.gif** from the server

2. the server sends back a 401 "Unauthorized" error status line, with a **WWW-Authenticate:** header saying what type of authentication is required, and usually a page containing the error message to be displayed to the user if the authentication isn't successful. Below is an **ngrep** trace of a request and response:

```
T 192.0.2.22:1926 -> 192.0.2.29:80 [AP]
  GET /ours/treasure-map.gif HTTP/1.1..Accept: application/vnd.ms-excel,
  application/msword, application/vnd.ms-powerpoint, image/gif, image/x
  -xbitmap, image/jpeg, image/pjpeg, */*..Accept-Language: en-gb..Accept
  -Encoding: gzip, deflate..User-Agent: Mozilla/4.0 (compatible; MSIE 5.
  5; Windows NT 4.0)..Host: mail..Connection: Keep-Alive....
##
T 192.0.2.29:80 -> 192.0.2.22:1926 [AP]
  HTTP/1.0 401 Unauthorized..Date: Tue, 24 Jul 2001 14:44:23 GMT..Server
  : Apache/1.0.3..WWW-Authenticate: Basic realm="Metro-Client"..Content-
  type: text/html....<HEAD><TITLE>Authorization Required</TITLE></HEAD>.
  <BODY><H1>Authorization Required</H1>.This server could not verify tha
  t you.are authorized to access the document you.requested.  Either you
  supplied the wrong.credentials (e.g., bad password), or your.browser
  doesn't understand how to supply.the credentials required.<P>.</BODY>.
```

The response says that the type of authentication is **Basic** (i.e. username and password) and that the **Realm** is "Metro-Client." A *realm* is a name that tells the user which set of usernames and passwords this authentication request refers to. Here, the particular server has a set of usernames and passwords for clients of the machine Metro. In a large organization, there might be different Web servers in departments and sub-departments, and the realms might be named after these subdivisions; e.g. a realm "Finance" might indicate that to access this web page you must give a username from the list that's specific to the finance department Web servers can tie in their user authentication with other mechanisms, such as Windows domains (Chapter 20) or RADIUS (Module 27.8).

3. the browser realizes the error message means authentication is required. Instead of displaying an error message, it displays the authentication dialog (Figure 14.20), which includes the realm so the user knows which of their many usernames and passwords to use

4. the user enters the username and password, which are read by the browser. The browser then re-issues the request for the page to the server, but includes an extra header, **Authorization:**, which contains the authentication information the user typed, and the type of authentication being used. In our example, as shown in Figure 14.21, the authentication type is **Basic**, as requested by the server, and the information following is the username and password, separated by a colon, all converted to base64 encoding. (See the Notes for how to un-encode base64 data.)

Figure 14.20
Authentication
dialog

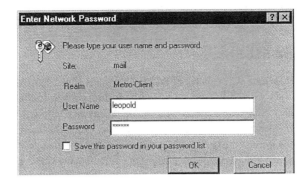

5. if the authentication is successful, the server returns the requested page; otherwise it returns the 401 Unauthorized status code again. The browser re-issues the authentication dialog, and the cycle is repeated. After a certain number of failures (usually three) the browser gives up and displays the error page returned in the 401 Unauthorized response (Figure 14.22).

If the user requests other protected pages in the same "realm," the browser retrieves it without asking you to authenticate. It appears that you have "logged on" to the Web server and that it knows who you are. However, this is *not* the case at all – the server doesn't handle "logins" or maintain state information. What's happening is much simpler: the client is including the **Authorization:** header in *every* request it sends for URLs that begin with the same path as the one that first caused the server to demand authentication.

```
T 192.0.2.22:1927 -> 192.0.2.29:80 [AP]
  GET /ours/treasure-map.gif HTTP/1.1..Accept: application/vnd.ms-excel,
    application/msword, application/vnd.ms-powerpoint, image/gif, image/x
    -xbitmap, image/jpeg, image/pjpeg, */*..Accept-Language: en-gb..Accept
    -Encoding: gzip, deflate..User-Agent: Mozilla/4.0 (compatible; MSIE 5.
    5; Windows NT 4.0)..Host: mail..Connection: Keep-Alive..Authorization:
    Basic bGVvcG9sZDpibG9vbXMK....
```

Figure 14.21 tcpdump trace of **Basic** authentication showing Base64 – encoded password

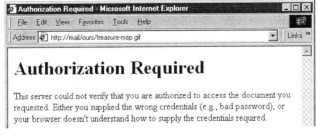

Figure 14.22 Error displayed by browser when authorisation fails

14.18 Miscellaneous Web topics

HTTPS and SSL

SSL (*Secure Sockets Layer*) is an encryption system that runs over TCP. *HTTPS* is HTTP secured by SSL; its well-known port is 443, and its protocol scheme in a URL is **https**. SSL uses public-key encryption (see Notes) for the client to verify that the server it's connecting to really is who it says it is, using a *digital certificate*. Once the client and server are conversing, they exchange a *secret*, i.e. a *secret* key, that they then use to encrypt further communications using symmetric-key encryption. The reason for this two-phase operation is that public-key encryption uses very large keys, which are very CPU-intensive, so this is used only for the preliminary phase. Once the secret has been exchanged, symmetric encryption is used because it's very much faster, and is suitable for encrypting large data transfers.

Retrieving Web pages automatically

In Module 14.2 we explained that a browser doesn't have to be a graphical program and that there are several non-graphical browsers. Because these run from the command-line, you can use them non-interactively in a script, to retrieve and store pages, e.g. to search them for particular content, or use them as a local copy of a Web site (assuming that you're not breaching someone's copyright), etc.

The **lynx** character-terminal browser has a "-dump" option – retrieve the specified page, print it on the standard output, and then exit. For example, to capture a specific image file from a site and save it locally, you could use something like

```
lynx -dump http://www.sun.com/pics/sunlogo.gif > stolen.gif
```

wget is a non-interactive "browser" or program to retrieve pages. It is available for Linux and other versions of UNIX. It lets you retrieve individual pages, or recursively retrieve whole sites or directories.

We use **wget** in a script that is run automatically twice a week to retrieve the national lottery results and see if we are now fantastically rich:

```
lynx  -dump "http://lottery.merseyworld.com/" > /tmp/lot
/usr/local//bin/extract-lottery-result.pl < /tmp/lot > /tmp/result
mailx  -s 'lottery result' fred@example.com < /tmp/result
```

We use another script that runs every five minutes to retrieve pages from our important Web servers, to make sure they are up and running; if the retrieve fails, the script mails an alert to the administrators. This is much better than just **ping**ing the server since **ping** will respond even when the machine is in a half-crashed state. Below is an extract from a **wget** session retrieving a whole sub-tree of a Web site. In this case we want to get the Linux "SSL Certificates HowTo" which consists of many separate Web pages. We give **wget** the URL of the main document, and then specify option "-r" (recursive). **wget** then retrieves this document and all the links within it. (**wget** has extra options to prevent it following links to other sites, or links higher up within this site, etc.)

```
alice% wget -r www.linuxdoc.org/HOWTO/SSL-Certificates-HOWTO/index.html

--10:17:43--  http://www.linuxdoc.org:80/HOWTO/SSL-Certificates-HOWTO/index.html
           => 'www.linuxdoc.org/HOWTO/SSL-Certificates-HOWTO/index.html'
Connecting to www.linuxdoc.org:80... connected!
HTTP request sent, awaiting response... 200 OK
Length: 2,669 [text/html]

    OK -> ..                                              [100%]

10:17:44 (15.07 KB/s) - 'www.linuxdoc.org/HOWTO/SSL-Certificates-HOWTO/index.html'

--10:17:44--  http://www.linuxdoc.org:80/HOWTO/SSL-Certificates-HOWTO/c16.html
           => 'www.linuxdoc.org/HOWTO/SSL-Certificates-HOWTO/c16.html'
Connecting to www.linuxdoc.org:80... connected!
HTTP request sent, awaiting response... 200 OK
Length: 2,517 [text/html]

    OK -> ..                                              [100%]

10:17:45 (13.73 KB/s) - 'www.linuxdoc.org/HOWTO/SSL-Certificates-HOWTO/c16.html'

--10:17:45--  http://www.linuxdoc.org:80/HOWTO/SSL-Certificates-HOWTO/x18.html
           => 'www.linuxdoc.org/HOWTO/SSL-Certificates-HOWTO/x18.html'
Connecting to www.linuxdoc.org:80... connected!
HTTP request sent, awaiting response... 200 OK
Length: 1,732 [text/html]

    OK -> .                                               [100%]

10:17:45 (20.88 KB/s) - 'www.linuxdoc.org/HOWTO/SSL-Certificates-HOWTO/x18.html'
```

MS-Outlook retrieves messages from Hotmail via an internal HTTP connection – you don't have to use a Web browser yourself at all.

Lynx (or a similar tool) is sometimes used embedded within programs to retrieve data via HTTP. For example, if you are installing extra software on a Debian Linux system using a suitably configured version of **APT** (Advanced Package Tool) it compares the version of the package that you have on your CD-ROM with a remote repository; if your CD-ROM version is out of date, APT downloads the latest version using HTTP. All this happens so transparently that if you don't look carefully at the screen, you won't even notice that APT has been using the Web.

14.19 Troubleshooting an HTTP connection

To troubleshoot an HTTP connection, break down the whole process into small steps (exactly as your browser is doing internally) and test each individually.

1. Resolve the Web server name

Use **nslookup** or **host** to resolve the server's name to an IP address:

```
host www.aw.com
```

If you can't resolve the server's name, the problem may well be at the server site.

2. Start a sniffer

We start both **ngrep** and **tcpdump** because they are good at different things. **ngrep** is good for showing the headers in an HTTP conversation, whereas **tcpdump** is better for seeing the overall packet flow. For example, assuming our client machine is Alice, the Web server is using the well-known port, and the server's IP address is 1.2.3.4:

```
ngrep port 80 and host 1.2.3.4
tcpdump port 80 and host 1.2.3.4
```

We use the IP number rather than the symbolic name, because if the name has multiple IP numbers (e.g. **www.ibm.com**) we might end up using a different IP address for each of **ngrep**, **tcpdump**, and **telnet**, because of the round-robin operation of the DNS on successive queries.

3. Check basic connectivity from client to server

Use the troubleshooting checklists from Part 1 to make sure your client can reach the server – that basic routing is OK, that your Internet connection and theirs are up, etc. If you can **ping** the server successfully, that shows that almost everything is OK. If you can't **ping**, you can't be sure anything is wrong – their firewall may have **ping**s blocked, or their server may deliberately not respond to **ping**s; however, failure to **ping** is suspicious, so proceed with caution to the next step.

4. Connect to the server using telnet

```
telnet 1.2.3.4 80
```

Make sure you use the same IP number as in step 2 above.

If the server has multiple IP numbers, check each in turn, because your problem may be due to the failure of one server out of many. This will show up as an intermittent problem, because sometimes the DNS will return the address of the failed machine as the IP number, and sometime the addresses of the other (good) machine(s). Make sure that **telnet** has fully connected, i.e. on Linux it says "Connected to *ipaddr*, Escape character is …" or on Windows the title bar of the **telnet** window shows the destination address.

If you can't **telnet** but can **ping**, then the server software on the server machine is probably dead (or being rebooted, or …). In our experience, about 70% of Web problems come down to this.

5. Issue a simple GET request

You want to be sure that the server listening on port 80 at the far end really is a Web server, so retrieve the home page:

```
GET /
```

If you don't get a page – even if it is an error page – there's a problem with their Web server.

6. Issue a full request

If the server replied with the home page, request the page you were really trying to retrieve when the problem occurred. You can use a simple request because it looks like there is only one Web site on this server:

```
GET /full-pagename
```

If the server gave you a "Web site not found" type of error (indicating that there are multiple Web sites on this single IP address), you will have to use a full request:

```
GET /full-pagename HTTP/1.1
host: www.example.com
```
                                                              blank line to terminate

If the server returns the page correctly, it looks like your browser is at fault. If the request fails, make sure that you entered the pagename correctly, because it may be case-sensitive.

7. Check your browser settings

If you reach this point, your browser is suspect.

a. first, exit all copies of your browser and restart. We've noticed some browsers "remember" when they have tried to resolve a name using the DNS and it has failed due to a temporary problem; even when the DNS is working correctly again, the browser thinks it knows best and won't retry

b. try to connect to the site, and closely observe the browser's status messages (usually displayed in a status line at the bottom of the browser window, as shown in Module 14.14)

c. if you have the **lynx** character-based browser, try retrieving the page with it, because it gives good informational messages as it proceeds

d. force a re-load of the page using `Ctrl-F5` or `Shift-Reload` (c.f. Module 14.16)). If the page loads correctly, there may be a cache problem, either in your client or on a proxy server

e. if you can, change your client not to use a proxy server, and re-try

f. temporarily disable all caching in your client ("always check that page is up to date") and delete temporary/cached files to make sure. Then retry.

Summary

- the Web uses the HTTP protocol to transfer Web pages from server to client browser

- the client browser requests pages from servers and interprets and displays the pages it receives in return. Most browsers use a full, windowed GUI but there are text-only browsers too

- most Web pages contain HTML, which can contain hyperlinks to allow the user to jump to a different page, on this server or another one

- HTTP runs over TCP and uses well-known port 80

- an HTTP conversation – like SMTP – consists of plain-text commands and responses. However, unlike SMTP, HTTP can transfer arbitrary binary data safely without any special encoding because it knows it's using a TCP connection

- in versions 1.0 and 1.1 of HTTP, client and server send headers in their requests and responses, to give information about their capabilities and about the data requested/returned

- HTTP uses MIME to specify content types and sizes

- HTTP/1.0 uses a separate TCP connection for each request/reply, but HTTP/1.1 can use a single connection for multiple request/reply transactions

- HTTP/1.1 can handle multiple Web sites on a single IP address by using the **Host:** header that is included in the client request

- the name of a "Web site" is just the IP address of the server handling that site, which is usually retrieved using a DNS query. A single name often has multiple IP numbers, which allows load-sharing across multiple Web servers

- Web pages can be static files on the server, or can be generated dynamically by the server in response to user input included in the client request

- Web proxy servers are often used for performance, security or logging/control reasons

- Web browsers usually cache pages they have downloaded. You can configure how caching operates in your browser if you need to

- Web servers can require the user to authenticate when they access certain parts of a Web site. Authentication information is usually sent in an **Authorization:** header in the request, with the user/password information base-64 encoded

- Web traffic can be sent securely encrypted between client and server using the HTTPS protocol

- you can troubleshoot a Web connection by issuing commands manually using **telnet** and watching the traffic using **tcpdump** or **ngrep**.

What's next?

In the next chapter we introduce the second widely used transport protocol, UDP (the first one was TCP). After that we look at some more applications and related higher-level protocols.

Notes and further reading

The HTTP protocol

The original HTTP/0.9 spec is at:

❑ **http://www.w3.org/Protocols/HTTP/AsImplemented.html**

HTTP was invented at CERN (the European Centre for Nuclear Research) and they have a history of its development, with lots of links to other sources:

❑ **http://ref.cern.ch/CERN/CNL/2001/001/www-history/**

The specifications for HTTP are:

❑ **RFC-1945 May-1996** *Hypertext Transfer Protocol – HTTP/1.0*

❑ **RFC-2616 June-1999** *Hypertext Transfer Protocol – HTTP/1.1*

which is where to look up the different HTTP headers if you need to. (A few headers were added in later RFCs.)

❑ **RFC-2396 August 1998** *Uniform Resource Identifiers (URI) – Generic Syntax*

We haven't dealt with servers at all. However, it's worth mentioning that compared with the browser the server is very simple – it just has to accept a TCP connection, read a few headers, and reply with a chunk of data (the Web page). The client is very complex because of its need to handle many different forms of graphics, user interaction with multiple windows, JavaScript and Java executable code, etc. Here's an indication of how large a project a Web browser really is. Netscape made the source code for their browser public, and Mozilla.org (**http://www.mozilla.org**) was set up to handle the development with contributions from hundreds of developers and testers – on the open-source model like Linux. But even with full access to the source code it took about two years before the project really took off and started delivering the expected goodies – very much longer than anticipated.

For curiosity, here are some tiny, and/or weird, implementations of HTTP servers. They are, respectively, a tiny server, written in C (150 lines of code), a Shell script server, and a server written in Postscript (for people with strange brains):

❑ **http://www.acme.com/software/micro_httpd/**

❑ **http://jester.vip.net.pl:8081/**

❑ **http://www.pugo.org:8080/**

The PostScript server is of course just a curiosity, but the micro server in C can be genuinely useful as a special-purpose server to embed in your own applications, etc.

Dynamic Web pages

In the early days of the Web, all Web pages were "static," i.e. you received the contents of a normal file that resided on the Web server. To make the Web usable as a general interface to applications, some method is needed to allow the Web server to call other programs, and to pass data – that you have entered in your Web browser – to those programs. The standard mechanism for this is called *CGI* (*Common Gateway Interface*). This is a fancy name but it is in fact very simple. The simplest and clearest introduction to CGI scripts that we've seen is:

❏ **http://snowwhite.it.brighton.ac.uk/~mas/mas/courses/html/html3.html**

which includes some excellent examples. For a more general overview of CGI, see:

❏ **http://hoohoo.ncsa.uiuc.edu/cgi/overview.html** *The Common Gateway Interface*

The Web server recognizes if a requested page is dynamic from the server's configuration and the URL specified. For example, a common arrangement is that URLs of the form **http://***servername***/cgi-bin/***pagename* means "run the CGI script called *pagename.*" On Microsoft Web servers, Active Server pages usually have a URL that ends in **.asp.**

Java and JavaScript and ActiveX programs work differently. JavaScript code is often embedded in the text of an HTML page and is introduced by the special **<script>** HTML tags. Java and ActiveX programs are specified as links within a page using the special **<applet>** and **<object>** tags.

Proxies

❏ **http://spywaresucks.org/prox/index.html** *The Proxomitron – a Universal Web Filter*

❏ **http://www.flaaten.dk/prox** *The Proxomitron*

❏ **http://www.sankey.ws/proxomitron.html** *Introduction to the Proxomitron*

Microsoft's Internet Explorer supports WPAD (Web Proxy Autodiscovery Protocol) for automatic proxy configuration:

❏ **http://www.microsoft.com/technet/prodtechnol/ie/reskit/ie5/part5/ch21auto.asp** [IE 5.x > Resource Kits] *Chapter 21 – Using Automatic Configuration and Automatic Proxy*

The following note describes a problem in WPAD but also includes a clear description of how it works:

❏ **http://www.securiteam.com/windowsntfocus/3O5PTQAQAA.html** *Patch Available for the "WPAD Spoofing" Vulnerability*

WPAD was not approved by the IETF as an Internet standard:

❏ **http://www.ietf.org/proceedings/99nov/46th-99nov-ietf-35.html**

❏ **http://www.ietf.org/iesg/iesg.99-08-12**

Browser caching

❏ **MS-KB-Q201535** *Internet Explorer Does Not Check for Newer Versions of Web Pages*

❏ **MS-KB-Q263070** *How Internet Explorer Cache Settings Affect Web Browsing*

Authentication

You can encode and un-encode base-64 data using the Linux program **mimencode**. Like many UNIX programs, this will either read the standard input direct from your keyboard (type Ctrl-C to terminate), or you can use the echo program to pipe a string to it. Examples of both are shown below. Decoding is very similar, but you give the encoded data as input and give the "-u" un-encode option to **mimencode**. The example we've used is from the headers in Module 14.17.

```
alice% mimencode
leopold:blooms
bGVvcG9sZDpibG9vbXMK
^C
alice%

alice%  echo leopold:blooms | mimencode
bGVvcG9sZDpibG9vbXMK
```

SSL

The SSL specification and related documents:

❏ **http://www.netscape.com/eng/ssl3/**

For an introduction to symmetric and public-key (asymmetric) cryptography, see

❏ **http://www.garykessler.net/library/crypto.html** Gary Kessler's *An Overview of Cryptography*

Character-based browsers – retrieving Web pages automatically

❏ **http://lynx.browser.org/** – the Lynx text browser

❏ **http://www.gnu.org/software/wget/wget.html** – GNU Wget, a free software package for retrieving files using HTTP, HTTPS, and FTP

Appendices

Appendix 17: HTTP/1.1 server response codes

15 UDP and other protocols

Introduction

UDP is the second widely used transport protocol. Like TCP it uses ports and provides end-to-end connectivity between client and server applications. It is a small and efficient protocol, but unlike TCP, it does not guarantee delivery – applications have to implement their own error recovery mechanisms if they need them. This makes it suitable for some applications but not for others.

15.1 UDP is a connection-less and "unreliable" transport protocol

The end-user applications that we've looked at so far (SMTP, POP, and IMAP e-mail, HTTP Web browsing, the **telnet** application itself) all use TCP as their transport:

- there are usually multiple transfers between client and server, involving an ongoing session rather than the exchange of a single packet. The effect of one command or request depends on what occurred earlier in the client/server conversation (e.g. if you delete a file **abc.txt** in an FTP session, exactly which file is removed depends on what directory you were in at the time, which is determined by your earlier commands)

- they often exchange large amounts of data.

In this chapter we consider a different transport, UDP (*User Datagram Protocol*). In some ways, UDP is similar to TCP:

- UDP is a transport protocol: it deals with communication only between the two end-points (e.g. the client application on your machine, and the server application on the remote machine). Intermediate routers don't bother with the UDP data in the packets they are forwarding – the routers operate only at the lower-down IP or network layer (Figure 15.1).

- UDP uses ports to distinguish between traffic for multiple UDP applications on the same machine, and to send the correct packets to the appropriate application. (This is called *demultiplexing*.) UDP and its port provides the interface between the application program and the IP networking layer. We discuss ports in more detail in Module 15.3.

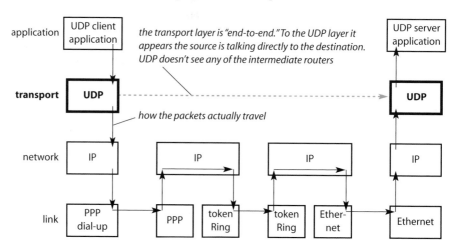

Figure 15.1 Operating at the lower-down network layer

UDP differs from TCP in some important respects:

- UDP is "datagram-oriented," TCP is session-oriented. A *datagram* is a self-contained packet of information; UDP deals with individual datagrams or packets sent from client to server, or vice versa

- UDP is *connection-less.* The client doesn't establish a connection to the server before it sends its data – it just sends the data straight away

- UDP is "unreliable" in the formal network sense:
  - packets can get lost. UDP itself can't detect this, so …
  - the application program – client or server – (as opposed to the TCP/IP stack itself) has to detect lost packets and handle retransmission, etc. Applications often just wait until a timeout elapses, and then try again
  - packets can get corrupted. UDP packets contain a checksum of all the data in the packet. This lets UDP detect when a packet has been corrupted. If this happens, the packet is dropped, and as usual it's the application that has to detect this and retransmit as necessary.

    This checksum operation can be switched off, and some applications do this for performance reasons. However, as this means either that corrupted packets aren't detected, or the application layer must perform its own data integrity checks, it's a false economy.

  A less derogatory term than "unreliable" is "best effort." UDP does its best to deliver the packets but delivery is not guaranteed.

- because UDP is datagram-oriented and at the protocol level each packet stands alone, it has no concept of out-of-order packets, which in turn means it doesn't need sequence numbers on packets

- since it was first developed, TCP has been enhanced with very sophisticated mechanisms for controlling the rate of flow over its connections, to avoid congestion and excessive packet loss. Because UDP only sends single, stand-alone packets, it doesn't need any of the elaborate control mechanisms. That makes it easier and smaller (in terms of lines of code, and memory) to implement, but also makes it unsuitable for transferring large amounts of data.

If an application is implemented using UDP instead of TCP, the application itself must provide lost-packet detection, retries, etc.

UDP inherits its connection-less and unreliability properties from IP. You can think of UDP as a very thin transport layer placed above IP to give applications access to IP's basic networking facilities, without adding very much extra functionality other than ports and checksums. (By contrast, TCP is also a transport layer but it does very much more than basic IP packet communication.)

In the next module we explain why some applications use UDP, in spite of its apparent deficiencies.

15.2 Applications that use UDP

An obvious question is why use a connection-less, unreliable protocol like UDP when we have TCP, which is reliable and seems to do everything we need? The answer is that UDP is cheaper than TCP in almost every respect:

- UDP is a small, easy-to-implement protocol, unlike TCP, which is now huge. (RFC-768, the standard for UDP, is only three pages long.) UDP is small because it adds very little, apart from ports, to the underlying IP protocol

- because UDP is small, it can fit in special-purpose devices with limited memory, or in expensive flash or programmable read-only memory (PROM) used to boot up devices over the network. (This is less important now than a few years ago when memory was much more expensive.)

- because UDP is less complex than TCP it uses less CPU

- because UDP is connection-less, a client can send information to a server with very little overhead. By contrast, establishing a TCP connection consumes time and network resources. UDP is ideal where a client sends small amounts of information infrequently to one or more servers

- a UDP datagram can be sent to the broadcast address to request a service where the client doesn't know in advance where the server is. TCP can only connect between specific, individual addresses.

As a result, we can say that, broadly, UDP is suitable for:

- small data transfers

- intermittent transfers, e.g. where a client contacts a server very rarely, but where there may be a very large number of clients per server

- multicast or broadcast applications, which increasingly includes audio and video multimedia.

On the other hand, TCP is better where the client and server:

- exchange large amounts of data

- exchange information frequently, typically having an ongoing two-way "conversation."

Some applications that use UDP are listed below.

DNS

The DNS client and server use UDP to exchange queries and requests. If DNS used TCP for normal requests, the root servers would have to keep millions or tens of millions of TCP connections open all the time, one for each site's DNS server that ever issues a DNS query.

We didn't mention in Chapter 7 that DNS uses UDP, but this didn't interfere with our explanation because we were able to view DNS's operation in terms of packets. We can now say that these packets were in fact DNS datagrams rather than raw IP packets.

You may have noticed, if you looked in the **/etc/services** file (Linux) or **C:\WINNT\system32\drivers\etc\services** file (NT) that DNS can use TCP or UDP. It uses UDP for all its normal queries and responses. It uses TCP only for zone transfers – copying all the DNS data for a whole domain, usually to a backup server – because this requires a lot of information to be exchanged in a short amount of time. Very rarely it will also use TCP for normal queries that are very large.

DHCP (Chapter 16)

The DHCP client broadcasts a request using UDP to find a DHCP server. The client couldn't open a TCP connection to a server because not only does it not know the server's address, at this stage (when it's booting) it doesn't even have an IP address.

Microsoft Windows Networking (Part 3)

Clients broadcast UDP packets to find other Windows machines on the network, and to resolve machine names. We discuss this further in Part 3, where we will also see that UDP's unreliable nature (its inability to guarantee delivery) can cause significant problems.

TFTP – Trivial File Transfer Protocol

TFTP is like FTP (Module 17.2), which you're probably familiar with, but much simpler. In the past it was used widely for booting diskless workstations, and for uploading and downloading firmware to special-purpose devices such as routers, firewalls and other network devices, and some still use it as a last resort. Its great advantage is that it's very small because it doesn't use the large TCP protocol. The IP, UDP, and TFTP code can be stored in non-volatile memory, making it suitable for booting. Its disadvantages are its limited set of commands and that it doesn't use any authentication at all – making it a security hole.

Syslog – the system logger

Syslog (Module 17.12) allows applications on any machine on the network to send a log message to a log server on a single central machine, instead of writing lots of separate log files on each of the client machines. Messages are sent to the log server using UDP. It uses UDP because logging involves sending relatively few data, infrequently, and because hundreds of clients may log to a single server, so full TCP connections would be too costly.

NFS – the Network File System

NFS (Module 17.14) gives client machines transparent access to files and directories on a file server. It can operate over UDP or TCP. TCP is best for use over wide-area networks where packets are more likely to be dropped or corrupted. However, on a LAN, NFS usually uses UDP. While UDP is "unreliable," in practice on a LAN not many packets are dropped, so NFS works fine, with less overhead than with TCP. Moreover, when NFS was first developed in 1985, UDP was able to transfer large amounts of data quicker than TCP.

(To improve NFS's performance, some vendors switched off the UDP checksums at the operating system kernel, i.e. for *all* UDP. However, as we explained in the previous module, this can lead to corrupt data, both in NFS and in other protocols.)

traceroute

traceroute (Module 3.9) sends UDP packets. It expects that there won't be a server at the other end, so trying to establish a TCP connection would be wasteful and pointless.

15.3 UDP ports

Conceptually, UDP ports are almost identical to TCP ports (Module 10.4):

- particular *well-known port numbers* are allocated by convention to particular services. The server for a particular service listens on the appropriate well-known port. For example, the DNS server listens on port 53, treats any incoming requests on that port as DNS queries requests and processes them accordingly. (See the inside front cover for a fuller list of port numbers.)

- the client specifies the *destination port* when it sends a request to the server. By specifying the specific port number, the client is saying what service is required. For example, Bob uses Alice's DNS server by sending to her UDP port 53

- the client listens on an ephemeral port, and includes its port number as the *source port* in the request. The server sends its reply (or replies) to this port on the source machine, and the client reads the replies from it

- in TCP, the combination (N_1, P_1, N_2, P_2) of source and destination IP and port numbers is a unique reference that specifies a TCP connection. UDP is connection-less, so a listening client port isn't "connected to" a port on a server, and in fact any machine can send to the client's listening port, just as any client can send to a server's port. (In fact there's no difference between client and server listening ports in UDP. In TCP what distinguishes client and server is that the client connects to the server, thereby establishing the connection.) Consequently, the client has to make sure that any "replies" on its listening port really are related to the request it sent. This is why DNS uses identifiers (Module 7.8).

    The incoming port number is what UDP uses to demultiplex the packets coming in from the IP layer and pass them up to the respective applications in the application layer (upper part of Figure 15.2). This is an important function of the transport layer, because it's not provided by the network (IP) layer lower down.

To see which ports are being listened to, use the **netstat** command. You can optionally restrict the output to UDP, using the "**-u**" option (Linux) or "**-p udp**" option (Windows-NT). As before, "**-n**" prints addresses as IP numbers, and "**-a**" shows all active ports; otherwise, servers listening for incoming data are not shown:

```
netstat -n -a -u                                    Linux
netstat -n -a -p udp                              Windows
```

(On Linux, "**-p**" gives the name of the program that is listening on this port. There's no similar standard tool for Windows, but see the Notes.)

Relation between UDP and TCP port numbers

UDP ports are completely separate from the TCP ports. The port numbers in a UDP packet are used only by the UDP part of the stack, and similarly the port numbers in a TCP packet are processed only by TCP. However, if a service can run over UDP and TCP, then the same well-known port number has been chosen for both, purely for convenience. You can see this by looking at your **/etc/services** file (Linux) or **C:\WINNT\system32\drivers\etc\services** file (NT).

The lower part of Figure 15.2 shows diagrammatically how UDP and TCP are separated in the stack. When a transport protocol passes data down to the IP layer to be transmitted, it sets a special IP protocol number field in the header of the IP packet to say which protocol is being used. The protocol number for UDP is 17. When the packet arrives at the destination machine, the IP layer looks at the protocol number, and passes the packet up to the appropriate protocol in the transport layer. This process of taking a single incoming stream (the IP packets from the link layer) and separating it out into its multiple constituent streams to pass up to the transport layer is called demultiplexing.

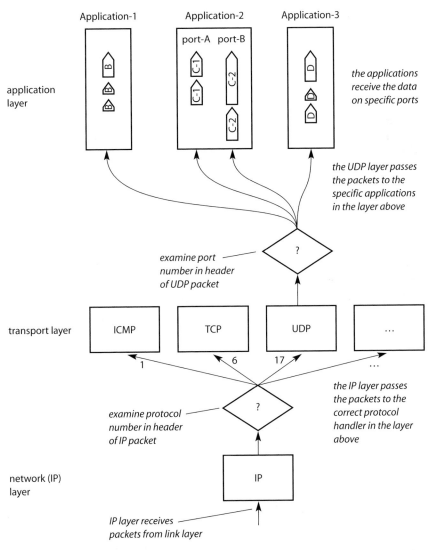

Figure 15.2 IP demultiplexes on IP protocol number and UDP demultiplexes on UDP port number

15.4 How the protocols relate to each other

We have introduced several protocols so far. Some (ARP, ICMP for **ping**) we covered quite informally, emphasizing the practical aspects rather than the formal protocol description. Now that we have covered the two important transport protocols, TCP and UDP, we can put all the different protocols into context. Figure 15.3 shows where in the stack the various protocols sit. Figure 15.4 shows how they are related, and how they interact. We have included some protocols that we'll be covering later – NetBIOS for Microsoft Windows Networking (Part 3) and ESP (used in VPNs, Chapter 27). We've also shown the Novell IPX and SPX protocols in the diagram, just to show how they provide equivalent but different functionality to the TCP/IP protocols.

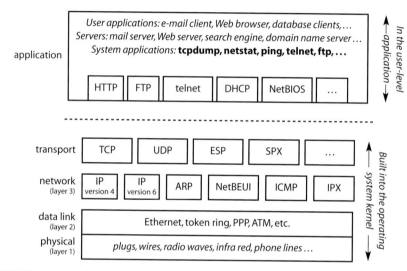

Figure 15.3 The protocol stack

To recap what we said about the functions of the various layers:

- the **link layer** (e.g. an Ethernet LAN segment) is responsible for moving packets from one machine to another that is connected directly to it on the same wire – it handles a single hop

- the **network layer** moves packets from the source machine to the destination machine, via any intermediate routers on the path. All routing is handled at this level.
  This layer also includes ARP and ICMP because they don't really fit anywhere else. ARP acts as an intermediary so that IP can obtain the MAC addresses from the link layer. ICMP uses IP so perhaps ICMP ought to be in the layer above IP; on the other hand, ICMP definitely isn't a transport protocol. (It just goes to show that a model is only a model. Use it when it helps you understand what's happening; forget about it if it causes you problems.)

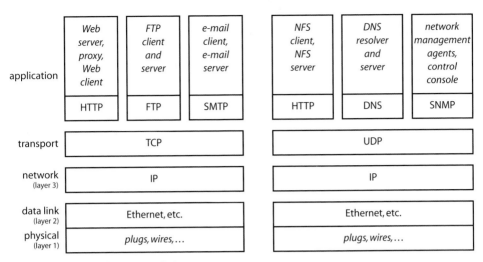

Figure 15.4 How the protocols interact

- the **transport layer** provides end-host to end-host data communication, and isn't involved on the intermediate routers. The Internet transports are UDP and TCP, which provide ports as a way for the application above to interface with the network layer below. In addition TCP provides a lot of extra functionality, including reliable (guaranteed) delivery, and connection-oriented sessions.

All the above layers are either in the hardware or built into the operating system. The final layer is different:

- the **application layer** is separate from the operating system, and the protocols at this layer are usually included in the application by means of subroutines or libraries. In addition to the code for the network protocols, the applications of course contain the code to do what the user wants – interact with a database, or handle e-mail, or browse Web pages.

Summary

- like TCP, UDP is a transport protocol. It connects applications end to end and plays no part in routing, which it leaves to the lower IP (network) layer
- UDP is a connection-less datagram-oriented protocol. It sends single packets between client and server and does not establish an ongoing connection
- UDP is "unreliable" (best-effort). Packets can get lost or out of order and UDP won't notice, won't try to retransmit, and won't inform the application. Any error-recovery required has to be implemented by the application itself, usually by means of re-transmitting if it hasn't received a response after a particular timeout period
- UDP is a compact, easy-to-implement protocol. It is suitable for applications that have only intermittent, ad-hoc or small data transfers, and applications that need to broadcast, e.g. to locate a particular service. Common applications that use UDP are the DNS, DHCP, Microsoft Windows Networking, Syslog, and NFS file sharing
- UDP uses port numbers to identify which application the packets are destined for. UDP and TCP port numbers are completely unrelated although if a service is capable of running over both, the same well-known port number is allocated to each (by convention only).

What's next?

In the next chapter we look at DHCP – the Dynamic Host Configuration Protocol. This runs over UDP and is used for automatically setting the TCP/IP and related configuration details of your machines.

Notes and further reading

The specification for UDP is only three pages long:

❑ **RFC-768 UDP August 1980** *User Datagram Protocol*

As usual, Stevens gives a good description of what UDP does and how it works.

Applications that use UDP

❑ *Stevens UNIX Network Programming* Volume 1 (1990, Prentice Hall PTR)

contains a detailed discussion of when UDP might be used instead of TCP, and the programming consequences of doing so. In particular see Module 20.4 *When to use UDP instead of TCP* and Module 20.5 *Adding Reliability to a UDP Application.*

The RADIUS dial-up authentication service uses UDP instead of TCP; the reasons for this are discussed explicitly in Module 2.3 of

❑ **RFC-2058 January 1997** *Remote Authentication Dial-in User Service (RADIUS)*

The most recent version of NFS runs over TCP, not UDP:

❑ **RFC-3010 December 2000** *NFS version 4 Protocol*

❑ **http://www.nluug.nl/events/sane2000/papers/pawlowski.pdf** *The NFS Version 4 Protocol*

Troubleshooting UDP applications

When troubleshooting our TCP e-mail and Web applications we were able to use **telnet** as a test client, because they all use TCP as the transport. There is no convenient tool that we can use in the same way for UDP, because UDP doesn't use plain-text command strings like TCP since UDP doesn't provide sessions and conversations like TCP. Instead, most UDP data are encoded in a compact, binary form in the UDP datagram, and it's not easy to generate correctly formed packets by hand. However, a useful approach is:

- use the specific application to test out the service, e.g. **host** or **nslookup** for DNS

- use **tcpdump** to make sure that what is going down the wire makes sense. **tcpdump** often gives you most or all of the information you need, because UDP applications typically involve very few packets and small amounts of data

- if you have access to the server, check the status of the port you are interested in, and make sure the port is being handled by the correct application. To do this use **netstat** with options "**-u**" (show only UDP), "**-a**" (show all active ports), "**-p**" show the server program names.

  That works only on Linux. For Windows, the **Fport** tool provides similar information. See

  ❑ **http://www.foundstone.com > R&D Labs > Tools > Intrusion Detection**

  ❑ **http://www.foundstone.com/rdlabs/tools.php?category=Intrusion+Detection**

- for advanced debugging, consider **netcat** (Module 17.4) which can function as a UDP client or a UDP server.

Appendices

Inside front cover: assigned TCP and UDP port numbers
Appendix 18: IP protocol numbers

16 | DHCP – automating your TCP/IP client management

Introduction

DHCP lets you configure the hosts on your network automatically. When a machine boots, it broadcasts a request to a DHCP server, which replies with the IP address, netmask, and other parameters that the host should use. This greatly simplifies IP address management, and network management generally.

16.1   Why DHCP is needed

DHCP is the *Dynamic Host Configuration Protocol*. It allows a machine to obtain its IP address, netmask, and other network configuration settings from a *DHCP server* at boot-time, rather than having them hard-coded in configuration files or the Windows Registry on the local host. It lets you add a host to your network very quickly and automatically. You don't have to define any configuration settings for the host at all once your DHCP server is up and running. When the client boots up, it broadcasts a request and waits for a DHCP server to reply with its network configuration parameters (Figure 16.1). The communication between client and server depends entirely on broadcasts, because until the conversation has completely finished, the client doesn't have a valid IP address.

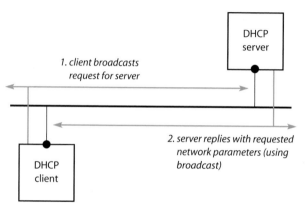

Figure 16.1 At boot time, DHCP client uses broadcasts to communicate with the server

DHCP is used widely, especially on large networks, to minimize the effort of managing IP addresses and other network settings.

An IP address that a host receives via DHCP is called a *dynamic IP address*, in contrast to an address that is configured manually, which is called a *static IP address*.

Significant reasons for using DHCP are:

1. static IP addressing on a network is time-consuming and error-prone:

   • you have to keep a record of all the static IP addresses that you allocate. When fire-fighting or installing a new machine under pressure, it's easy to forget to note the IP address you've allocated, and then later on you may allocate the same address to another host. Resolving a case of duplicate IP addresses wastes a lot of effort; it's often a long time before you even realize that this is the cause of the problems that users are reporting

   • you must ensure consistency of netmask, default gateway, DNS server settings, etc. across the whole network. For example, if you make a typo in the netmask, the newly installed machine may only be able to see part of your network

   • if your network is sub-netted, when you move a host from one sub-net to another – e.g. from one side of your building to the other – you may have to change its IP address, netmask, and default gateway

- if you are traveling with a laptop and want to plug in to the network at the site you are visiting, you have to configure all your IP settings. (Even finding someone who can tell you which settings to use can be a big job.) From the site administrator's point of view, transient users are hard to manage: they have to be allocated an IP number when they arrive, and the number has to be de-allocated when they leave

- network settings also have to be changed:

  - when you first connect your site's LAN to the Internet, if you weren't already using legal addresses specifically allocated to your organization. Most sites get their legal addresses only when they join the Internet, so this is a common occurrence

  - if you alter your network to use Network Address Translation (NAT, Module 23.2) instead of public IP addresses

  - when you change to a new ISP, because your public IP addresses are normally allocated to you by your ISP

  - when you add extra services to your network. For example, if you install a second DNS server for reliability, you have to add these extra DNS server details to every host on your network. Or, if you are using Microsoft Windows Networking, and decide to use a WINS server (Chapter 19), you must configure all Windows hosts with the IP address of the WINS server

  DHCP and dynamic addresses overcome all these problems

2. diskless machines must of necessity obtain all their configuration parameters from elsewhere, as they cannot store them locally. This was important when graphical workstations first came on to the market; disks were very expensive and running diskless workstations was a cost-effective way to implement a distributed network. Diskless operation remains necessary for thin-client devices such as Windows terminals (for Windows NT Server Terminal Edition) and X windows system (Module 17.6) terminals.

DHCP servers are now deployed very widely. In fact they are built as standard into many network devices such as firewalls, leased-line and ISDN routers, etc.

ISPs also need to allocate IP addresses dynamically to users connecting via dial-up modems, dial-up ISDN or ADSL connections. This is important because the Internet is running out of public IP addresses and there just aren't enough IP addresses to give every dial-up user a permanent address specific to themselves. However, because only a small proportion of an ISP's dial-up users are connected at any one time, the ISP can share a small number of IP addresses amongst a much larger number of users, by allocating addresses dynamically each time a dial-up user connects. While this may not involve DHCP, in Module 16.6 we outline how ISPs allocate IP addresses dynamically.

In the next module we explain in detail how the DHCP client and server interact.

16.2   How DHCP works (1)

DHCP uses UDP as its transport. The DHCP server listens on UDP well-known port 67. The DHCP client broadcasts to UDP port 67, and the server replies to the client on UDP well-known port 68. The full conversation is shown in Figure 16.2.

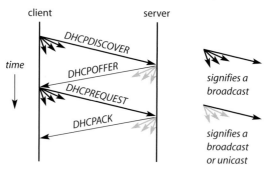

Figure 16.2 DHCP conversation between client and server

1.   the client first broadcasts a DHCPDISCOVER request. As the client doesn't have an IP address yet, it uses 0.0.0.0 as its source address

2.   one or more servers respond to client's MAC address, with a DHCPOFFER reply. To reduce broadcast traffic, some servers (but not Windows-NT's DHCP server) unicast the reply, even though the client has no configured IP address yet. They do this by explicitly setting the client's MAC address as the Ethernet destination in the packet. However if the client set the *broadcast* flag (see Figure 16.3) in the DHCPDISCOVER packet, indicating it can't receive unicast packets before if has configured its IP address, the server must broadcast the reply.

3.   the client accepts one server's offer by broadcasting a DHCPREQUEST containing the IP address of the server being accepted; that server then knows that it has been chosen to service the rest of the DHCP conversation. Any other servers that replied can see from the client's DHCPREQUEST that they have *not* been chosen, and take no further part

4a.   the chosen server replies with a DHCPACK (DHCP acknowledgment), which is broadcast or unicast depending on the server and the value of the broadcast flag, as in (2) above.

4b.   the client sets its network parameters to the values received.

```
0.0.0.0.68 > 255.255.255.255.67:  ...  DHCP:DISCOVER ...
212.140.133.22.67 > 255.255.255.255.68:  ...  DHCP:OFFER ...
0.0.0.0.68 > 255.255.255.255.67:  DHCP:REQUEST ...
212.140.133.22.67 > 255.255.255.255.68:  ...  DHCP:ACK ...
```

Below is a **tcpdump** trace of the whole conversation, heavily edited:
Because of the number of different fields in the packets, **ethereal** is better than **tcpdump** for looking at the details. (See Web Appendix 19 for a list of DHCP fields and the abbreviations **tcpdump** uses for them.) **ethereal** shows DHCP details as *Bootstrap Protocol (BOOTP)*, and many documents and your **services** file show the DHCP ports as "BOOTP server" and "BOOTP client" or a similar abbreviation. As explained in the Notes section, this is because DHCP is an enhancement of BOOTP and is backward compatible with it.

The **ethereal** trace (Figure 16.3) illustrates several features of the conversation:

1. each packet specifies its message type (DISCOVER, OFFER, REQUEST, or ACK)

2. the client includes its Ethernet address in its initial request to the server as its *client identifier*. This uniquely identifies the client host because Ethernet addresses are globally unique

3. the client sends a *parameter request* list indicating the network settings it wants values for. DHCP uses *option numbers* (rather than alphabetic names) in request and reply packets between client and server. The option numbers are defined in the DHCP RFCs and are summarized in Web Appendix 19

   The list of options that a client requests depends on the DHCP client software that it's using. The client in Figure 16.3 is a Windows-NT server, which is why the parameters it has requested include NetBIOS (Windows Networking) settings. A Linux client would have requested a different set

4. the client may preserve some information about its configuration, either from a previous DHCP session, or, as in this case, from manual configuration: the hostname **TIMEPCNT** was configured manually, using **Control Panel > Network**.

```
⊞ User Datagram Protocol
⊟ Bootstrap Protocol
     Boot Request
     Hardware type: Ethernet
     Hardware address length: 6
     Hops: 0
     Transaction ID: 0x4407d141
     Seconds elapsed: 0
     Broadcast flag: 0
     Client IP address: 0.0.0.0 (0.0.0.0)
     Your (client) IP address: 0.0.0.0 (0.0.0.0)
     Next server IP address: 0.0.0.0 (0.0.0.0)
     Relay agent IP address: 0.0.0.0 (0.0.0.0)
     Client hardware address: 00:50:da:e4:61:34
     Server host name not given                          1. message type
     Boot file name not given
     Magic cookie: (OK)
     Option 53: DHCP Message Type = DHCP Discover
   ⊟ Option 61: Client identifier                        2. unique identifer
        Hardware type: Ethernet                             for this client host
        Client hardware address: 00:50:da:e4:61:34
     Option 12: Host Name = TIMEPCNT
   ⊟ Option 55: Parameter Request List                   3. options requested
        1 = Subnet Mask                                      by this client
        15 = Domain Name
        3 = Router
        44 = NetBIOS over TCP/IP Name Server
        46 = NetBIOS over TCP/IP Node Type
        47 = NetBIOS over TCP/IP Scope
        6 = Domain Name Server
     End Option
     Padding
```

Figure 16.3 ethereal trace of a DHCP request

In the next module we look at the rest of the client/server interaction.

16.3 How DHCP works (2)

The previous module described the initial DHCPDISCOVER request that the client sent to the server. Below is the server's DHCPOFFER reply:

```
Client IP address: 0.0.0.0 (0.0.0.0)
Your (client) IP address: 212.140.133.85 (212.140.133.85)
Next server IP address: 0.0.0.0 (0.0.0.0)
Relay agent IP address: 0.0.0.0 (0.0.0.0)
Client hardware address: 00:50:da:e4:61:34
Server host name not given
Boot file name not given
Magic cookie: (OK)
Option 53: DHCP Message Type = DHCP Offer
Option 1: Subnet Mask = 255.255.255.128
Option 58: Renewal Time Value = 1 day, 12 hours
Option 59: Rebinding Time Value = 2 days, 15 hours
Option 51: IP Address Lease Time = 3 days
Option 54: Server Identifier = 212.140.133.22
Option 15: Domain Name = uit.co.uk
Option 3: Router = 212.140.133.29
Option 6: Domain Name Server = 212.140.133.19
End Option
Padding
```

1. the server is offering address 212.140.133.85 (**Your (client) IP address** field.)

2. the server has filled in values for the options requested by the client

3. the client doesn't get the IP address forever: it only gets a fixed-term *lease* on it. (The length of lease is usually a configuration option in the server.) The server replies with the duration of the lease and a *renewal time* when the client should contact this server again and ask if it can renew (i.e. extend) the lease. This allows a client to keep the same IP address for as long as it needs. The server also specifies a *rebinding time*: if the client was unable to renew the lease from the original server, after the rebinding time it should try to renew its lease on this IP address from any available DHCP server.

When the client receives the DHCPOFFER, it confirms to this server that it wants this address, by sending a DHCPREQUEST. Finally, the server acknowledges that with a DHCPACK and records that this client now has a lease on this IP address. On receiving the DHCPACK, the client sets its network parameters to the values the server gave it.

We haven't shown the detailed contents of the DHCPREQUEST and DHCPACK packets – apart from the message type field they are almost identical to the others.

Exercise: use **ethereal** to examine all four packets in a DHCP session.

DHCP allocates the same IP address to the same client each time, if possible

While it is crucial that DHCP address allocation works automatically, on private networks it's desirable that individual machines keep the same IP address all the time, even when they reboot, because many logging mechanisms use the IP address to identify the user or department. DHCP facilitates this in several ways:

- as discussed above, the client periodically renews its lease on its IP address, so that it keeps the same address at least until it is rebooted. A lease renewal consists of only two packets, a DHCPREQUEST and DHCPACK. As we see below, these packets are not broadcast: both client and server have valid IP addresses and so can communicate normally:

```
212.140.133.85.68 > 212.140.133.22.67:  ... C:212.140.133.85 DHCP:REQUEST ...
212.140.133.22.67 > 212.140.133.85.68:  ... DHCP:ACK ...
```

- when an existing lease is being renewed, or where the client has a record of the lease it had last time, it can attempt a shorter conversation. The client starts by sending its DHCPREQUEST (instead of the usual DHCPDISCOVER) containing the details of its previous lease. If the same server is prepared to let the client have the same lease, it replies with a DHCPACK and the conversation is complete, having used only two packets (below) instead of the usual four for the full conversation.

   Note that unlike a renewal, which also takes only two packets, this communication relies on broadcasts, because until the conversation is complete the client doesn't know whether it's allowed to use the IP address from its previous lease:

```
0.0.0.0.68 > 255.255.255.255.67:  ... DHCP:REQUEST  ...
212.140.133.22.67 > 255.255.255.255.68:  ... DHCP:ACK ...
```

- after a client shuts down, the server can preserve a record of the IP address it had allocated to this client. When the client reboots and sends its initial DHCP request, the server can check the Ethernet address/client identifier field, and re-allocate the same IP address as last time, if it's available. Servers can decide not to re-use a previously allocated address and instead keep it for re-use by the original client later, as long as the server has a large enough pool of IP addresses available to satisfy new clients. Only if the server runs out of addresses does it have to allocate the same address to a different client. In this way the server can keep client IP addresses as unchanging as possible over very long periods of time, while still providing fully-automatic operation

- sometimes, you have to be able to allocate an address permanently to a host, e.g. your DNS or WINS (Module 19.4) server, so that you can enter its IP number in the configuration files of other hosts. DHCP supports *manual address allocation* to let you do this. Typically, on the server you enter the Ethernet address of the client and the IP address to be allocated, and this address is reserved for that client. Allocating fixed addresses in this way is better than configuring the IP address manually on the client, because you keep *all* your IP address allocations within DHCP, so you don't have to maintain a separate, manual list of permanently allocated ones.

16.4   Lab – configuring a client to use DHCP (Windows)

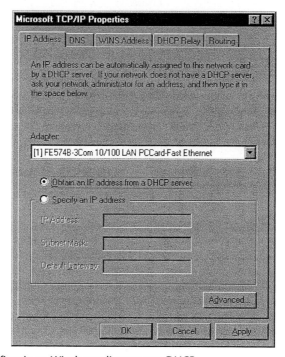

Figure 16.4 Configuring a Windows client to use DHCP

Configuring Windows to use DHCP is simple as can be. In **Control Panel > Network > Protocols > TCP/IP > Properties > IP Address**, tick the **Obtain an IP address from a DHCP server** box (Figure 16.4). Windows prompts you to confirm that you want to use DHCP. After you confirm and as soon as you press **OK** or **Apply** in the **TCP/IP Properties** dialog, Windows attempts to retrieve its settings via DHCP (which you can see by starting **tcpdump** before you press **Apply**.) As usual, check that Windows has applied the settings by running **ipconfig/all** or **wntipcfg > More Info**; both programs also tell you the IP address of the DHCP server that allocated the address to the client, when the lease was obtained, and when it is due to expire (Figure 16.5). (**wntipcfg** comes in the NT 4.0 Resource Kit.)

If Windows doesn't find a DHCP server on the network after about two minutes, it gives an error message saying the DHCP client could not obtain an IP address. (During this time the machine doesn't have a valid IP address but you're not aware of this because the PC hasn't given its error message yet; trying to use your network in this period can be very confusing.)

Figure 16.5 wntipcfg (or **winipcfg**) shows your DHCP lease details

Releasing or renewing the DHCP lease

If you need to free up an IP address that a DHCP machine has been using (e.g. when you're removing a PC permanently, or when you need to check out DHCP's operation) you can *release* the lease using the **Release** button in **wntipcfg** (Figure 16.5). **Release All** does the same thing, but for all NICs, not just the one selected.

You can renew a lease using **Renew** or **Renew All**. This gets a new lease if the PC didn't have one to start with.

ipconfig lets you perform the same operations from the command-line, using its "**/release**" and "**/renew**" options. For further information, enter "**ipconfig /?**".

Troubleshooting

If DHCP doesn't work on any machine, check out your DHCP server. If DHCP fails to work only on a particular machine, configure that machine to use a specified, static IP address instead of obtaining one via DHCP. If TCP/IP networking fails even with a static address, the fault isn't with DHCP – there's something wrong with the TCP/IP software stack or the network card.

16.5   Lab – configuring a client to use DHCP (Linux)

Configuring your Linux DHCP settings is easy. However, finding out which settings to configure in the first place is much more complicated. The problem is that the configuration files to modify to use DHCP settings are not only specific to your distribution of Linux, they also depend on whether you're using a "normal" network card or a PCMCIA one, and commonly any one of three different DHCP clients can be installed:

1. **pump** written by RedHat. (The name is a joke: a "pump", like a "boot," is something you wear on your foot, and the "boot protocol" was the precursor to DHCP.)

2. **dhclient** from the Internet Software Consortium

3. **dhcpcd** ("DHCP client daemon"). Don't confuse this with **dhcpd**, which is the DHCP *server* from the Internet Software Consortium.

Which client should you use? If one is already installed and it works properly, that's obviously the easiest. Otherwise, opinion seems split fairly evenly between the three clients: as **pump** was written by RedHat, it will probably be well integrated on RedHat distributions; **dhclient** is highly configurable and well supported; **dhcpcd** has been around a long time and is well described in Linux HOWTO documents. If we had to choose one, we'd go for **dhclient**, because of who develops it, its adherence to the protocol standards, and comments from experienced network administrators.

How DHCP works on Linux

The DHCP client runs as an application-level program: even though it's configuring some fundamental aspects of your operating system's kernel operation, it doesn't need to run as kernel-level code itself. This makes sense when you think that all the client really does is:

- send and receive a few UDP packets
- extract values from the DHCP ACK reply
- apply these values to the system, in effect just like **ifconfig** or **route** does.

A slight complication is that the client does have to handle DHCP leases, so every so often it has to contact the server to renew the current lease. For this reason, the client runs as a "daemon," i.e. an application running on its own in the background, not connected to any terminal. (That explains the name of the **dhcpcd** client, even though it's confusing at first sight.)

Details of leases are recorded in a text file. Even if this machine reboots in the meantime, the DHCP client can use this information when it next requests a lease from a DHCP server. This makes it possible for a machine to keep the same IP address for long periods even though the address is dynamically allocated, as we explained in Module 16.3.

The leases file is called something like **dhclient.leases** or **dhcpcd-***interface***.info**, typically to be found in **/var/dhcp** or **/var/database** or **/etc/dhcpc**.

Configuring your system to use DHCP

There are two parts to DHCP configuration: telling your system which client to run, and setting configuration options for that client.

1. **specifying which DHCP client your system is to run**

   You must edit your system's startup files to cause your chosen DHCP client program or daemon to run when your system boots up. Typically this step only involves setting a variable to indicate whether a particular client is to be used, e.g.

   ```
   DHCLIENT="n"                                don't run dhclient
   PUMP="y"                                     do run pump
   ```

   or

   ```
   BOOTPROTO="dhcp"
   ```

   or that the default DHCP client configured on this machine is to be used:

   ```
   iface eth0 inet dhcp
   ```

   However, the precise settings depend on your Linux distribution and version – see Appendix 6.

2. **settings specific to your chosen DHCP client**

   The usual configuration files for each of the three clients are:

   > /etc/pump.conf
   >
   > /etc/dhclient.conf
   >
   > /etc/dhcpc/config

   All three DHCP client systems will work in most cases with no special configuration options and usually work fine even if the configuration file isn't present at all (although we have found that because of bugs, the file sometimes has to be present even if its empty).

   Connecting to a cable network provider with DHCP is a special case: you may have to configure your DHCP hostname option. With **dhclient** use **send hostname** … , with **dhcpcd** set option **-h** in **/etc/dhcpc/config**, and with **pump** use argument **-h** or the hostname option in **/etc/interfaces**. (See the manpages for details.)

Viewing, releasing, or renewing leases

pump has options **--status**, **--release** and **--renew**. Recent versions of **dhcpcd** (1.3.18-p17+) have option **-n** to renew a lease. With older versions you have to use something like:

```
dhcpcd -k ; dhcpcd              release this lease; then start again and get a new one
```

but this does cause your machine to have no IP address at all for a tiny while, which causes open connections to be dropped. Recent versions of **dhclient** have option **-r** to release a lease but don't have an explicit "renew" command.

Troubleshooting

As with Windows, if DHCP doesn't work on a particular machine, try static addressing. If that fails too, then there is something wrong with the stack or the NIC.

16.6 Large networks: DHCP relay; ISP dial-up addresses

Using DHCP on a bigger network: DHCP relay

When a DHCP client is starting up, it doesn't know its own netmask, let alone its IP address, so when it broadcasts, the only broadcast address it can use is the 255.255.255.255 limited broadcast address. In Module 4.10 we said that this is visible only on the local wire segment, and is never forwarded by a router. So how can you use a single DHCP server for a large, routed network? (You don't want lots of separate DHCP servers because you'd no longer have a single, centralized point for managing your IP addresses.) *DHCP relay* addresses this issue (Figure 16.6).

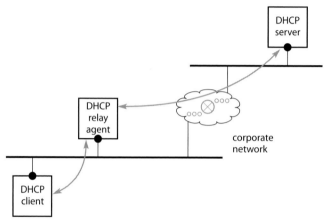

Figure 16.6 Relay agent permits DHCP over multiple segments

- on each separate network segment, you run a *DHCP relay agent,* which you configure so it knows the IP address of the real DHCP server. (A DHCP relay agent is often included in purpose-built routers)

- when a DHCP client broadcasts on its local segment, obviously the real DHCP server doesn't see the broadcast, because it's on a different segment. However, the DHCP relay agent *does* see the local broadcast. It takes the request, and passes it to the real DHCP server

- the real DHCP server processes the request and sends the reply back to the relay agent

- the relay agent receives the response and broadcasts it on its local wire, so the DHCP can receive it.

DHCP relay is built into some routers, so you may not have to run anything extra on your network to use it. Software relay agents are also available for Windows-NT and Linux.

How ISPs use dynamic addresses

So far we have discussed using DHCP on a private network. ISPs also need to allocate IP addresses dynamically to dial-up users. There just aren't enough IP addresses to give every dial-up user a unique, permanent address, but because only a small proportion of an ISP's dial-up users are connected at any one time, the ISP can share a small number of IP addresses amongst a much larger number of users.

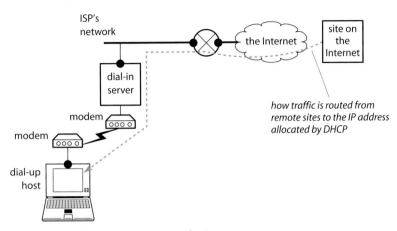

Figure 16.7 How a dial-up PC connects to the Internet

Figure 16.7 shows schematically how a dial-up PC connects to the Internet. The dial-up software on the PC must be configured to accept an address allocated by the dial-in server. (Figure 16.8 shows the dial-up TCP/IP settings from a Windows-NT host.)

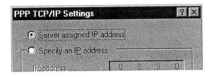

Figure 16.8 Dial-up TCP/IP settings from a Windows-NT host

The PC dials in to the ISP and attempts to log on (in fact authenticate with the dial-in server). The ISP's dial-in server verifies the logon, and allocates an IP address from its pool to the PC. The PC accepts the IP address and initializes its dial-up TCP/IP link with this address.

Note that this is *not* DHCP, although it is similar. The PC is given the IP address only for this connection session; it isn't given a lease on the address, and there are no renewal, rebind, or lease times. The PC is using dial-up connection software, not a DHCP client. Finally, the PC couldn't use DHCP even if it wanted to, because modems and an ordinary phone line give you a point-to-point connection to your ISP. Your dial-up machine and the ISP's server are the only things on this connection, and it doesn't support UDP broadcasts, which are essential for DHCP. (However, the dial-in servers themselves may obtain the IP addresses for allocating to dial-ups from an internal DHCP server, so that one pool of addresses can be shared without any clashes across multiple dial-in servers. In this case it is the dial-in servers that are the DHCP clients.)

Connections over cable modems or DSL are different. Your cable or DSL modem is in effect connected to an internal network of your ISP, along with the cable modems of all the other subscribers in your area. This is very much like an Ethernet, but using a different link layer and physical media, and DHCP is often used for address allocation on this type of connection.

Summary

- DHCP lets you configure automatically the three fundamental networking parameters on machines on your network. This is necessary for diskless machines and very convenient for other machines. It greatly simplifies network management

- by allocating and re-using addresses from a pool, DHCP can share a small number of addresses among a large set of machines that are not all in use at the same time

- the DHCP client and server converse using UDP broadcast packets. The full conversation consists of four packets: DISCOVER, OFFER, REQUEST, ACKNOWLEDGE

- the server allocates an IP address to a client for a fixed lease time. Near the expiry time, a client can ask the server to renew its lease. Even when a client shuts down, the server will normally not allocate this address to another client unless it runs out of available addresses. This enables clients to keep the same IP address over very long periods

- DHCP broadcast packets can't pass through routers. To allow DHCP to work on routed networks, DHCP relay agents pass DHCP broadcasts to the full DHCP elsewhere on the network, and in turn broadcast the replies they receive, allowing the DHCP client to hear the reply.

What's next?

The next chapter looks at many other commonly used protocols and how they work.

Notes and further reading

The almost-original DHCP RFC is very readable and understandable, giving background on why DHCP is necessary, its design criteria, and how it works:

❑ **RFC-1541 October 1993** *Dynamic Host Configuration Protocol*

This has now been superseded by:

❑ **RFC-2131 March 1997** *Dynamic Host Configuration Protocol*

For notes on using DHCP with Linux, with the **dhcpcd** client:

❑ **http://www.linuxdoc.org/HOWTO/mini/DHCP/index.html**

The current DHCP standard can server only class-ful routes, i.e. the netmask for the route is derived from the class A, B, or C type of the address specified. As this isn't adequate nowadays when almost everyone uses classless (CIDR) addressing, an amendment to the DHCP standard has been proposed to include classless route as a DHCP option.

A dated (1999) but very good FAQ:

❑ **http://www.dhcp-handbook.com/dhcp_faq.html** *DHCP FAQ*

Notes on DHCP and current developments are on:

❏ http://www.dhcp.org/

A book from the guys who developed DHCP:

❏ **Ralph Droms and Ted Lemon** *The DHCP Handbook. Understanding, Deploying, and Managing Automated Configuration Services* (1999, Pearson Higher Education)

DHCP implementations

Version 3 from the Internet Software Consortium, which includes both client and server:

❏ http://www.isc.org/products/DHCP/

❏ http://www.isc.org/products/DHCP/dhcp-v3.html

❏ http://www.nominum.com/resources/faqs/dhcp-faq.html *DHCP FAQ*

❏ http://arsinfo.cit.buffalo.edu/FAQ/faq.cgi?pkg=ISC%20DHCP *ISC DHCP Server FAQ*

You can configure which DHCP options Linux clients request, but for Windows there is a small set of supported options; all you can do is remove some of these by editing the Registry, but it's hard to think why you would ever want to do this. See:

❏ **MS-KB-Q121005** *DHCP Options Supported by Clients*

❏ **MS-KB-Q187742** *Methods of Setting DHCP Options*

For an overview of setting up a basic DHCP server configuration, see Web Appendix 20.

DHCP's predecessors – RARP and BOOTP (historical interest only)

In the early days, diskless workstations obtained their IP addresses from a server using the RARP (*Reverse ARP*) protocol. A workstation broadcast a RARP request on the local Ethernet, and the packet of course contained the machine's MAC address. A RARP server that heard the request looked up its database of MAC-address/IP-number mappings (usually stored in the file **/etc/ethers**), and if the sender's MAC address was in the database the server replied with the corresponding IP number. As RARP uses broadcasts, it's not routable and therefore is limited to a single Ethernet segment.

BOOTP (Boot Protocol) goes further than this. It can serve lots of parameters – not just IP address, netmask and default gateway settings – including details of which printers to use, etc., although many of BOOTP's parameters aren't very relevant to today's networks. DHCP is more extensible and flexible, doesn't require manual configuration of a database of client addresses which BOOTP does, and allocates an addresses for a fixed lease period so it can be reclaimed and reused for another machine if the client goes away.

What if my DHCP server fails?

You can run more than one DHCP server, but to give you the redundancy you want the servers must exchange details of what addresses they have each leased out so that if one fails, another can take over. At the time of writing there is no final standard for this, but a standard for the *DHCP Failover Protocol* is very close to being agreed and the ISC DHCP v3 server supports a current version of the protocol. If you don't have servers that handle failover in some way, there are a couple of workarounds you can employ:

1. make your lease times long enough so that if a server does fail, most clients have a long enough lease to give you time to fix or replace the server, and ...

2. run a second server with a pool of addresses that doesn't overlap the main server's. This can handle any requests for new leases when the first server is down. This second server can run all the time and have just as big a pool as the first server, in which case they share the load. Or you can configure it with a very small pool, and keep the server software disabled for normal running; when the first server fails, enable the server software on the second machine, which only takes a few seconds (as long as this machine is switched on, of course).

Windows-NT 4.0 DHCP servers don't replicate automatically. See:

❑ **MS-KB-Q193819** *Errors When Using Directory Replicator to Backup DHCP Database*

Dial-up and DHCP

❑ **MS-KB-Q160699** *Understanding DHCP IP Address Assignment for RAS Clients* (Note that this isn't DHCP combined with PPP-dial-up to an ISP.)

How DNS ties in with DHCP

It's easy to allocate a fixed IP number to servers, as we explained in Module 16.3, and then you can enter this IP number in your DNS database with its name, because you know it will never change. For hosts with IP numbers that aren't manually allocated and specially reserved like this, there are implementations that combine DNS and DHCP: when the DHCP server allocates an IP address to a name, it automatically creates corresponding entries in the DNS database. Windows-2000 and the ISC DHCP server both support dynamic DNS:

❑ **http://technet.microsoft.com** *TechNet Home* > **Products & Technologies > Windows 2000 Server > Resource Kits > Part 2 > Chapter 6 – Windows 2000 DNS**

❑ **http://www.isc.org/products/DHCP/**

Appendices

Appendix 6: making network settings permanent – Debian Linux
Web Appendix 19: DHCP options summary
Web Appendix 20: setting up a DHCP server

17 Other applications and their protocols

Introduction

This chapter gives an overview of many network applications and protocols. A common theme is that these applications provide something as a network service (rather than as a facility available only on the local machine, or built in to the end-user application). For the more important ones, we explain briefly how they work, and give an example of their use. The aim is to show you how useful some of these facilities can be, and to give you pointers if you need to explore further.

17.1 daytime, echo, discard, **and** chargen **services**

We start this chapter with four little network services that are useful for testing (and for very little else), which we'll need later in the chapter. These are all client/server protocols, and all are available on UDP as well as TCP. Their well-known ports are:

Service	Port
daytime	13
echo	7
chargen	19
discard	9

daytime the server ignores any input that the client sends, and returns the time and date from the server machine, as a text string (below, edited to save space, and to show lines from the server indented):

```
bob# telnet 192.0.2.17 daytime
     Mon Jul 30 10:43:17 2001
```

echo the server returns exactly what the client sends (below). To terminate, press Ctrl-C in Linux **telnet**, or use menu **File > Exit** on Windows **telnet**.

```
bob# telnet 192.0.2.17 echo
Connected to 192.0.2.17.
Escape character is '^]'.
abc
     abc
def
     def
^C
bob#
```

chargen character generator – it ignores your input completely; instead it generates a constant stream of lines and sends them to you, giving one-way traffic from the remote host to you (below). To exit you have to terminate your **telnet** client, as above.

```
lindeb# telnet 192.0.2.17 chargen
 !"#$%&'()*+,-./0123456789:;<=>?@ABCDEFGHIJKLMNOPQRSTUVWXYZ[\]^_`abcdefg
!"#$%&'()*+,-./0123456789:;<=>?@ABCDEFGHIJKLMNOPQRSTUVWXYZ[\]^_`abcdefgh
"#$%&'()*+,-./0123456789:;<=>?@ABCDEFGHIJKLMNOPQRSTUVWXYZ[\]^_`abcdefghi
#$%&'()*+,-./0123456789:;<=>?@ABCDEFGHIJKLMNOPQRSTUVWXYZ[\]^_`abcdefghij
$%&'()*+,-./0123456789:;<=>?@ABCDEFGHIJKLMNOPQRSTUVWXYZ[\]^_`abcdefghijk
%&'()*+,-./0123456789:;<=>?@ABCDEFGHIJKLMNOPQRSTUVWXYZ[\]^_`abcdefghijkl
&'()*+,-./0123456789:;<=>?@ABCDEFGHIJKLMNOPQRSTUVWXYZ[\]^_`abcdefghijklm
```

discard is the opposite of **chargen** – the server swallows all its input silently. (So if you are clever enough to connect a **chargen** server at one end of a connection to a **discard** server at the other, you can generate one-way traffic over the network for as long as you want.)

These little services are ideal for testing: they make use of all your IP routing, DNS name resolution, and TCP and/or UDP, but impose virtually no load on your server machine, and need almost no software. We use these services frequently when installing new machines. We can check that a lot of the network infrastructure is working just by connecting to, for example, the **daytime** service. These services are also particularly useful when installing a firewall before any server machines have been installed on the LAN (Module 24.8).

To enable these services on Windows-NT, install the Simple TCP/IP Services network service in **Control Panel > Network > Services** (Figure 17.1). You can control them from **Control Panel > Services**.

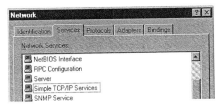

Figure 17.1 Installing the Simple TCP/IP Services on Windows-NT

To enable these services on Linux, ensure their names and port numbers are in the **/etc/services** file (Figure 17.2) and that the file **/etc/inetd.conf** (Figure 17.3) contains entries for the ones you want, and that they are not commented out. (As we explain in Appendix 20, if you change **inetd.conf** you must use the **HUP** signal to tell the **inetd** process to re-read the file.)

```
echo            7/tcp
echo            7/udp
discard         9/tcp           sink null
discard         9/udp           sink null
daytime         13/tcp
daytime         13/udp
qotd            17/tcp          quote
chargen         19/tcp          ttytst source
chargen         19/udp          ttytst source
```

Figure 17.2 Service names and port numbers (Linux)

```
we don't want ──────   echo      stream  tcp   nowait  root  internal
UDP echo and           #echo     dgram   udp   wait    root  internal
we don't use           #chargen  stream  tcp   nowait  root  internal
chargen at all ──────  #chargen  dgram   udp   wait    root  internal
                       discard   stream  tcp   nowait  root  internal
                       discard   dgram   udp   wait    root  internal
```

Figure 17.3 Comment-out unwanted services to disable them

On Linux these services are implemented in **inetd** itself, rather than as separate programs, because they are so small.

You can also use these services over UDP instead of TCP (Module 17.4).

The Notes at the end of the chapter give information on some other services.

17.2 FTP – File Transfer Protocol

Before the World Wide Web became popular, *FTP* (*File Transfer Protocol*) was *the* way people retrieved data from remote sites. It was one of the three big applications. (The other two were e-mail and **telnet** – for accessing remote applications and information services.) Increasingly, HTTP is used instead of FTP for interactive transfers of individual files, but FTP is still used for non-interactive transfers, for batch transfers of multiple files or whole directories. Even within browsers, **ftp://** URLs are still common – so understanding how FTP works is worthwhile.

Below we show a very simple FTP session. The client on Bob connects to the server on Alice and transfers the file **/tmp/x** from the server to the current directory on the client:

```
bob% ftp alice
Connected to alice
    220 ProFTPD 1.2.0pre10 Server (Debian) [alice]
Name (alice:niall): fred
    331 Password required for fred.
Password: xxx
    230 User fred logged in.
    Remote system type is UNIX.
    Using binary mode to transfer files.
ftp> get /tmp/x
    local: /tmp/x remote: /tmp/x
    200 PORT command successful.
    150 Opening BINARY mode data connection for /tmp/x (29 bytes).
    226 Transfer complete.
    29 bytes received in 0.00 secs (45.0 kB/s)
ftp> quit
    221 Goodbye.
bob%
```

FTP client programs are usually large, because FTP supports so many features, necessary to address the particular needs of users in the early days of the Internet. Below we show some of the user commands in a Linux command-line client:

```
bob# ftp
ftp> help
Commands may be abbreviated.   Commands are:
!          debug        mdir        sendport      site
$          dir          mget        put           size
account    disconnect   mkdir       pwd           status
append     exit         mls         quit          struct
. . .
```

Clients with a graphical user interface are widely available now, especially on Windows, and most Web browsers let you retrieve files using FTP. However, we are not going to spend much time on how to use FTP; we concentrate on its network features instead.

FTP uses TCP as its transport. It has two well-known ports:

FTP data port	20
FTP control port	21

The commands and status information are sent over the *control port*; the requested files, etc. are transferred on the separate *data port*. RFC-959, the standard for FTP, illustrates a typical FTP set-up, as shown in Figure 17.4. The user types commands such as "**get /tmp/x**" into

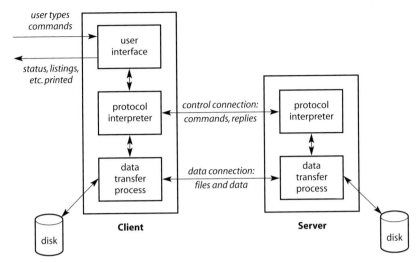

Figure 17.4 Typical FTP implementation

the part of the client program that handles the user interface (or, if it's a GUI client, the user clicks on buttons, filenames, etc.). This part of the program communicates the user's instructions to the "protocol interpreter" (PI) – a separate part of the program that sends FTP protocol commands to the server, and interprets responses from the server. The PI also controls the "data transfer process" (DTP) component, instructing it as to when to connect to the server, which IP address and port number to connect on, which files to transfer, etc. The actual file data, directory listings, and so on are transferred over the data connection.

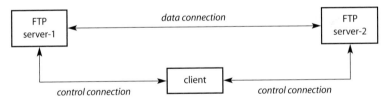

Figure 17.5 Client controls third-party transfer between two other machines

The FTP protocol can handle "third-party" transfers, from one remote server to another remote server, controlled by a client elsewhere (Figure 17.5), which is why the control and data connections are separate. Nowadays this isn't particularly useful but on the early Internet, before personal computers or workstations were invented, it was used a lot. Often the computer your terminal was connected to was limited in power, and any heavy computation had to be carried out on another machine. Using third-party FTP, you transferred your data from, say, a host controlling lab equipment where experimental data were generated, to a powerful machine to analyze the data. (Then you **telnet**ed to the powerful machine to run your analysis programs.) Not all clients and servers provide a user interface that lets you specify third-party transfers.

In the next module we look at how the FTP connections are established, and a problem caused by having more than one connection.

17.3 How FTP connections are established

A typical FTP session consists of two phases (Figure 17.6):

1. the user specifies to the client which server and port to connect to. The client establishes the control connection. The user logs in, negotiates any transfer parameters with the server (e.g. binary or text mode transfer), and sets any local parameters (whether to print "**#**" marks for every *n* data blocks transferred, etc.)

2. the user requests a file transfer (from server to client or vice versa). The data connection has to be established now. The procedure is:

   a. the client opens an ephemeral port and listens on it, waiting for the server to connect

   b. the client sends the FTP **PORT** command, telling the server the number of the port the client is listening on.

   c. the server connects to that port and the connection is established

   d. the data are transferred over the connection

   e. the connection is closed.

Phase 2 is repeated for each transfer (each file or directory listing), using a new data connection each time.

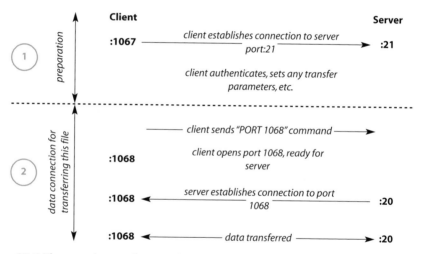

Figure 17.6 The two phases of a typical "active mode" FTP session

We can see the connections using **netstat** (with appropriate option to show only TCP connections, for convenience):

```
netstat -n -t                                          Linux
netstat -n -p tcp                                      Windows-NT
```

Opposite we show the **netstat** output, edited to save space (i) when the client logged in, (ii) during transfer of file-1, (iii) during transfer of file-2, and (iv) when the file transfers were completed. You can see that the control connection (marked "C" in the figure, connecting

```
bob# netstat -n -t
      Proto Recv-Q Send-Q Local Address      Foreign Address   State
C     tcp        0       0 192.0.2.19:1067   192.0.2.17:21     ESTABLISHED

      bob# netstat -n -t
D1    tcp        0       0 192.0.2.19:1068   192.0.2.17:20     ESTABLISHED
C     tcp        0       0 192.0.2.19:1067   192.0.2.17:21     ESTABLISHED

      bob# netstat -n -t
D2    tcp        0       0 192.0.2.19:1073   192.0.2.17:20     ESTABLISHED
C     tcp        0       0 192.0.2.19:1067   192.0.2.17:21     ESTABLISHED

      bob# netstat -n -t
C     tcp        0       0 192.0.2.19:1067   192.0.2.17:21     ESTABLISHED
```

ports :1067 and :21) persists throughout, but different data connections (**D1** = :1068/:20 and **D2** = :1073/:20) are used for each transfer and then terminate.

The way the data connection is established causes problems when the connection is through a firewall, from an internal client to an external server. The data connection is established from outside the firewall (the server) to inside (the client) on a more or less random port (:1068 here). The firewall doesn't know whether this is the second phase of a genuine FTP session that an internal client established or an outside hacker trying to break in and consequently many firewalls block it.

To overcome this problem, the FTP server can operate in *passive mode* (as opposed to *active mode*, that is what we described above):

- the client issues a **PASV** command (instead of a **PORT** command)
- the server opens on an ephemeral port, r, and listens for the client to connect
- the server tells the client the number of the port it's listening on
- the client connects to that port.

The rest (Figure 17.7) is as with active mode. The firewall is now happy, because the connection was established from inside, so it can't be a hacker. We'll now explore FTP in detail using **telnet** as a client, but to do that we need a new tool, **netcat**, which we describe in the next module.

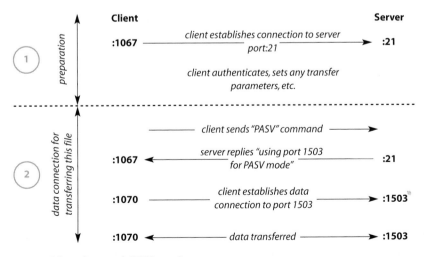

Figure 17.7 A "passive mode" FTP session

17.4 netcat (or nc) – the TCP/IP Swiss army knife

This module and the next are very detailed. Skip them on first reading if you don't use FTP a lot.
At its simplest **netcat** is like **telnet**:

- it connects to a TCP server that's listening on a port
- it reads the input you type and sends it to the server
- it receives the output that the server returns on the connection, and prints it.

However, **netcat** differs from **telnet** in three important ways:

a. it can listen on a port for incoming connections, and respond to them. In this mode it acts like a server. By contrast, **telnet** always acts as a true client and can only connect to a port that's already listening

b. it avoids **telnet's** complexity (fancy options for special modes, terminal handling, etc., which we haven't covered, as they don't relate to its network functionality)

c. it can use UDP as its transport instead of TCP.

That gives us four possible modes, which we examine below.

netcat is available for Linux and Windows. See Appendix 19 for more details and its manpage. (The name is confusing. It's referred to as **netcat** but the program, manpage, etc. are all called **nc**.)

1. nc as TCP client (replacement for telnet)

You can use **netcat** to connect to SMTP servers, HTTP servers, etc. as we did in earlier chapters. For example:

```
alice# nc mail1.microsoft.com smtp
220 inet-vrs-01.redmond.corp.microsoft.com InterScan VirusWall NT ESMTP 3.
```

(One thing you probably *won't* be able to do is logon to a remote system on the **telnet** port. The **telnet** server goes through a preliminary terminal and parameter negotiation with the client, and doesn't issue the login prompt until that has succeeded, and **netcat** doesn't bother with this by default. However, if your **netcat** version supports the "**-t**" option, it gets round this problem.)

2. nc as TCP server

This is the mode that we need in the next module. Use options "**-l**" (listening mode, i.e. server) and "**-p** *portnum*" (port number to listen on), e.g.

```
nc -l -p 80
```
                                                    may not work if Web server already running

listens on port 80, i.e. can be used as a dummy or test Web server, at least to detect incoming connections. (If you have another process, such as a real Web server, already listening on port 80, **netcat** will fail because it won't be allowed access to port 80.) Check that **netstat** is doing what you expect with "`netstat -n -l -t -p`" (Linux: option "`-p`" shows program name, below), "`netstat -n -a -p tcp`" (Windows):

```
alice# netstat -l -t -n -p
Proto Recv-Q Send-Q Local Address    Foreign Address  State    PID/Program
tcp       0      0 0.0.0.0:80        0.0.0.0:*        LISTEN   30298/nc
```

When a client establishes a connection to this port, **netcat** prints what the client sends, and sends to the client anything you type (Figure 17.8), so you are acting as a manual Web server. We'll use **netcat** in this mode as a test server when installing a firewall in Chapter 24.

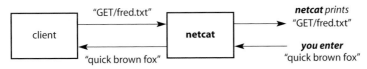

Figure 17.8 Using **netcat** as a "manual Web server"

3. nc as UDP client

You can tell **netcat** to use UDP instead of its default TCP by specifying the "`-u`" option. Below we show a **netcat** "conversation" – it's not a connection, because UDP is connection-less – talking to the UDP daytime server. Every time you enter a line, it is sent to the server, which ignores what you sent but sends the current date/time as a reply. To exit you have to terminate the **netcat** client, in this case with Ctrl-C.

```
bob# nc -u alice daytime
      the quick
Mon Jul 30 13:11:02 2001
      brown fox jumps
Mon Jul 30 13:11:03 2001
^C
bob#
```

The **netcat** distribution includes a tiny front-end program called **data** to help you construct "binary" encoded packets, typically for use with UDP (Appendix 19).

4. nc as UDP server

Use options "`-u`" (UDP), "`-l`" (listening, i.e. server), and "`-p *portnum*`" (port number to listen on), e.g. mode

   `nc -u -l -p echo`   *may not work if UDP echo server on this machine*

listens for incoming UDP echo requests. **netcat** as usual prints whatever the client sends and replies with whatever you type. By typing back in what **netcat** prints you are acting as an **echo** server. (But there are, one hopes, better ways to employ your time.)

   In the next module we use **netcat** to retrieve the output from an FTP server.

17.5 Lab – two FTP sessions using telnet as client

We're going to run two FTP sessions by hand using **telnet** and **netcat** to illustrate in practice the difference between active and passive modes. We'll start with passive mode, because it's easier. In the diagrams we've inserted extra lines to show the time sequence in which we entered commands and received replies. Long lines are wrapped. Lines for the second clients are indented a lot. The conversations below illustrate:

- the end-user commands that you type to your FTP client's user interface component (e.g. "**put**", "**get**", "**ls**", "**rename**") aren't what goes over the wire. The on-wire commands are four-character strings, like the SMTP and POP commands we saw earlier. You can get a list of the user commands by connecting to the FTP server and entering **HELP**. (You don't have to enter username and password first.)
- the response codes from the server are like the HTTP response codes, e.g.

Code	Meaning
125	Data connection already open; transfer starting
200	Command OK
331	User name OK, need password
421	Service not available, closing control connection
501	Syntax error in parameters or arguments

RFC-959 lists all the response codes and their meanings.

1. Passive mode

We use two separate **telnet** connections to replicate the actions of an FTP client. The sequence of actions (Figure 17.9) is:

a. connect to the FTP server using **telnet**. This is the control connection

b. login to the FTP server, giving the username and password

c. send the **PASV** command to tell the server to use passive mode

d. **telnet** prints the server's reply, which is in the format $a,b,c,d,p1,p2$, where $a.b.c.d$ is the server's IP address and $(p1 \times 256 + p2)$ is the port number it's going to open for the client – in this example $(4 \times 256 + 12) = 1036$

e. leaving **telnet** running in another window or on another terminal, connect another **telnet** session to the server on the port we just calculated, 1036. It sits waiting for the server to connect. This is the data connection

f. in **telnet-1**, enter the FTP on-wire command to retrieve the file, "**RETR/tmp/j**". This is sent over the control connection to the server …

g. … which sends the contents of file **/tmp/j** to our **telnet-2** over the data connection, and then terminates the connection.

2. Active mode

The sequence is very similar to passive mode, but instead of the client sending the **PASV** command, it sends a **PORT** command saying which port the *client* will be listening on; to make the calculations easy we have specified port $(10 \times 256 + 0) = 2560$. At that point we have to use **netcat**, with options "**-l**" (listen) to open and listen on the client port, for the server to connect, for the data connection. Option "**-v**" (verbose) gives us more information about what's happening (Figure 17.10).

```
a.  bob# telnet alice ftp
        Connected to alice.example.com.
            220 alice FTP server (Version 6.2/OpenBSD/Linux-0.10) ready.
b.  USER fred
            331 Password required for fred.
    PASS xxxxxx
            230 User fred logged in.
c.  PASV
d.      227 Entering Passive Mode (192,0,2,17,4,12)
e.                              bob# telnet alice 1036
                                Connected to alice.example.com.
f.  RETR /tmp/j
            150 Opening ASCII mode data
        connection for '/tmp/j' (128 bytes).
g.                              'Twas brillig, and the slithy toves
                                Did gyre and gimble in the wabe;
                                All mimsy were the borogoves,
                                And the mome raths outgrabe.
                                Connection closed by foreign host.
                                bob#
        226 Transfer complete.
    QUIT
        221 Goodbye.
        Connection closed by foreign host.
    bob#
```

Figure 17.9 Using two **telnet** connections for FTP passive-mode transfer

```
bob# telnet alice ftp
    Connected to alice.example.com.
    220 ProFTPD 1.2.0pre10 Server (Debian) [alice.example.com]
USER fred
    331 Password required for fred.
PASS xxxxxx
    230 User fred logged in.
PORT 192,0,2,17,10,0
    200 PORT command successful.
                            bob# nc -v -l -p 2560
                            listening on [any] 2560 ...
RETR /tmp/j
    150 Opening ASCII mode data connection for /tmp/j (128 bytes).

                            connect to [192.0.2.19] from [192.0.2.17] 20

                            'Twas brillig, and the slithy toves
                            Did gyre and gimble in the wabe;
                            All mimsy were the borogoves,
                            And the mome raths outgrabe.
                            bob#

    226 Transfer complete.
QUIT
    221 Goodbye.
    Connection closed by foreign host.
bob#
```

Figure 17.10 Using **telnet** and **nc** for FTP active-mode transfer

17.6 X window system

The X window system (it's a window system called "X," not a system called "X Window") is the base on which all Linux graphical workstations are built. It is also available for almost every UNIX platform, and many others too, including Windows and Macintosh, and many handheld computers and PDAs (personal digital assistants). On some systems, especially Windows, it is a chargeable extra, usually supplied by third-party vendors.

The current (and only foreseeable) version of X is X11.

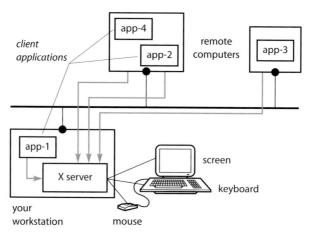

Figure 17.11 Unique features of the X window system

As window systems go, X has some unique features, illustrated in Figure 17.11:

- it is a client/server system, from the ground up
- the *display server* (or *X server*) controls the graphics display, keyboard, and mouse
- the *client* is the application program that:
  - sends *requests* to the server to draw lines and characters on-screen
  - receives *events* from the server, containing mouse movements/clicks, and keyboard input

  In other words, the server is on the workstation you're sitting at, and the client is the application that may be running locally on the same workstation, or remotely on another machine on the network. You can think of it as the client sending pictures of its windows across the network, to be displayed on the server's screen. (The terminology seems backward compared with, for example, file servers and Web servers, where the server part is remote. However, if you remember that the server is something that provides a service and accepts requests from clients to do things – display graphics in this case – it makes sense.)
- there's no difference between a local client application and a remote one, Both of them use exactly the same protocol; the requests and events travel over the wire in one case and via a local inter-process communication method in the other

- because all X clients are inherently networked, you can use a remote application just as easily as a remote one. This makes remote system administration of Linux systems very easy, and no special coding is necessary to make the management applications accessible remotely.

To start an application running on a remote machine, displaying back to the X server on your own desktop, you often use the **rsh** command (Module 10.11) either explicitly or via some graphical front end. The example below starts the X clock application on Bob, displaying back to the X server on your workstation, Alice:

```
alice% rsh bob xclock -display alice:0 &
```

X runs over TCP. Its well-known ports are 6000–6063, so it's easily traced with **tcpdump**. (The reason for the large number of ports is that you can have multiple displays on a single machine, and each display needs a port of its own.) We run an X server on our Windows PCs, and then display windows from our Linux boxes to the server on the local PC, allowing us to run both our Windows and Linux examples on the same screen and capture the screen-dumps for inclusion in this text. The following code extract shows an excerpt of a **tcpdump** trace; the packets are small because they relate to mouse movements, which require very few data – a few bytes to specify the current mouse position.

```
xserver.6000 > xclient.1604: P [tcp sum ok] 3393:3425(32) ack 1640 win 8760
xserver.6000 > xclient.1604: P [tcp sum ok] 3425:3457(32) ack 1640 win 8760
xclient.1604 > xserver.6000: . [tcp sum ok] 1640:1640(0) ack 3457 win 16060
xserver.6000 > xclient.1604: P [tcp sum ok] 3457:3489(32) ack 1640 win 8760
xserver.6000 > xclient.1604: P [tcp sum ok] 3489:3521(32) ack 1640 win 8760
xclient.1604 > xserver.6000: . [tcp sum ok] 1640:1640(0) ack 3521 win 16060
xserver.6000 > xclient.1604: P [tcp sum ok] 3521:3553(32) ack 1640 win 8760
xserver.6000 > xclient.1604: P [tcp sum ok] 3553:3585(32) ack 1640 win 8760
```

An interesting implementation of an X server is an *X terminal*, which was the first example of the "thin client" system architecture. The terminal consists of an X server and network software, packaged with the CPU and memory to run it on, mouse, keyboard, network interface, and a minimal operating system. Applications don't run in the terminal itself, but on a host at the other end of the wire. Terminals don't have any disks or files that can be damaged by a sudden failure of the electricity supply – after a power failure, you just switch on again.

Which user interface?

Another unusual feature of X is that the user interface – the look and feel of applications – isn't built into the base window system. X is a low-level layer and applications are typically built using standard function libraries or *toolkits* that provide a particular look and feel. On UNIX systems, CDE (Common Desktop Environment) is common, with the older Motif and OpenLook look-and-feels still running on many machines. On Linux, GNOME and KDE provide desktop environments and development libraries for new applications (see Notes). **ethereal** (Chapter 13) uses the GNOME look-and-feel.

17.7 LDAP – Lightweight Directory Access Protocol; overview

Many applications on the network require information about users and other resources, e.g. user IDs and passwords are needed to control access to an application and its data. Some applications need more information, e.g. an e-mail client needs the user's full name, names of mail servers, and various other preferences; a calendar application needs the basic user information too, but also needs to know which department the user belongs to, which office they are in, and whether they are a manager (who can schedule meetings for their staff); the human resources (HR) application also needs to know the person's position in the organization, but in addition records more private information such as social security numbers, salary, etc.

This information is typically stored in some form of database specific to the application. Obviously, this gets complicated as more and more applications are added – one user ends up with multiple usernames and passwords in different places, and each application has its own isolated "island" of information, often duplicating information used elsewhere by other applications (Figure 17.12). This imposes an ever-increasing maintenance load on the system administrators, and leads to errors or inconsistencies in the data.

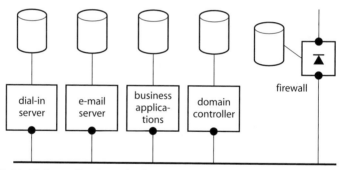

Figure 17.12 Multiple applications duplicate lists of usernames, passwords etc

LDAP (Lightweight Directory Access Protocol) begins to solve this problem. Instead of separate databases for each application, a single, central *directory* is maintained, containing all the information for all applications. This is made available as a network service (Figure 17.13), not as an application or file local to one machine.

All the applications now retrieve information from the one directory, using LDAP. For example, when a new employee joins the organization, the HR department creates a record for them in the directory, and the HR application automatically creates a username for them on the network and gives them access to the applications they need to perform their job, based on their department and job function. The organization's network starts to function as a single, integrated entity.

LDAP was originally implemented as a front-end to X.500 (which implemented the *Directory Access Protocol (DAP)*, the directory service for OSI). However, X.500 is a big, heavyweight protocol, and when LDAP was implemented as a directory service in its own right, it was called *lightweight* in contrast. LDAP runs over TCP, on well-known port 389.

LDAP is used for storing information about all aspects and components of a network, not just users. Microsoft Windows-2000's Active Directory uses LDAP extensively, as does

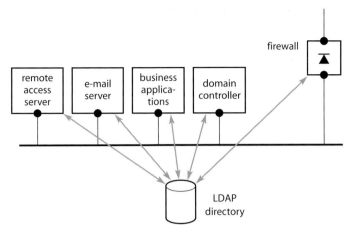

Figure 17.13 An LDAP directory stores usernames, passwords, etc., centrally

Novell's NDS (Novell Directory Services, now called eDirectory), and the Netscape (iPlanet) suite of Web, e-mail and other servers. The Distributed Management Task Force (DMTF) is working on standards for the "Directory-Enabled Network" (DEN) so that management information for all components of the network can be stored centrally, but accessed from anywhere. Many new applications are now "directory-enabled."

In Figure 17.13 we've shown the LDAP directory providing information to many different applications and servers. Increasingly, however, LDAP is used to export information from one server to a client application or to another server. Figure 17.14 shows a common scenario. A firewall (or similar application or device) has a security policy that specifies what Internet access individual users are permitted. Instead of duplicating the user database, the firewall relies on the domain controller or Active Directory (Windows) or other authentication or login service, and retrieves user information from it using LDAP, to control what individual users may do.

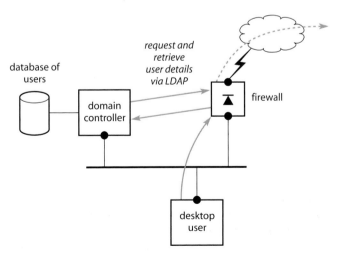

Figure 17.14 Firewall uses LDAP to query Windows domain controller for user information

17.8 LDAP – directories and database considerations

What is an LDAP "directory"? The concept of a directory evolved from things like phone directories – a list of people, and information relating to each of them, in a specific order so that the directory can be searched to find the information needed. An LDAP directory contains information (with a specification of what type of data it is), in a particular order (like the phone book) so it can be searched or browsed, e.g.

- I want Fred Bloggs' e-mail address
- list all e-mail addresses containing Bloggs
- is there a color printer on the LAN near me?

An LDAP directory is made up of *entries*. An entry is a collection of *attributes*. Each attribute has a type and one or more values. The type specifies whether single or multiple values are allowed, and what the format of the data is. For example, a phone number attribute would probably allow multiple values, a **surname** attribute has a text-string value, and a **photoID** attribute might contain a GIF image as a binary object.

Entries are stored in a hierarchy in the directory, just like files are stored in a hierarchy on a disk. Each entry's full name, its *distinguished name* (DN), is made up of the name of this node in the *directory information tree* (DIT), followed by the names of all its parent nodes. All DNs are unique, so any entry can be specified unambiguously. For example, in a directory ordered by "common name" within organizational unit (i.e. department) within organization within country, an entry might be

cn=Niall Mansfield, ou=R&D, o=UIT Cambridge, c=GB

Directories in the LDAP sense are quite general and can contain almost any information, although:

- they are still most often used for user-related information – usernames, passwords (which can be encrypted), phone numbers, public encryption keys, etc.
- they contain information that is structured in some way, and is searchable (e.g. by username or by e-mail address)
- they are not suited for information that is not structured and searchable
- directories are used almost entirely for lookups rather than updates (reading as opposed to writing) and are optimized for this, so that, for example, looking up an e-mail address for someone is very fast. Some LDAP directories don't implement elaborate transaction-oriented database operations for updates because they occur so rarely.

Because LDAP is a network service, the directory can be used from outside your LAN. (You should make sure suitable security mechanisms are in place, of course. Even internally, access control and data encryption are needed both to prevent unauthorized changes, and to preserve confidentiality, e.g. of personal details or passwords.) This allows a large organization to maintain a single, organization-wide user database for access control, per-user application data, etc. This simplifies what have historically been the awkward problems of user management:

- users who are visiting from some other site. They need to use resources on this LAN (printers, file servers, etc.) but they also need to access their applications at their own site over the network

- travelling users who are accessing the internal network over the Internet from a hotel room or from customer sites.

However, keeping a single directory in one place could cause serious problems – it would be a single point of failure for the organization's whole network. If the directory failed, every application in every office would probably fail too. To overcome this, LDAP allows *replication*. The same information is duplicated to several servers, but in a controlled way, so that data consistency is maintained, and different copies of the same data cannot be modified independently.

To allow different sites to operate as autonomously as possible while still not duplicating information, LDAP also allows *referrals* from one directory to another. For example, a head office runs the LDAP server that contains the root of the LDAP directory tree and details for all users who work at HQ. However, departments at other sites run their own servers, containing the details for their users. Then the HQ directory refers to the other servers for their information. This gives devolved or delegated management of data – so the data are managed where they are generated – but a single integrated view of all the data is still available via the main LDAP server. (This is conceptually similar to how the DNS databases are distributed and devolved by delegation.)

LDAP defines how information is retrieved or sent to an LDAP server, but it doesn't specify how data are stored within the server. LDAP can be used to allow data held within a proprietary database to be accessed easily by other applications, e.g. a Lotus Notes database can make lists of e-mail addresses and usernames accessible to a third-party Internet mail server via LDAP.

To facilitate manual exchange of data between different types of LDAP servers, the *LDAP Data Interchange Format (LDIF)* has been defined, which specifies a text file format so that one server can import a file of data written by another server. Below is an LDIF file containing two entries:

```
dn: cn=Barbara J Jensen, o=University of Michigan, c=US
cn: Barbara J Jensen
cn: Babs Jensen
objectclass: person
sn: Jensen

dn: cn=Jennifer J Jensen, o=University of Michigan, c=US
cn: Jennifer J Jensen
cn: Jennifer Jensen
objectclass: person
sn: Jensen
jpegPhoto:: /9j/4AAQSkZJRgABAAAAAQABAAD/2wBDABALD
 A4MChAODQ4SERATGCgaGBYWGDEjJROoOjM9PDkzODdASFxOQ
 ERXRTc4UG1RV19iZ2hnPk1xeXBkeFxlZ2P/2wBDARESEhgVG
. . .
```

17.9 Lab – using LDAP to find e-mail addresses

The examples in this module use Outlook Express. Netscape Communicator's facilities are very similar, although the menus and buttons are of course different.

Many e-mail clients, including Outlook, Netscape and Eudora, support LDAP for looking up e-mail addresses. Some clients even include a list of public LDAP directories (although most of these pre-configured directories don't exist any longer). Currently Bigfoot still works, and you can use it to experiment with LDAP, although it's hard to know who is or isn't going to be listed in it. More realistically, if you already run your own internal LDAP server, you can use this facility to look up people in your own or related organizations.

In Outlook Express, to show which services are already configured, use menu **Tools > Address Book > Tools > Accounts** (Figure 17.15).

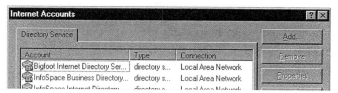

Figure 17.15 Outlook Express's Directory Service

To add a new directory that you want to use, click on **Add**, which runs an "Internet Connection wizard:"

1. enter the hostname of the LDAP server you want to use, e.g. **ldap.bigfoot.com**

2. usually you ignore the tickbox **This** [LDAP] **server requires me to log on**. However, if your server does require logon, tick the box and the wizard will ask you for your username and password

3. if you tick the **Check e-mail addresses** box, every e-mail address you use when sending a message will be checked against this directory, which is probably *not* what you want, unless this directory is an internal corporate address book for your whole organization

4. Click on **Finish**.

You can modify details for the account you set up by highlighting it in the list and clicking on the **Properties** button, to give the dialog shown in Figure 17.16a. You can change the port number to connect to, and some details of the search function, using the **Advanced** dialog (Figure17.16b).

To use a directory service to look up an address, when sending a message, click on the image of a book beside the **To:** box (Figure 17.17a). This gives the **Select Recipients** dialog (Figure17.17b). Click the **Find** button, to give the **Find People** dialog (Figure 17.17c). Enter the name you want to search for, and click on the name that you want in the results returned. The name is inserted into your address book, where you can use it as normal.

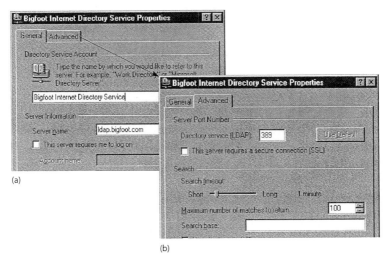

Figure 17.16 Modifying account details

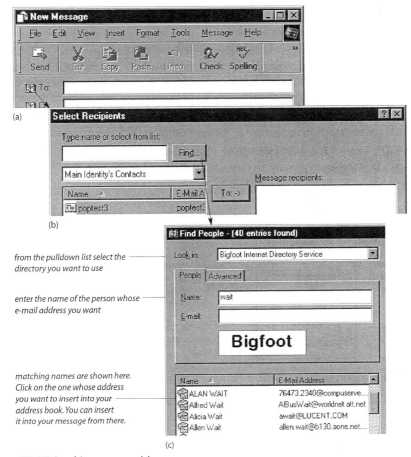

from the pulldown list select the
directory you want to use

enter the name of the person whose
e-mail address you want

matching names are shown here.
Click on the one whose address
you want to insert into your
address book. You can insert
it into your message from there.

(c)

Figure 17.17 Looking up an address

17.10 SNMP – Simple Network Management Protocol

SNMP is under-valued. While it's both simple and powerful, it has been wrapped in mystique because it's used by huge and expensive "enterprise" systems, and as a result has been under-used. You can use it simply and inexpensively, as we show.

SNMP (Simple Network Management Protocol) is used to manage or control *network elements* (hosts, routers, switches, firewalls, etc) from a *management station*. Each network element contains an SNMP *agent* that the management station communicates with:

- SNMP views the state of a machine as a set of variables or *managed objects.* The management station sends commands to the agents to query or update specific variables, and the agents reply

- the management station listens for *traps* – information that agents send without being asked, usually because something important has happened, or a problem has occurred.

SNMP runs over UDP, so it doesn't impose a heavy load on the network, or on the devices that use it. Its well-known ports are 161 for requests from manager to agent, and 162 for traps (Figure 17.18).

SNMP provides only a few basic operations on the management variables:

- **GET**: the management station requests the value of a variable from an agent, and the agent responds with that value

- **GET-NEXT**: the management station requests the value of the next variable after the one specified, and the agent responds with the ID of the variable and the variable's value. This lets the manager retrieve multiple values in a table variable (e.g. the multiple addresses of an IP interface). It also allows the management station to get a complete list of the variables the agent has, and their values, by starting at the root of the variable tree (see below)

- **SET**: the management station sets a value for some variable on an agent

- **TRAP**: when the agent has something important or unexpected to report, it traps, i.e. sends an unsolicited message to the management station.

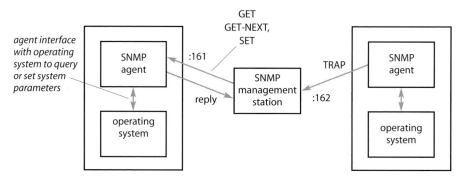

Figure 17.18 SNMP components

MIB – Management Information Base

Conceptually, SNMP variables are organized in a tree structure (Figure 17.19). Different devices need different sets of variables to describe and control them, e.g. the variables needed by an NT server are very different from those needed by a switched hub. Collections of related variables – typically specific to a device or class of devices – are defined in *MIB modules*, which make up subtrees of the tree. The whole, abstract tree is called the *Management Information Base (MIB)*. MIB modules are often informally (and confusingly) referred to as "MIBs." A MIB module specifies the variables, their types, what values they can take, and whether they can be set or are read-only. MIB modules are defined in a standard text-file format, and the management station can load specific modules in order to manage specific devices, even if it knows nothing about them in advance; it may use a *MIB compiler* to verify the contents of the module file, and to convert it into an internal format for ease of processing.

Each node has a numeric ID and a textual name. Like files in a directory tree, the full *object ID (OID)* of a variable is made up of the name of the ID of the variable's node, preceded by the IDs of all its parent nodes. The structure of the top levels in the tree (Figure 17.19) is defined in standards documents; all the OIDs you'll deal with in SNMP begin with the prefix 1.3.6.1. (**iso.org.dod.internet.**)

The **mgmt** subtree is used to identify "standard" objects, defined in RFC-1213. The **experimental** subtree is used to identify objects being designed by working groups of the IETF, which may move to **mgmt** if they become a standard. The **private** subtree is used to identify objects defined by organizations other than standards bodies. The **enterprises** subtree beneath **private** is used, among other things, to permit vendors of networking subsystems to register models of their products, and to create their own proprietary variables. Because each vendor registers their own unique node under the **private.enterprises** node (e.g. 3Com's node is 1.3.6.1.4.1.43 and our own – UIT's – is 1.3.6.1.4.1.12062) all names are guaranteed to remain globally unique.

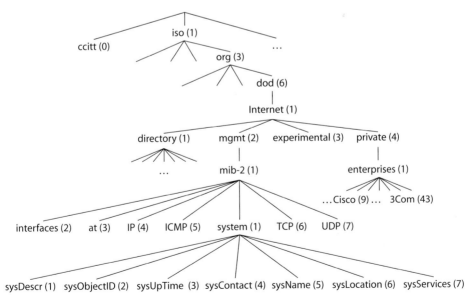

Figure 17.19 The SNMP MIB

17.11 Lab – using SNMP

In this module we use some easily accessible command-line tools to explore SNMP:

- Linux: the UC Davis SNMP tools, which are distributed freely
- Windows-NT: the SNMP utilities included in the NT Server 4.0 Resource Kit.

These simple tools emphasize that using SNMP need not be a huge and expensive project.

We're going to look at some standard variables in the **system** subtree. These all have the prefix: **iso.org.dod.internet.mgmt.mib-2.system** (1.3.6.1.2.1.1.):

Name	ID
sysDescr	1
sysObjectID	2
sysUpTime	3
sysContact	4

Name	ID
sysName	5
sysLocation	6
sysServices	7

The details of these variables or objects are explained in full in RFC-2578, but briefly, they describe the name of the machine, who looks after it, where it is, etc. One other point we must mention is that SNMP has security mechanisms to prevent unauthorized people examining or changing settings. In version 1 of SNMP, authorization consists of sending a password, called the *community string*. This is sent "in clear" (not encrypted) in the request, so it can easily be seen with a sniffer and is therefore a security hole, which SNMP version 2 overcomes by adding authentication. In these examples below on a basic network where security hasn't been configured, we will use the default community string **public** to gain access.

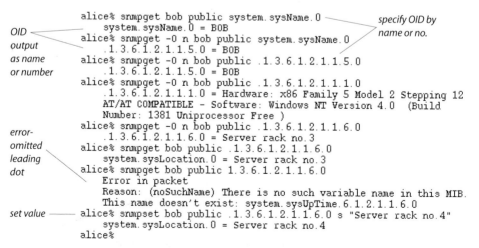

```
                alice% snmpget bob public system.sysName.0              specify OID by
                    system.sysName.0 = BOB                               name or no.
OID             alice% snmpget -O n bob public system.sysName.0
output              .1.3.6.1.2.1.1.5.0 = BOB
as name         alice% snmpget -O n bob public .1.3.6.1.2.1.1.5.0
or number           .1.3.6.1.2.1.1.5.0 = BOB
                alice% snmpget -O n bob public .1.3.6.1.2.1.1.1.0
                    .1.3.6.1.2.1.1.1.0 = Hardware: x86 Family 5 Model 2 Stepping 12
                    AT/AT COMPATIBLE - Software: Windows NT Version 4.0  (Build
                    Number: 1381 Uniprocessor Free )
error-          alice% snmpget -O n bob public .1.3.6.1.2.1.1.6.0
omitted             .1.3.6.1.2.1.1.6.0 = Server rack no.3
leading         alice% snmpget bob public .1.3.6.1.2.1.1.6.0
dot                 system.sysLocation.0 = Server rack no.3
                alice% snmpget bob public 1.3.6.1.2.1.1.6.0
                    Error in packet
                    Reason: (noSuchName) There is no such variable name in this MIB.
                    This name doesn't exist: system.sysUpTime.6.1.2.1.1.6.0
set value       alice% snmpset bob public .1.3.6.1.2.1.1.6.0 s "Server rack no.4"
                    system.sysLocation.0 = Server rack no.4
                alice%
```

Figure 17.20 snmpget on Linux

To retrieve the value of a variable, we use **snmpget** (Linux – Figure 17.20) or **snmputil get** (NT – Figure 17.21), followed by the name of the host we're interrogating, the community string, and the ID of the object whose value you want. (Note that an OID must begin with a dot, or you get an error.) We also set a value using **snmpset** (Linux only – the NT tools don't let you set variables).

error –
omitted
leading dot

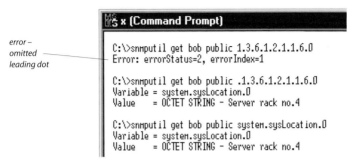

Figure 17.21 snmputil get on Windows-NT

Note that when we specify a variable, we append an *instance* value to its OID. For example, the OID of the **sysName** variable is 1.3.6.1.2.1.1.5, but when **get**ting it we specified 1.3.6.1.2.1.1.5.**0**. The instance here is zero because this is a simple, scalar variable and not an array. Instances are necessary to allow tables of values to be referenced. The Notes give more information on arrays and instances; for now, just remember that each simple variable must have an instance of zero appended – otherwise you'll get an error message when you try to reference it.

Looking at a trace for a couple of these commands, using "**`tcpdump -s200 port snmp`**" ("**-s200**" to capture enough bytes to show all the detail) we see that the protocol is very simple indeed, and what happens on the wire reflects very closely the commands we issued:

```
alice.2214 > bob.161:   GetRequest(32)   .1.3.6.1.2.1.1.6.0
bob.161 > alice.2214:   GetResponse(44)  .1.3.6.1.2.1.1.6.0="Server rack no.3"
alice.2214 > bob.161:   SetRequest(48)   .1.3.6.1.2.1.1.6.0="Server rack no.4"
bob.161 > alice.2214:   GetResponse(44)  .1.3.6.1.2.1.1.6.0="Server rack no.4"
```

Using **ethereal** on the same commands, we can see exactly what the packets contain, in the figure shown below.

The Notes at the end of the chapter give you pointers on how to explore SNMP in more depth.

17.12 Other useful services – Syslog; LPR printing

Syslog – the system log service

When desktop workstations started to take over from centralized minicomputers and mainframes, it was desirable to capture log and status files centrally, instead of storing them on the originating workstation. Syslog provides this service (Figure 17.22). Syslog also provides a way for server processes – that aren't attached to any terminal or screen – to log alerts or information messages.

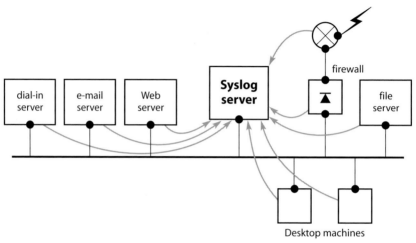

Figure 17.22 Syslog server collects log information from many hosts

What the Syslog server does with incoming messages is controlled by a configuration file: it can log classes of messages in different files, send them to other processes, or write them on the console or specified users' terminals. Syslog is standard on Linux, and many Linux and UNIX applications log to the Syslog service. Third-party versions of Syslog are available for Windows, but few if any Windows applications log to the Syslog service, so Windows Syslog servers are useful only for collecting logs from UNIX machines and other appliances (firewalls, routers, etc). on your network.

Syslog runs over UDP, with well-known port 514. Conventionally, you define the name **loghost** in your DNS, to point to the Syslog server. You can exercise Syslog, to trace what happens, using either the **logger** tool on Linux, or more primitively using **netcat**, with option "**-u**" (use UDP). In the example below, our server is on Loghost (which is a DNS CNAME alias for Alice), which saves all messages in the file **/var/log/sys-info**.

```
bob# nc -u loghost 514                          ———— Bob sends a message
This is a test message —————————                     to the Syslog server
^C

                                                     verify that the server
alice# tail /var/log/sys-info ————————          ———— has logged the
                                                     message to file,
...                                                  using tail, which
Aug  1 10:29:11 bob This is a test message           shows the last lines
alice#
```

The Syslog mechanism is often used with firewalls to record activity for later analysis. Often the server receiving the firewall log is not the site's main Syslog server, but is a special server that processes the logs and produces reports on who is using what, etc. Below we show a typical firewall log entry, broken into several lines for clarity.

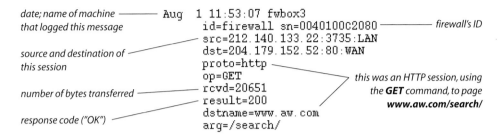

```
Aug  1 11:53:07 fwbox3
     id=firewall sn=0040100C2080
     src=212.140.133.22:3735:LAN
     dst=204.179.152.52:80:WAN
     proto=http
     op=GET
     rcvd=20651
     result=200
     dstname=www.aw.com
     arg=/search/
```

date; name of machine that logged this message — *firewall's ID*
source and destination of this session
number of bytes transferred
response code ("OK")
*this was an HTTP session, using the **GET** command, to page **www.aw.com/search/***

LPR printing – "lineprinter"

On versions of Linux and UNIX derived from Berkeley UNIX, to print a file you use the command **lpr**. The **lpr** subsystem manages printing on the local machine: it spools print files, and transmits them to the printers on the local machine. However, **lpr** can also handle network printing: it lets you configure a printer queue on your machine that sends the print file over the network to a printer on a remote machine (Figure 17.23).

In the past, printers were usually attached to a host machine, which handled the networking. However, nowadays many printers have networking hardware and software built in (right-hand side of Figure 17.23), or are connected to the LAN using a special-purpose print-server box that provides the networking hardware and software (centre of Figure 17.23).

lpr uses TCP as its transport and its well-known port is 515.

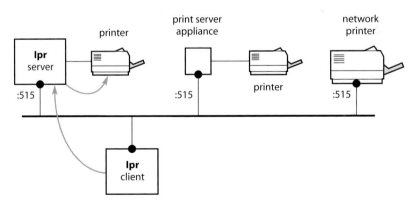

Figure 17.23 Network printing with **lpr**

The **lpr** protocol is conceptually very simple. The client connects to the server and says which printer (more precisely, which printer queue) it wants to print on. If the client isn't authorized, the server terminates the session. Otherwise the client transfers the contents of the file to be printed. Then the server queues the file for printing on the specified local printer.

17.13 NTP – Network Time Protocol

NTP (the *Network Time Protocol*) keeps computer clocks synchronized with each other. You can use it to:

- make sure all the computers on your network show the *same* time
- make sure they are all showing the *correct* time, by synchronizing them with an accurate, external reference server.

Keeping accurate time throughout your site is a good idea for many reasons:

- you can accurately correlate events in different log files on different machines, e.g. if you suspect a security breach and want to check a sequence of actions across your site
- file backup applications need to know when a file has changed, to decide whether it needs to be backed up
- when you use networked file systems, such as NFS (in the next module) or Microsoft Windows Networking (Part 3), there are at least two potentially different clocks involved – one on the client and one on the server. If the server is ahead of the client, a file could appear to have been modified some time in the future
- network performance monitoring – how long does each hop take as a packet is routed across the network?
- caches of Web pages use the current time to decide whether a page in the cache is up to date and may be used, or is out of date and must be retrieved again.

Real-world applications, such as air-traffic control, process control in factories, and financial trading where, for example, stock prices are changing with time, obviously need accurate time-keeping too.

NTP works by noting the time it takes for packets to travel between client and server, and estimating the error involved:

The client sends an NTP message to the server; the time according to the client's clock (T_c) is 520. The server receives the message, and records when it arrived, according to its own clock (T_s =700). The server processes the packet and responds, giving both its current time (T_s =730) and when it received the packet (T_s =700). This message arrives at the client at TC = 590. The total round trip time is (590 – 520) = 70. However, the server had the packet for (730 – 700) = 30, so the network-only round trip time = (70 – 30) = 40. Therefore, the approximate time for a single trip from server to client is 40/2 = 20. Therefore, the message that arrived at T_c = 590 was sent by the server at T_c = (590 – 20) = 570. This means T_c 570 is the same as T_s 730, i.e. the client's time is slow by (730 – 570) = 160 units. NTP on the client adjusts the clock to correct this. By default, small time adjustments – less than half a second or so – aren't made all in one go, but little by little over a long period, so that time doesn't suddenly jump, which could upset some applications. Instead, the clock is speeded up/slowed down as appropriate, until it has reached the correct time, and then it's reset to run at the normal rate. Larger time adjustments are made in a single step (because adjusting gradually would just take too long).

NTP doesn't just synchronize this machine against one other. NTP servers and clients are arranged in layers or *strata*. At the top are *reference clocks* – very accurate physical clocks, e.g. using radio signals from a national standard clock, atomic clocks, clocks obtaining time from the GPS (Global Positioning System). These are also called stratum-0 clocks. A stratum-1 NTP server is connected directly to a reference clock. (There are very few public stratum-1 servers, and they are only for use by stratum-2 servers that serve hundreds of clients.) Stratum-2 servers connect to at least one stratum-1 server; for more accuracy, they should connect to several servers. (There are a few hundred public stratum-2 servers, and many ISPs have stratum-1 or stratum-2 servers exclusively for use by their customers.) Stratum-3 servers are NTP servers that take their reference from stratum-2 servers, stratum-4 take it from stratum-3, and so on:

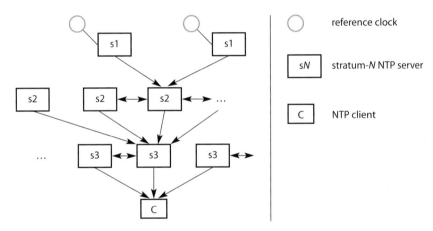

NTP on a machine takes input from all the servers it communicates with in the stratum above and analyzes it statistically to reject any values that are obviously wrong, and to get a more accurate estimate of the true time. A server usually also communicates with other servers in the same stratum and shares time information with them, to provide resilience in case network connections break.

Machines, especially desktops, can run an NTP client instead of a server. This receives time information from servers but the servers never take any time information from the client. A server can typically service hundreds (but not thousands) of servers in the stratum below it. Clients are less consumptive to serve.

The typical accuracy for a clock maintained by NTP over the Internet is tens of milliseconds.

It's a good idea to use NTP across your site so you can easily relate **tcpdump** timestamps with times in log files, etc. Otherwise you'll almost certainly have differences of seconds or minutes between machines, making it almost impossible to cross-reference one with another.

17.14 NFS – the Network File System

NFS was developed by Sun Microsystems in 1985. It transparently gives a client machine full access to files on a file server elsewhere on the network (Figure 17.24). NFS was developed because diskless UNIX workstations were becoming available and some form of network-based file storage was required. (NFS also facilitates sharing data, applications, configuration information, etc.) It's available on almost every UNIX system, and Linux comes with both the client and server software. It's also available for MS-Windows, but both client and server are extra-cost options.

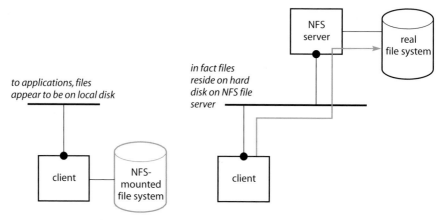

Figure 17.24 NFS makes remote file systems appear to be local

An application program accesses the files as though they are on a local disk; it can read and modify them in place (unlike FTP, where you can copy a file over the network, but when you modify your local copy, the original of course remains unchanged). NFS is similar in functionality to Microsoft Windows Networking. A Windows "share" is the equivalent of an NFS-mounted remote file system. As with Windows Networking, the server doesn't have to be a dedicated machine – you can use the file sharing as a convenient way to get permanent or occasional access to files on a desktop workstation on the LAN.

NFS can run over UDP or TCP. LAN NFS configurations use UDP by default. At first sight this is surprising, because UDP is not connection-oriented and is unreliable in the formal network sense. UDP was chosen because it has less overhead than TCP, and when NFS was first developed, UDP had better performance than TCP for transferring large amounts of data. Moreover, as we have discussed (Module 15.2), UDP on a LAN doesn't lose many packets, so NFS works well in practice. However, TCP's performance has been greatly improved over the years, so it can now sensibly be used for NFS on a LAN. NFS is sometimes used over a WAN, in which case it really does make sense to use TCP, because packets are much more likely to be dropped or corrupted.

Surprisingly, NFS servers are *stateless* – they don't maintain any information about clients that are "connected." Instead, the client maintains all the information about an NFS connection. If a server fails or the network fails, when the server is available again it's fully operative: it doesn't have to worry about what clients were connected, because the clients just keep retrying their requests until the server responds again. (This is the cause of the "NFS server not responding" messages that NFS users know and hate.)

Because the server maintains no state, all requests from client to server must be complete in themselves. On a regular (non-NFS) file, the OPEN system-call tells the operating system to create a chunk of state information for how this file is being used by this process. For example, when the process READs some data, the operating system remembers which was the last byte read; on the next READ, the operating system knows that it should continue reading from where it left off last time.

However, in NFS the server does none of this, because it's stateless. Consequently, all requests from the client have to include full details of what file is being operated on, whether it's a READ or WRITE operation, the offset in the file where the operation is to start, and so on. The NFS client software on the client machine maintains all this state about the file, so that applications on the client machine can use file OPEN, READ, WRITE, and CLOSE operations as usual and don't have to distinguish between remote NFS file and regular, local files.

The client and server use a unique NFS *filehandle* to refer to a file. The filehandle contains whatever the server needs to specify a file uniquely; on UNIX systems it's usually made up of the IDs of the disk partition the file is on, plus its file number ("inode number") within that partition. The client includes the filehandle in every NFS request to the server. Figure 17.25 shows (more schematically than accurately) how the client and server interact when a file is opened. The client operating system sends an NFS **lookup** request to the server, to check that the file exists and that this client and user are allowed to access it in this mode (read-only, or read–write, etc.). If the server's access controls permit, the server returns the file's filehandle so the client can access it thereafter. The client operating system stores the filehandle and other file details for use in subsequent NFS read or write requests to the server.

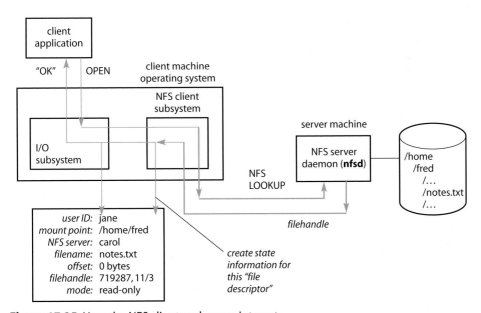

Figure 17.25 How the NFS client and server interact

17.15 NFS – implementation details

You can skip this module and the next if NFS isn't relevant to you.

In the next module we're going to use **ethereal** and **tcpdump** to look at some NFS operations over the wire. However, before we do that we need to explain how an NFS client mounts an NFS file system from a remote NFS server. We also explain a significant NFS security problem.

Mounting an NFS file system; the portmapper

(If you're familiar with Microsoft Windows Networking, NFS mounting is equivalent to mapping a network drive with Windows Explorer or "**net use.**")

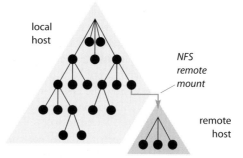

Figure 17.26 NFS mounting a remote directory

When you NFS *mount* a remote directory from your local machine, you can access all files in that directory and below it – in effect you have spliced that directory sub-tree onto the file system of your local machine's tree (Figure 17.26). For example, when you issue an NFS mount command from Alice like

```
mount -t nfs carol:/datadir /home/fred/mydata
```

the directory **/datadir** on Carol, and all files and directories below it, are accessible on Alice, as **/home/fred/mydata/**... The functions of the **mount** operation are:

- to verify that the requested directory exists
- to implement file-access controls for the server's file systems. On Linux NFS servers, the file **/etc/exports** specifies which file systems may be mounted, by which users, from which remote machines
- assuming everything is OK, to return the filehandle of the mounted directory so that it and everything under it can be accessed using the basic NFS protocol.

The mount protocol is separate from the basic NFS protocol. On Linux it is implemented as the **mountd** daemon. It usually runs over TCP (although it can run over UDP) and uses a port of its own. The ports often used are:

	UDP	**TCP**
NFS	2049	2049
mount service	1027	1024

We say "often" because both services can use other ports instead, by means of the *portmapper*. Web Appendix 22 describes the portmapper in detail, and why it's used, but we'll explain it briefly here:

- instead of using a well-known port, NFS and mount servers (and many other applications) listen on an ephemeral port, i.e. any port that currently happens to be free

- each server then contacts the portmapper server on the same machine, on the portmapper's well-known port (111), to tell it which service it's running (e.g. NFS or **mount**) and on which port. In this way the portmapper on a machine builds up a list of the services running on that machine

- when an NFS client wants to contact the NFS or mount server on a particular machine, the client first contacts the portmapper on that machine, and asks what port number the particular service is running on. The portmapper replies with the port number

- the client opens the service on that port number, and uses the service in the normal way.

NFS filehandles and security

Filehandles pose a security problem because of how NFS operates.

When an application opens a regular file (on a local disk), the operating system verifies that this user has permission to access this file, and then records the fact that this application has opened the file. Later, when the application requests a read or write action on the file, the operating checks that the application has the file open in the appropriate mode, before permitting the action to proceed. In other words, most of the permission checking happens when a file is opened; if an application has an open file, it is implicitly permitted to perform certain actions on the file.

However, an NFS server is stateless, and there is no NFS "open" operation. The closest equivalent is **lookup**; as we explained in the previous module, **lookup** causes the server to verify that user X on machine Y is allowed to access this file in mode M, and if so the server returns the filehandle for the file. This is where the problem occurs: the server assumes that if a client has a filehandle, then it is allowed access to the file; the server doesn't keep a record of who it gave a filehandle to in the past. If any client has a filehandle and requests an operation on it, the server will perform the requested operation.

As we'll see in the next module, you can sniff NFS operations on the wire using **tcpdump**, and can see which filehandle corresponds to which file. All you need then is a modified NFS client and you can access that file, even though you never opened it, and never mounted the file system it's on.

While some NFS servers overcome this problem by performing access checks on each operation, the same type of issue applies to the mount procedure. If you can sniff the filehandle for the root of a mounted file system, you can then access the file system, even though you haven't mounted it, thus by bypassing all the security checks that are performed at the mount stage. Cheswick & Bellovin (see Notes) mention someone who has a list of root filehandles stuck on the wall of his office!

Newer versions of the NFS protocol address these issues.

17.16 Lab – sniffing an NFS session

We're going to look at what happens on the wire when we NFS mount a directory on a remote system, and then read a file on that system. We'll use both **ethereal** and **tcpdump** because each shows some aspects of NFS more clearly than the other.

We ran **tcpdump** with options "`-s 200`" to capture enough of the packet to show all the detail we'll need, and "`-v  -v`" to show more information about NFS packets. (We edited the **tcpdump** output; we removed lines that **ethereal** shows adequately, wrapped long lines, and added line numbers to match the corresponding **ethereal** output.)

The traces are of the following actions:

1. from Alice, NFS mount Carol's **/tmp** directory as local directory **/mnt**.

2. on Alice, view the file **notes.txt** (using the command "`cat /mnt/notes.txt`")

This involves:

- using the portmapper to discover which port Carol's mount server is listening on
- NFS mounting the file system
- "opening" the file
- reading the contents of the file.

The traces show each of these operations clearly:

1,2   ask Carol's portmapper which port the mount service is running on. It's running on TCP 1024. (We haven't shown this in the figure, but you can see it by clicking on **ethereal**'s line 2 and expanding the packet in the protocol-tree window.)

3–9   connect to the NFS-mount service on Carol's port 1024, and mount the remote directory, using a TCP session

10,11   use Carol's portmapper again to find out which port NFS is on (2049 as usual)

12–15   termination of TCP session used for mount

16,17   get file and protection attributes of root of mounted sub-tree

18,19   perform an NFS **lookup** on the file **notes.txt**: in response to the client application's OPEN call. Return **notes.txt**'s filehandle to the client

20,21   read the file **notes.txt** and return the data it contains.

Notes:

- in line 19 **tcpdump** shows the components of the NFS filehandle. (The "nodeid" is the Linux inode number of the file **notes.txt** on Carol.) However, **ethereal** doesn't show filehandle details – it just says "opaque data"

- in NFS packets **tcpdump** doesn't show the port number. Instead it shows the client's request ID, which the client uses to relate NFS replies with the requests sent (e.g. in lines 16 and 17 the request ID is 3781236016).

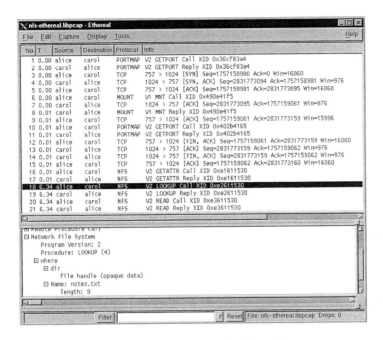

```
16 alice.3781236016 > carol.2049: 100 getattr fh Unknown/1
   (ttl 64, id 45427, len 128)
17 carol.2049 > alice.3781236016: reply ok 96 getattr
   DIR 41777 ids 0/0 sz 4096  (ttl 64, id 33532, len 124)
18 alice.3798013232 > carol.2049: 116 lookup fh Unknown/1
   "notes.txt" (ttl 64, id 45440, len 144)
19 carol.2049 > alice.3798013232: reply ok 128 lookup fh Unknown/1
   REG 100644 ids 0/0 sz 501 nlink 1 rdev 35c3 fsid 802 nodeid 1839d
   a/m/ctime 997971025.000000 997971017.000000 997971017.000000
   (ttl 64, id 33569, len 156)
```

Tip: to trace NFS mount and file accesses to a particular NFS server (Bob, say) you'll probably need to find the port numbers for the mount and NFS services. The trace below shows how you run the **rpcinfo** command from Alice to interrogate Bob's portmapper for its list of known services. (See Web Appendix 22 for more detail.)

```
alice% rpcinfo -p bob
   program vers proto   port
    100000   2   tcp    111    portmapper
    100000   2   udp    111    portmapper
    100024   1   tcp    734    status
    100003   2   udp   2049    nfs
    100005   1   udp   1027    mountd
    100005   1   tcp   1024    mountd
   . . .
```

Summary

- the **daytime, echo, chargen,** and **discard** little services are useful for testing
- FTP is the traditional way to transfer files over the network:
    - it runs over TCP
    - it uses separate control and data channels
    - client and server exchange command and control information as plain text strings on the control channel
    - normally it is the server that establishes the data connection to the client. This causes problems with firewalls, which can be overcome by using passive mode
- the **netcat** (or **nc**) tool is useful for testing FTP and many other services
- X is a client/server window system used on Linux and almost every UNIX version, and on many other platforms
- LDAP allows directories of users, passwords, e-mail addresses, machine details, and other information to be retrieved over the network from a central database. LDAP is at the core of Windows-2000 Active Directory and many other user/configuration management systems
- SNMP lets you remotely monitor and manage machines and devices on your network
- Syslog is the system logging service; messages are logged to a central server instead of to a local file
- **lpr** is the Linux/UNIX network-based printing service
- NTP lets you synchronize the clocks on your machines across the LAN, WAN, or Internet
- NFS is the Linux/UNIX filesharing system. It lets a client machine mount a directory that lives on a remote NFS server and access its files as though they were on a local disk.

What's next?

We've reached the end of Part 2, which covered the common TCP/IP applications and their protocols, which are used on almost every platform. In Part 3, we look at Microsoft Windows Networking – what it is, how it works, and how it ties in with the rest of your TCP/IP network.

Notes and further reading

Daytime, echo, chargen, discard

There are many other services listed in a typical **/etc/services** (Linux) or **C:\winnt\system32\ drivers\etc\services** file (NT) that are rarely used. Some, such as **qotd** ("quote of the day") were and still are merely curiosities. Others, like **webster** (server for Webster's dictionary) shared an expensive resource to many machines over the network, and have been largely supplanted by equivalent facilities on the Web. Still others (**finger, netstat, systat**) gave information on users and systems, but are not often used now, both because they can give information to potential hackers and because there are other ways for legitimate users to get the information they need.

inetd

❑ **Linux manpages: inetd(8), inetd.conf(5), services(5)**

The program **xinetd** ("extended **inetd**") is a popular replacement for **inetd**. It offers extensive logging, access control, limits on the number of child processes (to prevent denial-of-service attacks), and many other features. See:

❑ **http://www.xinted.org/** *xinted* home page

FTP

The specification for FTP is

❑ **RFC-959 October 1985** *File Transfer Protocol (FTP)*

The early sections are readable and give some useful background, and its Module 4.2 lists the response codes.

Most publicly accessible FTP servers allow you to logon as user **anonymous** and ask you to give your full e-mail address as password. The username **ftp** is the same as **anonymous** and is much quicker to type.

Increasingly HTTP is used instead of FTP for file downloads, but FTP is sometimes used in preference to HTTP because:

- for the server administrator, it's easier to just copy a file into an FTP directory than having to build and maintain an HTTP page containing a link to the file. (Some HTTP servers let you list the contents of a directory (below), which diminishes this advantage.)

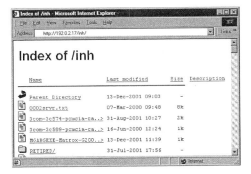

- FTP can do multiple transfers. For example, you can download all PDF files using the FTP command "**mget *.pdf.**" (**mget** means "multiple get")
- if an FTP transfer breaks in mid-session, some clients and servers let you restart from where you left off instead of from the beginning of the file again, which is ideal if the files being transferred are very large.

netcat

❑ **http://freshmeat.net/projects/netcat/**

❑ **http://www.atstake.com/research/tools/index.html**

❑ **http://www.uit.co.uk/practcp/netcat.pdf** *Netcat tutorial*

X Window System

For a detailed description of what X is and how it works, see our book:

❑ **Niall Mansfield** *The Joy of X – An Overview of the X Window System* (1993, Addison-Wesley)

Good starting points for exploring Linux X resources, Gnome, and KDE are:

❑ http://www.linuxdoc.org/HOWTO/XWindow-User-HOWTO-11.html

❑ http://www.kde.org

❑ http://www.gnome.org

❑ http://www.linuxdoc.org/LDP/lame/LAME/linux-admin-made-easy/using gnome.html *GNOME Installation and Configuration*

❑ http://www.linuxdoc.org/LDP/lame/LAME/linux-admin-made-easy/using-kde.html *KDE Installation and Configuration*

❑ http://www.gtk.org *The GIMP Toolkit,* which is a multi-platform toolkit for creating graphical interfaces

X now runs on handheld computers:

❑ http://www.handhelds.org/

and IBM even have it running on a wrist-watch (that runs Linux!).
A related system is VNC ("virtual network computing"):

❑ http://www.uk.research.att.com/vnc/

which is used widely for remotely managing Microsoft Windows systems. It lets you connect to a Windows system from another Windows system or a Linux/UNIX box running X and display the full screen of the remote system, and use all its capabilities.

LDAP

❑ **RFC-2251 December 1997** *Lightweight Directory Access Protocol (v3)*

Much of the original work on LDAP was done at the University of Michigan. Their site still has some historical information:

❑ http://www.umich.edu/~dirsvcs/ldap

but this has been superseded by the OpenLDAP project:

❑ http://www.openldap.org

and some of our examples are from that distribution.

Microsoft's Active Directory:

❑ http://www.microsoft.com/windows2000/techinfo/howitworks/activedirectory/adarch.asp *Active Directory Architecture*

❑ http://www.labmice.net/ActiveDirectory/default.htm

Novell's eDirectory or NDS (Novell Directory Services):

❏ **http://developer.novell.com/nds/ndsldap.htm**

For the DEN (Directory Enabled Network) and other directory initiatives:

❏ **http://www.dmtf.org/standards/standard_den.php**

❏ **http://www.opengroup.org/directory/** *Directory Interoperability Forum.* See under "white papers".

SNMP

The standard for SNMP is:

❏ **RFC-1157 May 1990** *A Simple Network Management Protocol*

A lot of work on SNMP has been done at the University of California at Davis (UC Davis). The project page (which used to be at **http://ucd-snmp.ucdavis.edu**) has been renamed to **net-snmp**, available at:

❏ **http://net-snmp.sourceforge.net/**

Stevens, Chapter 25 gives a good overview of SNMP. Other good books are hard to find; many books seem to have a small amount of real body text and huge appendices listing MIBs that are better left in machine-readable files. The "SNMP FAQ" available on the net isn't a good introduction – you have to know what SNMP is about for it to be very useful:

❏ **ftp://rtfm.mit.edu/pub/usenet/comp.protocols.snmp/comp.protocols.snmp_ SNMP_FAQ_Part_1_of_2**

❏ **ftp://rtfm.mit.edu/pub/usenet/comp.protocols.snmp/comp.protocols.snmp_ SNMP_FAQ_Part_2_of_2**

but the FAQ about the UC Davis tools at **http://net-snmp.sourceforge.net/** above is helpful. There's a great tutorial at:

❏ **http://www.netcom-sys.com/techdocs.html** *SNMP For Dummies*

although it refers quite a bit to the Optivity network management software from Nortel Networks.

For an explanation of all the SNMP node numbers (all the 1.3.6.2. ... stuff), see:

❏ **http://www.iana.org/assignments/smi-numbers**

and for a listing of the private enterprise numbers, see:

❏ **http://www.isi.edu/in-notes/iana/assignments/enterprise-numbers**

MIB-II is defined in:

❏ **RFC-1213 March 1991** *Management Information Base for Network Management of TCP/IP-based internets: MIB-II*

MIB modules are written in *ASN.1 (Abstract Syntax Notation 1)* described in:

❏ **RFC-2578 April 1999** *The Structure of Management Information Version 2 (SMIv2)*

The Windows-NT SNMP tools are included with the NT 4.0 Resource Kit. These include the basic but useful **snmpmon** tool. This lets you specify a set of SNMP variables on particular hosts, and it monitors them (retrieves their values) periodically; you can execute arbitrary commands depending on the results, e.g. to send an alert or e-mail, or remove temporary files from a directory if the machine is running short of disk space, etc.

Lots of system and network administrators write their own tools from scratch to monitor and control various aspects of their systems (e.g. monitor disk space, check network connections, etc.). Instead of re-inventing the wheel, consider using SNMP instead. It *will* take you longer initially, but very soon it will save you a lot of time and make your tools more portable and more generally useful.

We haven't covered SNMP traps. Agents have to be pre-configured with the address of the management station – there's no discovery mechanism to enable an SNMP "client" machine to find the management station automatically. (But it can be configured with DHCP.) On NT, **snmputil trap** listens for traps.

SNMP has only four commands: **get** and **set**, which we used, **trap**, which we discussed above, and finally **get-next**. **get-next** returns the value (and OID) of the variable after the one you specified. By specifying the root of the tree, and repeatedly **get-next**ing, you can retrieve the whole tree, without knowing what's in it or how it's made up. This is one of the features that makes SNMP so powerful. It lets you browse the MIB tree and get any information you're interested in. Linux includes the command **snmpwalk**, which uses **get-next** repeatedly to retrieve all the values in the sub-tree below the variable you specify. Below, we show **snmpwalk** output for the **system** node. **get-next** is also essential for handling arrays that you don't know the size of.

```
alice% snmpwalk -O n bob public system
.1.3.6.1.2.1.1.1.0 = Hardware: x86 Family ...  Software: Windows NT Version 4.0
.1.3.6.1.2.1.1.2.0 = OID: .1.3.6.1.4.1.311.1.1.3.1.3
.1.3.6.1.2.1.1.3.0 = Timeticks: (663334843) 76 days, 18:35:48.43
.1.3.6.1.2.1.1.4.0 =
.1.3.6.1.2.1.1.5.0 = BOB
.1.3.6.1.2.1.1.6.0 = Server rack no.4
.1.3.6.1.2.1.1.7.0 = 76
alice%
```

There's a good graphical SNMP tool for Microsoft Windows called **getif** ("get interface information") available from:

❏ **http://www.wtcs.org/snmp4tpc/**

Syslog

Even though Syslog is very old, it has only recently been documented as an RFC:

❏ **RFC-3164 August 2001** *The BSD Syslog Protocol*

which gives a lot of readable background. **syslog** and similar services can be critical in logging and monitoring systems, but Syslog over UDP doesn't give the sender any feedback on whether the message has been logged successfully. A recent RFC specifies how **syslog** can be run over a reliable (TCP) connection, and with enhanced data integrity and security:

❏ **RFC-3195 November 2001** *Reliable Delivery for Syslog*

Syslog can collect a huge amount of information, and to make the most of it you need some form of automatic processing, e.g. to raise an alert when a particular warning message occurs, or a specific type of event is logged. An easily configured tool of this type is **Xlogmaster**:

❏ **http://www.gnu.org/software/xlogmaster/**

While this is still available for download, it's not being developed further. Even so, it's very useful as it stands. A Windows version of the **syslog** server, with extra analysis features, is produced by:

❏ **http://www.kiwi-enterprises.com**

This is commercial software, but they also make a free version available.

Other log analysis tools:

❏ **http://www.cert.dfn.de/eng/logsurf/** *Logsurfer Homepage*

❏ **http://www.counterpane.com/log-analysis.html** *Log Analysis Resources*

❏ **http://www.oit.ucsb.edu/~eta/swatch/** *SWATCH: The Simple WATCHer*

❏ **http://www.psionic.com/products/logsentry.html** *LogSentry (formerly Logcheck)*

lpr

❏ **RFC-1179 August 1990** *Line Printer Daemon Protocol*

lpr is the standard printing system on Linux. It's also available on Windows-NT as the **Microsoft TCP/IP Printing** network service.

NTP

The standards for NTP are:

❏ **RFC-1305 March 1992** *Network Time Protocol (Version 3) Specification, Implementation and Analysis*

Some of the diagrams and tables are messed up in that text version. A more readable version is

❏ **ftp://ftp.isi.edu/in-notes/rfc1305.pdf**

A lighter-weight version of NTP, suitable for less demanding applications, is called *SNTP (Simple Network Time Protocol)*, described in:

❏ **RFC-2030 October 1996** *Simple Network Time Protocol (SNTP) Version 4 for IPv4, IPv6 and OSI*

Most of the work on NTP has been done by David Mills at the University of Delaware:

❏ **http://www.eecis.udel.edu/~mills/database/brief/overview/overview.htm**

❏ **http://www.ntp.org**

Alas, we find much of the documentation on NTP incomprehensible and have never come across a good tutorial or overview. However the above overview is reasonably understandable.

To find NTP servers that you're allowed use, ask your ISP or see **http://www.ntp.org.** For other time-related information, including some live-time displays, see:

❏ **http://tycho.usno.navy.mil** *Time Service Department U.S. Naval Observatory* The Official Source of Time for the Department of Defense and the Standard of Time for the United States

For Windows systems only, you can synchronize one machine with another (*masterbox*, say) using the **net time** command. On the "client", enter the command

```
net time \\masterbox /set /yes
```

NFS

The original RFC describing NFS gives some interesting background on its design:

❏ **RFC-1094 March 1989** *NFS: Network File System Protocol Specification*

❏ **RFC-3010 December 2000** *NFS version 4 Protocol*

For filehandles as a security hazard see the book:

❏ **William Cheswick and Steven Bellovin** *Firewalls and Internet Security: Repelling the Wily Hacker* (1994, Addison-Wesley)

To allow files to be updated in a controlled way, they must be "locked" while they are being updated. NFS uses the "NFS lock manager" server, usually called **lockd** or **rpc.lockd** to handle this.

NFS has been ported to a wide range of machines and operating systems, and around 1990 it was *the* way to share files and data across a heterogeneous network. On UNIX/Linux-only networks, NFS is still the shared file system of choice. However, to share files between Linux/UNIX and Windows, a free, and excellent, alternative is Samba (Module 22.4).

Appendices

Appendix 19: **nc** (**netcat**) manual page in full
Appendix 20: controlling network services
Web Appendix 22: the RPC portmapper service

Part 3

Microsoft Windows Networking on a TCP/IP network

Introduction

Most real-world networks contain Microsoft Windows machines, and increasingly they contain Linux and UNIX machines too. Windows Networking is very different to the TCP/IP networking we've covered so far. It was developed separately and uses its own protocols and mechanisms, layered on top of and separate from TCP/IP, for much of its basic operation, including:

1. name resolution
2. logon and user authentication
3. "browsing" the network to automatically find lists of available machines and resources.

The challenge is to make these two very different worlds operate well on the same network, and to apply to Windows Networking the same investigative and diagnostic approach we've used for everything else.

In the five chapters in this part of the book, we give an overview of the major architectural features of Windows Networking, then cover in detail name resolution, authentication, and browsing, and finish off with a brief chapter on using Windows Networking in practice.

18   MS-Windows Networking – introduction

Introduction

This chapter introduces Microsoft Windows Networking. Windows Networking was developed separately from TCP/IP, running on different network systems, and only relatively recently was it made to run over TCP/IP too. Consequently it's architecture and how it's implemented differ greatly from the "real" Internet protocols that we've seen elsewhere in the book. We also cover the Windows Network Monitor, a packet sniffer that's very similar to **ethereal** and that comes as standard on NT.

18.1   An overview of Microsoft Windows Networking

Microsoft Windows Networking is a specific set of protocols that Windows computers (and some others) use to share resources on a LAN or a WAN. It was developed in the early days of networking with the aim of making it easy for a small "workgroup" of users to:

- find out what resources (printers, file servers) are available on the network, by allowing users to "browse the network"

- share files and printers

- make all this happen without any pre-configuration or dedicated servers.

You should be able to install Windows on a PC and as soon as you connect it to the LAN the sharing mechanisms should work automatically. You don't have to configure dedicated file servers: my desktop PC can share files with your desktop. The PCs on the LAN share resources as a *peer-to-peer network*, although with the advent of NT, dedicated file servers and a client/server oriented network architecture are used very widely.

Windows Networking is different from other Internet protocols

Microsoft Windows Networking is a whole separate world from the other network protocols that we deal with in this book:

- it was originally developed on top of other network systems long before TCP/IP became dominant. It was made to run over TCP/IP afterwards

- it was developed commercially, without the wide exposure to comment, criticism, and improvement that is a feature of the Internet and its RFCs

Because it grew up in this self-contained way, separately from the "real" Internet protocols that evolved together on the Internet in a fairly consistent fashion, it has significant differences from TCP/IP:

- it doesn't use different ports for different network operations; instead, almost everything works over ports 137, 138, and 139. As we'll see, this makes deciphering what's happening on the wire much more difficult

- names not IP numbers, are the primary reference for resources. This isn't too surprising when you recall that Microsoft Windows Networking can operate over non-IP networks where there just aren't any IP numbers

- it is still used over other, non-TCP/IP networks and therefore can't rely on TCP/IP components, even when it's running over TCP/IP. For example, to resolve names, Windows Networking can't rely on DNS – it has to use some mechanism that works on non-TCP/IP networks too. (However, DNS is mandatory for Active Directory; Windows-2000 networking is now starting to abandon the non-TCP/IP networking systems!)

- documentation that describes how the Microsoft Windows Networking protocols evolved in the way they did, can be very hard to find. Very detailed system descriptions are almost non-existent. (Because of this we've included more detail in the chapters in this part of the book than we would otherwise have done, to make the information more accessible.)

In addition, some of the topics are complex, and involve a lot of network traffic, so working through them using a sniffer isn't easy. For all these reasons we have found it hard (coming from a TCP/IP background) to get to grips with Windows Networking. It does things very differently, and your knowledge of the Internet protocols isn't as applicable and doesn't help you understand Windows Networking as much as you'd like. To make things easier for you we've tried to make these chapters "as simple as possible but no simpler" (as Einstein suggested).

What we cover

We cover Windows Networking only over TCP/IP, mostly because this book is about TCP/IP networks, but also because the other networking systems that Windows Networking can run over are dying out.

Our emphasis is on how Windows Networking fits into a TCP/IP network, and explains it from the point of someone who's either new to networking, or has come from a TCP/IP and/or UNIX background. Windows Networking is a huge subject in itself, and we don't cover how to plan, implement, and manage global Microsoft-based networks. But we do aim to give you a firm grounding in how these networks work. We show the similarities and differences between Windows Networking and TCP/IP and use the same approach to understand what's happening on the wire, and to troubleshoot problems.

We've concentrated on the Windows-NT 4.0's Windows Networking because:

- Windows-NT is by far the most commonly deployed system for Windows networks. While most desktop machines are still running Windows-98 or Windows-95, the overall network architecture used is Windows-NT

- NT is the foundation for Windows-2000 ("Win-2K") and XP. Although we don't cover Win-2K and XP explicitly, everything we describe here works almost identically on those systems (apart from Active Directory, which is new in Win-2K)

- networks using only Windows-9x are now relatively uncommon. Apart from that, we and our customers have found Windows-9x very much less reliable than NT, especially in the networking area. Even small sites often prefer to use NT or Win-2K servers to obtain greater reliability, in spite of the higher initial cost (the reduced cost of support often makes up for that)

- Win-2K and XP are now being rolled out, but very few sites have switched over completely and most still have a large number of older systems

- Win-2K and XP support the NT style of networking for compatibility.

What we cover is relevant to networks of all sizes, from small, single-segment LANs, to multi-segment LANs (i.e. LANs with local routers) and to WANs where there are several sites connected via the Internet, perhaps using VPN (virtual private networks, Chapter 27). We give an overview of Windows Networking's implementation and architecture, NetBIOS name resolution (Windows' equivalent of the DNS), authentication and NT "domains" (logging on to the network), browsing the network – to find other machines and resources, and finally practical advice on using Windows Networking. We've covered the topics in this order because that's how they are used: logging on to a domain uses name resolution, and browsing the network only happens after you've logged on (and it too uses name resolution).

18.2 Microsoft Windows Networking – architecture

Microsoft Windows Networking is often called *NetBIOS (Network Basic Input Output System)* networking. NetBIOS is the layer in the Windows Networking stack that interfaces between the Windows Networking applications up above and whatever network system is being used lower down – TCP/IP, or Novell, etc.

Windows Networking uses NetBIOS for file transfer and name resolution and so on. It doesn't use FTP or NFS or any of the other Internet application-level protocols (although it can make limited use of DNS in certain circumstances, Module 19.7). This is different from NFS, used for file sharing on Linux and UNIX: NFS provides only file sharing and leaves other protocols to handle other aspects of the machine's network operation, whereas Windows Networking deals with it all itself.

NetBIOS is a layer in the stack – an application program interface. NetBIOS uses the *SMB (Server Message Block)* protocol for sharing files and printers over the network, and sending alert messages between logged-on users. (The terms "SMB" and "NetBIOS" and "Windows Networking" are often used incorrectly as though they were synonymous.) SMB is used on many different but compatible network implementations on many different operating systems and network systems: Microsoft Windows Networking (i.e. for Windows-9x, NT, 2000 and XP), Microsoft Windows for Workgroups (i.e. networking for Windows version 3.1, the predecessor to Windows-95), LAN Manager (for Windows and for UNIX), IBM LAN Server, DEC Pathworks and the DECnet network system, 3Com's 3+Open, although many of these are no longer used widely.

Figure 18.1 shows the relationship of the different components of the system on NT. This illustrates how NetBIOS runs over many different networking layers, as mentioned in the previous module. We have shown the Novell and DECnet components only for comparison, and won't mention them again. We're not interested in NetBEUI either: it's an old protocol that we don't need, although because it often causes confusion we explain it in the Notes. (Note that Figure 18.1 shows the Windows versions of **ping** and **telnet** as NetBIOS applications: they can use Windows Networking – instead of or as well as DNS – to resolve names, as we'll see in Chapter 19.)

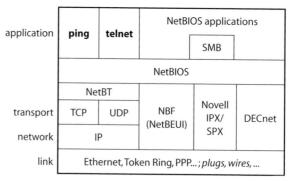

Figure 18.1 The network components of Windows-NT

We're only really interested in NetBIOS running on TCP/IP networks. On Windows-NT this is called *NetBT* or *NBT (NetBIOS over TCP/IP)*.

Several features flow naturally from Windows Networking's origins and design:

- because it was designed for single-LAN "workgroups," it relies heavily on broadcast packets. Since broadcasts don't work across routers and therefore don't work over the Internet, this causes difficulties where we have large LANs or multi-site networks using Windows Networking (Modules 19.3 and 22.2).

- because Windows Networking can be used over many different network systems, it can't rely on TCP/IP components even when it's running over TCP/IP. For example, to resolve names, Windows Networking can't rely on DNS – it has to use some mechanism that works on non-TCP/IP networks too. (If the rest of your network uses the Internet protocols, some of Windows Networking looks like re-inventing the wheel.)

- NT uses *bindings* to control which components in one layer connect with components in other layers. This lets you choose which lower-level protocols and which network cards an upper-layer service or protocol can use (Module 18.5). Bindings are applied in a specific order, so two systems with the same network components but a different binding order can behave differently

- because the different network systems do things in different ways, it's recommended that you use only one lower-layer protocol on your network where possible. Otherwise:

  - different sets of machines can behave inconsistently, e.g. when you look at the set of network resources from one machine using Windows Explorer you could get only a subset of the resources visible from another machine. This could happen because one machine uses NetBIOS over TCP/IP when it's accumulating the list of resources on the network, whereas a machine with NetBEUI would only see other NetBEUI machines

  - you might use a different binding order for the protocols on different machines, e.g. if a name **alice** is to be resolved, one machine might resolve it using DNS, giving one result, and a different machine might resolve it on Novell, giving a different result

  - performance suffers because many different alternatives have to be tried, e.g. if you have many name resolution systems running, and you look up the name of a non-existent machine, each resolution system has to be tried in turn, and any timeouts involved in each system have to expire before your machine can really know that the name is invalid. This may take three or four times as long as necessary, and involves a lot of extra traffic on the network as well. (This is sometimes why Windows users complain about slow performance.)

  - extra protocols can be a security hole, e.g. if you run NetBEUI on your systems it can provide a "back door" around your TCP/IP-based firewall and other security systems

  - troubleshooting becomes very difficult – there are many more components and configuration settings that you have to check.

18.3   Windows Networking implementation

In the following chapters we're going to cover three big areas of Windows Networking:

1. Machine and resource names

Windows Networking uses names, not IP numbers, as its primary reference for machines and other resources. This is the complete opposite of TCP/IP, where a machine's IP number is the important thing and hostnames are almost an afterthought. Whereas an IP network can work perfectly well (if less conveniently for human users) without names, Windows Networking depends entirely on names for its basic operation:

- it uses unique names for PCs and for users, e.g. my PC's name is **pc29** and I am logged on to it with username **administrator**
- it uses "group names" for certain network services or resources. A group name is shared by all machines that offer that service or resource.

Because names are fundamental to the operation of the system, how they are resolved is crucial. There are two main ways that names are resolved to machine addresses (to IP numbers in our case):

a. using broadcast packets. Let's say our PC is booting, and it's been configured with the name **alice**. It broadcasts asking if there's a machine **alice** already on the network. If there's no reply, it assumes the name is OK and the PC then operates as **alice**. (If some other machine says it is using the name, we'll have to reconfigure and reboot our PC.) If Alice then wants to contact another Windows machine, Bob, she broadcasts a query for the name **bob**. If there is a **bob** on the network, he replies, giving his IP address

b. using WINS (Windows Internet Name Service). Each machine as it boots registers its name and IP number with the WINS server, and any time it wants to get the address of another machine it queries the WINS server.

We cover name resolution in detail in Chapter 19.

2. Authentication and security

Authentication and security are an important part of Windows Networking that was enhanced a lot in Windows-NT. NT introduced the concept of a security "domain" – a set of machines sharing a single database of usernames, passwords, and authorization information that controls who may use what and how.

Domain-based security provides "single sign-on:" you logon to the network once, and that logon is used to control all your accesses to resources – on this machine and elsewhere on the network. All authorization checks are performed transparently: even if this machine has to log you on to another one, it does so automatically by itself, without prompting for your username and password again.

Chapter 20 covers NT domains, authentication, and security.

3. Browsing the network to find machines and other resources

"Browsing" is the process Windows Networking uses to find out what resources are available on this network. To achieve this automatically without any manual configuration or special servers, Windows uses an elaborate system in which machines hold "elections" on the network, to decide which one should provide a particular service. In this case, the machines elect a "browse master:" its job is to accumulate a list of resources on the local network. Then, when any machine on the network wants to find the list of resources, it queries the browse master and gets the list of available resources in return. This is how Windows Explorer displays the **Network Neighborhood** list of machines and printers on your network.

We cover Windows Network browsing in Chapter 21.

In addition to those three big areas, we devote Chapter 22 to using Windows Networking.

NetBIOS programs, "real" TCP/IP programs, and hybrid programs

Some Windows applications are obviously NetBIOS programs because they deal with NetBIOS networking. For example, **net use, net view**, and Windows Explorer are all intimately bound up with Windows Networking, and use NetBIOS networking. **ethereal** on the other hand lives in the TCP/IP part of Windows-land and doesn't use NetBIOS or Windows Networking at all.

There are other programs – especially "standard" TCP/IP applications that Microsoft has ported to Windows – that are hybrids. **ping** and **telnet** are good examples. While their primary function (sending ICMP packets, or connecting to a remote host) must operate using TCP/IP, their name resolution uses both NetBIOS and TCP/IP (DNS) resolution. For example, I can, as you'd expect, use commands like:

```
C:\> ping www.microsoft.com
```

and the name **www.microsoft.com** is passed to DNS for resolving, but I can also use **ping** even if I don't have DNS running on my network at all. For example,

```
C:\> ping bob
```

will work on a Windows-only (no-DNS) LAN because **ping** will use NetBIOS to resolve the name if DNS resolution doesn't succeed. (In fact, if the resolver on your PC isn't configured correctly, DNS resolution may not even be attempted, and if **bob** is a UNIX machine that can't be resolved using NetBIOS, the **ping** could fail.)

We'll mention this point again when we deal with name resolution in Chapter 19, and also in Appendix 22.

18.4 Windows Networking implementation over TCP/IP

Windows Networking uses the following TCP/IP ports for almost everything:

NetBIOS name services	connection-less	UDP port 137
NetBIOS datagram service	connection-less	UDP port 138
NetBIOS session service	connection-oriented	TCP port 139

These ports are usually used for both source and destination. A very few operations use Microsoft RPCs (remote procedure calls); these initially connect to the DCE endpoint locator in order to find out which port a particular service is running on, and then connect to that port; accordingly you can't tell in advance which port number will be used. (C.f. the Linux portmapper, Module 17.5.)

Microsoft DCE endpoint locator ("portmapper")	connection-oriented	TCP port 135

The "session" service is for operations like file copies, etc. These are machine-to-machine and run over TCP, for the reasons discussed in Module 15.2. The other services have to run over UDP because they require one of the following:

- broadcasts, e.g. when finding a particular service, or querying for a name
- "multicasts," where the same packet has to be sent to multiple machines, e.g. to all the members of NetBIOS group name ABC. (Recall that TCP provides only connections with exactly two ends; it doesn't support the multiple ends that support multicasting and broadcasting require.)

Figure 18.2 illustrates schematically a NetBIOS multicast to members of a NetBIOS group:

- at the NetBIOS level this is a multicast
- however, at the UDP and Ethernet levels it's implemented as a broadcast packet.

The packets are broadcast on the wire, so each machine on the LAN receives and reads the packet. Only NetBIOS machines are listening on the correct port; other machines will discard the packet silently. Each NetBIOS machine checks the NetBIOS destination address in the packet contents; if this machine is part of the specified group, NetBIOS passes the packet up to the application; otherwise it discards it silently.

We'll explain the port usage and communication mechanisms used by the various services as we go along.

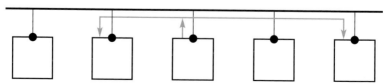

Figure 18.2 NetBIOS multicast

NetBIOS session service

NetBIOS session service connections run over TCP connections. A single TCP connection can support multiple simultaneous NetBIOS session connections (i.e. multiple NetBIOS sessions are *multiplexed* over a single TCP connection). When NetBIOS needs to open a new session connection, e.g. between Alice and Bob, it first checks to see whether it already has a TCP connection open between these two machines. If so, it opens the new NetBIOS session on top of the existing TCP/IP connection; if not, it establishes a new TCP connection between Alice and Bob and then opens the new NetBIOS session on top of that.

Because of this, it's difficult to decipher NetBIOS session traffic using **tcpdump**. We find it much easier to use either **ethereal** or Windows Network Monitor (which we introduce in Module 18.6). They make it easy to look deep into the packet contents, making it possible to trace a NetBIOS session over its lifetime.

You can display a list of sessions currently connected to your PC using the commands:

display remote hosts as IP numbers	nbtstat -s
display remote hosts as names	nbtstat -S

as illustrated below. (You can't display the list for a remote host).

```
    Command Prompt

C:\> nbtstat -s
                 NetBIOS Connection Table
Local Name          State     In/Out  Remote Host          Input   Output
-------------------------------------------------------------------------
ALICENT    <00>  Connected    Out   BOBNT       <20>      3KB      3KB
ALICENT    <00>  Connected    Out   DENNISNT    <20>      1KB      1KB
ALICENT    <00>  Connected    Out   HAL9000-NT  <20>      1KB      1KB
ALICENT    <03>  Listening
ALICENT    <03>  Listening
```

An aside: getting help on Windows commands

Windows Help contains manpage-like descriptions of command-line programs such as **net use**, **nslookup**, etc. They often have three associated topics (all listed as "untitled"): examples, notes on usage, and a description of the command syntax. For example, use **Start > Help > Find**, enter "**net use**," double-click on the **net use command** index entry, and then **Display** the topics listed.

You can also get help at the command line:

```
net help
```

lists the various sub-commands within "net." To get more information about a sub-command, e.g. for "**net view**," you have two options:

```
net view /?                                    syntax summary
net help view                              detailed help message
```

To get more information about an NT network error message, enter:

```
net helpmsg msg-num
```

(although we rarely find that this gives you any more detail than the original message).

18.5   Windows Networking implementation – NT Services

The most obvious use of Microsoft Windows Networking is sharing files, so we'll look at how that is implemented using NT Services.

An NT Service is a chunk of code that provides a specific piece of functionality. You can think of some of the network Services as the equivalent of specific servers that run as application-level programs on Linux, e.g. the **Simple TCP/IP Services** service provides the **daytime, echo, chargen**, and **discard** services (Module 17.1).

You control Services using **Control Panel > Services** (Figure 18.3). With the **Startup** button, you can specify whether the particular Service is started automatically when the system boots, or has to be started manually, or is disabled. The Services shown are those which have been installed. You can add or remove network Services (which are the only ones we're interested in) using **Control Panel > Network > Services**. (This **Control Panel** function is conceptually similar to Linux's **inetd**, which controls which network-based servers are to be run.)

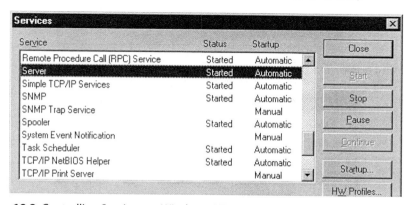

Figure 18.3 Controlling Services on Windows-NT

Workstation Service

The client component of Windows Networking is the Workstation Service, which implements the client side of file sharing. Workstation is implemented with a user-level component in the program **Services.EXE** (the *Service Control Manager*) with another part that resides in NT's kernel, **Rdr.sys**, the *redirector*. The redirector intercepts systems calls from the client application to the operating system to perform a file operation (open, read, write, etc.) on a file that isn't local, i.e. resides on a remote machine. The redirector forwards (redirects) the request to the remote machine, and handles any networking and data transfer involved. Conceptually this is similar to the role of the client subsystem in NFS (Module 17.14).

Server Service

The server component of Windows Networking is the Server Service. As with Workstation, it has a user-level component, again in **Services.EXE**, and a kernel-resident part, **Srv.sys**. Figure 18.4 shows how Workstation and Server interact to provide remote file access over the network.

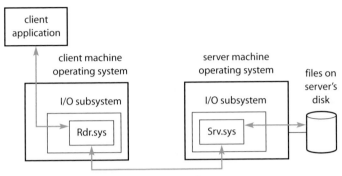

Figure 18.4 How Workstation and Server Services interact

Services and bindings

Some network Services are the equivalent of server applications on Linux. Others are embedded in NT's kernel, e.g. **Rdr.sys** and **Srv.sys**. Irrespective of where the code executes (in user space or kernel) a Service sits at a fairly high level in the network stack – above IP, Novell, NetBEUI, etc. – and this is where bindings (c.f. Module 18.2) come into play. A binding specifies a connection between either:

- a Service and what NT calls a protocol (really a protocol family, e.g. TCP/IP or Novell), or …
- an NT protocol and an adapter (network card).

Figure 18.5 illustrates diagrammatically the concept of bindings. Service-X can run over proto-A or proto-B. Proto-A only operates over adapter-1, but proto-B can communicate using both adapters. Service-Y uses only proto-C, on adapter-3 only. For example, Service-X might be Workstation, operating over TCP/IP on adapters-1 and -2, and over Novell on adapter-1 only. Service-Y might be Server, run over NetBEUI on its own adapter-3, providing service for ancient legacy machines. **Control Panel > Network > Bindings** lets you view and modify the bindings and the order in which they're applied. Normally you never have to bother with this, because bindings are configured by the installation program when you install the network components. However, in the example of Figure 18.5, if you wanted to ensure that Service-X uses proto-B first in preference to proto-A, you could use **Control Panel > Network > Bindings** to do it.

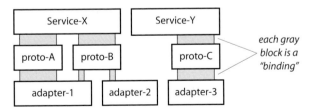

Figure 18.5 Bindings

In the following chapters we'll meet other Services providing other parts of Microsoft Windows Networking functionality. (See the Notes for information on the common Services and how they are implemented as processes.)

The rest of this chapter introduces our last sniffer, Windows Network Monitor, which we will need later to look at Windows Networking traffic.

18.6   Lab – the Windows Network Monitor, overview

This module and the next four introduce our final packet sniffer/protocol analyzer – the Microsoft Windows Network Monitor ("Netmon"). It's similar to **ethereal** but it knows more of the detailed internals of Windows Networking, so it gives a more complete interpretation of the traffic. Other advantages are: (a) it handles non-TCP/IP protocols; (b) you can use it on dial-up PPP connections; (c) Windows-NT includes it as standard, so you can use it in emergencies or on other people's machines when you don't have the other sniffer installed (or aren't allowed to install them). Its disadvantages are that it can only look at packets sent to the machine its running on, you can't view the list of packets "live" during capture, and it's harder and slower to use than the other tools.

(An enhanced version of Network Monitor comes with the Microsoft Systems Management Server product. As most people don't have this, we restrict ourselves to the standard version. The enhanced version does let you capture traffic for all machines, i.e. in promiscuous mode, and you can connect your Network Monitor window to a "Network Monitor Agent" on a remote machine to view the packets captured there rather than captured on your own PC. Several menu items and buttons in the standard version are "grayed out" and inaccessible because they relate only to the enhanced version.)

How to install Windows Network Monitor

Network Monitor is a Network Service. Install it from **Control Panel** > **Network** > **Services** > **Add** in the usual way.

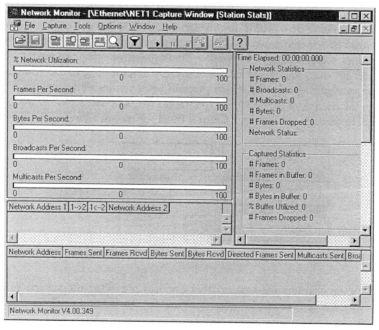

Figure 18.6 Network Monitor's initial window

Using Windows Network Monitor

Start it from the **Start** button > **Programs** > **Administrative Tools (Common)** > **Network Monitor**, to give its initial window (Figure 18.6).

- when it starts, Network Monitor isn't capturing
- before you start capturing, you can define a *capture filter* to capture only specific packets of interest (Module 18.7)
- when you are capturing, the statistics displays are updated, but you can't look at the list of packets captured
- when you stop capturing you can look at the list of packets, and you can optionally apply a *display filter* to limit which packets are displayed (Module 18.7).

To start capturing

- click on the ▶ icon (or use menu **Capture > Start**). The statistics in the right-hand window pane update on the fly as packets are captured.

To stop capturing

- click on the ■ icon menu (or use **Capture > Stop**) to just stop, or click on 🔳 (or use **Capture > Stop and view**) to stop and also view the packet list.

Viewing the packet list

The displayed list initially consists of only a single pane containing the packet list. If you double-click on a packet line, you get the three-pane display (Figure 18.7) with a layout and operation almost identical to **ethereal**'s. Double-clicking again reverts to the single-pane display.

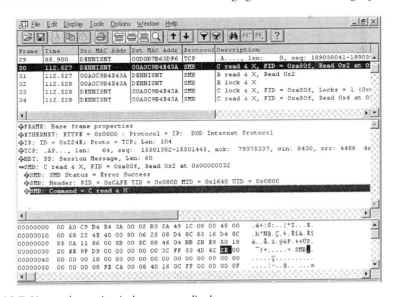

Figure 18.7 Network monitor's three-pane display

18.7 Lab – Network Monitor – capture filter by protocol

A capture filter tells Netmon which packets you want to capture; any packets that don't match the filter are not captured, reducing the amount of work that Netmon has to do, and reducing the size of the capture file. (Netmon's capture file size is limited by the amount of memory on your PC, so reducing the file size can sometimes be important.) Netmon's capture filter is conceptually the same as **ethereal**'s "**-f**" option, or the filter expression you type at the end of a **tcpdump** command line.

Netmon lets you filter by:

1. address (IP or MAC address)
2. protocol
3. detailed contents of the packet, e.g. "byte 4 = 123" (although we won't cover this).

You can't specify a TCP or UDP port number in a capture filter. (But once you've captured traffic on all ports, you can view traffic on only a specific port, by using a display filter at view-time, which we cover in the next module.)

To define a capture filter selecting by particular protocol(s):

1. click on the ▼ icon or use menu **Capture > Filter** to give the **Capture Filter** window (Figure 18.8). The initial setting captures everything to and from your machine

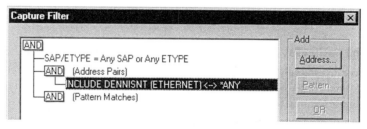

Figure 18.8 Network Monitor's Capture Filter window

2. to select by protocol, double-click on the **SAP/ETYPE** line to give the window shown in Figure 18.9. By default it captures all packets, i.e. all are enabled.

   To select, for example, only ARP or ICMP packets:

   i. click **Disable All**. All the protocols jump down into the **Disabled Protocols** from the **Enabled Protocols** pane

   ii. from the list of protocols, select **ARP** and click **Enable**. Do the same for **IP**. There are two points to note here: first, you can't select only ICMP in a capture filter. In fact your "protocol" options are very limited. You have to capture more than you really want and then zoom in on what you want later, using a display filter. Second, you may see that different protocols are shown as **ETYPE** or **SAP** or both. These relate to two different types of "Ethernet" (see Notes): if you have a choice, choose both, which is what you will do to capture IP.

   Press **OK**, which displays the revised Capture Filter (Figure 18.10)

   iii. press **OK** again, and the filter will be used as soon as you start capturing.

3. to capture, use menu **Capture > Start** as before.

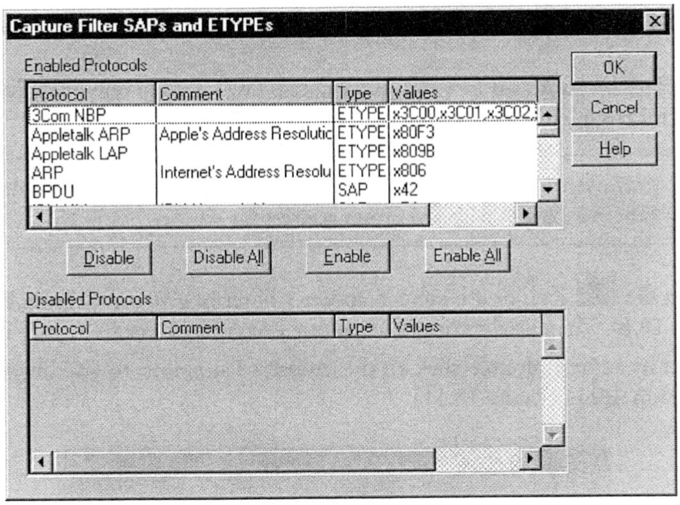

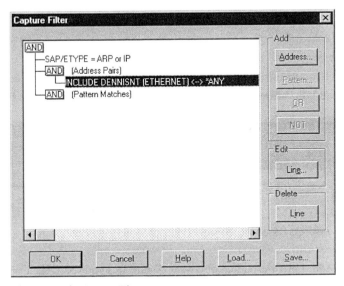

Figure 18.9 Filtering by protocol

AND **and** OR **operators in filters**

A logical operator **AND/OR** groups all the branches that are connected to the base of the operator's box representation in the window. For example, Figure 18.10 means (SAP/ETYPE = ARP or IP) AND (INCLUDE DENNISNT...). The only **AND** that matters here is the left-most one; the other two have no effect because they contain at most one item. (There's a larger example, with both **AND** and **OR** in Module 18.9.)

Figure 18.10 The revised Capture Filter

18.8 Lab – Network Monitor – capture filter by address

Specifying a filter by address is easy but longwinded. (We've really only included this module and the next for completeness.)

> **Warning:** don't use the "**ANY GROUP**" address. It does *not* mean "any machine." (It means any Ethernet packet with the **group address** bit set. See Notes.)

1. click on the 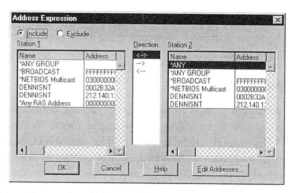 icon or use menu **Capture > Filter** to give the **Capture Filter** window (Figure 18.8). The initial setting is to capture everything to or from your machine

2. to select by address, double-click on the (**Address Pairs**) line, to give the **Address Expression** dialog (Figure 18.11)

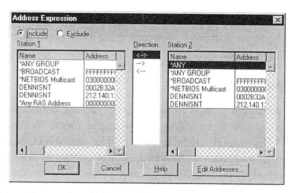

Figure 18.11 Address Expression dialog

Let's say we're interested only in traffic to/from IP address 192.0.2.5. If we've used this address before, it will be shown in the list of addresses, so we can jump to step 4 below

3. if we haven't used this address before, we must first add it to our list of addresses:

   i.   click on **Edit Addresses** to give the **Address Database** dialog (Figure 18.12).

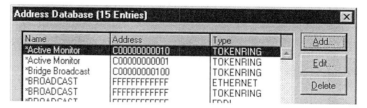

Figure 18.12 Address Database dialog

   ii. click **Add**. Enter the address you want (Figure 18.13). Press **OK.**. The address you entered now shows in Address Database. Click **OK** to return to the **Address Expression** dialog (Figure 18.14), where you'll see that the address you entered is now shown in the **Station 2** pane

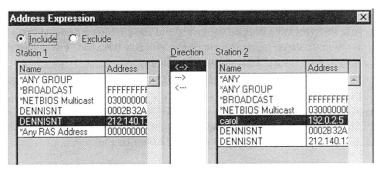

Figure 18.13 Entering address Information

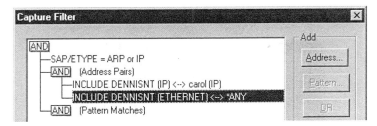

Figure 18.14 Selecting traffic between **DENNISNT** and **Carol**

4. in the **Address Expression** dialog (Figure 18.14), click on the remote machine (**Station 2**) whose traffic you're interested in (**carol** in this example). Select the **Direction** you want (i.e. whether you want only packets where **carol** is the destination, or the source machine, or either). Under **Station 1**, select the IP address of your own PC (**dennisnt**, 212.140... in this case). Click **OK** to display the capture filter as it stands now (Figure 18.15). (That the left and right panes of the display are different reflects the fact that this version of Netmon can only capture packets to and from this machine.)

5. We don't want the highlighted "**DENNISNT** <-> ANY" line so remove it using the **Delete Line** button (not shown). Press **OK** again, and the filter will be used as soon as you start capturing. To capture, use menu **Capture > Start** as before.

Figure 18.15 Updated Capture Filter

18.9 Lab – Network Monitor – display filters

Once you have stopped capturing, you have a set of packets that you can display. The whole packet list is displayed by default, but you can display selected packets only by defining and applying a display filter. (Conceptually this is identical to Ethereal's display filters, Module 13.4.) Display filters are the only way you can filter by port in Netmon.

We'll create and use a display filter: Assume we have captured a packet list and want to display only ICMP and ARP packets:

1. make sure that you have stopped capturing and are displaying a packet list. If all is correct, the main menu bar at the top of the Window will read "**File – Edit – Display** …", instead of the usual "**File – Capture – Tools** …"

2. click on the 🔽 icon to give the **Display Filter** window (Figure 18.6). By default, the filter displays all protocols and all addresses. You can selectively filter on protocol, address, or both, or by "property" – you can select any field from the packet and specify values to match. The range of protocols is much larger than for capture filters and by choosing the right protocol you can effectively filter by port.

Figure 18.16 Display Filter window

> **Warning:** the labels on the buttons in the dialog, and therefore their actions, change depending on what line is selected.

---

3. select the "Protocol == Any" line

4. press button **Edit Expression** (not shown) to give the **Expression** dialog (Figure 18.17)

5. press **Disable All**; all the protocols jump from the **Enabled Protocols** pane to the **Disabled Protocols** pane

6. select **ARP_RARP** and press **Enable**

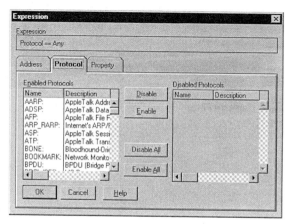

Figure 18.17 Display-filter expression dialog

Figure 18.18 Updated Display Filter

7. press **OK**, giving you the filter shown in Figure 18.18. Now we have to include ICMP packets in the filter

8. press button **Add Expression**, to give the expression dialog again. This time it will display the last expression you edited, suggesting that you're going to modify your previous setting, but that's not how it works: it just displays the previous values as a (confusing) convenience in case your next expression might be similar

9. press **Disable All**; then select **ICMP**, press **Enable** and press **OK.**, giving the filter shown in Figure 18.19.

Figure 18.19 ICMP Protocol added to filter

There's a problem here: it says show packets that are both ICMP and ARP, whereas it ought to say ICMP *or* ARP:

i. highlight the "Protocol == ARP_RARP" line

ii. press the **OR** button, which inserts an OR line

iii. drag the "Protocol == ICMP" line onto the OR line, giving the filter we want (Figure 18.20).

Figure 18.20 Our desired filter – match ICMP *or* ARP

We could have achieved the same result differently by double-clicking on the AND line in Figure 18.18 to change the operator to an OR, and then deleting the "ANY <-> ANY" line, or by enabling both ICMP and ARP together back in step 6. We did it the long way to show how to insert operator (AND, OR) lines.

> **Warning:** it's very easy to forget step 5 ("disable all"), and just enable the protocols you're interested in. As these are already enabled (as part of "all enabled"), it has no effect.

Setting up filtering by address is very similar. However, when you double-click on the "ANY <-> ANY" line (or select it and press **Edit Expression**), you get an address dialog almost identical to the **Capture Filter** one in the previous module.

18.10 Windows Network Monitor – tips and tricks

> **Tip:** a quick way to create or modify a display filter is to select an appropriate packet in the packet list pane and double-click on it to get the protocol tree pane. Then, very much like we did with Ethereal (Module 13.6), select an appropriate line in the tree display, right-click on it, and select menu item **Add to Filter**. Then edit as you wish.

> **Tip:** when editing a display filter, you can drag and drop lines within the filter window.

If you really want to specify an explicit port number, you have to drill down into the **Property**.

As with **tcpdump** and **ethereal**, you can run several instances of Netmon simultaneously on the same machine, each capturing a different set of packets. The separate instances do not interfere with each other.

Using capture files

Having captured a set of packets, you can save it to disk, using menu **File > Save As** (Figure 18.21). Note that you can save just a specified range of records, and you can optionally apply the display filter to the packet list (by ticking the **Filtered** box) and save only the filtered list.

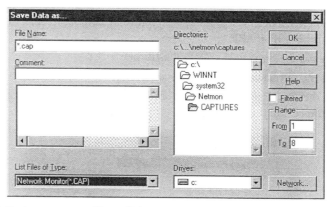

Figure 18.21 Saving a capture file to disk

We find saved capture files particularly useful where we've captured on one machine – a server, say – but want to analyze the packets back on our own PC; we just copy the file across.

If you have the SMS version of Netmon, you can often avoid saving and copying capture files. The SMS version lets you connect Netmon on your PC to a Netmon *agent* on another machine (Figure 18.22). The Netmon Agent Service must be installed and started on the remote machine. You can start it remotely from your own PC using the **sc** command in the NT Resource Kit. For example,

```
C:\> sc \\bob start nmagent
```

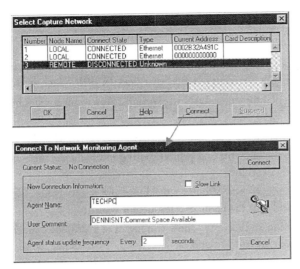

Figure 18.22 Connecting to a remote Netmon agent

Exchanging capture files with ethereal and tcpdump

ethereal can read Netmon's **.cap** files. This lets you capture with Netmon, then browse and analyze the results in **ethereal** (or vice versa):

capture with Netmon, view with ethereal: we find this very useful where we've asked a customer to save a capture file, and they send it to us for analysis. Usually they don't have **tcpdump** or **ethereal**, and it's easier for them to use Netmon instead. This mode is also ideal when you're working on site and don't have **ethereal** available, or are using a machine that you're not allowed to install it on

capture with ethereal, view with Netmon: this is the way we often explore aspects of Windows Networking. We capture using **tcpdump** or **ethereal** – because they let us specify capture filters much more easily, they can display the packet list on the fly as it's being captured, and they can capture in promiscuous mode, which Netmon can't. Then, in **ethereal** we save the packet list in Microsoft Network Monitor format as *name*.cap, read this into Netmon, and analyze the results there.

tcpdump doesn't have a file-format conversion facility, so if you capture using **tcpdump**, you have to read the capture file into **ethereal** to convert it before viewing it with Netmon. Similarly, **tcpdump** can't read Netmon's **.cap** files either, so if you want to view a Netmon capture using **tcpdump**, you must first use **ethereal** to convert it to **libpcap** format – the format used by **tcpdump** (and **ethereal**'s default format).

Summary

- Windows Networking is different from other Internet protocols because it developed separately, using networking systems other than TCP/IP – such as Novell and NetBEUI:
  - it was designed for single-LAN workgroups. As a result it relies heavily on broadcast packets
  - it uses names, not IP numbers, as the definitive reference to a machine or a resource
- in addition to the basic file and printer sharing mechanisms, there are three major parts to Windows Networking:
  - a. name resolution – how Windows machines and resources are named, and how my machine finds out the name of a resource it wants to use
  - b. authentication and security – how you logon to a Windows system, and how it controls your access to resources
  - c. browsing the network – automatically retrieving lists of machines and resources that are available on the network. This is crucial to making Windows Networking easy to use on a small workgroup that doesn't have a dedicated system administrator
- on NT, Windows Networking over TCP/IP is called NBT. It uses UDP ports 137 and 138, and TCP port 139 for almost everything
- much of NT's networking is implemented as and controlled by "NT Services." Bindings specify which lower-level networking system (e.g. TCP/IP or Novell or NetBEUI) a service is to run over
- the Windows Network Monitor is a graphical packet sniffer very like **ethereal**:
  - the standard version of Netmon captures only packets for this machine and can't capture promiscuously
  - Netmon is better than **ethereal** or **tcpdump** for displaying the contents of Windows Networking traffic.

What's next?

In the next chapter we cover Windows Networking's mechanisms for name resolution, because names and how they are resolved are fundamental to everything in Windows Networking.

Notes and further reading

Microsoft Windows Networking in general
The RFCs describing NetBIOS over TCP/IP are:

❑ **RFC-1001 March 1987** *Protocol Standard For a NetBIOS Service on a TCP/UDP Transport: Concepts and Methods*

❑ **RFC-1002 March 1987** *Protocol Standard For a NetBIOS Service on a TCP/UDP Transport: Detailed Specifications*

RFC-1001 is very readable and explains the ideas behind the implementation. RFC-1002 gives very low-level specifications of packet formats, etc. and you'll probably never want to look at it. Interestingly, Microsoft's own NT implementation doesn't conform 100% to these specs: in particular the NetBIOS Datagram Distribution (NBDD) service doesn't exist.

For an overview of Microsoft's implementation of TCP/IP:

❑ **ftp://ftp.microsoft.com/bussys/winnt/winnt-docs/papers/tcpimp2.exe** *Microsoft Windows NT 3.5/3.51/4.0: TCP/IP Implementation Details. TCP/IP Protocol Stack and Services, Version 2.0*

We've found Microsoft's own publications to be the best source of detailed information on Windows Networking. In particular, the Resource Kits for the various operating systems contain in-depth (although not comprehensive) discussions on many aspects of Windows Networking. The paper editions of the Resource Kits (which you can buy from a bookstore) contain both the printed manuals and many extra software tools. We've found these tools very useful in understanding how things really work.

❑ **Microsoft Windows NT Server resource kit for Windows NT Server version 4.0** (1996, Microsoft Press) (which we refer to from now on as "the Resource Kit.")

The Resource Kit documents are available online. The NT 4.0 version is:

❑ **http://www.microsoft.com/technet/prodtechnol/winntas/reskit/default.asp**

For higher-level (less nitty-gritty) documents, the *Windows NT Server Concepts and Planning Guide* is good:

❑ **http://www.microsoft.com/technet/prodtechnol/winntas/proddocs/concept/front.asp**

(We often have difficulty finding this if we don't have the full URL to hand. On the Microsoft TechNet site, follow the links: **TechNet > Products and Technologies > Windows NT Server > Product Documentation.**)

Other useful sources of information are the Microsoft TechNet site in general:

❑ **http://www.microsoft.com/technet/**

and the Microsoft Knowledgebase:

❑ **http://support.microsoft.com**

which is a database of technical notes, usually relating to bugs or other problems. (The Knowledgebase articles are occasionally reviewed and updated, so unlike the RFCs, you can't use them to trace the history of a feature and see what influenced its development over time.) The Knowledgebase is excellent for very specific questions ("your Windows XYZ system misbehaves when ABC; to work around that …"). However, on all the Microsoft sites we've found it hard to locate articles that provide an overview of a technology area but are still technically oriented. For that type of information we've found the third-party "NT FAQ" site:

❑ **http://www.ntfaq.com**

to be especially good for articles describing concepts and for answering broader questions like "why would I want to do X?" or "how would I configure my network to do Y?"

Windows-2000, much more than NT 4.0, is an architecture truly designed for the Internet. CIFS (*Common Internet File System*) is Microsoft Windows Networking for the Internet. It hasn't been adopted as an IETF Internet standard and discussion on the net seems to have languished for a couple of years, but this appears to be the future direction for Microsoft file- and print-sharing systems, and getting full documentation of how it works remains a problem. See:

❑ **http://www.theregister.co.uk/content/53/24490.html** *Why Microsoft's EU 'concession' is no concession at all*

"Peer-to-peer networking" is increasingly being used on the Internet, as a way to avoid over-loading of popular servers in the usual client/server model of interaction. It refers to end-user machines interacting directly with one another rather than acting as clients to dedicated servers – Napster is (or was?) an example, as are Gnutella and KaZaA. Both on the Internet and in Windows Networking the key idea is that client machines can automatically discover and use resources instead of being pre-configured to use specific servers. For more information:

❑ **http://www.peer-to-peerwg.org**

❑ **http://www.computer.org/internet/v6n1/** **Jan/Feb-2002** IEEE Internet Computing *Peer-to-Peer Networks in Action*

NetBIOS and NetBEUI

We only mentioned NetBEUI to suggest you don't use it unless you have a good reason to. Nowadays almost nobody needs it, so if you don't know whether you need it or not, the chances are you don't. (You can always disable it for a couple of weeks on your own machine and see if anything breaks. And even if NetBEUI is being used, it can easily be that NetBIOS over TCP/IP could perform the same functions for you.) A common source of confusion is that NetBEUI stands for NetBIOS Extended User Interface. Ignore that – on NT, NetBEUI and NetBIOS are completely separate and different things.

If you run NetBEUI on your systems it can provide a "back door" around any TCP/IP-based security systems you have in place (Module 24.8). It can also cause name resolution problems (see Chapter 19, Notes). Ideally use only a single protocol, i.e. TCP, and not IPX and not NetBEUI.

For a comparison of TCP/IP, IPX/SPX and NetBEUI see:

❑ **MS-KB-Q128233** *Comparison of Windows NT Network Protocols*

The **NetBIOS Interface** NT Service is *not* the whole NetBIOS networking subsystem – only a very small part of it. It's a specific service that lets you configure very low-level details of the bindings of protocols to network adapters, which typically you have to do only for non-Microsoft applications, such as Lotus Notes. Most Microsoft applications don't require it although it's impossible to get a definitive list of which ones do use it (and if you disable it and try to use RAS for dial-up networking, you'll get an **Error 720**). For secure installations many people do disable it.

NT Services

The Resource Kit contains a couple of useful tools. **sclist** lists the services on this machine, and their status. You can use it to view the list of services on a remote machine too. (**sclist**'s help-message says option **-m** lists only stopped services; in fact the option is **-s**.) The **sc** ("service controller") command lets you interact with the Service Controller and the NT Services. Its sub-command **sc qc** ("query configuration") shows which process a service runs in, its dependencies on other services, and some other details.

Windows Network Monitor

For a detailed tutorial, see:

❑ **http://www.microsoft.com/technet/prodtechnol/winntas/proddocs/concept/xcp10.asp**

Some of Netmon's dialogs for filters, etc. show things at a lower level of detail than you'd like. For example, the **ANY GROUP** address means any packet with the "group" bit set in its MAC address. (If you really want to, see Perlman, page 25 for details. Even better, forget about it and never use this address.) Another instance is in the protocol filter dialog: some protocols, including IP, are shown in two variants, one with **ETYPE** and a second with **SAP**. These refer to different variants of "Ethernet" packets. (C.f. IEEE 802.3 v. DIX, Notes, Chapter 2.) To find out what yours is, run NetMon without any filter and see whether your packets are **ETYPE** or **SAP** and use whatever you see. (Again, see Perlman, page 30, for details if you must.)

You can distinguish between the SMS version and the ordinary version using the menu **Help > About**. The ordinary version shows "v4.00.349," with the name "Retail ..." in the window title-bar, whereas the SMS version shows "v4.00.351" and has "SMS Retail ..." in the title-bar.

The SMS version lets you re-send packets by selecting them in the packet list window and using menu **Tools > Transmit Frame**. Menu **Transmit Capture** lets you re-send the whole packet list.

If you have SMS, you can install its version of Netmon without the rest of SMS. Find the Netmon **setup.exe** program on the SMS or BackOffice CD, typically in a directory called **\Nmext\Disk1**. Then run this **setup** program.

Appendices

Appendix 22: name resolution order in Windows

19 Windows Networking – name resolution

Introduction

NetBIOS names are fundamental to Windows Networking because names, not IP numbers, are its primary reference for machines and resources on the network. A machine "registers" a name when it is prepared to offer a particular resource or service. It can register the name using broadcast packets, or using a special name registration server called WINS – the Windows Internet Name Service. Other machines also use broadcasts or WINS to resolve names in order to access the corresponding resources. However, a machine can also use several other mechanisms to resolve names, which can be useful in particular circumstances.

19.1 NetBIOS names and name resolution – overview

Microsoft Windows Networking (or NetBIOS) uses names as its primary reference for machines and services, in contrast to TCP/IP, which uses IP numbers to identify machines. As we mentioned in Module 18.1, this is because Windows Networking can work over many different networking systems, not just TCP/IP, and whatever mechanism it uses must work on all these different systems. Because of this, Windows Networking works very differently from the Internet protocols we cover elsewhere in this book, as we'll see here and in the following chapters.

Of course, when Windows Networking runs over TCP/IP, NetBIOS names must be resolved to IP numbers for the basic UDP and TCP communications mechanisms to operate. How Windows Networking resolves names is what this chapter is about.

Before we even explain properly what NetBIOS names are, we'll look briefly at how they are resolved. For now, let's assume we're dealing with the NetBIOS name of a PC, Bob, say. Your PC is Alice, and you want to use some resource on Bob. Alice needs to find out Bob's IP address.

Because we're now in Windows Networking land, which was designed to operate in small workgroups without any central servers and without any pre-configuration, things work very differently to what we're used to:

- name resolution and other name-related functions work using broadcast UDP packets. (It has to be UDP because TCP doesn't allow broadcasting.)
- when your PC boots up, it reads its name (Alice) from its configuration in the Windows Registry. Before it can say "I am Alice", it has to check whether there is already a machine called Alice on this network:
  - your PC broadcasts several "name claim requests" to its local subnet, saying "I want to call myself Alice. Is that OK?" (These are also called "name registration requests" but "name claim" is more descriptive of what actually happens.)
  - if no other PC replies saying "No, *my* name is Alice, so you can't have that name," the PC decides it's called Alice. (Rigorous, isn't it?)
- now Alice wants to find out Bob's IP address:
  - Alice broadcasts a "name query" request
  - Bob replies with his IP number.

NetBIOS names are used to identify machines, groups of machines (usually a set of servers providing a specific Windows Networking function), users, and NT-domains (Chapter 21). We look at the types of names in more detail in the next module.

Implementation of NetBIOS name resolution

(From now on we'll refer to TCP/IP hostnames as "DNS-names," to distinguish them from NetBIOS names.)

There are in fact six different methods of NetBIOS name resolution:

1. broadcasts, as outlined above
2. WINS, the "Windows Internet Name Server." This is a bit like a DNS server, but handling all the special features of NetBIOS names that we'll see in the next module.

3. using the DNS to resolve NetBIOS names (not DNS names)

4. the **hosts** file

5. the **LMHOSTS** file

6. an internal cache of names already looked up.

Originally, broadcasting was the only mechanism available. The others were added at different times for performance reasons and to handle the more complex networks that were being used, with routers and WAN/Internet links.

PCs can use different subsets of the six resolution methods and in different orders, depending on how they are configured. We cover that configuration in Module 19.5, along with why you would want each different configuration option and when to use it. First we'll explain what each method is and how it works, in Module 19.3 onwards.

The nbtstat **command**

nbtstat ("NetBIOS status) displays the "name table" for a machine, i.e. the list of names that the machine has registered. **nbtstat** has three different name-display options (as well as other options that we'll see later):

show my own <u>n</u>ame table	nbtstat -n
show name table for hostname *name*	nbtstat -a *name*
show name table for IP number *a.b.c.d*	nbtstat -A *a.b.c.d*

The "A" in "**-a**" and "**-A**" stand for *adapter status*, which is an old NetBIOS term for "the list of NetBIOS names that the specified machine owns". Figure 19.1 shows typical **nbtstat** listings. (Notice that we don't prefix machine names with \\ here; if you say, for example, "**nbtstat -a \\hal9000-nt**" you'll get an error.)

```
Command Prompt

C:\> nbtstat -n
             NetBIOS Local Name Table
    Name               Type         Status
---------------------------------------------------
ALICENT        <00>  UNIQUE      Registered
TEST-NTD       <00>  GROUP       Registered
ALICENT        <03>  UNIQUE      Registered
ALICENT        <20>  UNIQUE      Registered

C:\> nbtstat -a hal9000-nt
            NetBIOS Remote Machine Name Table
    Name               Type         Status
---------------------------------------------------
HAL9000-NT     <00>  UNIQUE      Registered
HAL9000-NT     <20>  UNIQUE      Registered
TEST-NTD       <00>  GROUP       Registered
TEST-NTD       <1C>  GROUP       Registered
TEST-NTD       <1B>  UNIQUE      Registered
TEST-NTD       <1E>  GROUP       Registered
HAL9000-NT     <03>  UNIQUE      Registered
ADMINISTRATOR  <03>  UNIQUE      Registered
TEST-NTD       <1D>  UNIQUE      Registered
.._MSBROWSE__.<01>  GROUP       Registered
```

Figure 19.1 Typical **nbtstat** listings

19.2 NetBIOS names

Superficially, NetBIOS names look like DNS names. For example, in Windows Explorer's Network Neighborhood, or the equivalent **net view** command (Figure 19.2), machines on our LAN are listed by name. These are NetBIOS names because they are the names of machines participating in Windows Networking.

Figure 19.2 net view command

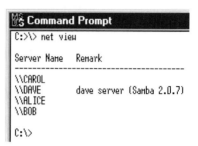

However, the resemblance between DNS names and NetBIOS names is only superficial. Internally there are profound differences between them, which reflect the fact that NetBIOS and TCP/IP are very different networking systems:

1. the DNS namespace is hierarchical, the NetBIOS namespace is flat. In other words, DNS names are arranged in a tree (e.g. **pc29.sales.example.com**), whereas NetBIOS names consist of a single, simple name, (e.g. **pc29**)

2. DNS names can be of almost any length. NetBIOS names that you enter must be 15 characters or less

3. NetBIOS names are used to name resources on machines and on the network, not just the machines themselves. Internally, whenever a NetBIOS name is used to refer to a resource, it's exactly 16 characters long; it's padded out with spaces to 15 characters, and an extra, 16th character is appended to specify what type of name or what service this is. For example, to connect to the Server Service on machine **snodgrass**, the NetBIOS name used is

   snodgrass■■■■■■ [20]

where each ■ indicates a space, and [20] is a single byte containing the hexadecimal value 20 (to indicate we want the Server Service on **snodgrass**). For brevity we often write this as:

   snodgrass<20>

Conceptually this 16th character is reminiscent of a TCP or UDP port, because it specifies the particular service on a machine that's required. For example, the following two names differ only in their suffix, but have very different functions:

ex-ntd<1b>	unique	the domain master browser (Module 21.6)
ex-ntd<1c>	group	list of domain controllers (Module 20.5)

Appendix 21 lists the 16th-byte suffix characters and what they are used for. We'll also explain them in the body of the text as we go along.

4. there are two types of NetBIOS names:

   i. *unique names*

   ii. *group names*

A unique name identifies a single resource, e.g. the Server Service on an individual PC. If machine **bob** is running the Server Service, Bob registers the name **bob<20>**. If he isn't running Server, he does *not* register **bob<20>** and any attempt to resolve that name will fail. A group name identifies a set of resources. A group name can be used in two different ways:

   i. when this name is resolved, it returns a list of IP numbers. For example, resolving **ex-ntd<1c>** gives the list of domain controllers for the domain called **ex-ntd**. This type of group is called an *Internet group type* (Windows itself uses only one group of this type – the **<1c>** group of domain controllers)

   ii. a PC can send a packet to all the members of a group (without first having to find out the list of members). For example, the command

```
net send /domain:ex-ntd "fire drill in 2 hours"
```

sends a message to all PCs in the domain **ex-ntd**, which it addresses as **ex-ntd<00>**. This type of group is called a *normal group*

In other words, a group name can be either a list of machines or a name shared by many machines.

The type of a name (unique or group) is specified as part of the definition of the particular 16th-byte suffix. In most cases you can tell directly from the suffix whether the name is unique or group, e.g. *name*<20> is always unique. However, with some suffixes you can tell only by usage or context, e.g. <00> is used to specify the unique name of a PC, but it's also used as a group name for all the machines that belong to a domain:

domain name **<00>**	group	all members of *domain name* register this name
computer name **<00>**	unique	this PC's name

NetBIOS computer names are often prefixed with a double backslash, as in

```
\\alice
```

to indicate that this is a machine name and to distinguish it from an ordinary filename in contexts where either may occur, e.g.

```
copy \\alice\myfiles\abc.dat myabc.dat          "alice" is a machine name
rename alice alice.txt                          "alice" is a filename
```

The \\ isn't part of the name but is only a delimiter.

In the rest of this chapter we concentrate on how names are registered and resolved, and ignore what the names are being used for. We discuss what the different names are, what they are used for, and why, in the chapters after this. In particular, browsing the resources on the network (Chapter 21) makes use of name resolution, but is separate from it.

In the next module we look at the various methods NetBIOS uses for resolution.

19.3 Method 1: broadcasts

Every node (machine) on a Microsoft Windows network has its own unique name. This is the name that you configure as the **Computer Name** in the **Control Panel > Network > Identification** window, or when you installed the Windows software on the PC in the first place. This name uses suffix <00> and – like any other name – must be explicitly *registered*.

Name registration (name claim)

Registration is also called *name claim*, which is a much more explanatory term when used on a network that's using broadcasts. The machine broadcasts a *NAME REGISTRATION REQUEST* on its local wire, to the IP sub-net broadcast address, on port 137. All the other PCs on the same sub-net hear this request. Then:

- if one of them has already registered the name itself, it sends back a *NEGATIVE NAME REGISTRATION RESPONSE* to the PC that is trying to register this address and the registration fails. If the name in question is the PC's computer name, it will have to be reconfigured with a different name and rebooted

- if no other PC sends back a negative response, the requestor is free to have this name so it says to itself "I have succeeded, this name belongs to me."

Below is the Ethereal trace of a PC booting (IP address 192.0.2.35, name ALICENT). After checking that no other machine is using its IP address, the PC issues four NB (NetBIOS) name claim (name registration) requests. These are sent to the sub-net broadcast address (192.0.2.127 here, because our netmask is 255.255.255.128). The total elapsed time was 5½ seconds (not shown). Because no other machine has replied to the name claim, the PC sets its name to ALICENT.

Source	Destination	Protocol	Info
00:50:da:e4:61:34	ff:ff:ff:ff:ff:ff	ARP	Who has 192.0.2.35? Tell 192.0.2.35
00:50:da:e4:61:34	ff:ff:ff:ff:ff:ff	ARP	Who has 192.0.2.35? Tell 192.0.2.35
00:50:da:e4:61:34	ff:ff:ff:ff:ff:ff	ARP	Who has 192.0.2.35? Tell 192.0.2.35
192.0.2.35	192.0.2.127	NBNS	Registration NB ALICENT <00>
192.0.2.35	192.0.2.127	NBNS	Registration NB ALICENT <00>
192.0.2.35	192.0.2.127	NBNS	Registration NB ALICENT <00>
192.0.2.35	192.0.2.127	NBNS	Registration NB ALICENT <00>

The following trace shows the trace of a PC booting with a name (BOBNT) that's already in use on another PC (192.0.2.31). The existing PC responds that it's already using the name **BOBNT**, and the booting PC can't register (claim) the name for its own use.

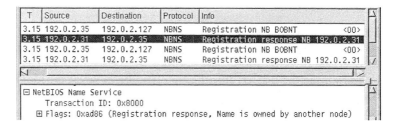

T	Source	Destination	Protocol	Info
3.15	192.0.2.35	192.0.2.127	NBNS	Registration NB BOBNT <00>
3.15	192.0.2.31	192.0.2.35	NBNS	Registration response NB 192.0.2.31
3.15	192.0.2.35	192.0.2.127	NBNS	Registration NB BOBNT <00>
3.15	192.0.2.31	192.0.2.35	NBNS	Registration response NB 192.0.2.31

```
⊟ NetBIOS Name Service
     Transaction ID: 0x8000
     ⊞ Flags: 0xad86 (Registration response, Name is owned by another node)
```

That's the procedure when a PC claims a NetBIOS unique name. If the name is a group name, more than one PC may legitimately claim it – after all, a group name is a shared name. If a PC that has registered a group name hears a claim request broadcast for that group name, it does nothing, thus permitting the requestor to claim the group name too and become part of that group.

The trace below shows that a PC when booting, having registered (claimed) its own computer name, then goes on to register itself as a member of its domain (**UIT** in this case). By drilling down into the packet, **ethereal** shows you that UIT<00> is a group name (but we haven't included this detail for lack of space).

Source	Destination	Protocol	Info	
192.0.2.35	192.0.2.127	NBNS	Registration NB ALICENT	<00>
192.0.2.35	192.0.2.127	NBNS	Registration NB UIT	<00>
192.0.2.35	192.0.2.127	NBNS	Registration NB UIT	<00>
192.0.2.35	192.0.2.127	NBNS	Registration NB UIT	<00>
192.0.2.35	192.0.2.127	NBNS	Registration NB UIT	<00>

Name resolution

The opposite of name registration is *name query*, also called *name resolution*. When a PC wants to resolve a NetBIOS name to an IP number, it broadcasts a name query request on the subnet broadcast address, port 137. If another PC has already claimed (registered) this name, its responds with its IP address to the requestor; otherwise, the requestor knows that there is no PC with this name.

The trace below shows ALICENT **ping**ing a non-existent host BOB. ALICENT broadcasts three name queries for BOB and gives up. Then we **ping** again, for the correct name this time – BOBNT. ALICENT broadcasts the name query, and gets a name query response from BOBNT immediately, saying his IP address is 192.0.2.31, and the **ping** proceeds.

Source	Destination	Protocol	Info	
192.0.2.35	192.0.2.127	NBNS	Name query NB BOB	<00>
192.0.2.35	192.0.2.127	NBNS	Name query NB BOB	<00>
192.0.2.35	192.0.2.127	NBNS	Name query NB BOB	<00>
192.0.2.35	192.0.2.127	NBNS	Name query NB BOBNT	<00>
192.0.2.31	192.0.2.35	NBNS	Name query response NB 192.0.2.31	
192.0.2.35	192.0.2.31	ICMP	Echo (ping) request	
192.0.2.31	192.0.2.35	ICMP	Echo (ping) reply	

Relying on broadcasts like this seems strange in the context of the Internet protocols we've looked at so far – there seems plenty of opportunity for things to go wrong, and the broadcasts generates network traffic and an extra load on every machine on the local wire. However, this mechanism appears more sensible in the context of a small workgroup. It works without any central server to register names, and without any pre-configuration (apart from naming the PC when Windows was installed on it) so it's ideal for the small workgroups that NetBIOS was originally designed to handle. On the other hand, it works only on a network where every machine can broadcast to every other one, i.e. a single Ethernet segment. Routers don't pass broadcasts, so if the network contains routers, e.g. on a large LAN or a WAN or on a virtual private network (Chapter 27) – name registration and resolution using broadcasts won't work. To get over that problem, NetBIOS can use a "NetBIOS name server," which we cover in the next module.

19.4 Method 2: WINS – the NetBIOS name server

The obvious problem with name resolution using broadcasts is that it's limited to the local network segment since routers don't pass broadcast packets. So if Alice was on one sub-net, and Bob on another, they would not be able to resolve each other's name. (Even if routers did pass broadcasts, on a large network the broadcast traffic from thousands of PCs would have a significant effect on performance.) To overcome this, *WINS* (the *Windows Internet Name Service*) was introduced with Windows NT 3.5.

WINS is a client/server system:

- you explicitly configure each client (manually or via DHCP) with the IP address of one or more WINS servers

- when a client wants to register (claim) a name, it sends a name registration request to the WINS server. WINS returns the registered details if it succeeded or else reports a failure. Below is the **ethereal** trace of ALICENT registering with the WINS server on 212.140.133.7:

```
212.140.133.35  212.140.133.7   NBNS   Multi-homed registration NB ALICENT       <00>
212.140.133.7   212.140.133.35  NBNS   Registration response NB 212.140.133.35
```

- when a client wants to query a name, it sends the name query directly to the WINS server, which resolves it or reports a failure

- all requests and replies are sent using UDP. The request and reply are not broadcast; they're sent directly to the server and client IP address, respectively

- the source and destination port are always 137.

In some respects WINS is like a DNS server for NetBIOS. However, you don't have to enter names before using them, names have suffixes and are not hierarchical, and the WINS server only deals with your organization's network.

Because WINS uses one-to-one ("unicast") UDP transmission, it can work over a network containing routers (Figure 19.3) and therefore across the Internet. Another advantage is that it cuts down on the number of broadcasts on the local sub-net.

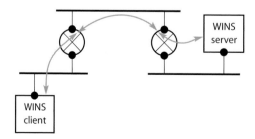

Figure 19.3 WINS is routable

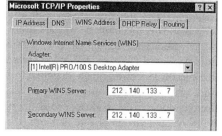

Figure 19.4 Configuring the WINS client

WINS client configuration

(We cover the client first because you may be using WINS yourself on your own PC even if you're not administering it.)

You configure the client using **Control Panel > Network > Protocols > TCP/IP > WINS Address** (Figure 19.4); reboot your PC for the settings to take effect.

You can specify the IP addresses of both a **Primary WINS Server** and a **Secondary WINS Server**. The secondary server is queried if the primary doesn't respond, or if the primary responds saying it does not have the name in its database. (In the case where the primary didn't respond, the secondary server will be used first in future resolution attempts. Periodically the WINS client will see whether the primary is available again, and if so, will switch back to it.) If neither WINS server can be contacted, the PC will attempt to resolve the name using broadcasts (assuming your PC is configured suitably – Module 19.10).

> **Tip**: if you configure a primary, always configure a secondary too, even if it's the same address as the primary.

This makes your system more resilient. NetBIOS name resolution runs over UDP, and packets can get dropped or delayed, especially if your WINS server is at a remote site on the Internet, or if you're using VPN (Chapter 27). By configuring the secondary server, you get six bites at the cherry: if your PC can't contact the primary after three attempts, it tries the secondary three times as well. We've found that on VPN especially, this can make all the difference between having a working system and a frustrating half-working mess.

> **Warning**: don't forget to configure the WINS server addresses on the WINS server machine itself.

Below is the trace of ALICENT querying BOB (non-existent) and BOBNT (which does exist). Note that when the primary returns a negative response, the client tries the secondary (at the same address in this example) and after its negative response the client tries yet again, using broadcasts.

```
94.09 212.140.133.35    212.140.133.7      NBNS   Name query NB BOB              <00>
94.10 212.140.133.7     212.140.133.35     NBNS   Name query response
94.10 212.140.133.35    212.140.133.7      NBNS   Name query NB BOB              <00>
94.10 212.140.133.7     212.140.133.35     NBNS   Name query response
94.10 212.140.133.35    212.140.133.127    NBNS   Name query NB BOB              <00>
94.85 212.140.133.35    212.140.133.127    NBNS   Name query NB BOB              <00>
95.60 212.140.133.35    212.140.133.127    NBNS   Name query NB BOB              <00>
112.6 212.140.133.35    212.140.133.7      NBNS   Name query NB BOBNT            <00>
112.6 212.140.133.7     212.140.133.35     NBNS   Name query response NB 212.140.13%
112.6 212.140.133.35    212.140.133.31     ICMP   Echo (ping) request
112.6 212.140.133.31    212.140.133.35     ICMP   Echo (ping) reply
```

19.5 WINS server configuration

WINS is an NT network Service. You install it from **Control Panel > Network > Services > Add** and select **Windows Internet Name Service**.

In its simplest configuration, WINS runs happily on its own and needs no pre-configuration. Any WINS client machines that have been configured to use this server send name registrations, queries, etc. to it, and it responds.

You can configure and interrogate the WINS server using **WINS Manager** (Figure 19.5). If you haven't installed the WINS server on this machine, there won't be an entry for WINS Manager in your **Start** button menus, but the program may nonetheless be on your machine. If so, you can run it from the Command Prompt as **winsadmn.exe**. This is handy because WINS Manager lets you connect to WINS servers running elsewhere on the network: you add WINS servers to the Manager's list using menu **Server > Add WINS Server ...** and then select from the list to connect to that machine's WINS server.

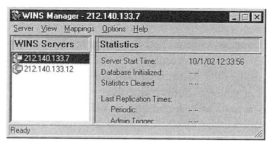

Figure 19.5 WINS Manager – initial window

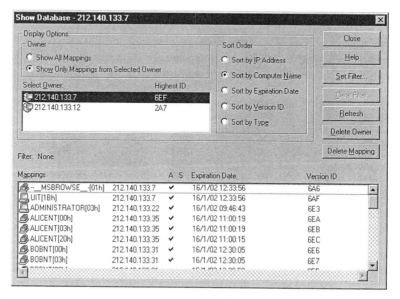

Figure 19.6 WINS manager – Show Database window

You can list the contents of the WINS server's database using menu **Mappings > Show Database** (Figure 19.6).

For a large network, the number of entries is correspondingly large, and WINS Manager's small display is hard to use. If you just need to look at one machine's entries, you can use the **Set Filter** button to restrict your view. Alternatively, you can use the program **winsdmp.exe** from the NT 4.0 Resource Kit. Figure 19.7 shows a partial **winsdmp** listing; the funny characters are the 16th-byte suffixes we mentioned in Module 19.2, which display oddly because they're outside the normal printable range.

```
██ Command Prompt

C:\>winsdmp 192.0.2.7
[2 owner(s) found]
[1] 192.0.2.12 (Highest ID = 2a7h)]
[Reading records in the range 0h - 7cfh ... 8 records found]

192.0.2.12,"TEST-NTD      ",0,17,1,0,0,7,0,1001065488,1,10.1.1.34,
192.0.2.12,"HAL9000-NT    ♥",3,17,0,0,0,667,0,1001065488,1,192.0.2.12,
192.0.2.12,"HAL9000-NT    ",20,17,0,0,0,668,0,1001065488,1,192.0.2.12,
192.0.2.12,"HAL9000-NT    ",0,17,0,0,0,669,0,1001065488,1,192.0.2.12,
192.0.2.12,"TEST-NTD      ▲",1E,17,1,0,0,670,0,1001065488,1,192.0.2.12,
192.0.2.12,"TEST-NTD      ←",1B,17,0,0,0,671,0,1001065488,1,192.0.2.12,
192.0.2.12,"TEST-NTD      ∟",1C,17,2,0,0,672,0,1001065488,1,192.0.2.12,
192.0.2.12,"HAL9000-NT¬¬¬¬¬¬",BF,17,0,0,0,679,0,1001662583,1,192.0.2.12,
```

Figure 19.7 A partial **winsdmp** listing

The Resource Kit contains another command-line tool, **winscl.exe**, that you can use to interrogate the server and control many aspects of its operation; see Web Appendix 25 for details. **winscl** is a horrible program to use, but:

- it lets you send very specific name queries to WINS servers, giving you more control than if you just **ping** the name
- the way it displays groups is clearer than WINS Manager's.

You can stop or start the WINS server from **Control Panel > Services**, or from the command line, using the **net** command:

```
net start wins
net stop wins
```

although you're unlikely ever to want to do this except when testing, or exploring how name resolution operates.

19.6 Other WINS issues: non-WINS clients; database replication

Integrating WINS and non-WINS clients

If a machine on the network can't use WINS (because it runs a very old version of Windows or a non-Windows operating system), you have two options for integrating it with WINS:

1. define a *static mapping* for the machine's address, using WINS Manager's menu **Mappings > Static Mappings**. This is also useful during testing, e.g. to create a dummy name that you know exists only in WINS and not in any other name resolution system

2. if the machine uses NetBIOS broadcasting, you can set up any NT machine on this LAN segment to act as a WINS *proxy agent* (Figure 19.8.)

   - the client broadcasts as usual

   - the proxy agent hears the broadcast, and forwards the client's request to the WINS server. (As usual the WINS doesn't have to be on this LAN segment, because the proxy forwards the request using unicast UDP, i.e. it doesn't broadcast the request but sends it specifically to the WINS server's IP address.)

   - the WINS server responds, sending its reply to the proxy

   - the proxy then broadcasts the reply on its local LAN segment, and the non-WINS client hears the broadcast reply.

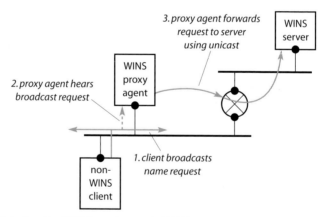

Figure 19.8 Relaying NetBIOS broadcasts via WINS proxy

You should have only one or two proxy agents per LAN segment, because each one will forward the requests to the server and with multiple proxy agents you're multiplying the network traffic and the load on the WINS server. (For efficiency you really only want one proxy, but for resilience you want two.)

You can't enable WINS Proxy Agent via the **Control Panel** – you have to edit the Windows Registry (see Notes). **ipconfig** and **wntipcfg** both show whether WINS proxy is enabled on this PC.

Multiple WINS servers and database replication

We explained in Module 19.4 that you really need WINS if you're going to use Microsoft Windows Networking over a network that includes routers. The WINS server then becomes an essential component of your network; if the server fails, you lose some of your network's functionality. Accordingly, you need multiple WINS servers for resilience. You'll probably want multiple servers for performance reasons too: there's a limit to how many clients a WINS server can handle, and in any case you don't want your name queries and replies to travel all the way back and forth across your large network. So you can run several WINS servers, perhaps one at each office or site (Figure 19.9).

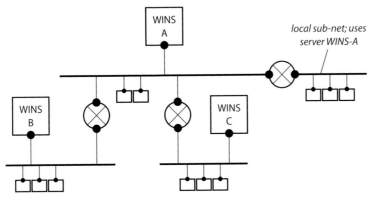

Figure 19.9 Running several WINS servers on different segments

When you have multiple servers, each maintains its own database of registrations, etc. that it knows about. If you did nothing more, you'd end up with multiple, inconsistent views of the network. To overcome this, WINS servers support *replication*. You configure each server with one or more *replication partners* to exchange its database contents with:

- a server can be configured to be a *pull partner*, or a *push partner*, or both, of another server
- an individual replication occurs in a single direction only:
  - a push partner sends updates about its own database to another server
  - a pull partner receives updates from another server

  so that if A is pushing, and B is pulling, B finds out about all modifications to A's database, but A doesn't learn anything about B's. To make sure that A stays in synch with B and vice versa, you have to define two replications:

  i. A pushes to B, B pulls from A
  ii. B pushes to A, A pulls from B

- you specify how often each replication is to take place, e.g. replications between servers on the same site might happen frequently (every ten minutes or so) whereas between sites on different continents, much less frequent replication would probably be fine.

Replication explains why WINS Manager's **Mappings > Show Database** has the option **Show Only Mappings from Selected Owner**. It lets you hide entries that a server has obtained by replication from other servers, so you can see which registrations this server has handled itself.

19.7 Method 3: using the DNS as NetBIOS name server instead of using WINS

If you use WINS for the Windows PCs on your network and DNS for your Linux and other machines, you are running two separate systems, doubling your system management and maintenance load. Wouldn't it be nice to run only one and avoid all the extra work? You can't use WINS for non-Windows systems generally, but you *can* use DNS to resolve NetBIOS names, and in a suitably configured network this lets you avoid running WINS.

To use DNS for NetBIOS name resolution, set **Control Panel > Network > Protocols > TCP/IP > WINS Address > Enable DNS for Windows Resolution** = YES (Figure 19.10).

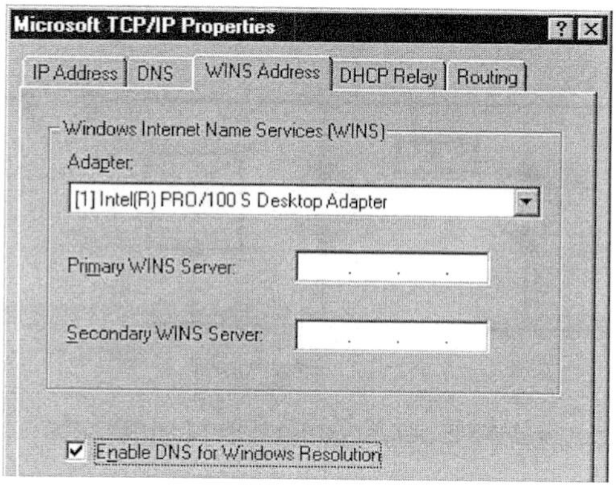

Figure 19.10 Enabling DNS for Windows name resolution

When the client wants to resolve a NetBIOS name, **frednt** say, it sends a normal DNS query to its configured DNS server. If the DNS lookup is successful, the client uses the returned IP number.

> **Warning:** don't forget to configure the DNS settings on this client so that it knows which DNS server to contact. If you haven't configured (enabled) DNS on this client, ticking **Enable DNS for Windows Resolution** will have no effect.

There are several points to note about this resolution method:

1. assuming your DNS client is configured normally, with either the DNS **domain** defined or a **Domain Suffix Search Order** specified, the DNS queries will be for names like, for example, **frednt.example.com** and **frednt.sales.example.com**; any 16th-byte suffix in the NetBIOS name is ignored, and the part of the name after the first dot is irrelevant – any old DNS domain name will do. If *any* lookup succeeds, the NetBIOS resolution succeeds and uses the IP number returned in the DNS reply

2. when DNS successfully resolves a name for NetBIOS, the DNS result is cached, which is not what you're used to with DNS. Unfortunately Windows-NT 4.0 doesn't give you any way to look at this cache or to clear it out (although Windows-2000 does – use **ipconfig/displaydns**) and diagnosing what's happening isn't easy. The result is kept in

the cache for the time-to-live (TTL) duration returned in the DNS result, which is
often 24 hours.

The trace below shows a **host** program lookup on Linux, showing that the TTL for
hostname **badxxx** is 60 seconds. The hostname exists but the host doesn't, deliberately.

```
alice% host -v badxxx.example.com
Query about badxxx.example.com for record types A
Query done, 1 answer, authoritative status: no error
badxxx.example.com     60      IN      A       192.0.2.5
. . .
```

Now from a Windows PC, Dave, we try to view the shared resources on **badxxx**, using
the command "**net view \\badxxx.**" The trace for this is shown below, lines 1–11. We
repeated the command after about 20 seconds; we see the DNS query is not repeated
(lines 15–19). Finally, after about 80 seconds we tried again. This time (lines 23–29)
the DNS lookup is issued, as expected, because we've exceeded the TTL and the entry
has been removed from the cache.

The **ping** requests are generated automatically by the resolution system on Dave.
(We've filtered out ARPs and several other packets where Dave unsuccessfully sends a
NetBIOS query to **badxxx** for a list of its resources.)

No.	Time	Source	Destination	Protocol	Info	
1	0.00	dave	192.0.2.127	NBNS	Name query NB BADXXX	<20>
2	0.74	dave	192.0.2.127	NBNS	Name query NB BADXXX	<20>
3	1.49	dave	192.0.2.127	NBNS	Name query NB BADXXX	<20>
6	2.24	dave	carol	DNS	Standard query A badxxx.example.com	
7	2.25	carol	dave	DNS	Standard query response A 192.0.2.5	
10	2.25	dave	192.0.2.5	ICMP	Echo (ping) request	
11	4.27	dave	192.0.2.5	ICMP	Echo (ping) request	
15	23.7	dave	192.0.2.127	NBNS	Name query NB BADXXX	<20>
16	24.4	dave	192.0.2.127	NBNS	Name query NB BADXXX	<20>
17	25.2	dave	192.0.2.127	NBNS	Name query NB BADXXX	<20>
18	25.9	dave	192.0.2.5	ICMP	Echo (ping) request	
19	28.3	dave	192.0.2.5	ICMP	Echo (ping) request	
23	79.2	dave	192.0.2.127	NBNS	Name query NB BADXXX	<20>
24	79.9	dave	192.0.2.127	NBNS	Name query NB BADXXX	<20>
25	80.7	dave	192.0.2.127	NBNS	Name query NB BADXXX	<20>
26	81.4	dave	carol	DNS	Standard query A badxxx.example.com	
27	81.4	carol	dave	DNS	Standard query response A 192.0.2.5	
28	81.4	dave	192.0.2.5	ICMP	Echo (ping) request	
29	83.9	dave	192.0.2.5	ICMP	Echo (ping) request	

3. don't confuse this with the normal DNS lookup that Windows TCP/IP programs such
   as **ping** and **telnet** perform. Here we're talking about resolving NetBIOS names.
   Windows treats NetBIOS names and DNS names differently. (In practice you rarely
   have to worry about this distinction, but we explain it in more detail in Appendix 22.)

19.8 Methods 4, 6: HOSTS files and NetBIOS cache

Method 4: HOSTS – the TCP/IP hosts file

The **hosts** file is common to TCP/IP implementations on just about every platform. As we mentioned in Module 8.1, it predated the DNS, and originally held the names and IP addresses for all the hosts on the Internet. Nowadays it just contains a set of local hosts and hosts of special local interest, and is really of use only if you don't use DNS at all, or for testing.

The **hosts** file is located in "**C:\WINNT\system32\drivers\etc\Hosts**"; note that it has no filename extension.

> **Tip**: make sure your Windows Explorer options (menu **View > Options > View**) are configured to **Show all files** and **Hide file extensions for known file types** = No, so that you can see exactly what the filename is.

The format of the file is

 IP-number   tab/spaces   hostname

e.g.

 192.0.2.54   alice   # this is a Linux server

You can enter comments by preceding them with a "**#**".

The **hosts** file is enabled for NetBIOS name resolution only if **Enable DNS for Windows Resolution** = YES. However, we recommend you don't enter anything in the file apart from the default entry, which maps the name **localhost** to **127.0.0.1**, and otherwise don't use the file at all – it only confuses things (e.g. if you have a name in **Hosts**, when you try to resolve that name, the value from **Hosts** is used in preference to DNS or WINS or broadcast name resolution, which is almost certainly not what you want).

You can't disable **hosts** for DNS name resolution.

Method 6: the NetBIOS name cache

(We cover this topic out of order – i.e. before the **LMHOSTS** file – because **LMHOSTS** interacts with the cache, and we'll need the cache manipulation tools when we cover **LMHOSTS**.)

When NetBIOS has resolved a name, it keeps a record of the name and its IP address in its internal *NetBIOS name cache* for a certain amount of time. When NetBIOS next comes to resolve a name, it first checks the cache, and if the name is in there it uses the cached value. This reduces the name resolution traffic on the network and the load on WINS servers.

When a name is entered in the cache, its *lifetime* is set to 11 minutes. (NT's internal setting says ten minutes, but a bug causes an extra minute to be added.) After that time has elapsed, it's removed from the cache, and if the name has to be resolved again, NetBIOS will have to resort to WINS or broadcasts again.

You can manipulate the contents of the cache using the **nbtstat** ("NBT status") command:

view the cache	nbtstat -c
clear (Reload) the cache	nbtstat -R
show resolution statistics	nbtstat -r

Clearing the cache is called "reloading" because it also causes any static entries defined in the LMHOSTS file (see next module) to be reloaded.

Figure 19.11 illustrates the cache in operation. First, we look at the starting state of the cache: it has two entries. Then we **ping** BOBNT (which we know is a NetBIOS name – because we didn't enter it in the DNS.) Looking at the cache again immediately, we see BOBNT is now present, with a lifetime of 660 s (11 minutes). Some time later we look at the cache again, and see that the lifetime of all the entries has decreased by a minute.

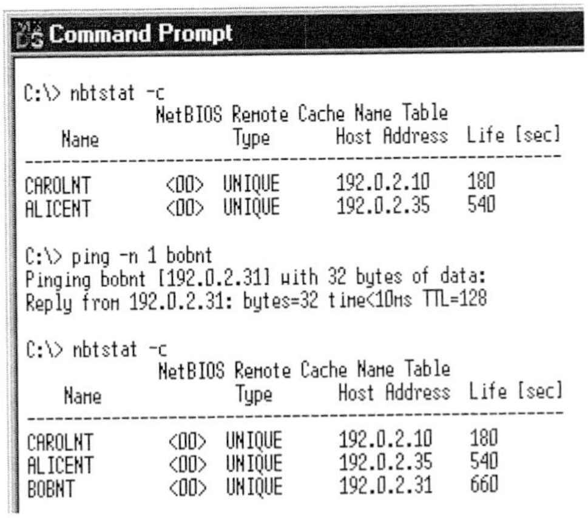

Figure 19.11 The NetBIOS name cache in operation

Note that **nbtstat** doesn't show names resolved using DNS, even though NetBIOS does cache DNS lookup results.

19.9 Method 5: LMHOSTS – the LAN Manager hosts file

This module describes only the syntax of the LMHOSTS file, not the purpose of the entries. Later on when you need to configure this file, we'll explain exactly what entries to make.

The **Lmhosts** file is the LAN Manager (NetBIOS) analog of the **hosts** file and is conceptually similar – it provides static mappings of names to IP numbers. However, it is separate from **hosts** because it's used only by NetBIOS and also provides extra functionality, as we'll see below.

Lmhosts is useful where you are not running WINS and need to contact NetBIOS PCs that are not on your local wire, e.g. on a large LAN with routers, or over the Internet, especially where you are using VPNs (Chapter 27).

Lmhosts is located in "**C:\WINNT\system32\drivers\etc\Lmhosts**"; again note that it has no filename extension.

> **Warning**: make sure your Windows Explorer does *not* **Hide file extensions for known file types**. NT ships with a sample file called **Lmhosts.sam**; if you can't see the file extensions, you might think this file is **Lmhosts**. (Not doing this cost someone a lot of work – they thought their **Lmhosts** file was active, and spent days debugging a non-existent problem with their network.)

You control whether **Lmhosts** is to be used in name resolution using **Control Panel > Network > Protocols > TCP/IP > WINS Addresses**:

- activate **Lmhosts: Enable LMHOSTS lookup** = YES (reboot needed)
- if you have a file somewhere else containing **Lmhosts** entries and you want this to *overwrite* your existing **Lmhosts** file (if any), click on **Import LMHOSTS** and follow the dialog.

The format of the file is similar to **hosts**, but after the hostname you can optionally enter a 16th-byte NetBIOS suffix, and/or extra "keywords" to control how this line is to be interpreted. Comments can be entered by preceding them with a "**#**"; the special keywords are also preceded with a "**#**", so that old versions of software that don't understand the keywords view them as comments and ignore them.

Let's look at a typical example. We want to specify that machine **CAROLNT** is the domain controller for our domain **EX-NTD**:

```
192.0.2.66 CAROLNT #DOM:EX-NTD                          only half-correct
```

The "**#DOM**" keyword is followed by a colon and the domain name says this is the domain controller. By default, **LMHOSTS** is read *every time* WINS or DNS or broadcast resolution fails, which is inefficient for entries like domain controllers, which are needed often. You can append another keyword, "**#PRE,**" which "preloads" the entry into NetBIOS's internal cache of names; at resolution time, if the name is in the cache, NetBIOS doesn't have to read **LMHOSTS**, which speeds things up considerably. Thus our domain controller line is:

```
192.0.2.66 CAROLNT #PRE #DOM:EX-NTD                          correct
```

You can force NetBIOS to re-read the file using "**nbtstat -R**" (re-load) and check that the file has been processed correctly using **nbtstat**'s "**-c**" option (Figure 19.12).

Notice the entries that have been created for 192.0.2.66:

- <00>: its PC name is **CAROLNT**
- <20>: this name is used to contract **CAROLNT**'s Server Service, i.e. if you want to share files on Carol

**Figure 19.12
nbstat's "-c"
option**

```
  Command Prompt                                      _ □
 C:\> nbtstat -c
                  NetBIOS Remote Cache Name Table
          Name          Type     Host Address    Life [sec]
       -------------------------------------------------------
       CAROLNT      <03> UNIQUE    192.0.2.66        -1
       CAROLNT      <00> UNIQUE    192.0.2.66        -1
       CAROLNT      <20> UNIQUE    192.0.2.66        -1
       EX-NTD       <1C> GROUP     192.0.2.66        -1
```

- <03>: **CAROLNT**'s Messenger Service, i.e. if you want to send messages or alerts to Carol, e.g. using **net send**.

All the above are unique NetBIOS names. A fourth, group entry has been created, saying that 192.0.2.66 is part of the **EX-NTD<1C>** group, i.e. that 192.0.2.66 is a domain controller for domain **EX-NTD**.

The lifetime of -1 shows that the entries are pre-loaded and will remain in the cache until the PC shuts down.

If you don't enter an explicit 16th-byte suffix, NetBIOS creates the three entries listed above, i.e. <00>, <03>, and <20>. To explicitly enter a 16th-byte suffix, enter the name in double quotes, pad it out with spaces to 15 bytes long, and then insert the suffix using the C programming language notation \0x*HH* where *HH* is the two-hexadecimal-digit value. For example, to specify another domain controller for **EX-NTD**, you might use the line

```
192.0.2.68 "EX-NTD████████\0x1c" #PRE
```

where ■ is a space.

Tip: to make it easy to see that you have the correct number of spaces, enter on the preceding line the comment shown below:

```
#          123456789 123456
192.0.2.68   "EX-NTD       \0x1c"  #PRE
```

Tip: after editing **LMHOSTS**, always reload and check the name cache using **nbtstat -R** to make sure the changes you made are correct.

Tip: put all #PRE entries at the bottom of **Lmhosts** and remove all the standard comments. The #PRE entries need to be read only once, so the effort of reading to the bottom of the file once is a tiny overhead. On the other hand, other name resolutions that read the file don't have to process these entries before they get to the entries they really want, so it speeds up all other name resolutions that use **LMHOSTS**. (However, in most cases, the only entries in the file are #PRE entries, in which case it doesn't matter.)

Tip: use uppercase for all machine and domain names in **Lmhosts**. There have been bugs where entries were processed case-sensitively.

19.10 "Node type" and NetBIOS name resolution order

A PC's configuration determines which resolution methods it uses, and in which order. There are four different configurations, and these are given special names. (We've never found these names helpful. It's hard to find out exactly what each does, and the names are not very descriptive. However, we have no choice but to use the standard names). Almost always your machine will be configured as one of the first two types:

b-node   "broadcast:" uses broadcasts and doesn't use WINS at all

h-node   "hybrid:" tries WINS first, and if that fails tries broadcasts.

The other, less frequently met types are:

p-node   "point-to-point:" contact WINS server directly (using unicast UDP) and doesn't use broadcasts at all

m-node   "mixed:" tries broadcast first, and if that fails tries WINS.

All the types also use the NetBIOS name cache and **hosts** file, and may use **LMHOSTS** and/or DNS if they have been enabled. The table below shows the order in which the different methods are attempted. We'll explain the effects of the different node types, and why you'd choose one instead of another, in the next module.

	H-node	**P-node**	**M-node**	**B-node**
first	NetBIOS name cache			
	WINS	WINS	broadcast	broadcast
	broadcast		WINS	
	LMHOSTS file (*if enabled*)			
	hosts file			
last	DNS (*if enabled*)			

ipconfig/all (below) and **wntipcfg > More info** show your node type (which applies to the whole machine, not to an individual network adapter).

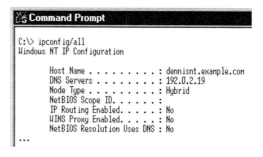

```
C:\> ipconfig/all
Windows NT IP Configuration

        Host Name . . . . . . . . . : dennisnt.example.com
        DNS Servers . . . . . . . . : 192.0.2.19
        Node Type . . . . . . . . . : Hybrid
        NetBIOS Scope ID. . . . . . :
        IP Routing Enabled. . . . . : No
        WINS Proxy Enabled. . . . . : No
        NetBIOS Resolution Uses DNS : No
...
```

Warning: there is an added complication to all this. In different circumstances Windows sometimes regards a name either as a NetBIOS name or as a DNS name. The order above applies to NetBIOS names; for details of DNS name resolution order, see Appendix 22. (See also the note on NetBIOS v. "real" TCP/IP programs, Module 18.3.)

How to specify which resolution methods to use

Windows-NT defaults to B-node. If you enable WINS, the type is set to H instead.
To use something other than B or H types, you have to set the node type explicitly, either by using DHCP or by editing the Windows Registry (see Notes).

Verifying name resolution order

You can easily use **tcpdump** or **ethereal** to check what's happening on the wire by running the command **net view badxxx** on Dave, where the name **badxxx** isn't configured anywhere, so the PC will try in turn every resolution method it's configured to use. The figures below show what happens:

a. on B-node (i.e. no WINS)

b. on H-node (i.e. WINS server **bob** specified) but no DNS server numbers configured

c. on H-node, with DNS configured to use server Carol, and **Control Panel > Network > Protocols > TCP/IP > Properties > WINS > Enable DNS for Windows Resolution** = YES.

(We use **net use badxxx** instead of **ping badxxx** because of the difference between DNS and NetBIOS names mentioned above.)

(a)

Time	Source	Destination	Protocol	Info
0.00	dave	192.0.2.127	NBNS	Name query NB BADXXX
0.74	dave	192.0.2.127	NBNS	Name query NB BADXXX
1.49	dave	192.0.2.127	NBNS	Name query NB BADXXX

(b)

0.00	dave	bob	NBNS	Name query NB BADXXX
0.00	bob	dave	NBNS	Name query response
0.00	dave	bob	NBNS	Name query NB BADXXX
0.00	bob	dave	NBNS	Name query response
0.00	dave	192.0.2.127	NBNS	Name query NB BADXXX
0.74	dave	192.0.2.127	NBNS	Name query NB BADXXX
1.49	dave	192.0.2.127	NBNS	Name query NB BADXXX

(c)

0.00	dave	bob	NBNS	Name query NB BADXXX	<20>
0.00	bob	dave	NBNS	Name query response	
0.00	dave	bob	NBNS	Name query NB BADXXX	<20>
0.00	bob	dave	NBNS	Name query response	
0.00	dave	192.0.2.127	NBNS	Name query NB BADXXX	<20>
0.74	dave	192.0.2.127	NBNS	Name query NB BADXXX	<20>
1.49	dave	192.0.2.127	NBNS	Name query NB BADXXX	<20>
2.25	dave	carol	DNS	Standard query A badxxx.example.com	
2.30	carol	dave	DNS	Standard query response, Name error	
2.30	dave	carol	DNS	Standard query A badxxx.sales.example.com	
2.36	carol	dave	DNS	Standard query response, Name error	

As an exercise use **ping** instead of **net use** and see whether the order is different. Change your node type to M and see the effect.

19.11 Choosing a node type

What are all the different node types for, and why would you choose one instead of another? The answers to these questions involve the evolutionary history of Windows Networking, and how nodes are typically deployed.

First of all, the four node types represent all possible permutations of WINS and broadcasting. The P, M, and B types were defined in RFC1001. The H type was defined with the advent of Windows-NT. (You will sometimes see references to, for example, "modified B-node." This just means that this version of the software can handle **Lmhosts/hosts** files too, although that behavior isn't defined in RFC-1001. All recent Windows systems are "modified.")

B-node

B-nodes (broadcast only) are suitable for a small network:

- without any WINS servers
- without any routers (except perhaps a router connecting to the Internet).

We say "small" because using broadcast only on a network with a large number of machines will affect performance badly.

However, if this network connects to Windows machines at other, remote sites via the Internet, another node type might be better (although we'll see in Module 22.2 that using **Lmhosts** might be adequate for a network of this type).

H-node

H-nodes use WINS first, and fall back to broadcasts if WINS fails to resolve the name.

The node type defaults to B-node but if you enable WINS the type changes to H-node, so in practice, most nodes are either B or H. This works well for a typical installation:

- when the network is small and WINS isn't in use, all the nodes are B, and Windows Networking works well without any specialized configuration. This is ideal, because many small networks don't have a specialized network manager to configure anything more elaborate

- as the network grows, a WINS server or two is introduced, and the clients nodes are configured to use it, making them change from B-node to H-node. WINS is used in preference to broadcasts, so operation is efficient as long as the WINS servers are running properly. If there is a problem with WINS, or a new PC is introduced and WINS hasn't been enabled ("Oops, I forgot"), broadcasts still work and the network continues to run OK.

P-node

P-nodes use WINS only. They are suitable for networks where WINS is installed and is running well. If WINS can't resolve the name, the resolution fails, and broadcasts are never used. This means the user gets a message saying the name is invalid much more quickly, without having to wait for several broadcasts to go unanswered.

M-node

This is the most rarely used node type. It broadcasts first, and only if that fails does it try WINS. It's suited to a network where most of the name resolutions will be handled successfully by local broadcasts, but some others will need to be passed to a WINS server. Examples of such a network are:

- a self-contained workgroup within a larger office. This workgroup might be on its own LAN segment connected to the main office via a router (Figure 19.13). Most of the network traffic stays within the workgroup, but occasionally the users need to access resources on the main network, e.g. file servers or printers, and they use WINS to resolve the names of these resources

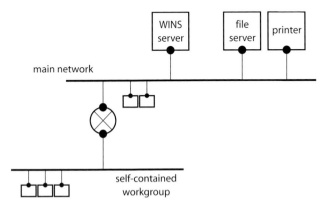

Figure 19.13 Using M-node for a self-contained workgroup

- a self-contained network at a small office that occasionally needs to connect over the Internet to Windows machines at the head office or other branches. WINS isn't used locally – perhaps because there are only a few machines and a printer or two. However, the machines do use the domain controller at head office to control access, and they occasionally need to access file servers or other resources at head office too. (This is almost a special case of the first example.)

Occasionally, Microsoft recommends you use M-node type to solve certain logon problems (see Notes).

RFC-1001 recommends you don't mix B-nodes with M- or P-nodes. Where some nodes are registered by broadcast and others with a WINS server, you could end up with different and inconsistent views of your network when you come to browsing (Chapter 21).

19.12 Troubleshooting NetBIOS name resolution

The hardest thing with NetBIOS name resolution is understanding what it's supposed to be doing, i.e. knowing what is correct behavior and what isn't. That's what the earlier part of this chapter was about.

Next, remember that name resolution and browsing the network (Chapter 21) are different. Browsing uses its own servers ("browse masters") that accumulate a list of the network resources, and return this (the "browse list") to clients that request it, e.g. in Windows Explorer or **net view**. Browsing does call on name resolution to locate the browse masters but otherwise is completely separate.

Finally, remember that name resolution is only one phase of a network operation – resolving a name to an IP number. If connecting to a share on another PC fails, it may be that the name is resolving correctly and the problem lies in the connect-to-share operation. (Just like not being able to retrieve a Web page from a dead server: DNS is resolving successfully, for example, **www.example.com**, but the Web server at that address isn't responding.) So it's important to recognize what name resolution is doing, and to separate out its function from the other components of Windows Networking. As usual, to do this we rely heavily on **tcpdump** (or **ethereal** or Netmon), looking for name resolution traffic on the wire.

Warning: a PC's node type determines how this PC *resolves* names; it does *not* affect how this PC *answers* name queries. (This can be confusing if you're solving a network problem under pressure). In particular, if my node type is H and WINS is running, I will always register names on WINS, but if you send a broadcast name query for my name, I'll see it on the network and reply to you, giving you my IP number.

Tip: the best sniffer for this type of work is **ethereal**: it shows NetBIOS traffic clearly and it can collect packets in promiscuous mode, so you don't have to install it on the PC you're investigating (Alice, say) which might be possible. More importantly, you can capture promiscuously and see the whole picture from one place whereas Netmon can only see traffic to and from Alice: if Alice is using broadcasts and there's a WINS proxy on the network, Network Monitor won't show you the traffic between the WINS proxy and the WINS server. **tcpdump**'s display of Windows Networking traffic is horrible and verbose; we only use it to confirm traffic flow but never to examine the content of the traffic.

Troubleshooting tips for name resolution

As with everything so far, our approach is to understand what ought to be happening, and then trace each step of the network conversation with a sniffer. When something happens that isn't what you expect, you have a pointer to where the problem is. To verify that name resolution is working correctly, especially if you're not familiar with Windows Networking, you have to work slowly and methodically. The first step is to find out exactly what's happening on your network.

Let's say your PC is Alice and you want to resolve the name **bobnt**:

1. collect all the relevant configuration details for your PC. We've included a worksheet for this in Appendix 23, which you can photocopy

2. from the table in Appendix 23, write down the order of name resolution steps that this node type uses

3. print listings of **Lmhosts** and **hosts** files

4. run your chosen sniffer on Alice or at some point where it can see all the relevant traffic

5. on Alice, you now want to force two name resolutions:

   i. a name that doesn't exist anywhere, to exercise each name resolution method. We use the name **badxxx**.

   ii. the name that you're investigating (**bobnt** in our example)

   First run the command

   ```
   nbtstat -a badxxx
   ```

   When the resolution is finished (successful or failed), note the last packet shown in your sniffer, and then run

   ```
   nbtstat -a bobnt
   ```

6. when the resolution is finished, clear the NetBIOS cache and run the command again, and when that resolution is finished, stop your sniffer.

   ```
   nbtstat -R
   nbtstat -a bobnt
   ```

If the name you're testing is a real one, remember that it may be in the NetBIOS name cache; if it is, it will be resolved, but you'll see no packets on the wire.

(If the application causing your name resolution problem is a "real" TCP/IP program and not a NetBIOS program, use **ping** instead of **net view**. True-blue TCP/IP programs use DNS-names instead of NetBIOS names, so the resolution order is different – see Appendix 22.)

Here are some specific points that often cause problems:

1. if you're using an **Lmhosts** file:

   • don't forget to include #PRE or you won't see the entry in **nbtstat -c**

   • don't forget to run **nbtstat -R** (not -r) to force the file to be reloaded

   • always use uppercase for host and domain names, and keywords like #PRE and #DOM

2. if you have different netmasks on PCs on the same LAN segment, their sub-net broadcast addresses will be different, so they won't hear each others' broadcasts and B-node and similar resolution will fail. See also the Warning regarding broadcast addresses in Chapter 4's Notes.

3. remember, there is a difference in resolution order between DNS names and NetBIOS names (see Appendix 22)

4. if you are running any other protocol in addition to TCP/IP (e.g. running NetBEUI or Novell) they may interfere with name resolution and make it much more complicated. Don't run any protocols that aren't essential

5. if you're using Samba, its **nmblookup** tool (Module 22.4) gives you much more precise control, and more feedback, than NT's **nbtstat** over how the test name query that you issue is resolved.

Summary

- Windows Networking uses names as its primary reference for machines and resources
- a NetBIOS name contains not just a machine or domain or username, but also a special suffix that specifies what type of resource this name refers to. There are individual names and two types of group names
- a machine registers a name when it is prepared to offer a particular type of resource. Registration can be done by broadcasting a "name claim" request on the local network, or by registering the name with a WINS server
- Windows Networking uses six different methods to resolve names that have been registered:
  1. broadcasts: this machine broadcasts a "name query" request and the owner of the name replies. Because this uses broadcast packets, it can only work on the local network segment
  2. WINS: this machine sends a name resolution request to a WINS server. The server replies with the resolution details. This uses only unicast UDP packets so it can work over a WAN or the Internet. You can run multiple WINS servers for resilience and performance; you should configure the servers to replicate their databases to one another
  3. DNS: you can use the DNS to resolve NetBIOS names. This can give you a unified name resolution system for all your machines, not just Windows PCs
  4. the **hosts** file: don't use it
  5. the **Lmhosts** file: you can enter static entries, with their 16th-byte suffixes, in a machine's **Lmhosts** file. This is useful when you are running a network containing routers but are not using WINS, for testing, and for overcoming particular network problems
  6. the internal NetBIOS name cache. You can view the contents of the cache, or cause it to be cleared and re-load its static (**Lmhosts** file) entries with the **nbtstat** command
- a machine's NetBIOS node type determines which resolution methods are used and in which order
- the **nbtstat** command lets you view the names a particular machine has registered.

What's next?

The next chapter explains how you logon to a Windows-NT machine or to a Windows-NT "domain." We'll see that the logon mechanisms have to make use of the name resolution that we've just covered, to locate a logon server to authenticate your logon.

Notes and further reading

Name resolution is also called *name discovery*. We don't use that term because we find it confusing: the name is already known and it's the address that has to be discovered.

See the Notes in Chapter 18 for general references on Microsoft Windows Networking. RFC-1001 in particular gives an excellent and readable explanation of how NetBIOS name resolution works using broadcasts and also using a WINS-like name server. The Resource Kit *Networking Guide* is also good, but takes too much for granted. The Samba documents give good insights into name resolution, in particular:

❑ **NetBIOS.txt** *Definition of NetBIOS Protocol and Name Resolution Modes* in the Samba distribution or at

❑ **http://www.samba.org/samba/ftp/docs/textdocs/NetBIOS.txt**

We've ignored NetBIOS *scope* completely. It's a way to have separate NetBIOS "universes" on the same wire; machines with one NetBIOS scope can't communicate (and can't even "see") machines with a different scope. Microsoft recommend that you don't use it.

The resource kit contains three useful tools. We already mentioned **winsdmp** and **winscl** in Module 19.5. The third is **winschk**, which checks out your WINS configuration. It lets you verify that specified names are in specific WINS databases, check that your WINS replication configuration is OK, and continually monitor for WINS replication communications failures.

NetBIOS name types

❑ **MS-KB-Q119495** *List of Names Registered with WINS Service*

❑ **MS-KB-Q314104** *A List of Names That Are Registered by Windows Internet Naming Service*

The following is a much longer list:

❑ **MS-KB-Q163409** *NetBIOS Suffixes (16th Character of the NetBIOS Name)*

For an explanation of "normal group" versus "Internet group," see:

❑ **MS-KB-Q140064** *WINS Static Entry Descriptions*

❑ **WINS Manager Help**, search for **Using Type Options** and view the link **Internet Group Type**

We have concentrated on computer and domain names in this chapter, but usernames are also registered in NetBIOS, as *username<03>*. This lets Windows send a message or alert to a particular user very easily. *username<03>* resolves to the IP number of the computer that *username* is logged onto, so Windows can send the message directly to that computer. Windows doesn't have to do an exhaustive search of each machine to see if the user is logged on there.

WINS architecture and implementation

Microsoft's white paper on WINS is very readable and informative:

❑ **ftp://ftp.microsoft.com/bussys/winnt/winnt-docs/papers/winswp.doc**

For information about running multiple WINS servers, how to estimate the load, and decide on the number and location of servers, and configuring database replication between them:

❑ **Resource Kit, Chapter 8**

WINS client configuration

❏ **MS-KB-Q150737** *Setting Primary and Secondary WINS Server Options*

❏ **MS-KB-Q173525** *WINS Client May Switch Primary and Secondary WINS Servers*

Multi-homed (i.e. with more than one IP address) WINS server can cause problems:

❏ **MS-KB-Q185786** *Recommended Practices for WINS*

The following article describes a problem you can have with WINS, although it's also interesting for the insight it gives on how WINS systems replicate:

❏ **MS-KB-Q168076** *WINS Fails to Converge*

WINS proxy agent

❏ **MS-KB-Q121004** *WINS Proxy Agent Functionality*

❏ **MS-KB-Q164765** *How to Enable WINS Proxy Agent in Windows NT 4.0*

❏ ftp://ftp.microsoft.com/bussys/winnt/winnt-docs/papers/tcpimp2.exe *Microsoft Windows NT 3.5/3.51/4.0: TCP/IP Implementation Details. TCP/IP Protocol Stack and Services, Version 2.0*

WINS database replication – "tombstoning" and "scavenging"

In Module 19.6 we explained that if you have multiple WINS servers, they replicate entries from one to another. You can explicitly delete an entry for a name on a WINS server, using **WINS Manager** (below). However, if the entry had previously been replicated to other servers, the entries on those servers will not be deleted. Worse, those servers may replicate

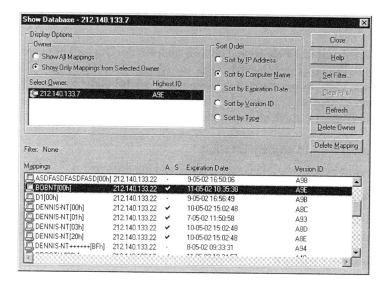

back to this server the entry you just deleted. To avoid this, instead of "deleting" the entry, you *tombstone* it. This marks it as extinct, so the server will never use the entry to reply to a NetBIOS name query from a client. However, the entry is not physically removed, but can be replicated in its tombstoned state to other servers, which in turn mark it as extinct. This prevents the deleted entry being replicated back to the original server and ensures that the entry is eventually marked as extinct on every WINS server on the network. When you attempt to remove an entry, WINS Manager will ask you whether you want to perform a simple delete or a tombstone.

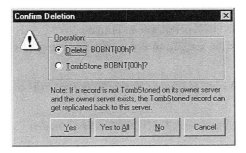

The WINS server automatically *scavenges* its database periodically, to physically remove extinct items that have been replicated across the whole network, so preventing the database growing forever.

NetBIOS name cache

❏ MS-KB-Q236901 *NetBIOS Remote Name Cache Time-Out Is 60 Seconds Off*

LMHOSTS file

Using **Lmhosts** is not resilient:

❏ MS-KB-Q163949 *Workstation Using LMHosts Fails to Logon if Domain Controller Unavailable*

See also the references for **Lmhosts** in the Notes for Chapter 20.

Node type and name resolution order

❏ MS-KB-Q160177 *Default Node Type for Microsoft Clients*

For a (relatively unlikely) example of when you might use an M-node type, see:

❏ MS-KB-Q181171 *Secure Channel Manipulation with TCP/IP*

To set the node type automatically, you can either configure the PC using DHCP, which has a setting for node type:

❏ MS-KB-Q121005 *DHCP Options Supported by Clients*

or you can write a small script:

❑ **MS-KB-Q167640** *Automatically Changing the Node Type of a Windows NT Workstation*

To set the node type manually, modify the Windows Registry key **NodeType**:

❑ **MS-KB-Q160177** *Default Node Type For Microsoft Clients*

The key is **HKEY_LOCAL_MACHINE\System\CurrentControlSet\Services\Netbt\Parameters\Node Type**; values 1, 2, 4, and 8 correspond to B-node, P-node, M-node, and H-node, respectively. You only need to do that if you want to set the type to P-node or M-node; NT defaults to B-node and enabling WINS changes the type to H-node.

You can also modify the resolution order without changing the node type, using the **ServiceProvider** Registry key:

❑ **MS-KB-Q139270** *How to Change Name Resolution Order on Windows 95 and Windows NT*

❑ **MS-KB-Q187709** *Windows NT 4.0 Domain Name Resolver Caches Responses Regardless of Registry Setting*

❑ **MS-KB-Q173941** *Windows NT DNR Does Not Cache Short Names*

❑ **MS-KB-Q171567** *Windows NT 4.0 ServiceProvider Priority Values Not Applied*

❑ **MS-KB-Q172218** *Microsoft TCP/IP Host Name Resolution Order* describes the difference between "host name resolution" (i.e. DNS name resolution) and NetBIOS-name resolution.

❑ **MS-KB-Q198550** *SP4 Changes DNS Name Resolution*

❑ **MS-KB-Q230744** *Windows NT 4.0 SP4 DNR Client Does Not Send Unqualified DNS Queries*

Module 19.7 explained that NetBIOS name resolution can use DNS. An added complication is that if you are running a Microsoft DNS server, you can configure the DNS server to look up WINS if the name to be resolved isn't found in the DNS. For more information see Web Appendix 26.

Appendices

Appendix 21: NetBIOS names and suffixes
Appendix 22: DNS and NetBIOS name resolution order in Windows
Appendix 23: Windows name resolution worksheet
Web Appendix 25: Summary of WIN SCL.EXE commands
Web Appendix 26: Microsoft DNS can use WINS

20 Windows Networking – logon and domains

Introduction

This chapter explains how Windows Networking uses "domains" to control user logons and access to resources, and how in logging on to the domain your PC interacts over the network with a "domain controller," which performs the actual validation of your logon.

We cover these topics in a lot of detail – certainly more than you need in day-to-day operations, (a) because it's hard to get this information elsewhere, and (b) so that when something goes wrong you can understand what the error messages really mean and use an intelligent approach in resolving your problem. You can skip Modules 20.5–20.10 on first reading if you wish.

20.1 Overview of NT domains and security

What we cover in this chapter

- what a domain is and how Windows-NT security is based on it
- what happens when you press Ctrl-Alt-Del to get the logon dialog
- the components of the system that are involved in logon, etc.
- local login, where the user is logging on to the domain controller machine itself, or is logging on to a machine itself rather than to the domain
- how passwords are stored securely
- network logon:

  1. locating a DC to handle the logon, e.g. where I'm logging on at my desktop PC, and the logon has to be validated by a DC
  2. sending the password securely to the remote DC

- how logon ties in with control of access to network resources.

In other words, we're concerned with how you *authenticate* yourself to the system (prove you are who you say you are) and when you have authenticated, how the system *authorizes* you to access specific resources but not others.

What a domain is

- an NT domain has no connection whatsoever with a domain in the DNS sense of the word; we'll use the term "NT domain" to avoid ambiguity where necessary
- an NT *domain* is a number of computers using the security mechanisms and sharing a common database of usernames, passwords, and (some) access-control information
- NT domains provide centralized security management. You can think of the domain as a single entity from the security point of view: a user has a single account, and they logon to the domain, not to an individual computer. They can logon from any computer in the domain (unless the administrator specified otherwise.)
- a domain provides *single sign-on*. Having logged on to your account, your logon information is obviously used to control what resources on the local machine you can access, and how. But the logon information is also used automatically when you use resources on other computers in this domain, without you having to logon again. To handle this, the domain's security database contains details of all your access rights, in addition to your username and password, of course
- the PCs in a domain don't have to be physically adjacent – they can be spread over a WAN, e.g. on an organization's global network with many branches in different countries. (The reverse of this is that you can have multiple domains on the same wire. This isn't usual, but may be needed for testing or when two separate companies occupy the same office, perhaps after a merger or before a split.)

Before NT domains were invented – and even today, if you don't use domains – a group of PCs running Microsoft Windows Networking form (or belong to) a "workgroup:" each computer is standalone and manages its own security information; they just share a common network, and exchange information about which public resources (shares, printers) they office. You specify whether your NT machine is a member of a domain or workgroup, and which one, when you install the operating system on your machine. The domain or workgroup name is shown in **Control Panel > Network > Identification** (Figure 20.1). The **Change** button lets you alter these settings (Module 20.5).

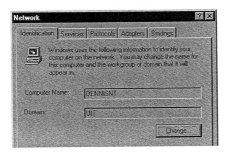

Figure 20.1 Setting your PC's NT-domain name

Domain controllers

A machine that holds and manages the security database for an NT domain is called a *domain controller* (DC). For reasons of performance and resilience, there can be more than one DC; depending on the size of your network, you might have one per LAN, or per network segment, or even more than one per LAN if you are running a multi-branch network (Figure 20.2). However, there is only one DC that holds the authoritative version of the database, and this is called the *primary domain controller (PDC)*; the others are called *backup domain controllers (BDCs)*. Module 20.12 covers domain controllers in more detail.

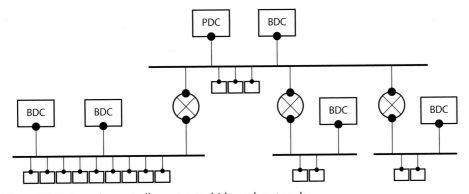

Figure 20.2 Domain controllers on a multi-branch network

20.2 The logon prompt and local and network logons

1. when Windows-NT boots, its starts a *logon process* called **WinLogon**. **WinLogon** takes control of the keyboard, so that no Trojan-horse programs can intercept what you type and steal your username and password. Then **WinLogon** waits until …

2. you type Ctrl-Alt-Del (the *secure attention sequence* or *SAS*). **WinLogon** brings up the NT logon window (Figure 20.3).

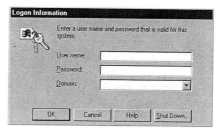

Figure 20.3 Windows-NT logon window

3. you enter your name, password, and domain
4. the logon process, **WinLogon**, passes the details entered to the rest of the security sub-system for validation (Figure 20.4).

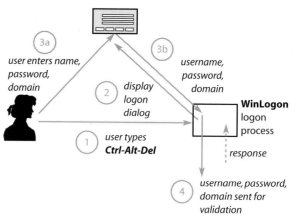

Figure 20.4 Validation process

5a. if you're logging on to the local machine (Figure 20.5), the security sub-system compares the username and password you entered with those in its security database, and allows or rejects the logon accordingly.

5b. if you're logging on to the domain, the mechanism used is much more complicated (Figure 20.6). The **Netlogon** process on your local PC sets up a secure communications channel with a domain controller and transmits the logon details to the domain controller for validation

6. if the details you entered agree with the database, the login is authorized, **WinLogon** is informed, and it creates your normal desktop. If your details are not correct, you get a message (Figure 20.7) and the logon window remains on screen for you to try again.

In the following modules we look at each of the above steps in more detail.

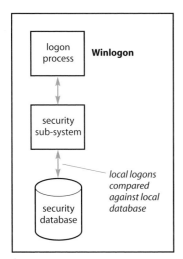

Figure 20.5 Logging on to the local machine

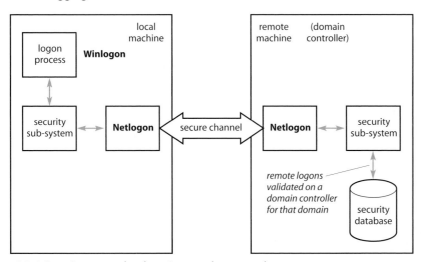

Figure 20.6 Logging on to the domain over the network

Figure 20.7
Logon message

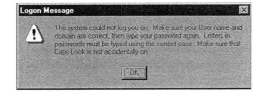

20.3 Local logon. Encrypting the password

In this module we concentrate on local logon – where you're logging on to the machine you're sitting at. This occurs in two situations:

- the PC is a domain controller (DC) for the domain that you're logging on to, e.g. you entered **EX-NTD** in the logon Window's **Domain** field, and this PC is a DC for **EX-NTD**
- you aren't logging on to a domain, but just to the local machine. You'd do this for one of two reasons:
  i. this PC is not part of a domain, i.e. NT was installed on this PC as a "standalone server"
  ii. you want to logon to the local machine itself rather than the domain it belongs to, e.g. if your PC is **BOBNT** and it has been installed on a member of the **EX-NTD** domain, when you're logging on, the **Domain** pull-down menu includes **BOBNT** as one of the available "domains", so that you can logon locally.

     Even if you normally logon to a domain, you can always logon locally instead. Indeed, it's essential to be able to do this, in case a network configuration problem is preventing your PC communicating with its DC; you must fix the configuration problem before you can logon to the domain, so you logon locally to reconfigure. (Often you will be able to use "cached credentials" – see Module 20.5 – to logon to the domain even when there is a problem; however there are circumstances where this isn't an option and local logon is essential.)

What happens for a local logon is:

1. **WinLogon** has received the logon details you entered, as described in the previous module
2. **WinLogon** passes the logon details and the name of the *authentication package* that is to be used for validation to the rest of the security subsystem for validation (Figure 20.8). It is the *Local Security Authority (LSA)* component of the security sub-system that manages the rest of the logon. (You can see the LSA running as the process **LSASS.EXE** in NT's Task Manager.)

   An authentication package is specified because NT allows different packages to be used for different purposes. For example, authentication systems based on fingerprints, or a retina scan, or a smart-card reader would use their own logon process and a special, specific authentication package. The default package used by **WinLogon** is *MSV1_0*, Microsoft Authentication Package V1_0 (and it's the only one we cover).

3. the LSA passes the logon details to the specified authentication package, MSV1_0 in this case

4. MSV1_0 is divided into two parts:
   - the top half first encrypts the password (see below). Then it decides on the basis of the domain you specified whether this machine can validate the password, i.e. whether this is a local logon. Here we're assuming it is local. (We cover network logons in the next module.)
   - the *bottom half* contacts the *Security Account Manager (SAM)* on this machine, and requests this user's encrypted password, which is held in the security-information database, also known as the *SAM database*

5. if the encrypted password calculated by the top half matches the encrypted password
    retrieved from the SAM database, the LSA informs **WinLogon** that the login has
    succeeded, and **WinLogon** creates your normal desktop.

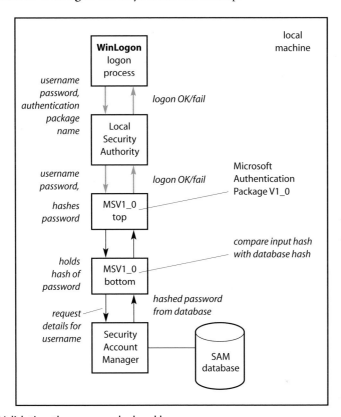

Figure 20.8 Validating the password – local logon

Encrypting ("hashing") the password

The Security Account Manager (SAM) manages the security database containing usernames,
passwords, and access rights. The SAM doesn't store the password "in clear" in its database;
instead, it stores an encrypted version, so even if an intruder steals the database file, they still can't
find out a user's password. (The same is true on Linux. Users' passwords are encrypted, and
stored in the **/etc/passwd** or **/etc/shadow** file; they are never stored in clear.) The encrypted version of the password, also called a *hashed version* or *hash*, is produced by encrypting a constant
using the clear-text password as key. This gives a fixed-length hash, which is stored in the SAM.
(The password itself isn't encrypted directly because the encrypted result would give a clue to the
length of the plaintext (unencrypted) password. The advantage of the hash, is that it's always the
same length, and therefore gives a potential cracker no information about the password length.)

In fact NT stores two versions of the password: a relatively weak hash that is compatible
with LAN Manager and older Microsoft Windows Networking versions such as Windows-95
and Windows-98, and a much stronger NT-only encrypted version (see Web Appendix 28).

20.4 Logon over the network – overview

In the previous module we saw that the top half of the MSV1_0 authentication package decides, on the basis of the domain name you specify in the logon window, whether a local or network logon is required. (The logon is local if the domain name you enter is the local computer's name, or if you're sitting at a domain controller machine for this domain and logging on to its domain.)

However, in most cases when you logon at a machine, it is a logon to the domain, and this machine doesn't itself validate the logon. Instead, it has to performs a *network logon*: it has to send the logon over the network to a domain controller for validation, because only domain controllers keep a copy of the security database. (For now we'll assume you're logging on to the domain that your PC belongs to. You can also logon at a PC to a different domain, as we explain in Module 20.9.)

Logon over the network involves the following steps:

1. when the PC you're sitting at PC boots up, it:
   a. locates a domain controller for its domain
   b. creates a "secure channel" to that domain controller and the PC (as distinct from any user) authenticates itself to the domain controller

   All this happens in the background, and you're not aware of it when it works properly. However, there can be occasional problems, so we explain the process in detail in Module 20.5. This step occurs only once, when the PC boots up, i.e. before the user logon itself occurs and even before the logon dialog box is presented.

You press Ctrl-Alt-Del to bring up the logon dialog and enter your username, password, and domain. Then:

2. your PC's **Netlogon** service:
   a. encrypts the username and password logon information
   b. sends the logon information over the secure channel (Figure 20.9.)

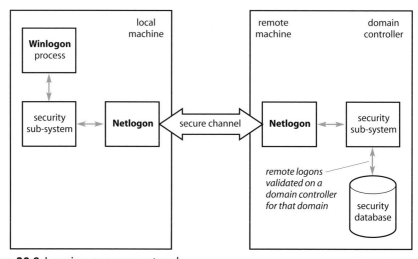

Figure 20.9 Logging on over a network

3. the domain controller checks to see if you entered the correct details and replies to your PC

4. your PC's **Netlogon** receives the OK/fail response from the domain controller and passes it up to **Winlogon**. **Winlogon** starts your desktop or re-issues the logon prompt as appropriate.

All fours steps are managed by the **Netlogon** NT Service, which is started when the machine is booted. Don't confuse **Netlogon** with **WinLogon**: **WinLogon** handles the initial Ctrl-Alt-Del dialog, whereas **Netlogon** handles communications between a local PC and a DC, and between DCs.

Tracing logon traffic on the network

You'll find that sniffing packets on the wire for network logon isn't easy, for a couple of reasons:

1. much of the logon traffic is encrypted, so even Microsoft's own Network Monitor isn't able to look into the packets and decode their contents

2. logons use the NetBIOS session service, where multiple NetBIOS sessions are multiplexed over a single TCP connection and even a new NetBIOS session may be created over an existing TCP connection. Consequently you can't necessarily use the normal SYN/SYN-ACK/ACK and FIN/ACK/FIN/ACK sequences to recognize the start and end of a session. We haven't used any NetBIOS connection-oriented (TCP) services before, so we have never met this problem. (All the NetBIOS name resolution and WINS traffic used the NetBIOS datagram service, i.e. UDP.)

But in spite of all that our tools are still helpful:

• Netmon analyzes Windows Networking traffic in more detail and more accurately than **ethereal**

• **ethereal** gives a reasonably detailed analysis of network logon traffic. (And it's under constant development and is improving all the time as more and more becomes known of the internal operation of Windows Networking.)

20.5 Logon over the network (1a) – "discover" a domain controller

Let's assume your PC is AliceNT, that AliceNT is a member of domain **EX-NTD**, and you're logging on to **EX-NTD** from AliceNT. AliceNT locates a domain controller for **EX-NTD** using a mechanism called "discovery." This uses the domain controller NetBIOS <1c> group-name – **EX-NTD<1c>** in our example. All DCs when they boot up register themselves as members of this group. When a PC issues a NetBIOS name query for this group, it receives in reply a list of (up to 25) names of machines that are members of this group.

1. if AliceNT uses WINS, she sends a directed name query to a WINS server for group **EX-NTD<1c>**; otherwise she broadcasts the name query.
   AliceNT receives a list of **EX-NTD**'s domain controllers in reply

2a. AliceNT broadcasts a **netlogon** request to *domainname*<1c>. (Note this is a logon request; what we had in step 1 above was only a name query.)

2b. AliceNT also sends a directed (i.e. non-broadcast) **netlogon** request to each of the DCs in the list she obtained in step 1

3. AliceNT picks the DC that responds first, and uses it to handle the remainder of the logon procedure.

This process is called *discovery*. You can see that in fact it consists of two related actions: find a list of suitable DCs, and then choose one from that list.

On a large, routed network with many domain controllers, you want discovery to give you a DC that is close to you in networking terms, so that communication between you and the DC is fast. The initial broadcast in step 2a ensures that DCs on the local wire (i.e. very close in network terms) are more likely to be chosen first. Even if step 2a fails, the DC chosen is still likely to be close, because the first machine to respond in step 2b will probably be a close one. Moreover, the list sent back by WINS is specially ordered:

- the PDC is listed first even though it may be near or far away
- next are any DCs that registered directly with this WINS server. These are likely to be near, because you usually configure your PC to use a nearby WINS server, for efficiency
- finally are any other DCs that WINS knows about from replication with other WINS servers, which are likely to be further away.

If in spite of all this your PC isn't discovering a nearby DC but ends up using a distant one instead, it may cause problems with logon and access to resources on the network. If that happens, you can explicitly control which DC your machine should use (see Notes).

If Netlogon can't find a domain controller; cached credentials

When you logon to a domain from a PC, **Netlogon** keeps a copy on the PC of your logon information (username, password, access rights, …). On subsequent logon attempts, if **Netlogon** can't find a domain controller (e.g. because they are all down, or because this PC has been disconnected from the network for some reason), **Netlogon** will be able to log you on using *cached credentials*, giving you this message as it logs you on:

> **Logon Message: A domain controller for your domain could not be contacted. You have been logged on using cached account information.**
> **Changes to your profile since you last logged on may not be available.**

You must previously have logged in from this PC, to this domain, as this user. Otherwise the appropriate credentials won't have been cached on this machine and the logon will fail after waiting a couple or minutes or so, with the message:

> **Logon Message: The system cannot log you on now because the domain EX-NTD is not available.**

If you run a sniffer during this, you can see the PC sends about 60 packets in all, repeatedly trying to locate a domain controller, before it gives up.

By default, the last ten logons on this PC are stored. You can set this number to zero for maximum security, or increase it if you frequently use your PC disconnected from the network (see Notes).

For comparison, here is the standard message you receive when you give an incorrect username or password:

> **Logon Message: The system cannot log you on. Make sure user your username and domain are correct, then type your password again. Letters in passwords must be typed using the correct case. Make sure that Caps Lock is not accidentally on.**

Now we move on to the next stage of logon over the network – how your PC authenticates itself to the domain controller.

20.6 Logon over the network (1b) – the computer account

At this point AliceNT has chosen a domain controller for the **EX-NTD** domain; now her **NetLogon** needs to communicate with **NetLogon** on the chosen DC to validate the logon information. In order to do this, AliceNT first has to authenticate herself to the DC. Note that this is the PC authenticating itself to the domain controller, *not* the user logging on. (Most people find this surprising at first because it all happens behind the scenes and you're not normally aware that it's happening.)

For AliceNT to authenticate to the DC, she must have a *computer account* in this domain. Before we look at the logon step in the next module we have to explain what this computer account is.

Adding a computer to a domain – the "computer account"

For a machine to use NT domain-based security, it must be made a member of the domain ("added to the domain"). Internally this means that:

   a. an account for machine AliceNT (in our example) is added to the directory of accounts on **EX-NTD**'s domain controller. Note that this is a special account for the computer itself, not for any users who might use the workstation. The account information and password are, as usual, stored on the PDC, and replicated to any BDCs. The workstation itself also keeps a copy of its password. The end-user never enters or even sees the computer account password – the passwords are all automatically generated and maintained by NT itself. The computer account is sometimes called the *workstation trust account*

   b. AliceNT is configured to say she belongs to the domain **EX-NTD**. (A machine can only belong to one domain at a time.)

There are three ways to add a computer to a domain:

   1. when the NT software is installed on the PC (AliceNT) in the first place

   2. using **Control Panel > Network > Identification > Change …**
   Figure 20.10(a), (b) shows the machine AliceNT's domain being changed from **TEST-NTD** to **EX-NTD**. When you do this, as well as telling AliceNT that its domain is now **EX-NTD**, the domain controller for **EX-NTD** must be told that AliceNT is now a member, i.e. an account for AliceNT has to be created, so tick the **Create a Computer Account in the Domain** checkbox. The account details you specify in the dialog are *not* the computer account details – you never ever see them. The details you enter are for a normal user account, in the new domain; this user must be privileged enough to create the machine account on the DC so you usually specify the **Administrator** account

   3. on the **EX-NTD** domain controller run **Start > Programs > Administrative Tools (Common) > Server Manager**. Use menu **Computer > Add to Domain** to give the dialog in Figure 20.10(d). This creates the computer account in the domain. (You can do the same thing from the command line using **net computer \\alicent /add**.) Now you must walk over to AliceNT and tell her that her domain is **EX-NTD**. You do this using **Control Panel > Network > Identification > Change …** as in step 2 above; the only difference is that a machine account already exists now, so you don't have to tick the **Create a Computer Account in the Domain** checkbox. A PC's domain membership

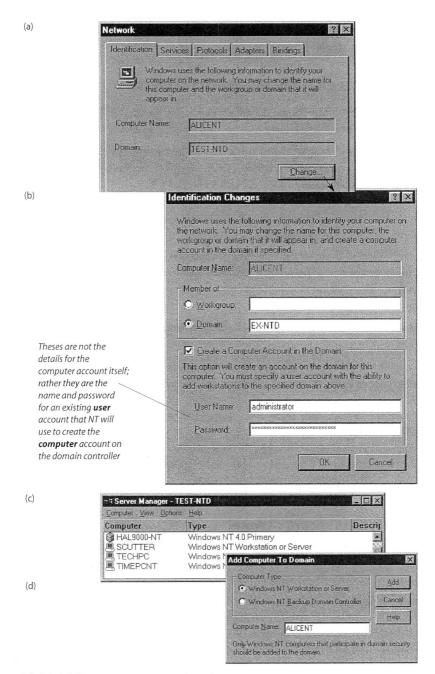

(a)

(b)

Theses are not the details for the computer account itself; rather they are the name and password for an existing **user** account that NT will use to create the **computer** account on the domain controller

(c)

(d)

Figure 20.10 Adding a computer to a domain

is typically configured when the PC is first added to the network and never changed during its lifetime, so this computer account creation action happens very rarely.

20.7 Logon over the network (1b contd) – PC authenticates and creates a secure channel

PC authenticates itself to the domain controller

At this point AliceNT has chosen a domain controller for the **EX-NTD** domain, she has a computer account in **EX-NTD**, and now she must logon to the domain:

- AliceNT opens a NetBIOS Session Service connection to the DC that she has just chosen. As we mentioned in Module 20.4, NetBIOS session connections run over TCP, and are persistent. This is the first example we've seen of NetBIOS using a connection-oriented TCP service

- over this session connection, the DC issues a *challenge* to AliceNT, consisting of a fixed-length nonce (string of random bytes)

- when AliceNT receives the challenge she encrypts it with her own copy of the computer account password and sends the result as her *response* to the challenge

- the DC also encrypts the challenge, but using the DC's own copy of the computer account password

- if the two calculations match, the challenge/response succeeds.

That's only one side of the authentication – AliceNT has proved to the DC that she is who she says she is. AliceNT also sends her own challenge to the DC, in exactly the same way, in order that she can know that the DC really is the machine it's supposed to be.

If both challenge/responses are OK, the logon is successful – AliceNT has authenticated herself with the DC and vice versa – and AliceNT then goes on to establish a secure connection to the DC.

The reason for using the challenge/response mechanism is that the password is never sent in clear over the network. The next module shows in some detail how the challenge/response is also used in validating the username and password.

Establishing the secure channel

AliceNT and the DC now set up what NT calls a *secure Netlogon channel* or a *secure communications channel*, which they will use when exchanging the username and password information to validate the user logon in the next module.

AliceNT and the DC now negotiate encryption parameters. They agree on a *session key* – a dynamically generated temporary encryption key that both of them use to encrypt/decrypt traffic from one to the other over the secure channel. The session key only lasts as long as the session stays up; when a new session is established, a new session key is created too.

Before NT 4.0 Service Pack 4 the "security" of the channel was minimal – it really meant only that the two ends of the channel knew who was at the other end. Now, however, traffic is encrypted by default (to prevent eavesdropping) and/or digitally signed (to prevent/detect modification). The following Registry settings (see Notes) control the operation of the secure channel:

SignSecureChannel: all outgoing secure channel traffic should be digitally signed

SealSecureChannel: all outgoing secure channel traffic should be "sealed", i.e. encrypted

RequireSignOrSeal: don't send any traffic over a "secure" channel that isn't very secure. Without this, if a DC didn't support the improved encryption, the old, less secure method could be used, leaving a security hole.

The high-encryption version of NT 4.0 uses 128-bit keys for this secure-channel encryption, whereas previous versions used less secure 40- or 56-bit keys.

Once the secure channel has been established between AliceNT and the DC, they keep it open permanently, ready to use whenever it's needed for logons. If the connection is lost for any reason, the channel will be re-established when it's needed again.

If this PC can't authenticate to the domain controller for the specified domain – typically because it hasn't been configured as part of this domain, or because the name of this PC has been changed but the DC hasn't been notified of it, you get the message:

Logon Message: The system cannot log you on to this domain because the system's computer account in its primary domain is missing or the password on that account is incorrect.

Working through the steps in the previous module to add this computer to the domain will usually solve this problem, and the Notes refer you to a specific Microsoft Knowledgebase article. More generally, you can use some of the tools below to solve this sort of the problem, and the Microsoft Knowledgebase has many articles on related topics.

Tools related to secure channels

The following tools are included in the NT 4.0 Resource Kit:

netdom.exe: (Domain Manager): a command-line tool that lets you reset (re-establish) the secure channel from a machine to a domain controller (and manage computer accounts)

nltest.exe: (NetLogon tester?): this command-line program's **/SC_QUERY** and **/SC_RESET** let you query and reset the secure channel from a server to a domain controller. (It has many other options too.)

dommon.exe: (Domain Monitor): a GUI program that monitors and displays the status of domain controllers and servers in your domain, and of their secure channels to domain controllers of other, trusted domains.

20.8 Logon over the network (2) – sending the password securely

At this point in the logon cycle, AliceNT has a secure channel open to a domain controller that she chose to handle the logon. Now the DC has to validate the logon. Figure 20.11 shows all the components involved, apart from the actual logon dialog window created by **WinLogon**.

AliceNT could send the username and password "in clear" over the secure channel for validation. However, as we mentioned in the previous module, the secure channel hasn't always been very secure. Instead, AliceNT could send the hashed password, which would prevent an eavesdropper finding out the password; however, the eavesdropper could capture the hashed password, and using specially modified software (which *is* available from hacker sites), could impersonate the user, without actually knowing the clear-text password. To overcome these problems, NT again uses a challenge/response mechanism:

1. when AliceNT connects to the DC, the DC sends her a *challenge*, which is a 16-byte *nonce* (random number). A new challenge is generated for each logon attempt so it doesn't matter if an eavesdropper catches the challenge (or the response, below) because it's only valid for this one logon attempt

2. AliceNT encrypts the challenge with the hashed version of the password that the user entered, and returns this as its *response* to the DC

3. the DC receives the response and encrypts the challenge it sent, using its own copy of this user's hashed password, retrieved from the SAM database on the DC, and compares this with the response received from AliceNT

4. if the values are the same, the user gave the correct password so the logon succeeds; otherwise it fails, AliceNT's **WinLogon** gives an error message, and waits for the user to re-enter username, password, and domain.

In fact, NT replies with two different responses to each challenge because of the two different versions of the hashed password that are maintained in the SAM database (Module 20.3):

1. LM (LAN Manager) challenge/response

2. NTLM (NT LAN manager) challenge/response.

NTLM has been enhanced further to use longer encryption keys and to provide extra security in its transmission; this enhanced version is called NTLMv2. You can control which variants may be used or must be used by setting values in the NT Registry; in particular, you can completely disable the use of LM authentication which is a security hole. (See Web Appendix 28 for more detail.)

When you've logged on, the PC registers the NetBIOS name *username*<03>, e.g. **Fred Bloggs<03>**. This is used when you **net send** messages to users.

You can see which username and domain you've logged in as by pressing Ctrl-Alt-Del to display the **Windows NT Security** dialog.

That completes our coverage of how a user logs on to the domain that their PC is a member of. In the next module we look at some other types of logon.

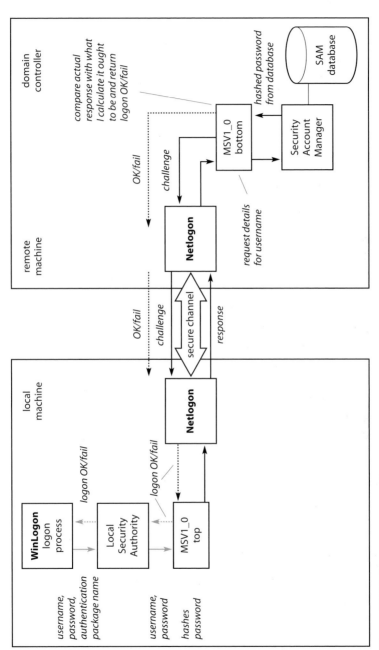

Figure 20.11 Logon components

20.9 Different logon types: terminology (1)

We have included this section because the terms used for different types of logon can be confusing.

In Module 20.3 we covered local logon, where you, sitting at AliceNT, log on to AliceNT and not to a domain, or you logon to domain **EX-NTD** while sitting at one of **EX-NTD's** domain controllers.

Pass-through authentication is when the local workstation doesn't complete the logon validation on its own, but passes over it over to a domain controller elsewhere on the network. This occurs in three situations:

1. **You logon to this PC's domain**

   This is an *interactive logon* – i.e. where the system gives you a logon dialog – to a domain, where you logon from a workstation that isn't a domain controller, to this PC's domain (e.g. user **Fred Bloggs** logs in from PC **AliceNT** to domain **EX-NTD**). As we saw in detail earlier in this chapter, the logon is passed for authentication to one of **Ex-NTD's** domain controllers:

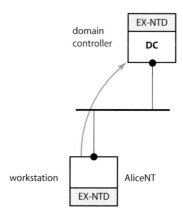

2. **You logon to a different domain**

   This is an interactive logon from a workstation in one domain to a different domain (e.g. user **Fred Bloggs** logs in from PC **AliceNT** to domain **TEST-NTD**). The logon is passed to one of **EX-NTD's** domain controllers, which in turn passes it to one of **TEST-NTD's** domain controllers:

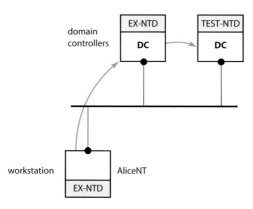

For domains to work in this way (i.e. users in one domain are allowed to access machines and other resources in the other domain), *trust relationships* have to be set up between the domains. You set up a trust relationship using **Start > Programs > Administrative Tools (Common) > User Manager for Domains** and then use menu **Policies > Trust Relationships**. For more details on interdomain trusts and this type of logon, see the Notes. We continue with the terminology for Logon types in the next module.

20.10 Different logon types: terminology (2)

3. **Using a resource on another machine**

This is a *remote logon* (as opposed to an interactive one) where you have already logged on to a domain, and then access a resource (file or printer) on another machine, **fileserv**, say. The access request that **AliceNT** sends to **fileserv** contains your credentials (username **Fred Bloggs**, password, domain **EX-NTD**). **fileserv** has to authenticate you, and passes your credentials to a domain controller for **fileserv**'s domain. If **fileserv**'s domain is **EX-NTD**, the authentication happens as we've already described:

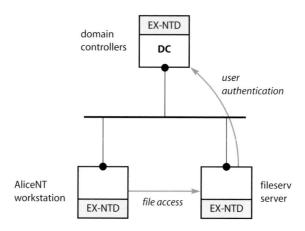

However, if **fileserv**'s domain is **TEST-NTD**, say, the **TEST-NTD** domain controller passes the authentication request through to an **EX-NTD** domain controller for authentication, and when it gets the result back, passes it on to **fileserv**:

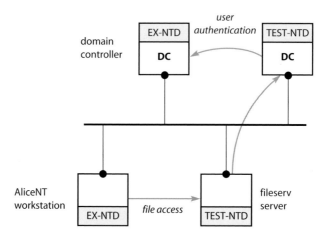

This logon is transparent to you: the system doesn't give a logon dialog and you don't have to enter your username or password. (An exception is when using Windows Explorer > **Tools** > **Map Network Drive** and in the **Connect As**: box you explicitly specify a different username to the one you logged on as: you'll be prompted for a password. The same applies when you explicitly specify a username to the **net use** command, as in, for example, "**net use x: /user:test-ntd\fred \\alicent\datafiles**").

Be warned that the above terms are often used loosely: some people use "pass-through authentication" exclusively for the second or third cases above.

20.11 Logon and controlling access to network resources

When you have logged on successfully, your logon account controls which resources you may access. Here we give a (very brief) summary of the internal mechanisms used to implement this.

1. when the MSV1_0 authentication package retrieves the hashed password from the SAM database (local logon in Module 20.3, network logon in Module 20.8) it also retrieves from the database the *security ID (SID)* for your username, and SIDs for all groups that you belong to. A security ID is a unique number used to represent a user or group; you can think of it as a numeric name

2. MSV1_0 returns all these SIDs to the LSA (Local Security Authority) on the machine you're sitting at (logging in from)

3. the LSA creates an *access token* containing all the SIDs and a list of all the associated user rights

4. the LSA passes the access token to **WinLogon**

5. **WinLogon** runs your desktop (usually starting with Windows Explorer) and the access token is attached to that process

6. any process that you start after this also inherits a copy of the token.

All the above happens when you logon.

Now, when one of your processes attempts to use a resource on the local machine, e.g. read a particular file:

7. the *Security Reference Monitor* component in the NT kernel checks your access token against the *access control list (ACL)* for the resource, and decides whether you are allowed to access it. An ACL is simply a list saying which users and groups are allowed to do what with this resource; you modify a file's ACL, for example, using the **File > Properties** dialog for the file in Windows Explorer (Figure 20.12).

Figure 20.12
Modifying a file's
access control list

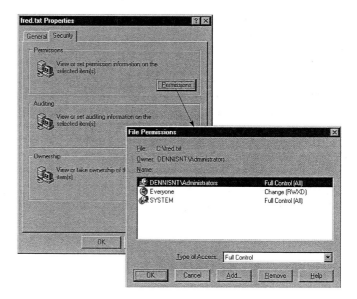

When one of your processes accesses a resource on a remote machine:

8a. the workstation sends your credentials (username, hashed password, domain) to that machine, which validates the logon again, using remote logon as described in the previous module, and creates a new access token. it stores this locally and passes a reference to it, in the form of a *User Identifier (UID)* back to the workstation

8b. whenever the workstation accesses another resource on that remote machine, it includes a copy of the UID in the request, so that the remote machine doesn't have to perform another validation.

Mapped network drives

Mapping a network drive is the Windows Networking equivalent of mounting a shared NFS file system: it lets you access files on a remote system as though they were on a disk on your local PC. To map a network drive, you can either use the Windows Explorer menu **Tools > Map Network Drive** dialog, or **net use** from the command line, e.g.:

```
net use r: \\bobnt\rchives          map rchives share on bobnt to local drive R:
```

Accessing a network drive is little more than an instance of accessing any remote resource. As usual the account you logged on to must have access rights for the remote shared file system that you are connecting to, or the mapping will fail. (For more on mapped network drives, which are also known as "shares," see Module 21.1. See also the Notes in Chapter 22 regarding the "Guest account;" this can allow you to access resources on other machines that would otherwise be forbidden to you.)

Share-level security

Before NT-style domain security was developed for windows, access to remote shares (network file systems) was controlled by *share-level security.* The share is optionally protected by a password. If a network user can supply the correct password, they are allowed to access the share and all files in it. Microsoft doesn't recommend relying on this security scheme alone, because of the low security it provides.

By contrast, NT domain user-level security can give much finer-grained control, letting you specify the permissions a user has for each file (as long as the file system on the server is NT's NTFS type rather than the old DOS FAT type). However, as Microsoft point out, "permissions for access through a shared directory that is on an NTFS volume operate in addition to NTFS permissions set on the directory and files. Shared directory permissions specify the maximum access allowed over the network." For example, if the share permissions are set to read-only, even if the user-level permissions on a file on the share are set to "full control," you will be unable to write to that file.

20.12 Domain controllers

Domain controllers manage the security for an NT domain. They:

- authenticate users logging on, as we described throughout this chapter. (For this reason they are also known as *logon servers*.)
- store and maintain the SAM (Security Account Manager) database.

As we've already mentioned, there are two types of domain controller:

1. **Primary domain controller (PDC)**

   A domain can have only one PDC. This hold the master copy of the database, and all modifications to the database have to be made on the PDC.

2. **Backup domain controllers (BDCs)**

   A domain can and often does have more than one BDC. BDCs hold a read-only copy of the SAM database, so they can authenticate users, allowing them to logon even if the PDC is not available. However, changes to the SAM database can't be made on a BDC so changes to user accounts can be made only if the PDC is available.

BDCs are used for two reasons:

- resilience, so users can still logon when the PDC isn't available
- performance: the logon load is shared across all the DCs. In a multi-site network you might have a BDC at each site so that logons can be handled locally without having to travel across the WAN. (A large or important site might even have several local BDCs, for performance and resilience.)

Figure 20.13
Configuring user
rights

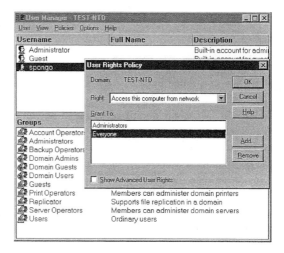

The SAM database; database replication

The SAM database contains all the details for each user:

- username and (hashed) password

- when they are allowed logon (you can restrict users so they can logon only at certain times of day)
- which machines they're allowed logon to
- whether they are allowed logon over a dial-up link
- what *rights* this user has, e.g. **Load and unload device drivers**, or **Shut down the system**, etc. (You configure these rights using **Start > Programs > Administrative Tools (Common) > User Manager for Domains** and then menu **Policies > User Rights Policy**, Figure 20.13.)
- what *groups* this user is a member of. Rights are usually allocated by groups for ease of maintenance (e.g. allocate appropriate rights to the "Server Operators" group, and then add users to that group, rather than adding rights to users directly).

This information can be updated only on the PDC, and therefore any changes made must somehow be copied to the BDCs, so that all the copies of the database are consistent. This *database synchronization* (or *replication*) works as follows:

- the PDC checks every five minutes to see whether, for example, **User Manager for Domains** or **Server Manager** has changed any account in the database
- if there are any changes, the PDC informs each of the BDCs
- each BDC establishes a secure channel to the PDC and pulls down any changed data that it needs

The SAM database contains four types of accounts:

1. user accounts, which we have just described
2. computer accounts (workstation trust accounts), used when a machine in this domain connects to one of the domain's DCs (Module 20.6)
3. *server trust accounts*, used to set up secure channels for database replication between this domain's BDCs and its PDC
4. *interdomain trust accounts*, used when a DC in this domain wants to talk to a DC in another, trusted domain, e.g. for pass-through logon, where a user is interactively logging on to that other domain, or is using a resource on one of that domain's machines (cases 2 and 3 in Module 20.9).

The **netdom**, **nltest**, and **dommon** tools (Module 20.7) let you explore and modify the domain controller structure and replication on your network.

Promoting a BDC if the PDC fails

If the PDC fails for any reason (e.g. it crashes, or it has to be closed down) your network can still operate, but you can't make any changes to accounts. If the outage is brief, it probably doesn't matter, but if the PDC is down for a long time, you can *promote* one of your BDCs to be the new PDC, so that your network is fully functional. When the original PDC comes back again, you can demote the temporary PDC back to a BDC, and have the same configuration as before (see Notes).

Summary

- Windows-NT Networking security is based on NT domains
- an NT *domain* is a number of computers using the security mechanisms and sharing a common database of usernames, passwords, and (some) access-control information
- NT domain security provides single-sign-on
- domain controllers validate user logons. There must be one and only one primary DC. There can be zero or more backup DCs. Any DC can handle a logon but account information can be updated only on the primary DC
- you can logon locally to a machine rather than to its domain. This type of logon is handled entirely on the local machine by its security sub-system. Your username and password are checked against those held in the Security Account Manager database
- when you logon to the domain:
    - your PC uses "discovery" to find a DC to handle the logon
    - your PC establishes a secure channel to the chosen DC
    - your PC's **Netlogon** service encrypts your username and password and sends them to the DC for validation
    - the DC compares them against those held in its Security Account Manager database and allows/denies logon
    - on your PC, **Netlogon** receives the allow/deny from the DC and informs **WinLogon**. If logon is allowed, **WinLogon** starts your desktop
- each member PC in a domain has a "computer account" in the domain, used to prove to the DC that this machine really is who it says it is
- NT can use many different challenge/response systems to verify passwords. Passwords themselves are not sent over the wire
- your logon account controls which resources you are allowed to access on this machine and elsewhere on the network. When you access a resource on a different machine, it performs a pass-through authentication of your logon details with a domain controller. This is transparent to the user – you are not prompted for your username and password
- BDCs periodically replicate copies of the accounts database from the PDC.

What's next?

In the next chapter we look at Windows Networking's "browsing." This has nothing to do with Web browsing – it's how Windows PC automatically get a list of machines and resources on the network, e.g. as shown in Windows Explorer's Network Neighborhood.

Notes and further reading

> **Tip:** we use the suffix "-NTD" (for "NT Domain") in all domain names that we create, to make it clear that this is an NT domain name. This is particularly useful on large, multi-platform networks that use many different name resolution systems. For example, on our internal network we have NIS for Sun machines, DNS for Linux and other UNIX machines, and Windows Networking, each of which has its own idea of what a "domain" is. We made the common mistake of calling our domains after our organization – just plain "UIT." If we see a DNS resolution for "UIT," it's very hard to tell what has originated the query. But if we see a query for "UIT-NTD" we know exactly where it's come from.

For summaries of conversations involved in logons (although these are now a little out of date because since NT 4.0 Service Pack 4 network logon traffic is usually encrypted) see:

❏ **http://technet.microsoft.com > Products and Technologies > Windows NT Server > Plan > NT Server Capacity Planning**

To capture a lot of the network conversations we used when writing this chapter we used **ethereal**, because specifying capture filters in **ethereal** is so much easier than in Netmon. Then, still using **ethereal**, we saved the capture files in Netmon format, and then analyzed them using Netmon, which gives a much more detailed analysis of Windows Networking traffic.

Many of the Samba documents give a clear description of various aspects of Windows Networking. In your Samba distribution, see the files:

❏ **cifsntdomain.txt,**	**NT_Security.txt,**
DOMAIN_CONTROL.txt,	**NTDOMAIN.txt,**
DOMAIN_MEMBER.html,	**NetBIOS.txt,**
DOMAIN_MEMBER.txt,	**PROFILES.txt,**
DOMAIN.txt,	**security_level.txt,**
ENCRYPTION.txt,	**UNIX-SMB.txt,**
NT4_PlainPassword.reg,	**Win95_PlainPassword.reg,**
NT-Guest-Access.txt,	**WinNT.txt**

Many of these files are also available on:

❏ **http://www.samba.org/samba/ftp/docs/textdocs/**

For a good overview of Windows authentication, see:

❏ **MS-KB-Q102716** *User Authentication with Windows NT*

which covers:

- how passwords are stored in the SAM database
- user authentication with the MSV1_0 authentication package
- pass-through authentication.

Other relevant articles are:

❏ **MS-KB-Q172931** *Cached Logon Information*

❏ **MS-KB-Q314108** *How to Write an LMHOSTS File for Domain Validation and Other Name Resolution Issues*

❑ **MS-KB-Q180094** *How to Write an LMHOSTS File for Domain Validation and Other Name Resolution Issues*

❑ **MS-KB-Q262655** *Primary Domain Controller (PDC) Names Entered in LMHOSTS File Are Case-Sensitive*

❑ **MS-KB-Q266729** *Netlogon Behavior in Windows NT 4.0*

Discovery and secure channels

You can control which DC a machine establishes its secure channel with by setting your node type to M-node, or using settings in the **Lmhosts** file, or using the **setprfdc**, **nltest**, or **netdom** tools:

❑ **MS-KB-Q181171** *Secure Channel Manipulation with TCP/IP*

❑ **MS-KB-Q158148** *Domain Secure Channel Utility – Nltest.exe*

❑ **MS-KB-Q183859** *Integrity Checking on Secure Channels with Domain Controllers*

How to solve the "missing computer account" problem:

❑ **MS-KB-Q175024** *Resetting Domain Member Secure Channel*

The logon authentication itself

Logon uses RPCs (remote procedure calls) – one machine specifies a subroutine or system call that's to be executed on a remote machine. If the traffic weren't encrypted you'd be able to see RPC calls for **NetrServerReqChallenge**, **NetrServerAuthenticate2**, **NetrSamLogon**, and **NetrSamLogoff** functions in your Netmon traces, and old documentation – before logon traffic encryption was introduced – still shows some of these.

Different types of logon

For an explanation of the different types, how they work, and some examples:

❑ **Resource Kit, pages 90–93**

❑ **MS-KB-Q122422** *Example of Remote Logon with Windows NT Server*

LM, NTLM, and NTLMv2 authentication methods

❑ **MS-KB-Q147706** *How to Disable LM Authentication on Windows NT*

Replication between PDC and BDC

❑ **MS-KB-Q173882** *Netlogon Synchronization Errors*

❑ **MS-KB-Q149664** *Verifying Domain Netlogon Synchronization*

In spite of the following article's title, it discusses the whole process of promoting and demoting a BDC when your PDC fails:

❑ **MS-KB-Q167248** *How to Demote to BDC When Two PDCs are Present*

Trusted and trusting domains

"Trusts" are a way of separating groups of users into separate domains but still giving them the convenience of domain-logon's single sign-on. If we have two domains, **A-NTD** and **B-NTD**, we can tell B to trust A. Then, if a user who belongs to A tries to logon to a machine in B or use a resource on one of B's machines, a domain controller in B will perform a pass-through logon to one of A's controllers. If that DC says the logon is OK, B trusts it, and allows the user access.

Trusts are one-way. Above we said that B trusts A, but that doesn't mean that A trusts B; if we want that, we explicitly have to tell A to trust B. Many trusts are set up as two-way but one-way trusts have their uses. For example, a branch office might trust HQ, but HQ doesn't trust the branch office (because they have an incompetent network manager, say). Then the HQ folks can logon to branch office machines, to perform system maintenance, etc., but the incompetent branch-office guy can't get at HQ's network.

Using trusts lets each office have its own domain controllers and avoids the replication across the WAN that you would have with a single domain used in all branches. It also avoids any problems of machines trying to logon to a DC across the WAN instead of using a local DC (except, of course, for pass-through authentications).

You administer trusts in **User Manager for Domains > Policies > Trust Relationships**

Logon types

In Modules 20.9 and 20.10 we explained the different scenarios in which pass-though authentication is used. A different type of authentication is needed in the less common case where the network (or at least the target machine, whose resources are being used) isn't using domain-based security at all:

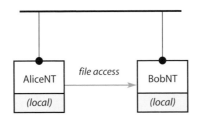

In this case, AliceNT sends the username, password, and domain name (that you initially logged on with on AliceNT) to BobNT. BobNT then validates the username and password against his own, local SAM database. No domain controller is used in this remote logon. This type of logon is useful where BobNT is a server outside your main network and does not participate in the main network's domain security, e.g. BobNT might be a server on a demilitarized zone of a firewall (Module 24.6).

In Module 20.9 we mentioned that you can explicitly specify a username when mapping a network drive with **net use**. However, when you (on AliceNT) use resources on another machine (BobNT, say), only one set of credentials can be in use at a time. For example, if you try the following:

```
net use x: \\alicent\datafiles /user:fred
net use y: \\alicent\textfiles /user:mike
```

you'll get an error message "System error 1219 has occurred. The credentials supplied conflict with an existing set of credentials." For further information see:

❑ **MS-KB-Q106211** *Err Msg: The Credentials Supplied Conflict with an Existing...*

❑ **MS-KB-Q173199** *Multiple Credentials in a Single Windows NT Session*

Windows-9x

Windows-9x is primarily a workgroup operating system, but it can use NT domain security if the "workgroup" name is set to the name of the NT domain you want to operate in. The workgroup/domain is set in two places:

1. in **Control Panel > Network > Identification**, set the **Workgroup** value to *your NT domain*
2. in **Control Panel > Network > Configuration > Client for Microsoft Networks**, set:
   - Log on to Windows NT domain = YES
   - Windows NT domain = *your NT domain.*

Windows-9x doesn't support the **/user:***name* option in **net use**.

Troubleshooting

Windows Networking authentication, unlike every other topic in this book, is difficult to diagnose using a sniffer, for many reasons:

- it's very complex
- it's badly documented
- a lot of the interesting traffic is encrypted

and we haven't shown network traces because of their sheer size. (An NT server booting up can generate about 250 packets even before you logon.)

But all is not lost. First, many logon problems are really name resolution problems that prevent logon from working correctly. Troubleshooting name resolution is relatively straight-forward, and if you know it's working properly, you have narrowed down the possible causes of your logon difficulties.

Secondly, you can make things easier for yourself by setting up a test network. Even if you can't reproduce the exact problem on the test network, it will give you invaluable practical experience and understanding. Initially the network should contain only a single workstation, a PDC, and a sniffer. For simplicity disable WINS on both client and server. Use only a single domain on the test network. For safety use a dummy domain name like **EX-NTD**. (You can use your real domain name, but using a test domain name is safer in case this machine inadvertently finds its way back onto your real network and then tries to act as its PDC.) Disable any network services you don't need, to minimize chatter on the wire. (RAS is particularly noisy. Remove DNS and DHCP too.) Experiment on the test network, and you will soon (or soon-ish) get to recognize patterns of network traffic that represent domain controller discovery and logon. Try logging on with the client disconnected from the wire; reconnect, and try again with the PDC disconnected. Add a BDC. Add a second domain and explore pass-through authentication.

Finally, you can assume that everything's fine, and if you run into problems search the Microsoft Knowledgebase and/or Google for a solution. Even if you do adopt this approach, the background you covered in this chapter will make your search very much easier.

For a list of event IDs that appear in the Event Log, and typical causes, see:

❏ **MS-KB-Q150518** *NetLogon Service Fails When Secure Channel Not Functioning*

For example, "event ID 5721 means that your PC's computer account (workstation trust account) isn't in the domain's database."

Appendices

Web Appendix 28: Windows password hashes

21 | Windows Networking – browsing the network

Introduction

Windows Networking "browsing" lets your machine automatically obtain a list of other machines, printers, and NT domains on your network, which you can view in Windows Explorer's **Network Neighborhood**. The browse system works without any manual pre-configuration. We explain the mechanisms that allow it to do this, and how browse clients interact with browse servers to retrieve the lists of resources on the network.

21.1 Overview

In Microsoft Windows Networking, *browsing* means automatically finding a list of the resources (domains, servers, printers) on the network. Most of the information displayed in the **Network Neighborhood** of Windows Explorer (Figure 21.1) is obtained from the browse service.

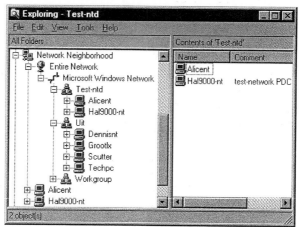

Figure 21.1 Network Neighborhood shown in Windows Explorer

The **net view** command displays browse-service information directly (Figure 21.2) and in Module 21.5 we explain some important differences between Explorer and **net view**.

```
Command Prompt

C:\> net view
Server Name          Remark
-------------------------------------------------------
\\ALICENT
\\HAL9000-NT         test-network PDC


C:\> net view /domain:UIT
Server Name          Remark
-------------------------------------------------------
\\DENNISNT
\\GROOTLX            grootlx server (Samba 2.0.7)
\\SCUTTER
\\TECHPC

C:\>
```

Figure 21.2 The **net view** command also shows Network Neighbourhood information

Browsing in this sense has nothing to do with Web browsing – Windows Networking browsing was around for years before the Web was invented. Browsing is one of the big advantages of Windows Networking, and follows on from the design goal of making networking easy, especially in a small workgroup on a site that doesn't have a specialist network administrator. Without any pre-configuration, the browse system automatically accumulates a list of the network's machines and their resources, and makes it available to other machines.

Browsing is separate from name resolution. However, as we'll soon see, to perform its function, browsing has to make extensive use of NetBIOS name resolution, especially in networks containing routers.

Browsing is also separate from logon and authentication and authorization; a machine name can be displayed in Network Neighborhood even if you don't have any rights to access that machine.

Browsing architecture

Windows Networking browsing is a client/server system:

- when a client PC boots up, it broadcasts its name on the local network segment
- a special browse server, called a *browse master* (or *master browser*), hears the broadcast and adds the PCs name to its *browse list* – the list it maintains of resources on this network segment. Usually there are also backup browse servers (*backup browsers*) on the segment, and the browse master periodically replicates the browse list to the backup browsers
- the first time a client wants to display its Network Neighborhood, it broadcasts a NetBIOS name query for browse servers on the local network segment, and selects one server from the list returned.

  Then it establishes a NetBIOS session connection to the selected server (on TCP port 139), and requests the browse list. The server returns the browse list to the client, and the client displays it in its Network Neighborhood.

You can see that, in principle, browsing is very simple. But to make it work automatically, without any pre-configuration whatsoever, and in today's routed IP networks, things becomes a lot more complicated, e.g.

- which machines act as browse masters and browse servers?
- how does my machine find a list of browse masters and servers?
- what happens if a browse master goes down?
- Figures 21.1 and 21.2 show browse lists for domains **TEST-NTD** and **UIT**, illustrating that browsing can work across domains. How does that work?
- if browsing depends on broadcast packets, how can my PC get a view of all my organization's network, and not just my local segment?

We cover all these issues in the following modules. We'll just mention here that the browse server function doesn't require a dedicated machine. Just about any machine can act as a browse server, although domain controllers and Windows NT Server PCs (as opposed to Windows NT workstation) are given priority, so usually the function is indeed performed by what we think of as a "server."

21.2 The client announces itself to the server(s)

Let's assume that we're booting up AliceNT on an existing network, and that browse servers are already functioning.

As soon as AliceNT has finished registering her names (to WINS, or via broadcast name claims) she announces herself to the browse master on her local segment. The large Windows Network Monitor trace (Figure 21.3 – labels match the items below) illustrates:

A. the announcement uses the NetBIOS datagram service, which in turn uses UDP

B. the source and destination ports are always 138

C. the packet is a UDP broadcast to the sub-net broadcast address (212.140.133.127 in this case, because our netmask is 255.255.255.128)

D. from the NetBIOS point of view, the announcement is broadcast to the **TEST-NTD<1d>** NetBIOS unique name ("the browse master for **TEST-NTD** on the local segment"). Note that the client doesn't try to use WINS or anything else to resolve it – it doesn't want to know because it's much easier to broadcast to it.

E. the announcement contains details about the type of machine this is. In Module 21.7, we'll see how the four "browser" fields in the "Server Type" summary are used.

When the browse master receives the announcement, it adds this machine's name into its browse list, i.e. into its accumulated database of machines on the network.

Notice in Figure 21.3 that the BROWSER protocol has no field for this machine's domain name. The only place the domain is specified is in the NBT Destination name, which means that only the browse master for the **TEST-NTD** domain will receive this packet, which is how it knows that AliceNT belongs to **TEST-NTD**.

What this trace doesn't show (but you can easily observe on your own network) is that:

- the client repeats its announcement after 4, 8, and 12 minutes, and every 12 minutes after that, as shown in the **ethereal** trace below. (The "time" field is "seconds since previous packet".)

- the client doesn't know whether anyone hears its announcements. It just shouts out its name and hopes someone is listening. (However, the server-side of the browse system operation has a lot of redundancy built into it, so it's unlikely that no browse master at all would be available, as we see in Module 21.7.)

X The Ethereal Network Analyzer				_ □ X
File Edit Capture Display Tools				Help

No.	Time	Source	Destination	Protocol	Info
66	0.000	212.140.133.35	212.140.133.127	BROWSER	Host Announcement ALICENT
80	237.5	212.140.133.35	212.140.133.127	BROWSER	Host Announcement ALICENT
107	477.1	212.140.133.35	212.140.133.127	BROWSER	Host Announcement ALICENT
181	718.9	212.140.133.35	212.140.133.127	BROWSER	Host Announcement ALICENT
217	721.1	212.140.133.35	212.140.133.127	BROWSER	Host Announcement ALICENT

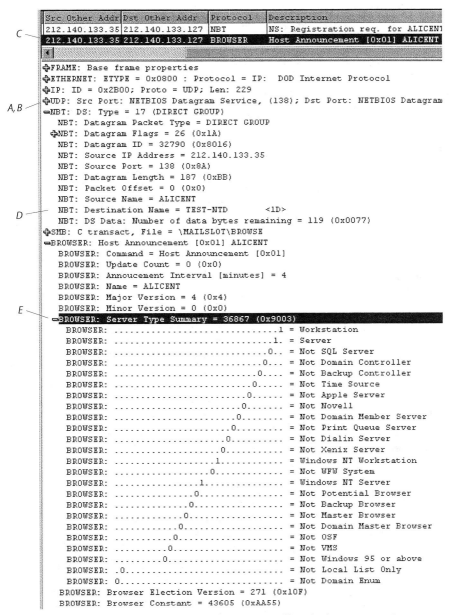

```
    Src Other Addr  Dst Other Addr   Protocol   Description
    212.140.133.35  212.140.133.127  NBT        NS: Registration req. for ALICENT
C   212.140.133.35  212.140.133.127  BROWSER    Host Announcement [0x01] ALICENT

    ⊕FRAME: Base frame properties
    ⊕ETHERNET: ETYPE = 0x0800 : Protocol = IP:  DOD Internet Protocol
    ⊕IP: ID = 0x2B00; Proto = UDP; Len: 229
    ⊕UDP: Src Port: NETBIOS Datagram Service, (138); Dst Port: NETBIOS Datagram
A,B ⊟NBT: DS: Type = 17 (DIRECT GROUP)
      NBT: Datagram Packet Type = DIRECT GROUP
     ⊕NBT: Datagram Flags = 26 (0x1A)
      NBT: Datagram ID = 32790 (0x8016)
      NBT: Source IP Address = 212.140.133.35
      NBT: Source Port = 138 (0x8A)
      NBT: Datagram Length = 187 (0xBB)
      NBT: Packet Offset = 0 (0x0)
      NBT: Source Name = ALICENT
D     NBT: Destination Name = TEST-NTD       <1D>
      NBT: DS Data: Number of data bytes remaining = 119 (0x0077)
    ⊕SMB: C transact, File = \MAILSLOT\BROWSE
    ⊟BROWSER: Host Announcement [0x01] ALICENT
      BROWSER: Command = Host Announcement [0x01]
      BROWSER: Update Count = 0 (0x0)
      BROWSER: Annoucement Interval [minutes] = 4
      BROWSER: Name = ALICENT
      BROWSER: Major Version = 4 (0x4)
      BROWSER: Minor Version = 0 (0x0)
E    ⊟BROWSER: Server Type Summary = 36867 (0x9003)
      BROWSER: ............................1 = Workstation
      BROWSER: ...........................1. = Server
      BROWSER: ..........................0.. = Not SQL Server
      BROWSER: .........................0... = Not Domain Controller
      BROWSER: ........................0.... = Not Backup Controller
      BROWSER: .......................0..... = Not Time Source
      BROWSER: ......................0...... = Not Apple Server
      BROWSER: .....................0....... = Not Novell
      BROWSER: ....................0........ = Not Domain Member Server
      BROWSER: ...................0......... = Not Print Queue Server
      BROWSER: ..................0.......... = Not Dialin Server
      BROWSER: .................0........... = Not Xenix Server
      BROWSER: ................1............ = Windows NT Workstation
      BROWSER: ...............0............. = Not WFW System
      BROWSER: ..............1.............. = Windows NT Server
      BROWSER: .............0............... = Not Potential Browser
      BROWSER: ............0................ = Not Backup Browser
      BROWSER: ...........0................. = Not Master Browser
      BROWSER: ..........0.................. = Not Domain Master Browser
      BROWSER: .........0................... = Not OSF
      BROWSER: ........0.................... = Not VMS
      BROWSER: .......0..................... = Not Windows 95 or above
      BROWSER: .0........................... = Not Local List Only
      BROWSER: 0............................ = Not Domain Enum
      BROWSER: Browser Election Version = 271 (0x10F)
      BROWSER: Browser Constant = 43605 (0xAA55)
```

Figure 21.3 Network Monitor trace: host announces itself to the browser service

In the next module we look at how a client finds a browse server and requests the browse list.

21.3 How the client locates a browse server

At this point the PC has booted and announced itself to whatever browse servers are listening on the local network segment. Now we want to browse the network. This is a two-stage process:

1. find a browse server
2. request the browse list from the server.

Locating a browse server

To locate a browse server, the client uses one or two special NetBIOS names:

domainname<1d>: as we'll see in Module 21.7, the machine that is acting as the browse master on a network segment registers itself as part of the NetBIOS name group *domainname*<1d>. This group is specific to the local network segment and therefore identifies the browse master on this segment, the *segment master browser (segMB)*. It's specific to this segment in that each segment has its own segMB, and because packets are only ever sent to it by broadcast. Even if you try to resolve it using WINS, WINS will reply with the segment's sub-net broadcast address, so you'll end up broadcasting anyway

domainname<1b>: on a multi-segment network, i.e. a network containing routers, you have many <1d> browse masters for a domain, one per segment. One of these performs a special role, of coordinating all the others, and it's called the *domain master browser (domMB)*. This role is always fulfilled by the primary domain controller. The domain master browser registers itself as the NetBIOS unique name *domainname*<1b>. The domMB acts as the segMB on its own segment.

Figure 21.4 illustrates how segMBs and the domMB are distributed over the network.

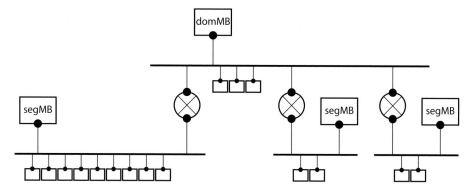

Figure 21.4 How segMBs and the domMB are distributed over the network

Now let's see how the client uses the <1b> and <1d> names to locate a browse server. For simplicity we'll assume that our client is called AliceNT and our domain is **TEST-NTD**.

1. AliceNT issues a NetBIOS name query to resolve the domain master browser, i.e. **TEST-NTD<1b>**, and notes the result (below). This is usually done shortly after the PC boots:

Src Other Addr	Dst Other Addr	Protocol	Description
212.140.133.35	212.140.133.127	NBT	NS: Query req. for TEST-NTD <1B>
212.140.133.13	212.140.133.35	NBT	NS: Query (Node Status) resp. for TEST-NTD

2a. AliceNT broadcasts a browser protocol **GetBackupList** request to **TEST-NTD<1d>**, which is received by whatever local machine happens to be acting as browse master. In spite of its name, the **GetBackupList** requests a list of *all* the browse servers on this segment for this domain, not just the backup servers

2b. if **TEST-NTD<1b>** resolved OK in step 1, AliceNT sends a **GetBackupList** request to the domain master browser as well. (This request is unicast or "directed," i.e. not broadcast.)

   The reason for this step is that it allows AliceNT to find a browse server on another sub-net if there isn't one on her local segment. (Of course, for this to work, AliceNT must be running WINS, because if the domMB is on another segment, the only way AliceNT can resolve its name, **TEST-NTD<1b>**, is via WINS – broadcasts won't work.)

3. AliceNT receives the list of servers in reply. (She doesn't care if she gets two replies.) In the trace below, the query has returned only a single server name, HAL9000-NT, because our test network is very small; in real life the list would probably be much longer, and AliceNT would choose three browse servers at random from the list, for use in the next step in the browsing process, which we cover in the next module.

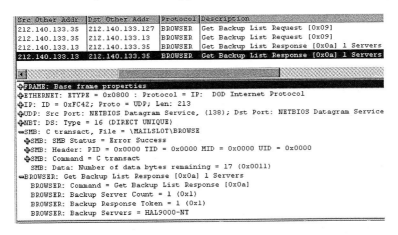

21.4 Retrieving the browse list

AliceNT now has a list of browse servers on her local segment. Each of these has the browse list for AliceNT's domain. All that remains for her to do is request and retrieve the information, which she does as follows:

1. AliceNT chooses one of the browse servers from her list of three, and establishes a NetBIOS session connection (TCP port 139) to it if she doesn't have one open already. In our case AliceNT only knows of one browse server, HAL9000-NT, so she uses that:

   a. she resolves the name **HAL9000-NT<20>** to IP address 212.140.133.13. (She connects to **<20>**, the Server NT Service – or equivalent on other operating systems – which is what accepts NetBIOS session connections.) This is shown in lines 141 and 142 of Figure 21.5, which is displaying exactly the same trace data that we had in the previous module. However, here we've used **ethereal** instead of Network Monitor because it shows the browse list retrieval more clearly. In the figure we've again shown the **GetBackupList** requests and responses (lines 138–140) that we saw in the previous module so you can get a feel for the whole conversation.

   b. AliceNT's NetBIOS establishes the TCP connection (Lines 143–145). You probably recognize the SYN, SYN/ACK, ACK three-way handshake by now. (This step may not happen if NetBIOS already has a TCP connection between AliceNT and HAL9000-NT, because multiple NetBIOS sessions can be multiplexed over a single TCP connection.)

   c. AliceNT opens the NetBIOS Session Service (NBSS) connection (lines 146–151)

2. now that AliceNT has an open connection to the browse server, she sends a **NetServerEnum2** ("enumerate servers") request for the browse list (line 152)

3. the server replies with the **NetServerEnum2** response, containing the browse list for this domain (line 153).

You can see the browse list in the protocol tree pane. It says it has two entries, and then lists them, ALICENT and HAL9000-NT.

This illustrates three important features of browsing:

1. the browse list contains information for a single domain only – for **TEST-NTD** in our example here. We'll see how we can browse more than one domain in the next module.

2. the browse list contains a list of machines but does *not* contain a list of shares (file systems that can be mapped/mounted from other systems) even though Windows Explorer make it appear that it does. Obtaining the list of shares is handled differently (see next module).

3. the browse list does *not* contain the machines' IP numbers – only their names. This means that to connect to a machine you see in Windows Explorer, you still must be able to resolve its name, using NetBIOS name resolution.

In the TCP/IP context, that's surprising, but it seems reasonable when you remember that NetBIOS has to work over many different network systems, not just TCP/IP, and therefore it's unlikely that anything so network-system-specific as IP numbers would be visible at such a high level of the NetBIOS system as the browse list.

However, the browse list does contains a little detail for each machine, including the server description – e.g. "test-network PDC," which shows in the **Comment** field in Windows Explorer and in the **Remark** field in **net view**.

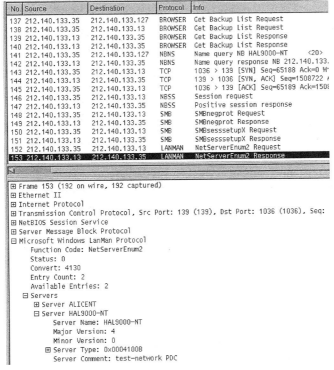

No.	Source	Destination	Protocol	Info
137	212.140.133.35	212.140.133.127	BROWSER	Get Backup List Request
138	212.140.133.35	212.140.133.13	BROWSER	Get Backup List Request
139	212.140.133.13	212.140.133.35	BROWSER	Get Backup List Response
140	212.140.133.13	212.140.133.35	BROWSER	Get Backup List Response
141	212.140.133.35	212.140.133.127	NBNS	Name query NB HAL9000-NT <20>
142	212.140.133.13	212.140.133.35	NBNS	Name query response NB 212.140.133.
143	212.140.133.35	212.140.133.13	TCP	1036 > 139 [SYN] Seq=65188 Ack=0 W
144	212.140.133.13	212.140.133.35	TCP	139 > 1036 [SYN, ACK] Seq=1508722 /
145	212.140.133.35	212.140.133.13	TCP	1036 > 139 [ACK] Seq=65189 Ack=150{
146	212.140.133.35	212.140.133.13	NBSS	Session request
147	212.140.133.13	212.140.133.35	NBSS	Positive session response
148	212.140.133.35	212.140.133.13	SMB	SMBnegprot Request
149	212.140.133.13	212.140.133.35	SMB	SMBnegprot Response
150	212.140.133.35	212.140.133.13	SMB	SMBsesssetupX Request
151	212.140.133.13	212.140.133.35	SMB	SMBsesssetupX Response
152	212.140.133.35	212.140.133.13	LANMAN	NetServerEnum2 Request
153	**212.140.133.13**	**212.140.133.35**	**LANMAN**	**NetServerEnum2 Response**

```
⊞ Frame 153 (192 on wire, 192 captured)
⊞ Ethernet II
⊞ Internet Protocol
⊞ Transmission Control Protocol, Src Port: 139 (139), Dst Port: 1036 (1036), Seq:
⊞ NetBIOS Session Service
⊞ Server Message Block Protocol
⊟ Microsoft Windows LanMan Protocol
      Function Code: NetServerEnum2
      Status: 0
      Convert: 4130
      Entry Count: 2
      Available Entries: 2
    ⊟ Servers
      ⊞ Server ALICENT
      ⊟ Server HAL9000-NT
            Server Name: HAL9000-NT
            Major Version: 4
            Minor Version: 0
          ⊞ Server Type: 0x0004100B
            Server Comment: test-network PDC
```

Figure 21.5 ethereal trace: retrieving the browse list

21.5 Client browsing more than one domain

We said in the previous module that the retrieved browse list contains details for a single domain only. How then does Windows Explorer show information from multiple domains?

To explain this, first let's look at the **net view** command. This is a command line semi-equivalent of Windows Explorer; it's advantage is that makes it easier to see exactly what's happening. We'll start with three basic variants of the command:

```
net view                          get and display the browse list for my domain
net view /domain                  get and display the list of domain names
net view /domain:dname            get and display the browse list for domain dname
```

(You must leave a space between "view" and "/domain.") These commands reflect very closely how browsing works internally (and are what we used to generate the network traffic in the previous module.) In Figure 21.6 (run on AliceNT, who is part of the **TEST-NTD** domain), you can see that **net view** without any arguments displays only the machines in this domain.

```
Command Prompt

C:\>net view
Server Name        Remark
------------------------------------------------------
\\ALICENT
\\HAL9000-NT       test-network PDC

C:\>net view /domain
Domain
------------------------------------------------------
TEST-NTD
UIT
WORKGROUP

C:\>net view /domain:uit
Server Name        Remark
------------------------------------------------------
\\DENNISNT
\\GROOTLX          grootlx server (Samba 2.0.7)
\\SCUTTER
\\TECHPC
```

Figure 21.6 net view without arguments

Displaying information for other domains is a two-step process:

1. retrieve a list of domains (**net view /domain**)
2. then for each domain, list the machines within it (**net view /domain:**dname).

You can see the outputs for these commands too in Figure 21.6. Our test network has two real domains (**UIT** and **TEST-NTD**); the **WORKGROUP** domain is a hangover from some Samba (Module 22.4) machine.

Figure 21.7, which is a slightly different view of the same data from the previous module, shows the traffic in response to **net view /domain** and **net view /domain:uit** commands. In this example, AliceNT isn't using WINS.

> **Lines 184–185** get the list of domain names from my browse master. (The **NetServerEnum2** request can be used to get a list of domains as here, or a list of servers as we saw in the previous module, by specifying appropriate flags in the request.)

Line 187: broadcast a request for the list of **UIT**'s browsers. This is sent to **UIT<1d>**, i.e. to domain **UIT**'s segment master browser

Line 188: AliceNT looks for domain **UIT**'s domain master browser (but no reply was ever received, for reasons unknown)

Line 191: 212.140.133.7 **UIT**'s PDC and therefore domMB replies to line 187's request with a list of browse servers

Lines 192–193: AliceNT chooses one server name (TECHPC in this case) from the list of servers she has just received, and resolves its name to an IP number. Then …

Lines 194–203: she establishes a NetBIOS session (NBSS) connection to the chosen browse server (TECHPC, 212.140.133.7)

Lines 204–205: AliceNT finally asks for the browse list (of servers in domain UIT) and receives the information in reply.

No.	Source	Destination	Protocol	Info
184	212.140.133.35	212.140.133.13	LANMAN	NetServerEnum2 Request
185	212.140.133.13	212.140.133.35	LANMAN	NetServerEnum2 Response
187	212.140.133.35	212.140.133.127	BROWSER	Get Backup List Request
188	212.140.133.35	212.140.133.127	NBNS	Name query NB UIT <1b>
191	212.140.133.7	212.140.133.35	BROWSER	Get Backup List Response
192	212.140.133.35	212.140.133.127	NBNS	Name query NB TECHPC <20>
193	212.140.133.7	212.140.133.35	NBNS	Name query response NB 212.140.133.7
194	212.140.133.35	212.140.133.7	TCP	1035 > 139 [SYN] Seq=64244 Ack=0 Win=
195	212.140.133.7	212.140.133.35	TCP	139 > 1035 [SYN, ACK] Seq=28887888 Ac
196	212.140.133.35	212.140.133.7	TCP	1035 > 139 [ACK] Seq=64245 Ack=288878
197	212.140.133.35	212.140.133.7	NBSS	Session request
198	212.140.133.7	212.140.133.35	NBSS	Positive session response
199	212.140.133.35	212.140.133.7	SMB	SMBnegprot Request
200	212.140.133.7	212.140.133.35	SMB	SMBnegprot Response
201	212.140.133.35	212.140.133.7	SMB	SMBsesssetupX Request
203	212.140.133.7	212.140.133.35	SMB	SMBsesssetupX Response
204	212.140.133.35	212.140.133.7	LANMAN	NetServerEnum2 Request
205	212.140.133.7	212.140.133.35	LANMAN	NetServerEnum2 Response

```
⊞ Frame 185 (170 on wire, 170 captured)
⊞ Ethernet II
⊞ Internet Protocol
⊞ Transmission Control Protocol, Src Port: 139 (139), Dst Port: 1034 (1034), Seq: 1199750E
⊞ NetBIOS Session Service
⊞ Server Message Block Protocol
⊟ Microsoft Windows LanMan Protocol
     Function Code: NetServerEnum2
     Status: 0
     Convert: 0
     Entry Count: 3
     Available Entries: 3
   ⊟ Servers
     ⊞ Server TEST-NTD
     ⊞ Server UIT
```

Figure 21.7 ethereal trace: **net view /domain** and **net view /domain: uit**

21.6 Different types of browse server

Up to now we've concentrated on browsing as seen by the client. We now have to look at two issues concerning browse servers:

1. how does a machine decide whether to become a browse server? How does a browse server decide whether it ought to act as a segment master browser, or even the domain master browser?

2. all the browse operations we've seen depend on broadcasting to announce a PC's presence on the segment and to find a browse server. How can this be extended to a LAN that contains routers, where broadcasts are limited to the local segment?

To answer these questions we must first look at the different types of browse servers you can have.

Types of browse server

A PC can play four (or five) different server roles in the browsing system:

1. *segment master browser*: there can be only one of these per network segment. It listens on a segment for announcements (from machines in its domain only) and from those announcements builds up the browse list for the local segment. It can also service **GetBackupList** and **NetServerEnum2** get-browse-list requests from clients on this segment

2. *backup browsers*: these don't accumulate the browse list themselves. (In fact, they can't: announcements are made to *domainname*<1d>, which is a unique NetBIOS name that only the segMB has registered, so only the segMB can hear the announcements.) Instead, every 15 minutes or so they retrieve a copy of the current browse list from the segment master browser. However, backup browsers can and do service get-browse-list requests from clients on this segment. This improves the performance of the system, which is one function of backup browsers. Their other function is to be able to take over from the segment master browser if it fails

3. *potential browsers*: these aren't acting as browse servers at all, but if the segment master browser or some of the backup browsers fail, they may become browse servers if necessary. Most Windows PCs are potential browsers. In the next module we'll see how potential browsers can change state and become backup or master browsers

4. *domain master browser*: there can be only one of these per domain, irrespective of how many network segments there are. It communicates periodically with each of the segment master browsers on each of the network segments and retrieves their segment-specific browse lists. It merges these into a single browse list covering the whole domain, which it sends back to each segment master browser. In this way, every segment can get a complete browse list for the whole network.

    The PDC always acts as the domain master browser. The domain master browser registers the NetBIOS unique name *domainname*<1b> (which, incidentally, is often used to find the PDC, even though strictly it's only the domain master browser)

5. *non-browser*: this never, ever becomes a browse server.

There is no NetBIOS group name to identify backup browsers on this segment – you can only find out which they are by asking the segMB for a list of them. All potential browsers do register <1e> as explained in the next module. However, if you ask WINS to resolve <1e>, it gives you 255.255.255.255 to force you to broadcast to the group name as usual. (The Samba **nmblookup** tool is great for exploring this type of issue – you can issue specific queries and explicitly see the results.)

Replication from master to backup servers

We haven't explained yet how a machine decides which role it's to fulfill, but for now, let's assume we have a browse master and a population of backup browsers, and see how they interact. The mechanism is very simple:

- every 12 minutes, each backup browser contacts the segment master browser (they locate it by broadcasting to *domainname*<1d>)
- using *NetServerEnum* calls the backup browser asks the segMB for:

  a. the latest browse list of servers in this domain

  b. the latest list of domain names

- the segMB replies with the lists. The reply isn't just a set of changes or updates since last time; the list is returned in its entirety every time.

Figure 21.8 shows a backup browser, 212.140.133.35, regularly contacting the segMB, 212.140.133.13, and on each iteration requesting the two lists. (The "T" field is time since the packet on the preceding line.)

T	No.	Source	Destination	Protocol	Info
720.0	11	212.140.133.35	212.140.133.13	LANMAN	NetServerEnum2 Request
0.004	12	212.140.133.13	212.140.133.35	LANMAN	NetServerEnum2 Response
0.001	13	212.140.133.35	212.140.133.13	LANMAN	NetServerEnum2 Request
0.003	14	212.140.133.13	212.140.133.35	LANMAN	NetServerEnum2 Response
720.1	15	212.140.133.35	212.140.133.13	LANMAN	NetServerEnum2 Request
0.005	16	212.140.133.13	212.140.133.35	LANMAN	NetServerEnum2 Response
0.001	17	212.140.133.35	212.140.133.13	LANMAN	NetServerEnum2 Request
0.003	18	212.140.133.13	212.140.133.35	LANMAN	NetServerEnum2 Response
720.0	19	212.140.133.35	212.140.133.13	LANMAN	NetServerEnum2 Request
0.004	20	212.140.133.13	212.140.133.35	LANMAN	NetServerEnum2 Response
0.001	21	212.140.133.35	212.140.133.13	LANMAN	NetServerEnum2 Request
0.003	22	212.140.133.13	212.140.133.35	LANMAN	NetServerEnum2 Response
720.0	23	212.140.133.35	212.140.133.13	LANMAN	NetServerEnum2 Request
0.008	24	212.140.133.13	212.140.133.35	LANMAN	NetServerEnum2 Response
0.001	25	212.140.133.35	212.140.133.13	LANMAN	NetServerEnum2 Request
0.003	26	212.140.133.13	212.140.133.35	LANMAN	NetServerEnum2 Response

```
⊟ Microsoft Windows LanMan Protocol
      Function Code: NetServerEnum2
      Status: 0
      Convert: 4130
      Entry Count: 2
      Available Entries: 2
   ⊟ Servers
      ⊞ Server ALICENT
      ⊞ Server HAL9000-NT
```

Figure 21.8 ethereal trace: periodic replication of browse and domain name lists to segMB

In the next module we'll see how a machine decides which role it is to fulfill.

21.7 Deciding which PC takes on which role; elections

There are Windows Registry settings (see Notes) to make a PC a non-browser, or to make it a *preferred master browser* (i.e. it wants to be either the master browser or at least a backup browser). Unless it's a non-browser, it's automatically a potential browser, at least. In this module we explain what happens when a potential browser PC starts up, and in the next module we show a line-by-line trace.

When our PC starts:

1. it announces its presence to *domainname*<1d> – as every machine does

2. because it may become a browser later on, it registers as part of the NetBIOS group *domainname*<1e>, which is the *browser election group*

3. it broadcasts a **RequestAnnouncement** browser request to *domainname*<1d>. This asks the segMB (for *domainname*, on the local segment) to announce itself, which is how our PC finds the segment browse master.

What happens next depends on whether our PC got a reply in step 3. Let's assume there's no reply (e.g. we're just building our network and this is the first machine to be added, or the segment browse master is down):

4. our PC forces a *browser election* in order to nominate a new segment browse master. It does this by sending a browser **Election (Force)** request, broadcasting it to *domainname*<1e> which is heard only by browsers and potential browsers (see step 2 above).

   domainname<1e> is treated specially by WINS (if you are running it). When a PC asks WINS to resolve *domainname*<1e>, WINS returns the IP address 255.255.255.255, so the PC then broadcasts to this address whatever it was going to send to <1e>. This ensures the election stays local to the sub-net, which is what we want. Remember, it is the *segment* master browser that we're electing

5. each browser and potential browser, including our PC, joins in the election by replying with an **Election** packet containing details of this machine's operating system and current browser role, coded as a 4-byte number called its *election criteria*.

   The election criteria are encoded so that Windows NT Server machines have priority over other operating systems, then NT Workstation, then Windows-9x, so that server machines are most likely to win the election. For machines with the same operating system, priority is given to the PDC, then a preferred master browser, then an existing master browser, and finally a backup browser. Figure 21.9 shows the election criteria values for an NT 4.0 server currently acting as both segMB and domMB

6. every machine participating in the election compares its own election criteria with the criteria in all the **Election**s received from other machines. The one with the highest value of the criteria wins, becomes the segment browse master, sends a few more **Election**s just to make sure that everyone has heard, registers itself as *domainname* <1d> (segMB), and finally announces itself as the segment browse master. If things are working correctly, there will be no responses to these **Election**s because all the other machines realize this machine has the best criteria.

```
    BROWSER: Command = Election [0x08]
    BROWSER: Election Version = 1 (0x1)
  ⊕BROWSER: Election Criteria = 536940462 (0x20010FAE)
    ⊕BROWSER: Election OS Summary = 32 (0x20)
       BROWSER: .......0 = Not WFW
       BROWSER: ......0. = Not used
       BROWSER: .....0.. = Not used
       BROWSER: ....0... = Not used
       BROWSER: ...0.... = Not Windows NT Workstation
       BROWSER: ..1..... = Windows NT Server
       BROWSER: .0...... = Not used
       BROWSER: 0....... = Not used
     BROWSER: Election Revision = 271 (0x10F)
    ⊕BROWSER: Election Desire Summary = 174 (0xAE)
       BROWSER: .......0 = Not Backup Browse Server
       BROWSER: ......1. = Standby Browser Server
       BROWSER: .....1.. = Currently Master Browser Server
       BROWSER: ....1... = Domain Master Browse Server
       BROWSER: ...0.... = Not used
       BROWSER: ..1..... = Transport Running WINS Client
       BROWSER: .0...... = Not used
       BROWSER: 1....... = Windows NT Advanced Server
    BROWSER: Server Up Time [DD:hh:mm:ss] 3:20:47:56
    BROWSER: Election Server Name = HAL9000-NT
```

Figure 21.9 Network Monitor trace: **Election** criteria values

In fact, what we've just described is an over-simplification:

a. to reduce the amount of network traffic, in step 5 machines delay a certain amount of time before sending their **Election** details. The current browse master replies to the **Election (Force)** after 1/10 of a second; backup browsers delay randomly for 2/10–6/10 of a second and others delay for 8/10–3 seconds. Then …

b. while waiting to send its own **Election**, if a PC hears one from another machine that indicates the other PC would be elected, this PC doesn't bother sending its own **Election**, because it knows it's going to lose the election and sending its own **Election** would only waste network bandwidth and processing power on other machines.

These two features mean that the existing segMB will broadcast first, and unless a better candidate has just joined the network, the existing segMB will win the election immediately, so there will be very little election traffic in practice.

The above describes the case where our PC got no reply to its **Request Announcement** in step 3. If our PC does hear the segMB reply with an **Announcement**, our PC compares the segMB's criteria (which are included in the **Announcement**) against its own criteria; if our PC's criteria are worse, there's no point forcing an election, so our PC just announces itself as a potential browser and joins in the browsing system as normal.

Elections also occur (i) when a preferred master browser PC boots, (ii) when any PC boots and can't find a segment master browser, (iii) when a backup browser tries to contact the master and it's not available, and (iv) when a master browser closes down gracefully (because it forces an election as it goes).

In the next module we look at the trace of an election line by line.

21.8 Lab – line-by-line trace of an election

```
X alicent-isdomainmaster-boot-election.netmon - Ethereal
File  Edit  Capture  Display  Tools
No.  T    Source           Destination      Protocol  Info
  61 11.8 212.140.133.35   212.140.133.127  NBNS      Registration NB ALICENT          <03>
  62 12.6 212.140.133.35   212.140.133.127  NBNS      Registration NB ALICENT          <03>
  63 17.6 212.140.133.35   212.140.133.127  NBNS      Registration NB ALICENT          <20>
  64 18.4 212.140.133.35   212.140.133.127  NBNS      Registration NB ALICENT          <20>
  65 19.2 212.140.133.35   212.140.133.127  BROWSER   Host Announcement ALICENT, Workstation,
  66 19.2 212.140.133.35   212.140.133.127  NBNS      Registration NB TEST-NTD         <1e>
  69 19.9 212.140.133.35   212.140.133.127  NBNS      Registration NB TEST-NTD         <1e>
  70 20.7 212.140.133.35   212.140.133.127  NBNS      Registration NB TEST-NTD         <1e>
  71 21.4 212.140.133.35   212.140.133.127  NBNS      Registration NB TEST-NTD         <1e>
  72 22.2 212.140.133.35   212.140.133.127  BROWSER   Request Announcement
  73 22.2 212.140.133.35   212.140.133.127  BROWSER   Local Master Announcement HAL9000-NT,
  74 22.2 212.140.133.35   212.140.133.127  BROWSER   Browser Election Request
  75 22.2 212.140.133.35   212.140.133.127  BROWSER   Host Announcement ALICENT, Workstation,
  76 22.3 212.140.133.13   212.140.133.127  BROWSER   Browser Election Request
  77 23.3 212.140.133.13   212.140.133.127  BROWSER   Browser Election Request
  78 24.3 212.140.133.13   212.140.133.127  BROWSER   Browser Election Request
  79 25.3 212.140.133.13   212.140.133.127  BROWSER   Browser Election Request
  80 26.1 212.140.133.13   212.140.133.127  BROWSER   Become Backup Browser
  81 26.1 212.140.133.35   212.140.133.127  BROWSER   Request Announcement
  82 26.3 212.140.133.13   212.140.133.127  BROWSER   Local Master Announcement HAL9000-NT, Wc
  98 26.5 212.140.133.35   212.140.133.127  BROWSER   Host Announcement ALICENT, Workstation,

⊞ Internet Protocol
⊞ User Datagram Protocol
⊞ NetBIOS Datagram Service
⊞ Server Message Block Protocol
⊟ Microsoft Windows Browser Protocol
     OpCode: Become Backup Browser
     Browser to Promote: ALICENT
```

Figure 21.10 ethereal trace: AliceNT booting

Figure 21.10 shows the trace for AliceNT booting (filtered to exclude packets that aren't relevant to browsing). We have configured AliceNT's Windows Registry setting so that she will become a backup browser at least (see Notes). She is not using WINS.

Lines 61–64: (separate from browsing) AliceNT registers her NetBIOS names for Messenger Service (**<03>**) and Server Service (**<20>**) as usual

Line 65: this is the start of AliceNT participating in the browse system. She announces her presence so that the segMB can add her computer's name to the browse list.

Lines 66–71: she is a potential browser at least, so she registers as part of the **TEST-NTD<1e>** (browser election) group, so that she will be able to hear elections if she needs to.

Lines 72–73: she checks that there is a segMB present (by asking it to announce itself) and hears the reply from 212.140.133.13 saying that it is the segMB.

Line 74: because we configured her Windows Registry to be a backup browser at least, she forces an election

Line 75: she announces herself as a potential browser. (You can't see that detail in the figure because the line is truncated, but if you run **ethereal** yourself you will see it clearly, both in the packet list display and in the protocol tree pane.)

Line 76: HAL9000-NT (212.140.133.13), the current browse master, joins in the election and broadcasts its election criteria

Line 77: no-one else has replied to the election, so HAL9000-NT believes that it has won the election. (AliceNT has seen that HAL9000-NT beats her, so she doesn't bother sending her **Election** at all.)

Lines 78–79: HAL9000-NT still believes it's going to win the election and sends a few more confirming **Elections** If HAL9000-NT had not been the segMB already, i.e. if another machine had previously won an election, HAL9000-NT would now register itself as *domainname* <1d> to identify itself to other machines as the current segMB. However, as HAL9000-NT was already the segMB before this election started, it has no need to register itself as a *domainname* <1d> again.

Line 80: HAL9000-NT is now the browse master, and instructs AliceNT to become a backup browser. The protocol tree pane shows the detail of how HAL9000-NT tells AliceNT to do this.

Line 81: AliceNT configures herself as a backup browser, and sends an **Announcement Request** to check that there is a browse master. (You'd think she could remember this from Line 73, but it appears that the browser code internally is divided into separate chunks for the "client," "backup browser," etc. roles and there's no communication between them.)

Line 82: HAL9000-NT announces itself as the segment master browser

Line 98: AliceNT announces herself as a backup browser. HAL9000-NT hears this and adds AliceNT to its list of backup browsers.

The election is finished, HAL9000-NT is the segMB and AliceNT is acting as backup browser. The browse system is back to a steady state again, where all the browse servers know of one another and act accordingly, handling client requests, etc.

The browse system aims to have one backup browser for every 32 machines on the local segment. The segMB counts how many different machines have announced themselves, and for every 32, it instructs one to become a backup, as in line 80 above.

(A better name for an election packet would be a "bid" packet, because one machine doesn't elect another; it merely announces its own bid, and if nobody else bids higher, it knows it has been elected. This is like participating in an auction to buy something without an auctioneer. If I make a bid and nobody bids within a "reasonable amount of time" after me, I know I have purchased the item and go and pay the vendor.)

Note: Netmon shows election packets slightly differently to **ethereal**. Netmon distinguishes between an **Election (Force)** packet to initiate an election, and an **Election** bid packet in response to the **Force**. **ethereal** just shows them all as **Elections** in the packet list pane (but of course you can see the full detail for each in the protocol tree pane).

21.9 Multiple-segment browsing and the domain master browser

Segment master browsers hear all **Announcement**s from PCs on the local LAN segment, and build up their browse list from these. But if your network contains routers, and therefore consists of several segments, you end up with several disjointed, partial browse lists – one for each segment. How are these combined?

This is where the domain master browser comes in:

- each segment master browser (i.e. the segment master browser on each of the network segments) contacts the domain master browser every 15 minutes. It knows who the domMB is by resolving the NetBIOS name *domainname*<**1b**>. Because the domMB is on a different segment to the segMB, this name resolution can't use broadcasts, so how does it work? For browsing to function in this type of network, you must configure your system in one of two ways:

  a. use WINS. We saw in Chapter 19 that WINS operates perfectly well over multiple segments, because it uses directed (unicast) UDP instead of broadcasts. The domMB can register itself with WINS (no matter where the WINS server is) and the segMBs can query the WINS server (no matter where it is) so cross-segment resolution is no problem

  b. add an entry to each segMB's **Lmhosts** file to tell it where the domMB is. We know the primary domain controller always acts as the domMB, so we use its IP address. For Windows-NT enter, for example:

    ```
    192.0.2.13 bobnt #PRE #DOM:EX-NTD
    ```

    naming **bobnt** as the PDC; the browser realizes that it can use this as the domMB address too. Windows-95 machines aren't as clever, so you have to add an explicit <**1b**> entry in addition, e.g.

    ```
    192.0.2.13 bobnt #PRE #DOM:EX-NTD
    192.0.2.13 "EX-NTD■■■■■■■■■\0x1b" #PRE
    ```

    where each ■ indicates a space. (We sometimes find that it's necessary to add this on NT also.)

- from each segMB that connects to the domMB, the domMB retrieves the segment-specific browse list. It merges all these into a single browse list covering the whole domain, which it sends back to each segment master browser. In this way, every segment can get a complete browse list for the whole network.

Because the segMBs contact the domMB every 15 minutes, it can take up to about 45 minutes for the browse lists across all the segMBs to reach a steady state and be fully synchronized, each having a full browse list for the whole network. And of course, if a PC is switched off or dies, the same length of time can elapse before every segMB gets the updated browse list that doesn't contain this machine. During this time, PCs on other segments will see the PC in their Network Neighborhoods, even though it's been switched off. (See Web Appendix 27 for detailed examples of how browse lists synchronize over multiple segments.)

Multiple domains – how one domain learns about others

Elections, segMBs, and domMBs all relate to a single domain only. (Recall that all elections, and conversations between client and master browsers, use *domainname*<xx> to locate the relevant machines.)

Browse masters for one domain discover the presence of other domains on the network in two ways:

1. The special NetBIOS group name <01><02>__MSBROWSE__<02><01> is registered by all segMBs. This name is local to a segment, and even if it's registered with WINS, WINS will return the address 255.255.255.255 for it, so any machine trying to contact it will in fact broadcast locally. Every 12 minutes, each segMB broadcasts to this address a *Domain Enum* or *Domain Announcement* (Figure 21.11) containing the name of this domain, i.e. every 12 minutes the segMB for one domain will hear domain announcements from every other domain's local segMB on this wire, discovering both the domain name and the address of its local segMB. The segMBs propagate this other-domain information back to their respective domMBs just as they do with their browse lists, and the domMBs propagate it out to each of their respective segMBs. Consequently, all segMBs end up with a complete list of all domains on the network, even if some domains are present on only a few of the segments. (To be precise, browse servers for domain A will learn about domain B and vice versa only if there is at least one segment, somewhere on the network, that contains a browse server for A and a browse server for B.)

2. if all the machines are using WINS, each domMB sends a special request to WINS, asking for a list of domain master browsers. (This is like a wildcard request for *<1b>, but in fact a special RPC call is used to retrieve the information. You can perform the same operation yourself using the **GD** option of the **winscl.exe** command in the NT 4.0 resource kit.)

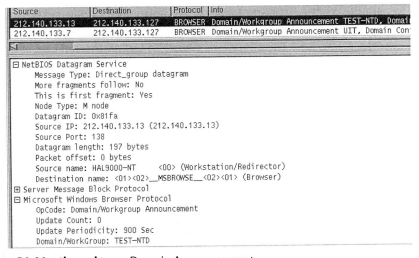

Figure 21.11 ethereal trace: Domain Announcement

21.10 Miscellaneous

Browsing and NT Services

The NT Service **Browser** is in fact the "server" side of browsing – the component that partici-pates in elections, etc. and acts as segMB or domMB as necessary. This is implemented in the user-level **Services.exe** process. There is also a kernel-level component to browsing in **Rdr.sys**.

If your machine is acting only as a browse client, you don't need the **Browser** Service and your machine will work fine without it. However, as the resilience of your browsing depends on having enough backup browse servers, etc., you shouldn't normally disable **Browser**.

Browsing and accessing shares

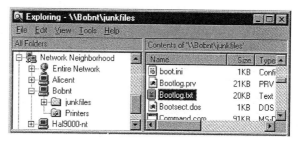

Figure 21.12 Information about remote machine BobNT

In Windows Explorer you can click on a machine in Network Neighborhood (or use **net view** *\\hostname*) to display the list of shares and printers on that machine. For example, Figure 21.12 shows Windows Explorer on AliceNT displaying information about remote machine BobNT. However, in Module 21.5 we said that listing the shares on a machine isn't part of the browse serv-ice, so what's happening here? The answer is that AliceNT does *not* obtain the list of BobNT's resources from the browse service, i.e. from a browse server. Instead, she connects directly to BobNT and uses an RPC call to retrieve the list of shares. You can see this in the trace in Figure 21.13. The top pane shows all the packets generated after we clicked on BobNT in Explorer:

Lines 66–67: AliceNT (.35) resolves BobNT's NetBIOS name to his IP address (.31) using the WINS server (.7)

Lines 68–69: ARP request/reply generated by the next step ...

Lines 70–72: establish TCP connection from AliceNT to BobNT in order to ...

Lines 73–77: establish NetBIOS session connection from AliceNT to BobNT

Lines 78–79: ARP request/reply generated by next step ...

Lines 80–86: pass-through logon from AliceNT to PDC (.13)

Lines 87–92: send RPC from AliceNT to BobNT to retrieve list of resources. The tree pane shows packet 92, and the hex pane shows its contents. You can see the list of shares in the ASCII dump.

```
Fr Src Other Addr  Dst Other Addr  Protoc Description
66 212.140.133.35  212.140.133.7   NBT    NS: Query req. for BOBNT
67 212.140.133.7   212.140.133.35  NBT    NS: Query (Node Status) resp. for BOBNT,
68                                 ARP_RA ARP: Request, Target IP: 212.140.133.31
69                                 ARP_RA ARP: Reply, Target IP: 212.140.133.35 Tar
70 212.140.133.35  212.140.133.31  TCP    ....S., len:    4, seq:      56784-56787,
71 212.140.133.31  212.140.133.35  TCP    .A..S., len:    4, seq:      69391-69394,
72 212.140.133.35  212.140.133.31  TCP    .A...., len:    0, seq:      56785-56785,
73 212.140.133.35  212.140.133.31  NBT    SS: Session Request, Dest: BOBNT
74 212.140.133.31  212.140.133.35  NBT    SS: Positive Session Response, Len: 0
75 212.140.133.35  212.140.133.31  SMB    C negotiate, Dialect =
76 212.140.133.31  212.140.133.35  SMB    R negotiate, Dialect # = 7
77 212.140.133.35  212.140.133.31  SMB    C session setup & X, Username = administr
78                                 ARP_RA ARP: Request, Target IP: 212.140.133.13
79                                 ARP_RA ARP: Reply, Target IP: 212.140.133.31 Tar
80 212.140.133.31  212.140.133.13  SMB    C NT create & X, File = \NETLOGON
81 212.140.133.13  212.140.133.31  SMB    R NT create & X, FID = 0x1809
82 212.140.133.31  212.140.133.13  MSRPC  c/o RPC Bind:          UUID 12345678-1234-
83 212.140.133.13  212.140.133.31  MSRPC  c/o RPC Bind Ack:      call 0x1  assoc grp
84 212.140.133.31  212.140.133.13  MSRPC  c/o RPC Request:       call 0x1  opnum 0x2
85 212.140.133.13  212.140.133.31  MSRPC  c/o RPC Response:      call 0x1  context (
86 212.140.133.31  212.140.133.35  SMB    R session setup & X, and R tree connect &
87 212.140.133.35  212.140.133.31  SMB    C NT create & X, File = \srvsvc
88 212.140.133.31  212.140.133.35  SMB    R NT create & X, FID = 0x800
89 212.140.133.35  212.140.133.31  MSRPC  c/o RPC Bind:          UUID 4B324FC8-1670-
90 212.140.133.31  212.140.133.35  MSRPC  c/o RPC Bind Ack:      call 0x1  assoc grp
91 212.140.133.35  212.140.133.31  MSRPC  c/o RPC Request:       call 0x1  opnum 0xF
92 212.140.133.31  212.140.133.35  MSRPC  c/o RPC Response:      call 0x1  context (
```

```
⊕TCP: .AP..., len:   404, seq:      69878-70281, ack:       57735, win: 7810, src: 1
⊕NBT: SS: Session Message, Len: 400
⊕SMB: R transact TransactNmPipe (response to frame 91)
⊕MSRPC: c/o RPC Response:       call 0x1  context 0x0  hint 0x140  cancels 0x0
```

```
00000120 00 00 49 00 50 00 43 00 24 00 00 00 FF FF 0B 00   ..I.P.C.$... ..
00000130 00 00 00 00 00 00 0B 00 00 00 52 00 65 00 6D 00   ..........R.e.m.
00000140 6F 00 74 00 65 00 20 00 49 00 50 00 43 00 00 00   o.t.e. .I.P.C...
00000150 44 00 03 00 00 00 00 00 00 00 03 00 00 00 43 00   D.............C.
00000160 24 00 00 00 00 00 0E 00 00 00 00 00 00 00 0E 00   $...............
00000170 00 00 44 00 65 00 66 00 61 00 75 00 6C 00 74 00   ..D.e.f.a.u.l.t.
00000180 20 00 73 00 68 00 61 00 72 00 65 00 00 00 0A 00   .s.h.a.r.e......
00000190 00 00 00 00 00 00 00 00 0A 00 00 00 6A 00 75 00   ..........j.u.n.
000001A0 6B 00 66 00 69 00 6C 00 65 00 73 00 00 00 01 00   k.f.i.l.e.s.....
```

Figure 21.13 ethereal trace: retrieving the list of shares

This illustrates clearly that the only involvement of the browse service was to let AliceNT know of the existence of a machine BobNT in the first place, and illustrates a couple of other significant points about browsing:

- the browse list contains only names. The client (AliceNT) that receives the browse list still has to resolve the name "BobNT" before she can access resources on the remote machine (BobNT) (c.f. Module 21.4).

- you can access resources on machines without browsing to them. For example, if AliceNT knew already that the BobNT existed, and had a share called **junkdirs**, she could just run the command, e.g.

```
type \\bobnt\junkdirs\bootlog.txt
```

to see the contents of a file. The browser wouldn't even have to be running. This also illustrates that you can use shares without explicitly mapping a drive. However, often we map the drive first, using **Windows Explorer > Tools > Map Network Drive** or the command-line equivalent, e.g.

```
net use J:\\bobnt\junkdirs
type J:bootlog.txt
```

21.11 **What** Find Computer **does**

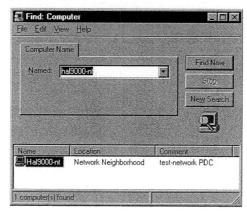

Figure 21.14 Find Computer dialog

The Windows Explorer menu **Tools > Find > Computer** (Figure 21.14) looks for a computer *that is participating in Windows Networking* and that may or may not be displayed in the browse list. How exactly it does this depends on your machine's and your network's configuration. The following describes **Find**ing from AliceNT, who is a member of **TEST-NTD** and isn't using WINS or DNS:

1. **when you enter a name:**

   a. AliceNT retrieves the browse list for her domain from her segMB. If the name is in the browse list, AliceNT displays it *without trying to resolve it.* That means that the machine may not currently be accessible even though it's displayed, e.g. if it closed down in the last 15 or 30 minutes, it may not yet have been removed from the browse list. Only when you click on the found name does AliceNT try to resolve. Figure 21.15 shows the trace generated when we looked for HAL9000-NT from AliceNT.

   Because AliceNT only looks at the browse list for her own domain, if the machine belongs to another domain, AliceNT won't be able to find it using this mechanism

   b. if the name isn't in the browse list, AliceNT tries to resolve the name, using whatever name resolution methods she was configured with, e.g. if NetBIOS name resolution is enabled, AliceNT tries to resolve *name*<20> and to connect to it, using the NetBIOS session service. Note the <20> suffix (the **Server** NT service); if the machine isn't running Server, you won't be able to **Find** it. (You won't be able to find a Windows-9x machine unless it is sharing files or printers.) This explains how you might be unable to **Find** a machine but still **ping** it successfully using its NetBIOS name: **ping** is resolving *name*<00>, not *name*<20>. This circumstance can easily arise if the machine you're **Find**ing is a non-Server and has been disconnected from the wire for a long time, or has just booted up:

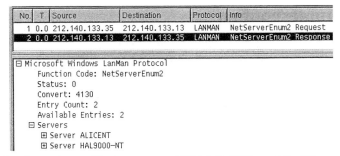

No.	T	Source	Destination	Protocol	Info
1	0.0	212.140.133.35	212.140.133.13	LANMAN	NetServerEnum2 Request
2	0.0	212.140.133.13	212.140.133.35	LANMAN	NetServerEnum2 Response

```
⊟ Microsoft Windows LanMan Protocol
     Function Code: NetServerEnum2
     Status: 0
     Convert: 4130
     Entry Count: 2
     Available Entries: 2
  ⊟ Servers
     ⊞ Server ALICENT
     ⊞ Server HAL9000-NT
```

Figure 21.15 ethereal trace: **Find computer HAL9000-NT** from **AliceNT**

- if it belongs to your domain and is on another segment, its name won't have rippled across to your segMB yet, but if you try again after 15 or 30 minutes or so – multiples of the browse servers' replication frequency – it will be **Find**able

- if it belongs to another domain, its name won't be in your segMB's browse list

2. **when you enter an IP number**

    a. AliceNT retrieves the browse list for her domain from her segMB as before, and looks up the IP number *as a string.* This is for the weird and not recommended case where the PC's name (not it's IP number) is, for example, 1.2.3.4. (If you do this sort of thing it will cause you problems, but the weird name will show in Network Neighborhood!)

    b. AliceNT then tries to create a NetBIOS session connection to the IP address specified, looking for the Server service. Because it doesn't know the target machine's *name*, the connection attempt is to the special name *SMBSERVER<20>. If that succeeds, **Find** displays the IP number as found

    c. if a route exists from AliceNT to the IP address (which means either that the address does exist on the local sub-net, or else its address is on a different sub-net and AliceNT can't tell whether it exists), AliceNT then sends a directed NetBIOS name query for the special name "*" followed by 15 <00>s, which is a NetBIOS adapter status query on an IP number. (It has to use the wildcard name because it doesn't have the real NetBIOS computer name, only its IP address.)

Tip: you can call up the **Find Computer** dialog from outside Windows Explorer by pressing Ctrl-WindowsKey-F. (WindowsKey-F without Ctrl calls up the **Find Files** dialog.)

Tip: you can call use wildcard expressions in the **Find Computer** by name dialog, e.g. "*NT" and "*SRV*". "*" on its own lists all the machines in your segMB's browse list.

21.12 Troubleshooting

There's a good guide to troubleshooting Windows Networking browsing in the Microsoft White Paper on browsing, summarized in a Microsoft Knowledgebase article. See the Notes for full details, but in brief, if a machine is not appearing in the browse list, you trace step by step from that machine's segment:

- first, is it a real problem? Or has the machine just joined the network and it's taking time for its name to ripple across the browse servers on the various segments of your network?
- does the machine appear in that segment's segMB's browse list?
- is segMB replicating the entry to the PDC?
- is the PDC replicating the entry to your own segment's segMB?
- is your segMB replicating the entry to backup browse servers on your segment (because you may be obtaining the browse list from a backup browser rather than the segMB)?

We also include a few extra notes and tips here.

Tools

1. **net view** and **net view /domain:***domainname* show the current browse lists for your own domain, and a specified other domain. What these don't tell you is which browse server your machine is using

2. the NT 4.0 Resource Kit program **browmon.exe** is a GUI program that shows the domains (Figure 21.16a) and browse servers with their browse lists (Figure 21.16b) that the browse system knows about, and details of each browse server's role (Figure 21.16c)

3. another NT 4.0 Resource Kit program, **browstat.exe**, is very useful. It's a command-line program and unfortunately is very awkward to use. However, it does let you retrieve lists of master and backup browsers, and interrogate the browse list on a specific browse server (see Appendix 24 for details)

Notes

1. remember, as we explained in Module 21.4, that even if the name of a machine is displayed in your Network Neighborhood, you still have to resolve that name before you can access the machine (because the browse list doesn't contain the IP numbers of the PCs). This explains how it's possible for two common problems to occur:

   a. a machine name appears in Network Neighborhood, but you can't resolve it. This can occur very easily if the machine has closed down but the browse system hasn't noticed yet. (Even when a client is shut down gracefully, it doesn't tell the browse master.)

b. you can access a machine by name, but it doesn't appear in Network Neighborhood. Again, this can occur easily because of the time intervals for browse list updates. If a machine has booted up, it may take up to 45 minutes for it to be included in all the browse lists across the network.

2. if possible, do *not* use more than one networking system on your Windows machines (e.g. don't use NetBEUI or Novell IPX in addition to TCP/IP). The browse functions on the network are specific to a networking system, so you could get different browse masters and different, incomplete or incompatible browse lists on the different underlying network systems

3. if the segMB dies and there are no other backup or potential browsers on the segment dies, the browse service fails. Even if there is a backup browser, the browse service can be disrupted for a few minutes – it takes a while before the backup browser takes over the role of segMB and the clients have to work out what's happened and switch to the new segMB

4. if the domMB (i.e. the PDC) dies, then the segMBs for this domain on other segments can only see the machines on their local segments, and eventually the browse lists that these segMBs hold will only contain their local machines' names.

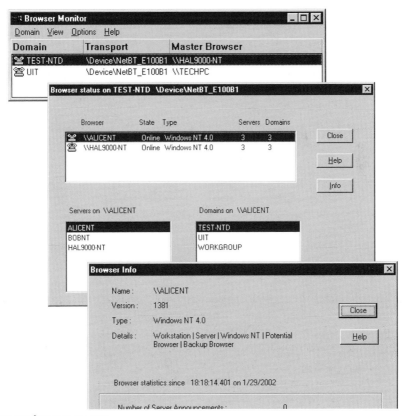

Figure 21.16 browmon.exe

Summary

- Windows Networking browsing means automatically finding a list of the machines and resources on the network. It has nothing to do with Web browsing. You view browse lists in Windows Explorer's **Network Neighborhood** or using the **net view** command
- the browse system works automatically without any manual pre-configuration
- when a PC boots, it announces itself to the browse system by broadcasting to *domainname*<1d>, the segment master browse server, which adds this machine's name to the browse list
- when a PC wants a list of machines and resources:
  - it gets a list of browse servers from the segment master browser, and chooses one from the list
  - from the chosen server requests both the browse list for this domain, and a list of domains. These requests use the NetBIOS session service (TCP port 139)
- the browse system doesn't use dedicated servers. Almost any machine can act as a browse server and machines on the network hold elections to decide which machines should take on the various browse server roles:
  - the segment master browser accumulates the browse list for this segment
  - the domain master browser combines all the per-segment browse lists into a complete list for the whole domain, which it periodically sends back to each segment masters browsers. The PDC is always the domain master browser
  - on each segment, backup browse servers regularly obtain the browse list and the list of domains from their segment master browser. Backup browsers can service browse list request from clients but don't accumulate entries into the browse list: only the segment master browser does that
  - many potential browsers are prepared to take on the above roles if an existing browse server fails
- one domain's browse servers learn about other domains from "domain announcements," which each segment master browser periodically broadcasts to the special <01><02>__MSBROWSE__<02><01> NetBIOS group name
- delays are a feature of browsing, because of the fixed replication intervals (all about 12–15 minutes) between the various servers. It can take about half an hour for a PC that's just joined the network to be known on every segment, and about an hour before a machine that has closed down to be removed from the browse lists everywhere
- the **Find Computer** tool is useful for locating a machine that hasn't yet been added to the browse list (because the machine has only recently started up, or because you have browsing problems).

What's next?

The next chapter is our last one devoted to Microsoft Windows Networking. It covers many small aspects of using Windows Networking, and Samba, and explains the configuration changes necessary to run Windows Networking over a network containing routers – which brings together many of the issues we've discussed already.

Notes and further reading

To explore browsing, build a simple test network containing a single browse "client," a PDC, and a sniffer. Disable WINS to start with. Use only a single domain on the test network. Experiment with the client's Registry configuration: make it a non-browser initially, so that it's forced to use the PDC as its browse server and you can see the browse traffic (e.g. for **net view**) on the wire. Then change it to a preferred browser, so it will become a backup browser and then you can watch the replication process on the wire. Experiment with the tools we mentioned in Module 21.12, so you can use them with comfort on your live network.

Even though the browse function in Windows-2000 and XP works completely differently – it's based on Active Directory – everything we've covered here is still relevant because all NT 4 and Win-9x systems do it "the old way," which will remain important as long as you are running any legacy systems (or Samba).

For a little history, see:

❏ **http://alternic.net/drafts/drafts-l-m/draft-leach-cifs-browser-spec-01.txt**

(This may be available at other sites, but because it's an "expired" Internet (IETF) draft, it may not always be easy to find.) It outlines how the browser architecture changed from early versions of LAN Manager, through Windows for Workgroups, and Windows-NT.

Many documents on the Web and elsewhere incorrectly say that *domainname*<1b> is a group; it is unique, as you can confirm if you run **nbtstat -n** on your PDC.

Browse system architecture

The original RFC gives a lot of useful and understandable background, although current implementations may not agree exactly with the RFC:

❏ **RFC-1001 March 1987** *Protocol Standard For a NetBIOS Service on a TCP/UDP Transport: Concepts and Methods*

For a good insight into how the browse system works, see:

❏ **http://www.cmu.edu/computing/ccg/wins/ntbrowse.doc** or

❏ **http://www.microsoft.com/TechNet/prodtechnol/winntas/deploy/prodspecs/ntbrowse.asp** *Microsoft Windows NT Browser* White Paper by R. Dan Thompson IV and Randy McLaughlin

For a good overview of how browsing over multiple network segments works, in your Samba distribution, see the file:

❏ **BROWSING.txt**

also available on:

❏ **http://www.samba.org/samba/ftp/docs/textdocs/**

Different browser roles

❏ MS-KB-Q102878 *Information on Browser Operation*

Troubleshooting

For a description of the problems of using more than one protocol on a PC, again see the Samba documentation, in particular the file:

❏ **BROWSING-Config.txt**

For a troubleshooting checklist, see the Microsoft Browser White Paper above, or the summary, which is included in:

❏ MS-KB-Q188305 *Troubleshooting the Microsoft Computer Browser Service*

The White Paper mentioned earlier lists the Registry parameters used by browsing. In particular, you can force this machine to not be a browser at all, by setting **MaintainServerList** = False (instead of its default, which is "Auto"). You can make a machine a preferred master browser by changing **IsDomainMaster** from "False" to "True." If you do force a machine to be "not a browser," you will get an Event Log message on booting, along the lines of "Event ID: 7024. Source: Service Control Manager. The Computer Browser service terminated with service-specific error 2550."

If you're using Samba, the following may be relevant:

❏ MS-KB-Q168821 *Domain Browsing Issues with Samba Servers*

Windows-9x and browsing

Windows-9x browsing is controlled by the **Client for Microsoft Networks**. This PC doesn't appear in the browse list unless:

- in **Control Panel > Network > Configuration** the network component **Client for Microsoft Networks** is installed
- **Control Panel > Network > Configuration > File and Print Sharing** has either **I want to be able to give others access to my files** or **I want to be able to able to allow others to print to my printers** enabled (i.e. unless you're going to share something, you don't show on the network's list of resources).

Appendices

Appendix 24: the BROWSTAT command
Web Appendix 27: synchronizing browse lists

22 | **Using Windows Networking**

Introduction

This chapter covers a number of small topics, and explains what you need to do to make Windows Networking operate over a network containing routers. We also introduce Samba, an implementation of Windows Networking for Linux and other non-Windows systems.

22.1 Using Windows Explorer

Shares – mapped network drivers

A *share* is a directory – with all its subdirectories and file – on one PC that other PCs are allowed to access over the network. It is often a whole disk but it doesn't have to be. It's the Windows equivalent of a Linux NFS-shared file system. On the machine where the shares physically reside, they are shown with a "hand symbol" in Windows Explorer (Figure 22.1).

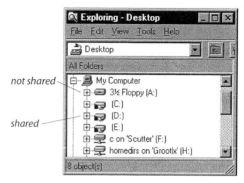

Figure 22.1 Shares in Windows Explorer

To set up the server-side of a share, i.e. to make a drive on this machine accessible to others:

1. the **Server** NT Service must be running. (It is, by default).

2a. in Windows Explorer:

    i. select the drive or the subdirectory within the drive that you want to share, and use menu **File > Properties > Sharing** (or right-click on the drive name) to bring up the **Sharing** dialog

    ii. click on **New Share** and enter a name for the share. When sharing a drive, many people give the share the same name as its drive, but you can give it a longer, more meaningful name, which is helpful for less expert users. For example, use **reports** instead of **F**

    iii. using **Permissions**, specify the access rights you want to allow other people to have to your drive

2b. alternatively, you can use **net share** from the command line. The format of the command is **net share** *sharename=driveletter:pathname*, e.g.

```
net share reports=D:\data\reps
```

makes the directory tree **D:\data\reps** available as the share called **reports**. You can set the permissions using the **cacls** command.

To use a share from a client machine:

1a. in Windows Explorer, use menu **Tools > Map Network Drive**, or …

1b. use **net use** from the command line, e.g. on BobNT you might say

```
net use R: \\alicent\reports
```

In command-line commands and elsewhere, you reference a share as *\\servername\sharename*, as in the example above; you reference files on a share as *\\servername\sharename\filename*, e.g.

```
type \\alicent\reports\abc.txt
```

That also illustrates that you can use shares without explicitly mapping a drive using "UNC" notation. You could have performed the same thing more longwindedly using the following commands:

```
net use R: \\alicent\maildirs
type R:abc.txt
net use R: /delete
```

Network drive mappings can be *persistent* – re-instated every time you boot – or not. To make a mapping persistent, with **net use** append the option **/persistent:yes**, or in Windows Explorer, tick the **Reconnect at Logon** box. The flag indicating whether this mapping is persistent is recorded in the Windows Registry.

List your mapped drives with Windows Explorer, or **net use** (Figure 22.2):

```
Command Prompt                           _ □

C:\> net use
Status  Local  Remote              Network
-----------------------------------------------------------
OK      R:     \\BOBNT\rchives      Microsoft Windows Network
OK      S:     \\BOBNT\samples      Microsoft Windows Network
OK      T:     \\DAVENT\tempfiles   Microsoft Windows Network
```

Figure 22.2 net use

In the Notes we list several tips on using Windows Explorer.

22.2 Lab – using Windows Networking over a routed network

As you'll have gathered by now, Windows Networking relies heavily on broadcast packets on the local network segment for its basic operation. This will not work once your network extends beyond a single segment, e.g. where:

- you've grown your network and introduced internal router(s)
- this site is connecting to another over the Internet using Windows Networking (e.g. a branch office connecting to HQ, or even a single dial-up user connecting from home to the office, but needing to use domain logon and browsing, and printing on the office printers).

In these configurations, broadcast packets can't reach all the Windows machines on the network, so you have to ensure that a machine can locate in some other way any resources it needs (e.g. domain controller for logon, and browse master for browsing). The two common alternatives are, as we've already described, making static entries in the **Lmhosts** file, or using WINS, which is usually easier and much more maintainable.

The best way to work through the issues involved in using Windows Networking over a routed network is to experiment with a small test network (Figure 22.3) and get that working. Then you can start expanding your real network.

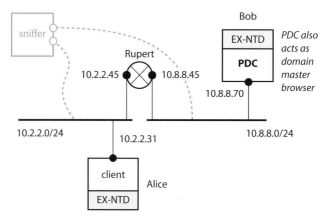

Figure 22.3 Small test network to explore Windows Networking in a routed environment

1. cable up the network shown in Figure 22.3. Use UTP hubs to connect the client to the router machine, and the router machine to the PDC. (You could use UTP cross-over cables instead, but then you won't be able to sniff the traffic easily, which you'll certainly want to do.)

2. configure the IP addresses and routing so that Alice can see Bob and vice versa. (For convenience we've shown suitable IP addresses, but use representative addresses from your own network if you prefer.)

3. check that you can **ping** from each machine to every other, by IP number.

We'll assume that Bob is set up to act as the PDC for NT-domain **EX-NTD**. (You can use your own domain name, although using a test domain name is safer in case this machine inadvertently finds its way back onto your real network and then tries to act as its PDC!)

4. set Alice's NT-domain to **EX-NTD**, to match Bob's

5. on Alice *and on* Bob, disable LMHOSTS lookup, remove any WINS server addresses, and remove any DNS server addresses

6. reboot Alice and Bob, so you're sure of the starting configuration

7. plug in your sniffer to watch traffic from Alice to Rupert

8. logon to Alice, user=Administrator, domain=Alice (i.e. local logon, because you won't be able to do a domain logon, or if you can, it will be using cached credentials). You'll probably have to wait about 35 seconds for your logon prompt. What happens after logon depends on Alice's browse system configuration, but what follows is typical:

   - start Windows Explorer, and click on Network Neighborhood. After about 10 seconds, the branch will expand

   - click on Entire Network to show the sub-branch Microsoft Windows Network

   - click on Microsoft Windows Network. After about 15 seconds, the **EX-NTD** branch is displayed

   - click on **EX-NTD**. After about 15 seconds, you get the error "EX-NTD is not accessible. The list of servers for this workgroup is not currently available"

   The traffic from Alice is all broadcast to the sub-net broadcast address (10.2.2.255) as she tries, unsuccessfully, to locate the PDC and the domain browse master.

Now you want to configure Alice so her Windows Networking can operate past the router. First, try it with **LMHOSTS**, and then use WINS instead:

A. on Alice, enable **LMHOSTS** lookup. Create or edit the **LMHOSTS** file itself, to contain only this entry:

```
10.8.8.70 bob #DOM:EX-NTD #PRE
```

and reboot. Now you can logon from Alice to the domain. Browse the network too, and you ought to see Bob in your Network Neighborhood. (If not, add the **<1b>** entry to your **LMHOSTS** file

```
10.8.8.70 "EX-NTD■■■■■■■■\0x1b" #PRE
```

where each ■ is a space, re-load it using **nbtstat -R**, check with **nbtstat -C**, and then browse again.) Check the browse system status with **browstat status -v**

B. on Bob, make sure the WINS NT Service is running, and that Bob himself uses his own WINS server for name resolution. Reboot.

On Alice, disable **LMHOSTS** lookup, and enter Bob's IP number as Alice's Primary and Secondary WINS server addresses. Reboot. You should now be able to logon from Alice to the domain, and browse. (How many minutes does it take for Alice to appear in Bob's browse list?)

22.3 Troubleshooting

We included some troubleshooting tips in the specific chapters on name resolution, authentication/logon, and browsing. Here we give some broader guidelines in case you have a problem.

General points

- look at your logs:
  - the Windows NT **Start > Programs > Administrative Tools (Common) > Event Viewer** records error and information messages
  - NT has three different logs: **System, Application**, and **Security**. You select which one to display using menu **Log**. You often need to look at all the logs when you're tracing a problem
  - **Event Viewer** lets you look at the event logs on remote machines as well as your own, using menu **Log > Select Computer**
  - the Resource Kit Documentation Help files list event IDs and messages that may give you pointers to the cause of the problem, but we've found it's usually quicker and more informative to search on the Internet instead, e.g. using Google
- note carefully any error messages from logon, browsing, etc. and keep a record of them in a file. When you've resolved the problem, enter in the file the cause and solution for the problem on your particular network.
- as always, use a sniffer. Sniffing name resolution and browsing traffic is fairly easy, because there aren't too many packets involved in a typical conversation. Logons are harder: booting and successfully logging on to a PC typically involves about 250 packets. If you try to limit the packets you capture using a filter, be careful that your filter does allow everything you need to see, because a PC may talk to:
  - WINS servers (primary and/or secondary)
  - PDC and/or BDC, for the PC's own domain, and other domains too if you have them
  - segment browse master and backup browse servers
  - domain master browser if this PC is participating in browser elections

  Sometimes it's easier to build a small test network and recreate and solve the problem on that first.
- remember that name resolution and browsing are separate, but name resolution problems often show up when you click on a name in Network Neighborhood and can't connect. Sniffing will show you whether it's really a resolution problem, or whether the name is resolving correctly and the problem lies in the "connect-to-share" stage.
- remember that many NetBIOS sessions can be multiplexed over a single TCP connection. Even if a new NetBIOS session is created, it may use an existing TCP connection so if you're sniffing the wire you may not see the TCP three-way handshake (SYN, SYN/ACK, ACK) that you might otherwise expect.

- modify and simplify your configuration to isolate the cause of the problem. This can cut down on the network traffic you have to look at and bypass several components of Windows Networking; and if the problem goes away when you alter a setting, you have a good pointer to where the problem is:
  - use the **Lmhosts** file. Disable WINS, enable **Lmhosts** lookup, and insert an entry for the troublesome name if you can't seem to resolve it properly, or insert an entry for your PDC if you're having logon problems. Sniffing will show you if your PC is then attempting to use the address it found in **Lmhosts**
  - remove the **Lmhosts** entries and make sure your PC is using WINS. You can see clearly on the wire if your machine is using WINS to resolve – whether it's a troublesome PC name, or the name of the PDC or domain master browser or a segment master browser
  - if sniffing shows that your PC is connecting correctly to a domain controller, and the logon is still failing, check the logs on that machine to see why.

(If your PC can't logon to the domain, you may have to logon locally in order to be able to make some of these configuration changes.)

General tips

- if you mess around with your PDC it may not work properly. Don't let anybody use it as their desktop workstation, and only run other server-type applications on it (DNS, DHCP, etc.)
- don't change the name of your NT domain. Any domains we create now always end in "-NTD." (We found this out the hard way, and called our internal domain **UIT**: if we see a DNS name resolution for **uit** we can't tell immediately whether it's for our NT domain or our DNS domain name.)
- do use WINS, and on WINS client PCs always enter an IP number for both secondary and primary WINS servers. If you've only one WINS server, enter its IP number as the secondary server too
- don't enter any hostnames and addresses in the **hosts** file. It will only cause confusion and maintenance problems
- use only one networking system on a PC if you can. Don't use NetBEUI unless you really have to; it's out of date, it confuses name resolution and network browsing, and it can provide a backdoor around any TCP/IP-based firewall and security systems you've installed
- if you're used to Linux or UNIX, remember that Windows stores configuration settings, etc. in the Windows Registry
- systems processes usually show in uppercase in Windows NT Task Manager, in case you're looking for them.

22.4 Samba

Samba (so called because it provides SMB file and printer sharing) is a superb free software implementation of Windows Networking for Linux/UNIX. It includes:

- NetBIOS name resolution
- SMB file sharing
- domain authentication
- network browsing.

Both client-side and server-side are included, so you can:

- access files on Microsoft Windows PCs from your Linux machines
- access files on your Linux machines from Microsoft Windows PCs.

This allows you to share the same data to both Linux and Windows users, without having to duplicate them. If you keep your data on Linux Samba servers, then you don't need to install any extra software on any of your desktop machines (Figure 22.4). Windows PCs see the Samba server as a Windows Networking file server, included in their browse list as normal, and Linux users can access the server using NFS (Module 17.14). In Appendix 26 we explain how we use this type of configuration to share our central archive of software to all the machines on our network.

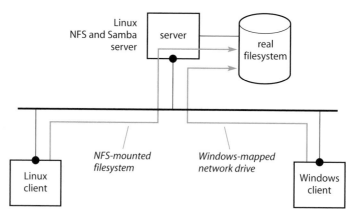

Figure 22.4 Using Samba and NFS to share the same files to Linux and Windows

As well as saving you effort and money – not having to buy or install client software for your desktops – we've found this approach also leads to more reliable networks: the less software you have to install on Windows machines the better, especially "intrusive" networking software that has to work at a low level within the operating system. An alternative approach used widely in the past was to install commercial, third-party NFS software on the Windows PCs. While this works, it can be expensive, and we've often found that low-level software like this can be troublesome, especially on earlier versions of Windows.

Our experiences with Samba have been very good: it works reliably, it performs well, the documentation is helpful (although written mostly for a technical audience), and it has some useful tools. Surprisingly, we've found it easier to gain an understanding of Windows

Networking internals using Samba than using NT. In particular, because of the architecture and packaging of Linux/UNIX systems, it's more obvious what's installed and what isn't, making it easier to see which components of the system are interacting with what.

Samba's nmblookup **tool**

nmblookup is a mixture of a Linux version of **nbtstat** and a NetBIOS equivalent of DNS's **nslookup**. It lets you do things you can't do with any other tool, e.g. it gives you very precise control over how you perform NetBIOS lookups.

The simplest form of the command is:

```
nmblookup name
```

which attempts to resolve *name* using NetBIOS broadcasts. For example:

```
alice% nmblookup bobnt
querying bobnt on 212.140.133.127
212.140.133.31 bobnt<00>
```

Source	Destination	Protocol	Info
212.140.133.17	212.140.133.127	NBNS	Name query NB BOBNT <00>
212.140.133.31	212.140.133.17	NBNS	Name query response NB 212.140.133.31

You can use the wildcard "*" as the name, to show all names. Or you can append a 16th-byte NetBIOS suffix using the notation **#XX**, e.g.

```
alice% nmblookup uit#1d
querying uit on 212.140.133.127
212.140.133.7 uit<1d>
```

Instead of broadcasting, you can use a WINS server to resolve, with options **-R** ("recursive") and **-U** *serveraddr* ("unicast"). For example, to use the WINS server on .7:

```
alice% nmblookup -U 212.140.133.7 -R bobnt#20
querying bobnt on 212.140.133.7
212.140.133.31 bobnt<20>
```

You can do "adapter status" queries by name or number – the direct equivalents of **nbtstat**'s -A and -a options:

```
nmblookup -S name
nmblookup -A ip-num
```

nmblookup lets you look for segment master browsers, either for a specific domain by name, or by looking for browsers that have registered the special __**MSBROWSE**__ name:

`nmblookup -M ex-ntd`	*lookup master for **ex-ntd***
`nmblookup -M -`	*lookup all masters (using __**msbrowse**__)*
`nmblookup -M`	*wrong – must specify a name*

There are also options -**d** to give debug information and -**T** to resolve all IP numbers returned from a query using DNS (for comparison with their NetBIOS names). See the Notes for example **nmblookup** output.

Summary

- you manage shares (mapped network drives) using Windows Explorer or the **net use** command

- to use Windows Networking over a routed network you must use WINS (or at least the **Lmhosts** file) to enable machines to resolve names and locate resources on other network segments, because the basic broadcast packet mechanisms don't work across routers

- Samba is an excellent implementation of Windows Networking for non-Windows systems, especially Linux and UNIX.

What's next?

That's the end of our coverage of Windows Networking (apart from Windows dial-up networking; see Chapter 26). It's a whole world to itself, which can be difficult to get to grips with because of its complexity and because it's very different "philosophically" from the other Internet protocols we cover throughout the book. We have explained the low-level mechanisms that Windows Networking uses – for name resolution, logon/authentication, and browsing. We found that the best way to really understand the system is to take each part of it in isolation, ideally by building a simple a network and experimenting with each component, and watching the traffic on the wire using a combination of **ethereal** and Windows Network Monitor. This experience will help you get your live system working correctly and overcome the problems you will inevitably meet.

In Part 4, the next and final part of the book, we move on and bring together everything you've learned so far – in commissioning your Internet connection and securing your site against hackers.

Notes and further reading

Tips for Windows Explorer

- we always use drive letter **Z:** for our CD-ROM drive – so it's the same on all machines and doesn't clash with other drives. (You assign drive letters using Disk Administrator.)

- always enable menu **View > Options > View > Show All Files** and always disable **Hide File Extensions for Known File Types**, especially when you're working on **HOSTS** and **LMHOSTS** files (c.f. Module 19.8)

- you can start Windows Explorer from anywhere by pressing WindowsKey-E

- we always copy shortcuts for **Control Panel** and **Control Panel > Network** into our **Start** button menu. You can use the **Start** menu by pressing the WindowsKey on its own

- when organizing files, you can run more than one copy of Windows Explorer, making it easy to drag and drop files from one place to another

- to start Explorer from the command line, to view a specific directory, e.g.

```
explorer D:\ntreskit\telnet , /e            don't omit the comma
```

- there are shortcut keys within Explorer to speed up navigation:
  - Ctrl-G brings up the **Go To Folder** dialog. In that dialog, Ctrl-F4 drops down the pull-down menu of previous locations you've gone to
  - in the left-hand pane, RightArrow expands the selected branch of the directory tree. LeftArrow moves to the parent directory; LeftArrow a second time collapses the current branch. In the right-hand pane, the Space key selects a branch, the Enter key expands that branch, and Backspace collapses a branch.

Licensing

Licensing is a significant cost issue in building a Windows network. Each client machine that accesses a Windows-NT server as a server must have a "client access license" (CAL). This applies irrespective of the client's operating systems – even if it's Mac or a Linux box, you need a CAL for it. For this reason, some organizations that use Windows-9x on desktops use Linux machines as their central servers, running Samba to give client access, and so avoiding the need for large numbers of CALs. This type of network configuration is becoming increasingly popular, and there are frequent articles in the trade press on large commercial and government organizations that have implemented it successfully. (We haven't included any URLs because news articles tend to go out of date and be removed very quickly.)

Samba

❑ http://www.samba.org

In 2000, a separate development effort called "Samba TNG" ("the next generation") split off from the main Samba project. This was an amicable split for good technical reasons: the purpose was to allow some experimental approaches to Windows networking to be tried out, and to re-engineer much of the code into a library form that would be easier to use in different applications. However, this could not be done within the main Samba project, where stability of the final code is the primary requirement, so it was necessary to launch a separate development thread. For more information, see:

❑ http://www.samba-tng.org/faq.html *Samba TNG*

Here are two small examples of Samba's **nmblookup** output:

```
alice% nmblookup -M uit
querying uit on 212.140.133.127
212.140.133.7 uit<1d>
alice% nmblookup -M -
querying ^A^B__MSBROWSE__^B on 212.140.133.127
212.140.133.7 ^A^B__MSBROWSE__^B<01>
212.140.133.19 ^A^B__MSBROWSE__^B<01>
```

> **Warning:** because NetBIOS depends so heavily on broadcasts, it's crucial that a Samba machine is configured with the correct broadcast address for the network it's connected to. For example, in the **nmblookup** listing above, **alice** is connected to the network 212.140.133.0/25, i.e. with netmask 255.255.255.128 and broadcast address 212.140.133.127. If her broadcast address were incorrectly set to 212.140.133.255, **nmblookup** (and the rest of Samba) would not work properly. See also the Warning regarding broadcast addresses in Chapter 4's Notes.

Security

Now that we've covered Windows authentication and name resolution and browsing, here's a hacker document that shows how those mechanisms can be used to attack your system. It gives an interesting sideways look at NT's operation:

❏ **http://packetstormsecurity.org/groups/rhino9/wardoc.txt**

Windows Explorer shortcuts

❏ **MS-KB-Q126449** *Keyboard Shortcuts for Windows*

The Guest account

In Module 18.1 we explained that Windows peer-to-peer networking was designed to make it easy to access resources on other machines on the network. However, in the 20 years since Windows Networking has developed, security has become a major issue – on internal LANs as well as the Internet – and allowing automatic unrestricted access to machines is no longer seen as a good thing to do. The NT domain-based security of Chapter 20 now gives you fine-grained control over access to resources on your machines. However, you can use the *Guest account* to allow access to people who don't have a normal user account, or an account in the relevant domain. The Guest account does not require a password. On Windows NT the Guest account is disabled by default; enable it if you wish, in **User Manager for Domains**.

Assuming the Guest account is enabled, you can logon as Guest except on a domain controller. This logs you on locally to the machine you're sitting at, and you have whatever permissions the administrator granted to Guest.

However, the Guest account is used in another way too – for a network logon. Let's say you have logged on at your machine, using your normal domain account or an account on your machine. Then you try to access resources on another machine but your logon account doesn't give you permission to do so. If the Guest account is enabled on the machine you're trying to access, and it doesn't have a password defined for it, you are logged on to that machine as Guest, even though the username you specified in the original logon dialog was not "Guest." For more information, see:

❏ **http://www.microsoft.com/technet/treeview/default.asp?url=/TechNet/prodtechnol/ winntas/proddocs/concept/xcp02.asp** *Windows NT Server Concepts and Planning Guide: Chapter 2 – Working with User and Group Accounts*

Appendices

Appendix 26: organizing your software downloads on Windows and Linux.

Part 4

Connecting to the Internet, and Internet security

Introduction

We covered the main TCP/IP applications in Part 2, and Windows Networking in Part 3, so by now you have a good basic understanding of what happens under the hood in much of your day-to-day network operation.

In this part of the book we bring together many of the topics we've covered already, in order to connect your internal network to the Internet, using both permanently-on, leased-line connections and dial-up links.

Nowadays, security is an integral part of connecting to the Internet. Most organizations regard their Internet connection as mission-critical, and consequently firewalls, Internet anti-virus protection, and other security mechanisms are essential.

Because of the huge variety of Internet connection types, network configurations, firewalls, and other security systems, we can't cover every possible combination exhaustively. Instead, our aim is to relate the concepts involved to the material we've covered so far, and show how you can use the same methodical diagnostic approach to understand and troubleshoot your Internet-connected network.

23 Connecting your site to the Internet

Introduction

In this chapter we look at the issues involved in connecting up a typical site to the Internet. Increasingly, sites want to (or must) use network address translation (NAT), so we explain that first. Then we explain step by step how to plan the work involved in connecting to the Internet and the basic tests you need to perform at each stage.

23.1 First steps – deciding what you need

Let's say you're about to connect a site (something like that in Figure 23.1) to an ISP to provide Internet access to and from your site. The first thing you have to do is work out what you need. Here are the decisions you have to make; we'll discuss these in the rest of the chapter:

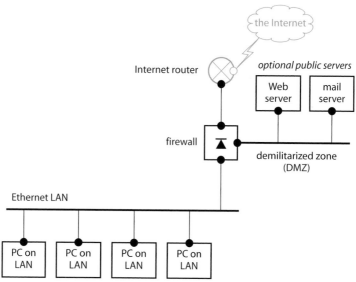

Figure 23.1 Connecting a site to the Internet via an ISP

a. do you need any servers at your site to be accessible from the Internet, e.g. your own Web, e-mail, or DNS servers? Or will you host them elsewhere, or use your ISP's offerings?

b. do you need "always on" access (leased line, ADSL) or is occasional dial-up access adequate (ISDN or a modem)? Dial-up connections can usually be configured to bring up the connection to your ISP automatically when there is outgoing traffic, e.g. when you send an e-mail message or start to surf the Web. (See Web Appendix 29 for information on types of Internet connections.)

c. do you need static (fixed) external IP addresses to be allocated to your site, or can you work with dynamically allocated addresses?

d. what Internet bandwidth will you need?

e. will you use network address translation (NAT – which we cover in the next module) or will all your internal machines have valid public IP addresses?

f. will you buy and install your own Internet router, or will your chosen ISP provide, install, and manage it for you?

g. do you need a backup Internet connection in case your primary connection fails?

h. you *will* need a firewall of some kind to protect you from hackers. Will you buy and install your own, or have it provided by your ISP, or by a third-party company?

(We defer firewall and other security issues until later chapters.)

The questions above are inter-related. If you run a publicly accessible Web or e-mail server at your site:

- you will need a static IP address for it, to be entered in the DNS, so that users on the Internet can connect to your server (but see the Notes for possible exceptions)

- you will need always-on access so that when an outsider attempts to connect to your site, your Internet connection is up. (You might be able to use ISDN instead, but only if your ISP is prepared to dial your site to bring up the Internet connection whenever there is inbound traffic for you.)

- you may want to locate the servers on a "demilitarized zone" separate from your main network (as explained in Chapter 24); this will influence your choice of firewall.

The alternative to running your own servers is to have them hosted elsewhere, e.g. at your ISP or at a dedicated hosting site. This reduces your system administration load, gives you a wider choice of suitable connection types, and may give a faster and more reliable service if your ISP has the necessary infrastructure. On the other hand, if you need to link your Web server to a database that you are running internally, e.g. for an e-commerce application, you may have to set up a VPN link (Chapter 27) to your hosting site, which adds effort and expense. Using your ISP's e-mail services is more straightforward; the ISP may include e-mail service as part of their standard offering, or at least run a backup mail server for you. Then, if you have a dial-up connection, mail sent to your site when you are not connected is queued at the ISP, for you to retrieve when your connection comes up.

Your bandwidth requirements are determined by the number of users at your site, what they do, and what your business is. If you have 1000 users e-mailing large spreadsheets to customers and suppliers, you will need more bandwidth than a site with ten users who only occasionally surf the Web. If you want to set up an e-commerce site, what level of business, and therefore how many connections to your Web server, do you expect?

Of course, many decisions involve cost, which in turn depends on the country you are in, whether you're in a big city or a remote rural location, etc. For example, in many UK cities, an ADSL always-on connection is cheaper to install than ISDN; ADSL involves no extra phone charges, gives you 10 or 20 times the bandwidth of ISDN, and may offer you static IP addresses, so it's hard to see why you would choose ISDN. On the other hand, if you're in a remote location in a developing country with poor telecomms infrastructure, you might be unable to get even ISDN, and have to make do with a dial-up link.

We assume that your Internet router is provided by and configured by your ISP. This is usually the case with small sites, and it's increasingly common with large sites too. We've found that it's certainly the best way to get started. When your network is up and running and stable, you can consider installing and configuring your own router (see Notes) but there is a lot to be said for giving your ISP responsibility for the router as well as the connection itself. It avoids the far too common "our line is OK, the problem is your router" scenario.

In the next module we look at NAT, how it works, and why you might want it.

23.2 Network Address Translation (NAT) – overview

Network Address Translation (NAT) lets you use IP addresses inside on your LAN that are different to those visible from outside on the Internet (Figure 23.2). Usually, many internal addresses are translated into a single outside address. Some form of NAT device (firewall or router with NAT built in, or a server running NAT software) sits between your site and the Internet, and it translates the addresses in the packets passing through it. NAT is also called *IP masquerading*, especially on Linux.

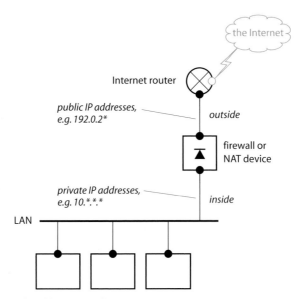

Figure 23.2 Network Address Translation

With NAT you usually use the private class A, B, and C addresses that we mentioned back in Module 4.2.

There are many reasons to use NAT:

- your ISP may give you only 4, 8, or 16 static public IP addresses (some of which will be taken up by network and broadcast addresses, your firewall and router.) If you have more machines than this, or if your network is likely to expand in the future, you will need NAT

- your ISP may not give you any static addresses at all – only a dynamic address for the external port of your router – so you must use NAT to isolate the inside addresses from the (occasionally changing) outside addresses. With NAT, the addresses of your LAN machines remain constant, irrespective of the dynamic external address your ISP happens to assign you at any one time. In this case, the router and NAT system, shown as separate devices in Figure 23.2, are combined

- you want to use the private non-routable address ranges. These let you accommodate an internal network of any size, and are essential for large sites. However, even small sites use them for the greater flexibility they give you in sub-netting your internal network

- if you are not connecting to the Internet immediately, you should use the private address ranges internally. If you do connect later, you won't have to renumber (change the IP addresses of) your internal machines. (If you use an arbitrary range of IP addresses instead, when you join the Internet your internal addresses will clash with the real owner of the numbers you used, and nobody will be able to route to you. You'll have to renumber.)

- by using NAT with private address ranges, you can change to a new ISP with minimal changes to your LAN. It also simplifies using a separate, backup connection to the Internet (Module 23.12).

How NAT works

As a packet from the LAN passes through the NAT device, the packet is actually modified: the NAT device translates the internal IP address (e.g. 10.1.1.1) to an external address (e.g. 192.0.2.78). Usually all the internal addresses are mapped to a single external address – the external address of the NAT device, although this may be configurable, depending on what NAT device you're using. Figure 23.3 shows a typical NAT network, illustrating how the source address of outgoing packets are translated as they move through the NAT device. In Module 23.4 we explain in detail how addresses are translated.

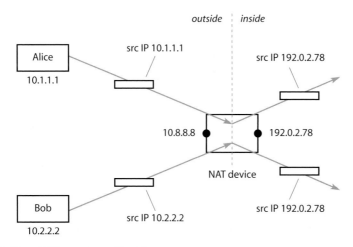

Figure 23.3 How NAT translates IP addresses

Default gateway when using NAT

When you use NAT on your inside network (your LAN), the default gateway setting for LAN machines is the internal IP address of the NAT device (firewall, or router). For example, in Figure 23.3, the default gateway settings for Alice and Bob are 10.8.8.8.

23.3 Consequences of using NAT

Using NAT has several consequences:

- to the "outside" (i.e. as seen from the Internet) all the internal machines share a single IP address, and appear to be a single machine. Because of this:
  - packets returning to the site in reply to requests from internal machines (e.g. packets in reply to HTTP requests to external Web sites) must somehow be routed to the internal machine they relate to, using more than just the IP number
  - if Dave wants to initiate a connection from the Internet, e.g. to a mail server on Bob, some mechanism must be used to distinguish which internal machine is the actual destination

  In both cases just specifying the visible, public, destination address (192.0.2.78) isn't enough, because all the LAN machines share it. And in the second case, Dave can't specify Bob's internal address either, first because Dave doesn't know what it is, and second because the 10.* addresses are private and you can't route to them over the public Internet. Port translation and one-to-one NAT solve these problems, as explained in the next module

- packets are modified in transit by the NAT device, changing at least the IP source/destination addresses. Some protocols (e.g. FTP, Microsoft Windows Networking, and the H.323 videoconferencing standard used by Microsoft's NetMeeting® product, among others) embed IP addresses in the payload or body of their packets, not just in the packet headers. If the NAT device doesn't understand the details of the protocol and translate all instances of source/destination IP address, the protocol won't work across the NAT device. This explains why some NAT systems are better than others.

  Figure 23.4 illustrates this. A NetBIOS packet is sent from the internal network to an external machine. NetBIOS datagram packets duplicate the source IP number within the packet. When NetBIOS on the external PC replies, it sends the reply packet to the IP address within the NetBIOS part of the packet, *not the IP address in the packet header*. If the NAT device translates only the IP number from the packet header, as shown on the right of the figure, the reply will be sent to the wrong destination, and the machines will be unable to communicate

- when you use VPN (Chapter 27), the data in the packet are encrypted. The NAT device can't modify the encrypted data (because it doesn't know how to decrypt them). The IP address is usually included in the encrypted data, so just as above, the system can't work. However, you can get over this problem if the VPN encryption and the NAT translation are carried out by the same device, and this solution is used widely in practice, often by using a firewall that provides NAT and VPN features in addition to basic security

- it may improve the security of your site. As we explained above, it is difficult or impossible for an external hacker to initiate connections to internal machines unless you have deliberately made them accessible. However, for machines that you have made accessible, NAT of itself gives you no security protection at all. And, any traffic in transit can still be sniffed or interfered with.

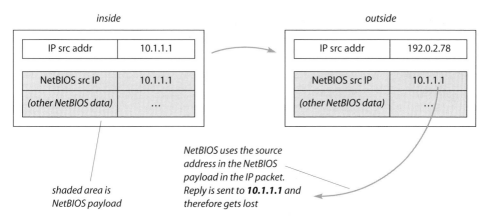

Figure 23.4 Some NAT systems don't translate IP addresses embedded in the body of the packet

Renumbering your network to use NAT

You will have to renumber (change the IP addresses) all of the machines on your network if you change from non-NAT to NAT, or even if you don't use NAT but were using someone else's IP addresses on your LAN before you connected to the Internet. Renumbering is straightforward but can be time-consuming:

- manually changing each machine's IP address, netmask, and default gateway takes at least 15 minutes per machine, by the time you've rebooted, checked that it's working, and noted the IP address used in your site records.

  Using DHCP can reduce this time dramatically. You can ask all your users to shut down their machines one evening; then you change the DHCP server settings, and when the users switch on again in the morning they automatically pick up the new settings. However …

- some servers and other applications may have IP numbers embedded in configuration files, e.g. an application may specify that only machines in the range *a.b.c.d–w.x.y.z* can use a particular service. You'll have to find and change all such configuration settings that include your old IP numbers. For this reason sites often renumber over a weekend: they make the changes quickly on Friday night and spend the rest of the weekend tracking down configuration issues that are affected by the change.

23.4 NAT – port translation; one-to-one NAT

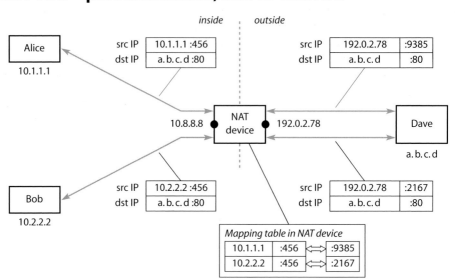

Figure 23.5 Port translation distinguishes between multiple connections

Port translation

In our example network (Figure 23.5), all packets arriving from outside are addressed to 192.0.2.78; how does the NAT device decide which internal machine they are really destined for? It uses *network port translation (NPT)*, also called *port address translation (PAT)* or *network address and port translation (NAPT)*, to do this. (NAT is often assumed to include PAT – the usage of the terminology isn't very strict.)

When an outgoing packet for a new combination of *source address + source port* passes through the NAT device, the device creates and stores a new mapping entry. Not only does it translate the source address, to 192.0.2.78 in Figure 23.5, but it also translates the source port – to a new port number that isn't in use. E.g. port 456 on 10.1.1.1 is translated to port 9385. Now when a packet arrives from outside, addressed to 192.0.2.78, port 9385, the NAT device looks up the port number in its internal mapping table. It sees that 9385 really refers to port 456 on 10.1.1.1. translates the IP number and port accordingly, and passes the packet on to Alice. Similarly, when a packet arrives from outside addressed to 192.0.2.78 but on port 2167, the NAT device translates this to 10.2.2.2 port 456 and passes it to Bob.

In this way – dynamically mapping each combination of internal address and port to a unique outside port number on the same outside IP address – the NAT device can distinguish unambiguously between packets for any internal machine.

Port translation and initiating connections from outside

How can Dave on the Internet initiate a connection, to an e-mail server, say, on Bob on the LAN? Specifying "destination IP = 192.0.2.78 port 25" doesn't work, because Alice also appears to have that address. Dave can't specify "destination IP =10.2.2.2 port 25" either because he doesn't know the internal IP number. (Even if he did, packets can't be routed to it over the Internet since it's a non-routable private address.)

If the external address on the NAT device is allocated dynamically by the ISP, there is no solution to this problem: you just can't have publicly accessible servers on such a network. You either have to change to an ISP who will give you static IP addresses, or else host your servers at some other site. This is one of the issues to consider when choosing an ISP.

However, if the external address on the NAT device is static – so that you can tell remote users what it will always be, and can include it in the DNS entries for your site – there are two possible solutions.

1. Statically map an external port number to one specific internal IP address

We want to run an e-mail server on Bob, behind the NAT device. When an external user tries to send to us, they will be connecting to 192.0.2.78 port 25. If we can set up the static mapping entry shown below, it works exactly as we want. The outside IP address is the same as in all the other (dynamic) mapping entries, i.e. 192.0.2.78. All incoming connections to port 25 are passed on to port 25 on 10.2.2.2, i.e. to Bob, which does exactly what we want:

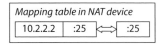

Many NAT devices provide this facility; some demand that the inside and outside port numbers are the same, whereas others let you specify them explicitly. This facility is called *mapped IP addresses* or *virtual IP* or *virtual servers*; there's no single, unambiguous term for it.

2. One-to-one NAT (static NAT)

So far all the NAT mapping entries we've referred to have been for one outside address – the outside address of the NAT device, 192.0.2.78. Some devices have a feature called *one-to-one NAT* (also called *static NAT*), which lets you have more than one outside address. Let's say we wanted our internal e-mail server to have a different outside address. In other words, we'd like to define the mapping entry shown below:

Mapping table in NAT device

| 10.2.2.2 | any | ⟺ | 212.140.133.2 | any |

Here we have a "one-to-one" mapping between an outside IP address and an inside address. Any traffic that comes in to IP address 192.0.2.2 is passed to 10.2.2.2, irrespective of what port it comes in on, and the port number is not translated at all. This is in complete contrast to normal NAT, where it is *only* the incoming port number that is used to distinguish between all packets coming in to the single address (192.0.2.78). Many NAT devices, but not all, offer one-to-one NAT.

23.5 Planning your implementation

We covered NAT first because the decision "to NAT or not to NAT" affects so many of the subsequent steps in your implementation. Now let's go back and start at the beginning!

Sign up with an Internet service provider (ISP)

The first thing you need to do is sign up with an ISP. Depending on what country you are in, the delay in having any necessary telecomms lines (leased line, ADSL, ISDN) installed may be much greater than the ISP's delivery time, so start this ball rolling as soon as you possibly can. *Always* plan for "unexpected" delays (e.g. on one connection here in Cambridge a large telecomms supplier promised us a link in three weeks, but in fact took nearly six weeks).

When choosing an ISP, compare your requirements (Module 23.1) with the offerings from ISPs in your area, and choose the best match to your particular needs. Make sure the support offered by the ISP covers what *you* want. If this is your first Internet connection, paying extra for good responsive support is probably a good idea, whereas if you have a lot of experience, you might be happy with a technically competent ISP with terrible support.

Choose your domain name, and register it. Your ISP may do this for you or will tell you how to go about it.

Now let's assume you have just signed up with an ISP, your telecomms links have been installed, and there's a router at your site ready for you to connect into, i.e. you have everything shown in Figure 23.6, plus your domain name, and the IP addresses that your ISP allocated to you if you have static addresses. Where do you go from here?

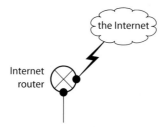

Figure 23.6 What you connect your site to

Implementation overview

The following is an overview of the steps involved. We've already covered much of the technical detail, e.g. how to configure a host for network connectivity, how to test DNS, etc.; the purpose of this module is to discuss some of the decisions you have to make for your particular installation and to give you a checklist of all the tasks so you can plan your implementation. The steps are:

A. draw a sketch-map of your planned network

B. allocate your IP addresses

C.   configure your router's NAT settings if it's providing NAT

D.   install your cabling

E.   install a **tcpdump** diagnostic PC and a separate dial-up PC for testing

F.   install and test basic Internet connectivity on a single LAN PC

G.   configure the test PC for DNS, and test DNS operation

H.   install your firewall

J.   configure your DHCP server if you want to use DHCP

K.   add one or two more PCs to your LAN and test again

L.   install public DNS server if required

M.   install internal, private DNS server if required

N.   install internal e-mail server if required

P.   install all your other LAN PCs and internal servers

Q.   draw up contingency plans.

Implications of a firewall

You have to test your basic Internet connectivity before you install your firewall, so your implementation divides broadly into three phases:

i.   set up and test basic connectivity

ii. install firewall and adjust network as appropriate to take account of the firewall

iii. continue configuring your LAN, which is now your live network.

While you really ought to install a firewall before your network goes live, some sites don't, usually for reasons of cost or lack of expertise. If that's what you choose to do, you just omit phase ii: the configuration used during the basic testing phase is your live network.

Any machines connecting to the Internet before the firewall is installed may be compromised (hacked). It's unlikely, because they won't be connected for long, but it is possible. Make sure they have anti-virus protection running, disable any services you don't need (especially e-mail clients and servers and Web servers), and if you're paranoid, rebuild the machines from scratch as soon as your testing is finished.

We don't cover firewalls until the next chapter, because some people won't bother with a firewall, and because you have to get your connection up and working first before you install a firewall. If you do plan to implement a firewall, skim through the rest of this chapter – so you know where you intend to go – and read the next chapter in full before coming back here and starting your implementation.

Because your firewall may be performing NAT for you, and because NAT affects your initial implementation and testing, we have to take account of the firewall in the next module when we look at specific testing approaches for different types of Internet connection. After that we start on the implementation proper.

23.6 Internet connection types, NAT, firewalls, and LAN: IP addressing for preliminary testing

Broadly, ISPs provide three different types of Internet connection, from an addressing point of view. The type you've got affects how you test and implement your network:

1. you are allocated at least one public, static IP address. On your LAN you have the choice of using public addresses or of NATing – which is usually performed by the firewall (or other NAT system) on the LAN side of the router. (You could have the router perform the NATing, if it supports it, in which case follow the instructions just as for case 2 below. However, if you do that, you lose the benefit of public addresses.)

2. no static IP addresses, router does NAT. (Typical examples: ISDN connection, cable modem, or ADSL for home use.)

3. no static IP addresses, router does *not* NAT, but allocates IP address to a single machine on the LAN using DHCP. (Almost always for home use.)

Figure 23.7 shows how you allocate addresses on your LAN for the preliminary testing of your Internet connection. The important point is that in case 1 you'll use static public addresses (1a, Figure 23.7), in case 2 you'll use NATed private addresses on your LAN during testing (2a) and in case 3 you'll have to use DHCP on a single test PC on your LAN (3a). We'll ignore case 3 from now on – for testing it's like case 1 with a single machine, and for live running it's very like case 2 with NAT provided by the internal firewall (but make sure your firewall can act as a DHCP client!).

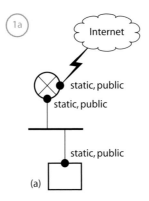

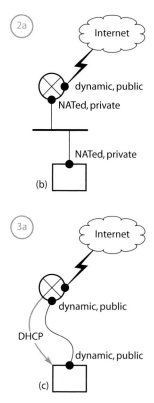

Figure 23.7 Allocating addresses to your Internet router and your LAN

In the next Module we'll look at how to allocate addresses when we've finished testing and inserted our firewall into the network.

23.7 IP addressing for the live network

In the previous module we explained how to handle public/private addressing for the preliminary testing of your Internet connection. In this module we assume your connection has been tested and is working OK. You now have to insert your firewall into your network and configure your IP addressing for live running.

1. At least one public, static IP address

There are two variants here:

i.   many public, static IP addresses. You may choose to use NAT or not. If you do, the NATing will be performed by your firewall. (Typical examples: ADSL for business use, permanent leased line.)

ii. a single, public, static IP address. If you want more than one machine on your LAN (and we assume you will), you must use NAT, performed by your firewall; otherwise, this is just a small instance of (i) above. (Typical examples: analog dial-up or ADSL for home use.)

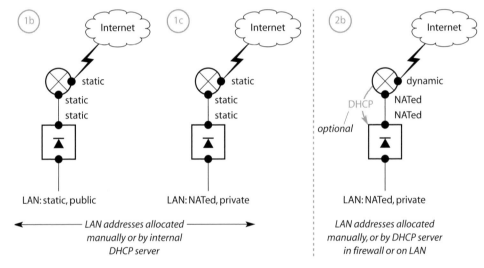

Figure 23.8 Allocating IP addresses to machines on your live LAN

All the machines use the static, public addresses during testing (1a, Figure 23.7). If you're not going to use NAT, adding the firewall (1b, Figure 23.8) is very easy because you continue to use the numbers from testing. If you do implement NAT, it becomes active only after you add your firewall, so you will have to renumber your test machines after the firewall is installed (1c, Figure 23.8). However, as we install only one or two machines for testing, this is a very small job.

If you have only one address, you will have to omit step K (Module 23.9 – adding extra machines) from your testing until you add a firewall (1c Figure 23.8). For reasons of space we won't treat this as a special case any more – it's just an instance of case (i) with NAT.

If you chose (probably unwisely) not to implement a firewall, then your test configuration (1a or 2a) will be your final, live configuration too.

2. No static IP addresses

Because the machines on your LAN use NATed addresses during testing, there's no need to change the addresses when you go live. Your Internet router almost certainly gives you the option to specify what the NATed, private address range is for your LAN, and may even be able to act as a DHCP server for internal machines. Choose a range of private addresses that you can configure in your Internet router, or use the router's pre-configured range if you have to.

If you install a firewall later:

- you can allocate the firewall's external address manually from the range of internal addresses your router is configured with. Alternatively, it may be able to get its external address by DHCP server from the router (2b, Figure 23.8).

- you can allocate the addresses to the LAN machines manually, or using a DHCP server – in the firewall if it has one, or else on the LAN.

Now that you know which IP addresses you'll be using in the preliminary testing phase, we get started on constructing the network, in the next Module.

23.8 Implementation (1)

A. Draw a sketch-map of your planned network

Draw your network as you expect to implement it and add the IP numbers you expect to allocate. (See Appendix 9 for an example.)

B. Allocate your IP addresses for testing

By now you know the range of IP addresses ("LAN-IP-range"), and the netmask ("LAN-netmask") you'll be using on your LAN – either the static range your ISP allocated, or the NAT range you will configure on your router for in step C below.

LAN-IP-range	___ . ___ . ___ . ___
LAN-netmask	___ . ___ . ___ . ___
LAN-default gateway = IP address of router's internal interface	___ . ___ . ___ . ___

C. Configure your router's NAT settings if it's performing NAT

(This applies only if you have what we called connection type 2 in the previous module – no static IP addresses at all. If you will be using NAT but have static IP addresses, skip this step, because you use non-NATed addresses for the first phase of testing.)

You want to tell your router the range of IP numbers that you'll be using on your private (internal) network. These are specified by the LAN-IP-range and LAN-netmask in step B above.

Most routers nowadays have a Web interface, and we've found that configuring NAT isn't a big deal. With a modern device with a good user interface, it might take you less than half an hour, including finding and reading the relevant documentation. (With a bad user interface and bad documentation it could take you days.)

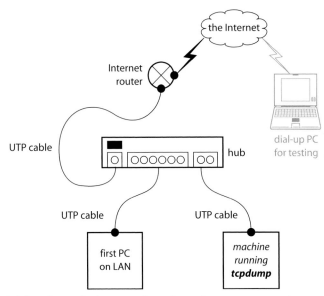

Figure 23.9 Cabling for preliminary testing of your Internet connection

D. Install your cabling

Nowadays this will almost certainly be 10/100Mbps UTP Ethernet, although gigabit Ethernet and wireless networking are becoming affordable and popular. Assuming you're using UTP, for performance reasons you'd use a switch rather than a hub (c.f. Module 2.8 and Appendix 3), but to make network testing and debugging easy, a non-switched hub is much better. The best compromise is to buy a small hub, use it for your preliminary installation (Figure 23.9), and when everything is working replace it with a switch. You'll need the hub later on anyway, for day-to-day testing and debugging as we described in Chapter 2. And, for tracing just the traffic to/from the Internet, you can insert the hub between the Internet router and the switch; this lets you see all Internet traffic but doesn't slow down your LAN.

E. Install a tcpdump **diagnostic PC and a separate dial-up PC for testing**

We always make the mistake of thinking everything will work first time and forget this step. In fact things never work first time, so it's much quicker to put your diagnostic tools in place right from the beginning: it saves you time and gives you great confidence when you can see exactly what's happening on the wire.

    a. set up a PC running **tcpdump** (Figure 23.9) It doesn't matter what its network settings are, because it's only listening on the wire, never sending. (You can use this to impress your managers too. "Look, there's our very first e-mail packet going out to the Internet.")

    b. set up a stand-alone PC with a dial-up connection to the Internet. You will use this to test that your site can be accessed from the Internet. It's best if the ISP you use for this dial-up is *not* the same one as you use for your main connection, so that your tests exercise more of the Internet. (If you use the same ISP for both, the connection from the ISP to the rest of Internet could be broken; you could still dial in and connect to your own main site, but not be able to connect to other sites, and you wouldn't know why.)

23.9 Implementation (2)

F. Install and test basic Internet connectivity on a single LAN PC

At this point you only need to configure the three magic settings:

i. static IP address: choose one from LAN-IP-range (from step B). Make sure you don't use the same address as your router. Even if you are going to use DHCP later on, allocate the IP address manually for this test, to reduce the number of variables

ii. netmask = LAN-netmask (from step B)

iii. default gateway = LAN-default-gateway (from step B).

Verify that you can:

a. **ping** yourself, on both the loopback address (127.0.0.1) and the address you just configured on your PC

b. **ping** the internal interface of the router

c. **ping** a site on the Internet. (You have to specify an IP number, not a hostname, as you haven't configured DNS yet. Your ISP has probably given you the IP numbers of their DNS or mail servers: pick one of them to **ping** if you can't find any others easily. And remember that some sites don't allow **ping**. If in doubt, check using your stand-alone dial-up connection that the site you choose does respond to **pings**.

Using your stand-alone dial-up PC, connect to the Internet. Now, from this dial-up PC:

d. **ping** the test PC you've just installed on your LAN. (This won't be possible if you're using NAT without special configuration of your NAT system.)

e. if the LAN PC is running any server (e.g. **daytime**, **telnet**, etc.) attempt to connect to that service

f. if your ISP has set up DNS for you, use **nslookup** or **host** to check that the DNS entries you expect really are present. Let's assume your domain is **example.com** and your ISP has set up MX entries for mail servers for you, and also an entry for a Web server, your tests will be something like:

```
nslookup -q=mx example.com
nslookup www.example.com
```

If you're not using the ISP's DNS for your public server addresses (if you have any public servers), you'll have to defer these tests until step L or M.

If any of these tests fail, you will have to check out what's happening as we explained in Part 1; **tcpdump** will help you isolate where the problem lies.

G. Configure the test PC for DNS, and test DNS operation

Configure the PC on the LAN to use the DNS server(s) at your ISP, and test it using **ping** (or **nslookup** or **host**). For example:

```
ping www.uit.co.uk
ping www.debian.org
ping www.aw.com
```

H. Install your firewall

This is covered in detail in Chapter 24. However, for convenience you might like to record the following settings here or on your network sketch. (The LAN-default-gateway may be the router's internal address, or the firewall's internal address, depending on your firewall model, and whether you're using NAT or not – see Chapter 24 for details.)

firewall's external interface address	___ . ___ . ___ . ___
firewall's external interface netmask	___ . ___ . ___ . ___
firewall's internal interface address	___ . ___ . ___ . ___
firewall's internal interface netmask	___ . ___ . ___ . ___
LAN-IP-range (private if NAT)	___ . ___ . ___ . ___
LAN-netmask	___ . ___ . ___ . ___
LAN-default-gateway	___ . ___ . ___ . ___

If your firewall is NATing, NAT becomes active now, so you have to renumber any test machines (which are behind the firewall) and repeat the tests listed in step F above.

From here on, your network is protected, so anything you install can remain as part of your live network.

J. Configure your DHCP server if you want to use DHCP

Using DHCP is so easy and has so many advantages that you should certainly use it unless you have a tiny site. If you don't have a router or other device that provides DHCP, you can easily run a DHCP server on a server machine. If you won't be installing that until later, you can use static addressing on your LAN for now and switch to DHCP later with very little effort. Whether you use DHCP or not affects nothing else in your implementation, so do whatever makes life easier for you.

- change the PCs on the LAN to use DHCP
- repeat the tests from step H above.

K. Add one or two more PCs to your LAN and test again

Connect one or two more PCs to your LAN and configure them. Then:

- check that all PCs on the LAN can contact each other
- repeat all the earlier tests (a–f in step F) for the new machines.

This verifies that your LAN is working correctly, that you can connect out to machines on the Internet, and that users on the Internet can connect in to you.

23.10 Implementation (3)

L. Install public DNS server if required

Do you need to run your own DNS server, or will you rely on your ISP for DNS? As we discussed in Modules 8.12 and 7.3, this depends on the size of your site, and on what servers you provide for public access from the Internet. If you are a tiny site with no servers at all, the public DNS (i.e. visible on the Internet) needs to contain only the MX records for the mail servers for your domain name. And if you are a tiny site you will almost certainly use your ISP's mail servers for sending and receiving mail, so your ISP can easily run your DNS for you and save you a lot of trouble. Similarly, if you have one or two public Web or other servers, your ISP's DNS can easily accommodate these. On the other hand, if you are running a large site or a big e-commerce operation, you may want the immediate control that running your own DNS servers give you (and you will probably have all the necessary resources too).

Check that your public DNS is accessible, both from a PC on your LAN and also from your stand-alone dial-up PC.

M. Install internal, private DNS server if required

You may need an internal DNS to map the names of internal machines to their IP addresses. We have found that very few small or medium-sized sites need this. Until recently, even large sites that used Microsoft systems exclusively ran internal DNS because Microsoft Windows Networking has its own (NetBIOS) system for name resolution. However, with Windows-2000 internal DNS is more common. Internal DNS is also helpful where you have a UNIX-based or mixed network, and where you run several internal services that you want to be able to address by name. For example, it's much less error-prone to enter **mailsrv.uit.co.uk** when configuring an e-mail client than having to remember **10.47.183.205**. Even though they could manage without it, many small Linux/UNIX users prefer to run internal DNS because of the convenience it gives.

Configure your LAN PCs to use the internal DNS and check that they can access it correctly.

N. Install internal e-mail server if required

To send e-mail you have to make use of an e-mail server. If you don't run your own internal e-mail server, messages are sent via your ISP's server, even if you are sending to the person sitting at the desk beside you. And messages can be sent and received only when your Internet connection is up, so if you are using a dial-up connection, internal e-mail can be slow and unresponsive, and costs real money in phone charges. On the other hand, if you have an always-on leased line or ADSL connection, the fact that e-mail to the next desk travels out to the ISP and back in again matters very little, as it's reasonably fast and doesn't cost anything extra. So how do you decide? Our experience suggests that if any of the following is true, you need an internal server of your own:

- you have an intermittent dial-up connection
- internal e-mail is mission-critical in your organization. By running an internal server your internal mail traffic is no longer dependent on your Internet connection, router, or firewall, so you have removed several potential points of failure

- you have large volumes of internal e-mail. If these went out and in again on your connection they would use a lot of bandwidth
- you have large volumes of external e-mail. Your ISP may complain or charge extra for handling all your messages
- you use a combined e-mail, scheduling, and diary system such as Microsoft Exchange. (ISPs usually only provide basic SMTP and POP servers.)

Configure your LAN PCs to use the internal e-mail server and check that they can access it correctly and that you can send and receive e-mail.

P. Install all your other LAN PCs and internal servers

We've left this until last, because you want to minimize the exposure of your machines to hackers until your firewall is in place. Repeat step H above for each machine. You now have a working LAN connected to the Internet, protected by a firewall.

Q. Draw up contingency plans

Your Internet connection (or at least Web access and your e-mail) is probably mission-critical to your organization. You need to work out what to do if any of the following happen:

- your Internet connection goes down because of:
    - a problem in your telecomms link to your ISP
    - a problem at your ISP
    - your Internet router fails
    - your firewall fails
- your e-mail server fails.

Most of these can be got over with a good maintenance or swap-out agreement with the equipment suppliers, and maybe a backup Internet connection of some kind. However, 99% of small and medium-sized businesses fail to carry out this planning step until it's too late.

We often find that when buying and setting up an Internet connection, organizations cut costs to the minimum and will not pay for any redundancy or contingency precautions. Then when something does fail, they scream blue murder when they see hundreds of users doing nothing for half a day because they can't get any e-mail or access information on the Web. Point out to management the cost – in lost business and lost productivity – of a connection failure; if they decide not to pay for the necessary backup systems it's their own fault. (But make sure you get their decision in writing.)

23.11 Other ways to connect your site to the Internet

You might want to connect a whole site (and not just a single computer) to the Internet using a modem and a dial-up telephone line. (We cover dial-up connections for a single computer in Chapter 26.) Typical uses are setting up a temporary connection for a site, connecting a very small site that only needs intermittent access, or connecting from a small home-office network.

Our experience is that this is often more trouble than it's worth – dial-up phone connections are always troublesome. If you can, use ADSL or cable access instead: they're much better and no more expensive in the long run. But sometimes you might *have* to use dial-up and here are some pointers on how to go about it.

Microsoft Windows Internet connection sharing (ICS)

Windows-98, ME, 2000, and XP have a feature called *Internet connection sharing (ICS)*. The Windows machine dials up as normal, but it also acts as a NAT device so that other machines on the LAN can use it as their Internet router (Figure 23.11) and as a DHCP server to your small network if you want it to.

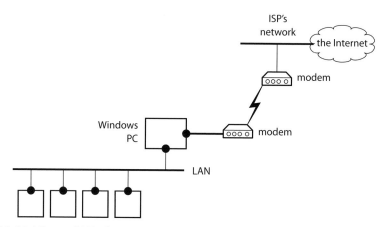

Figure 23.10 Microsoft Windows Internet connection sharing

The disadvantage of this configuration is that your Windows PC is completely exposed to the Internet and is difficult to secure. It's much easier to protect your site if you have a firewall (or just a router with some in-built security features) between *all* your machines and the Internet, whereas in Figure 23.11 you can't insert anything between the Windows PC and the Internet.

Windows NT Server 4.0 doesn't include this feature, but the NT 4.0 Small Business Server provides the same type of facility.

Router connected via a modem

You can connect a router to the Internet via an ordinary dial-up modem. This used to be quite complex and possible only on high-end routers but now hardware manufacturers offer combined modem-and-router boxes for a few hundred dollars.

These new systems are easy to set up and, like any router, they have the advantage that you can hide all vulnerable machines on the LAN behind a firewall (Figure 23.12).

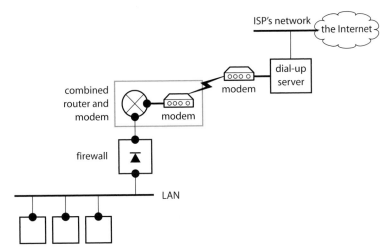

Figure 23.11 Combined router-and-modem devices make it easy to insert a firewall in front of your LAN

23.12 Backup Internet connections

For many organizations, their Internet access and e-mail are mission critical (even though management often doesn't realize it!). Many ISP's can provide a router with two Internet interfaces – one for a leased line which is used by default, and another for ISDN which is used as a backup in case the other goes down (Figure 23.12).

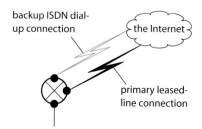

Figure 23.12 Router with two Internet interfaces

VRRP (Virtual Router Redundancy Protocol)

However, the configuration in Figure 23.12 has two draw-backs:

1. the router is a single point of failure

2. your ISP is a single point of failure. If their internal networks fail, you lose your Internet connectivity.

To overcome these problems, you can use two routers, running *VRRP (Virtual Router Redundancy Protocol)*. The Figure below shows a very simple example of a VRRP configuration:

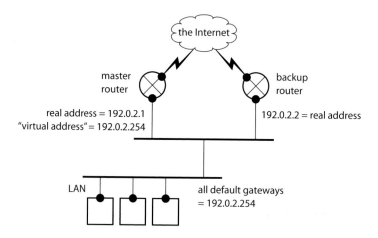

- the two routers run VRRP

- one router acts as master, the other as backup

- each router has its own real IP and MAC address, as usual. These are used for managing the routers, and for the routers to talk to one another.
- the master also responds to the "virtual router" IP and MAC addresses, 192.0.2.254 and *a:b:c:d:e:f*, say, for our example
- the master and backup constantly talk to each other using VRRP, each checking that the other is up and running
- in normal running, the backup router performs no routing function – none of the LAN machines forward it any packets to route.
- when the master router fails, the backup router detects this and takes over the routing function. It will now respond to the virtual router IP address 192.0.2.254 and the virtual router MAC address *a:b:c:d:e:f*, exactly the same as the master router. The LAN machines don't even know that this has happened, and the LAN users function as normal. The typical length of interruption on the network – before the backup takes over the routing – is less than a second.

The above is an over-simplification of VRRP. In practice you would probably share the load across both routers, using each as the backup for the other. You can have more than two routers, and you can connect each to more than one Ethernet switch so that you don't have a switch as a single point of failure either.

A cheap backup Internet connection

VRRP and high-availability switch configurations are too expensive and complex for most small and medium sites. A cheaper approach is to use a cheap cable modem or ADSL connection as backup for your primary connection (Figure 23.13). This only works if you're using NAT provided by a box (e.g. firewall) behind the router, i.e. if your LAN IP addresses don't depend on your external router address. When your primary connection fails, manually switch the firewall connection from the primary router to the ADSL router, and change the firewall's default gateway accordingly. This only takes five minutes, but gives you a very usable backup, at very little cost and you can use different ISPs for your two connections, to give an extra level of backup. (Of course your public servers – which use IP addresses from your primary ISP – will not be visible over the backup line; but see the Notes for a possible solution.)

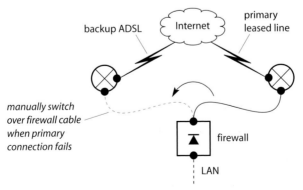

Figure 23.13 Using ASDL as a cheap backup connection for your main Internet connection

Summary

- as soon as you decide that you're going to connect your site to the Internet, work out what your precise requirements are before you choose an Internet service provider. One of your first decisions is whether to use network address translation (NAT)
- NAT lets you use IP addresses inside on your LAN that are different to those visible outside on the Internet:
  - this is useful if you have been allocated only a few public IP addresses or if you want a large internal IP address range for convenience in sub-netting
  - NAT usually maps all internal IP addresses to a single external address. Some systems also let you map individual internal machines to individual external addresses; this is often used to make servers publicly visible on the Internet
  - when you implement NAT on an existing network you usually have to renumber the IP addresses of your LAN machines
  - most NAT systems include Port Translation too
- when you have decided on your requirements, plan your implementation and work out in detail what IP numbers you'll allocate to which machines on your network. How you do this depends very much on whether you will be using a firewall and/or NAT
- implement your plan, testing each installed component on the way
- in certain circumstances, connecting your site to the Internet using a dial-up link can be useful.

What's next?

This chapter hasn't covered the security issues involved in connecting your site to the Internet, so we cover firewalls in the next chapter, and other security systems in the chapter after that.

Notes and further reading

In Module 23.1 we said you need static IP address(es) if you want any server(s) to be publicly visible on the Internet. Strictly this isn't true: you can use *dynamic DNS* to make a dynamic address visible through the DNS. There are two variants of this.

1. Windows-2000's DNS allows machines on the network to update their DNS entries automatically. Of course, for these addresses to be visible on the Internet, you must be running your own public DNS server, and *it* must have a static address. For more information see:

   ❏ **http://technet.microsoft.com** *TechNet Home* > **Products & Technologies > Windows 2000 Server > Resource Kits > Part 2 > Chapter 6 – Windows 2000 DNS**

2. there are many sites on the Internet that allow home users to register their dynamic addresses with a DNS server, so that a home machine name can be resolved via the public DNS. For information search for "dynamic DNS" on Google.

Appendix 25 contains a checklist that we use to remind us what tests we need to do when connecting a site to the Internet, and to record the results on.

If you own your Internet router ...

In Module 23.1 we assumed that your ISP has supplied and configured your Internet router. However, some sites – especially smaller ones using ISDN – buy their own routers. Most routers nowadays have a Web interface, and configuring them – at least the basic settings – is straightforward. (In fact the hardest thing is working out what you need to set and what you can leave as it is.) Depending on your router, configuration consists of something like this:

1. *configure a PC to talk to the router box*. A router typically comes with a 192.168.x.x. address and you need to configure your PC's IP settings to match, so the two can talk, ideally using a Web interface, or (for old-style routers) via **telnet**

2. *configure the LAN (inside) interface.* You need to tell the router it's IP address and netmask (which also determines the range of IP addresses on the LAN). Once these settings take effect you can reset your PC to its normal IP settings

3. *configure the WAN (outside) interface.* Specify the external IP address and netmask (or configure the router to obtain an address via DHCP or whatever your ISP has told you to do). Typically the only routing you need is to set your router's default gateway to the address of your ISP's router (which the ISP will have told you about), i.e. you send all your packets to them, and they can do all the fancy routing – which is what you pay them for

4. *security settings.* Make sure nobody from outside can logon to or change settings on your router. (ISPs often configure routers the other way round; users on the *LAN* aren't allowed to configure them so their customers can't mess up their settings.)

5. *management settings.* Enable and configure SNMP, Syslog or other logging, etc.

NAT

❑ **RFC-1335 May 1992** *A Two-Tier Address Structure for the Internet: A Solution to the Problem of Address Space Exhaustion* was the first RFC to mention NAT

❑ **RFC-1631 May 1994** *The IP Network Address Translator (NAT)*

For a note on the consequences of using NAT, see:

❑ **MS-KB-Q172227** *Network Address Translators (NATs) Can Block Netlogon Traffic*

For a non-exhaustive list of NAT-able applications, see:

❑ **http://www.tsmservices.com/masq/**

("masq" stands for IP masquerading, i.e. NATing.) This site isn't the clearest and has a lot of information devoted to games, but it can give you helpful pointers on using an application with NAT in case you run into problems.

In Japan they have NATed NAT (i.e. even the external addresses allocated to a site might be NAT, private addresses). There IP address space is so tight because of the popularity of Internet-enabled mobile phones and PDAs.

Changing your ISP

If you run your own public e-mail or Web servers, if you change your ISP, your IP numbers will change, so on your new connection your servers will have new IP addresses. However, even after you've switched to your new ISP and your new DNS entries are published, some DNS servers out on the Internet will have your servers' old IP addresses in their cache until their TTL expires. During this period, any of those DNS servers' clients will try to send e-mail to your old mail server address, or access your old Web server, which are no longer reachable. You can minimize this problem by reducing the TTL setting for your old DNS entries, to one hour, say, instead of the typical 24 hours. Do this (or ask your old ISP to do it for you if they run your DNS) several days in advance of your switch-over date.

Other ways to connect your site to the Internet

❑ **MS-KB-Q234815** *Description of Internet Connection Sharing* (ICS) lists the components of Microsoft's ICS as including:

- a simplified DHCP server (or "Allocator") to serve the IP address, gateway, and DNS server settings to
- DNS Proxy, to resolve names on behalf of the LAN PCs. This forwards queries to your ISP's DNS servers
- NAT. The ICS PC acts as a NAT device for the internal PCs
- auto-dialer, which automatically dials up to the ISP when there is any traffic.

In Module 23.12 we explained how you can use a cheap cable or ADSL connection as a backup for your main Internet link. In the configuration we described, your public servers (on your DMZ or on the LAN) won't be visible. You can even get over this if you run your own DNS server and are prepared to do a little more manual reconfiguration when you need to swap over from one link to the other. For details, see Web Appendix 30.

In Module 26.12 we mention that dial-up links (using SLIP or PPP) can be used to link small offices or even remote workgroups. While this is still feasible, the cost and ease of Ethernet, and wireless networking for longer distances, mean it's less used now.

VRRP

❑ **RFC-2338 April 1998** *Virtual Router Redundancy Protocol*

Cisco have a proprietary protocol that provides a similar function to VRRP:

❑ **http://www.cisco.com/warp/public/619/3.html** *Hot Standby Router Protocol (HSRP): Frequently Asked Questions*

Appendices

Appendix 3: Ethernet hubs and switches
Appendix 9: example of working network diagram
Appendix 25: worksheet for testing a new Internet connection
Web Appendix 29: types of Internet connection
Web Appendix 30: cheap backup for an Internet connection

24

Firewalls

Introduction

This chapter explains what firewalls are, how they work, and the features they may offer. It includes notes on choosing, implementing, and troubleshooting your firewall system.

24.1 What a firewall is and why you want one

"When you're connected to the Internet, the Internet is connected to you."

Your Internet connection is an open two-way channel; when you are connected to the Internet, any machine on the Internet can reach your machines. Therefore it can use any service running on your desktop PCs or servers – Microsoft Windows Networking (your shared files and printers), e-mail, **telnet**, NFS, your company database, etc. – unless you explicitly prevent it. Some services are protected by usernames and passwords, but operating systems and applications often have security holes that let a malign hacker bypass these basic checks. Or, the hacker may be able to install a "Trojan horse" program or sniffer to capture your passwords, and then use your servers posing as a legitimate user.

This is where a firewall comes in. It's a single, secured point of entry and exit for your network: *everything* passes through here and *nothing* comes in or out anywhere else. It blocks access to your network at the perimeter of your site (Figure 24.1). Because the packets are blocked before they even reach the machines that are running your services, they protect you from (many of) the vulnerabilities in your applications and operating systems.

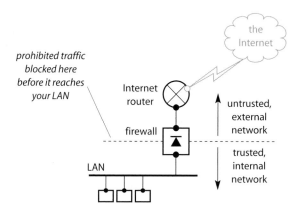

Figure 24.1 A firewall is a single point of entry/exit on your network

At their most basic, firewalls block particular TCP/IP source/destination address/port combinations. For example, your mail server (IP number 192.0.2.66) listens on port 25, and your Web server (192.0.2.77) listens on port 80. Your firewall might have rules like:

```
allow source=any  dest=192.0.2.66 destport=25
allow source=any  dest=192.0.2.77 destport=80
deny source=any   dest=any
```

These allow only Web connections to your Web server, and e-mail connections to your mail server. But there are complications. The rules as they stand don't allow any traffic out at all: your users can't surf the net, and worse still, it's no use allowing packets to come in to your Web server if the reply packets can't get out. Firewalls have to take account of issues like these.

Even when we solve that problem, there's a further complication. We are allowing Web traffic in to our Web server; if our Web server has any security holes (and at the time of writing, we've just had the Code Red and Nimda worms, which have caused significant problems worldwide by exploiting Web server vulnerabilities) hackers can still exploit them. So our firewall, or something else, has to be clever enough to handle this problem. We explain how in this chapter and the next.

Other important features of a firewall are:

- alerting you to hacker attacks, so you can take immediate evasive action if required

- logging your Internet activity. Because all access is through this one point, monitoring your firewall lets you track all your Internet traffic.

"Nobody will want to hack me"

If you think nobody wants to hack you, you're wrong – very wrong. In the old days, sites were usually hacked only because they were special in some way (a bank, a prestige defense establishment, a prominent Web site, a company with information needed by a competitor…). Nowadays people hack just for fun. There are automated tools that scan whole chunks of the Internet, looking for vulnerable machines. Hackers with no technical skill ("script kiddies") download and use these tools. If you're on the net and vulnerable, you'll be hacked – not because you're special (the hacker may not even know you exist) but just because you're vulnerable. Moreover, many viruses and worms spread automatically. Some worms use the e-mail address books on compromised machines to find names of new machines to attack: you may get hacked just because your e-mail address is in the e-mail address book of someone else who got hacked earlier. (This is how the Nimda worm infected nearly 500,000 systems in less than two days.)

There are lots of interesting (and frightening) statistics:

- the "2001 Computer Crime and Security Survey" reported that 70% of the organizations surveyed said their Internet connections were frequently attacked, and 40% of them detected system penetration

- a Gartner Group report says: "By 2003, 50 percent of small and midsize enterprises (SMEs) will have been successfully attacked through the Internet. SMEs, most of which are ill-prepared to identify or respond to Internet attacks, should develop security measures as soon as possible"

- one of our customers is a small company (less than ten people) but still sees an average of five intrusion attempts every day

- another customer was hacked and all their machines virus-infected within two days of getting their ADSL connection, before they ordered their firewall. After six weeks they still hadn't cleared up all the mess. Apparently it's now common for ADSL connections to be hacked within a few days of installation.

Ask yourself what are the costs – in time, money, and adverse publicity – if your data are damaged or removed, or your Internet connection is brought down? If you're connected to the Internet, the Internet is connected to you, and you need a firewall.

24.2 How firewalls work (1) – packet-filtering firewalls; rule ordering

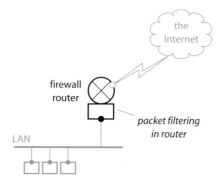

Figure 24.2 A basic packet-filtering firewall

Packet filtering

When firewalls were first developed, they were implemented using normal routers. A basic firewall is shown in Figure 24.2. The router performs the normal LAN-to-Internet routing function, but it's also configured to act as a *packet filter* with a set of rules to allow or deny packets based on their source and destination. A packet is filtered only on the information in its header; the content or payload of the packet is not examined. Figure 24.3 shows a set of packet filtering rules (from a real firewall, but with the IP numbers changed to protect the innocent) for a firewall of this type, illustrating some of its problems:

- it requires very detailed knowledge of the protocols, because you're working at a detailed, low level

- it's error-prone: if you put in a single rule in the wrong place, you may inadvertently open up the whole firewall, and never be warned of it.

Packet filtering is very fast, but because it only looks at each packet in isolation, it has significant limitations:

- it doesn't maintain any state about established TCP connections, so there are certain types of attack it can't block (see next module)

- it has difficulty handling FTP, because of FTP's multiple-port operation. Some firewalls can only handle passive-mode FTP because of this

- it doesn't handle user authentication (see next module), which requires the firewall to keep state information about authenticated users.

For these reasons, most firewalls now use stateful packet inspection, which we cover in the next module.

Ordering of security "permit/deny" rules

The packet filtering rules in Figure 24.3 are applied top-down. When the firewall/router receives a packet, it compares the packet headers against the first rule; if the packet matches, the action specified in the rule is performed ("permit" in this case) on the packet, and that's the end of that. However, if the first rule doesn't match, the packet is compared with the second rule. If that matches, it's actioned; otherwise the third rule is checked, and so on, until no rules are left. Usually there is an automatic, "deny-everything," catch-all rule inserted at the end (See the Notes for a diagram representing this graphically).

```
permit  172.16.204.3/32 10.1.1.5/32 UDP =123 In
permit  10.1.1.1/32                       Source  In
permit  10.1.1.5/32      UDP     =53       Source  In
permit  10.1.1.5/32      TCP     =53       Source  In
permit  10.1.1.254/32    TCP               Source  In
permit  192.168.5.29/32  TCP     >0        Source  In
deny    10.1.1.1/32      TCP     =23       Dest    In
permit  10.1.1.1/32                        Dest    In
permit  10.1.1.2/32                        Dest    In
permit  10.1.1.3/32      UDP     =53       Dest    In
permit  10.1.1.5/32      UDP     =53       Dest    In
permit  10.1.1.5/32      TCP     =53       Dest    In
permit  10.1.1.6/32      TCP     >1023   !=3751   !=6000   Dest   In
permit  10.1.1.7/32      TCP     >1023   !=3751   !=6000   Dest   In
permit  10.1.1.11/32     TCP     >1023   !=3751   !=6000   Dest   In
permit  10.1.1.12/32     TCP     >1023   !=3751   !=6000   Dest   In
permit  10.1.1.199/32    TCP     =21       Dest    In
permit  10.1.1.254/32    TCP               Dest    In
permit  10.1.1.240/28    TCP     =80       Dest    In
permit  10.1.1.192/26                      Source  In
permit  10.1.1.192/26                      Dest    In
permit  10.1.1.0/24      ICMP              Dest    In
permit  10.1.1.1/32                        Source  Out
permit  10.1.1.5/32      UDP     =53       Source  Out
permit  10.1.1.5/32      TCP     =53       Source  Out
permit  0.0.0.0/32                         Source  Out
permit  10.1.1.1/32                        Dest    Out
permit  10.1.1.5/32      UDP     =53       Dest    Out
permit  10.1.1.5/32      TCP     =53       Dest    Out
permit  10.1.1.192/26                      Source  Out
permit  10.1.1.192/26                      Dest    Out
permit  10.1.1.0/24                        Source  Out
deny    default
```

Figure 24.3 Packet-filtering rules

This "top-down, action-and-terminate when a rule matches" behavior is typical of almost every Internet security device – firewalls, routers, VPN systems, etc. If the device doesn't help you get the ordering correct, then you have a problem: it's easy to put a rule in the wrong place by accident, with surprising results, e.g. in Figure 24.3, if we had the "deny default" rule at the beginning instead of the end of the list, it would be actioned for every packet, so none of the other rules could ever take effect: our firewall would be acting as a very expensive and complex "air gap."

24.3 How firewalls work (2) – stateful packet inspection

A *stateful packet inspection (SPI)* firewall maintains a table of current activity, e.g. information about each TCP connection, and uses this information in conjunction with the packet's source and destination addresses/ports to decide whether the packet should be allowed or denied (blocked). Figure 24.4 illustrates how incoming traffic, even for the same port, is distinguished on the basis of whether it is part of an existing connection. By contrast, a packet filter would either allow traffic to port :1234 or deny it; it could not distinguish between the two cases shown, because it keeps no record (state information) about what happened in the past.

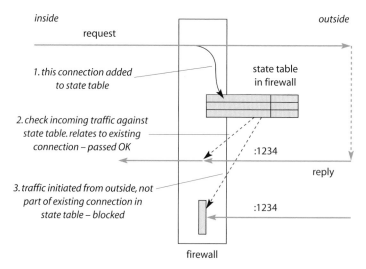

Figure 24.4 Distinguishing between internally and externally-initated connections

SPI firewalls have many advantages over basic packet filtering:

- they can allow reverse traffic automatically, without your having to enter specific rules. Consider an inside Web client connecting to a Web server outside on the Internet. The TCP connection will be from an ephemeral port (:1234, say) on the client, to port :80 on the server. With a packet filter you have a problem, because you won't know in advance what the ephemeral port is, and often just have to allow any incoming access to a whole range of ports that might be used as ephemeral ports by clients. By contrast, the SPI firewall records the ephemeral port number in its state table when the connection is first established through the firewall, and knows that only this Web server is allowed reply to this client on this port

- similarly, even though the firewall might "allow incoming Web connections to port 80 on internal server 192.0.2.55," if an incoming packet for that destination isn't part of an existing connection, e.g. if the connection hasn't completed the normal three-way TCP handshake (Module 10.8), the firewall can deny it. So even though port 80 has been "opened" on the firewall, incoming traffic to port 80 is subjected to many other checks before being permitted. By contrast, on a packet filter, an "allow traffic to port 80 on 192.0.2.55" is a "blanket" allow – anything to that port is permitted. This is an important distinction: there are hacker attacks that work by sending a packet that looks like it's in the middle of a TCP session. SPI firewalls can block these attacks but packet filters can't

- they can control UDP and ICMP traffic, even though these are connectionless, by creating "pseudo sessions." For example, the firewall can recognize an outgoing ICMP **ping** packet and record the source and destination, **ping** identifier and sequence number, etc. in its state table, and permit only incoming packets that are replies to this

- they can handle user authentication. An external user can connect to the firewall and authenticate ("logon") to it, and the firewall records this fact. It can then let this user access internal resources that are blocked to non-authenticated users. This allows external users to connect to private internal mail and Web servers from external sites, for instance.

In short, SPI firewalls give much finer control over your traffic than do packet-filtering firewalls. You will usually have far fewer rules too, which makes configuring them much easier and much less error-prone.

In the next module we look at an example of a hacker attempt being processed by a stateful packet inspection firewall, and see how – unlike packet filtering – SPI requires more memory resources as it handles higher levels of traffic.

24.4 Stateful packet inspection and resource usage

Let's look at a specific example of how an SPI firewall can block a particular type of attack, using its state information. A common *denial of service (DoS)* attack is the "SYN Flood." Here's how it works. When a TCP connection is being established, client and server go through the normal SYN, SYN/ACK, ACK three-way handshake (Module 10.8). When the server receives the initial SYN from the client, it replies with SYN/ACK and creates an entry in an internal table saying it's awaiting an ACK from the client to complete the connection establishment (Figure 24.5).

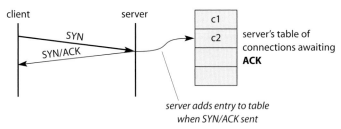

Figure 24.5 Server awaiting an ACK to complete connection establishment

When the client sends the answering ACK, the server removes the entry from the "awaiting ACK" table because the connection is now fully established (Figure 24.7).

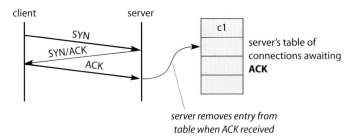

Figure 24.6 Connection established — three-way handshake completed

In a SYN flood, the attacker sends a large number of SYNs in quick succession and never completes the connection establishment. The server's internal table fills up (Figure 24.7) so it's unable to accept connections from any other, real clients. In this way it has denied service to legitimate users.

SPI firewalls can protect servers from this type of attack. Instead of passing the initial SYN through to the server, the firewall itself sends the SYN/ACK, and awaits the establishing ACK. If the client is legitimate and sends the ACK, the firewall then performs its own three-way handshake with the server (Figure 24.8); when that's complete, it passes all traffic from the legitimate client to the server as normal. However, if the client is a hacker attempting a SYN flood, the real server is never contacted; the firewall detects the attack, recognizing the abnormal load of incomplete connection establishments and discarding them. The firewall may also raise an alert to inform the network manager of the attack.

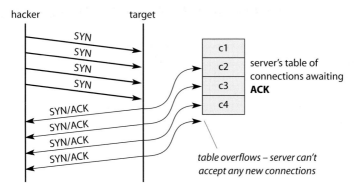

Figure 24.7 Internal table fills up

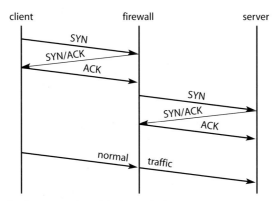

Figure 24.8 Firewall's three-way handshake with the server

Because the firewall must maintain state tables for each established TCP connection, for connections in the process of being established, and for UDP and ICMP packets, it can use a lot of memory. This is why you will often see a firewall advertised as "handling 5000 simultaneous connections" or similar. The busier your site, the more connections will be needed, so the firewall must have the memory and processing power to handle the likely volume.

24.5 How firewalls work (3) – application-level gateways

An *application-level gateway (ALG)* is a firewall program that runs at the application level of the TCP/IP stack, not at the IP packet level. ALGs are also called *application proxies* or *application-level proxies.* Figure 24.9 shows a client on the Internet connecting to one of our internal servers via an ALG firewall.

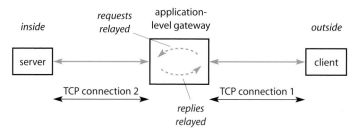

Figure 24.9 Separate TCP connections on either side of ALG firewall

- the client establishes a connection to the ALG
- the ALG connects to the server
- the ALG acts as a proxy on behalf of the client. It accepts requests from the client, analyzes them, and if they are acceptable according to the firewall's rules, re-issues them on the ALG's connection to the server. The ALG handles responses from the server in the same way.

With an ALG there are two separate TCP connections, as illustrated in Figure 24.9. This is fundamentally different from packet filter and stateful packet inspection firewalls where there is a single connection – from the client to the server – with the firewall acting almost as a router (Figure 24.10).

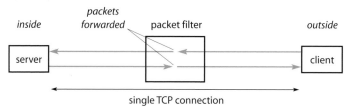

Figure 24.10 Non-ALG firewall acts almost as a router

With the ALG, packets from the client are not forwarded to the server – only the semantic information (protocol commands, etc.) extracted from the packets is relayed. Malformed packets sent from the client – either because of a faulty client implementation or because they are deliberately malformed as part of a hacker attack – can never reach the server.

Advantages of application-level gateway firewalls

- ALGs understand the application-level protocols being used, so they can check the meaning of requests and replies. Let's take some examples:
  - an early version of the **sendmail** mail server had a "backdoor" built in for debugging: if you used the **WIZ** (wizard) command, you could get root user (administrator) access. Because packet filters and SPI firewalls don't understand the SMTP protocol at this high level, they can't block valid but unwanted commands like this. Because the ALG does operate at the application level, it can easily block this type of request
  - ALGs can offer fine control over requests sent to a Web server. At the simplest level, the firewall could block certain URLs when requested by certain internal IP addresses. It could also block the Code Red worm's requests: they are valid according to the HTTP specs, but are recognizable because of the particular URL they request
  - you could allow FTP **GET** requests but block **PUT** requests, so Internet users can retrieve files from your FTP server but can't deposit virus-laden or other troublesome files.
- ALGs can give very detailed, protocol-specific logging.

Disadvantages of application-level gateway firewalls

- because of the amount of state information and the number of open connections they maintain, ALGs need more memory and processing power than packet filters or SPI firewalls. They may also be slower because of the extra load of extracting and validating the application-level semantics
- a separate proxy application must be provided within the firewall for each different protocol supported. When a new protocol or service is developed, there will usually be a delay before the firewall manufacturer releases a suitable proxy. For most people this delay won't matter, and anyway a generic proxy application can often be used as a stop gap. This will have no specific knowledge of the new protocol, but will allow it to operate through the firewall. Proxy programs are often only a few hundred lines of C program code, so they can be produced quickly
- (some old ALGs and proxies only worked with special versions of client applications or libraries that were aware they were using the ALG, but nowadays most ALGs are "transparent" giving the illusion that the client is connected directly to the server, and don't need any special client software.)

Hybrid firewalls

Hybrid firewalls are a mixture of stateful packet inspection for performance, and ALGs for fine control of specific protocols. Many modern firewalls are hybrids of this type.

If your firewall doesn't contain some ALG-like functionality, especially for e-mail and Web traffic, you should consider a separate security tool (program or appliance) to give you finer control (Chapter 25).

24.6 Using a demilitarized zone (DMZ) on a firewall

A *demilitarized zone (DMZ)* is a half-way-house network between the untrusted, external Internet and your trusted, internal LAN. It contains servers that are accessible from the Internet, e.g. the e-mail server that receives messages from the Internet, and the Web server that hosts your public Web site (Figure 24.11). The firewall allows outsiders on the Internet to access the servers on the DMZ but not any machines on your LAN.

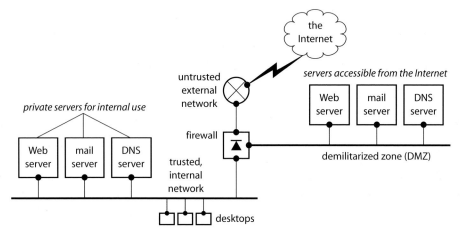

Figure 24.11 Demilitarized zone on a firewall for publicly-accessible servers

The purpose of a DMZ is to keep your public servers completely separate from your private LAN, in case the public servers are compromised. "Compromised?" you ask, horrified. "Does that mean the firewall doesn't give me 100% protection?" The answer is the one you really didn't want to hear: no firewall is 100%. Accepting that fact helps you secure your systems by encouraging you to take the approach, "OK, that protects us from ABC, but what if XYZ happens after that? Can we put in a second or third line of defense?" (This is called "security in depth.")

To protect your LAN, the firewall restricts traffic from DMZ to LAN, as well as from WAN to LAN. Then, if your Web server, say, is broken into, your LAN is still protected, because the intruder still has to go through the firewall to reach the LAN. But if your Web server lived on the LAN instead, and was broken into, the intruder would have a clear run from the Web server to everything else on your network. You *do* have to plan for this type of intrusion: e-mail and Web servers are notorious for having security holes in them.

Even though some access to the DMZ is allowed from the Internet, it is good practice to configure the firewall as restrictively as possible. Allow access only to the specific services you want to be accessible – HTTP and SMTP on a typical site – and block everything else. This accords with another general security principle: allow nothing at all initially, and then only open up as little as possible. This approach helps protect you from inadvertent misconfigurations. For example, let's assume your Web server is a Windows machine and it's running Microsoft Windows Networking. If the firewall allows access to this server, a hacker could connect to a share (shared file system) on your server and delete or change files. But if your firewall blocks everything except HTTP access, you are protected from this threat.

There are other precautions you should take with Internet-accessible machines:

- disable all network services that you don't need, for two reasons:
  a. if a service isn't running, nobody can connect to it
  b. all software has bugs, and many security holes arise from software bugs. The more software you run, the more bugs there are, and the more security holes you have
- physically remove all unnecessary software from your machine. If your machine is compromised, someone might try to start network services that you had previously disabled; if the software isn't there, they can't
- if you're running Windows-2000, use "Security Templates" (see Notes).

Different roles of DMZ servers and internal servers

Why does the site in Figure 24.11 have two servers of each type (Web, e-mail, and DNS)? The reason is they fulfill different purposes:

Web servers: the DMZ server provides the public Web site, accessible from the Internet. It's not normally accessed by internal users. The LAN Web server runs the internal intranet system, is accessed only by internal users, and contains private information (internal pricing, customer and supplier details, staff handbook, etc.)

E-mail servers: the DMZ server receives incoming mail from the Internet, passing it on to the internal e-mail server. It may also receive e-mail from internal users and send it over the Internet to its destination, and will need to interact with the DNS to locate the destination e-mail server for each message. The LAN e-mail server handles all internal e-mail, and may also include scheduling and other functions (e.g. MS-Exchange). It can operate even if the Internet connection is down.

In the next chapter we'll see that the DMZ e-mail and Web servers often have extra security functions such as scanning traffic for viruses, and/or checking the content of Web pages and e-mail messages for unsuitable or confidential material.

DNS servers: there are many difference scenarios where you'd have two separate servers. The most common is where the DMZ server is the primary DNS server for your site; its database holds the names and IP numbers of your public servers and nothing else, and machines on the Internet access it to resolve these addresses. The LAN DNS server holds completely different information – all the addresses of your LAN machines – and is used only by internal machines to access internal servers by name, e.g. **http://intrawebserv** or **int-mail-srv**. The LAN DNS server might use the DMZ server as a forwarder so that it never has to connect to a DNS server outside your site. (Recall the "split" or "shadow" server DNS configuration in Module 8.12.) This type of configuration reduces both the number of machines that need to pass traffic through the firewall and the number of your firewall rules.

Yet another general security guideline is to isolate one service from another as much as possible, so that if one is compromised, the others are still safe. This would lead you to run each DMZ service on a separate machine for security reasons. However, for cost reasons you might have to run multiple services on a single machine.

24.7 Choosing a firewall

Firewalls and security are two areas where we always advocate buying a product (even though free software packages are available) for the following reasons:

1. if your security matters at all, it's important to *know* that it really is doing what you think it is. Buying a firewall would be worthwhile just for the logging and alerting facilities, even if you ignored the protection it offers

2. nowadays you can buy a "firewall in a box," i.e. a hardware firewall appliance. For many people these are a better option than a firewall software package running on a PC or workstation (see below)

3. firewalls aren't ridiculously expensive any more. You can buy small appliances starting at about US$500

4. if you choose the right firewall, you can be up and running the same day.

However, if security isn't paramount, or if you have a lot of security expertise, or later on when you really know what you're doing and if you have the time, you could consider using the firewall facilities such as **ipchains** that are available free for Linux.

Below are some of the important factors to consider when choosing a firewall.

Basic security features

1. how secure is the firewall? That's a hard question for anyone to answer. Check out the fundamental features of the firewall: does it offer packet filtering, or stateful packet inspection, or application-level gateways/proxies? Look in the computer press for technical reviews on the firewalls you're interested in.

2. does it support VPN (Chapter 27)?

3. does it support NAT (Chapter 23)? Almost every firewall does nowadays. Combining NAT and VPN in the one box overcomes the problems that NAT has trying to modify packets that have already been encrypted by a separate VPN system (Module 23.3)

4. does it support URL blocking (Module 25.3)?

5. does it support virus scanning for Web, e-mail, and FTP traffic (Module 25.2)?

Other features

6. does it support only two Ethernet ports (for basic firewalling) or can it have a third port for implementing a DMZ, or even multiple DMZ ports?

7. does it have a high-availability option to let you run two firewalls in tandem, so that if one fails, the backup unit takes over automatically?

8. how easy is it to use? With some firewalls you need weeks of training before you can be confident using them. With others, a few hours will get you started. (We once had a customer who had a big complex firewall. They contacted us for help three years after the guy who installed it had left: they hadn't touched it in the meantime and didn't

know what it was doing) In practice, a well-administered simple firewall is much more secure than a badly configured sophisticated system that nobody understands.

9. if the firewall will be performing authentication, e.g. for users connecting via dial-up ISPs over the Internet, does the firewall support LDAP for accessing user databases? Does it support any other user-database management tools you might want (e.g. integration with your Windows-NT domains or Active Directory)?

10. what type of logging and reporting does it support? Can it use **syslog** to integrate its logs with the rest of your log-handling infrastructure? Does it integrate with third-party log analysis and reporting tools? Does it give full usage reporting or just exception reports? Can it alert you when it detects that you are being attacked? (See also Intrusion Detection Systems, Module 25.1.)

11. for small networks, having a 4- or 8-port UTP hub, and/or a DHCP server built into the firewall can be convenient.

Dedicated hardware appliance, or software firewall on a PC?

In our experience, dedicated hardware firewall appliances are often a better option than a firewall software package running on a standard PC or workstation:

- we've found that appliance firewalls are much easier to set up and to manage
- they save you the cost of a machine to run the software on
- they avoid a lot of the operating system (O/S) bugs and configuration problems that can affect software firewalls. As we said earlier, the more code you have, the more bugs you have, and NT and Linux are huge. You have to know what you're doing and *harden* the O/S, by removing as much as possible and modifying your configurations specially for security (see Notes). Appliances have a tiny O/S and no extra applications so they minimize the risks.

Performance considerations

12. can the firewall handle the throughput (Mb/s) of the Internet connection you are using, for normal (unencrypted) traffic and for VPN (Chapter 27) if you are going to use it?

13. how many simultaneous connections can the firewall handle? This is important for busy sites. Small sites could easily be handled within the 5000 connection limit of a small to medium-sized firewall, whereas large, busy, or e-commerce sites might need hundreds of thousands of connections

14. what speed are the Ethernet interfaces: 10Mb/s, 100Mb/s, or 1Gb/s? While most sites don't have an Internet connection anywhere near 10Mb/s, you may still want faster Ethernet if, for example, you have a Web server running on the DMZ, pulling a large amount of data from database servers on the LAN. On a general-purpose computer used as a firewall you can change you Ethernet cards to suit your network, but if you need a 1Gb/s card, be sure that the computer you're using can deliver the throughput you need.

24.8 Implementing a firewall

This module outlines how to implement a firewall on your network. Because firewalls vary so much, this is of necessity very general. First, some general points to note are:

- if you're using a general-purpose PC with firewall software (as opposed to a purpose-built appliance) *don't* run anything else on it:
    - many security holes arise from software bugs. All software has bugs. The more software you are running, the more bugs there are, and potentially the more security holes you have
    - if you're running your firewall on a Windows PC, adding an operating system Service Pack to fix a problem, e.g. with a Web server, could break your firewall
- firewalls are usually for TCP/IP protocols only. If you use IPX or NetBEUI, you may open up an unprotected backdoor from "outside" to "inside" because NetBEUI traffic bypassed the firewall code. Even NetBT (NetBIOS over TCP/IP) can be dangerous because it's a whole networking system in itself, making it easy to permit wider access than you intended. If you don't need Windows Networking on your firewall, disable and remove it
- don't allow any modems on your firewall. If a modem connects to the Internet, it provides a backdoor that bypasses all your firewall's security.

Implementation outline

1. read all the documentation before you start! (Nobody ever does, but it really helps to view the big picture before diving in.)

2. draw up a security policy – a document that says who needs to be able to do what, from where, and why (e.g. "internal e-mail server must be accessible from 192.0.2.64/224, our Edinburgh branch office, so they can pick up e-mail for their users"). Write down all your needs and decisions, and keep the document up to date as you change your security configs. This is a great help for new staff, and auditors love it too

3. draw a map of your network, and keep this with your security policy. (See Appendix 9 for an example diagram.)

4. if you're not using a ready-built appliance:
    - prepare your firewall PC by removing all unnecessary software. (Even better, start with a new PC or a re-formatted disk, and install only what you need. Then you *know* there's nothing else lying around from previous installations.)
    - install the firewall software

5. configure the firewall's network settings: IP and netmask for internal and external interfaces, and DMZ if you have one. It is at this point that you enable and configure NAT if you're using it. You also have to configure the firewall's default gateway, which will almost certainly be the address of the internal interface of your Internet router

6. configure the firewall's basic rules and logging:
   - enable detailed logging. (When the firewall is up and running OK you may want to decrease the verbosity of the logs.)
   - set the firewall to block everything, in and out
7. insert the firewall into your network
8. modify any settings on LAN machines that have to take account of the firewall. For example, if you've just enabled NAT, you'll have to renumber your LAN PCs. The default gateway for the LAN PCs depends on your configuration and firewall type, so you'll have to check your documentation. If you're using NAT, the default gateway is usually the firewall's internal interface address; without NAT, it could be either the firewall's internal interface, or the firewall's own default gateway. (See under "Proxy ARP" in the Notes for why there are two different possibilities.)
9. refine your firewall rules:
   - on paper, translate your security policy into a set of firewall rules
   - apply these rules to the firewall.

   We've usually found it's best to apply rules in stages. First allow outgoing **ping** traffic, and check that that part works correctly. Then allow other outgoing traffic, and check it, before allowing traffic initiated from outside. (This implicitly assumes that you're using an SPI firewall.) Finally, if you have a DMZ, configure it and apply any necessary rules.

   We use a checklist to remind us of what tests we need to do, and to record the results (Appendix 25).

   You will probably need to check that certain TCP services (e.g. HTTP, SMTP) are accessible from outside, but it's unlikely you have the necessary servers on your test "inside" PC. You can either enable the **daytime** service and modify your rules accordingly for testing, or alternatively run **netcat** on the inside machine – acting as a "manual" server listening on the appropriate port, as we described in Modules 17.5 and 17.4
10. when the firewall is behaving as you want it:
    - save its configuration settings to file, and store them on a safe machine on your LAN, *not* on the firewall. In the same location, save the firewall software (or firmware if it's an appliance). See Web Appendix 33 for the convention we use to make sure we have everything we need to restore our firewall configs
    - continue with your network implementation as described in Chapter 23.

Adding a firewall to an existing live network

If you're adding the firewall into an existing live network, it's often easiest if you build a small test network first, so you can familiarize yourself with the firewall without disrupting anyone else. Add one machine "outside" the firewall and one machine "inside," to simulate the WAN and LAN respectively. The outside machine will be the firewall's deft gateway and vice versa. Otherwise, configuration is almost exactly as described earlier.

When the firewall is working as you require, insert it into your live network, and continue as with step 8 above.

24.9 Troubleshooting with a firewall in place

As with the previous module, this module can give only a general approach rather than a detailed formula, because all firewalls are different.

Troubleshooting with a firewall is harder than normal networking because the firewall "interferes with" the traffic (which is its job after all). We say "troubleshooting with a firewall in place" rather than "troubleshooting your firewall" because often you don't know whether it's the firewall that's the problem, or whether something else is misbehaving. (The whole of this book grew out of troubleshooting firewall installations. It's ironic that this chapter is one of the shortest in the book, but we've often found that on a three-day project to install a firewall, only half a day is devoted to firewall setup/configuration/debug. The rest of the time is spent sorting out the customer's network and routing and DNS and Windows Networking.) If you understand your network thoroughly, you'll be able to diagnose whether a problem is really being caused by the firewall or whether it's a normal networking issue.

The key idea to keep in mind is that traffic can go only two ways through the firewall from outside (Figure 24.12): either the firewall passes it to the LAN, or the firewall drops it and shows the reason why. (We've assumed that we're sorting out a problem with incoming traffic; this is where most problems arise since many sites permit all outgoing traffic.). Then work through the steps below:

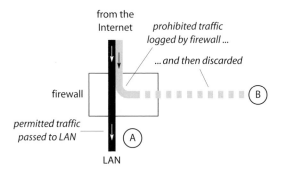

Figure 24.12 Possible paths through the firewall from outside

1. look at the firewall's logs to see whether it tells you straight away why the traffic was blocked. If not ...

2a. configure the firewall to give its most detailed logging, at least on the type of traffic or source/destination that you're having the problem with

2b. as well as logging, the firewall may have debugging options. But be careful – they can reduce performance significantly, e.g. enabling debug on one of our firewalls increases the time for a **ping** from about 5 milliseconds to 600 milliseconds. If you're troubleshooting a live firewall you may have to choose a very slack time or work out of hours

3a. run **tcpdump** between the firewall and router (A1, Figure 24.13) and ...

3b. ... run **tcpdump** inside the firewall also (A2, Figure 24.13). If you're paranoid, use two separate sniffer PCs; otherwise, you can use a single PC with two NICs. The danger is that your **tcpdump** PC could get hacked, because A1 is outside the firewall and unprotected. If the sniffer has a second interface on the trusted LAN, hackers could use it as a backdoor from outside to inside. A compromise is to connect your **tcpdump** machine using special UTP cables that have their transmit capability disabled (see Notes); the sniffer PC can then listen but not transmit, making normal TCP/IP networking impossible and making the PC unhackable. (This also means that you can only access it only via its own screen and keyboard – not across your network – until you change the cable.)

4. generate test traffic that illustrates the problem

5. look at the logs, and relate any messages to the **tcpdump** traces, and/or to any firewall debug outputs.

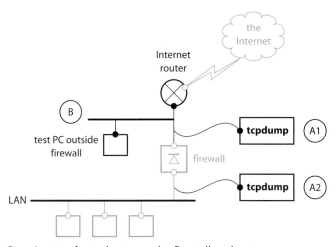

Figure 24.13 Running **tcpdump** between the firewall and router

Locating the problem *can* be very hard. Sometimes you're using VPN (Chapter 27); not only is VPN complex in itself, but it encrypts your data, making it even harder to see what's happening. Too often, the firewall's logging isn't sufficiently detailed, or just doesn't show the events you're looking for. NAT complicates things too: the packet you see coming in at A1 will have been modified by NAT when you see it at A2. To make things easier for yourself, ensure that the capture filters you specify for **tcpdump** are as precise as possible, so you can quickly focus in on the relevant data.

If you're still not getting anywhere, move an expendable PC onto the Ethernet segment between the firewall and the router (B, Figure 24.13). ("Expendable" because it's unprotected and may get hacked.) If the problem still occurs when communicating between this PC and the Internet, you know the firewall isn't causing it.

Summary

- a firewall is a secure single point of entry and exit for your network. It controls all traffic passing through it on the basis of rules you specify
- if you're connected to the Internet, you need a firewall
- there are several types of firewall – packet-filtering, stateful packet inspection, application-gateway (or proxy), and hybrid. Each has advantages in terms of performance, level of security, and ease of configuration
- a demilitarized zone is a half-way-house network between the external Internet and your internal LAN:
  - the DMZ is used for servers that are accessible from the Internet
  - the firewall controls traffic from the Internet to the DMZ and from the DMZ to your LAN, giving you an extra layer of protection should any DMZ server be compromised
  - servers on the DMZ (e.g. Web, HTTP, or DNS) usually fulfill a different role to servers running the same protocols on the internal LAN
- troubleshooting with a firewall in place is made harder because the firewall interferes with the traffic. Using two sniffers, one on the LAN inside the firewall and the second outside, often gives you the information you need to diagnose what's happening.

What's next?

The next chapter covers other security systems for your Internet gateway – the point of connection of your network to the Internet: filtering Web traffic on the basis of the URLs specified and on the content of pages, blocking spam e-mail, and virus-scanning. Depending on your systems, many of these may tie in with your firewall.

In Chapter 27 we cover VPN, which can improve the security of connections to your site from branch offices and from dial-up users.

Notes and further reading

Don't forget to include your firewall in the contingency plans you drew up in Module 23.10. We explain "personal firewalls," for single dial-up machines, in Chapter 27's Notes. In Module 24.6 we mentioned Win-2K's Security Templates. For more information see:

❏ http://www.microsoft.com/windows2000/en/server/help/sag_SCEwhatis.htm
Security Templates Overview

A few RFCs give general security guidelines. These are now dated, but the general approach is still valid:

❏ **RFC-2916 September 1997** *Site security handbook*

❏ **RFC-2504 February 1999** *Users' Security Handbook*

❏ **RFC-2828 May 2000** *Internet Security Glossary*

There are countless Web sites dealing with security. Three of the better ones are:

❏ **http://www.sans.org** The SANS (System Administration, Networking and Security) Institute

❏ **http://www.cert.org** the CERT® Coordination Center (which was originally the "computer emergency response team"

❏ **http://www.freefire.org/** *The Freefire Project* Click on "Tools" for a wonderful, comprehensive list of free security software

For statistics of the spread of the Code Red and Nimda worms, see:

❏ **http://www.caida.org/dynamic/analysis/security/code-red**

❏ **http://www.caida.org/dynamic/analysis/security/nimda/**

Other interesting sites include:

❏ **http://www.gocsi.com/prelea/000321.html** Complete the survey on one of the links to see the *2001 Computer Crime and Security Survey*

❏ **http://www3.gartner.com/resources/93300/93311/93311.pdf** *Gartner Research Indicates Small and Midsize Enterprises Are Vulnerable to Internet Attacks*

❏ **http://www.insecure.org/** An interesting site with enough hacker information to keep you awake at night

❏ **http://www.insecure.com/tools.html** *Top 50 Security Tools*

Firewalls

A FAQ on the type of traffic you're likely to see reported in your firewall logs:

❏ **http://www.robertgraham.com/pubs/firewall-seen.html**

That site plus another also tell you how to make receive-only Ethernet cables:

❏ **http://www.robertgraham.com/pubs/sniffing-faq.html#receive-only**

❏ **http://home.ie.cuhk.edu.hk/~msng0/sniffing_cable/**

For lots of material on firewalls and security, see:

❏ **http://rr.sans.org/firewall/firewall_list.php**

❏ **http://www.sans.org/infosecFAQ/firewall/DMZ.htm** *Designing a DMZ*

❏ **http://www.sans.org/top20.htm** *The Twenty Most Critical Internet Security Vulnerabilities*

❏ **MS-KB-Q259240** *XWEB: How to Configure OWA to Connect to Exchange Through a Firewall*

❏ **RFC-1919 March 1996** *Classical versus Transparent IP Proxies* – how application-gateway firewalls work

Ordering of security "permit/deny" rules

The figure below shows how security rules are applied in most security software and appliances. Rules are checked in order, from top to bottom. As soon as a rule matches, the action associated with this rule is performed, and processing terminates.

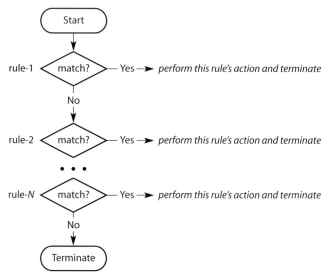

Figure 24.14 Checking all rules

Internal firewalls

Statistics indicate that about two-thirds of threats come from inside an organization – disgruntled employees and contractors, inadequately trained staff, etc. You can use extra firewalls *internally* to protect sensitive departments from other parts of your network. There are also distributed internal firewalls:

❑ http://www.uit.co.uk/ans.htm

Lighter reading

A detailed description by Bill Cheswick of prolonged hacker attacks on AT&T:

❑ ftp://ftp.research.att.com/dist/internet_security/berferd.ps *An Evening with Berferd In Which a Cracker is Lured, Endured, and Studied.* This is also included in …

❑ **W.R. Cheswick and S.M. Bellovin** *Firewalls and Internet Security* (1994, Addison-Wesley) The first edition is dated in terms of implementation but contains great (and frightening) descriptions of what the problems are. A second edition is due very soon.

❑ **Clifford Stoll** *The Cuckoo's Egg* (1990, Bodley Head) – how Stoll exposed an international spy ring selling secrets to the KGB. Stoll was running a central computer at a Berkeley lab, and was asked to trace an error in the computer user accounts. This began a hunt for a hacker who was infiltrating sensitive American networks.

Proxy ARP

Some firewalls use "proxy ARP," which we mentioned in Chapter 2's Notes. Let's say we've just added the firewall into the network shown below and that until now all the LAN PC's had 192.0.2.1 as their default gateway. None of the LAN PC's can now reach .1 directly – they broadcast ARPs but broadcast packets aren't transmitted through the firewall. We *could* change all our LAN PCs' configurations to use the firewall (192.0.2.2) as default gateway, but that is time-consuming. Some firewall manufacturers overcome this by using proxy ARP. The firewall knows that **.1** is on the outside, but when it hears an ARP request for **.1** from a LAN PC, the *firewall* sends the ARP reply, containing the firewall's MAC address. The LAN PCs send their 192.0.2.1 traffic to the firewall's MAC address and the firewall routes these packets to the real 192.0.2.1. Similarly, the router doesn't have to be told that only the firewall is now directly connected to it: the firewall can proxy ARP replies to any ARP requests that the router sends for machines on the LAN. In this way the firewall can just be dropped into the LAN with almost no changes to the internal machines. (This is sometimes called "ARP bridging.")

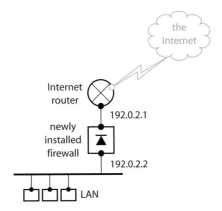

Appendices

Appendix 9: example of working network diagram
Appendix 25: worksheet for testing a new Internet connection
Web Appendix 33: conventions for saving firewall settings

25 Other security services

Introduction

Your firewall is only your first line of defense against hackers trying to enter your site from the Internet. You need finer-grained control over Web and e-mail and similar traffic: even if the Web or e-mail request is valid according to the protocol, it still might be an attempt to compromise your system. At best, it could be sending you junk e-mail. At worst, it could be an attempt to break into your Web server and take control of that machine, or a virus-laden e-mail message that could infect your whole network. Special proxy servers give you fine control over what traffic you allow and what traffic you block.

25.1 Proxy servers; other security components

Most firewalls nowadays use stateful packet inspection, as described in the previous chapter. In practice this usually means that:

- most services on internal machines are protected and outsiders can't connect to them, which is what you want …

- … but if you do permit connections to a particular service, that service is wide open and is vulnerable to any weaknesses in the server application providing the service.

Let's take a couple of examples:

1. if your SMTP server runs on port 25 on machine 192.0.2.4, a typical firewall rule will be "allow connections from any outside IP address to 192.0.2.4 port 25." What it does not check is that:

   - the mail message being sent to your server is for a destination that belongs to you. It may be a spam message being relayed via your server (c.f. Module 11.14).

   - the message is free from viruses

   - the SMTP conversation isn't trying to exploit a known weakness in your mail server

2. you probably allow Web clients to connect to your Web server, but don't verify the contents of the HTTP requests. This allows hackers to exploit holes in your Web server. For example, the Code Red worm requests the page **default.ida** followed by a long string of Xs or Ns and some other stuff that is easily recognizable, but very few firewalls check traffic at this application level.

Because of considerations like these, you will often reinforce your firewall's protection with extra security systems, either on your DMZ or your LAN or both. These systems typically operate as proxy servers, forwarding requests and replies between client and server. They also have extra code to ensure that requests:

- agree with the RFC or other specification for the applications

- are not exploiting a weakness in the protocol or the application

and any unacceptable traffic is blocked by the proxy (Figure 25.1).

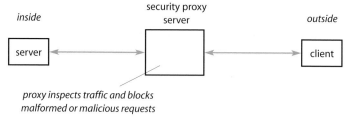

Figure 25.1 Proxy blocks unacceptable traffic

Using the examples above, once your security system is already handling the SMTP or HTTP protocol dialog, it needs only a small amount of extra code to check that the message really is for one of your users, or that the URL requested isn't part of a Code Red worm attack.

You should be careful about *all* services and applications that are accessible from the Internet. Because the most common publicly accessible services are e-mail and HTTP, we'll concentrate on them in the following modules. Below we cover a couple of other security-related topics.

Network Intrusion Detection Systems (IDSs)

We mentioned above that even though certain Web and e-mail requests are valid as far as the protocol specification is concerned, they can still be part of a hacker attack. *(Network) Intrusion Detection Systems (IDSs or NIDSs)* address this issue by watching the network traffic on the wire or at a particular host, looking for patterns of events or requests that may indicate an attack. The IDS has a database of *attack signatures* – patterns of activity that network managers have seen previously in attacks. They are stored in the database in a simple specification language. For example, a signature for the Sircam worm (which is carried by e-mail) in one IDS is:

```
alert tcp any any -> any 25 (msg:"Virus - Possible W32.Sircam.Worm@mm";
content: "I hope you like the file that I sendo you"; nocase; rev:2;)
```

and a signature for the Code Red work that attacks Microsoft Web servers is:

```
alert TCP $EXTERNAL any -> $INTERNAL 80 (msg: "IDS552/web-iis_IIS
ISAPI Overflow ida"; dsize: >239; flags: A+; content: ".ida?";)
```

When a signature is recognized, the IDS raises an alert to the administrator, or, depending on the system, may automatically modify your firewall or router configuration to block further traffic for the offending source.

Vulnerability and penetration testing

Your firewall plus the related security systems that we cover in this chapter will protect you from just about everything, you hope. But it's easy to make configuration mistakes, or to forget to undo a temporary change made to accommodate an urgent requirement. Or, there may be some plain old deficiencies in your security system. It is worthwhile having your security tested objectively.

Penetration testing involves running special software from outside your network, scanning all your IP addresses for accessible machines and services. It identifies where your perimeter security can be penetrated. (In other words it's a port scan and sweep, but run for your benefit – not by a hacker trying to damage your site.) Depending on the tester you use, when it finds an open service it may probe more deeply for specific vulnerabilities (e.g. that a guest account has no password, or that your Microsoft Windows Networking shared file systems are accessible, …) and report on these vulnerabilities.

You can obtain vulnerability and penetration testing software and run the tests yourself, or there are many third parties who offer a testing service.

25.2 Virus scanning and content filtering

Virus scanning

Nowadays about 80% of virus infections occur over the Internet. Viruses can be included in e-mail message attachments and Web pages and FTPed files.

Anti-virus best-practice suggests you should run three layers of anti-virus scanning:

1. at the entrance to your site from the Internet
2. on your file and Web and e-mail servers
3. on individual desktops.

For maximum protection, these should be independent systems from different manufacturers using different technology. That gives you different virus pattern-recognition engines and different update frequencies, so that if a virus does get through one level it may well be caught by the next. However, the cost and effort of maintaining three separate systems often mean that a single manufacturer's system is used throughout; many such systems have a management console that lets you administer all the different, distributed components from a single, centralized point. We'll look only at the first type of scanner here – the one at the entry to your Internet site.

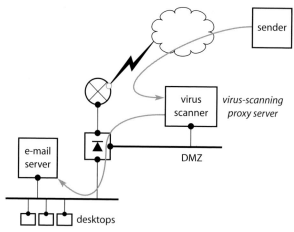

Figure 25.2 Virus-scanning proxy system handling incoming e-mail

Figure 25.2 shows a typical configuration for a virus-scanning proxy system handling e-mail. You configure your DNS so that your MX records point to the virus scanner, not to your real e-mail server. E-mail from the Internet comes in to the virus scanner, which is a full SMTP server (but of course doesn't contain non-SMTP functions like POP or IMAP, etc.). The virus scanner checks the received messages for viruses. What it does when it finds a virus depends on the package and how it's configured; typical options are to discard the message and inform the recipient, or remove the virus and forward the "disinfected" message to the recipient, or hold the message in a "quarantine" area so the system administrator can decide what to do with it later.

These virus scanners can usually handle HTTP and FTP traffic too. The user's client application (e.g. Web browser) is configured to use the virus-scanner as a proxy. The client sends the request to the proxy, which retrieves the page and virus-scans it, and then returns the scanned page to the client.

Content filtering (content scanning)

To perform virus scanning, the proxy server needs a full understanding of the relevant protocol. For example, to scan incoming Web pages, the scanner must be a Web proxy server, be able to handle all the different types of HTTP requests, and forward all the retrieved pages to the client. It also needs a full understanding of the different data encodings, so that embedded files as well as the top-level pages can be scanned correctly. Compressed archives such as Zip files or UNIX **tar** archives are often sent via HTTP, so the scanner must understand these formats, be able to extract the individual entries in the archives, and re-insert disinfected files into the archive when it has finished scanning.

Because the scanner already contains all this infrastructure, enhancing the system to scan for things other than viruses is relatively straightforward. Scanning systems now let you perform some or all of the following:

- block the Web page or discard the e-mail if it contains particular keywords (e.g. if an outgoing message contains "Here's a copy of my resume," or an incoming Web page contains the phrase "red hot teen girls" – you get the idea)
- discard particular attachment types, e.g. Visual Basic or executable programs
- limit Web download sizes, or defer sending large e-mail messages until night-time, to reduce the load on your Internet connection during busy periods
- define a whole security and usage policy, saying who can send what to whom, when, etc.

Systems like these are used primarily by organizations for their own financial, legal, religious, or other reasons to control what their users are allowed to access. There are other, similar systems that control Web downloads for the user's benefit. An example is the Proxomitron, which is highly configurable. Some of its options are:

- don't download banner advertisements (saves bandwidth and display time)
- remove pop-up windows
- automatically change fonts and colors on the page (e.g. if you have a sight disability or merely good taste)
- limit the information that a server can obtain from your browser about you and your PC
- remove specified types of JavaScript from pages, especially scripts that add advertisements or breach your privacy
- disable animation of GIF images (saves CPU on your browser).

Virus and content scanning does slow down traffic. Users can notice this on large HTTP transfers, but not with e-mail, as message receipt is not interactive.

25.3 Web URL filtering

Filtering on Web URLs is related to the content scanning we discussed in the previous module, but it works entirely differently. It controls access to Web pages on the basis of the URL string only, not by inspecting the content of the page the URL points to.

You configure your desktop HTTP clients to use the URL filter as their HTTP proxy. When a client requests a page, the filter system in the proxy looks up the URL in an internal database containing a huge number of URLs and their classifications, to find out what type of Web page the user requested (e.g. pages on **www.playboy.com** contain nudity and information on recreational drugs). If the administrator has forbidden this type of page, the user's request is blocked (shown at 2a in Figure 25.3), otherwise the request is honored (shown at 2b). The system doesn't even need to connect to the remote Web server because it's not checking the content of the page, merely its URL. To ensure nobody bypasses the filter, block all HTTP traffic (except to/from the filter machine) at your firewall.

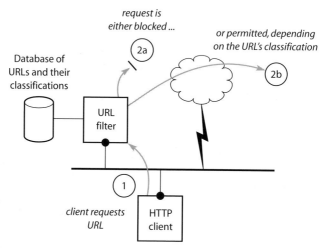

Figure 25.3 Request is either blocked or permitted, depending on classification of the URL in the database

The database is compiled and updated regularly by the manufacturer who has a large team of people looking at Web pages and classifying them appropriately. Because the database changes quickly, the URL filter system downloads a new copy automatically every night or every week.

As well as blocking obviously unsuitable material, these systems are useful for logging your organization's Web usage – for charging purposes or just to understand your network activity patterns better.

Some organizations control personal (non-work-related) surfing by blocking:

- advertisements
- instant messaging and chat
- streaming audio/video, MP3 sites
- shopping, share dealing
- "reality TV" sites

and contend that the saving in bandwidth means they need a significantly smaller (and cheaper) Internet connection than they would otherwise.

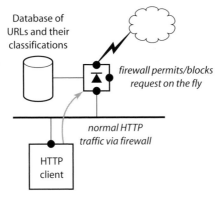

Figure 25.4 URL database held on firewall

Some firewalls have URL filtering built in. They can either maintain the database themselves (Figure 25.4), or merely detect the URL and pass it to the filter system for validation (Figure 25.5). The advantage of filtering in the firewall itself is the HTTP clients don't have to be configured to use the firewall as an HTTP proxy. Because the firewall sees all traffic, it can look into the HTTP request packets and perform the URL filtering on the fly.

The advantages of Figure 25.4's system over Figure 25.5's are:

- you don't need an extra server to run the URL filter

- there is no extra network traffic passed so no network traffic at all is required when deciding to accept/reject this URL.

But Figure 25.5's system probably gives you a wider range of filter systems to choose from, not just the one the firewall manufacturer supports.

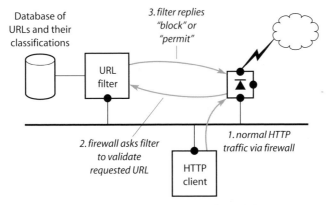

Figure 25.5 Passing the URL to a separate filter system for validation

25.4 E-mail: proxy and filtering servers

In Module 11.14 we mentioned the problem of open e-mail relays – e-mail servers that will accept and forward messages destined for any user at all (Figure 25.6):

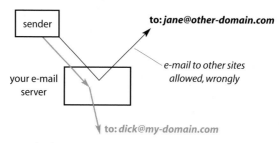

Figure 25.6 Open e-mail relay

whereas a correctly configured server will accept messages only for users at this site or set of sites (Figure 25.7).

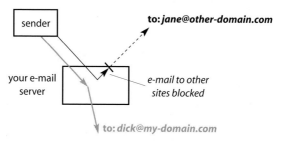

Figure 25.7 Correctly configured e-mail server — relay blocked

Even if your own e-mail server isn't an open relay, open relays at other sites can cause you problems, because they are used by spammers to send huge amounts of junk e-mail that waste your time and your network's resources.

There are tools to help you block mail from known spammers and mail from known open relays. Several organizations operate databases of spammers and open relays, which e-mail servers can use as follows:

- when an incoming SMTP connection is established, your server detects the sender's IP address
- your server looks up this IP address in one or more databases. If the address is listed as a spammer or open relay, your server drops the TCP connection so the message is never even received, and you don't waste any bandwidth receiving junk.

The best-know databases are:

RBL (Real-time Blackhole List): a list of known spammer addresses. The list is maintained by MAPS (Mail Abuse Prevention System), a not-for-profit organization in California dedicated to fighting spam

DUL (Dial-Up List): a list of known dial-up IP addresses (i.e. ranges of IP addresses dynamically assigned by ISPs to their dial-up users). Also run by MAPS. Even though most private (non-company) e-mail originates from dial-up PCs, all the usual e-mail client programs (Outlook Express, Netscape, Eudora, etc.) send their messages to the ISP's mail server to be forwarded. You receive the messages from the ISP's server; since its IP address isn't dynamic, it's not in the DUL list, so the message won't be blocked. Typically only spammers run a full mail server on a dial-up, dynamic IP address – in order to bypass their ISP's server and any spam controls the ISP imposes

ORBS (Open Relay Behavior-modification System or Open Relay Blocking System): a list of known open relays. In fact this service shut down in mid-2001, but we mention it because it became notorious and even got involved in legal disputes. After it closed, other organizations such as ORBZ (Open Relay Blackhole Zones) have offered a similar service

RSS (Relay Spam Stopper): a list of known open relays, similar in concept to ORBS but maintained by MAPS.

Unlike the URL filters in Module 25.3, your mail server doesn't download any of these lists. Instead, it uses DNS in a curious and interesting way to look up entries in the database. Let's say your mail server has received an SMTP connection over TCP from IP address 1.2.3.4, and it wants to consult the RBL list:

1. your server issues a DNS query, using your usual DNS servers (either your own or your ISP's) for the hostname **4.3.2.1.blackholes.mail-abuse.org**. (This *is* a name, and not an IP number, and it is performing a query for an A record.)

2a. if the DNS query succeeds, i.e. a record is found, this IP address is on the list and your server will drop the connection. (The IP address resolved is usually 127.0.0.2, which is never a real address on the outside Internet.)

2b. if the query fails, i.e. no record is found, the IP address isn't of a known Bad Person so your e-mail server processes the rest of the SMTP transaction.

The way the system works is that the **mail-abuse.org** site maintains a large DNS database of spammer and open-relay IP addresses. Let's take an example: assume that 192.0.2.66 is a known spammer address, but that 192.0.2.88 is a good network citizen. The **mail-abuse.org** people create a DNS A record in their database for the name **66.2.0.192.blackholes.mail-abuse.org**. This name is within their domain (**mail-abuse.org**) so it can't interfere with anything else, and only lookups for the full name will ever see it. Our other IP address, 192.0.2.88, isn't a spammer, so **mail-abuse.org** don't create an A record for it. Anyone who looks up the name **88.2.0.192.blackholes.mail-abuse.org** will get a lookup failure, indicating that this isn't a known spammer.

While this is an unusual way of using the DNS, it has the great advantage that no new protocol is required, and mail servers require very little modification to use it because they already contain all the DNS-handling code.

On a separate note, some sites block all incoming mail to their SMTP server except from their ISP's site. This avoids spamming and other attacks on their internal server, but it does slow down e-mail because all messages must be queued on the ISP's backup relay and then forwarded to the internal server.

Summary

- for security in depth, you need to augment your firewall with other security systems
- intrusion detection systems detect penetration attempts by recognizing a "signature" or pattern of events on the host or network
- penetration testing lets you scan your network for vulnerabilities accessible from the Internet
- special proxy servers can provide extra security, control, and logging over services such as e-mail, Web and FTP. They can
  - scan content for viruses and remove them or discard the message
  - scan downloaded or e-mailed content for confidential or offensive material
  - check a requested URL against a database that classifies Web pages for certain criteria and block undesirable pages. Because the check is on the URL string itself, the page doesn't have to be downloaded before it is blocked
- e-mail servers can use lists of known spammers and open relays to block junk e-mail.

What's next?

In the next chapter we look at dial-up networking for connecting to the Internet just for surfing, or for accessing your office LAN from outside. In the chapter after that we return to security and see how VPN can help you secure your dial-up links, and links to branch offices.

Notes and further reading

Security is now such a big issue that every IETF RFC issued has to include a "Security Considerations" section.

A security-related benefit of **syslog** (Module 17.12) is that it lets you store logs of sensitive machines on a different machine. That way, even if the machine is compromised, the hacker can't modify or delete the logs, so you still have the information to trace the intruder and if necessary to use it as legal evidence. You can even send logs to more than one logging machine for extra security.

Intrusion detection systems

❏ **http://www.snort.org/** *Snort – The Open Source Network Intrusion Detection System*

❏ **http://www.snort.org/docs/lisapaper.txt** A very readable overview of Snort, what it does, and how it works

❏ **http://www.snort.org/docs/idspaper/** *Insertion, Evasion, and Denial of Service: Eluding Network Intrusion Detection,* some of the problems faced by IDSs

Penetration testing and vulnerability scanning

There are many commercial scanning systems, but here are some free ones. (Note that this type of tool may be developed by security folks or by hackers.)

❑ **http://www.porcupine.org/satan/** *SATAN (Security Administrator Tool for Analyzing Networks)* – one of the oldest and best-known security scanners

❑ **http://www.hoobie.net/brutus/** *Brutus* A remote online password cracker

❑ **http://www.nessus.org/** *Nessus* – a free, powerful, up-to-date and easy to use remote security scanner

❑ **http://www.insecure.org/nmap/** *Nmap – Free Stealth Port Scanner For Network Exploration & Security Audits network mapper.* The main part of this site has lots of other security information of interest

❑ **http://www.cert.org/incident_notes/IN-99-01.html** *CERT® Incident Note IN-99-01 – "sscan" Scanning Tool,* which can be configured to automatically exploit vulnerabilities that it detects

❑ **http://packetstormsecurity.nl/Crackers/NT/l0phtcrack/** L0phtcrack is a password cracker for Windows. (Recent versions are full commercial products with significant license fees.)

Poor man's URL blocking

Let's say you want to block the Web site **ads.example.com** because it is a banner-ad site and you don't want to waste time and bandwidth downloading silly ads. Add the line:

```
127.0.0.1 ads.example.com
```

to your **hosts** file (in spite of what we said about **hosts** in Chapter 19). When your Web browser retrieves a Web page containing a link to **ads.example.com**, it will try to retrieve the ad image from 127.0.0.1, which is your own machine, which of course don't have the ad, so it will display it as a big red X or an "Action canceled" legend or similar. Ugly but fast. You can insert as many of these lines as you like in your **hosts** file.

E-mail filters

❑ **http://www.mailabuse.org** Follow the links for *RBL – Realtime Blackhole List, DUL – Dialup Users List and RSS – Relay Spam Stopper*

TCP wrappers

The "TCP wrappers" security tool is available for Linux and often comes as part of a standard distribution. This lets you log who uses what service on this machine. This is ideal if the service itself doesn't use **syslog** or keep a log file. You can also protect services by restricting who (i.e. which IP addresses) may access them. For example, you could have a rule specifying "only allow sub-net 10.5.5.5/25 to access the FTP server on this machine." You enter a list of "permit" rules in **/etc/hosts.allow** and "prohibit" rules in **/etc/hosts.deny**.

TCP wrappers is implemented as the **tcpd** daemon, which usually works in conjunction with the **inetd** super-server (Appendix 20).

> **Warning**: if TCP wrappers is installed and wrongly configured, it will block access to services that you think ought to be available to you.

To download the software and for more information:

❏ **ftp://ftp.porcupine.org/pub/security/**

❏ **ftp://ftp.porcupine.org/pub/security/tcp_wrapper.ps.Z** or **ftp://ftp.porcupine.org/pub/security/tcp_wrapper.txt.Z**

❏ **See the tcpd(8), hosts_access(5)** manpages in your Linux distribution, which may well include TCP wrappers.

Appendices

Appendix 20: controlling network services

26 Dial-up networking and PPP

Introduction

In this chapter we cover dial-up networking, connecting a single machine (as opposed to a whole LAN) to the Internet. Usually the purpose of the connection is to give Internet facilities to a person who's traveling or working from home, or to integrate a remote PC into the infrastructure on the HQ's LAN, and give the user access to resources on the LAN, such as printers, file servers, the corporate e-mail system, etc. We explain how to configure a PC to dial up to the Internet via an ISP, how to configure the necessary settings on your dial up PC, and the significant differences between dial-up and normal (Ethernet, LAN) connections.

26.1 Dial-up networking – overview

Up to now we've dealt with permanent, always-on connections. Most of these have been LAN-Ethernet connections, but others were permanent leased lines, ADSL links, etc. to the Internet. (We also mentioned ISDN links for connecting a site to the Internet, but as these are usually set up to dial on demand, they look much the same as an always-on connection to a user on the LAN.) In this chapter we look at connections via dial-up links, usually to the Internet, and primarily for single machines rather than networks of several machines. Typical scenarios where you need dial-up connections are:

1. occasional access to the Internet with a single PC from home or a hotel room or other remote location, using a dial-up ISP (Figure 26.1). For added security, this configuration is often used with virtual private networking (VPN; Chapter 27). You may also want to connect to your office network via the dial-up

2. dial-in from home or hotel room directly to your own office, not using an ISP at all (Figure 26.2). In this configuration, if you access the Internet, it is via your own LAN and then out again via your organization's Internet router.

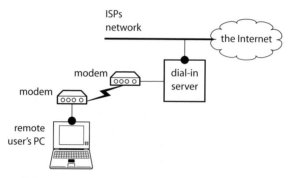

Figure 26.1 Using a dial-up ISP to access the public Internet

We won't cover the second scenario in much detail because:

a. the first one is much more common

b. scenario 1 combined with VPN can give you the same connectivity and more than scenario 2 with a lot less hassle. Table 26.1 compares the two approaches. In our experience, using an ISP is *much* easier, if only because managing dial-up connections and modems is always troublesome.

Later on, in Module 26.12, we outline some other scenarios that are useful although relatively rarely needed.

A dial-in connection from a single PC using an ISDN line and an ISDN modem (as opposed to an ISDN router) is almost identical to dial-up using a normal, voice (analog) phone line: the ISDN modem or terminal adapter behaves just like a modem as far as the PC is concerned (and even implements the usual modem "AT commands" to control the dial-up session). Accordingly, we'll say no more about ISDN, and in the rest of this chapter we will concentrate on scenario 1 above, and how it differs from the always-on connections we've used so far.

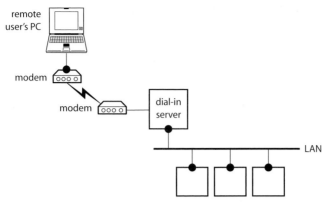

Figure 26.2 Using private dial-up to access the internal LAN

Dial-up connections are different

Dial-up connections differ in two important respects from Ethernet connections that we've been mostly concerned with, and from ADSL and other leased-line connections:

1. intermittent connectivity rather than always-on. When the dial-up connection is established, extra entries are added to your routing tables; the entries are removed when the connection is closed

2. a dial-up connection is *point to point*. It connects a single IP address at one end to another, single IP address at the other end. By contrast, Ethernet is a *broadcast medium* and can have many, many different machines connected to a single segment. On a point-to-point link, you can't broadcast – it doesn't make sense – and therefore any functionality that depends on broadcasts (ARP, Windows NetBIOS broadcast name queries, DHCP, etc.) can't work. PPP (the *Point-to-Point Protocol*) is nowadays almost always used for dial-up. This is the equivalent of Ethernet at the link layer of the protocol stack. You can run many different protocols, not just IP, over PPP (although that's not relevant to us here).

We only cover Windows dial-up, because it's used by the vast majority of dial-up systems. In the next module we summarize what's involved.

Table 26.1 Your own dial-up server v. using Internet dial-up via an ISP

Using your own dial-up server	Using an ISP for dial-up
you need extra, dedicated phone lines, dial-in servers, modems, etc.	no dial-up "infrastructure" needed. The ISP handles all the messy bits
complexity increases as you add users	scales up easily for many users
dial-up systems are hard to administer, and often error-prone	if you don't use VPN, there is almost no admin required (but without any security). Using VPN is now relatively easy
can be expensive, especially for overseas users or long-distance calls	usually cheaper, as users always dial the ISP's local point of presence
ensuring adequate security is non-trivial	VPN can give good security

26.2 Overview of Windows dial-up networking

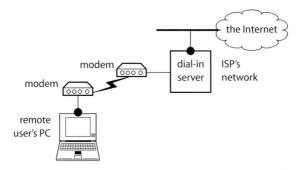

Figure 26.3 Basic dial-up connectivity — accessing the public Internet

There are two typical scenarios for Windows dial-up networking over the Interent:

1. *basic connectivity*: a home user connecting to the Internet, to surf the Web, send e-mail, etc. (Figure 26.3)
2. *professional use*: using your office network via a dial-up ISP link (Figure 26.4):
   - you dial up and connect to your ISP from a hotel room. (It could be from anywhere but we'll use "a hotel room" as shorthand for "single-user dial-up from a single PC at a remote site".)
   - you connect to your site ("HQ") and logon to your internal NT domain
   - you can browse the HQ network and use the resources on it – printers, file servers, Web and e-mail servers, etc – just as though you were working locally on the LAN.

In other words, the dial-up PC behaves as an integral part of your LAN. None of the steps in configuring dial-up is hard, but there are many, many different configuration screens, and it's easy to get lost if you're not used to them. We give a summary later on to help you navigate through them.

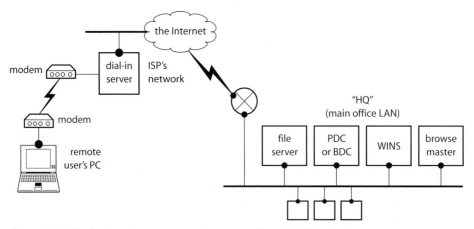

Figure 26.4 Professional use — accessing your private LAN via the Internet

Configuration overview – basic connectivity

To implement the configuration shown in Figure 26.3, you have to:

obtain a dial-up account with an ISP; connect your modem to your PC, and configure the PC for the modem. On NT this step can be combined with the next step; install dial-up software on your PC and configure it to use the modem from step B; configure your PC with the details of your ISP account (i.e. create "phonebook entries"); configure the PC's dial-up default gateway and other routing.

> **Tip:** don't use ISP-specific dial-up software – use the standard Windows tools instead. They're easier to maintain, you can see more easily what's happening, and you can troubleshoot your laptop almost like a normal, LAN-based machine. ISP-specific software often adds or modifies components (typically undocumented, of course), may break some of your existing configurations, and can be almost impossible to uninstall.

Configuration overview – connecting to HQ's office network

The initial steps are the same as above. In addition:

ensure your PC logs on to HQ's NT domain; because your PC is no longer on the HQ LAN, it can't send or receive broadcasts from the HQ machines, so it must use WINS (ideally) or LMHOSTS (at a pinch) to locate domain controllers, browse masters, etc. on the LAN, and for any other NetBIOS name resolution that's needed; configure your e-mail (and other applications) to use the internal servers at HQ. (We don't cover this any further – once your NetBIOS and/or DNS resolution are working correctly, accessing servers over dial-up is almost like on the LAN.)

> **Warning:** the network in Figure 26.4 provides no security (apart from NT domain username and password) to prevent unauthorized users entering your site. You will need VPN (see next chapter) and/or some other security mechanism to keep out intruders.

Obtain a dial-up account with an ISP

You have a Windows-NT laptop (or other PC) and want to surf the net from home. You've signed up with a dial-up ISP. They've given you the three essential pieces of information, and optionally a couple of other configuration settings to use:

your username; your password; a phone number to connect to.

Some ISPs may also give you:

a static IP address that your PC will use when dialing up (but 99% of dial-up accounts use a dynamically allocated address, not a static one); DNS server addresses for your PC to use for DNS name resolution. (They will probably give you a lot of other information too, but you don't need it).

In the next modules we install the modem, and configure the PC dial-out software.

26.3   Connect a modem to your Windows-NT PC

Your modem may already be built into the PC. Otherwise, if it's a PCMCIA card modem, plug it into a free slot, or if it's an external modem connect it to the PC using a modem serial cable.

To configure NT to use the modem:

1.   switch on the modem

2.   **Control Panel > Modems > General > Add** ... (Figure 26.5)

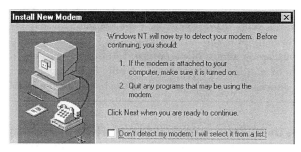

Figure 26.5 Install New Modem dialog

You can let NT find the modem automatically, or manually select the modem type from a list. Auto-detecting is very helpful because it tells you what communications port the modem is on. (Otherwise, we always have problems trying to find out what the port is.) However, auto-detecting often doesn't identify the modem type correctly, so we use a mixture of the two methods

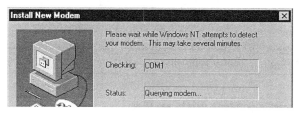

Figure 26.6 Auto-detecting the modem

3a. leave "**Don't detect** ..." unchecked and press **Next**; NT detects the modem (Figure 26.6).

3b. if the modem type displayed isn't correct (Figure 26.7a) click on **Change** and select the modem from the list (Figure 26.7b). This is the same dialog you get if you bypass auto-detection in the first place, except that NT will also ask you for the port details

4.   the installation completes (Figure 26.7c).

Configuring modem properties (optional)

From **Control Panel** > **Modems** you can configure two distinct sets of modem properties – one set specific to a particular modem, the other set applying to all modems:

1. select a modem from the list and press **Properties**. In the **General** tab you control whether the modem speaker is to be enabled. We always enable it (even though the noise is irritating) because it gives you early feedback on whether the call is succeeding – e.g. you can sometimes hear the far end's engaged tone. In the tab **Connection** > **Advanced** you can enable a logging to a file. Otherwise the default settings are usually fine

2. the **Dialing Properties** apply to all modems. The idea is you define one or more **Locations** that you call from (e.g. from the office, from home, from a small branch) and you specify the characteristics of the phone system at that place, e.g. whether you dial 9 to get an outside line, whether you need an area code, etc.) Personally we don't use these – we define a single location and insert a prefix 9 into the number as we dial if necessary, but the facility is useful for non-specialist users.

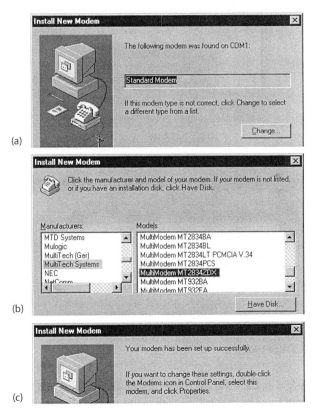

Figure 26.7 Modem set-up process

In the next module we move on and configure the dial-up software itself, and tell it to use the modem we've just added.

26.4   Install dial-up software on your PC

On NT the dial-up software is RAS – the Remote Access Service. (RAS also includes a server component – the PC acting as a dial-in server to receive calls from remote PCs dialing in to this site. We don't need that aspect of RAS, except for testing.)

1. install RAS from **Control Panel > Network > Services > Add > Remote Access Service**. When the installation starts, it asks you to insert the NT installation CD-ROM, and when the files are installed gives you the two dialogs shown in Figure 26.8. (If you hadn't installed any modems beforehand, it would prompt you to install one now, saying "There are no RAS capable devices to Add. Do you want RAS Setup to invoke the Modem Installer to enable you to add a modem?" If you choose not to install one, RAS will not be installed.)

2. select a modem from the list and press **OK** to give the dialog in Figure 26.9.

Figure 26.8
Installing RAS

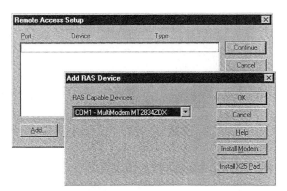

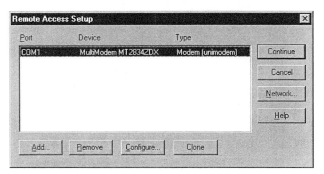

Figure 26.9 Selecting a modem

At this point the modem and the RAS software are installed. You now have to give RAS more information – that you will be dialing out on this modem, rather than receiving calls, details of the ISP you want to connect to, etc.

3. click **Configure** (Figure 26.10). Check **Dial out only** and click **OK**, which returns you to the Figure 26.9 dialog.

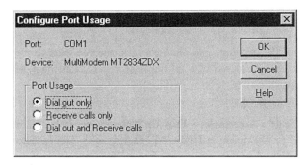

Figure 26.10 Configure Port Usage

4. click Network (in Figure 26.9 to give the dialog of Figure 26.11). Ensure only **TCP/IP** is checked. Press **OK**, which again returns you to the Figure 26.9 dialog.

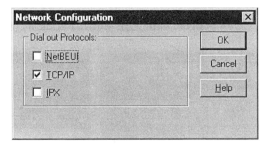

Figure 26.11 Remote access Network Configuration

5. click **Continue** in Figure 26.9. RAS tells you that it's installing and completes, returning you to **Control Panel > Network**. When you close **Control Panel**, NT will ask you to reboot.

If you ever need to change any of these settings, you can call up this dialog again using **Control Panel > Network > Services > RAS > Properties**.

Now RAS is installed, and it's ready to use the modem to dial out. The next step is to give it the details of your ISP accounts.

> **Tip:** in the next module we use the **Dial-Up Networking** tool (menu **Start > Accessories > Dial-Up Networking**). If you're going to be using it a lot, copy the short-cut to your **Start** menu. (The program that this uses, by the way, is called **Rasphone.Exe.**) Dial-Up Networking is often called "DUN" (pronounced like "done").

26.5 Configure PC with details of your ISP account

You can have several ISP accounts and choose which one you want to use when you dial up. Each account's details are entered in a "phonebook entry" of its own, which groups all the configuration settings together.

To create a phonebook entry:

1. select menu **Start > Accessories > Dial-Up Networking**. If you hadn't installed RAS already, you'd get the dialog in Figure 26.12a, but as we *have* installed RAS, but don't have any phonebook entries yet, we get Figure 26.12b.

2. press **OK** to give the dialog in Figure 26.13.

3. give the entry a name, check the **I know all about** … box and press **Finish**. This bypasses the phonebook wizard – create the entry manually instead so you see exactly what you're doing. This gives the dialog in Figure 26.14.

4. enter the ISP's phone number(s) and an optional comment. Select a modem to use for this connection. (The **Configure** button lets you disable the modem's speaker.)

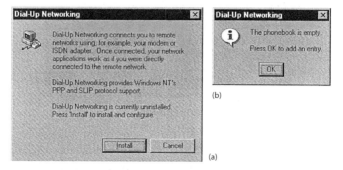

Figure 26.12 Starting **Dial-Up Networking**

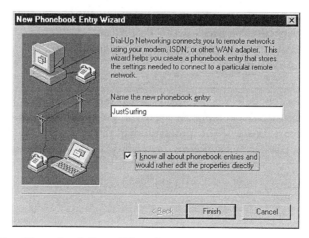

Figure 26.13 New Phonebook Entry Wizard

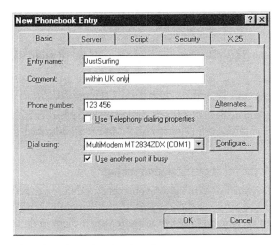

Figure 26.14 Bypassing the phonebook wizard

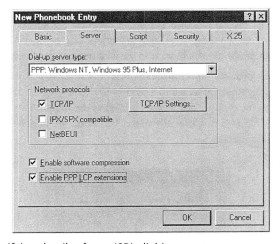

Figure 26.15 Specifying details of your ISP's dial-in server

5. select the **Server** tab to enter details of how this PC is to connect to this ISP (Figure 26.15). Ensure the server type is PPP and that only the TCP/IP protocol is checked. Also check the **Enable software compression** and **Enable PPP LCP extensions** to use the up-to-date software options which almost every server supports now. (For more information click the "What's this" tool – the "?" button at the top right of the window – over these options.)

6. click on the **TCP/IP Settings** button to enter IP addressing details, which we cover in the next module.

26.6   Configure PC with ISP TCP/IP addressing details

You just clicked on the **TCP/IP Settings** button to enter IP addressing details. There are two options:

6a. your ISP assigns your IP address dynamically (Figure 26.16).

6b. your ISP gives you a fixed IP address, and your dial-up software will use this address when it connects to the ISP (Figure 26.17). In the **IP address** box enter the address the ISP has given you.

Now continue with the other configuration settings:

7. almost certainly your ISP hasn't given you explicit DNS server addresses – normally the PC automatically configures these as part of its PPP connection setup. However, if you have been given specific DNS server addresses, enter them in the appropriate boxes.

    The WINS server addresses are only used in our second scenario, when we use this PC to connect to our HQ network

8. you usually leave **Use IP header compression** enabled. This uses "Van Jacobson IP header compression" (see Notes) to reduce the size of the packets sent over the (slow) PPP connection, without affecting its TCP/IP operation. This works with almost all modern servers, but if in doubt, try disabling it to see whether that fixes a problem you're having

9. the **Use default gateway on remote network** only matters if you have a LAN connection using a network card in addition to the dial-up connection. Checking the box means that the dial-up connection is used as the default gateway for this PC is, not the one configured in **Control Panel > Network**. We'll look at this setting in detail in Module 26.10.

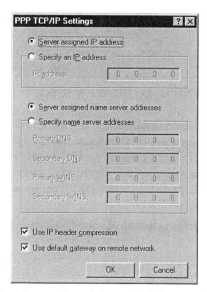

Figure 26.16 Your PC's IP address assigned dynamically by your ISP

You have now completed your phonebook entry (Figure 26.18) and are ready at last to use it to connect to your ISP. (Any time you want, you can go back and modify the phonebook entry using **More > Edit entry and modem properties.**)

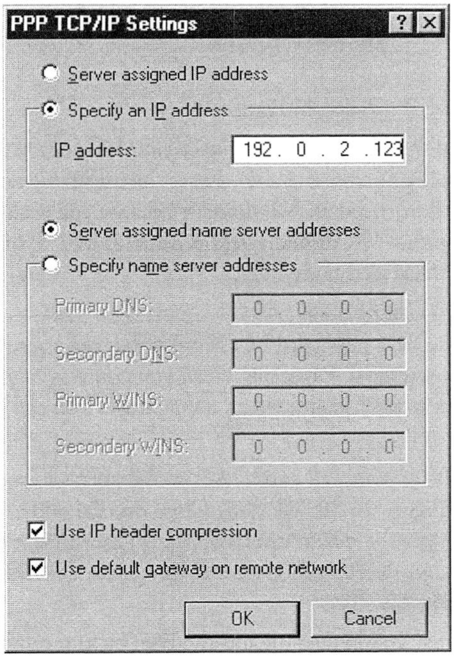

PPP TCP/IP Settings   ? X

  ○ Server assigned IP address

  ◉ Specify an IP address

    IP address: 192 . 0 . 2 . 123

  ◉ Server assigned name server addresses

  ○ Specify name server addresses

    Primary DNS: 0 . 0 . 0 . 0
    Secondary DNS: 0 . 0 . 0 . 0
    Primary WINS: 0 . 0 . 0 . 0
    Secondary WINS: 0 . 0 . 0 . 0

  ☑ Use IP header compression
  ☑ Use default gateway on remote network

     OK   Cancel

Figure 26.17 Your PC's IP address: fixed IP address specified

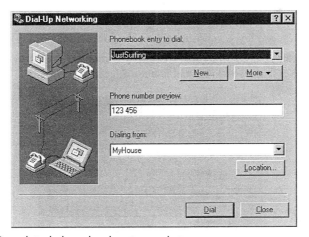

Dial-Up Networking   ? X

Phonebook entry to dial:

JustSurfing

  New...   More ▼

Phone number preview:

123 456

Dialing from:

MyHouse

  Location...

  Dial   Close

Figure 26.18 Completed phonebook entry ready to use

26.7 Dialing up

You're now ready to dial the ISP, using the phonebook entry (in the previous module) that you just created. (Later, you can get back to this dialog using menu **Start > Accessories > Dial-Up Networking**, or from **My Computer > Dial-Up Networking** in Windows Explorer or on the Windows Desktop.)

1. click on **Dial** to give the dialog in Figure 26.19

2. this is the logon information *for connecting to your* ISP (not to your local PC, and not to a domain controller at a remote site). Enter the username and password that your ISP gave you. You don't need an NT domain because you're not logging on to the ISP as an NT domain user. (The domain field is only needed if you are connecting to a private NT RAS server, see Figure 26.2.)

> **Tip:** we don't check the **Save password** box because that can cause the logon dialog to be hidden on subsequent attempts. Especially when you come to logging on to a domain as well as an ISP, it's easier to understand what's happening if you can see all the logon steps.

3. press **OK**. NT dials up your ISP and if all is well displays in succession each of the five status windows in Figure 26.20. We don't **Close on dial** and always **display this message** so that we get the maximum feedback on the current status of the connection. (We have to admit, we don't really trust dial-up systems!) Press **OK** to dismiss the **Connection Complete** window

4. you're now connected and logged on and the **Dial** button on the main **Dial-up Networking** window changes to **Hang Up** (Figure 26.21)

   Surf the net, send your e-mail, etc. Then …

5. to close down the connection, press **Hang Up**. NT asks you if you want to disconnect (Figure 26.22), and if you confirm, it drops the connection.

The next module tells you how you can continuously monitor the status of the connection, and the module after that gives some troubleshooting advice.

Figure 26.19 Enter the username and password for your ISP account

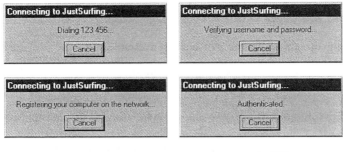

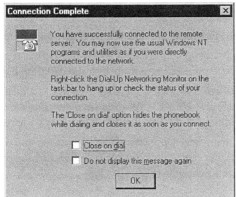

Figure 26.20 Successive status dialogs as your dial-up progresses

Figure 26.21 **Dial** button changes to **Hang Up** when connection is established

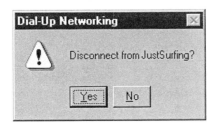

Figure 26.22 Closing down the dial-up connection

26.8 Monitoring the connection status

Before dialing up, or when the call has been established, you can use the **Dial-Up Networking Monitor** to give you more continuous information about the state of your call:

1. in your phonebook entry (Figure 26.18) select **More > Monitor status …** to give the dialog in Figure 26.23. You can leave this running for the duration of your call, watching the device **Condition** and making sure the **Bytes in** and **Bytes out** continually increase.

    The **Details** dialog (not illustrated) shows the IP address your ISP allocated to you, and the address of their dial-up server. The **Summary** tab (not illustrated) shows which dial-up links are being used

2. the **Preferences** tab (Figure 26.24a) lets you configure audio and visual status indicators:

    • we **Play a sound** for everything except data send/receive; it gives sufficiently useful feedback that we're prepared to put up with the irritating beeps and pips

    • the **Show status lights** configuration shown gives you a small **Dial-Up Networking** status window (Figure 26.24b): **TX** means transmitting data, **RX** receiving, **ERR** some error condition, and **CD** is carrier detect – the basic modem and line status.

    You can close the main **Dial-Up Networking Monitor** at any time without affecting anything else, and can open it again easily by double-clicking on the title-bar of the little **TX/RX/…** status window (Figure 26.25).

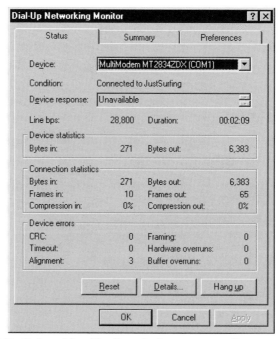

Figure 26.23 Dial-Up Networking Monitor displays current call status

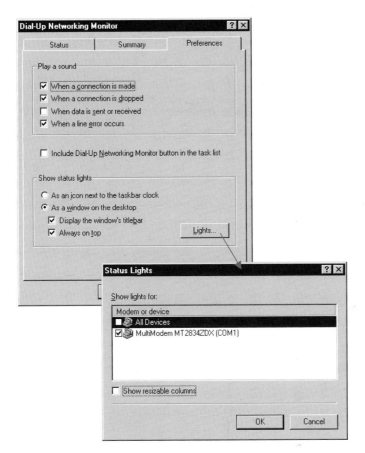

Figure 26.24 Dial-Up Networking Monitor Preferences tab

Figure 26.25 Show status lights, option **As a window on the desk top**

26.9 Troubleshooting

Software installation problems

Unfortunately, installing dial-up has many potential problems, which seem to be caused mostly by different pieces of software on this PC interfering with one another. The good news is that on a "clean" PC, which hasn't had lots of packages installed and uninstalled and reinstalled on it, installation usually behaves itself.

If you do have problems:

- as with any addition to NT, make sure you re-install your latest Service Pack after installing modems, dial-up networking, RAS, etc.

- note any error messages, log messages, or event log entries

- use the Knowledgebase on the Microsoft Web site. It has solutions to most problems (although finding them can be time-consuming)

- as a last resort, remove all your networking components ("protocols", i.e. TCP/IP networking, and network cards) and then reinstall. This sounds like a bigger job than it is. (We find the most time-consuming part is finding the correct network card drivers, but since we now archive them centrally, and keep a record of which driver is used on each machine, it's no longer a problem.)

Modem problems

If you installed the modem as we described (Module 26.3), it will be on the correct port and the correct type. If it's a very new model, you might want to download and install the latest drivers from the manufacturer's Web site.

You can test basic cabling and modem operation very simply using the **HyperTerminal** program that comes with NT. Let's assume our modem is on COM1:

1. menu **Start > Programs > Accessories > Hyperterminal > HyperTerminal**

2. HyperTerminal prompts you to set up a new connection, first asking for a name for the connection. Enter a name, e.g. "test COM1 modem"

3. HyperTerminal gives its **Connect to** dialog. The **Connect using** pulldown menu shows your modem, but also has an entry for **COM1**. Select **COM1**

4. HyperTerminal gives its **COM1 Properties** dialog, letting you set the serial port's speed, etc. Leave all the settings as they are, except perhaps the speed, which should match whatever you set in your DUN configurations. Press **OK** and you are now in HyperTerminal's terminal window, communicating directly with the modem: anything you type is sent to it, and anything the modem returns is printed in the window

5. we're going to operate the modem by hand, using the AT (attention?) modem commands, originally developed by Hayes but now a de-facto standard:

    a. type ATH1 ("off hook") followed by Enter. This is the equivalent of lifting the phone receiver. You should see the modem's **OH** indicator (if it has one) light up, and you'll hear the dial tone from your phone line. If you don't, check the cabling.

(It's easy to insert the modem jack into the phone socket but not make good electrical contact. Wiggle it about a bit and try again.) If it worked correctly, the modem replies with "OK," which is printed in HyperTerminal

b. assume you're in your office and that a nearby extension is 123. Enter ATDT123 ("dial, tone") followed by Enter. You should hear the modem dial the extension, which will ring (but won't answer unless there's a modem or fax on it). Eventually the modem gives up and replies "NO CARRIER." (You can abort the dialing by typing +++ (three plus signs))

c. enter ATH0 ("on hook") to hang up; the modem replies "OK"

6. exit HyperTerminal. Your modem, cabling, and basic software are OK.

There are two modem-related log files that may be of use to you. Both are created in the main NT directory (usually C:\WINNT):

ModemDet.txt: created by the auto-detection phase of modem installation
ModemLog*modemname***.txt:** created if you enabled modem logging (Module 26.3).

Problems connecting

If your modem is OK and is dialing out, but you can't connect to your ISP, the problem is usually one of these:

a. you're not dialing the correct phone number for the ISP (e.g. typo in number, or omitted prefix to get an outside line, or using outside-line prefix on a home line)

b. you have the wrong username and/or password

c. your modem is incompatible with your ISP's modem

d. your dial-up settings don't match the ISP's.

For cases (a) and (b), DUN will give you a message saying you can't connect. The message contains an error number (e.g. 678 in Figure 26.26) and a brief explanation; you can get a more detailed explanation by pressing **More Info**. See the Notes for a summary of what we usually find are the causes of the various error messages.

Figure 26.26 Getting **More Info** about an error number

Diagnosing cases (c) and (d) is more difficult. Check the connection details your ISP gave you and ask the ISP whether they support your modem. (If you're new to dial-up, check the ISP's Web page for recommended modems before you buy. Always go for popular brands and well-established models – these will have had their problems sorted out, unlike dirt-cheap or new bleeding-edge models.)

26.10 Configure the PC's dial-up default gateway and other routing

If your "laptop" (or other PC) doesn't have a LAN network connection, TCP/IP packets can only travel one way – over the dial-up link. If you do have a LAN connection as well (Figure 26.27), how does TCP/IP decide which route to use for packets that aren't for the local network?

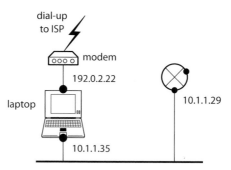

Figure 26.27 Dial-up link plus LAN connection

Figure 26.28 shows the routing tables for three different cases. We removed loopback, multicast and broadcast addresses, and the PC's own address from the routing tables to make things clearer. (The tables now look like Linux ones.) The three cases are, respectively:

a. before dial-up, or after disconnecting from dial-up.
   The default gateway is the LAN (Ethernet) one – 10.1.1.29

b. dialed up, with **Use default gateway on remote network** = NO
   Our dial-up connection address is 192.0.2.22, but the dial-up hasn't installed a default gateway of its own. In this configuration, any packets not destined for either the 10.1.1.* or 192.0.2.* networks are sent out via the Ethernet NIC's gateway, i.e. 10.1.1.29. This really means that you're using the dial-up only to connect to the 192.0.2.* network, which doesn't make sense if you're connecting to an ISP for surfing. It *does* make sense if your connection is to a dial-in server of your own or a partner organization's rather than an ISP's

c. dialed up, with **Use default gateway on remote network** = YES
   Dial-up has installed a default gateway this time – 192.0.2.22. In the routing tables this takes priority over the Ethernet NIC's gateway (10.1.1.29) because 10.1.1.29's **metric** has been changed by the dial-up software from 1 to 2. The metric is effectively a routing hop count: the lower the value, the better it is, so in this configuration, all packets not destined for 10.1.1.* or 192.0.2.* are sent via the dial-up. This is ideal for the case where you're working on a LAN that isn't connected to the Internet, and you're using your dial-up to reach the Internet from your PC. (This is, however, very insecure – your dial-up link is an unprotected link straight into your LAN.)

Most of the time these routing considerations aren't relevant, because most people either have their laptop connected to the office network, or are at home connected via dial-up, and never have both links active at the same time. However, when we look at a home machine connecting to the HQ network via a dial-up (Module 26.12) it will be important. (See Notes for what **PPP adapter NdisWan4** in Figure 26.28 means.)

```
D:\>ipconfig/all
Ethernet adapter El3c5741:
        Description . . . . . . . . : 3Com LAN PCCard
        IP Address. . . . . . . . . : 10.1.1.35
        Subnet Mask . . . . . . . . : 255.255.255.128
        Default Gateway . . . . . . : 10.1.1.29
PPP adapter NdisWan4:
        Description . . . . . . . . : NdisWan Adapter
        IP Address. . . . . . . . . : 0.0.0.0
        Subnet Mask . . . . . . . . : 0.0.0.0
        Default Gateway . . . . . . :

D:\>route print
    Net Addr        Netmask      Gwy Address    Interface   Metric
    0.0.0.0         0.0.0.0      10.1.1.29      10.1.1.35       1
    10.1.1.0   255.255.255.128   10.1.1.35      10.1.1.35       1
```
(a)

```
D:\>ipconfig/all
Ethernet adapter El3c5741:
        Description . . . . . . . . : 3Com LAN PCCard
        IP Address. . . . . . . . . : 10.1.1.35
        Subnet Mask . . . . . . . . : 255.255.255.128
        Default Gateway . . . . . . : 10.1.1.29
PPP adapter NdisWan4:
        Description . . . . . . . . : NdisWan Adapter
        IP Address. . . . . . . . . : 192.0.2.22
        Subnet Mask . . . . . . . . : 255.255.255.0
        Default Gateway . . . . . . :

D:\>route print
    Net Addr        Netmask      Gwy Address    Interface   Metric
    0.0.0.0         0.0.0.0      10.1.1.29      10.1.1.35       1
    192.0.2.0   255.255.255.0   192.0.2.22     192.0.2.22      1
    10.1.1.0   255.255.255.128   10.1.1.35      10.1.1.35       1
```
(b)

```
D:\>ipconfig/all
Ethernet adapter El3c5741:
        Description . . . . . . . . : 3Com LAN PCCard
        IP Address. . . . . . . . . : 10.1.1.35
        Subnet Mask . . . . . . . . : 255.255.255.128
        Default Gateway . . . . . . : 10.1.1.29
PPP adapter NdisWan4:
        Description . . . . . . . . : NdisWan Adapter
        IP Address. . . . . . . . . : 192.0.2.22
        Subnet Mask . . . . . . . . : 255.255.255.0
        Default Gateway . . . . . . : 192.0.2.22

D:\>route print
    Net Addr        Netmask      Gwy Address    Interface   Metric
    0.0.0.0         0.0.0.0      10.1.1.29      10.1.1.35       2
    0.0.0.0         0.0.0.0      192.0.2.22     192.0.2.22      1
    192.0.2.0   255.255.255.0   192.0.2.22     192.0.2.22      1
    10.1.1.0   255.255.255.128   10.1.1.35      10.1.1.35       2
```
(c)

Figure 26.28 Routing tables for three different dial-up configurations

26.11 Dial-up PC connecting to HQ's network

This is our second, more sophisticated scenario: you're in a hotel room and want to connect to your office network and use the resources on it. The sections below address three important issues. (We haven't included security. For a configuration like this you'd almost certainly use VPN – which we cover in the next chapter.)

Ensure your PC logs on to HQ's NT-domain

You are now logging on in three places, as shown in Figure 26.29:

1. logon to your PC before dialing up. This can either be a local logon to the PC's itself, or a logon to HQ's NT-domain used cached logon information. (Don't set **Logon using Dial-up Networking** to YES in the Logon dialog. It only confuses things.)

2. logon to ISP. You authenticate this PC to the dial-in server at the ISP site

3. logon to the NT-domain at HQ. (On NT this happens transparently as a pass-through logon when you access resources on the network. If you were running Windows-9x, you would have to configure **Log on to network** in the **Advanced Options** of the DUN Connection icon for this ISP, and in **Control Panel > Network > Client for Microsoft Networks > Log on to Windows** set **NT domain** = YES, and set **Windows NT domain** to your NT domain.)

There's nothing new here, but so many logons can be confusing.

You must also ensure that your laptop has a computer account on HQ's domain controller, and that the user's account (in **User Manager for Domains**) has **Grant dialin permission to user** = YES.

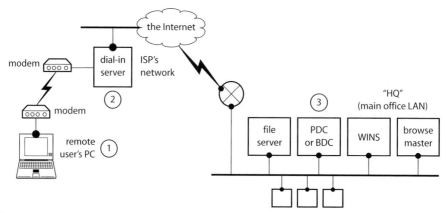

Figure 26.29 Three different logons in dialing up to your office LAN

NetBIOS name resolution and browsing

Your laptop is communicating with HQ over a network of routers, so NetBIOS mechanisms that rely on broadcasts for name resolution and browsing don't work. Instead, configure this machine to use the WINS servers at HQ (Module 19.4). (You could use an **Lmhosts** file instead – Module 19.9 – including in it entries for your PDC and any other machines you have to access, but WINS is much better.)

We've found the following to be helpful when building a network like this:

1. before you set up a laptop or other PC to operate over dial-up, use it on the LAN first. Make sure it operates correctly – that it can logon to the NT domain, browse, access printers and file servers, etc.

2. now move the laptop behind a router on the LAN. Make sure everything still works, now that NetBIOS name resolution and browsing can't use broadcasts – also the case when the PC is connecting over the Internet

   It's much easier to debug and troubleshoot name resolution, domain logon, etc. on a local PC in the privacy of your own workbench than trying to support a naive user by telephone at a distant site. You can bypass this step if you have to, but it saves a lot of problems for our users (which makes us look good!) and requires very little effort

3. remember, before you get browsing and name resolution working you can map network drives using **net use** (or the Windows Explorer equivalent):

   ```
   net use x: \\192.0.2.44\datadirs
   ```

Routing considerations

If you only use your laptop from a home or a hotel room, and it never lives on the HQ LAN, the only TCP/IP route for packets from your laptop to the LAN is via the dial-up link, which makes things very simple.

But now let's assume your laptop has a PCMCIA network card (NIC), which you use to connect to the HQ LAN when you're in the office. This configuration complicates things when you dial-up from home:

- the NIC's drivers are still active, and its routing information is in the PC's routing tables Figure 26.28 even though it isn't wired up to a network

- if you try to connect to, say 192.0.2.77, TCP/IP sees that you have a directly connected interface on this network, and routes the packets via the PCMCIA NIC, where of course they get lost.

There are three solutions to this:

1. (best) using **Control Panel > System > Hardware profiles** create a *hardware profile* in which the PCMCIA NIC is disabled. The easiest way to do this is:

   a. copy the **Original Configuration** profile as **Dial-up-only**, say,

   b. select **Dial-up-only > Properties > Network** and check **Network-disabled hardware profile.**

   c. rename the **Original Configuration** to something like **In-office-on-Ethernet**

   In future when the laptop boots, it will present a profile menu after the operating system menu, letting you choose between the **In-office-on-Ethernet** or **Dial-up-only** profiles. If you are dialing up, the NIC will be inactive and won't have any associated routing entries

2. (inelegant) pop out the PCMCIA NIC before booting your laptop at home. The drivers, etc. won't load because the PC thinks the device isn't working

3. (for sad heroes) when dialed-up from home manually delete the routing entries for the PCMCIA NIC.

26.12 Miscellaneous

Other dial-up scenarios

The two scenarios we covered in detail are dial-up to surf the net from home, and connecting to the HQ LAN from a hotel room using a dial-up ISP. Dial-up can be useful in other circumstances, to set up temporary or semi-permanent non-Ethernet connections within an organization, e.g.

- connecting home users to HQ, or connecting a remote office to HQ. By not using the Internet you can avoid some security issues. If the remote office or home users are close to the HQ, your phone company may have special arrangements (e.g. Centrex) that let one location phone another free, as though they were just extensions within the same office. That can make this a very cheap option
- building a small test network to check out dial-up systems and configurations (see below)
- connecting a machine with a broken network card, using a phone and modem, or a direct serial cable, to enable important data (or network drivers) to be transferred to or from the damaged system
- using a direct serial cable to connect a workgroup or department in a separate but adjacent building, e.g. across the road. (Stevens in his book describes how he used a SLIP link for this, although nowadays you'd probably use a wireless link instead of a serial cable.)
- using Microsoft's Internet Connection Sharing (ICS) to link several machines at one location (home or small office) to elsewhere, as described in Module 23.11.

In all these examples you're using a phone link with two modems or a direct serial cable to connect a dial-up system at one end to a dial-in server at the other end (Figure 26.30). We haven't covered setting up a dial-in server, but we give some references in the Notes. On NT, RAS includes a dial-in server, so if you've set up a dial-up RAS client, you will find the server side easy.

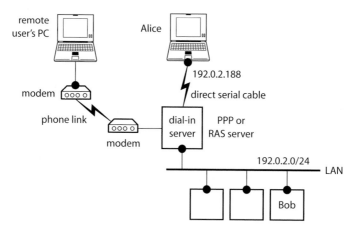

Figure 26.30 Connecting to your office LAN using a private dial-in server

Proxy ARP for dial-up servers

In the network in Figure 26.30, when the remote laptops are connected, how do the other machines on the LAN route packets to them?

We could set up explicit routing table entries on all our LAN PCs, or on our default gateway if we had one (which the network shown doesn't), but that would be tedious, and if the dial-up PCs are allocated dynamic addresses, we wouldn't be able to anyway. A much more elegant solution is if the dial-in server proxy ARPs for any of the laptops that it currently has connected. Let's say our LAN is 192.0.2.*, and the range 192.0.2.180–199 is dedicated to the dial-up server for allocating to its dial-in clients, as shown in Figure 26.30. Alice wants to communicate with Bob. She knows his address; her packets (with source address 192.0.2.188) are routed through the dial-in server to Bob. Now Bob has to reply. He has no special routing entry for 192.0.2.188 – it's just part of the directly connected LAN – so Bob ARPs for Alice. Here comes the clever bit: the dial-in server knows that 192.0.2.188 is connected to it, so the *dial-in server* sends an ARP reply to Bob, with the dial-in server's MAC address. Bob then sends his packets for Alice to the dial-in server, not aware at all that the server is acting as a router. When the server receives packets for Alice, it forwards them to her over the dial-up link.

Setting up a test "dial-up" system

You can set up a test PPP network not to run up large phone bills in two ways:

1. use two modems connected to two internal phone extensions in the same office – ideally both on your desk. Instead of dialing a chargeable call, dial one extension from the other

2. use a direct serial cable, instead of modems and phones, to connect the dial-up client and dial-in server. This doesn't tie up any phone extensions, and you can use it at home where you don't have several private extensions. You need to note a couple of points:

   - you have to use a special *null-modem* cable, or a straight-through cable with a null-modem attachment, to connect the two systems. A null modem contains no electronics at all – it just crosses some of the wires in the cables and connects some of the pins to make it appear like a real modem to the computer its connected to (Appendix 7)

   - the connection doesn't behave exactly as a modem/modem link. If your users use modems a lot, it's best to use modems for testing too, so use the two-internal-extensions approach in (1) above.

To set up this configuration you will need a PPP server of some kind. The easiest to set up is a RAS server on NT, because you've covered most of the work installing the dial-out part of RAS already. See the Notes for further information.

Summary

- dial-up connections are point to point. Nowadays they use PPP to connect to the ISP or other dial-in server

- for basic dial-up – just for surfing the Web, e-mail, etc. – the standard Windows dial-up software lets you configure all the network settings you need

- NT's Dial-Up Networking Monitor gives information about your connection status

- making a dial up connection creates extra routing table entries automatically. These are removed automatically when you drop the connection

- if you are dialing up an ISP in order to connect in to your office Windows Networking LAN, extra configuration is needed. You must:

  - set your laptop's NT domain

  - use WINS (or at least the **Lmhosts** file) to allow NetBIOS name resolution and browsing to operate across the routed network

  It is best to test out your laptop first on the LAN and behind a router before trying it out over a dial-up, to ensure that your Windows Networking configuration is correct

- if you use your laptop sometimes connected directly to the internal LAN and sometimes dialing-up via an ISP, you should create a Hardware Profile so that the laptop doesn't try to send packets via the PC's network card when you are dialing up (and disconnected from the LAN).

What's next?

In the next chapter we explore VPN, which lets you secure your dial-up connections and connections between branch offices by encrypting the traffic.

Notes and further reading

For laptops that move frequently between the office and home, wireless networking is convenient (if your office supports it), especially if you have a LAN at home.

PPP's predecessor was *SLIP (Serial Line IP)*. This supports only IP whereas PPP can support multiple protocols simultaneously over the same link. Unlike PPP, the IP addresses at both ends of the SLIP link have to be hard-coded. SLIP has now been superseded almost entirely by PPP. See Stevens Modules 2.4–2.6 for more information on SLIP (and a little bit of detail on PPP).

❏ **RFC-1661 July 1994** *The Point-to-Point Protocol (PPP)*

Van Jacobson header compression:

❏ **RFC-1144 February 1990** *Compressing TCP/IP Headers for Low-Speed Serial Links*

(Van Jacobson was one of the original developers of **tcpdump**, by the way.)

❑ RFC-2507 February 1999 *IP Header Compression*

❑ RFC-2508 February 1999 *Compressing IP/UDP/RTP Headers for Low-Speed Serial Links*

❑ RFC-2509 February 1999 *IP Header Compression over PPP*

Modem troubleshooting

See troubleshooting links on:

❑ http://www.modemsite.com/

❑ http://www.56k.com

❑ http://www.modemhelp.org

and a detailed paper, specific to US Robotics modems, at:

❑ http://infodeli.3com.com/docs/rapd/x2shoot4.pdf

Troubleshooting Dial-Up Networking

Microsoft's list of Dial-Up Networking error messages is:

❑ **Remote Access Service (RAS) Error Code List (Q163111)**

Or, you can lookup an error on our Web site:

❑ **www.uit.co.uk/resources > RAS errors**

which gives a fuller explanation of the error and what might have caused it.

Module 26.11 gave advice on how to prevent your "on-the-LAN" network settings interfering when dialing up from home to your office network. The reverse problem often occurs when you are using VPN. When you go back to the office and connect your machine to the LAN you cannot connect to any of the local machines, even though you have chosen the correct hardware profile (if you've set them up.) What's happening is that the VPN software on your laptop is encrypting your packets and trying to send them to a VPN box to forward to their destination. See Module 27.9 for how to overcome this.

Windows Network Monitor *does* work on dial-up connections. However, you can't (at the time of writing, at least) use Windump (or **ethereal**) on serial connections on Windows-NT and Windows-2000:

❑ http://netgroup-serv.polito.it/windump/misc/faq.htm)

Using Network Monitor on a dial-up-only machine is very straightforward – it defaults to monitoring the dial-up interface so you only have to start the program as normal. However, if you have both dial-up and Ethernet interfaces and want to monitor the dial-up traffic, you must explicitly tell Netmon to use the dial-up. Select menu **Capture > Networks ...** to give the **Select Capture Network** (below). Select the dial-up interface, which is the one that has a **Current Address** of all zeroes.

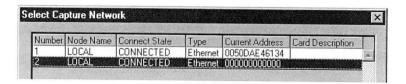

You must also change the capture filter (menu **Capture > Filter ...** , below) because Netmon has set the default filter to suit the LAN interface, not the dial-up one. Using the **Delete Line** button, remove the line "INCLUDE *hostname* (ETHERNET)<- ->*ANY," or change it to read "INCLUDE *ANY<- ->*ANY".

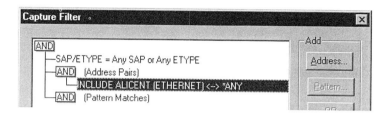

What NdisWan adapters **are**

Recall from Module 18.5 that the Windows-NT bindings tie an NT Service to a protocol family to an adapter. Because there is no physical adapter (network card) for dial-up networking, NT creates "pseudo adapters" to bind to, and these are called NdisWan. You can have multiple NdisWans; in fact, when you install RAS and enable both dial-in and dial-out, you'll see that two NdisWans have been created, one for dial-in and one for dial-out. (The "Ndis" part of NdisWan stands for "Network Driver Interface Specification" – the low-level interface that NT uses between the physical network card and the lower levels of the operating system.)

Building a test network

See Web Appendix 31 for details on setting up a RAS server on NT.

Dial-up on Linux

❑ http://www.linuxdoc.org/HOWTO/Serial-HOWTO.html

❑ http://www.linuxdoc.org/HOWTO/Modem-HOWTO.html

❑ http://www.stokely.com/unix.serial.port.resources/ppp.slip.html *"UNIX Serial Port Resources"*

❑ http://www.vlug.org/linux/links/Networking/PPP_-_SLIP/ Many links on PPP and SLIP

and on setting up a direct serial-cable connection:

❑ http://www.linuxdoc.org/HOWTO/Serial-Laplink-HOWTO/index.html

Dial-up on Windows-9x

Dial-up on Windows-9x is quite different, not least because Windows-9x's initial logon (to the local PC or the network) is different. The 9x DUN application keeps a directory with a separate "connectoid" (set of settings) for each different connection configuration, whereas on NT you have multiple phonebook entries within the single **rasphone.exe** application. While the configurations on the two systems are similar in many ways, the dialogs and how you get to them are sufficiently different to be confusing. (They confuse us at least.)

Appendices

Appendix 7: null modem wiring diagrams
Web Appendix 31: configuring a Windows dial-in server

27 VPN – virtual private networking

Introduction

VPN encrypts traffic so that eavesdroppers and hackers can't read it or modify it. It lets you secure links over the Internet, between sites, or from dial-up users accessing your internal network. We cover IPsec, which is the industry standard for VPN, and explain how it works and its various options, and outline how to set up and troubleshoot VPN links.

27.1 What VPN is and why you want it

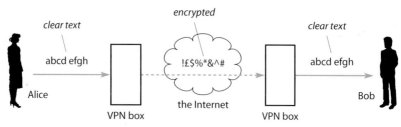

Figure 27.1 Virtual private networking

VPN (*virtual private networking* or a *virtual private network*) sends data securely over a public network such as the Internet by encrypting the traffic (Figure 27.1). Conceptually, VPN is simple: Alice sends her normal traffic to Bob via a VPN system of some kind. This encrypts the traffic and forwards it to another VPN system at Bob's site, where the traffic is decrypted again and finally received by Bob. Even though the traffic is sent over the Internet, because it's encrypted it is in effect private – it's "virtually private," and hence the name. The VPN is often viewed as a private, encrypted "tunnel" through the public Internet.

An important feature of VPNs is that to Alice and Bob, and to their applications, the VPN system is completely transparent: no applications have to be modified and no special libraries are needed. Often, users (and applications) don't even know a VPN is being used.

VPN scenarios

There are so many intruders on the Internet today that you need to protect your traffic from being modified, or stolen, or eavesdropped on, and you want to be sure that data that seem to come from someone you do business with really do come from them. There are many different circumstances where this is needed:

- traveling staff, connecting to HQ from a hotel room or a customer site
- system administrators troubleshooting or performing system maintenance from home
- other home workers
- remote offices and partner organizations communicating with HQ. By using the public Internet to exchange data, they can avoid the cost of private leased lines between the sites. This is especially important where offices are far apart or in different countries
- some manufacturers recommend you use VPN to connect all wireless users; otherwise hackers on the road outside your office might connect to your wireless network and in effect be connected to your LAN (see Notes).

VPN implementations and configurations

There are two typical VPN implementations, and they work slightly differently:

1. **"Gateway" implementation**

   (Sometimes called "bump in the wire" (BITW) because the VPN system runs in a separate piece of equipment at the edge of the protected network.) End-user machines (Alice and Bob in Figure 27.1) use the VPN device as their default gateway. It inspects the destination address of the packets and if they are destined for an address that VPN has been configured for, it encrypts the packets and forwards them.

   This system is often implemented in a firewall, where it can be combined with NAT so that even NAT traffic can be successfully VPNed. (C.f. Module 23.3.)

2. **"Client" or "host" implementation**

   (Sometimes called "bump in the stack" (BITS) because the VPN system runs in the client machine itself, effectively inserted in the protocol stack between the IP layer and the network drivers, e.g. Carol in Figure 27.2). The applications in the PC pass data to be sent down through the protocol stack, where the data are inspected by the VPN system, which encrypts and forwards as above.

The difference between the two systems is that the gateway implementation is completely transparent to desktop PCs, which require no modification or extra software at all – they just use the VPN system as their default gateway. This facilitates whole-site to whole-site VPN configurations (Figure 27.2, left-hand side). The client implementation on the other hand does require extra software to be installed on the client PC, and is usually used on a dial-up or other remote single machine (Figure 27.2, right-hand side) connecting in to HQ, which uses a gateway as before. (You can also have a client-to-client configuration without any gateway, but this is relatively rare.)

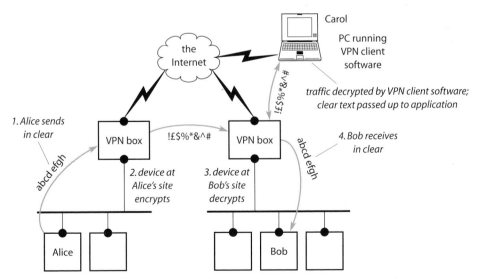

Figure 27.2 Alice and Bob using gateway VPN implementation, Carol using host implementation

27.2 IPsec – the IP security protocol

IPsec (IP Security Protocol) provides the whole framework needed for VPNs to operate. It includes mechanisms to specify:

- which destinations' packets are to be VPNed (e.g. Alice's VPN device is configured to say "traffic to Bob's network, 192.0.2.64/224, is to be encrypted") …
- whether the data are to be *transformed* in any way, e.g.
  - "authenticated" so you know that the person who claimed to send the data really did send them, and that they haven't been modified in the meantime, or
  - encrypted, or authenticated and encrypted, and which encryption algorithms (single-DES, ARC4, triple-DES, …) is to be used. IPsec doesn't define the encryption algorithms; it merely provides the framework in which these algorithms can be used, so it is straightforward for IPsec to make use of new or improved encryption algorithms as they become available. See the Notes for more information about encryption and cryptographic methods. (Encryption without authentication is a valid option but not a good idea because it's vulnerable to *man-in-the-middle attacks*, where an attacker inserts between the two parties and can intercept and alter their communications.)
- where the encrypted/authenticated packets are to be sent, e.g. in the example network in the previous module, Alice's site's VPN device sends packets destined for Bob not directly to Bob, but to Bob's site's *security gateway*, i.e. its VPN device, which then decrypts and forwards Bob's packets to him. By contrast, when Alice is communicating with Carol, Carol's packets are sent directly to Carol and not to a separate security gateway; Carol acts as her own security gateway.

IPsec uses the *AH (Authentication Header)* protocol for authentication-only, and the *ESP (Encapsulating Security Payload)* protocol for encryption-and-authentication. In a typical Internet configuration, you would normally encrypt and authenticate. However, you might use authentication-only on data that are already encrypted, or if there are legal restrictions on the use of encryption in a country you're operating in.

IPsec works at the IP layer of the protocol stack (Figure 27.3). The transformed ESP or AH packets are IP packets, with a source and destination address, so they can be routed over the network as usual; only the two end-points (the VPN devices) know about the encryption. This means you can secure *all* traffic between any two IP addresses – on the LAN, or WAN, or over the Internet. By contrast, if you use link layer encryption could operate only on a single LAN segment, and encryption used higher up in the stack, e.g. PGP for e-mail, protects only one application.

Key management

Encryption and authentication operate using cryptographic keys, and these keys must somehow be distributed securely to both ends of the VPN tunnel. IPsec defines two methods for managing keys:

1. *manual keying*: the system administrators somehow communicate the keys between themselves (e.g. by phone) and manually enter them into the VPN configs at either end

2. automated key management. Currently IPsec uses *IKE (Internet Key Exchange)* ("IKE" rhymes with "bike.")

Key exchange is a setup stage at the beginning of the communication between the two parties. It's short – IKE takes a few seconds or less, depending on the speed of the network and the power of the two systems. Once the keys have been exchanged, the main work of the VPN can proceed, sending and receiving packets encrypted/authenticated using the keys just set up. This part of the VPN link can last as long as required, e.g. a VPN between HQ and a branch site often stays up for months at a time.

IKE is really a more convenient replacement for the system managers at each end phoning each other to exchange keys; after that, the basic encryption of user data works the same, irrespective of how the keys were exchanged.

Figure 27.3 illustrates how IKE is separate from the ESP and AH part of IPsec. Whereas ESP and AH operate within the kernel of the operating system on the VPN box, IKE runs at the application level, and runs over UDP. In Linux implementations, IKE is handled by user-level daemons that handle key management, and they pass the keys down into the kernel for use by ESP and AH. In this respect the IKE daemons are very similar to routing daemons (Module 5.11).

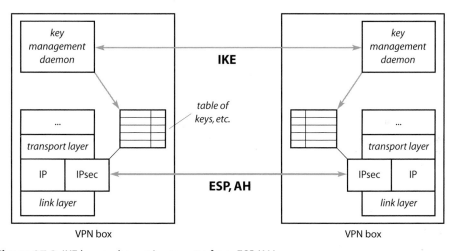

Figure 27.3 IKE key exchange is separate from ESP/AH

While VPNs are conceptually simple, there is an awful lot of detail, especially with IKE. There are excellent free software implementations of VPN for Linux, but for most sites it's more practical – at least initially – to buy a firewall or a VPN appliance instead (and they now cost as little as a few hundred dollars). In the rest of this chapter we assume that you are using such a box implementing firewalling and VPN software – either a purpose-built appliance or a dedicated PC with suitable software loaded.

In the next module we start with manual keying, because it's much simpler and introduces many concepts also used in IKE.

27.3 IPsec concepts – manual keying

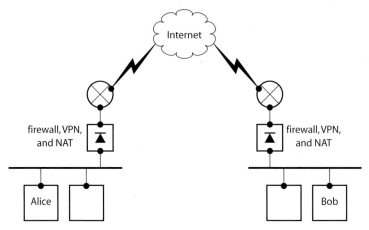

Figure 27.4 Site-to-site VPN system

Before we configure a VPN, we need to look in more detail at how IPsec works. Figure 27.4 shows a typical site-to-site VPN system. Figure 27.5 shows the same network simplified, ignoring routers other than the VPN boxes themselves, which act as their sites' default gateways. We're assuming the boxes also implement NAT, because that's the most common configuration in the real world.

To create the VPN between the two sites, each of the two VPN boxes needs at least the following information:

- the other's IP address. It is acting as the security gateway for its site
- the range of IP addresses "behind" the VPN box. If the destination address of a packet is within this range, then it should be sent through this VPN tunnel.

For example, we configure VPN box-A to say that any traffic for IP range 192.168.0.0/16 is to be sent to security gateway 1.2.3.87; we configure VPN box-B to say that traffic for 10.4.4.0/24 should go to 192.0.2.42. Notice that the packet destination addresses are the *private* (internal) ones, but that the security gateway addresses are real *public* ones on the Internet.

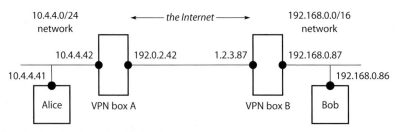

Figure 27.5 Simplified site-to-site VPN system

Now that the boxes know to send packets for each other's networks to one another, we have to configure them so they encrypt/authenticate the packets too:

- we'll use single-DES (Module 27.2) to encrypt and MD5 (Web Appendix 34) to authenticate the packets. (Single-DES isn't as secure as triple-DES; we've only used it because it keeps the keys shorter for our examples.)
- single-DES uses a 16-hex-digit key. On box A we'll use the key 1111111111111111 to encrypt what it sends to Bob's site. (We're using silly keys to make it easy to see what's happening. In real life, you'd use more random sequences of digits.)
- MD5 uses a 32-hex-digit key for authentication. On box A we'll use key 2222222222222222 2222222222222222 when sending to Bob's site.

When box B receives these packets it will only know that they came from 192.0.2.42 (box A), and has to know how to decrypt them. There could be several different tunnels from box A to box B, so we must somehow identify these ones in particular:

- we define an *SPI (Security Parameter Index)* for the Alice-to-Bob traffic. This is a fancy term but just means a numeric name that identifies the set of encryption parameters and keys we specified above. We'll use SPI = 5001. The VPN packets that box-A sends to box-B look like:

src IP	dst IP	proto	SPI	
192.0.2.42	1.2.3.87	(VPN)	5001	*encrypted payload*

- we now configure box-B saying that incoming packets from box A with SPI=5001 are to be decrypted and authenticated with the same keys and algorithms keys that we just configured on box A. We manually enter the SPI and the keys, etc. in box-B's configuration table.

That covers packets sent from Alice's site to Bob's. We now have to configure the system to handle packets sent from Bob's site to Alice's:

- on box-B we'll use the DES key 3333333333333333 to encrypt traffic sent to Alice's site, and key 4444444444444444 4444444444444444 to authenticate it (although some IPsec implementations will insist that you use the same keys for send and receive). We'll give this set of keys SPI=7438
- now we configure box-A to say that incoming packets from box-B with SPI=7438 are to use the keys we just configured on box-B.

That just about completes the configuration. A set of configuration settings like this on a VPN system is called an *SA (Security Association)*. An SA defines one end of a VPN between two systems. You can usually give an SA a name for convenience. For example, we might call the SA on box A **A-to-B** and on box B **Here-to-A**. The names are only for ease of reference by humans and don't really matter.

The SA doesn't include the destination IP range – in order that you can apply the same SA to several different sets of addresses. (In fact, IPsec says you should be able to select which packets the SA applies to not only on destination IP address, but also on port number and many other criteria.) That part of the configuration forms what is called an *SPD (Security Policy Database)*. In our simple example all traffic for a destination is VPNed, so our SPD will be very simple.

In the next module we summarize the configurations we created, and show how they are applied to traffic between Alice and Bob.

27.4 IPsec manual keying example

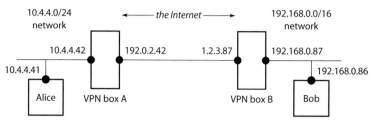

Figure 27.6

Table 27.1 summarizes the security association (SA) configurations on the two VPN boxes. The table shows clearly that the keys box B uses to encrypt incoming packets are the keys that box A encrypted them with when it sent them, and vice versa.

Table 27.1 Security association configurations

	VPN box A	VPN box B
SA name	A-to-B	here-to-A
IPsec keying mode	manual	manual
security gateway address	1.2.3.87	192.0.2.42
SPI on outgoing packets	5001	7438
encryption method	DES	DES
encrypt key	1111111111111111	3333333333333333
authentication method	MD5	MD5
authenticate key	2222222222222222 2222222222222222	4444444444444444 4444444444444444
SPI on incoming packets	7438	5001
decrypt method	DES	DES
decrypt key	3333333333333333	1111111111111111
authentication method	MD5	MD5
authenticate key	4444444444444444 4444444444444444	2222222222222222 2222222222222222

Table 27.2 shows our two very simple security policy databases (SPDs).

Table 27.2 Simple SPDs

	VPN box A	VPN box B
apply this SA	A-to-B	here-to-A
to packets destined for	192.168.0.0/16	10.4.4.0/24

Now let's see how this works in practice, when Alice pings Bob, i.e. she says "**ping 192.168.0.86:**"

- Alice's TCP/IP routes the ICMP **ping** packet travels to her default gateway, 10.4.4.42, because the destination is outside her directly connected local network
- the VPN system in 10.4..4.42 (box A) inspects the destination address, 192.168.0.86, sees that it's in the SPD, and therefore applies the specified SA for this address range:
  - the SA for this range is **A-to-B**
  - box A encrypts and authenticates the **ping** packet with the keys from **A-to-B**, i.e. encrypts with 1111111111111111 and authenticates with key 2222222222222222 2222222222222222
  - it creates a new packet with this encrypted/authenticated data as the payload, inserts the specified SPI (5001), and sets the destination address to the security gateway specified in **A-to-B**, i.e. 1.2.3.87. The source address of this packet is box A, not Alice, because Alice is hidden behind Box A. The final packet is shown simplistically below.

src IP	dst IP	proto	SPI	
192.0.2.42	1.2.3.87	(VPN)	5001	encrypted payload

- box A's TCP/IP routes this packet to its destination address, 1.2.3.87
- now box B receives this packet. It sees that it's a VPN packet and extracts the SPI, 5001
- it looks up SPI=5001 in its table of SAs, and finds it in the SA named **here-to-A**
- **here-to-A** says this packet should be decrypted with key 1111111111111111 and authenticated with key 2222222222222222 2222222222222222, so box B performs these actions
- the packet is now restored to what it was as it left Alice, i.e. as shown below:

src IP	dst IP	proto	payload
10.4.4.41	192.168.0.86	ICMP	**ping** request

- box B's TCP/IP routes this normal, unencrypted packet to its destination address, which is 192.168.0.86, i.e. to Bob
- Bob receives the **ping** request, and sends a **ping** reply to the sender's address, 10.4.4.41. Bob's TCP/IP routes this to his default gateway, because the destination isn't on his local, directly connected network. His default gateway is 192.168.0.87, i.e. box B – his site's VPN system
- box B then repeats all the steps that box A went through, so the **ping** reply is encrypted, sent to box A, decrypted, and finally forward to Alice, who is now happy because Bob replied to her **ping**.

Note that even though both Alice's and Bob's sites are using NAT, packets that travel through the VPN tunnel do *not* have their source/destination addresses translated: the whole packet is encrypted, and then decrypted, but otherwise unchanged. This fact is sometimes used to allow otherwise awkward protocols (i.e. that don't work through NAT) to pass into a NATed site without any problems.

27.5 VPN implementation details

Now we'll look in more detail at how a VPN configuration works in a wider context. Figure 27.7 shows the network we've just configured, but box A has a second VPN configured, to connect to network 172.16.16.0, and users at Alice's site also connect to other, non-VPN sites on the Internet – for normal Web surfing, sending e-mail, etc.

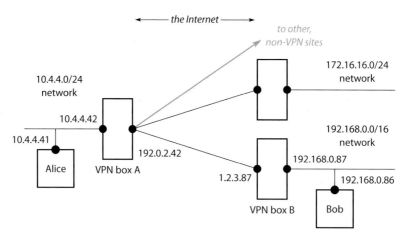

Figure 27.7 Alice's site configured to access several VPN and non-VPN sites

This is where the SPD (security policy database) comes in. When box A receives an outgoing packet from Alice, it inspects the packet contents and compares them against its SPD. If the packet's final destination (and port, etc.) match an entry in the SPD, box A transforms (i.e. encrypts) it and forwards it to the appropriate security gateway. In this respect box A is acting as a router, and the SPD is like a set of routing tables, but with extra VPN functionality added in.

If a packet from Alice doesn't match an entry in the SPD, box A doesn't modify the packet at all and just sends it on its way. In fact, SPDs have a third option (in addition to VPNing, and forwarding without VPNing) and that's to block the packet. This lets the VPN administrator restrict what users at Alice's site can do. For example, if Alice's site is a small branch, you might want its users only to be able to contact HQ (site 192.160.0.0, say) and maybe one other branch (172.16.16.0, say) but *not* be able to access the Internet directly. All external traffic should either be blocked, or more likely routed to HQ where virus-scanning, content-filtering, etc. is performed. Configurations like this let you use the Internet as a cost-effective way to connect remote sites to HQ, but to implement extra security mechanisms centrally – to minimize costs of licenses, server hardware, and system management. This configuration is especially useful for traveling laptops: you want to make sure that users don't collect viruses and all sorts of other rubbish by accessing the Internet in an uncontrolled way. Otherwise, when they subsequently connect to HQ over VPN they might infect your whole network.

Protocols for VPN

When Alice sends a **ping** request to Bob, the packet looks like:

src IP	dst IP	proto	payload
10.4.4.41	192.168.0.86	ICMP	***ping*** request

When the packet has been transformed by VPN, it looks like:

src IP	dst IP	proto	SPI	
192.0.2.42	1.2.3.87	(VPN)	5001	*encrypted payload*

The original packet, including its source and destination addresses and the field identifying it as ICMP protocol, has been encrypted; these encrypted data form the payload of the VPN packet. The new packet is no longer an ICMP packet. (It can't be, because ICMP doesn't use SPIs and doesn't contain encrypted payloads of variable lengths like VPN does.) In fact, VPN uses its own protocol types:

Protocol		
Name	**IP proto No.**	**Description**
ESP (Encapsulating Security Payload)	50	encrypted and authenticated
AH (Authentication Header)	51	authenticated only

Note that these are *protocol* numbers, *not* port numbers. You only have port numbers with TCP and UDP, and ESP and AH are separate protocols in their own right. (Recall from Module 15.3 that the IP protocol numbers for UDP and TCP are 6 and 17.) This distinction is important for understanding VPN, and for troubleshooting, as we'll see in Module 27.9.

You can easily see the protocol numbers (or names) in sniffer traces: below **tcpdump** shows the original **ping** packet travelling from Alice to box A:

```
10.4.4.41 > 192.168.0.86: icmp: echo request
```

Figure 27.8 is an **ethereal** trace of the encrypted packet sent from box-A to box-B: you can see the SPI (5001) in the packet, but the original ICMP payload and IP address information are encrypted, so **ethereal** can't see what they are.

Figure 27.8 ethereal trace of ESP encrypted packet

In the next module we move on to look at automated keying using IKE.

27.6 IKE – Internet Key Exchange (automated keying)

Manual keying is simple to configure. However, it has disadvantages:

- manually exchanging 32-digit hex keys (over the phone or however you choose to do it) is error-prone and/or insecure
- if you have 100 sites, to manually configure VPNs between each of them you have to set up 100 × 99 VPN tunnels (as each site has a tunnel to each of the other 99 sites). This isn't a very maintainable configuration
- if a hacker breaks your encryption, then they can read your future traffic and any traffic of yours that they've archived from the past, because the key never changes. And, the more you use a given key, the more data you're giving the hacker to analyze, to help them break the key.

IKE (*Internet Key Exchange*) addresses these issues. It provides a secure way to negotiate and exchange keys between sites, automatically, without any human intervention. Once the keys have been exchanged, they are used in security associations (SAs) just like with manual keying. In other words, setting up a VPN has two distinct parts:

a. exchange keys between the two ends of the VPN. This is done either manually or with IKE

b. use the keys to encrypt or authenticate the traffic over the VPN.

As well as making it easier to exchange keys, IKE has other advantages:

- because keys can now be exchanged automatically, you can automatically change keys ("rekey") frequently, e.g. every few hours
- by regularly changing keys, as long as the keys are generated in a particular way, you can have *perfect forward secrecy (PFS)* – breaking a key allows you to read only data encrypted with that key but doesn't makes it any easier to break earlier or later keys. So if a hacker breaks a key, they can read a few hours' worth of your traffic, but to read the next lot of traffic they have to break the new key from scratch. Breaking keys can take months or years, if it's possible at all, so you can see the big improvement in security that IKE can give you over manual keying.

How IKE works

IKE is divided into two *phases*. For simplicity we'll assume that we're still working with the same two VPN devices, box-A and box-B (Figure 27.7 in the previous Module).

Phase 1: box-A and box-B set up a secure (encrypted) communications channel between them and authenticate themselves to one another. This channel is only used by IKE, not by IPsec itself (i.e. ESP or AH) for transmitting the end-user packets.

Phase 2: over the channel established in Phase 1, IKE on the two boxes negotiates security associations and keys to be used by ESP or AH for sending the end-user packets.

Now both ends have agreed on SAs and keys, and they can encrypt/authenticate the users' packets, using ESP or AH, just as we saw with manual keying.

Multiple Phase 2 *exchanges* (i.e. conversations) can happen after a single Phase 1 exchange – because the channel set up in Phase 1 can be used repeatedly, reducing the overall amount of network traffic required.

In Phase 1, the two systems use the *Diffie-Hellman* key agreement method. This lets two parties converse over a public communications channel to negotiate a secret number, even if they don't have any shared secret information to begin with. Even though Eve the eavesdropper can listen in to the whole conversation, she won't be able to find out what the secret number is. (This sounds like magic but see the Notes for more information.) In IKE the two parties use the secret number they agreed as the encryption key for the rest of the IKE session.

IKE gets complicated because there are many different options in each phase. In Phase 1 the two parties can:

- authenticate using a *shared secret* (almost like a password) that both of them know, or using digital certificates and signatures, or using public-key encryption. With shared secrets, you still have to distribute them manually, which still isn't scalable to large numbers of sites. With public-key encryption or certificates, if Alice and Dave want to set up a VPN, they look up each other's public encryption keys (e.g. from a Secure DNS server or in a public LDAP directory of public keys) and can then use IKE as before. There is no longer any need to distribute keys or secrets manually

- use either *main mode* or *aggressive mode* to set up the secure channel. (Main mode hides the identities of the two parties from snoopers but aggressive mode uses fewer packets.)

- use different encryption and authentication algorithms, and different *groups* (used in the secret-number generation process) for the Diffie-Hellman exchange. There are currently five of these groups (named "1" … "5"). They are also called *Oakley groups* as they were used in the earlier Oakley protocol. (In fact IKE is a mixture of Oakley and ISAKMP – the Internet Security Association and Key Management Protocol.)

In Phase 2, the parties can:

- use different encryption and authentication algorithms

- have perfect forward secrecy (PFS) or not

- issue many *proposals* to one another, indicating which type of encryption algorithms each one is prepared to accept. The other party has to choose one of the proposals, and this specifies the details of the SA IKE will create. IPsec's ESP or AH then use this SA as before

- specify the *key lifetime*, i.e. the duration after which new keys ought to be renegotiated.

IKE runs over UDP, and uses port 500.

In the next module, we show the VPN settings for a Windows client.

27.7 IKE example

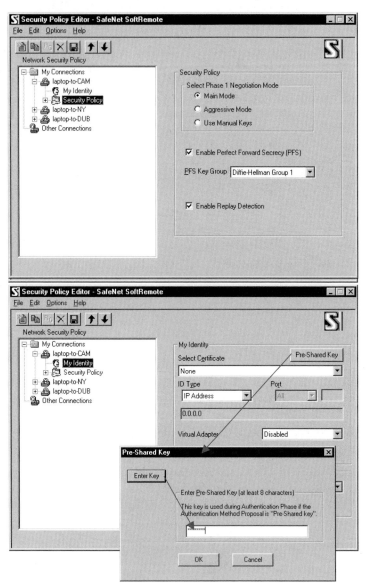

Figure 27.9 Dial-up VPN, IKE setup 1

Figures 27.9 and 27.10 show IKE settings for a Windows VPN client ('búmp in the stack' implementation) configured to VPN to several sites on the Internet. We chose a single-PC VPN system so that you can see the VPN settings clearly. (If we showed a firewall's VPN settings, they would be dependent on the firewall's NAT and other configuration details, which are not relevant to us here.)

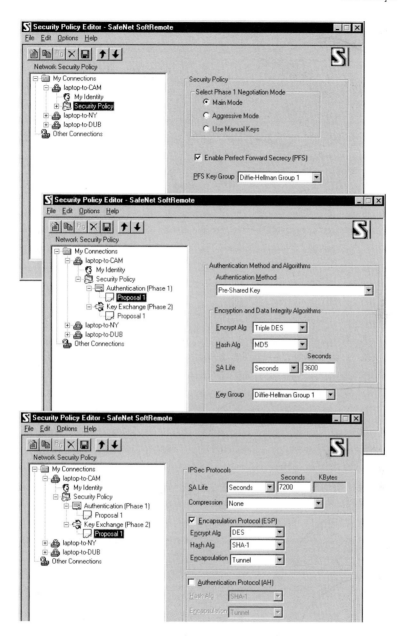

Figure 27.10 Dial-up VPN, IKE setup 2

27.8 Protecting dial-up VPN

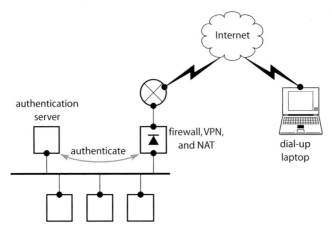

Figure 27.11 Using authentication to secure dial-up VPN

If Alice uses VPN software on her laptop, which you've pre-configured to connect to the HQ LAN (Figure 27.11), all traffic between the laptop and HQ's firewall is secured. Sounds good so far. But if a hacker physically steals Alice's laptop (or someone borrows it for a while), they have full access to the HQ LAN, just like they were connected to your Ethernet inside the firewall. You need to provide some extra security mechanism. There are several different options:

- username/password protection. Asking for a password before a VPN connection is established is an extra barrier to the thief
  - this password protection could be built into your VPN client software (although we haven't seen any that have this feature)
  - many firewalls, routers, and VPN boxes support RADIUS authentication, described below, where the VPN system receives the connection attempt from the laptop, but refers the authentication ("logon") request to a separate server for validation (Figure 27.11)
- *two-factor authentication* systems, where the user has a special smart-card or other type of device. This displays a special number that changes regularly (e.g. every minute). To logon, the user has to enter the currently displayed number, plus a password. The VPN system (or associated authentication server) also generates the same sequence of numbers internally, and when the user tries to log on, the server validates the password but also compares the number entered with the internally generated one. Only if everything matches is the logon allowed. The advantage of this system is that a thief has to obtain not just the smart-card device, but also the password, and that can't be physically stolen.

RADIUS – Remote Authentication Dial-In-User Service

RADIUS offers user authentication ("logging on") as a network service. As with LDAP, user-names and passwords and details of which resources each user is allowed access are stored on a central server. However, with RADIUS the authentication checking is performed on the RADIUS server, not on the client machine. (Some RADIUS servers store their user information in an LDAP directory, combining the benefits of both systems.) The client, e.g. the firewall or VPN box, encrypts the logon information that the user entered, and sends it to the server. The server checks whether the user has authenticated correctly, and replies to the client with either an Authentication Acknowledgement or an Authentication Reject message, which is also encrypted. RADIUS uses UDP; its official well-known port is 1812, although many implementations default to port 1645 for historical reasons.

RADIUS was originally developed to allow multiple remote-access servers to be controlled by a single authentication database. It's now also used widely by firewalls, routers, and VPN systems (Figure 27.12).

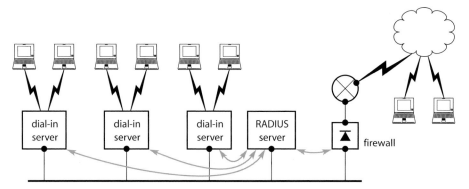

Figure 27.12 RADIUS server provides authentication to many devices

Other VPN security issues

An external laptop connected to your LAN via VPN appears (more or less) to be connected directly to your LAN, with the same ability to access resources as your local PCs. This can be dangerous: if the laptop isn't protected as above, you can't be sure who is using it. Even if the user is genuine, they may have connected to Internet sites or received e-mail that infected them with viruses, etc. and when they VPN in to HQ, they can easily infect your "protected" LAN. To guard against such problems you can restrict what the laptop user may do by (a) configuring their VPN software so they can only connect directly to HQ, ensuring all their Web surfing and e-mail is processed by the central HQ servers for virus scanning, content filtering, etc., and (b) giving them access only to the resources they need, but no more, both by restricting the traffic they are allowed to send through the VPN tunnel, and by using host-based security mechanisms on the LAN – on the servers in particular. In addition, you might use "personal firewall" software for laptops – as a product on its own or combined with VPN – that is becoming widely available now.

If you connect machines to the local LAN using wireless networking, you should consider treating them as "external" machines requiring VPN protection, etc. Otherwise, passing hackers might be able to connect to your LAN from just outside your building, using their wireless networking cards.

27.9 VPN troubleshooting

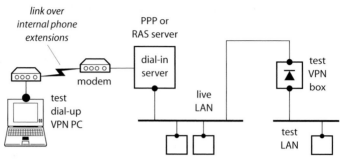

Figure 27.13 Test network for exploring dial-up VPN

As we mentioned in Module 27.6, VPN implementations differ widely for many reasons. What we give here are general tips that we've found useful with many different systems. (The overall approach is not unlike troubleshooting a firewall; see Module 24.9.)

It would be wonderful if every vendor included superb debugging tools in their products, but alas, they don't. Often you'll find that your VPN link doesn't work, but there are no error messages and no log messages. VPNs are often hard to get working for this reason and we have certainly had our share of problems.

- read all your log and error messages, at both ends of the VPN tunnel

- the best way we've found to set up VPN is to get it working on a test network integrated with your live LAN. We describe this in detail in the next module. To explore dial-up VPN and work through Windows Networking issues, etc. we also use a small, test network (Figure 27.13), similar to that described in Module 26.12. In this configuration our live LAN simulates the ISP's network and the Internet; the test dial-up connects over this to the test VPN box and test LAN, which are attached to our live LAN. This configuration lets us sniff packets and see what's happening everywhere

- use **tcpdump** of course! By tracing traffic just inside and just outside the VPN box (Figure 27.14) you can see traffic "in clear" reaching the VPN box and any transformed (ESP or AH, IP protocols 50 or 51) traffic heading to your Internet router. If you see transformed traffic leave your site, but none returning, you know that your own configuration is at least half correct. If you (or a colleague) can trace the traffic at the other end too, you can form a good view of what's happening and where the problem is likely to be

- manual keying is much easier to set up, because there are far fewer different options. It has no key-negotiation stage: if your keys and IP addresses are set up correctly, you'll see VPN traffic leave the VPN box as soon as you generate some test traffic from inside. We *always* start with manual keying; only when that's working do we try IKE. This is an example of the principle that it's best to start simple and get a basic configuration first. Then, and only then, should you start adding more complexity or sophistication: at each step verify that the system is still working, and if it isn't, your most recent change is usually what caused the problem

- for manual keying, we start with very simple keys that we can easily read and check over the phone. We use "0123456789abcdef" for a 16-digit key and the same thing repeated twice for a 32-digit key. (But make sure you change them to something less easily guessed as soon as the link is working!)

- ISPs often block the IPsec AH and ESP protocols by default. (It's more unusual to have IKE blocked, because it runs over UDP.) Before you even start installing your VPN, check that the ISPs at both ends allow protocols 50 and 51 (ESP, AH) and UDP port 500 (IKE) in and out of their networks

- many ISP services for home users (e.g. cheap or free phone calls to the ISP, and some ADSL or cable modem services) deliberately block ESP and AH, since they are only used by business customers. You may have to pay extra to have these blocks removed

- if you have your laptop set up to VPN to the office (e.g. to 10.*.*.*) and later bring it into the office and connect up to the LAN, traffic for 10.*.*.* will still be VPNed. (Typical symptoms are that ARPs succeed – **arp -a** shows other machines – but no other TCP/IP traffic is transmitted on the wire.) You need to either manually disable the VPN when on the LAN, or enable VPNing only on the dial-up interface (c.f. Module 26.10.)

- because IPsec is an evolving standard and IKE is very complex, not all implementations inter-operate with one another or support all options. This will become less of a problem in time, as implementations are tested and improved (and maybe IKE will be replaced with something better – see Notes). In the meantime, you may have to restrict yourself to option combinations that your VPN manufacturer recommends

- if you're using Microsoft Windows Networking over VPN, remember that your network now involves routers, so you'll have to use WINS (or an **LMHOSTS** file) if you want NetBIOS name resolution and network browsing to operate correctly (c.f. Module 26.11).

In the next module we explain how to integrate a test network with your live LAN, to simplify troubleshooting and to check out your configurations before you actually deploy them live.

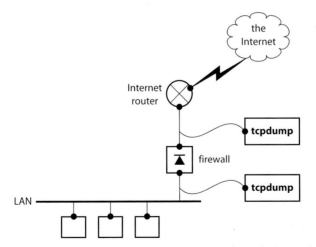

Figure 27.14 Use **tcpdump** outside your firewall to see encrypted VPN packets

27.10 Building a test network for VPN

A technique that saves us a huge amount of time is to "glue on" a test network to our live LAN. Let's say we're going to install a VPN firewall at our new office in New York ("NY"). Our aims are to:

- install the test firewall alongside the live network in Cambridge ("CAM"), so we can check out VPN, etc.
- configure the New York firewall/VPN fully, so it can be slotted into the real remote site without any extra configuration. We'll just courier it over to the new office, and have someone connect it up. We want to avoid sending an engineer over if possible.

However, there are many constraints:

- we're working on our live network, so CAM's Internet connectivity must not be disrupted for more than a minute or two at most
- the CAM router is managed by the ISP, and we can't alter it. Therefore we need another way to route traffic between the CAM and NY networks. We'll insert a temporary extra router to do this
- the NY firewall must be outside the live CAM firewall, so VPN and firewall rules for NY/CAM traffic are exercised
- the NY firewall must be inside CAM's ISP's router. It will have public IP addresses that really belong in NY; if any packets for these appeared on the network outside the CAM live router, they would be routed to NY.

We build the network shown in Figure 27.15 here in Cambridge. We've used a Linux box as the extra router; if you use an NT box instead, the steps are the same but the commands to apply the settings will of course be different.

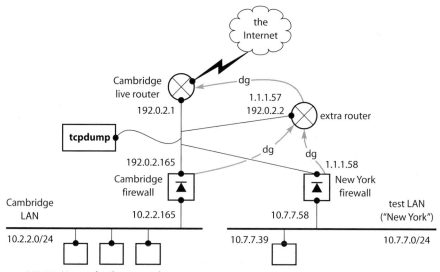

Figure 27.15 Home-built network

1. Configure the extra router:

- ensure IP forwarding is enabled:

```
echo 1 > /proc/sys/net/ipv4/ip_forward
```

- set its IP address to an unallocated one from the set of CAM public addresses. Its netmask should match the CAM firewall's external interface.

```
ifconfig eth0 192.0.2.2 netmask 255.255.255.0
```

- create a new interface **eth0:1** to match the real Internet router in NY:

```
ifconfig eth0:1 1.1.1.57 netmask 255.255.255.248 up
```

By choosing the IP address to match the real NY router, once we've configured the NY firewall, it can be installed in NY without any changes.

This is the crucial step: creating the interface automatically creates a routing table entry for the 1.1.1.57/29 network, so packets from CAM to NY will be sent to the NY firewall, which is exactly what we want

- set the default gateway to be the CAM live router (192.0.2.1) so that traffic for exterior sites can still get out

- connect the extra router into the network as shown. (It will have no effect until other components are changed.)

2. Configure the NY firewall:

- private (LAN) IP address = 10.7.7.58, netmask = 255.255.255.0 (or whatever IP address range you want to use in NY)

- public (WAN) IP address = 1.1.1.58 and netmask = 255.255.255.248 (or whatever your NY ISP has allocated)

- default gateway = extra router (1.1.1.57), so that packets can be routed between the NY and CAM networks.

3. Configure a small NY test LAN

Set up a machine on the test LAN, so we can **ping**, etc. and check out some of the rules, and ensure we have VPN connectivity, etc: IP address = 10.7.7.39, netmask = 255.255.255.0, default gateway = 10.7.7.58.

4. configure the live, CAM network use the extra router

Only when we do this is anything (apart from the test net) affected.

- we set the default gateway on the CAM firewall = extra router (192.0.2.2) instead of the CAM router. This allows traffic from the CAM network to route to the NY network.

Important: this works only because we're using NAT on the CAM LAN – all the LAN PCs use the *inside* interface of the CAM firewall as their default gateway. If you're not using NAT, their default gateway is almost certainly the live CAM firewall (192.0.2.1) and changing just the firewall's default gateway won't do what you need. You *could* change all the LAN PCs' default gateways manually, but you can do 99% of what you need by setting up a test PC on the CAM LAN, and set its default gateway explicitly = extra router (192.0.2.2). Then you can test connectivity and VPN between it and the NY LAN.

To remove the test network when you're finished, change the default gateway on the CAM firewall back to be the CAM live router (192.0.2.21) and physically disconnect the extra router, test network, etc.

Summary

- VPN secures traffic between:
  - two sites ("gateway implementation")
  - or (rarely) between two remote PCs ("host or client implementation")
  - or between a site and a remote PC
- most VPN systems use the IPsec IP security protocol
- IPsec uses the ESP protocol to encrypt/authenticate traffic, or the AH protocol if only authentication is needed. Encryption prevents an eavesdropper from reading the traffic, and prevents a hacker modifying the data without you knowing
- ESP and AH can each support many different algorithms for encryption and authentication
- both ends of the VPN "tunnel" must somehow obtain the encryption/authentication keys before they can exchange data over the tunnel
- IPsec supports two types of key management:
  1. manual keying. The administrators at both ends enter the keys manually (having agreed what keys to use beforehand, e.g. by phone or e-mail). Manual keying is easier to set up, but not so secure – if an encryption key is broken, all past and future traffic can be read
  2. automatic keying using IKE. Before sending any data across the tunnel, the ends automatically negotiate the keys to use. Over the lifetime of the VPN tunnel they may periodically "re-key," i.e. re-negotiate new keys to use. This can provide "perfect forward secrecy:" even if a hacker breaks one set of keys, they still can't read data encrypted with earlier or later keys. IKE is more complicated to configure than manual keying
- the VPN system on a dial-up laptop can contain all the keys, etc. necessary to connect into the HQ office LAN. To protect against theft of a laptop, you can use an extra layer of authentication and require the laptop user to logon when they connect in. You can use a RADIUS server or other authentication server on the LAN to implement this.

What's next?

Nothing, apart from the Epilog – you've reached the end!

Notes and further reading

❑ Kaufman, Perlman and Speciner's *Network Security: Private Communication in a Public World* (2002, Prentice Hall PTR)

Recently there have been several surveys of how organizations' wireless LANs have been accessible to anyone nearby on the street outside. (Finding accessible networks is known in the hacker world as *war-driving*, by analogy with the "war-dialing" of phone-phreaks in the 1960s and 1970s. To avoid such problems, some vendors suggest that you protect all wireless networking users – even those inside your building – with VPN. See:

❏ http://www.wardriving.com/doc/Wardriving-HOWTO.txt

❏ http://www.sundaytelegraph.co.uk/money/main.jhtml?xml=%2Fmoney%2F2002%2
F03%2F10%2Fccpring10.xml *Revealed: how a Pringles can cracked the City's most secret
networks*

❏ http://www.rsasecurity.com/newsletter/wireless/2002_winter/topstory.html Securing
Wireless LANs Follow the link "**a study of WLANs**" to get to the paper *Out of Thin Air,
A Wireless Security Survey of London*

❏ http://www.extremetech.com/print_article/0,3428,a=13880,00.asp *Exploiting and
Protecting 802.11b Wireless Networks*

IPsec generally

The Linux FreeS/WAN project has some of the most readable documents available on IPsec
and IKE. There's a great **glossary** and the **detailed table of contents** is a good place to start
when you're looking for IPsec-related material.

❏ http://www.freeswan.org/doc.html > *latest documentation tree*

The IPsec site has lots of pointers to standards and background material on encryption,
authentication, etc. (although much of it is formal, standards-oriented documentation, which
isn't the best way to get acquainted with something new):

❏ http://www.ietf.org/html.charters/ipsec-charter.html

For an overview of IPsec, see:

❏ **RFC-1825 August 1995** *Security Architecture for the Internet Protocol*

(RFC-1825 has been obsoleted by RFC-24.1, but the earlier version is more readable.) There
are many other RFCs dealing with VPN, but gosh, they are heavy going:

❏ **RFC-2401 November 1998** *Security Architecture for the Internet Protocol*

❏ **RFC-2402 November 1998** *IP Authentication Header*

❏ **RFC-2403 November 1998** *The Use of HMAC-MD5-96 within ESP and AH*

❏ **RFC-2404 November 1998** *The Use of HMAC-SHA-1-96 within ESP and AH*

❏ **RFC-2405 November 1998** *The ESP DES-CBC Cipher Algorithm With Explicit IV*

❏ **RFC-2406 November 1998** *IP Encapsulating Security Payload (ESP)*

❏ **RFC-2407 November 1998** *The Internet IP Security Domain of Interpretation for ISAKMP*

❏ **RFC-2408 November 1998** *Internet Security Association and Key Management Protocol
(ISAKMP)*

❏ **RFC-2409 November 1998** *The Internet Key Exchange (IKE)*

If you feel like an idiot when you try to read these RFCs and can't understand them, don't worry – you're in good company. For an interesting critique of IPsec by some well-known security experts, see:

❏ **http://www.counterpane.com/ipsec.pdf** *A Cryptographic Evaluation of IPsec*

which criticizes both the protocol design ("This is a typical committee effect ... it has a devastating effect on a security standard") and the documentation ("parts of the IPsec documentation are very hard to read ... essential explanations are missing ...").

The Virtual Private Network Consortium (VPNC) is the international trade association for manufacturers in the VPN market. Their site has interesting stuff on interoperability testing and interoperability conformance. They run interoperability "bakeoffs" too, and they have a list of current VPN-related Internet drafts, which give you an indication of where VPN is likely to go in the future. (The drafts are of course available on the IETF site (**www.ietf.org**) too, but it's harder to single out the VPN ones.)

❏ **http://www.vpnc.org**

❏ **http://www.vpnc.org/ids.html** *Internet Drafts*

IKE

IKE is hard. It's really about eight different protocols rolled up together because of all the various options. This makes it difficult for the developers to test their implementations, and makes good interoperability testing with other manufacturer's implementations a nightmare. This is why you sometimes have to choose a particular set of options to make one VPN system work with another. The security community are well aware of the problems, and are working to improve it.

❏ **http://www.ietf.org/internet-drafts/draft-ietf-ipsec-son-of-ike-protocol-reqts-00.txt** *Protocol Requirements for Son-of-IKE*

❏ **http://www.ietf.org/internet-drafts/draft-ietf-ipsec-jfk-00.txt** *Just Fast Keying (JFK)*

A discussion of what's wrong with IKE, but also one of the best overviews of how it works is:

❏ **Radia Perlman, Charlie Kaufman,** *Internet Computing,* **Nov/Dec-2000, pp50-56,** *Key Exchange in IPSec: Analysis of IKE*

❏ **http://www.counterpane.com/ipsec.pdf** *A Cryptographic Evaluation of IPsec*

Other VPN systems

As well as IPsec, there are two other widely used VPN systems:

1. *L2TP (Layer 2 Tunneling Protocol)*

    ❏ **RFC-2661 August 1999** *Layer Two Tunneling Protocol "L2TP"*

    ❏ **RFC-3193 November 2001** *Securing L2TP using IPsec*

2. *PPTP (Point-to-Point Tunneling Protocol)*

❑ **RFC-2637 July 1999** *Point-to-Point Tunneling Protocol (PPTP)* This RFC is informational only and does not specify an Internet standard.

❑ **http://www.counterpane.com/pptp.html** *Analysis of Microsoft PPTP Version 2*

IPsec will probably predominate, especially for multi-vendor VPNs. PPTP is a proprietary protocol that has also been implemented by many companies, especially Microsoft, but it's an older system and is falling out of favor and several security experts question how secure it is. Microsoft is also putting considerable effort behind L2TP, so L2TP with IPsec may become the default VPN system for Microsoft-only systems.

Cryptography

For an introduction to symmetric and public-key (asymmetric) cryptography, see:

❑ **http://www.garykessler.net/library/crypto.html** Gary Kessler's *An Overview of Cryptography*

❑ Web Appendix 34

RADIUS

The original RFC is very readable and explains why RADIUS was developed, how it operates, and why it uses UDP and not TCP:

❑ **RFC-2058 January 1997** *Remote Authentication Dial In User Service (RADIUS)*

❑ **http://www.freeradius.org** *The FreeRADIUS Server Project*

❑ **http://www.freeradius.org/related/** gives a list of other RADIUS servers

Secure DNS

Secure DNS is being developed. It has two aims: to prevent attacks on the DNS itself, and to act as a means for distributing public encryption keys, which is what concerns us here:

❑ **http://www.ietf.org/html.charters/dnsext-charter.html**

❑ **http://www.nlnetlabs.nl/dnssec/index.en.html**

Protecting dial-up VPN

- **personal firewalls**. A personal firewall is a small software firewall that protects the machine it runs on. These are particularly useful for single dial-up machines connected to the Internet, e.g. from a hotel room, where they don't have the protection afforded by a corporate firewall. Without the personal firewall, the machine is completely exposed to hackers, and if the machine is VPNed into the HQ network, it can provide a backdoor into that network for hackers.

  Different personal firewalls have different features. For corporate use, you should consider one that can be deployed and configured from a central management point, to reduce your support and management workload

- there are also "internal firewall" systems that protect all the machines on the LAN. These are being extended to handle external (home workers) and mobile (salespeople in hotel rooms) machines, so that all the organization's machines can be managed consistently and safely. These systems let you specify different rules for particular groups of machines, which not only lets you protect your dial-in PCs, but also lets you control very precisely what dial-in users are allowed access on the internal LAN. See:

  ❏ **http://www.uit.co.uk/ans.htm**

- here's a war story that shows how VPNs protect your network traffic in one way, but undermine your firewall in another. At a recent IETF (Internet Engineering Task Force) meeting, the Code Red worm was rampaging over the Internet. The sysadmins for the temporary network in the conference hotel scanned the connected machines, and found that about 20% of them had been infected by the worm. The worst bit was when delegates connected to their offices using VPN: the infection immediately spread from the infected laptops onto the head-office network. And that was an IETF meeting!

- some but not all VPN systems let you specify what traffic is allowed through a VPN tunnel, e.g. on a combined firewall/VPN system you can specify rules like "from dial-in VPN users allow HTTP access to Web proxy server 192.0.2.4 and e-mail access to mail server 192.0.2.99 but nothing else." This type of setting is also useful where you have set up a VPN tunnel to a customer or supplier or other partner organization: you want to give them access to specific services on one or two specific machines only – not unrestricted access to everything on your network.

Miscellaneous

- some VPN/firewall systems let you set up "hub and spoke" routing between a group of sites. Let's say you have ten sites. To have full VPN connectivity between each site, you'd have to set up nine VPN tunnels on each site (i.e. one to each of the other sites) making a total of 90 tunnels to configure. With hub and spoke, you just set up one tunnel from each branch to HQ; then, when branch A wants to talk to branch B, the packets from A are routed to HQ, which forwards them to B. This gives you full inter-branch connectivity with a minimum of configuration, at a cost of extra traffic through your HQ's Internet connection

- when designing a multi-branch network, it's usually a good idea to use NAT with the private address ranges, e.g. if you choose the 10.*.*.* range, you might allocate 10.1.*.* to HQ, 10.2.*.* to branch A, 10.3.*.* to branch C, etc. Each of these is a class-B-sized network itself (i.e. 65,536 IP addresses) so it gives you plenty of scope for easy sub-netting at branch level if you ever need it

- if you're using NAT and set up a VPN tunnel to another site, you are allowing your internal (private, NATed) IP numbers to communicate with their private, NATed IP numbers. What happens if you've used the 10.*.*.* addresses and so have they? Obviously, one of you can renumber your internal network, but that can be a very big job. An alternative is offered by some NAT/firewall systems, which lets you perform another NAT transformation on packets sent over a VPN tunnel. For example, our private addresses might be 10.1.1.*, but when we communicate with **example.com** over our VPN link, our addresses are NATed to 192.168.168.*.

Appendices

Web Appendix 34: encryption and cryptographic methods

Epilog

The key points to remember when running your networks are:

- TCP/IP is simple at heart. Apparently complex problems break down into a sequence of easily-understood steps
- the three fundamental networking parameters – IP address, netmask, and default gateway – determine 99% of a machine's TCP/IP behavior
- use a packet sniffer as soon as you think you have a networking problem. It's so easy that it invariably saves you time
- packets travel hop by hop across the network. Packets contain no routing information, only the destination IP address. Routers along the way forward the packet towards its destination on the basis of the entries in their routing tables
- when diagnosing a problem, trace the packet's progress hop by hop. Diagnosing a single hop is straightforward because it consists of two machines talking together on the same wire
- DNS converts IP numbers to hostnames and vice versa, but in many ways it's only a convenience – all routing, etc. operates exclusively with IP numbers
- TCP is a connection-oriented protocol that provides guarantees to deliver the data sent, and in the correct order. Many TCP applications – such as SMTP and POP e-mail, and the Web's HTTP – use plain-text commands and responses to exchange data between client and server
- UDP is a connection-less protocol and is "unreliable" – it doesn't guarantee delivery. Applications that use UDP must implement their own recovery procedures in case packets get lost. UDP is typically used for applications that need to broadcast, or need to send data only intermittently, or that need to send small volumes of data. DNS, DHCP, RADIUS, and Syslog are examples of UDP applications
- Microsoft Windows Networking is a world apart. It uses its own mechanisms for name resolution, authentication, and locating machines and resources on the network. Windows Network Monitor and **ethereal** can help you understand the Windows Networking traffic
- connecting your site to the Internet uses all the skills and understanding you gained earlier in the book. Fundamentally it involves adding a lot of extra routing to your network
- security is very important when you connect to the Internet. Firewalls provide your first line of defense, but you need other security systems for fine control over Web, e-mail, and other traffic
- VPN protects links from your branch offices or users dialing in via an ISP to your internal network.

Our final words:

To understand and diagnose your network: remember the three fundamental networking parameters, and watch the packets on the wire.

Bon voyage and happy networking!

Appendices

Appendix 1 Layers, the protocol stack, and network reference models

Figure A1.1 shows many of the common networking protocols. Each horizontal row is a *layer* and the whole is often referred to as the *protocol stack* or *TCP/IP stack* because each layer is stacked on top of the ones below.

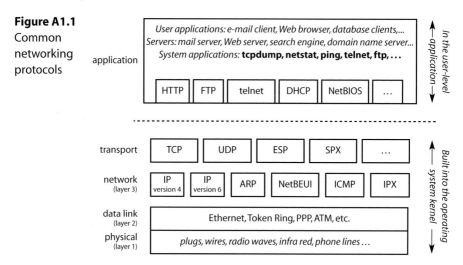

Figure A1.1 Common networking protocols

The easiest way to see what each layer does is to take an example. Consider the Web browser on your machine sending a request for a Web page to a Web server. The data flow might be as in Figure A1.2, which shows four machines making up an inter-network comprised of three networks. Let's look at each layer in turn.

The physical layer

This consists of your networking hardware – the cables, plugs, etc. and the Ethernet network card on a typical PC. This layer physically carries the electrical signal along the wire from one machine to another.

The link layer

The data link layer (often just the "link layer") is responsible for passing packets of data between two computers physically connected on the same wire. The most common type of connection on a LAN is Ethernet. Two other link-layer connection types are PPP (e.g. for dial-up Internet connections) and Token Ring. The link layer includes the drivers for your Ethernet network card but not the card itself. My link layer doesn't check whether the destination has received the packet I sent; as long as my Ethernet has successfully *transmitted* the packet, it doesn't care.

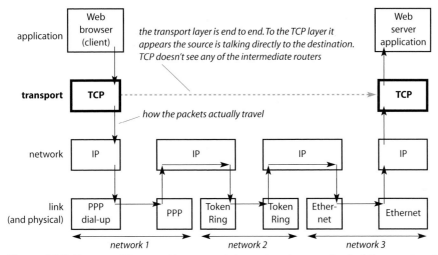

Figure A1.2 Four machines making up an inter-network comprised of three networks

Other important points to note are that this layer is only involved in sending between two machines (i.e. over a single hop) and that the machines are connected directly on the same wire. In Figure A1.2 there are three link-layer hops; from left to right these are PPP, Token Ring, and Ethernet.

The network layer (or IP layer)

This is responsible for getting packets all the way from the source machine to the final destination machine. This could be over a wide area network or through an inter-network as shown in Figure A1.2, not just over a single local wire. All TCP/IP routing (more precisely, all IP routing) operates at this level.

Given a packet, the IP layer forwards it to the next machine on its way towards the final destination. On that machine, the IP layer forwards it once more, towards the next successive machine, … etc. In other words, the IP layer moves a packet hop by hop from source machine to destination machine. That's why IP is called the "network layer" – it builds the distributed network.

If a packet gets lost, the IP layer doesn't notice and doesn't care. And once the packet has arrived at the destination machine, the IP layer considers its job done: it's up to higher layers to interface with applications.

A very important point to note from Figure A1.2 is that only the IP layer is involved in routing. As a packet travels across the Internet, the intermediate routers look only at the IP layer information – TCP, UDP, and other higher-level protocols are not involved at all. This was an important and deliberate decision in the design of the Internet. The routers, etc. that make up the backbone of the Internet – the part of the network between my site and yours – is relatively simple and has to deal only with the simple IP protocol. It is this simplicity that has allowed the development of entirely new applications and protocols; all the really complex stuff is in the applications at either end but the core of the network doesn't have to worry about any of that. To create a new application, we just have to make sure that the two machines at either end understand it; as long as you and I do that, we can get on with it without affecting anybody else. By contrast, if each router along the way had to understand all the higher-level protocols, introducing a new application (e.g. the Web) would be almost impossible, because the world-wide infrastructure would have to be changed before it could work, and experimentation would be stifled.

The transport layer

The transport layer is the hardest to understand – what does it do that the IP layer doesn't do? It's also called the *host-to-host* layer, which gives us a clue: it manages the end-to-end communication between this machine and the one its talking to. Unlike the IP layer, the transport layer comes into play only on the source machine and the final destination machine; the routers along the way don't even see it (or rather, they don't bother looking at it).

The best-known protocol at this layer is TCP, which provides reliable transmission of data between two hosts. As we explain in Chapter 10, to achieve this it has to keep track of lost or out-of-order packets, and re-transmits packets as necessary. The other common transport protocol is UDP (Chapter 15).

Another important function of this layer is to pass the different pieces of the incoming traffic to the respective applications they relate to; it uses the concept of *ports* for this (Modules 10.3 and 15.3).

Because this layer isn't involved in routing, when we are diagnosing a real network and are tracing packets on an intermediate router (i.e. not the source or destination host), we can ignore port and protocol and look at the IP details only. (It was years after we first saw this diagram that we realized its full significance. It explains the difference between the transport and network layer functions: one handles only the two ends, the other handles all the routing in between.)

The application layer

This provides the functionality the user wants – file transfer, Web browsing, database access, etc. The application-level protocols (HTTP, FTP, etc.) are implemented in the application program and are not part of the operating system. Just like the transport layer, the application layer operates only on the end-point machines (source and destination) and plays no role in the intermediate machines along the path.

In summary, we have:

physical	layer 1	electrical signals on a single wire
link	layer 2	packets, single hop, from this machine to the next
network (IP)	layer 3	routing over many hops, from source machine right to the destination machine
transport	layer 4	end-to-end (i.e. source host to destination host) for reliability and interfacing with multiple applications; ports
application		what the user wanted

It's difficult at first to appreciate the full significance of the different layers – especially the difference between transport and network. We suggest you re-read this appendix when you have finished Parts 1 and 2 of the book.

Network reference models

The layer names numbers in the table above are from the OSI "seven-layer model." We've only shown a few of the layers because the other OSI layers don't correspond to TCP/IP layers and don't give any useful insight. (In fact they just confuse things.)

The US Department of Defense (DOD) model is much more relevant to TCP/IP, but its terminology isn't widely used:

OSI layer name	DOD layer name
application	process/application
transport	host-to-host
network	Internet
link + physical	network access

❏ **RFC-942 February 1985** *Transport Protocols for Department of Defense Data Networks* (This RFC anticipated that the OSI protocols would conquer the world.)

Appendix 2 RFCs and Internet standards

From 1969, as TCP/IP was being developed, the researchers circulated documents giving information, and requesting feedback, on best practice and proposed standards. These documents were called *RFCs (requests for comments)*. As the Internet matured, the standards process became more formal, as we explain below, but the "RFC" name has been retained even though nowadays many RFCs define formal Internet standards.

Some RFCs are very technical, others are very readable. Unlike many "knowledgebase" systems, RFCs are never modified or updated once published. If an RFC really needs to be changed – because it contains an error (rare) or the standard has evolved over time (common) – a new RFC is issued that obsoletes the old one. As a result, the RFCs are a wonderful source of history, giving information on how and why particular TCP/IP features evolved.

RFCs are divided into several "tracks:"

Standards track:
for specifications that are intended to become Internet standards. These move through various *maturity levels*, from draft to proposed standard to full Internet standard as described below.

Best Current Practice RFCs (BCPs):
as RFC-2026 says, these are "*designed to be a way to standardize practices and the results of community deliberations. A BCP document is subject to the same basic set of procedures as standards track documents and thus is a vehicle by which the IETF community can define and ratify the community's best current thinking on a statement of principle or on what is believed to be the best way to perform some operations.*"

Non-standards track:
specifications that are not on the standards track are labeled with one of three "off-track" maturity levels: "experimental," "informational," or "historic," depending on their contents. These are not Internet Standards. For example, some consist of vendor-developed specifications that have been published as RFCs for the benefit of the networking community. Still others are purely humorous, e.g.

❏ **RFC-1149 1 April 1990** *A Standard for the Transmission of IP Datagrams on Avian Carriers* (the publication date is significant!)

(It's rumored that a company – whose leg had been pulled by some technical advisor – issued a request-to-tender for a system, and one of the requirements was RFC-1149 compliance. Some vendors responded to the tender claiming "compliance but only on April 1.")

Historic RFCs are typically standards that have been superseded by later RFCs, or RFCs that never became official standards – perhaps through lack of general interest.

A list of the RFCs that form the current Internet standards is published frequently – as an RFC itself. By convention its RFC number is a multiple of 100. For example, the current version (April 2002) is:

❏ **RFC-3000 November 2001** *Internet Official Protocol Standards*

This is also referred to as document STD1. A completely up-to-date list (updated daily) is available online at:

❏ **http://www.rfc-editor.org/rfc.html > Official Internet Protocol Standards**

There's interesting background and history on RFCs in:

❏ **RFC-2555 April 1999** *30 Years of RFCs*

"Which RFC do I want?" – indexes to RFCs

The official repository for RFCs is the RFC Editor's site:

❏ **http://www.rfc-editor.org/** *RFC Editor Homepage*

This has a link to the **RFC Database**, which contains many different indexes – by number in forward or reverse order, by type, etc. The link **Alternative RFC repositories** gives pointers to other sites with various indexing and searching capabilities.

RFC numbers are allocated sequentially, although occasionally special considerations apply, e.g. RFC-822 was obsoleted by RFC-1822 and RFC-2822. RFC-2468 (as in the children's rhyme "2–4–6–8. Who do we appreciate?") is a memorial to the late Jon Postel, who made great contributions to the Internet, not least in editing the RFCs for many years. And RFC-1984 relates to governments restricting the strength of encryption and security technology so they can decrypt anything they want. (C.f. "Big Brother" in George Orwell's novel *1984*.)

> **Tip:** because RFCs are issued as plain ASCII text, they are searched very easily using Linux's **grep**. We keep a full set of RFCs internally on our site. Searching these locally is much faster and more flexible than using someone else's Web site. We name the RFC files as **xxxx.txt**, e.g. **0822.txt**, **2555.txt**, etc., so that **grep** searches the files, and displays matches it finds, in numerical order. This makes it easy, for example, to find out when a particular term was first used in the RFCs.

Obtaining RFCs

RFCs are distributed free of charge. You can download them from the RFC Editor or the IETF sites:

❏ **http://www.rfc-editor.org/rfc.html** *RFC Database*

❏ **http://www.ietf.org** *The Internet Engineering Task Force* > **RFC Pages**

as well as countless other sites – just search for "RFCs" on any Web search engine.

We like the RFC Editor site because it lets you download collections of RFCs in groups of 500, as well as "all RFCs issued in the last 7 or 30 days," making it very easy to keep a complete, up-to-date set.

The Internet standards process

One of the most interesting but little known features of RFCs is how an "Internet standard" (a standards-track RFC) comes into being. The process is very different to other standards bodies' procedures. While some aspects of the process appear weird at first sight, it emphasizes that the purpose of standards is implementing working, robust, multi-vendor, inter-operable systems – and in fact the process has significantly helped the Internet's development. Here we're only giving the flavor of how things work; for more detail read:

❑ **RFC-3160 August 2001** *The Tao of IETF – A Novice's Guide to the Internet Engineering Task Force* (very readable)

❑ **RFC-2026 October 1996** *Best Current Practice: The Internet Standards Process – Revision 3* (more formal)

The RFC process is managed by the *Internet Engineering Task Force (IETF)*. This body is also slightly weird. It has no members, so you can't "join" it: anyone can participate by signing up to one of its mailing lists or attending one of its three-times-yearly conferences. People participate as individuals, not as representatives of their organization. The structure of the IETF is relevant to how RFCs are created so we'll give a potted summary here:

> **Working groups.** Most of the nitty gritty standards work is done by *working groups* (WGs) of the IETF, which focus on specific technology areas. WGs are created as necessary to achieve a certain goal – e.g. define a standard for some aspect of the Internet's operation – and often dissolve again when the task is finished. (For example, the SNMP WG concluded in 1991. If any new SNMP-related work arises, it will be handled by some other WG if it's relevant to their activity, or a new WG will be formed if required.) By having a close focus and potentially limited lifetime, WGs can fulfill their real tasks without too much bureaucracy. There are currently about 150 different WGs:
>
> > ❑ **http://www.ietf.org/html.charters/wg-dir.html** *Active IETF Working Groups*
> >
> > ❑ **http://www.ietf.org/html.charters/OLD/index.html** *Concluded Working Groups*
>
> Working groups are organized into "areas". An area covers a broad topic area, e.g. security, routing, applications, user services, etc. and has one or two area directors who know what all the WGs in their area are doing.
>
> **IESG (Internet Engineering Steering Group).** The IESG is made up of all the area directors and the chair of the IETF itself.

Now let's see how RFCs and standards tie in to that organization. Let's assume an existing or specially created working group has some particular issue to address. This is discussed by the WG participants on the WG mailing list, and maybe in WG sessions at the three-times-yearly IETF meetings too. The WG may produce zero or more *Internet drafts*. These are working documents describing work in progress, issued only for review and comment. They have no formal status at all, they are not archived, and they expire (often without trace) after six months. The current Internet drafts can be seen on:

❑ **http://www.ietf.org/ID.html** *Internet drafts*

When the WG believes the specification should be made a standard, it goes through three stages:

1. **Proposed Standard.** This is a complete and credible specification that a WG has reviewed in depth and is generally considered to be useful. A working implementation of the spec isn't required but often exists at this stage. This level is roughly equivalent to the full standards produced by other standards organizations. After six months, if approved by the IESG, the Proposed Standard can be elevated to the next stage, which is …

2. **Draft Standard.** For a specification to reach this level there must be two separate and independently developed implementations that cover all the option in the spec. This requirement helps overcome problems that occurred with other standards – where two implementations could be completely compliant with the standard but still not work with each other. During this stage the community gains operational experience with the specification, so that any ambiguities can be cleared up and any unnecessary elements can be removed. Draft standards are usually sufficiently mature that vendors can implement them in live-running environments. (Don't confuse a "Draft Standard" with an "Internet draft." They are completely different.)

3. **Standard (Internet Standard).** Many significant, separate implementations must have been produced and inter-operate. The specification is now highly mature and has gained general market acceptance.

A very important aspect of the whole process is that there is much public review and comment at each stage. Standards are not drawn up by a committee closed to public view: anyone can contribute. Interestingly, for a spec to be elevated to a level of standard, unanimous agreement is *not* required; instead, the emphasis is on "rough consensus and running code." The "running code" requirement ensures avoids "paper standards" that appear good at first glance but are ambiguous or flawed or lead to non-interoperable implementations. The "rough consensus" approach helps avoid the "camel is a horse designed by a committee" syndrome, where extra "options" are added to a standard to satisfy just one participant, in order to obtain a spurious unanimity. However, even if a WG does agrees unanimously that a spec should be made a standard, the IESG still has to approve it. The IESG contains experts in all the areas of the IETF and so is well equipped to notice if a spec in one area would have significant impact on another or affect the overall operation of the Internet itself. If necessary, the IESG can reject a spec, or request that certain aspects of it be modified to fit in better with the rest of the Internet standards and operational practices.

The "rough consensus" principle leads to another weird but practical feature of working group meetings: there are no formal votes. There are shows of hands, but the hands aren't counted: if the votes are so close that they need to be counted it's clear there is no real consensus. Another way of taking the opinion of the meeting is to hold a "hum." First, those in favor of the proposal hum audibly, then those against hum too; the loudest hum wins. (It has been suggested that members of more formal standards bodies would have apoplexy or heart attacks if they heard about this.)

Format of RFCs

The standard for the format of RFCs is:

❏ **RFC-2223 October 1997** *Instructions to RFC authors*

The primary format for RFCs is still plain ASCII text. The reason that other "fancier" formats are not favored is explained in:

❏ **http://search.ietf.org/internet-drafts/draft-rfc-editor-rfc2223bis-01.txt** *Instructions to Request for Comments (RFC) Authors*, which says:

❏ *The continued use of ASCII text for RFCs, despite the spread of "more modern" printing formats, is intermittently debated by the Internet community. The consensus continues to be that the great advantages of plain ASCII text – the ability to readily edit, cut-and-paste, and search documents, as well as the ubiquitous availability of tools for these functions – have made the ASCII choice a clear winner.*

While the official version of an RFC is ASCII, secondary versions can also be submitted in PDF or PostScript formats, because these are often easier to read and can include diagrams and graphs not reproducible in the basic ASCII format.

The Internet Research Task Force (IRTF)

The IRTF promotes research relevant to the evolution of Internet in the future. It has a small number of "research groups" that work long term on topics related to Internet protocols, applications, architecture, and technology. The current research groups are:

- Authentication Authorization Accounting Architecture
- End-to-End
- Group Security
- Internet Digital Rights Management
- Interplanetary Internet
- Network Management
- NameSpace
- Reliable Multicast
- Routing
- Services Management

For example, the **Interplanetary Internet** Research Group deals with:

❏ *"edge Internet" fragments [that] are generally untethered with respect to the Internet backbone and can range from single nodes with intermittent external connectivity to well populated subnetworks and internets with extremely constrained connectivity. Such fragments include remote terrestrial internets using wireless and satellite links, and in-situ internets deployed at off-Earth locations such as the surfaces and vicinities of other planets. Fragments of Internet may be found on space vehicles in transit from Earth to other planetary/solar system bodies, and may return to Earth or not, depending on the mission.*

❏ **http://www.irtf.org/** *IRTF Home Page*

Appendix 3 Ethernet hubs and switches

Wiring hubs and switches are used to connect computers by means of UTP (unshielded twisted pair) cabling.

With earlier wiring systems – thin Ethernet ("thin-net") and thick Ethernet ("thicknet") – a single cable runs throughout the building, and workstations are attached to this cable, using *Ethernet transceivers* for thicknet, and T-pieces for thin-net. The two dangling ends of the cable are fitted with *terminators*, for electrical signal transmission reasons. (In thin-net, the main cable consists of many smaller runs of cable joining up at the T-pieces; Figure A3.1. In thicknet, the cable is a single, very long piece of cable.)

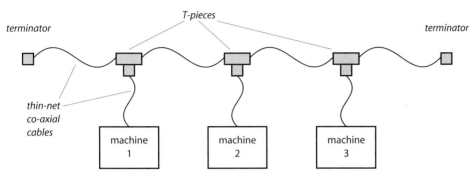

Figure A3.1 Thin-net wiring

Thin-net and thicknet networks are said to have a *bus* topology (Figure A3.2) – all the network signals travel over a single wire that every machine is connected to. If there's a break or a fault anywhere in the main cable, the whole network fails.

Figure A3.2
Bus topology

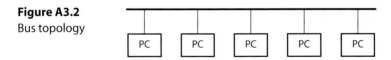

By contrast, UTP networks have a *star* or a *hub-and-spoke* topology (Figure A3.3). Each machine is connected by its own dedicated cable (often called a *patch cable*) to the central hub or switch. There is no longer a single "backbone" cable, and if an individual patch cable breaks, only that machine is affected – the rest of the network continues to work correctly. Figure A3.4 shows how a small UTP network is physically cabled up.

Figure A3.3 Star or
hub-and-space
topology

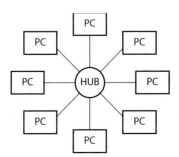

Figure A3.4
Cabling up a small
UTP network

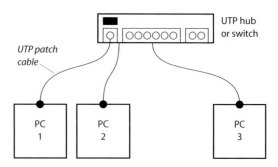

The fact that a break in one cable doesn't bring down the whole network is one big advantage of UTP over the other wiring systems. Another is that the hub or switch actively tests the *link integrity* of the connection from PC to hub. It sends pulses (about every 16 milliseconds for 10Mb/s Ethernet, or every 62 microseconds for 100Mb/s) to the network card in the PC, which responds appropriately if the link is OK. (These pulses are only for the benefit of the hub; your machine doesn't see them and they are not normal data exchanged between machines. The pulses are also used for *auto-negotiation*, so that the box can notice whether you've connected a 10Mb/s or a 100Mb/s network card at the other end and handle it appropriately.) Both hub and network card have an indicator lamp that is lit when the link is OK; it's easy to take this for granted, but it's a great diagnostic tool in its own right – as soon as you plug in a cable you have a positive indication that it's working correctly.

What hubs and switches really are

Hubs typically have 4, 8, 16, or 24 ports, so an obvious requirement is to connect several hubs (or switches) together to form a larger network. How do you do this? To answer that, we first have to look at what hubs and switches really are, and to do that it's easiest if we go back and look at old thicknet Ethernet again.

The Ethernet standard limits the length of cable you can have. If this isn't long enough for you (in a large building or a big network), you can use two separate cables (*segments*) connected using an *Ethernet repeater* (Figure A3.5).

Figure A3.5
Using an Ethernet
repeater

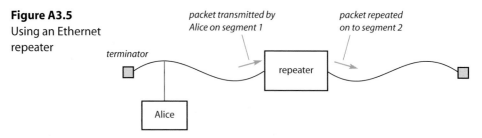

This is an active device (i.e. not a passive device like a plug or socket that contains no electronics). When a packet is transmitted on one segment, it arrives at the repeater, which then repeats the electrical signals bit by bit on to the other segment. You can have lots of repeaters in your network but you are limited by the *5–4–3 rule*: between any two machines on a 10 mb/s Ethernet you can have at most five segments and four repeaters, and only three of the segments can be populated, i.e. have non-repeater devices (such as PCs) connected to them for 100 mb/s Ethernet you are allowed only 2 repeaters.

In short, with repeaters, all packets are visible on every segment of the network. That lets you extend your network over greater distances, but it can also be inefficient. Consider the network in Figure A3.6, when Alice is sending to Bob.

Figure A3.6
An inefficient network

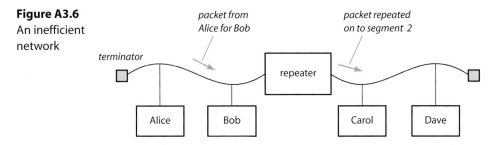

Bob can receive the packet from Alice because they are both on the same wire. However, the repeater still repeats the packet on to segment 2, even though there's no real need. Wouldn't it be nice if our box in the middle was clever enough to re-transmit to other segments only the packets that are required? Then, most traffic would remain local to a segment, so our network would be much less heavily loaded and could therefore accommodate a much larger number of machines. That's exactly what *Ethernet bridges* do (Figure A3.7).

Figure A3.7
The same network using an Ethernet bridge

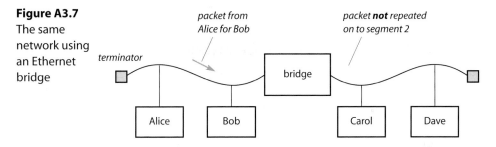

The bridge "learns" from the traffic it sees which MAC addresses are on which side of the bridge, so it knows that Alice and Bob are on the left segment, and Carol and Dave are on the right. If the bridge receives a packet on its left interface with destination address **bob**, the bridge knows that Bob is already on the left segment, so it doesn't have to forward the packet on to the right-hand segment. However, if a packet arrives from the left with destination address **dave**, the bridge knows that Dave is on the right-hand segment and does forward the packet. In this way, only traffic that really needs to pass through the bridge to the other side is actually forwarded. Bridges that operate like this are called *learning bridges*. (Before learning bridges were invented, you had to manually configure the bridge with a list of the addresses that were on either side.)

The 5–4–3 rule does *not* apply to bridges. There are limits on the number you can have in your network but these are rarely met in practice.

We have shown the repeaters and bridges with only two interfaces or *ports*, a left and a right. There are multi-port repeaters and bridges; they work in the same way but just handle more than two connected segments.

In fact, a four-port hub is just a four-port repeater, and an *n*-port switch is just an *n*-port learning bridge. Now let's see how that affects us in practice.

Practical aspects of hubs and switches

1. **Connecting multiple hubs/switches**

    - the 5–4–3 rule applies to hubs
    - you *can* connect hub to hub, or hub to switch. You use "ordinary" UTP cables. We say "ordinary" because you don't have to buy vendor-specific "hub-connecting" cables or anything like that. However, if you connect a normal port on one box to a normal port on another, you will need to use a cross-over UTP cable. This looks and costs the same as a normal (straight-through) cable, but has different internal wiring. (You can network two PCs directly using a cross-over cable, without a hub or switch. This is sometimes handy in an emergency, or for testing.)

    > **Tip:** mixing up cross-over and straight-through cables wastes time and causes needless confusion – you often think there's a problem with the PC instead of realizing you're using the wrong cable. We color-code our cables: we use red for all our cross-over cables and nothing else.

    Some devices have special "uplink" ports designed for connecting box to box, often with a switch that lets you choose "normal" or "uplink" mode. In uplink mode you can connect the boxes with a normal (straight-through) UTP cable; otherwise you need a cross-over cable. You're *not* limited to using these ports to connect boxes: as long as you use the correct cable type (cross-over or straight-through, as appropriate) you can connect from any port to any port on the boxes.

2. **Using** tcpdump (**or any other sniffer**)

    - because switches are bridges, they don't pass all the packets indiscriminately. If you're using **tcpdump** on one port of a switch, you won't see all the traffic for all the other ports. However, with a hub you will
    - if your network uses switches and you just want to sniff the traffic to one machine (Alice, say), the easiest way to do it is to connect Alice to a little hub instead, connect the hub to the switch, and plug your sniffer into the little hub. Figure A3.8 shows the before and after configurations

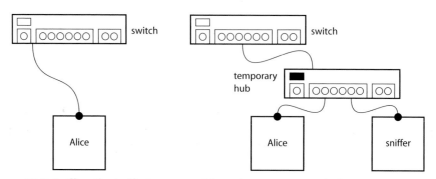

Figure A3.8 Sniffing the traffic to one machine using a temporary hub

- some "managed switches" (see below) can be configured so that all traffic is visible on all ports, or on a specific port (that you connect your sniffer to).

3. Dual-speed 10Mb/s and 100Mb/s hubs

Dual-speed hubs let you connect machines with a mixture of 10Mb/s and 100Mb/s network cards and the hub apparently treats all the machines the same, apart from connecting at different speeds. However, when you use a sniffer, there *is* a difference: the hub really acts almost like two separate devices – one handling the 10Mb/s machines, the other the 100Mb/s ones – connected by a switch. If your sniffer is on 10Mb/s and the machine you're sniffing is on 100Mb/s, the only packets you'll see are the broadcasts, which are of course visible over the whole network. (The two different sets of ports are sometimes said to be in different *collision domains* – traffic can be transmitted simultaneously on both without one interfering with the other. And in a switch, each pair of ports is in effect in its own collision domain.)

Terminology

The terms "hub" and "switch" are often applied loosely. Sometimes what we've called a switch is referred to as a "switched hub" (which is very confusing, so don't use that term).

Repeaters (hubs) operate at the electrical level of transmission, which is layer 1 in the OSI reference model (see Appendix 1) and are therefore sometimes called *layer-1 switches*. Bridges (switches) operate at the Ethernet/MAC address level, which is layer 2, and are called *layer-2 switches*. IP routers operate at the IP or networking layer of the stack, and are called *layer-3 switches* (although that term is often reserved for special, very fast routers, typically used only on LANs).

Managed hubs (or *switches*) support SNMP (Simple Network Management Protocol, Module 17.10) and can gather statistics and report errors over the network and so are ideal for very large networks or where integrity of the network is paramount. They can often be reconfigured over the network too, giving greater flexibility and reducing the cost of network management. Some give you the option of configuring the basic operation of the switch and make all packets on every port visible to one selected port. This can be very useful when you need to trace traffic using **tcpdump**; in this mode the switch is behaving more like a hub.

Stackable hubs can be linked together intimately (using special connectors) so they act and can be managed as a single unit. Because a managed hub (above) has to have an IP address so it can be accessed remotely, stacking several of them together saves on IP addresses and reduces the number of elements to be monitored and displayed in your network management applications.

Notes and further reading

For the best description we've ever come across of what repeaters and bridges are and how they work, see Perlman, Chapters 3 and 5. (And as she invented the "spanning tree algorithm" used in just about every bridge/switch, it's the best you can get.)

Appendix 4 tcpdump **command summary**

Appendix 5 contains the full manpage but you may find the summary here more convenient. (The manpage omits some options: our summary is derived from the program's source code, version 3.6, 12 December 2000.)

How to filter out just the packets you want to look at

By default, **tcpdump** prints details of *all* the packets it sees. On a busy network this can generate a huge amount of information, making it very difficult to see what you're looking for. You can tell **tcpdump** to show selected packets only. You can combine multiple selection criteria to give a very precise specification of what you want to see.

The tables below are for reference only – they contain a lot more detail than you need to get started. In the body of the book, whenever we use a new **tcpdump** feature we'll explain it. For now just quickly look over the range of options available, so you'll have an idea of the full range of **tcpdump**'s capabilities.

Selecting by address

Criteria	Select packets with ...
host *a.b.c.d* **host** *name*	this machine as source or destination IP address `tcpdump host 192.0.2.1`

ether host *a:b:c:d:e:f*
ether host *name*
	source or destination MAC address as specified (Module 5.12)
	`tcpdump ether host 08:00:20:0C:E4:E1`
	`tcpdump ether host RUPERT`

port *num* **port** *name*	this port as source or destination, e.g. HTTP traffic (port 80) `tcpdump port 80`

net *a.b.c.d* **mask** *nmask*
net *name* **mask** *nmask*
net *a.b.c.d/numbits*
	source or destination IP address in this range
	`tcpdump net 192.0.2.32 mask 255.255.255.240`
	`tcpdump net 192.0.2.32/28`

net *prefix*	again, select packets with source or destination IP address in this range, but using a non-standard notation: it matches if the specified prefix matches the IP address, e.g. any of "192", "192.0", "192.0.2" match (at least) all the addresses on the 192.0.2.0/24 network, but paradoxically, "192.0.2.0", which is our real network, address doesn't. The **net** notation is a very quick and handy way to enter a selection, e.g. `tcpdump net 192`
gateway *name*	packets forwarded via route with hostname name `tcpdump gateway rupert`
broadcast	packets sent using Ethernet broadcast

ether broadcast	`tcpdump broadcast`
ip broadcast	packets sent using any of the IP broadcast addresses

src ...
... src
	only match if the source address is as specified. This can be prefixed to **host**, **net**, or **port**, or appended to **ether**
	`tcpdump src net 10`
	`tcpdump src host 192.0.2.1`
	`tcpdump ether src BOB`

dst ... ... dst	only match if the destination address is as specified. This can be prefixed to **host**, **net**, or **port**, or appended to **ether**

Selecting by content

icmp
ip
tcp
udp
arp
	match only packets using the specified protocol
	`tcpdump arp`
	`tcpdump icmp`

ip proto *num*	match only packets using the specified protocol `tcpdump ip proto 50` *IP protocol 50 is ESP for VPN*

Combining multiple criteria

... and ...	match only if all criteria match
	`tcpdump arp and host 192.0.2.1`
	`tcpdump host 192.0.2.1 and port 80`
	`tcpdump host 192.0.2.1 and port 53 and udp`

... or ...	match if any of the criteria match
	`tcpdump arp or host 192.0.2.1 or src net 10`
	As shorthand, you can omit identical "qualifier lists".
	These are equivalent:
	`tcpdump src net 10 or 11 or 12`
	`tcpdump src net 10 or src net 11 or src net 12`

not ...	reverse the meaning of the match condition, e.g. `tcpdump not host 192.0.2.1` prints everything except traffic to/from that host. You often use this if you are on a networked machine and you want to exclude your own traffic from the trace
(...)	parentheses are used to group expressions, usually used with **and** and **or** `tcpdump arp and "(src net 10 or 12)"` We've used quotes to hide the parentheses from the shell, which would otherwise treat them as special characters. (Try it without and see what happens.)

Options for looking at the packets in different ways

Some options are needed only rarely and a few others are very obscure indeed. In the "N" (for Notes) column of the table, "0" = often used, "1" = useful occasionally, "2"=useful but rarely, and "3" = for experts; anything higher is for gurus.

Specify how addresses are printed

Criteria	Select packets with ...	N
-e	print Ethernet/MAC addresses as well as IP addresses	0
-a	print machine, network, and port addresses as names instead of numbers. (This is the default except in very weird cases, so you'll almost certainly never need to specify it.) This also affects MAC addresses printed with "**-e**"	3
-n	print machine addresses and ports as numerics, otherwise print them as names	0
-f	print "foreign" addresses (i.e. that aren't on our LAN) as numerics. This speeds things up because we don't have to look up these addresses in the DNS. We typically don't mind looking up *local* names in the DNS because they're usually cached and the lookup is very quick	0
-N	omit the domain part from names, e.g. machine **fred.example.com** is printed as **fred**	0

Specify how times are printed

-t	don't print time on the output lines `        tcpdump -t`	0
-tt	print time as unformatted timestamp (e.g. suitable for processing in a script). Output is like: `993480853.925946 192.0.2.17.1171 > 192.0.2.7.6000: …`	2

Specify which network interface to use

-i *interface*	use *interface* instead of the default interface `        tcpdump -i eth1` *sniff on eth1 – Linux* `        windump -i \Device\Packet_EL3c5741` *Windows-NT* You can specify **-i any** to capture simultaneously on all interfaces, but they will **not** be put into promiscuous mode	1
-D	list available interfaces `        windump -D` *Windows-NT only*	1
-p	*don't* put interface into promiscuous mode	2

Controlling the level of detail printed

-q	quiet or quick – print less information on each line	2
-v	verbose	0
-vv	very verbose	1
-vvv	very, very verbose	2
-x	print the contents of the packet in hexadecimal	1
-X	print the contents of the packet in ASCII as well as hexadecimal. (You get different results if you use it with or without -x (small x).)	1
-s *num*	grab a snapshot of *num* bytes instead of the default of 68 bytes. Use this to get more information about long packets, such as DNS replies	0

Miscellaneous

-F *filename*	read the selection criteria expression from *filename* instead of from the command line. Useful if the expression is long or complex, or if it includes lots of shell special characters, especially if you'll want to use it again `tcpdump -F webstuff.txt`	3
-c *num*	exit after receiving *num* packets, instead of waiting for the user to type Control-C	3
-l	make output "line buffered" for when you run **tcpdump** in a pipeline, when by default the output would be buffered in large chunks. This way, each line is output immediately it's ready so later programs in the pipeline can process it (or so you can see it)	1
-S	print TCP sequence numbers as absolute rather than relative numbers	3

How to interpret specific types of packet

-E *algorithm;secret*	for encrypted packets between virtual private networks (VPNs). Decrypt using the specified *algorithm* using *secret* as the secret key	3
-R	for ESP (VPN encrypted) packets: don't print reply information – assume RFC 1825–1829 ESP	9
-m *file*	load SNMP MIB module definitions from *file*	2
-u	print NFS handles undecoded	9
-T *type*	force the packets to be interpreted as *type*	3

Debugging

-d	show the pattern-matching code in a "human-readable" form	9
-dd	show the pattern-matching code as C program code	9
-ddd	show the pattern-matching code as decimal numbers	9
-O	don't run the pattern-matching code optimizer	9
-Y	run yacc debugging	9

Saving a trace to a file, reading from file

-w *outfile*	write packets to file *outfile* to be read and processed later	1
-r *infile*	read and process packets from file *infile* instead of from the network interface	1

Saving a trace to file and analyzing it later

There are several reasons why you might want to do this:

- there's lots of traffic – too much to look at, or you want to reduce the processing load on the **tcpdump** machine
- you want to analyze the information later
- you want to analyze the information in many different ways, or you're not yet sure how you will want to analyze it
- to avoid generating any extra traffic, which would clutter your traces. For example, when you're investigating the DNS itself (Chapter 7) use **-w** *file* when collecting the data, and then the **-r** *file* to process it later, so that **tcpdump** itself doesn't issue DNS queries during the capture.

Appendix 5 tcpdump **manpage in full**

NAME
       tcpdump – dump traffic on a network

SYNOPSIS
       tcpdump [–**adeflnNOpqRStuvxX**] [–**c** *count*]
                   [–**C** *file_size*] [–**F** *file*]
                   [–**i** *interface*] [–**m** *module*] [–**r** *file*]
                   [–**s** *snaplen*] [–**T** *type*] [–**w** *file*]
                   [–**E** *algo:secret*] [*expression*]

DESCRIPTION
       Tcpdump prints out the headers of packets on a network interface that match the
       boolean *expression*. It can also be run with the –**w** flag, which causes it to save the
       packet data to a file for later analysis, and/or with the –**b** flag, which causes it to
       read from a saved packet file rather than to read packets from a network interface.
       In all cases, only packets that match *expression* will be processed by *tcpdump*.

       Tcpdump will, if not run with the –**c** flag, continue capturing packets until it is
       interrupted by a SIGINT signal (generated, for example, by typing your interrupt
       character, typically control-C) or a SIGTERM signal (typically generated with the
       kill(1) command); if run with the –**c** flag, it will capture packets until it is inter-
       rupted by a SIGINT or SIGTERM signal or the specified number of packets have
       been processed.

       When *tcpdump* finishes capturing packets, it will report counts of:

              packets "received by filter" (the meaning of this depends on the OS on
              which you're running *tcpdump*, and possibly on the way the OS was con-
              figured – if a filter was specified on the command line, on some OSes it
              counts packets regardless of whether they were matched by the filter
              expression, and on other OSes it counts only packets that were matched
              by the filter expression and were processed by *tcpdump*);

              packets "dropped by kernel" (this is the number of packets that were
              dropped, due to a lack of buffer space, by the packet capture mechanism
              in the OS on which *tcpdump* is running, if the OS reports that informa-
              tion to applications; if not, it will be reported as 0).

       On platforms that support the SIGINFO signal, such as most BSDs, it will report
       those counts when it receives a SIGINFO signal (generated, for example, by typing
       your "status" character, typically control-T) and will continue capturing packets.

       Reading packets from a network interface may require that you have special privileges:

Under SunOS 3.x or 4.x with NIT or BPF:
> You must have read access to */dev/nit* or */dev/bpf**.

Under Solaris with DLPI:
> You must have read/write access to the network pseudo device, e.g. */dev/le*. On at least some versions of Solaris, however, this is not sufficient to allow *tcpdump* to capture in promiscuous mode; on those versions of Solaris, you must be root, or *tcpdump* must be installed setuid to root, in order to capture in promiscuous mode.

Under HP-UX with DLPI:
> You must be root or *tcpdump* must be installed setuid to root.

Under IRIX with snoop:
> You must be root or *tcpdump* must be installed setuid to root.

Under Linux:
> You must be root or *tcpdump* must be installed setuid to root.

Under Ultrix and Digital UNIX:
> Once the super-user has enabled promiscuous-mode operation using *pfconfig*(8), any user may capture network traffic with *tcpdump*.

Under BSD:
> You must have read access to */dev/bpf**.

Reading a saved packet file doesn't require special privileges.

OPTIONS

−a	Attempt to convert network and broadcast addresses to names.
−c	Exit after receiving *count* packets.
−C	Before writing a raw packet to a savefile, check whether the file is currently larger than *file_size* and, if so, close the current savefile and open a new one. Savefiles after the first savefile will have the name specified with the −w flag, with a number after it, starting at 2 and continuing upward. The units of *file_size* are millions of bytes (1,000,000 bytes, not 1,048,576 bytes).
−d	Dump the compiled packet-matching code in a human readable form to standard output and stop.
−dd	Dump packet-matching code as a C program fragment.
−ddd	Dump packet-matching code as decimal numbers (preceded with a count).
−e	Print the link-level header on each dump line.
−E	Use *algo:secret* for decrypting IPsec ESP packets. Algorithms may be **des-cbc**, **3des-cbc**, **blow-fish-cbc**, **rc3-cbc**, **cast128-cbc**, or **none**. The default is **des-cbc**. The ability to decrypt packets is only present if *tcpdump*

was compiled with cryptography enabled. *secret* the ascii text for ESP secret key. We cannot take arbitrary binary value at this moment. The option assumes RFC2406 ESP, not RFC1827 ESP. The option is only for debugging purposes, and the use of this option with truly 'secret' key is discouraged. By presenting IPsec secret key onto command line you make it visible to others, via *ps*(1) and other occasions.

–f   Print 'foreign' internet addresses numerically rather than symbolically (this option is intended to get around serious brain damage in Sun's yp server – usually it hangs forever translating non-local internet numbers).

–F   Use *file* as input for the filter expression. An additional expression given on the command line is ignored.

–i   Listen on *interface*. If unspecified, *tcpdump* searches the system interface list for the lowest numbered, configured up interface (excluding loopback). Ties are broken by choosing the earliest match.

       On Linux systems with 2.2 or later kernels, an *interface* argument of "any" can be used to capture packets from all interfaces. Note that captures on the "any" device will not be done in promiscuous mode.

–l   Make stdout line buffered. Useful if you want to see the data while capturing it. E.g., "tcpdump –l | tee dat" or "tcpdump –l > dat & tail –f dat".

–m   Load SMI MIB module definitions from file *module*. This option can be used several times to load several MIB modules into *tcpdump*.

–n   Don't convert addresses (i.e., host addresses, port numbers, etc.) to names.

–N   Don't print domain name qualification of host names. E.g., if you give this flag then *tcpdump* will print "nic" instead of "nic.ddn.mil".

–O   Do not run the packet-matching code optimizer. This is useful only if you suspect a bug in the optimizer.

–p   *Don't* put the interface into promiscuous mode. Note that the interface might be in promiscuous mode for some other reason; hence, '-p' cannot be used as an abbreviation for 'ether host {local-hw-addr} or ether broadcast'.

–q   Quick (quiet?) output. Print less protocol information so output lines are shorter.

–R   Assume ESP/AH packets to be based on old specification (RFC1825 to RFC1829). If specified, *tcpdump* will not print replay prevention field. Since there is no protocol version field in ESP/AH specification, *tcpdump* cannot deduce the version of ESP/AH protocol.

–r   Read packets from *file* (which was created with the -w option). Standard input is used if *file* is "-".

–S   Print absolute, rather than relative, TCP sequence numbers.

−s   Snarf *snaplen* bytes of data from each packet rather than the default of 68 (with SunOS's NIT, the minimum is actually 96). 68 bytes is adequate for IP, ICMP, TCP and UDP but may truncate protocol information from name server and NFS packets (see below). Packets truncated because of a limited snapshot are indicated in the output with "[|*proto*]", where *proto* is the name of the protocol level at which the truncation has occurred. Note that taking larger snapshots both increases the amount of time it takes to process packets and, effectively, decreases the amount of packet buffering. This may cause packets to be lost. You should limit *snaplen* to the smallest number that will capture the protocol information you're interested in. Setting *snaplen* to 0 means use the required length to catch whole packets.

−T   Force packets selected by "*expression*" to be interpreted the specified *type*. Currently known types are **cnfp** (Cisco NetFlow protocol), **rpc** (Remote Procedure Call), **rtp** (Real-Time Applications protocol), **rtcp** (Real-Time Applications control protocol), **snmp** (Simple Network Management Protocol), **vat** (Visual Audio Tool), and **wb** (distributed White Board).

−t   *Don't* print a timestamp on each dump line.

−tt   Print an unformatted timestamp on each dump line.

−ttt   Print a delta (in micro-seconds) between current and previous line on each dump line.

−tttt   Print a timestamp in default format proceeded by date on each dump line. −u Print undecoded NFS handles.

−v   (Slightly more) verbose output. For example, the time to live, identification, total length and options in an IP packet are printed. Also enables additional packet integrity checks such as verifying the IP and ICMP header checksum.

−vv   Even more verbose output. For example, additional fields are printed from NFS reply packets, and SMB packets are fully decoded.

−vvv   Even more verbose output. For example, telnet **SB ... SE** options are printed in full. With −X telnet options are printed in hex as well.

−w   Write the raw packets to *file* rather than parsing and printing them out. They can later be printed with the −r option. Standard output is used if *file* is "-".

−x   Print each packet (minus its link level header) in hex. The smaller of the entire packet or *snaplen* bytes will be printed.

−X   When printing hex, print ascii too. Thus if −x is also set, the packet is printed in hex/ascii. This is very handy for analysing new protocols. Even if −x is not also set, some parts of some packets may be printed in hex/ascii.

expression

selects which packets will be dumped. If no *expression* is given, all packets on the net will be dumped. Otherwise, only packets for which *expression* is 'true' will be dumped.

The *expression* consists of one or more *primitives*. Primitives usually consist of an *id* (name or number) preceded by one or more qualifiers. There are three different kinds of qualifier:

type   qualifiers say what kind of thing the id name or number refers to. Possible types are **host**, **net** and **port**. E.g., 'host foo', 'net 128.3', 'port 20'. If there is no type qualifier, **host** is assumed.

dir   qualifiers specify a particular transfer direction to and/or from *id*. Possible directions are **src**, **dst**, **src or dst** and **src and dst**. E.g., 'src foo', 'dst net 128.3', 'src or dst port ftp-data'. If there is no dir qualifier, **src or dst** is assumed. For 'null' link layers (i.e. point to point protocols such as slip) the **inbound** and **outbound** qualifiers can be used to specify a desired direction.

proto   qualifiers restrict the match to a particular protocol. Possible protos are: **ether**, **fddi**, **tr**, **ip**, **ip6**, **arp**, **rarp**, **decnet**, **tcp** and **udp**. E.g., 'ether src foo', 'arp net 128.3', 'tcp port 21'. If there is no proto qualifier, all protocols consistent with the type are assumed. E.g., 'src foo' means '(ip or arp or rarp) src foo' (except the latter is not legal syntax), 'net bar' means '(ip or arp or rarp) net bar' and 'port 53' means '(tcp or udp) port 53'.

['fddi' is actually an alias for 'ether'; the parser treats them identically as meaning "the data link level used on the specified network interface." FDDI headers contain Ethernet-like source and destination addresses, and often contain Ethernet-like packet types, so you can filter on these FDDI fields just as with the analogous Ethernet fields. FDDI headers also contain other fields, but you cannot name them explicitly in a filter expression.

Similarly, 'tr' is an alias for 'ether'; the previous paragraph's statements about FDDI headers also apply to Token Ring headers.]

In addition to the above, there are some special 'primitive' keywords that don't follow the pattern: **gateway**, **broadcast**, **less**, **greater** and arithmetic expressions. All of these are described below.

More complex filter expressions are built up by using the words **and**, **or** and **not** to combine primitives. E.g., 'host foo and not port ftp and not port ftp-data'. To save typing, identical qualifier lists can be omitted. E.g., 'tcp dst port ftp or ftp-data or domain' is exactly the same as 'tcp dst port ftp or tcp dst port ftp-data or tcp dst port domain'.

Allowable primitives are:

dst host *host*

> True if the IPv4/v6 destination field of the packet is *host*, which may be either an address or a name.

src host *host*

> True if the IPv4/v6 source field of the packet is *host*.

host *host*

> True if either the IPv4/v6 source or destination of the packet is *host*. Any of the above host expressions can be prepended with the keywords, **ip, arp, rarp,** or **ip6** as in:
>
> > **ip host** *host*
>
> which is equivalent to:
>
> > **ether proto ip and host** *host*
>
> If *host* is a name with multiple IP addresses, each address will be checked for a match.

ether dst *ehost*

> True if the ethernet destination address is *ehost*. *Ehost* may be either a name from /etc/ethers or a number (see *ethers*(3N) for numeric format).

ether src *ehost*

> True if the ethernet source address is *ehost*.

ether host *ehost*

> True if either the ethernet source or destination address is *ehost*.

gateway *host*

> True if the packet used *host* as a gateway. I.e., the ethernet source or destination address was *host* but neither the IP source nor the IP destination was *host*. *Host* must be a name and must be found both by the machine's host-name-to-IP-address resolution mechanisms (host name file, DNS, NIS, etc.) and by the machine's host-name-to-Ethernet-address resolution mechanism (/etc/ethers, etc.). (An equivalent expression is
>
> > **ether host** *ehost* **and not host** *host*
>
> which can be used with either names or numbers for *host* / *ehost*.) This syntax does not work in IPv6-enabled configuration at this moment.

dst net *net*

> True if the IPv4/v6 destination address of the packet has a network number of *net*. *Net* may be either a name from /etc/networks or a network number (see *networks(4)* for details).

src net *net*

> True if the IPv4/v6 source address of the packet has a network number of *net*.

net *net*

> True if either the IPv4/v6 source or destination address of the packet has a network number of *net*.

net *net* **mask** *netmask*

> True if the IP address matches *net* with the specific *netmask*. May be qualified with **src** or **dst**. Note that this syntax is not valid for IPv6 *net*.

net *net/len*

> True if the IPv4/v6 address matches *net* with a netmask *len* bits wide. May be qualified with **src** or **dst**.

dst port *port*

> True if the packet is ip/tcp, ip/udp, ip6/tcp or ip6/udp and has a destination port value of *port*. The *port* can be a number or a name used in /etc/services (see *tcp*(4P) and *udp*(4P)). If a name is used, both the port number and protocol are checked. If a number or ambiguous name is used, only the port number is checked (e.g., **dst port 513** will print both tcp/login traffic and udp/who traffic, and **port domain** will print both tcp/domain and udp/domain traffic).

src port *port*

> True if the packet has a source port value of *port*.

port *port*

> True if either the source or destination port of the packet is *port*. Any of the above port expressions can be prepended with the keywords, **tcp** or **udp**, as in:

> > **tcp src port** *port*

> which matches only tcp packets whose source port is *port*.

less *length*

> True if the packet has a length less than or equal to *length*. This is equivalent to:

> > **len <=** *length*.

greater *length*

> True if the packet has a length greater than or equal to *length*. This is equivalent to:

> > **len >=** *length*.

ip proto *protocol*

> True if the packet is an IP packet (see *ip*(4P)) of protocol type *protocol*. *Protocol* can be a number or one of the names *icmp, icmp6, igmp, igrp, pim, ah, esp, vrrp, udp*, or *tcp*. Note that the identifiers *tcp, udp*, and *icmp* are also keywords and must be escaped via backslash (\), which is \\ in the C-shell. Note that this primitive does not chase the protocol header chain.

ip6 proto *protocol*

> True if the packet is an IPv6 packet of protocol type *protocol*. Note that this primitive does not chase the protocol header chain.

ip6 protochain *protocol*

> True if the packet is IPv6 packet, and contains protocol header with type *protocol* in its protocol header chain. For example,

> **ip6 protochain 6**

> matches any IPv6 packet with TCP protocol header in the protocol header chain. The packet may contain, for example, authentication header, routing header, or hop-by-hop option header, between IPv6 header and TCP header. The BPF code emitted by this primitive is complex and cannot be optimized by BPF optimizer code in *tcpdump*, so this can be somewhat slow.

ip protochain *protocol*

> Equivalent to **ip6 protochain** *protocol*, but this is for IPv4.

ether broadcast

> True if the packet is an ethernet broadcast packet. The *ether* keyword is optional.

ip broadcast

> True if the packet is an IP broadcast packet. It checks for both the all-zeroes and all-ones broadcast conventions, and looks up the local subnet mask.

ether multicast

> True if the packet is an ethernet multicast packet. The *ether* keyword is optional. This is shorthand for 'ether[0] & 1 != 0'.

ip multicast

> True if the packet is an IP multicast packet.

ip6 multicast

> True if the packet is an IPv6 multicast packet.

ether proto *protocol*

> True if the packet is of ether type *protocol*. *Protocol* can be a number or one of the names *ip, ip6, arp, rarp, atalk, aarp, decnet, sca, lat, mopdl, moprc, iso, stp, ipx*, or *netbeui*. Note these identifiers are also keywords and must be escaped via backslash (\).

[In the case of FDDI (e.g., '**fddi protocol arp**') and Token Ring (e.g., '**tr protocol arp**'), for most of those protocols, the protocol identification comes from the 802.2 Logical Link Control (LLC) header, which is usually layered on top of the FDDI or Token Ring header.

When filtering for most protocol identifiers on FDDI or Token Ring, *tcpdump* checks only the protocol ID field of an LLC header in so-called SNAP format with an Organizational Unit Identifier (OUI) of 0x000000, for encapsulated Ethernet; it doesn't check whether the packet is in SNAP format with an OUI of 0x000000.

The exceptions are *iso*, for which it checks the DSAP (Destination Service Access Point) and SSAP (Source Service Access Point) fields of the LLC header, *stp* and *netbeui*, where it checks the DSAP of the LLC header, and *atalk*, where it checks for a SNAP-format packet with an OUI of 0x080007 and the Appletalk etype.

In the case of Ethernet, *tcpdump* checks the Ethernet type field for most of those protocols; the exceptions are *iso*, *sap*, and *netbeui*, for which it checks for an 802.3 frame and then checks the LLC header as it does for FDDI and Token Ring, *atalk*, where it checks both for the Appletalk etype in an Ethernet frame and for a SNAP-format packet as it does for FDDI and Token Ring, *aarp*, where it checks for the Appletalk ARP etype in either an Ethernet frame or an 802.2 SNAP frame with an OUI of 0x000000, and *ipx*, where it checks for the IPX etype in an Ethernet frame, the IPX DSAP in the LLC header, the 802.3 with no LLC header encapsulation of IPX, and the IPX etype in a SNAP frame.]

decnet src *host*

True if the DECNET source address is *host*, which may be an address of the form "10.123", or a DECNET host name. [DECNET host name support is only available on Ultrix systems that are configured to run DECNET.]

decnet dst *host*

True if the DECNET destination address is *host*.

decnet host *host*

True if either the DECNET source or destination address is *host*.

ip, ip6, arp, rarp, atalk, aarp, decnet, iso, stp, ipx, *netbeui*

Abbreviations for:

ether proto *p*

where *p* is one of the above protocols.

lat, moprc, mopdl

Abbreviations for:

ether proto *p*

where *p* is one of the above protocols. Note that *tcpdump* does not currently know how to parse these protocols.

vlan [*vlan_id*]

True if the packet is an IEEE 802. 1Q VLAN packet. If [*vlan_id*] is specified, only true if the packet has the specified *vlan_id*. Note that the first **vlan** keyword encountered in *expression* changes the decoding offsets for the remainder of *expression* on the assumption that the packet is a VLAN packet.

tcp, udp, icmp

Abbreviations for:

ip proto *p* **or ip6 proto** *p*

where *p* is one of the above protocols.

iso proto *protocol*

True if the packet is an OSI packet of protocol type *protocol*. *Protocol* can be a number or one of the names *clnp, esis, or isis*.

clnp, esis, isis

Abbreviations for:

iso proto *p*

where *p* is one of the above protocols. Note that *tcpdump* does an incomplete job of parsing these protocols.

expr relop expr

True if the relation holds, where *relop* is one of >, <, >=, =, !=, and *expr* is an arithmetic expression composed of integer constants (expressed in standard C syntax), the normal binary operators [+, −, *, /, & |], a length operator, and special packet data accessors. To access data inside the packet, use the following syntax:

proto [*expr* : *size*]

Proto is one of **ether, fddi, tr, ip, arp, rarp, tcp, udp, icmp** or **ip6**, and indicates the protocol layer for the index operation. Note that *tcp, udp* and other upper-layer protocol types only apply to IPv4, not IPv6 (this will be fixed in the future). The byte offset, relative to the indicated protocol layer, is given by *expr*. *Size* is optional and indicates the number of bytes in the field of interest; it can be either one, two, or four, and defaults to one. The length operator, indicated by the keyword **len**, gives the length of the packet.

For example, 'ether[0] & 1 != 0' catches all multicast traffic. The expression 'ip[0] & 0xf != 5' catches all IP packets with options. The expression 'ip[6:2] & 0x1fff = 0' catches only unfragmented datagrams and frag zero of fragmented datagrams. This check is implicitly applied to the tcp and udp index operations. For instance, tcp[0] always means the first byte of the TCP *header*, and never means the first byte of an intervening fragment.

Some offsets and field values may be expressed as names rather than as numeric values.

The following protocol header field offsets are available: icmptype (ICMP type field), icmpcode (ICMP code field), and tcpflags (TCP flags field).

The following ICMP type field values are available: icmp-echoreply, icmp-unreach, icmp-sourcequench, icmp-redirect, icmp-echo, icmp-routeradvert, icmp-routersolicit, icmp-timxceed, icmp-paramprob, icmp-tstamp, icmp-tstampreply, icmp-ireq, icmp-ireqreply, icmp-maskreq, icmp-maskreply.

The following TCP flags field values are available: tcp-fin, tcp-syn, tcp-rst, tcp-push, tcp-push, tcp-ack, tcp-urg.

Primitives may be combined using:

A parenthesized group of primitives and operators (parentheses are special to the Shell and must be escaped).

Negation ('!' or 'not').

Concatenation ('&&' or 'and').

Alternation ('ll' or 'or').

Negation has highest precedence. Alternation and concatenation have equal precedence and associate left to right. Note that explicit and tokens, not juxtaposition, are now required for concatenation.

If an identifier is given without a keyword, the most recent keyword is assumed. For example,

   not host vs and ace

is short for

   not host vs and host ace

which should not be confused with

   not (host vs or ace)

Expression arguments can be passed to *tcpdump* as either a single argument or as multiple arguments, whichever is more convenient. Generally, if the expression contains Shell metacharacters, it is easier to pass it as a single, quoted argument. Multiple arguments are concatenated with spaces before being parsed.

EXAMPLES

To print all packets arriving at or departing from *sundown*:

tcpdump host sundown

To print traffic between *helios* and either *hot* or *ace*:

tcpdump host helios and \(hot or ace \)

To print all IP packets between *ace* and any host except *helios*:

tcpdump ip host ace and not helios

To print all traffic between local hosts and hosts at Berkeley:

tcpdump net ucb-ether

To print all ftp traffic through internet gateway *snup*: (note that the expression is quoted to prevent the shell from (mis-)interpreting the parentheses):

tcpdump 'gateway snup and (port ftp or ftp-data)'

To print traffic neither sourced from nor destined for local hosts (if you gateway to one other net, this stuff should never make it onto your local net).

tcpdump ip and not net *localnet*

To print the start and end packets (the SYN and FIN packets) of each TCP conversation that involves a non-local host.

tcpdump 'tcp[tcpflags] & (tcp-syn|tcp-fin) != 0 and not src and dst net *localnet*'

To print IP packets longer than 576 bytes sent through gateway *snup*:

tcpdump 'gateway snup and ip[2:2] > 576'

To print IP broadcast or multicast packets that were *not* sent via ethernet broadcast or multicast:

tcpdump 'ether[0] & 1 = 0 and ip[16] >= 224'

To print all ICMP packets that are not echo requests/replies (i.e., not ping packets):

tcpdump 'icmp[icmptype] != icmp-echo and icmp[icmptype]!= icmp-echoreply'

OUTPUT FORMAT

The output of *tcpdump* is protocol dependent. The following gives a brief description and examples of most of the formats.

Link Level Headers

If the '-e' option is given, the link level header is printed out. On ethernets, the source and destination addresses, protocol, and packet length are printed.

On FDDI networks, the '-e' option causes *tcpdump* to print the 'frame control' field, the source and destination addresses, and the packet length. (The 'frame control' field governs the interpretation of the rest of the packet. Normal packets (such as those containing IP datagrams) are 'async' packets, with a priority value between

0 and 7; for example, '**async4**'. Such packets are assumed to contain an 802.2 Logical Link Control (LLC) packet; the LLC header is printed if it is *not* an ISO datagram or a so-called SNAP packet.

On Token Ring networks, the '-e' option causes *tcpdump* to print the 'access control' and 'frame control' fields, the source and destination addresses, and the packet length. As on FDDI networks, packets are assumed to contain an LLC packet. Regardless of whether the '-e' option is specified or not, the source routing information is printed for source-routed packets.

(N.B.: The following description assumes familiarity with the SLIP compression algorithm described in RFC-1144.)

On SLIP links, a direction indicator ("I" for inbound, "O" for outbound), packet type, and compression information are printed out. The packet type is printed first. The three types are *ip, utcp*, and *ctcp*. No further link information is printed for *ip* packets. For TCP packets, the connection identifier is printed following the type. If the packet is compressed, its encoded header is printed out. The special cases are printed out as *S+*n* and *SA+*n*, where *n* is the amount by which the sequence number (or sequence number and ack) has changed. If it is not a special case, zero or more changes are printed. A change is indicated by U (urgent pointer), W (window), A (ack), S (sequence number), and I (packet ID), followed by a delta (+n or -n), or a new value (=n). Finally, the amount of data in the packet and compressed header length are printed.

For example, the following line shows an outbound compressed TCP packet, with an implicit connection identifier; the ack has changed by 6, the sequence number by 49, and the packet ID by 6; there are 3 bytes of data and 6 bytes of compressed header:

O ctcp * A+6 S+49 I+6 3 (6)

ARP/RARP Packets

Arp/rarp output shows the type of request and its arguments. The format is intended to be self explanatory. Here is a short sample taken from the start of an 'rlogin' from host *rtsg* to host *csam*:

```
arp who-has csam tell rtsg
arp reply csam is-at CSAM
```

The first line says that rtsg sent an arp packet asking for the ethernet address of internet host csam. Csam replies with its ethernet address (in this example, ethernet addresses are in caps and internet addresses in lower case).

This would look less redundant if we had done *tcpdump –n*:

```
arp who-has 128.3.254.6 tell 128.3.254.68
arp reply 128.3.254.6 is-at 02:07:01:00:01:c4
```

If we had done *tcpdump –e*, the fact that the first packet is broadcast and the second is point-to-point would be visible:

```
RTSG Broadcast 0806 64: arp who-has csam tell rtsg
CSAM RTSG 0806 64: arp reply csam is-at CSAM
```

For the first packet this says the ethernet source address is RTSG, the destination is the ethernet broadcast address, the type field contained hex 0806 (type ETHER_ARP) and the total length was 64 bytes.

TCP Packets
(N.B.: The following description assumes familiarity with the TCP protocol described in RFC-793. If you are not familiar with the protocol, neither this description nor tcpdump will be of much use to you.)

The general format of a tcp protocol line is:

src > dst: flags data-seqno ack window urgent options

Src and *dst* are the source and destination IP addresses and ports. *Flags* are some combination of S (SYN), F (FIN), P (PUSH) or R (RST) or a single '.' (no flags). *Data-seqno* describes the portion of sequence space covered by the data in this packet (see example below). *Ack* is sequence number of the next data expected the other direction on this connection. *Window* is the number of bytes of receive buffer space available the other direction on this connection. *Urg* indicates there is 'urgent' data in the packet. *Options* are tcp options enclosed in angle brackets (e.g., <mss 1024>).

Src, dst and *flags* are always present. The other fields depend on the contents of the packet's tcp protocol header and are output only if appropriate.

Here is the opening portion of an rlogin from host *rtsg* to host *csam*.

```
rtsg.1023 > csam.login: S 768512:768512(0) win 4096 <mss 1024>
csam.login > rtsg.1023: S 947648:947648(0) ack 768513 win 4096 <mss 1024>
rtsg.1023 > csam.login: . ack 1 win 4096
rtsg.1023 > csam.login: P 1:2(1) ack 1 win 4096
csam.login > rtsg.1023: . ack 2 win 4096
rtsg.1023 > csam.login: P 2:21(19) ack 1 win 4096
csam.login > rtsg.1023: P 1:2(1) ack 21 win 4077
csam.login > rtsg.1023: P 2:3(1) ack 21 win 4077 urg 1
csam.login > rtsg.1023: P 3:4(1) ack 21 win 4077 urg 1
```

The first line says that tcp port 1023 on rtsg sent a packet to port *login* on csam. The S indicates that the *SYN* flag was set. The packet sequence number was 768512 and it contained no data. (The notation is 'first:last(nbytes)' which means 'sequence numbers *first* up to but not including *last* which is *nbytes* bytes of user data'.) There was no piggy-backed ack, the available receive window was 4096 bytes and there was a max-segment-size option requesting an mss of 1024 bytes.

Csam replies with a similar packet except it includes a piggy-backed ack for rtsg's SYN. Rtsg then acks csam's SYN. The '.' means no flags were set. The packet contained no data so there is no data sequence number. Note that the ack sequence number is a small integer (1). The first time *tcpdump* sees a tcp 'conversation', it prints the sequence number from the packet. On subsequent packets of the conversation, the difference between the current packet's sequence number and this initial sequence number is printed. This means that sequence numbers after the first can be interpreted as relative byte positions in the conversation's data stream (with the first data byte each direction being '1'). '-S' will override this feature, causing the original sequence numbers to be output.

On the 6th line, rtsg sends csam 19 bytes of data (bytes 2 through 20 in the rtsg → csam side of the conversation). The PUSH flag is set in the packet. On the 7th line, csam says it's received data sent by rtsg up to but not including byte 21. Most of this data is apparently sitting in the socket buffer since csam's receive window has gotten 19 bytes smaller. Csam also sends one byte of data to rtsg in this packet. On the 8th and 9th lines, csam sends two bytes of urgent, pushed data to rtsg.

If the snapshot was small enough that *tcpdump* didn't capture the full TCP header, it interprets as much of the header as it can and then reports "[|*tcp*]" to indicate the remainder could not be interpreted. If the header contains a bogus option (one with a length that's either too small or beyond the end of the header), *tcpdump* reports it as "[*bad opt*]" and does not interpret any further options (since it's impossible to tell where they start). If the header length indicates options are present but the IP datagram length is not long enough for the options to actually be there, *tcpdump* reports it as "[*bad hdr length*]".

Capturing TCP packets with particular flag combinations (SYN-ACK, URG-ACK, etc.)

There are 8 bits in the control bits section of the TCP header:

$$CWR | ECE | URG | ACK | PSH | RST | SYN | FIN$$

Let's assume that we want to watch packets used in establishing a TCP connection. Recall that TCP uses a 3-way handshake protocol when it initializes a new connection; the connection sequence with regard to the TCP control bits is

    1) Caller sends SYN

    2) Recipient responds with SYN, ACK

    3) Caller sends ACK

Now we're interested in capturing packets that have only the SYN bit set (Step 1). Note that we don't want packets from step 2 (SYN-ACK), just a plain initial SYN. What we need is a correct filter expression for *tcpdump*.

Recall the structure of a TCP header without options:

```
0                             15                              31
-------------------------------------------------------------------
|        source port          |        destination port       |
-------------------------------------------------------------------
|                    sequence number                          |
-------------------------------------------------------------------
|                  acknowledgment number                      |
-------------------------------------------------------------------
|  HL  |  rsvd  |C|E|U|A|P|R|S|F|        window size          |
-------------------------------------------------------------------
|       TCP checksum          |       urgent pointer          |
-------------------------------------------------------------------
```

A TCP header usually holds 20 octets of data, unless options are present. The first line of the graph contains octets 0–3, the second line shows octets 4–7 etc.

Starting to count with 0, the relevant TCP control bits are contained in octet 13:

```
0            7|              15|          23|          31
------------- | --------------- | ------------- | -----------
|  HL  |  rsvd |C|E|U|A|P|R|S|F|      window size           |
------------- | --------------- | ------------- | -----------
|             |    13th octet   |             |            |
```

Let's have a closer look at octet no. 13:

```
|               |
|---------------|
|C|E|U|A|P|R|S|F|
|---------------|
|7    5    3    0|
```

These are the TCP control bits we are interested in. We have numbered the bits in this octet from 0 to 7, right to left, so the PSH bit is bit number 3, while the URG bit is number 5.

Recall that we want to capture packets with only SYN set. Let's see what happens to octet 13 if a TCP datagram arrives with the SYN bit set in its header:

```
|C|E|U|A|P|R|S|F|
|---------------|
|0 0 0 0 0 0 1 0|
|---------------|
|7 6 5 4 3 2 1 0|
```

Looking at the control bits section we see that only bit number 1 (SYN) is set.

Assuming that octet number 13 is an 8-bit unsigned integer in network byte order, the binary value of this octet is

```
00000010
```

and its decimal representation is

```
7       6       5       4       3       2       1       0
0*2  +  0*2  +  0*2  +  0*2  +  0*2  +  0*2  +  1*2  +  0*2   = 2
```

We're almost done, because now we know that if only SYN is set, the value of the 13th octet in the TCP header, when interpreted as a 8-bit unsigned integer in network byte order, must be exactly 2.

This relationship can be expressed as

tcp[13] == 2

We can use this expression as the filter for *tcpdump* in order to watch packets which have only SYN set:

tcpdump -i xl0 tcp[13] == 2

The expression says "let the 13th octet of a TCP datagram have the decimal value 2", which is exactly what we want.

Now, let's assume that we need to capture SYN packets, but we don't care if ACK or any other TCP control bit is set at the same time. Let's see what happens to octet 13 when a TCP datagram with SYN-ACK set arrives:

```
|C|E|U|A|P|R|S|F|
|---------------|
|0 0 0 1 0 0 1 0|
|---------------|
|7 6 5 4 3 2 1 0|
```

Now bits 1 and 4 are set in the 13th octet. The binary value of octet 13 is

```
00010010
```

which translates to decimal

```
7       6       5       4       3       2       1       0
0*2  +  0*2  +  0*2  +  1*2  +  0*2  +  0*2  +  1*2  +  0*2   = 18
```

Now we can't just use 'tcp[13] == 8' in the *tcpdump* filter expression, because that would select only those packets that have SYN-ACK set, but not those with only SYN set. Remember that we don't care if ACK or any other control bit is set as long as SYN is set.

In order to achieve our goal, we need to logically AND the binary value of octet 13 with some other value to preserve the SYN bit. We know that we want SYN to be set in any case, so we'll logically AND the value in the 13th octet with the binary value of a SYN:

```
        00010010 SYN-ACK              00000010   SYN
AND     00000010 (we want SYN) AND 00000010 (we want SYN)
        --------                     --------
=       00000010              =     00000010
```

We see that this AND operation delivers the same result regardless whether ACK or another TCP control bit is set. The decimal representation of the AND value as well as the result of this operation is 2 (binary 00000010), so we know that for packets with SYN set the following relation must hold true:

((value of octet 13) AND (2))==(2)

This points us to the *tcpdump* filter expression

tcpdump -i xl0 'tcp[13] & 2 == 2'

Note that you should use single quotes or a backslash in the expression to hide the AND '&') special character from the shell.

UDP Packets
UDP format is illustrated by this rwho packet:

```
actinide.who > broadcast.who: udp 84
```

This says that port *who* on host *actinide* sent a udp datagram to port *who* on host *broadcast*, the Internet broadcast address. The packet contained 84 bytes of user data.

Some UDP services are recognized (from the source or destination port number) and the higher level protocol information printed. In particular, Domain Name service requests (RFC-1034/1035) and Sun RPC calls (RFC-1050) to NFS.

UDP Name Server Requests
(*N.B.:The following description assumes familiarity with the Domain Service protocol described in RFC-1035. If you are not familiar with the protocol, the following description will appear to be written in greek.*)

Name server requests are formatted as

src > dst: id op? flags qtype qclass name (len)

```
h2opolo.1538 > helios.domain: 3+ A? ucbvax.berkeley. edu. (37)
```

Host *h2opolo* asked the domain server on *helios* for an address record (qtype=A) associated with the name *ucbvax.berkeley.edu.* The query id was '3'. The '+' indicates the *recursion desired* flag was set. The query length was 37 bytes, not including the UDP and IP protocol headers. The query operation was the normal one, *Query*, so the op field was omitted. If the op had been anything else, it would have been printed between the '3' and the '+'. Similarly, the qclass was the normal one, *C_IN*, and omitted. Any other qclass would have been printed immediately after the 'A'.

A few anomalies are checked and may result in extra fields enclosed in square brackets: If a query contains an answer, authority records or additional records section, *ancount, nscount,* or *arcount* are printed as '[na]', '[nn]' or '[$n$au]' where n is the appropriate count. If any of the response bits are set (AA, RA or rcode) or any of the 'must be zero' bits are set in bytes two and three, '[b2&3=*x*]' is printed, where *x* is the hex value of header bytes two and three.

UDP Name Server Responses

Name server responses are formatted as

> *src > dst: id op rcode flags al nl au type class data (len)*

```
helios.domain > h2opolo.1538: 3 3/3/7 A 128.32. 137.3(273)
helios.domain > h2opolo.1537: 2 NXDomain* 0/1/0 (97)
```

In the first example, *helios* responds to query id 3 from *h2opolo* with 3 answer records, 3 name server records and 7 additional records. The first answer record is type A (address) and its data is internet address 128.32.137.3. The total size of the response was 273 bytes, excluding UDP and IP headers. The op (Query) and response code (NoError) were omitted, as was the class (C_IN) of the A record.

In the second example, *helios* responds to query 2 with a response code of non-existent domain (NXDomain) with no answers, one name server and no authority records. The '*' indicates that the *authoritative answer* bit was set. Since there were no answers, no type, class or data were printed.

Other flag characters that might appear are '–' (recursion available, RA, *not* set) and 'I' (truncated message, TC, set). If the 'question' section doesn't contain exactly one entry, '[*n*q]' is printed.

Note that name server requests and responses tend to be large and the default *snaplen* of 68 bytes may not capture enough of the packet to print. Use the –s flag to increase the snaplen if you need to seriously investigate name server traffic. '–s 128' has worked well for me.

SMB/CIFS decoding

tcpdump now includes fairly extensive SMB/CIFS/NBT decoding for data on UDP/137, UDP/138 and TCP/139. Some primitive decoding of IPX and NetBEUI SMB data is also done.

By default a fairly minimal decode is done, with a much more detailed decode done if -v is used. Be warned that with -v a single SMB packet may take up a page or more, so only use -v if you really want all the gory details.

If you are decoding SMB sessions containing unicode strings then you may wish to set the environment variable USE_UNICODE to 1. A patch to auto-detect unicode strings would be welcome.

For information on SMB packet formats and what all the fields mean see www.cifs.org or the pub/samba/specs/ directory on your favourite samba.org mirror site. The SMB patches were written by Andrew Tridgell (tridge@samba.org).

NFS Requests and Replies

Sun NFS (Network File System) requests and replies are printed as:

> *src.xid > dst.nfs: len op args*
> *src.nfs > dst.xid: reply stat len op results*

```
sushi.6709 > wrl.nfs: 112 readlink fh 21,24/10.73165
wrl.nfs > sushi.6709: reply ok 40 readlink "../var"
sushi.201b > wrl.nfs:
        144 lookup fh 9,74/4096.6878 "xcolors"
wrl.nfs > sushi.201b:
        reply ok 128 lookup fh 9,74/4134.3150
```

In the first line, host *sushi* sends a transaction with id *6709* to *wrl* (note that the number following the src host is a transaction id, *not* the source port). The request was 112 bytes, excluding the UDP and IP headers. The operation was a *readlink* (read symbolic link) on file handle (*fh*) 21,24/10.731657119. (If one is lucky, as in this case, the file handle can be interpreted as a major,minor device number pair, followed by the inode number and generation number.) *Wrl* replies 'ok' with the contents of the link.

In the third line, *sushi* asks *wrl* to lookup the name '*xcolors*' in directory file 9,74/4096.6878. Note that the data printed depends on the operation type. The format is intended to be self explanatory if read in conjunction with an NFS protocol spec.

If the –v (verbose) flag is given, additional information is printed. For example:

```
sushi.1372a > wrl.nfs:
        148 read fh 21,11/12.195 8192 bytes @ 24576
wrl.nfs > sushi.1372a:
        reply ok 1472 read REG 100664 ids 417/0 sz 29388
```

(–v also prints the IP header TTL, ID, length, and fragmentation fields, which have been omitted from this example.) In the first line, *sushi* asks *wrl* to read 8192 bytes from file 21,11/12.195, at byte offset 24576. *Wrl* replies 'ok'; the packet shown on the second line is the first fragment of the reply, and hence is only 1472 bytes long (the other bytes will follow in subsequent fragments, but these fragments do not have NFS or even UDP headers and so might not be printed, depending on the filter expression used). Because the –v flag is given, some of the file attributes (which are returned in addition to the file data) are printed: the file type ("REG", for regular file), the file mode (in octal), the uid and gid, and the file size.

If the –v flag is given more than once, even more details are printed.

Note that NFS requests are very large and much of the detail won't be printed unless *snaplen* is increased. Try using '**-s 192**' to watch NFS traffic.

NFS reply packets do not explicitly identify the RPC operation. Instead, *tcpdump* keeps track of "recent" requests, and matches them to the replies using the transaction ID. If a reply does not closely follow the corresponding request, it might not be parsable.

AFS Requests and Replies
Transarc AFS (Andrew File System) requests and replies are printed as:

> *src.sport > dst.dport: rx packet-type*
> *src.sport > dst.dport: rx packet-type service call call-name args*
> *src.sport > dst.dport: rx packet-type service reply call-name args*

```
elvis.7001 > pike.afsfs:
       rx data fs call rename old fid 536876964/1/1
       ".newsrc.new" new fid 536876964/1/1 ".newsrc"
pike.afsfs > elvis.7001: rx data fs reply rename
```

In the first line, host elvis sends a RX packet to pike. This was a RX data packet to the fs (fileserver) service, and is the start of an RPC call. The RPC call was a rename, with the old directory file id of 536876964/1/1 and an old filename of '.newsrc.new', and a new directory file id of 536876964/1/1 and a new filename of '.newsrc'. The host pike responds with a RPC reply to the rename call (which was successful, because it was a data packet and not an abort packet).

In general, all AFS RPCs are decoded at least by RPC call name. Most AFS RPCs have at least some of the arguments decoded (generally only the 'interesting' arguments, for some definition of interesting).

The format is intended to be self-describing, but it will probably not be useful to people who are not familiar with the workings of AFS and RX.

If the -v (verbose) flag is given twice, acknowledgement packets and additional header information is printed, such as the the RX call ID, call number, sequence number, serial number, and the RX packet flags.

If the -v flag is given twice, additional information is printed, such as the the RX call ID, serial number, and the RX packet flags. The MTU negotiation information is also printed from RX ack packets.

If the -v flag is given three times, the security index and service id are printed.

Error codes are printed for abort packets, with the exception of Ubik beacon packets (because abort packets are used to signify a yes vote for the Ubik protocol).

Note that AFS requests are very large and many of the arguments won't be printed unless *snaplen* is increased. Try using '-s 256' to watch AFS traffic.

AFS reply packets do not explicitly identify the RPC operation. Instead, *tcpdump* keeps track of "recent" requests, and matches them to the replies using the call number and service ID. If a reply does not closely follow the corresponding request, it might not be parsable.

KIP Appletalk (DDP in UDP)

Appletalk DDP packets encapsulated in UDP datagrams are de-encapsulated and dumped as DDP packets (i.e., all the UDP header information is discarded). The file */etc/atalk.names* is used to translate appletalk net and node numbers to names. Lines in this file have the form

```
number      name
1.254       ether
16.1        icsd-net
1.254.110   ace
```

The first two lines give the names of appletalk networks. The third line gives the name of a particular host (a host is distinguished from a net by the 3rd octet in the number – a net number *must* have two octets and a host number *must* have three octets.) The number and name should be separated by whitespace (blanks or tabs). The */etc/atalk.names* file may contain blank lines or comment lines (lines starting with a '#').

Appletalk addresses are printed in the form

```
net.host.port
144.1.209.2 > icsd-net.112.220
office.2 > icsd-net.112.220
jssmag.149.235 > icsd-net.2
```

(If the */etc/atalk.names* doesn't exist or doesn't contain an entry for some appletalk host/net number, addresses are printed in numeric form.) In the first example, NBP (DDP port 2) on net 144.1 node 209 is sending to whatever is listening on port 220 of net icsd node 112. The second line is the same except the full name of the source node is known ('office'). The third line is a send from port 235 on net jssmag node 149 to broadcast on the icsd-net NBP port (note that the broadcast address (255) is indicated by a net name with no host number – for this reason it's a good idea to keep node names and net names distinct in */etc/atalk.names*).

NBP (name binding protocol) and ATP (Appletalk transaction protocol) packets have their contents interpreted. Other protocols just dump the protocol name (or number if no name is registered for the protocol) and packet size.

NBP packets are formatted like the following examples:

```
icsd-net.112.220 > jssmag.2: nbp-lkup 190: "=:LaserWriter@*"
jssmag.209.2>icsd-net.112.220:nbp-reply 190: "RM1140:Laserwriter@*"250
techpit.2 > icsd-net.112.220: nbp-reply 190: "techpit:LaserWriter@*" 186
```

The first line is a name lookup request for laserwriters sent by net icsd host 112 and broadcast on net jssmag. The nbp id for the lookup is 190. The second line shows a reply for this request (note that it has the same id) from host jssmag.209 saying that it has a laserwriter resource named "RM1140" registered on port 250. The third line is another reply to the same request saying host techpit has laserwriter "techpit" registered on port 186.

ATP packet formatting is demonstrated by the following example:

```
jssmag.209.165 > helios.132: atp-req 12266<0-7> 0xae030001
helios.132 > jssmag.209.165: atp-resp 12266:0 (512) 0xae040000
helios.132 > jssmag.209.165: atp-resp 12266:1 (512) 0xae040000
helios.132 > jssmag.209.165: atp-resp 12266:2 (512) 0xae040000
helios.132 > jssmag.209.165: atp-resp 12266:3 (512) 0xae040000
helios.132 > jssmag.209.165: atp-resp 12266:4 (512) 0xae040000
helios.132 > jssmag.209.165: atp-resp 12266:5 (512) 0xae040000
helios.132 > jssmag.209.165: atp-resp 12266:6 (512) 0xae040000
helios.132 > jssmag.209.165: atp-resp*12266:7 (512) 0xae040000
jssmag.209.165 > helios.132: atp-req 12266<3,5> 0xae030001
helios.132 > jssmag.209.165: atp-resp 12266:3 (512) 0xae040000
helios.132 > jssmag.209.165: atp-resp 12266:5 (512) 0xae040000
jssmag.209.165 > helios.132: atp-rel 12266<0-7> 0xae030001
jssmag.209.133 > helios.132: atp-req* 12267<0-7> 0xae030002
```

Jssmag.209 initiates transaction id 12266 with host helios by requesting up to 8 packets (the '<0-7>'). The hex number at the end of the line is the value of the 'userdata' field in the request.

Helios responds with 8 512-byte packets. The ':digit' following the transaction id gives the packet sequence number in the transaction and the number in parens is the amount of data in the packet, excluding the atp header. The '*' on packet 7 indicates that the EOM bit was set.

Jssmag.209 then requests that packets 3 & 5 be retransmitted. Helios resends them then jssmag.209 releases the transaction. Finally, jssmag.209 initiates the next request. The '*' on the request indicates that XO ('exactly once') was *not* set.

IP Fragmentation
Fragmented Internet datagrams are printed as

> (**frag** *id:size@offset+*)
> (**frag** *id:size@offset*)

(The first form indicates there are more fragments. The second indicates this is the last fragment.)

Id is the fragment id. *Size* is the fragment size (in bytes) excluding the IP header. *Offset* is this fragment's offset (in bytes) in the original datagram.

The fragment information is output for each fragment. The first fragment contains the higher level protocol header and the frag info is printed after the protocol info. Fragments after the first contain no higher level protocol header and the frag info is printed after the source and destination addresses. For example, here is part of an ftp from arizona.edu to lbl-rtsg.arpa over a CSNET connection that doesn't appear to handle 576 byte datagrams:

```
arizona.ftp-data > rtsg.1170: . 1024:1332(308) ack 1 win 4096 (frag 595a:328@0+)
arizona > rtsg: (frag 595a:204@328)
rtsg.1170 > arizona.ftp-data: . ack 1536 win 2560
```

There are a couple of things to note here: First, addresses in the 2nd line don't include port numbers. This is because the TCP protocol information is all in the first fragment and we have no idea what the port or sequence numbers are when we print the later fragments. Second, the tcp sequence information in the first line is printed as if there were 308 bytes of user data when, in fact, there are 512 bytes (308 in the first frag and 204 in the second). If you are looking for holes in the sequence space or trying to match up acks with packets, this can fool you.

A packet with the IP *don't fragment* flag is marked with a trailing (**DF**).

Timestamps

By default, all output lines are preceded by a timestamp. The timestamp is the current clock time in the form

hh:mm:ss.frac

and is as accurate as the kernel's clock. The timestamp reflects the time the kernel first saw the packet. No attempt is made to account for the time lag between when the ethernet interface removed the packet from the wire and when the kernel serviced the 'new packet' interrupt.

SEE ALSO

traffic(1C), nit(4P), bpf(4), pcap(3)

AUTHORS

The original authors are:

Van Jacobson, Craig Leres and Steven McCanne, all of the Lawrence Berkeley National Laboratory, University of California, Berkeley, CA.

It is currently being maintained by tcpdump.org.

The current version is available via http:

http://www.tcpdump.org/

The original distribution is available via anonymous ftp:

ftp://ftp.ee.lbl.gov/tcpdump.tar.Z

IPv6/IPsec support is added by WIDE/KAME project. This program uses Eric Young's SSLeay library, under specific configuration.

BUGS

Please send problems, bugs, questions, desirable enhancements, etc. to:

tcpdump-workers@tcpdump.org

Please send source code contributions, etc. to:

patches@tcpdump.org

NIT doesn't let you watch your own outbound traffic, BPF will. We recommend that you use the latter.

On Linux systems with 2.0[.x] kernels:

packets on the loopback device will be seen twice;

packet filtering cannot be done in the kernel, so that all packets must be copied from the kernel in order to be filtered in user mode;

all of a packet, not just the part that's within the snapshot length, will be copied from the kernel (the 2.0[.x] packet capture mechanism, if asked to copy only part of a packet to userland, will not report the true length of the packet; this would cause most IP packets to get an error from **tcpdump**).

We recommend that you upgrade to a 2.2 or later kernel.

Some attempt should be made to reassemble IP fragments or, at least to compute the right length for the higher level protocol.

Name server inverse queries are not dumped correctly: the (empty) question section is printed rather than real query in the answer section. Some believe that inverse queries are themselves a bug and prefer to fix the program generating them rather than *tcpdump*.

A packet trace that crosses a daylight savings time change will give skewed time stamps (the time change is ignored).

Filter expressions that manipulate FDDI or Token Ring headers assume that all FDDI and Token Ring packets are SNAP-encapsulated Ethernet packets. This is true for IP, ARP, and DECNET Phase IV, but is not true for protocols such as ISO CLNS. Therefore, the filter may inadvertently accept certain packets that do not properly match the filter expression.

Filter expressions on fields other than those that manipulate Token Ring headers will not correctly handle source-routed Token Ring packets.

ip6 proto should chase header chain, but at this moment it does not. **ip6 protochain** is supplied for this behavior.

Arithmetic expression against transport layer headers, like **tcp[0]**, does not work against IPv6 packets. It only looks at IPv4 packets.

Appendix 6 Making network settings permanent – Debian Linux

This covers the latest "stable" release of Debian Linux (2.2.x). Versions of this appendix for other Linux distributions are available on our Web site.

The numbers in the headings below indicate the modules in the main text that refer you to this appendix.

The files used to store the settings permanently for PCMCIA cards are completely different from those for normal network cards. The reason is interfaces and their settings are dynamically installed when a PCMCIA card is inserted, and dynamically removed when the card is ejected. By contrast, a normal network card is assumed to be permanently installed. Accordingly, we cover the settings for a normal network card first, and afterwards point out where the PCMCIA configuration steps differ.

Normal network card

Disabling ping (Notes, Chapter 2)

Insert the line

```
echo1>/proc/sys/net/ipr4/icmp_echo_ignore_broadcasts
```

into the file **/etc/init.d/networking**, after the initial lines that begin with "#"

Basic network settings (Module 2.11)

The file **/etc/network/interfaces** (see the **interfaces**(5) manpage) contains a list of network cards and their configuration settings. At boot-time, the system runs the program **ifup**(8), which reads the values from the file and runs **ifconfig** and other programs to configure the interfaces to the specified values. Figure A6.1 shows the **interfaces** file for a typical machine:

Figure A6.1 interfaces file for a typical machine

```
# The loopback interface
iface lo inet loopback

# The first network card - entry created during Debian installation
iface eth0 inet static
      address 192.0.2.5
      netmask 255.255.255.0
      gateway 192.0.2.77
```

- lines beginning with # are comments and are ignored
- the keyword **iface** introduces this interface, and is followed by:
  - the name of the interface (**eth0** or **lo** here)
  - the type of network, which in our case is always **inet** (for Internet = TCP/IP) but could be **ipx** for Novell
  - the keyword **static** – allocate this explicitly specified address, rather than using some dynamically allocated address, e.g. if you're using DHCP (see below)
  - the IP address and netmask, introduced by their keywords

- with older versions of Linux you may have to define values for **network** and **broadcast**. (See **interfaces**(5) for details, and see also the Warning regarding broadcast addresses in Chapter 4's Notes.)
- other keywords, which we'll see below, are used to configure other settings related to this interface.

The **interfaces** file is also used by the companion program **ifdown**(8) for closing down interfaces, but you're unlikely ever to need this, except perhaps for testing.

Setting your default gateway – Linux (Module 3.5)

You define the permanent value for this machine's default gateway in the file **/etc/network/interfaces** too. Specify it using the **gateway** keyword, in the section of the file that relates to the first network card, as shown in Figure A6.1.

Configuring Linux to act as a router (Module 3.6)

The file **/etc/network/options** contains a list of options to be configured at system startup time. The default file contains the line:

```
ip_forward=no
```

To enable IP forwarding permanently – so this machine can act as a router – change that line to:

```
ip_forward=yes
```

Configuring multiple network cards (Module 3.7)

Configuring extra network cards is easy – just add sections for the extra interfaces into **/etc/network/interfaces**, naming them as **eth1**, **eth2**, etc. Figure A6.2 shows a file for a machine with three Ethernet cards.

Figure A6.2 interfaces file for a machine with three Ethernet cards

```
iface lo inet loopback

iface eth0 inet static
      address 192.0.2.5
      netmask 255.255.255.0
      gateway 192.0.2.77

iface eth1 inet static
      address 10.1.1.11
      netmask 255.255.255.0

iface eth2 inet static
      address 10.3.3.33
      netmask 255.255.255.0
```

If you have several network cards but they are of different types, you may have to load the necessary driver modules for second and subsequent cards. (The first card will have been handled when you were installing Debian.) The configuration details are entered in **/etc/modules** and **/etc/modutils/aliases**, and transferred by the system to **/etc/modules.conf**. For details see:

❑ **http://www.tldp.org/HOWTO/Ethernet-HOWTO.html** *Linux Ethernet-Howto*

❑ **http://www.scyld.com/network/** *Linux Network Drivers*

❑ **http://www.uit.co.uk/book/multiple-cards.pdf**

Adding routes (Module 5.3)

To add a route permanently you again use the **/etc/network/interfaces** file. Let's say the route we want to add is the one defined by the command:

```
route add -net 10.2.2.0 netmask 255.255.255.0 gw 10.1.1.22
```

We add this command to the **interfaces** file, prefixed by the keyword **up**. "**up**" indicates that this command is to be run after the relevant interface has been brought up. You can have several **up** lines for an interface; they are executed in turn. Figure A6.3 shows the **interfaces** file for the example network of Module 5.3.

Figure A6.3

Adding multiple routes for a single interface

```
iface lo inet loopback

iface eth0 inet static
        address 10.1.1.11
        netmask 255.255.255.0
        gateway 10.1.1.254
        up route add -net 10.2.2.0 netmask 255.255.255.0 gw 10.1.1.22
        up route add -net 10.0.0.0 netmask 255.255.0.0   gw 10.1.1.22
```

If the **interfaces** file is configured for more than one interface, add the **up** line to the interface whose sub-net includes the route's gateway. For example, if we were adding:

```
route add -net 10.2.2.0 netmask 255.255.255.0 gw 10.1.1.22
```

to the system in Figure A6.2, we would insert the **up** line into **eth1**'s section of the file.

The **interfaces** file also allows you to enter **down** lines for commands to be run just before the interface is taken down. We could add lines like:

```
down route delete -net 10.2.2.0/24 gw 10.1.1.22
```

to the file. However, the only time in normal running when we bring down the interface is when closing down the whole system, so **down** lines aren't really necessary in our case.

Configuring multiple IP addresses on one network card (Module 6.4)

Configuring multiple IP addresses on a single network card is straightforward too. For each extra address, insert an extra section into **/etc/network/interfaces**, naming them as *basename*:1, *basename*:2, ... , where *basename* is the name of the physical interface of the card. Figure A6.4 shows a file for a machine with two extra addresses for the **eth0** network card.

Figure A6.4

Configuring multiple IP addresses on the network card

```
# The loopback interface
iface lo inet loopback

# our only "real" network card
iface eth0 inet static
        address 192.0.2.5
        netmask 255.255.255.0
        gateway 192.0.2.77

# second addr on this network card
iface eth0:1 inet static
        address 10.2.2.222
        netmask 255.255.255.0

# third addr on this network card
iface eth0:2 inet static
        address 10.3.3.33
        netmask 255.255.255.0
```

DNS settings (Chapters 7 and 8)

In the main text we configured the DNS resolver by editing the file **/etc/resolv.conf**. These changes already persist across reboots of the system.

Setting the hostname (Module 8.14)

At boot time, Debian sets this machine's name to the value in the file **/etc/hostname**. For example, to set this machine's name to **dave** for the future, insert the name **dave** as the sole contents of the file **/etc/hostname**.

Name services switch (Module 9.4)

The file **/etc/nsswitch.conf** controls which methods are used to resolve hostnames, etc., and in which order. For example, if the file contains

```
hosts: files dns
```

when the resolver tries to resolve a host name, it will first read the **/etc/hosts** file, and if that doesn't contain the name we want it will then query a DNS server. For more detail see the **nsswitch.conf** manpage.

Configuring Linux to use DHCP (Module 16.5)

What we describe below is how DHCP works on a typical system with each of the three common DHCP clients. However, the interaction between your DHCP client and the rest of the system configuration may not be as clean as you'd like. Different versions may work slightly differently, especially if you have more than one client installed at the same time. Be warned!

Using pump as your DHCP client: in the file **/etc/network/interfaces** configure the interface(s) that are to use DHCP as type "**dhcp**" (Figure A6.5). This will start the client daemon at system startup time and the daemon will configure the interface(s).

```
iface lo inet loopback

iface eth0 inet dhcp
```

Figure A6.5 interfaces file configuring **eth0** to use DHCP

Using dhcpcd as your DHCP client: if **dhcpcd**'s own configuration file (**/etc/dhcpcd/config**) has a list of interfaces set in the variable **IFACE**, **dhcpcd** will start, and configure these interfaces. Alternatively, you can set **IFACE=none**, and instead configure the interface(s) as type "**dhcp**" in the file **/etc/networks/interfaces** (Figure A6.5). Then **ifup**(8) will start the client daemon at system startup time and the daemon will configure the interface(s).

Using dhclient as your DHCP client: the **dhclient** client daemon is started automatically at boot time, and finds all the network interfaces. Consequently there's no need to include any interface information in the file **/etc/networks/interfaces**. If you do include an interface in the file, e.g. as shown in Figure A6.5, you will end up with two copies of the client daemon running. (That's far from ideal, but fortunately it still works.)

On the following pages we cover the configuration for PCMCIA network cards.

PCMCIA network cards

The PCMCIA network interfaces are controlled by the script **/etc/pcmcia/network**, which in turn reads your particular settings from the file **/etc/pcmcia/network.opts**. **network.opts** is created by the Debian installation when you install the system, but you can edit the file yourself as required. Figure A6.6 shows a full example for a system that will have a single PCMCIA network card with a single IP address.

Figure A6.6
network.opts
file for a single
PCMCIA network
card

```
case "$ADDRESS" in
*,*,*,*)
        IF_PORT="auto"
        BOOTP="n"
        DHCLIENT="n"
        DHCPC="n"
        IPADDR="192.0.2.34"
        NETMASK="255.255.255.128"
        NETWORK="192.0.2.0"
        BROADCAST="192.0.2.127"
        GATEWAY="192.0.2.29"
        DOMAIN="example.com"
        DNS_1="192.0.2.19"
        DNS_2="192.0.2.39"
        DNS_3="192.0.2.59"
        ;;
esac
```

If you're using just a single PCMCIA card with a single interface, the only lines you have to edit or add are those that set the value of a variable, i.e. those containing "=".

Basic network settings (Module 2.11)

> **IF_PORT**: needed only if your PCMCIA card can't automatically detect the network transceiver type (e.g. Thick Ethernet, 10Mb/s UTP, …). Most cards can auto-detect
> **IPADDR, NETMASK**: the IP address and netmask for this interface
> **NETWORK**: the address of the network that this machine belongs to (Module 4.11). Not required for recent Linux versions
> **BROADCAST**: the broadcast address for the network that this machine belongs to (Module 4.10). (See the Warning regarding broadcast addresses in Chapter 4's Notes.)

The other lines in the file are explained below.

Setting your default gateway – Linux (Module 3.5)

In **network.opts** define **GATEWAY** to set the default gateway for this machine. As this applies to the machine as a whole and not a specific interface, it's usual to include its definition in the section for the first card that you will be using. If you have your system configured for multiple cards and you don't know the order in which they will be inserted, you can include the same **GATEWAY** setting in each of them.

Configuring multiple network cards (Module 3.7)

Configuring the settings for multiple PCMCIA network cards is easy. However, we must first explain a little more about how **network.opts** works. It's not a plain configuration file: it is in fact a shell script. The PCMCIA runs it at system startup time, or when a card is inserted or ejected, and passes to it the variable **$ADDRESS**, which specifies details of the card to be configured. **network.opts** uses **$ADDRESS** to select which settings are to be applied to a particular card: the case statement in the script matches **$ADDRESS** against patterns that you specify – one pattern per card that you will want configured. **$ADDRESS** consists of four fields separated by commas and no spaces:

    scheme,socket-number,instance-number,MAC-address

The contents of the fields are:

1. the PCMCIA "scheme," which we'll ignore. (It lets you set up different configurations for different environments. For example, you could have schemes for "at-home," "in-the-office," and "on-the-road.")
2. the PCMCIA socket number that the card occupies. **0** is the first socket, **1** the second, …
3. the device instance, for cards that have several physical interfaces. We'll ignore this too since most cards provide only one physical interface
4. this card's MAC (e.g. Ethernet) address.

By specifying patterns that match specific parts of **$ADDRESS** you can identify a particular card and configure it accordingly. For example, Figure A6.7a configures cards by socket number, whereas Figure A6.7b configures cards with specific MAC addresses.

Figure A6.7
Configuring
cards (a) by
socket number
and (b) with
specific MAC
addresses

```
case "$ADDRESS" in
*,0,*,*)
    # NIC in socket 0
    IPADDR=192.0.2.44
    NETMASK=255.255.255.0
    ;;
*,1,*,*)
    # NIC in socket 1
    IPADDR=192.0.2.77
    NETMASK=255.255.255.0
    ;;
esac
```

```
(b)  case "$ADDRESS" in
*,*,*,00:50:DA:E4:61:34)
    # our 3Com 574 10/100 card
    IPADDR=192.0.2.44
    NETMASK=255.255.255.0
    ;;
*,*,*,00:10:5a:8b:1f:86)
    # our 3Com 589 10Mb card
    IPADDR=10.2.2.222
    NETMASK=255.255.255.0
    ;;
esac
```

By contrast, the configuration in Figure A6.6 is intended to handle only a single card, so there is only one pattern – *,*,*,* – which matches any value of **$ADDRESS**.

Note that each pattern ends with ")" and the set of configuration items for a card is terminated with ";;".

Of course the settings for default gateway domain, searchlist, and DNS servers apply to the machine as a whole, not to a specific network card, so you typically define them only for the first card.

If you configure **network.opts** for only one card and then insert a second card, what happens depends on your precise configuration. If your only pattern is the default – *,*,*,* – both cards will use the same configuration, giving you the same IP address on each (unless you're using DHCP). If your pattern is more specific – e.g. *,**0**,*,* to configure only socket 0 – then the second interface will exist but will not be configured "up".

Adding routes (Module 5.3)

network.opts has a similar mechanism to the **interfaces** file's **up** and **down** lines, to run commands when an interface is brought up or down. However, the syntax is more complicated. When a PCMCIA interface is brought up, the PCMCIA subsystem executes the function **start_fn**, and it executes **stop_fn** just before it's brought down. You define these functions in **network.opts** to contain whatever commands you want run. Figure A6.8 shows an example, creating a route when the single interface is brought up, and removing it before it's brought down.

Figure A6.8 start_fn( ) adds a route for a particular card, and **stop_fn( )** deletes the route

```
case "$ADDRESS" in
*,*,*,*)
    IPADDR=192.0.2.44
    NETMASK=255.255.255.0
    start_fn()
    {
        route add -net 10.3.3.0 netmask 255.255.255.0 gw 192.0.2.22
        return;
    }
    stop_fn()
    {
        route del -net 10.3.3.0 netmask 255.255.255.0 gw 192.0.2.22
        return;
    }
    ;;
esac
```

If you don't dynamically insert or delete cards, you can omit the **stop_fn** because the only time the interface will be brought down is when you're shutting down your machine.

Configuring multiple IP addresses on one network card (Module 6.4)

To configure more than one address on a PCMCIA card, you again use **start_fn**. When the PCMCIA subsystem calls **start_fn**, it passes the name of the interface being configured in the variable **$DEVICE**, as, for example, **eth0** or **eth1**. You can use this to automatically derive names like **eth1:2** and **eth0:3** in your **start_fn**. Figure A6.9 shows **network.opts** for a single PCMCIA card with two extra IP addresses; we have kept the **route** command from the previous example to show that **start_fn** can contain many, relatively unrelated commands. Because we're using only one card we know that **$DEVICE** will be **eth0** so we could have hard-coded the device names as **eth0:1** and **eth0:2** but using **$DEVICE** is safer in case we use multiple cards later on. (Note that this has nothing to do with the "device instance" that we mentioned in item 3 on the previous page).

Figure A6.9 network.opts for a single PCMCIA card with two extra IP addresses

```
case "$ADDRESS" in
*,*,*,*)
    IPADDR=192.0.2.44
    NETMASK=255.255.255.0
    start_fn()
    {
        ifconfig $DEVICE:1 10.4.4.44 netmask 255.255.255.0
        ifconfig $DEVICE:2 192.168.168.44 netmask 255.255.255.0
        route add -net 10.3.3.0 netmask 255.255.255.0 gw 192.0.2.22
        return;
    }
    ;;
esac
```

> **Warning:** syntax errors in **network.opts** will cause program errors in the PCMCIA startup/closedown, because **network.opts** is a executable script. PCMCIA error messages and other output are logged to the **syslog** service (Module 17.12) and can usually be seen in the file **/var/log/syslog**, although this will depend on your syslog configuration. A typical message looks like:
>
>   … ./network: ./network.opts: line 12: syntax error near unexpected token ';'
>
> and your network will not have been initialized properly.

DNS settings (Chapters 7 and 8)

The PCMCIA subsystem dynamically modifies the **/etc/resolv.conf** file, according to the settings found in **/etc/pcmcia/network.opts**, so you can take two different approaches:

1. omit all DNS settings from **network.opts** and edit **resolv.conf** as normal
2. specify your DNS settings in **network.opts** so they are dynamically set with the rest of the configuration options for your PCMCIA card

As method 2 is the "official" way to do things, it's best to use it, if only for the sake of other administrators who may have to work on your machine. However, if your laptop isn't mobile and you use it in place of a normal desktop workstation, using method 1 is unlikely to cause you problems.

To configure the DNS resolver settings in **network.opts**, set the following variables:

DOMAIN: the name of the DNS domain that this machine belongs to, to be used as the **domain** setting in **resolv.conf**

SEARCH: the DNS searchlist to be used as the **search** setting in **resolv.conf**

DNS_1, DNS_2, DNS_3: any of these that you define are included as **nameserver** settings in **resolv.conf** (Module 7.3).

Setting the hostname (Module 8.14)

As for a normal network card, above.

Name services switch (Module 9.4)

As for a normal network card, above.

DHCP configuration – PCMCIA (Module 16.5)

There are two slightly different methods for configuring a interface to use DHCP, depending on which version of the PCMCIA software is included in your version of Linux. For both, enter the configuration details in **/etc/pcmcia/network.opts** file as usual in the section for the interface you're configuring. In newer versions (early 2000 onwards) you just set

```
DHCP="y"
```

and the PCMCIA sub-system looks in order for **dhcpcd**, then **dhclient**, and finally **pump**, and uses the first one it finds.

In the older version, configure as shown below to use the different DHCP clients:

Client	Set these variables
pump	PUMP="y" (*others don't matter*)
dhclient	DHCP="y" DHCLIENT="y" PUMP="n"
dhcpcd	DHCP="y" DHCLIENT="n" PUMP="n"

To tell which version you've got, look at the unmodified, installed **network.opts**. Only the older versions use specific **DHCLIENT** and **PUMP** variables. (If you've lost the original file, you can run **/usr/sbin/pcnetconfig** to recreate it. And if you can read shell scripts, looking at that file will tell you whether you've got the old or the new PCMCIA version.)

Of course, you should now omit from **network.opts** any settings that will be handled by DHCP. (If you leave the **IPADDR** variable defined, it will overwrite any settings that have been obtained via DHCP, which is almost certainly not what you want.)

You may need to set the variable **DHCP_HOSTNAME** if your ISP requires it.

We have found problems getting older versions of **dhclient** working with older versions of the PCMCIA software. We got over these by downloading the latest **dhclient** sources from the ISC site and building them ourselves, rather than using a pre-compiled package. We also found it helpful to use the most recent PCMCIA package from the Debian site.

Notes and further reading

Older versions of Debian (before release 2.2) used a different convention for configuration files and startup scripts. Instead of the **interfaces** file and the **ifup** and **ifdown** programs, the shell script **/etc/init.d/network** was run to configure interfaces and routes.

For PCMCIA information for Linux see:

❑ **http://pcmcia-cs.sourceforge.net/** *Linux PCMCIA Information Page*

❑ **http://pcmcia-cs.sourceforge.net/ftp/doc/** to download or view the latest PCMCIA "howto"

❑ **http://tldp.org/HOWTO/PCMCIA-HOWTO.html** the same as above but may not be quite up to date

When testing your PCMCIA configuration, you can use the commands "**cardctl eject**" and "**cardctl insert**" instead of physically ejecting and inserting your card(s) to see how a new configuration works. However, if you're using DHCP with PCMCIA we recommend you also do a full reboot to make sure you really do have the configuration that you want.

❑ **http://www.isc.org/products/DHCP/** to download **dhclient** client software

You may come across a problem when using a Linux client with a Microsoft DHCP server, where the string "\000" is appended to the **domain** or **search** values for the

resolv.conf file, which breaks name resolution on the DHCP client. Workarounds are to either:

- use a different DHCP server, or
- modify your DHCP client configuration so that the DNS values are manually overridden. For example, in **dhclient.conf** use the **supersede** statement to specify the correct values, as in

```
supersede domain-name "tech.example.com"
```

In **pump.conf** specify **nodns**, and manually insert the values you require in **resolv.conf**.

Appendix 7 UTP and null-modem wiring

RJ45 plug pin numbers

Pins are numbered from 1 to 8, from left to right, as you look at the plug from the front, with the clip above and the cable behind:

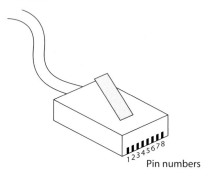

Pin numbers

Normal ("straight-through") UTP cable (RJ45 plugs)

Both ends are wired identically.

Pin No.	Wire Color
1	white, orange stripe
2	orange, white stripe
3	white, green stripe
4	blue, white stripe
5	white, blue stripe
6	green, white stripe
7	white, brown stripe
8	brown, white stripe

Cross-over UTP cable (RJ45 plugs)

End 1 is wired as above, but end 2 is wired differently.

End 1		End 2	
Pin No.	Wire Color	Pin No.	Wire Color
1	white, orange stripe	1	white, green stripe
2	orange, white stripe	2	green, white stripe
3	white, green stripe	3	white, orange stripe
4	blue, white stripe	4	blue, white stripe
5	white, blue stripe	5	white, blue stripe
6	green, white stripe	6	orange, white stripe
7	white, brown stripe	7	white, brown stripe
8	brown, white stripe	8	brown, white stripe

Special read-only UTP cable

To make a UTP cable that can receive but can't transmit, see:

❑ http://www.robertgraham.com/pubs/sniffing-faq.html#receive-only

❑ http://home.ie.cuhk.edu.hk/~msng0/sniffing_cable/

Null-modem serial cables

There are many variants for null-modem cables. These are the ones we've used. For others see:

❑ http://www.microsoft.com/windows2000/en/professional/help/sag_MODEconcepts_
133.htm *Null modem cabling*

DB9–DB25

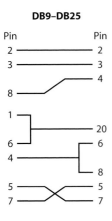

DB9–DB9

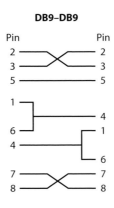

DB25–DB25

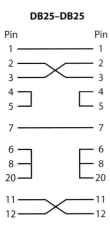

Appendix 8 Windows-NT route command manpage

Name

> **route** – display or modify this machine's routing tables

Synopsis

> **route** [-f] [-p] *command* *destination* **mask** *netmask* *gateway* **metric** *value* **if** *interface*

Options

> -f flush all "gateway" entries (i.e. not entries for directly connected networks). This may be used on its own or in conjunction with a *command*.
>
> -p used with the **add** command to make the specified route permanent (persist across reboots of the system). By default routes added are not persistent.

Commands

> **print** [*destination* [**mask** *netmask*]]
>
> > with no arguments, prints the entire routing table. With arguments *destination* or *destination* **mask** *netmask*, prints matching routes.
>
> **add** *destination gateway* [**metric** *value*] [**if** *interface*]
>
> **add** *destination* [**mask** *netmask*] *gateway* [**metric** *value*] [**if** *interface*]
>
> > creates a static route to *destination* via router *gateway*. If the **mask** arguments are given, the route is for a range of addresses specified by the combination of *destination* and *netmask*; otherwise it's for the single host with address *destination*. You can explicitly specify the network interface although usually that isn't necessary.
> >
> > The **metric** arguments can indicate a preference between routes that would otherwise be equally applicable; the higher the **metric** value, the less preferred the route.
>
> **delete** *destination* [**mask** *netmask*] [*gateway*]
>
> > delete all matching routes. If a deleted route was persistent it is deleted permanently, i.e. the deletion is persistent too.
>
> **change** *destination* [**mask** *netmask*] *gateway* [**metric** *value*] [**if** *interface*]
>
> > modify the specified route. Only one of the arguments should differ from the existing values, so that **route** can identify the entry you wish to change.

Notes

> 1. when you specify a range with *destination* **mask** *netmask*, the *destination* must be the network address (the lowest IP number in the specified range); otherwise you get an error, e.g. to create a route for the 16 addresses 10.1.2.22/240, the correct command is:
>
> > **route add 10.1.2.16 mask 255.255.255.240 192.0.2.77**
>
> whereas
>
> > **route add 10.1.2.22 mask 255.255.255.240 192.0.2.77**
>
> complains "The route addition failed: 87"
>
> 2. *destination* and *gateway* can be specified as host names instead of IP numbers
>
> 3. you can use wildcards in *destination*: * matches any string of characters, and ? matches any one character.

Appendix 9 Example of working network diagram

This is a diagram we drew on-site when implementing a customer's network. The IP numbers have been changed to protect the innocent. The notation *num-1* ≡ *num-2* indicates 1-to-1 NAT (mapped) IP addresses.

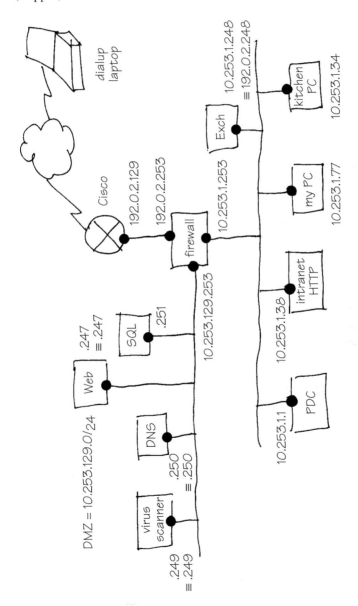

Appendix 10 Our on-site toolkit

Hubs

- 3 × Ethernet hubs (four-port) plus transformers

Laptop computers, etc.

- 1 × laptop PC, usually running Linux
- 1 × laptop PC, usually running Windows-NT
- 3 × PCMCIA Ethernet adapters

Both laptops are in fact configured as "multi-boot:" they each have full installations of Windows-NT, Windows-98, and Linux and at boot time we can choose which operating system to run. We normally use a Linux machine with two PCMCIA cards as our sniffer (and it can act as a temporary router if necessary), and we use the Windows PC for Web browsing, sending test e-mails, etc.

Modem

- external modem with transformer
- modem-to-phone connector
- modem-to-PC cable

Cables

- 6 × 50-cm straight-through UTP cables of different colors
- 1 × cross-over UTP cable (red)
- 25pin–25pin serial cable to connect to serial port of firewall appliances
- 25pin–9pin serial cable adapter
- 3 × gender changers (one each: M/M, M/F, F/F)

Documentation

- **tcpdump** manpage (on Linux PC)
- test matrix (Appendix 25) several copies

Software

- **tcpdump**
- **ethereal**
- **Windows Network Monitor**
- the three latest versions of the firewall software/firmware if we're installing a firewall
- VPN client for Windows-98 and Windows-NT
- WinZip, **gzip**, and **tar**, for unpacking software distributions

Miscellaneous

- labels – for labeling cables and hubs during testing

Appendix 11 nslookup **manpage in full**

NAME

>   nslookup – query Internet name servers interactively

SYNOPSIS

>   nslookup [-option ...] [host-to-find | -[server]]

DESCRIPTION

>   Nslookup is a program to query Internet domain name servers. Nslookup has two modes: interactive and non-interactive. Interactive mode allows the user to query name servers for information about various hosts and domains or to print a list of hosts in a domain. Non-interactive mode is used to print just the name and requested information for a host or domain.

ARGUMENTS

>   Interactive mode is entered in the following cases:
>
>   a) when no arguments are given (the default name server will be used),
>
>   b) when the first argument is a hyphen (-) and the second argument is the host name or Internet address of a name server.
>
>   Non-interactive mode is used when the name or Internet address of the host to be looked up is given as the first argument. The optional second argument specifies the host name or address of a name server.
>
>   The options listed under the "set" command below can be specified in the .nslookuprc file in the user's home directory if they are listed one per line. Options can also be specified on the command line if they precede the arguments and are prefixed with a hyphen. For example, to change the default query type to host information, and the initial timeout to 10 seconds, type:
>
> ```
>     nslookup -query=hinfo -timeout=10
> ```

INTERACTIVE COMMANDS

>   Commands may be interrupted at any time by typing a control-C. To exit, type a control-D (EOF) or type exit. The command line length must be less than 256 characters. To treat a built-in command as a host name, precede it with an escape character (backslash). An unrecognized command will be interpreted as a host name.

host [*server*]

> Look up information for *host* using the current default server or using *server*, if specified. If *host* is an Internet address and the query type is A or PTR, the name of the host is returned. If *host* is a name and does not have a trailing period, the default domain name is appended to the name. (This behavior depends on the state of the **set** options **domain**, **srchlist**, **defname**, and **search**.)

> To look up a host not in the current domain, append a period to the name.

server *domain*

lserver *domain*

> Change the default server to *domain*; **lserver** uses the initial server to look up information about *domain*, while **server** uses the current default server. If an authoritative answer can't be found, the names of servers that might have the answer are returned.

root   Changes the default server to the server for the root of the domain name space. Currently, the host ns.internic.net is used. (This command is a synonym for "**lserver ns.internic.net**".) The name of the root server can be changed with the "**set root**" command.

finger   [*name*] [> *filename*]

finger   [*name*] [>> *filename*]

> Connects with the finger server on the current host. The current host is defined when a previous lookup for a host was successful and returned address information (see the "**set querytype**=A" command). The *name* is optional. > and >> can be used to redirect output in the usual manner.

ls [*option*] *domain* [> *filename*]

ls [*option*] *domain* [>> *filename*]

> List the information available for *domain*, optionally creating or appending to *filename*. The default output contains host names and their Internet addresses. *Option* can be one of the following:

-**t** *querytype*
> lists all records of the specified type (see *querytype* below).

-**a**   lists aliases of hosts in the domain; synonym for "-**t** CNAME".

-**d**   lists all records for the domain; synonym for "-**t** ANY".

-**h**   lists CPU and operating system information for the domain;
synonym for "-**t** HINFO".

-**s**   lists well-known services of hosts in the domain; synonym for
"-**t** WKS".

When output is directed to a file, hash marks are printed for every 50
records received from the server.

view *filename*
> Sorts and lists the output of previous **ls** command(s) with more(1).

help

?   Prints a brief summary of commands.

exit   Exits the program.

set *keyword*[=*value*]
> This command is used to change state information that affects the lookups.
> Valid keywords are:

all   Prints the current values of the frequently-used options to **set**.
Information about the current default server and host is also
printed.

class=*value*
> Change the query class to one of:
> IN   the Internet class
> CHAOS   the Chaos class
> HESIOD   the MIT Athena Hesiod class
> ANY   wildcard (any of the above)
> The class specifies the protocol group of the information.
> (Default = IN; abbreviation = **cl**)

[**no**]**debug**
> Turn debugging mode on. A lot more information is printed
> about the packet sent to the server and the resulting answer.
>
> (Default = **nodebug**; abbreviation = [**no**]**deb**)

[**no**]**d2**   Turn exhaustive debugging mode on. Essentially all fields of
every packet are printed.

> (Default = **nod2**)

domain=*name*

Chance the default domain name to *name*. The default domain name is appended to a lookup request depending on the state of the **defname** and **search** options. The domain search list contains the parents of the default domain if it has at least two components in its name. For example, if the default domain is CC.Berkeley.EDU, the search list is CC.Berkeley.EDU and Berkeley.EDU. Use the "**set srchlist**" command to specify a different list. Use the "**set all**" command to display the list.

(Default = value from hostname(1), /etc/resolv.conf, or LOCALDOMAIN; abbreviation = **do**)

srchlist=*name1/name2/...*

Change the default domain name to *name1* and the domain search list to *name1*, *name2*, etc. A maximum of 6 names separated by slashes (/) can be specified. For example,

```
set srchlist=lcs.MIT.EDU/ai.MIT.EDU/MIT.EDU
```

sets the domain to lcs.MIT.EDU and the search list to the three names. This command overrides the default domain name and search list of the "**set domain**" command. Use the "**set all**" command to display the list.

(Default = value based on hostname(1), /etc/resolv.conf, or LOCALDOMAIN; abbreviation = **srchl**)

[no]defname

If set, append the default domain name to a single-component lookup request (i.e., one that does not contain a period).

(Default = **defname**; abbreviation = **[no]defname**)

[no]search

If the lookup request contains at least one period but *doesn't* end with a trailing period, append the domain names in the domain search list to the request until an answer is received.

(Default = **search**; abbreviation = **[no]sea**)

port=*value*

Change the default TCP/UDP name server port to *value*.

(Default = 53; abbreviation = **po**)

querytype=*value*

type=*value*

Change the type of information query to one of:

A	the host's Internet address.
CNAME	the canonical name for an alias.
HINFO	the host CPU and operating system type.
MINFO	the mailbox or mail list information.
MX	the mail exchanger.
NS	the name server for the named zone.
PTR	the host name if the query is an Internet address; otherwise, the pointer to other information.
SOA	the domain's "start-of-authority" information.
TXT	the text information.
UINFO	the user information.
WKS	the supported well-known services.

Other types (ANY, AXFR, MB, MD, MF, NULL) are described in the RFC-1035 document.

(Default = A; abbreviations = **q**, **ty**)

[no]recurse

Tell the name server to query other servers if it does not have the information.

(Default = **recurse**; abbreviation = **[no]rec**)

retry=*number*

Set the number of retries to *number*. When a reply to a request is not received within a certain amount of time (changed with "**set timeout**"), the timeout period is doubled and the request is resent. The retry value controls how many times a request is resent before giving up.

(Default = 4, abbreviation = **ret**)

root=*host*

Change the name of the root server to *host*. This affects the "**root**" command.

(Default= **ns.internic.net.**; abbreviation= **ro**)

timeout=*number*

Change the initial timeout interval for waiting for a reply to *number* seconds. Each retry doubles the timeout period.

(Default = 5 seconds; abbreviation = **ti**)

[**no**] **vc**   Always use a virtual circuit when sending requests to the server.

(Default = **novc**; abbreviation = [**no**] **v**)

[**no**] **ignoretc**

Ignore packet truncation errors.

(Default = **noignoretc**; abbreviation = [**no**] **ig**)

DIAGNOSTICS

If the lookup request was not successful, an error message is printed. Possible errors are:

Timed out

The server did not respond to a request after a certain amount of time (changed with "**set timeout**=*value*") and a certain number of retries (changed with "**set retry**=*value*").

No response from server

No name server is running on the server machine.

No records

The server does not have resource records of the current query type for the host, although the host name is valid. The query type is specified with the "**set querytype**" command.

Non-existent domain

The host or domain name does not exist.

Connection refused

Network is unreachable

The connection to the name or finger server could not be made at the current time. This error commonly occurs with **ls** and **finger** requests.

Server failure

The name server found an internal inconsistency in its database and could not return a valid answer.

`Refused`
> The name server refused to service the request.

`Format error`
> The name server found that the request packet was not in the proper format.
> It may indicate an error in **nslookup**.

FILES

`/etc/resolv.conf`	initial domain name and name server addresses
`$HOME/.nslookuprc`	user's initial options
`/usr/share/misc/nslookup.help`	summary of commands

ENVIRONMENT

`HOSTALIASES`	file containing host aliases
`LOCALDOMAIN`	overrides default domain

SEE ALSO

`named`(8), `resolver`(3), `resolver`(5); RFC-1034, "Domain Names – Concepts and Facilities"; RFC-1035, "Domain Names – Implementation and Specification".

AUTHOR

Andrew Cherenson

Appendix 12 host **manpage summary**

The following is a summary of only the most commonly used options and arguments. For full details, see the **host** manpage on your Linux system.

NAME

> **host** – query nameserver about domain names and zones

SYNOPSIS

> host [-v] [-a] [-t querytype] [options] name [server]
>
> host [-v] [-a] [-t querytype] [options] -l zone [server]
>
> host [-v] [options] -A host
>
> host [options] -x [name ...]
>
> host [options] -X server [name ...]

DESCRIPTION

> **host** looks for information about Internet hosts and domain names using the DNS.
>
> By default, the program simply converts between host names and Internet addresses. However, with the -t, -a, and -v options, it can be used to find all of the information about domain names that is maintained by the domain name server system.
>
> The arguments can be either host names (domain names) or numeric Internet addresses.
>
> The default action is to look up the associated host name for an IP number, and vice versa.
>
> For single names without a trailing dot, the local domain is automatically tacked on the end. Thus a user in domain "nikhef.nl" can say "host nikhapo", and it will actually look up "nikhapo.nikhef.nl". In all other cases, the name is tried unchanged. Single names with a trailing dot are considered top-level domain specifications, e.g. "nl."
>
> Note that the usual lookup convention for any name that does not end with a trailing dot is to try first with the local domain appended, and possibly other search domains. (As of BIND 4.9, names that have embedded dots but no trailing dot are first tried "as is" before appending search domains) This convention is not used by this program.
>
> The actual suffix to tack on the end is usually the local domain as specified in the **/etc/resolv.conf** file, but this can be overridden.

ARGUMENTS

The first argument is normally the host name (domain name) for which you want to look up the requested information. If the first argument is an Internet address, a query is done on the special "reverse mapping" domain to look up its associated host name.

If the -l option is given, the first argument is a domain zone name for which a complete listing is given. The program enters a special zone listing mode, which has several variants.

The second argument is optional. It allows you to specify a particular server to query. If you don't specify this argument, default servers are used, as defined by the **/etc/resolv.conf** file.

EXTENDED SYNTAX

If the -**x** option is given, it extends the syntax in the sense that multiple arguments are allowed on the command line. An optional explicit server must now be specified using the -**X** option as it cannot be given as an ordinary argument any more. The -**X** option implies -**x**.

The extended syntax allows no arguments at all, in which case the arguments will be read from standard input. This can be a pipe, redirection from a file, or an interactive terminal. Note that these arguments are the names to be queried, and not command options. Everything that appears after a "#" or ";" on an input line will be skipped. Multiple arguments per line are allowed.

COMMONLY USED OPTIONS

-**v** list information in "verbose" format. (Without this option, the ttl and class fields are not shown.) Also the contents of the "additional information" and "authoritative nameservers" sections in the answer from the nameserver are printed, if present. Normally these sections are not shown.

-**vv** very verbose

-**t** querytype: allows you to specify a particular type of resource record information to be looked up. Supported types are listed below. The wildcard may be written as either ANY or *. Types may be given in upper or lower case. The default is type A for regular lookups, and A, NS, and PTR for zone listings.

-**a** is equivalent to -**t** ANY. Note that this gives you "anything available" (currently cached) and not "all defined data" if a non-authoritative server is queried.

SPECIAL MODES

The following options put the program in a special mode:

-**l** zone: generates the listing of an entire zone.

-**A** enters a special address check mode.

COMMON OPTIONS

The following options can be used in both normal mode and domain listing mode.

-d turns on debugging. Nameserver transactions are shown in detail. Note that **-dd** prints even more debugging output.

-q be quiet and suppress various warning messages (the ones preceded by "!!!"). Serious error messages (preceded by "***") are never suppressed.

-T prints the time-to-live values during non-verbose out-put. By default the ttl is shown only in verbose mode.

-Z prints the selected resource record output in full zone file format, including trailing dot in domain names, plus ttl value and class name.

OTHER OPTIONS

The following options are used only in special circumstances.

-r causes nameserver recursion to be turned off in the request.

-R normally querynames are assumed to be fully qualified and are tried as such, unless it is a single name, which is always tried (and only once) in the default domain. This option simulates the default BIND behavior by qualifying any specified name by repeatedly adding search domains, with the exception that the search terminates immediately if the name exists but does not have the desired querytype. The default search domains are constructed from the default domain by repeatedly peeling off the first component, until a final domain with only one dot remains.

-u forces the use of virtual circuits (TCP) instead of datagrams (UDP) when issuing nameserver queries.

-V prints just the version number of the host program, and exits.

DEFAULT OPTIONS

Default options and parameters can be preset in an environment variable HOST_DEFAULTS using the same syntax as on the command line. They will be evaluated before the command line arguments.

QUERY TYPES

See full manpage.

WARNING and ERROR MESSAGE

See full manpage.

EXIT STATUS

The program returns a zero exit status if the requested information could be retrieved successfully, or in case zone listings or SOA checks were performed without any serious error. Otherwise it returns a non-zero exit status.

AUTHOR

This program is originally from Rutgers University.

Rewritten by Eric Wassenaar, NIKHEF, <e07@nikhef.nl>

Appendix 13 Base64 encoding

Base64 encoding lets you transform arbitrary 8-bit data into a series of printing characters without losing any information. This is used in e-mail and other applications to allow binary data to be transmitted safely over links that might not be able to handle binary data otherwise.

Here's how Base64 works:

- split the input into chunks of three characters at a time (i.e. 24 bits)
- divide each 24-bit chunk into four pieces of 6 bits each. The number of different values that can be stored in 6 bits is $2^6 = 64$ (hence Base64)
- look up each 6-bit value in the table below, and output the corresponding character. (In the table heading, **I** means "input", **O** means "output".)
- if the last input chunk consists of only one or two bytes (i.e. only 8 or 16 bits) it's padded out with four or two 0-bits respectively, to make it up to a multiple of 6-bits, and the output is padded at the end with two or one "=" characters, respectively.

I	O	I	O	I	O	I	O
0	A	17	R	34	i	51	z
1	B	18	S	35	j	52	0
2	C	19	T	36	k	53	1
3	D	20	U	37	l	54	2
4	E	21	V	38	m	55	3
5	F	22	W	39	n	56	4
6	G	23	X	40	o	57	5
7	H	24	Y	41	p	58	6
8	I	25	Z	42	q	59	7
9	J	26	a	43	r	60	8
10	K	27	b	44	s	61	9
11	L	28	c	45	t	62	+
12	M	29	d	46	u	63	/
13	N	30	e	47	v		
14	O	31	f	48	w		
15	P	32	g	49	x		
16	Q	33	h	50	y		

Examples

Let's take an example, with the input string "**Cat**". The output is **Q2F0** generated as follows:

input, shown as characters	C	a		t
input, decimal equivalent	67	97		116
input, convert to binary	01000011	01100001		01110100
break into 6-bit chunks	010000	110110	000101	110100
convert to decimal	16	54	5	52
base64 output from table	Q	2	F	0

Here's another example, not a multiple of three characters in length, so padding will be necessary at the end:

Input: **Cats**

Output: **Q2F0cw==**

The first four output characters are derived exactly as above, because the first three input characters are identical. The rest of the output is generated as follows:

input, shown as characters	s			
input, decimal equivalent	115			
input, convert to binary	01110011			
pad with 0-bits to multiple of 6-bit chunks	01110011	0000		
break into 6-bit chunks	011100	110000		
convert to decimal values	28	48	*pad*	*pad*
base64 output from table	c	w	=	=

Base64 output is about 33% bigger than the original, which is what you'd expect when you use a full 8-bit character in the output to represent 6 bits of the input.

Notes and further reading

❑ **RFC-1113 August 1989** *Privacy Enhancement for Internet Electronic Mail.* This was the first description in the RFCs of Base-64 encoding, although it isn't called that; it's referred to as "printable encoding."

Base64 as such is described in:

❑ **RFC-1521 September 1993** *MIME (Multipurpose Internet Mail Extensions) Part One*

❑ **RFC-2045 November 1996,** *Internet Message Bodies*

Appendix 14 Nested MIME attachments

This is based on an example in RFC-2046. If the content of Figure A14.1 is sent as a message, it's seen in Outlook Express as shown in Figure A14.2. Figure A14.3 shows how the delimiters structure the message into multiple and nested attachments.

Figure A14.1

Contents of a message with nested MIME attachments

```
MIME-Version: 1.0
From: fred@example.com
To: jim@example.com
Date: Sat, 23 Mar 2002 12:15:17 +0000 (GMT)
Subject: A multipart example
Content-Type: multipart/mixed; boundary=unique-boundary-1

This is the preamble area of a multipart message.
Mail readers that understand multipart format
should ignore this preamble.

If you are reading this text, you might want to
consider changing to a mail reader that understands
how to properly display multipart messages.

--unique-boundary-1

This is the first attachment.

(Note that the blank between the boundary and the start of the text in
this part means no header fields were given and this is text in the
US-ASCII character set.)

--unique-boundary-1
Content-type: text/plain; charset=US-ASCII

This could have been part of the previous part, but illustrates
explicit versus implicit content-type specification for body parts.

--unique-boundary-1
Content-Type: multipart/parallel; boundary=another-separator

--another-separator
Content-Type: audio/basic
Content-Transfer-Encoding: base64

       [audio data goes here]

--another-separator
Content-Type: message/rfc822

From: jane@example.com
To: mary@example.com
Subject: hi!
Date: Fri, 22 Mar 2002 12:34:56 +0000 (GMT)
Content-Type: Text/plain; charset=ISO-8859-1
Content-Transfer-Encoding: Quoted-printable

Hello Mary.

--another-separator
Content-Type: image/jpeg
Content-Transfer-Encoding: base64

       [image data goes here ...]

--another-separator--

--unique-boundary-1
Content-type: text/enriched

This is <bold><italic>enriched.</italic></bold>
<smaller>as defined in RFC 1896</smaller>

Isn't it
<bigger><bigger>cool?</bigger></bigger>

--unique-boundary-1--
```

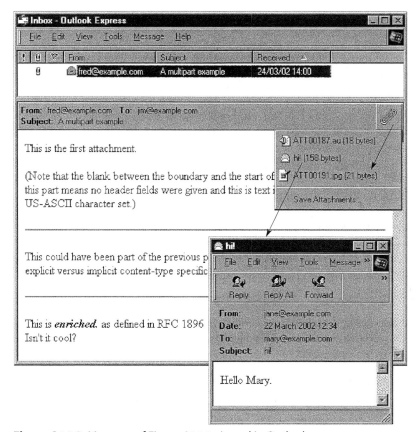

Figure A14.2 Message of Figure A14.1 viewed in Outlook express

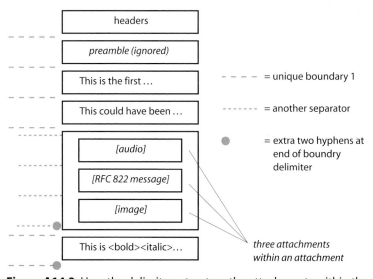

Figure A14.3 How the delimiters structure the attachments within the message

Appendix 15 Example of an IMAP session

In Figure A15.1 we connect, using **telnet**, to the IMAP well-known port on server Bob. As with POP and SMTP examples, we have indented the server's responses for clarity and truncated some of the lines to save space.

A difference from POP and SMTP is that when you enter an IMAP command, you have to prefix it with a *tag* – a text string used as a label. (You can use any old strings, as long as each is unique within this session.) When the IMAP server responds to a command, it prefixes the output with that command's tag, to indicate what the output relates to. This is necessary because the IMAP client/server interaction is asynchronous, i.e. the responses to commands are not necessarily output in the same order as the input commands, and you can enter another command before an earlier command completes. The reason for this is that some IMAP commands (e.g. large searches) can take a long time, and the server may not respond immediately, but *will* allow you to enter further commands. Commands that output multiple lines display an asterisk ("*") as the tag on all output lines except the last, which displays the input tag as usual, followed by **OK** if the command succeeded, or **BAD** if it failed.

Here's a line-by-line explanation of the session in Figure A15.1:

- **a1** login as user **bex15** and give the password. (**a1** is the first unique tag we decided to use.) The server replies that we have logged in OK, prefixing the response with the same tag that we input – **a1**

- **a2** **SELECT** specifies the mailbox we want to use, **/htiw/imap/mbox** in this case. The server replies that this mailbox contains three messages, and gives other details too

- **a3** **SEARCH** this mailbox for any messages whose SUBJECT header contains the word "elephants" and whose FROM header contains "snit". We could have specified extra criteria just by appending them, e.g. SUBJECT "elephants" TO "**fred@aw.com**" NOT FROM "**bex8@uit.co.uk**" The server replies with the numbers of the matching messages – numbers 2 and 3 in this example

- **a4** **FETCH** messages 2 and 3 and list the headers we specified

- **a5** tell me the MIME structure of message 1. (We've edited the output to show the structure more clearly. Normally this isn't seen by humans so its visual formatting is unimportant.)
  This message is a **multipart/mixed** with a text attachment and a GIF file attachment

- **a6** retrieve only the first (plain text) attachment of message 1. This attachment reads "This message has one line of text and a small GIF image attached."

- **a7** logout.

```
alice# telnet bob imap
Trying 192.0.2.63..
Connected to localhost.
Escape character is '^]'.
 * OK localhost IMAP4rev1 v12.264 server ready
a1 login bex15 xxx
 a1 OK LOGIN completed
a2 SELECT /htiw/imap/mbox
 * 3 EXISTS
 * 0 RECENT
 * OK [UIDVALIDITY 995036481] UID validity status
 * OK [UIDNEXT 4] Predicted next UID
 * FLAGS (\Answered \Flagged \Deleted \Draft \Seen)
 * OK [PERMANENTFLAGS (\* \Answered \Flagged \Deleted \Draft \Seen)] Permane
 a2 OK [READ-WRITE] SELECT completed
a3 SEARCH SUBJECT "elephants" FROM "snit"
 * SEARCH 2 3
 a3 OK SEARCH completed
a4 FETCH 2,3 (BODY[HEADER.FIELDS (DATE FROM TO SUBJECT)])
 * 2 FETCH (BODY[HEADER.FIELDS ("DATE" "FROM" "TO" "SUBJECT")] {142}
From: "Trudo von Snit" trudo@example.com
Date: Fri, 13 Jul 2001 15:51:46 +0100
To: bex15@uit.co.uk
Subject: Mice are desktop elephants

 )
 * 3 FETCH (BODY[HEADER.FIELDS ("DATE" "FROM" "TO" "SUBJECT")] {167}
From: "Trudo von Snit" trudo@example.com
Date: Fri, 13 Jul 2001 15:52:31 +0100
To: bex15@uit.co.uk
Subject: Assembler programmers hunt elephants on their knees

 )
 a4 OK FETCH completed
a5 FETCH 1 (BODYSTRUCTURE)
 * 1 FETCH
    (BODYSTRUCTURE
       (
          ("TEXT" "PLAIN" ("CHARSET" "us-ascii") NIL NIL "7BIT" 67 1 NIL
          ("IMAGE" "GIF" ("NAME" "dir.gif") NIL NIL "BASE64" 188 NIL NIL
       "MIXED" ("BOUNDARY" "PART-BOUNDARY=.21010713154504.ZM5863.dennis")
       )
    )
 a5 OK FETCH completed
a6 FETCH 1 (BODY[1])
 * 1 FETCH (BODY[1] {67}
This message has one line of text and a small GIF image attached.
 )
 a6 OK FETCH completed
a7 LOGOUT
 * BYE bob.uit.co.uk IMAP4rev1 server terminating connection
 a7 OK LOGOUT completed
Connection closed by foreign host.
alice#
```

Figure A15.1 Example of an IMAP session using **telnet** as the client

Appendix 16 Installing ethereal; ethereal field names

The **ethereal** Web site, for downloads and documentation, is:

❏ **http://www.ethereal.com** *Ethereal – sniffing the glue that holds the Internet together*

A helpful user manual is available:

❏ **http://www.ethereal.com/docs/user-guide/** *Ethereal User's Guide*

Installing ethereal on Linux

As with most software tools nowadays, you have two choices for installation: either download the source code, build it, and install from that, or download and install from a binary package ready-built for your version of Linux. For **ethereal** we've always chosen the binary package route because it's very quick and easy. On the other hand, if you want the very latest version, you usually have to build from source; fortunately this is usually very easy. The **ethereal** Web site has binary packages for half a dozen different Linux versions, and you can find version-specific packages on the usual sites for your particular Linux distribution.

For details on building and installing on Linux, see Chapter 2 of the Ethereal User's Guide:

❏ **http://www.ethereal.com/docs/user-guide/** > **2. Building and Installing Ethereal**

Installing ethereal on Windows

Building **ethereal** from source on Windows is not well documented, so it's best to install from a binary package, downloadable from:

❏ **http://www.ethereal.com/distribution/win32/** *Win32 Binary Distribution*

As the above Web page points out, you will also need the **Winpcap** packet capture library, obtainable from the same people who produce **Windump**, the Windows version of **tcpdump**:

❏ **http://winpcap.polito.it/** *WinPcap: the Free Packet Capture Architecture for Windows*

As well as downloads and documentation, the site has a useful FAQ:

❏ **http://winpcap.polito.it/misc/faq.htm**

ethereal's fields names and display filters

As Module 13.4 explained, **ethereal** uses its own syntax and field names in display filters, which are different from capture filters. In general, display filter expressions are made up of fields, logical (comparison) operators, and values. A field is specified by a protocol name, and usually the name of a field within that protocol. A typical example is:

```
tcp.dstport ne 6000
```

Tables A16.1 and A16.2 show the protocols and field names we use most often.

Table A16.1 Commonly used **ethereal** protocol names

Protocol	Description
arp	ARP
esp	Encapsulated Security Payload (VPN)
eth	Ethernet
frame	a "pseudo-protocol" to allow you to reference packet numbers and capture times. Of course these are not included in Ethernet packets but are stored with the packets in the capture file
ftp	FTP
http	HTTP
icmp	ICMP messages
ldap	LDAP
lpd	LPD printing
lanman	LAN Manager (Microsoft Windows Networking)
browser	network browsing (Microsoft Windows Networking)
netlogon	Network Logon (Microsoft Windows Networking)
netbios	NetBIOS (Microsoft Windows Networking)
nbns	NetBIOS name service (Microsoft Windows Networking)
nbss	NetBIOS session service (Microsoft Windows Networking)
nfs	Network File System
telnet	telnet

Table A16.2 Commonly used **ethereal** field names

Field	Description
esp.spi	Security Parameter Index (VPN, Module 27.3)
eth.addr	MAC address (Ethernet) source or destination
eth.dst	destination MAC address (Ethernet)
eth.src	source MAC address (Ethernet)
eth.len	Ethernet packet length
eth.type	packet type (0800 = IP, 0806 = ARP) (Module 2.4)
frame.number	the frame number (packet number) in the packet list
icmp.type	ICMP message type (3 = destination unreachable, 11 = TTL exceeded, 8 = **ping**/echo request, 0 = **ping**/echo reply)
ip.addr	IP address, source or destination
ip.dst	IP destination address
ip.src	IP source address
ip.proto	IP protocol number (see Appendix 18)
tcp.dstport	TCP destination port
tcp.srcport	TCP source port
tcp.port	TCP port, source, or destination
udp.dstport	UDP destination port
udp.srcport	UDP source port
udp.port	UDP port, source, or destination

For a full list of protocols and field names, see the **ethereal** manpage, which is included as a real manpage in the Linux distribution, as an HTML file in the Windows distribution, and online at:

❏ **http://www.ethereal.com/ethereal.1.html** HTML version

❏ **http://www.uit.co.uk/book/ethereal-manpage.pdf** PDF version

Specifying fields in a packet by byte number

Instead of the *protocol-name.field-name* syntax that we used above, you can specify a component field in a packet directly, as a specific numbered byte or group of bytes, e.g.

```
icmp[0]                                               byte 0
eth[12:2]              2 bytes starting at byte 12, i.e. bytes 12 and 13
```

The byte number referred to is within this protocol's part of the packet, not the packet as a whole, e.g. **icmp[0]** refers to the first byte of the ICMP data, whereas **eth[0]** is the very first byte of the packet as it appeared on the wire. Figure A16.1 illustrates this, showing how the ICMP data are encapsulated within an IP packet, which in turn is encapsulated in an Ethernet packet. The **icmp[...]** construct "doesn't see" the IP or Ethernet bytes preceding the ICMP data.

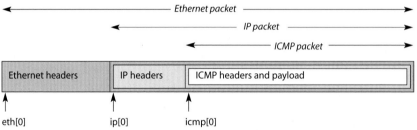

Figure A16.1 ICMP data encapsulated within an IP packet encapsulated within an Ethernet packet

Logical operators

Use logical operators for comparisons. You can specify them using either symbols or alphabetic abbreviations:

eq	==	equal
ne	!=	not equal
gt	>	greater than
lt	<	less than
ge	>=	greater than or equal to
le	<=	less than or equal to

Specifying values

integers: you can specify integers using decimal, octal, or hexadecimal notation, e.g. the following three display filter expressions are equivalent:

```
icmp.type == 11          decimal 11
icmp.type == 013         octal 013 = decimal 11
icmp.type == 0xb         hex 0xb = decimal 11
```

IP addresses: you can specify IP addresses as dotted-decimal IP numbers or as host names, e.g.

```
ip.addr == 192.0.2.56
ip.addr == bob.example.com
```

You can use CIDR notation to check whether an IPv4 address is contained in a certain sub-net. For example, assuming **bob.example.com** has address 192.0.2.25, either of these display filters will match any address in the 192.0.2 class-C network:

```
ip.addr == 192.0.2.0/24
ip.addr == bob.example.com/24
```

text strings: you specify text strings values in double quotes, e.g.

```
mount.path == "/datafiles"
```

groups of bytes: specify groups of bytes (and Ethernet addresses) as hex numbers separated by colons, dots or hyphens, e.g.

```
eth.dst == ff:ff:ff:ff:ff:ff   destination is Ethernet broadcast address
bootp.hw.address == 0-50-da-e4-61-34
```

If you're comparing a byte string containing only a single byte, the manpage says you have to specify the value using the syntax for integers, above. Consequently, if you were entering a hex value you would prefix it with 0x, as in:

```
icmp.[0] == 0xb          what the manpage says
```

On older versions of **ethereal**, that is necessary. However, on new versions, the string is automatically taken as hex, as in:

```
icmp.[0] == b           new versions only – right
icmp.[0] == 11          new versions only – wrong: 11 hex = 17 decimal
```

Appendix 17 HTTP/1.1 server response codes

This appendix is based on RFC-2616 June 1999 *Hypertext Transfer Protocol – HTTP/1.1*. The section numbers in the table refer to sections in RFC-2616 and give an explanation of the respective response (or status) code.

The first digit of the status code defines the class of response, as shown in the table below. The last two digits do not have any categorization role (i.e. there are no conventions like "40x is a minor error, 41x is a major error").

The response descriptions in the table (what the RFC calls "reason phrases") are only recommendations – they may be replaced (e.g. by local-language equivalents) without affecting the protocol.

Informational – request received, continuing process		
100	Module 10.1.1	Continue
101	Module 10.1.2	Switching Protocols
Success – action successfully received, understood, and accepted		
200	Module 10.2.1	OK
201	Module 10.2.2	Created
202	Module 10.2.3	Accepted
203	Module 10.2.4	Non-Authoritative Information
204	Module 10.2.5	No Content
205	Module 10.2.6	Reset Content
206	Module 10.2.7	Partial Content
Redirection – further action must be taken to complete the request		
300	Module 10.3.1	Multiple Choices
301	Module 10.3.2	Moved Permanently
302	Module 10.3.3	Found
303	Module 10.3.4	See Other
304	Module 10.3.5	Not Modified
305	Module 10.3.6	Use Proxy
307	Module 10.3.8	Temporary Redirect
Client Error – the request contains bad syntax or cannot be fulfilled		
400	Module 10.4.1	Bad Request
401	Module 10.4.2	Unauthorized
402	Module 10.4.3	Payment Required
403	Module 10.4.4	Forbidden
404	Module 10.4.5	Not Found

405	Module 10.4.6	Method Not Allowed
406	Module 10.4.7	Not Acceptable
407	Module 10.4.8	Proxy Authentication Required
408	Module 10.4.9	Request Timeout
409	Module 10.4.10	Conflict
410	Module 10.4.11	Gone
411	Module 10.4.12	Length Required
412	Module 10.4.13	Precondition Failed
413	Module 10.4.14	Request Entity Too Large
414	Module 10.4.15	Request-URI Too Large
415	Module 10.4.16	Unsupported Media Type
416	Module 10.4.17	Requested Range Not Satisfiable
417	Module 10.4.18	Expectation Failed
Server Error – the server failed to fulfill an apparently valid request		
500	Module 10.5.1	Internal Server Error
501	Module 10.5.2	Not Implemented
502	Module 10.5.3	Bad Gateway
503	Module 10.5.4	Service Unavailable
504	Module 10.5.5	Gateway Timeout
505	Module 10.5.6	HTTP Version Not Supported
Extended error messages		
xxx	*see below*	

HTTP status codes are extensible, i.e. a server can generate response codes other than the ones listed in the table. HTTP applications are not required to understand the meaning of all registered status codes, although such understanding is obviously desirable. However, applications must understand the class of any status code, as indicated by the first digit, and treat any unrecognized response as being equivalent to the x00 status code of that class, with the exception that an unrecognized response must not be cached. For example, if an unrecognized status code of 431 is received by the client, it can safely assume that there was something wrong with its request and treat the response as if it had received a 400 status code. In such cases, user agents should present to the user the entity returned with the response, since that entity is likely to include human-readable information that will explain the unusual status.

Appendix 18 IP protocol numbers

The table below shows a sub-set of the assigned IP protocol numbers. For a full list see:

❏ **http://www.iana.org/assignments/protocol-numbers** *Protocol Numbers*

No.	Name	Description
1	ICMP	Internet Control Message Protocol
2	IGMP	Internet Group Management Protocol
6	TCP	Transmission Control Protocol
8	EGP	Exterior Gateway Protocol
9	IGP	*any private interior gateway*
17	UDP	User Datagram Protocol
46	RSVP	Reservation Protocol
47	GRE	General Routing Encapsulation
50	ESP	Encapsulating Security Payload
51	AH	Authentication Header
115	L2TP	Layer Two Tunneling Protocol
135–254	Unassigned	
255	Reserved	

Note that these are *not* port numbers. As we explain in Module 27.5, you only have port numbers in TCP and UDP packets – with IP protocol numbers 6 and 17 respectively.

To illustrate this, consider Alice sending a UDP packet to a DNS server on machine Bob over a VPN tunnel (Figure A18.1). The packet that Alice sends has:

- IP protocol-number 17, because it's UDP
- UDP port-number 53 because it's to a DNS server.

VPN box A encrypts Alice's packet and sends the result in an ESP packet over the VPN tunnel to Bob's site. For the ESP packet:

- IP protocol number = 50, because it's ESP
- (no port number, because this is not a TCP or UDP packet).

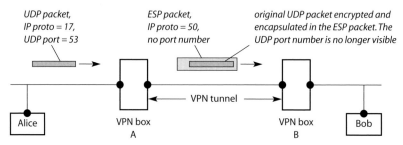

Figure A18.1 Sending an IP packet to a DNS server over a VPN tunnel

Appendix 19 nc (netcat) **manpage in full**

NAME

    nc – TCP/IP swiss army knife

SYNOPSIS

    nc *[-options] hostname port[s] [ports] ...*
    nc *-l -p port [-options] [hostname] [port]*

DESCRIPTION

    netcat is a simple unix utility which reads and writes data across network connections, using TCP or UDP protocol. It is designed to be a reliable "back-end" tool that can be used directly or easily driven by other programs and scripts. At the same time, it is a feature-rich network debugging and exploration tool, since it can create almost any kind of connection you would need and has several interesting built-in capabilities. Netcat, or "nc" as the actual program is named, should have been supplied long ago as another one of those cryptic but standard Unix tools.

    In the simplest usage, "nc host port" creates a TCP connection to the given port on the given target host. Your standard input is then sent to the host, and anything that comes back across the connection is sent to your standard output. This continues indefinitely, until the network side of the connection shuts down. Note that this behavior is different from most other applications which shut everything down and exit after an end-of-file on the standard input.

    Netcat can also function as a server, by listening for inbound connections on arbitrary ports and then doing the same reading and writing. With minor limitations, netcat doesn't really care if it runs in "client" or "server" mode – it still shovels data back and forth until there isn't any more left. In either mode, shutdown can be forced after a configurable time of inactivity on the network side.

    And it can do this via UDP too, so netcat is possibly the "udp telnet-like" application you always wanted for testing your UDP-mode servers. UDP, as the "U" implies, gives less reliable data transmission than TCP connections and some systems may have trouble sending large amounts of data that way, but it's still a useful capability to have.

    You may be asking "why not just use telnet to connect to arbitrary ports?" Valid question, and here are some reasons. Telnet has the "standard input EOF" problem, so one must introduce calculated delays in driving scripts to allow network output to finish. This is the main reason netcat stays running until the *network* side closes. Telnet also will not transfer arbitrary binary data, because certain characters are interpreted as telnet options and are thus removed from the data stream. Telnet also emits some of its diagnostic messages to standard output, where netcat keeps such things religiously separated from its *output* and will never modify any of the real data in transit unless you *really* want it to. And of course telnet is incapable of listening for inbound connections, or using UDP instead. Netcat doesn't have any of these limitations, is much smaller and faster than telnet, and has many other advantages.

OPTIONS

–g gateway	source-routing hop point[s], up to 8
–G num	source-routing pointer: 4, 8, 12, ...
–h	Display help.
–i secs	delay interval for lines sent, ports scanned
–l	listen mode, for inbound connects
–n	numeric-only IP addresses, no DNS
–o file	hex dump of traffic
–p port	local port number (port numbers can be individual or ranges: lo-hi [inclusive])
–q seconds	Quit after EOF is detected on stdin and after a delay. "-q 0" makes "nc" quit as soon as EOF is detected.
–r	randomize local and remote ports
–s addr	local source address
–t	Enable telnet negotiation
–u	UDP mode
–v	verbose [use twice to be more verbose]
–w secs	timeout for connects and final net reads
–z	zero-I/O mode [used for scanning]

COPYRIGHT

Netcat is entirely my own creation, although plenty of other code was used as examples. It is freely given away to the Internet community in the hope that it will be useful, with no restrictions except giving credit where it is due. No GPLs, Berkeley copyrights or any of that nonsense. The author assumes NO responsibility for how anyone uses it. If netcat makes you rich somehow and you're feeling generous, mail me a check. If you are affiliated in any way with Microsoft Network, get a life. Always ski in control. Comments, questions, and patches to hobbit@avian.org.

BUGS

Efforts have been made to have netcat "do the right thing" in all its various modes. If you believe that it is doing the wrong thing under whatever circumstances, please notify me and tell me how you think it should behave. If netcat is not able to do some task you think up, minor tweaks to the code will probably fix that. It provides a basic and easily-modified template for writing other network applications, and I certainly encourage people to make custom mods and send in any improvements they make to it. Continued feedback from the Internet community is always welcome!

Some port names in /etc/services contain hyphens – netcat currently will not correctly parse those, so specify ranges using numbers if you can.

SEE ALSO

/usr/doc/netcat/README.gz

AUTHOR

This manual page was written by Joey Hess <joeyh@master.debian.org> and Robert Woodcock <rcw@rcw.oz.net>, cribbing heavily from Netcat's README file.

Netcat was written by a guy we know as the Hobbit, or _H* <hobbit@avian.org>.

Appendix 20 Controlling network services

This appendix is oriented towards Linux more than Windows NT. In Linux, networking components are much more clearly identifiable and separate from one another than in Win-NT, where they appear as one big lump. (And seeing how Linux does things makes it easier to understand what the NT subsystems are doing, at least conceptually.)

TCP/IP uses lots of individual server programs to provide both services for users (SMTP, HTTP, FTP, …) and system services used by other programs (DHCP, DNS, …). How are these controlled? What starts them? How long do they run for? That's what we cover in this appendix. In particular:

1. we explain how servers run as "daemons", i.e. processes running in the background, not connected to a terminal or screen
2. two files, **/etc/services** and **/etc/inetd.conf**, control many of the network services running on your system
3. finally, we look at the **inetd** "super-server" program that controls and runs many of the services.

1. Servers and daemons

A *daemon* is a process running on its own "in the background," i.e. not connected to any terminal and not controlled by a human user. Daemons are used to provide specific services to users or to other parts of the system.

Most TCP/IP server software runs as daemons. We'll consider an HTTP/1.0 Web server as an example. The server listens on its well-known port, 80, for incoming connections. When a client browser connects, the server accepts the connection, and runs the session. This prompts us to ask two more, inter-related questions:

1. what happens when the session is finished – does the server "start over" or does it exit?
2. how does the server handle multiple sessions simultaneously?

Figure A20.1 shows how a Linux TCP server operates: it waits, listening for incoming connections and *spawns* (creates a new and identical) child process for every new connection, using the **fork** system call. (See the Notes below for more information.) The children run independently and concurrently, and terminate when they have finished servicing their respective clients. This type of server is called a *concurrent server* (Figure A20.2a). Having a separate process handle each client connection makes sense because TCP connections stay open for minutes, or hours, or days.

If the server doesn't spawn a new child each time, but instead waits until it finishes servicing one client before servicing the next, it's called an *iterative server* (Figure A20.2b). This is fine if it only takes a very short time to service each client. In fact, this is often the case for UDP servers, so they are often implemented as iterative servers. Client servicing is usually brief, and there is no ongoing session: as soon as the (small) UDP response is sent, the server is ready to handle the next UDP request. However, if client requests require a lot of processing, the server couldn't reliably handle multiple incoming connections – e.g. on a busy Web server – and a concurrent design would have to be used instead.

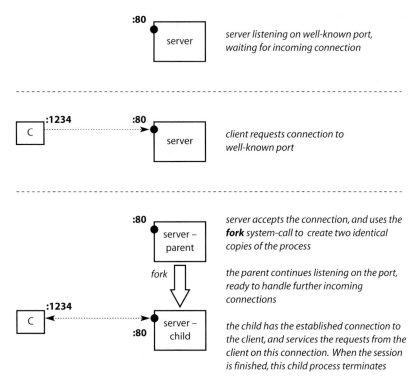

:80

server

*server listening on well-known port,
waiting for incoming connection*

:1234

C

:80

server

*client requests connection to
well-known port*

:80

server –
parent

*server accepts the connection, and uses the
fork system-call to create two identical
copies of the process*

fork

*the parent continues listening on the port,
ready to handle further incoming
connections*

:1234

C

:80

server –
child

*the child has the established connection to
the client, and services the requests from the
client on this connection. When the session
is finished, this child process terminates*

Figure A20.1 Operation of a Linux TCP server

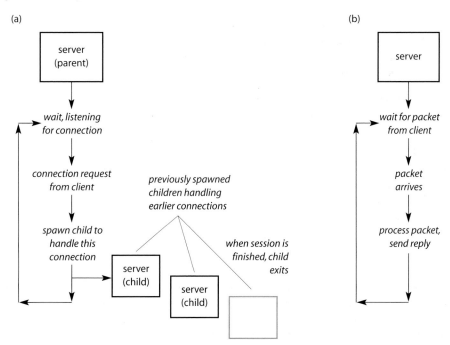

(a)

server
(parent)

*wait, listening
for connection*

*connection request
from client*

*previously spawned
children handling
earlier connections*

*spawn child to
handle this
connection*

server
(child)

server
(child)

*when session is
finished, child
exits*

(b)

server

*wait for packet
from client*

*packet
arrives*

*process packet,
send reply*

Figure A20.2 (a) Concurrent server; (b) iterative server

2. The /etc/services **file**

This file lists the port numbers corresponding to named network services. Just as the DNS makes it easy to use names instead of IP numbers for hosts, **/etc/services** lets you use names instead of numbers for ports. Figure A20.3 shows an annotated excerpt from the file on one of our Linux systems. Names are case sensitive, and fields are separated by tabs or spaces. Text after a "#" is treated as comment.

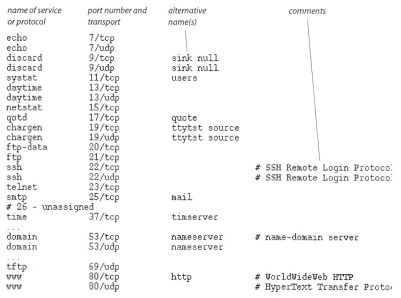

```
name of service      port number and    alternative                    comments
or protocol          transport          name(s)

echo                 7/tcp
echo                 7/udp
discard              9/tcp              sink null
discard              9/udp              sink null
systat               11/tcp             users
daytime              13/tcp
daytime              13/udp
netstat              15/tcp
qotd                 17/tcp             quote
chargen              19/tcp             ttytst source
chargen              19/udp             ttytst source
ftp-data             20/tcp
ftp                  21/tcp
ssh                  22/tcp                                            # SSH Remote Login Protoco!
ssh                  22/udp                                            # SSH Remote Login Protoco!
telnet               23/tcp
smtp                 25/tcp             mail
# 26 - unassigned
time                 37/tcp             timserver
...
domain               53/tcp             nameserver                     # name-domain server
domain               53/udp             nameserver
...
tftp                 69/udp
www                  80/tcp             http                           # WorldWideWeb HTTP
www                  80/udp                                            # HyperText Transfer Proto!
```

Figure A20.3 Excerpt from the **/etc/services** file on a Linux system

Applications that use ports read this file to translate between port names and numbers. This is how, for example, you can say **telnet http** instead of **telnet 80**, and how **tcpdump** prints port names in its output:

```
alice.2796 > bob.uit.co.uk.www: . ack 1 win 8760 (DF)
```

Notice that some of the names are not what you expect, e.g. DNS is called **domain** or **nameserver**, not **dns**. You can edit the file and insert your own aliases for these names (but even if you do add extra aliases, we recommend that you keep the original name in the file too, as other programs may rely on it).

Many services have entries for both UDP and TCP transports, for the same port number. As we mentioned in Module 15.3, UDP and TCP ports are completely separate. When the protocols were being developed, the well-known UDP and TCP port numbers for a given service could have been made different, but for convenience the same ones were always chosen for both. You only need the entry in **/etc/services** if you are going to use the service in question; otherwise you can delete it (or more usually, comment it out). Many of the UDP entries are historical and can be removed, e.g. the UDP entries for HTTP and POP3. And, except on test systems you could remove **echo**, **discard**, **systat**, **daytime**, and **chargen** on UDP and TCP. (Leaving unnecessary entries in the file uses no resources, so most people don't bother editing the file but it is good security practice to disable or remove anything you don't need.)

3. The inetd "super-server" and the /etc/inetd.conf file

A server machine can be providing many different services simultaneously, e.g. one of our internal machines provides more than 30. Running 30 large processes even when there's no network activity is a waste of CPU, memory, and processes, so instead of running a separate server for each service, Linux runs a single "super-server" that listens on all the necessary ports simultaneously. This server is called **inetd** ("Internet daemon") and the file **/etc/inetd.conf** controls which ports it listens on. Below is a line from our **inetd.conf** with the important fields annotated. (See the **inetd.conf**(5) manpage for details of other fields.)

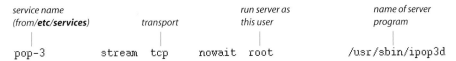

```
service name                              run server as            name of server
(from/etc/services)        transport      this user                program
    |                          |              |                        |
pop-3              stream    tcp      nowait  root          /usr/sbin/ipop3d
```

The service name is exactly as entered in **/etc/services**, and **inetd** looks up the name in that file to find out which port to listen on, and whether it's a UDP or TCP port. (If you spell the service name incorrectly, your server won't be run.) When **inetd** starts up, it listens on all the specified ports, waiting for connections, as shown below: the **netstat -n -p -a -t** command shows which programs are listening on which ports. (-t: TCP; -a: all, including listening ports; -n: print ports as numbers rather than names; -p: show name of program using this port.)

```
tcp  0   0 0.0.0.0:113     0.0.0.0:*       LISTEN    215/inetd
tcp  0   0 0.0.0.0:79      0.0.0.0:*       LISTEN    215/inetd
tcp  0   0 0.0.0.0:110     0.0.0.0:*       LISTEN    215/inetd
tcp  0   0 0.0.0.0:109     0.0.0.0:*       LISTEN    215/inetd
tcp  0   0 0.0.0.0:119     0.0.0.0:*       LISTEN    215/inetd
tcp  0   0 0.0.0.0:143     0.0.0.0:*       LISTEN    215/inetd
tcp  0   0 0.0.0.0:25      0.0.0.0:*       LISTEN    215/inetd
tcp  0   0 0.0.0.0:512     0.0.0.0:*       LISTEN    215/inetd
tcp  0   0 0.0.0.0:513     0.0.0.0:*       LISTEN    215/inetd
tcp  0   0 0.0.0.0:514     0.0.0.0:*       LISTEN    215/inetd
tcp  0   0 0.0.0.0:43      0.0.0.0:*       LISTEN    215/inetd
tcp  0   0 0.0.0.0:23      0.0.0.0:*       LISTEN    215/inetd
tcp  0   0 0.0.0.0:37      0.0.0.0:*       LISTEN    215/inetd
tcp  0   0 0.0.0.0:13      0.0.0.0:*       LISTEN    215/inetd
tcp  0   0 0.0.0.0:9       0.0.0.0:*       LISTEN    215/inetd
tcp  0   0 0.0.0.0:7       0.0.0.0:*       LISTEN    215/inetd
```

When **inetd** receives an incoming connection request, **inetd** uses the port number it came in on to decide which server program to run to service the connection. **inetd** accepts the connection call and forks as already described; the child process then executes the respective server program to service the client connection.

The trace below shows **inetd** continuing to listen for incoming POP3 connections, having already spawned a server (**ipop3d**) to handle an incoming request:

```
tcp  0   0 127.0.0.1:110 127.0.0.1:3773  ESTABLISHED 14368/ipop3d
tcp  0   0 0.0.0.0:110    0.0.0.0:*       LISTEN   215/inetd
```

(If the service isn't configured in **inetd.conf**, **inetd** won't be listening on the port, so any incoming connections will be refused, unless a separately configured server for that service is already running.)

Managing servers from **inetd**, instead of starting them all individually, has several advantages:

- only one daemon process runs, waiting for connections, so fewer resources are used
- the **inetd.conf** file makes it easy to enable or disable a service
- the code to accept incoming connections, forking, and handling multiple connections is in **inetd** only. The individual servers are smaller and less complex; they only need to handle a single connection, and when that's finished they terminate. That makes it easier to write a robust and secure server application.

Using **inetd** does impose a slight performance disadvantage: a server process has to be started before it can begin to handle the request. Consequently, servers handling large numbers of connections (e.g. Web and e-mail) are often *not* started via **inetd**. Instead these servers are started directly by the system start-up scripts at boot time.

There are a couple of other features you may see in **inetd.conf**:

- instead of a program-name argument, some services are shown as "internal". These are small services built into the **inetd** program itself rather than run as separate servers because they require so little code to handle them:

```
echo     stream tcp  nowait root   internal
chargen  stream tcp  nowait root   internal
discard  stream tcp  nowait root   internal
```

- some servers are run not directly but under the control of yet another super-server program called **tcpd**, the "TCP Wrappers" daemon:

```
telnet stream tcp   nowait root /usr/sbin/tcpd   /usr/sbin/in.telnetd
imap   stream tcp   nowait root /usr/sbin/tcpd   /usr/sbin/imapd
pop-3  stream tcp   nowait root /usr/sbin/tcpd   /usr/sbin/ipop3d
```

tcpd provides access-control security, and logging, to any number of servers. When access for the incoming connection has been validated, **tcpd** runs the specific server (which was specified as the argument to the **tcpd** program in the **inetd.conf** line) to handle the request. (For a little more detail on TCP wrappers see the Notes to Chapter 26.)

Modifying the inetd.conf file

By default, **inetd** only reads its configuration when it starts, so if you make any changes to the file, **inetd** won't notice them. You can force **inetd** to re-read the **/etc/inetd.conf** file by sending it the hangup "HUP" signal (with "**kill -HUP** *processid*" where *processid* is inetd's process number).

Windows NT analogs of the Linux components

The internal operation of Windows is very different from Linux and UNIX and often there is no direct correspondence between their components. However, NT does have a **services** file, C:\WINNT\system32\drivers\etc\services.

NT doesn't use **inetd**; instead, servers are controlled from **Control Panel > Network > Services** and **Control Panel > Services**, and settings, etc. are stored in the NT Registry.

Services.exe is the "Service Controller" or "Service Control Manager". It starts all the services on NT. (It was called **Lmsvcs.exe** before Windows-NT 3.5.) Some NT system services are implemented as separate processes of their own, but others are run as part of the Service Control Manager process to minimize the use of resources (like the Linux **daytime** and **echo** servers are implemented as part of **inetd**). Because these services are part of **Services.exe**, you can't see them in the NT Task Manager or Performance Monitor.

To list the services on your system, use **Control Panel > Services**. Or, from the Command Prompt, you can use several better tools that are included in the NT 4.0 Resource Kit:

> **sclist** (service controller list): list the services on a machine:
>
> ```
> sclist                          list services on local machine
> sclist bob                      list services on remote machine bob
> ```
>
> The listing shows both the full "Display Name" of the service, and its shorter "Key Name" (Figure A20.4).

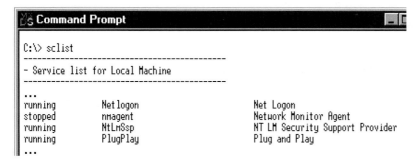

Figure A20.4 sclist shows names and status of services

> **sc** (service controller): this communicates directly with **Sevices.exe** and can give you very detailed information on a particular service.
>
> > The full syntax (most of which you don't need) is given by:
> >
> > ```
> > sc /?                           show help message
> > ```
> >
> > The most useful display we've found is:
> >
> > ```
> > sc qc servicename               "query configuration"
> > ```
> >
> > which shows which other services, etc. this one depends on, and what process this service runs as (Figure A20.5).

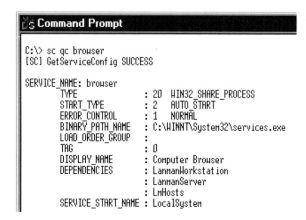

Figure A20.5 sc qc shows detailed configuration information for a service

The standard tool to list running processes is the NT Task Manager (**Ctrl-Alt-Del > Task Manager**, or right-click on the taskbar and then select **Task Manager**). The **Applications** tab shows end-user applications that you started manually or automatically; the **Processes** tab shows all the running process, including end-user applications and system programs.

However, tools included in the NT 4.0 Resource Kit are much more informative, and easier to use when exploring the system in depth:

> **tlist** (task list): without any arguments this lists the running processes, with their names and process IDs.
> With an argument of a process ID, it lists the modules (libraries) used by this process.
> With option "**/t**" it displays the process list in a tree format, showing the child/parent relationships of the processes.
>
> **pulist** (process and user list): again lists the running processes and the user who initiated them. Its great advantage is that you can list the processes on other machines, not just your own.
> (For example, "**pulist \\bob**" from Alice.)

Notes and further reading

❑ **Stevens**, Module 18.11 on TCP server design; Module 11.12 on UDP server design

❑ **Stevens** *Unix Network Programming* (1998, Prentice Hall) for concurrent/iterative servers, **inetd** implementation, and process forking. Especially Chapter 27.

❑ **Linux manpages: inetd**(8), **inetd.conf**(5), **services**(5), **tcpd**(8), **fork**(2)

The program **xinetd** ("extended inetd") is a popular replacement for **inetd**. It offers extensive logging, access control, limits on the number of child processes (to prevent denial-of-service attacks), and many other features. See:

❑ **http://www.xinetd.org/** *xinetd* home page

Appendix 21 NetBIOS names

Internally, all NetBIOS names are 16 characters long, formed by:

a. padding the ordinary name with spaces, to make it 15 characters long

b. appending a special sixteenth-byte suffix to specify what type of name this is. The different values of this byte are shown in Table A21.1.
By convention, these byte values are shown in hexadecimal, in angle brackets.

There are different types of names:

1. **individual names:** these typically resolve to the IP number of the computer that has registered that name. For example, if machine **bob** (whose IP address is 192.0.2.204, say) is running the Server NT service, when NetBIOS resolves the name **bob<20>**, the answer is 192.0.2.204.

2. **group names:** there are two different types of group names, which behave very differently. The Microsoft documentation isn't very clear on the differences, but here's how they work:

   a. **normal group names:** each member of the particular group registers the group name. These are used in two different ways, depending on what the particular group is:

      i. transmit to the group without trying to resolve the name first. This is the way all normal applications use normal group names.
      The client broadcasts a UDP packet to the sub-net broadcast address and in the packet gives the NetBIOS group name as the destination. Only machines on the local sub-net that have registered this group name will accept and process the packet. For example, a NetBIOS browse server can communicate with all other browse servers for domain **EX-NTD** by broadcasting to the normal group name **EX-NTD<1e>**, which is how browser elections take place. Similarly, if you use the command net **send** *domainname text* to send a message to all users in a domain, the client doesn't attempt a resolution – it just broadcasts to group name *domainname*<00>.

      ii. a client can try to resolve the name first, and then communicate with one or more of the IP addresses that are returned. Standard Windows programs don't usually do this but it may happen when you use a diagnostic tool (e.g. **nbtstat** or **nmblookup**).
      If a client does try to resolve such a name using WINS, the IP address returned is 255.255.255.255, i.e. the limited broadcast address, so that when the client sends its UDP packet to this name, it is in fact broadcast.

   b. **Internet group names:** an Internet group name *does* resolve to a list of IP numbers of members of this group, i.e. the addresses of machines that have registered this name. The list of domain controllers for a domain, i.e. group name *domainname*<1c> is a group of this type. By resolving this name a machine can get a list of DCs (typically to choose one which it will communicate with).
   The only Internet group used by standard Windows applications is the <1c> group, although you could write applications that define their own Internet group names and use them for their own purposes.

Table A21.1 NetBIOS names and suffixes

Base name	Suffix	Type	Service	Resolves to	Notes
domain-name	<00>	G		*not normally resolved*	each PC in this domain registers this name
computername	<00>	U	Workstation	*computername's IP number*	this is the PC's "computer name"
computername	<03>	U	Messenger	*computername's IP number*	
username	<03>	U	Messenger	IP number of computer that *username* logged onto	
computername	<06>	U	RAS server	*computername's IP number*	
domain-name	<1b>	U	Browser	IP number of domain master browser for this domain	this is always the PDC and is often used to locate the PDC, even in non-browse-related operations
domain-name	<1c>	G		list of IP numbers of *domain-name's* domain controllers	
domain-name	<1d>	U	Browser	IP number of segment master browser	One per domain per segment
domain-name	<1e>	G	Browser	*not normally resolved*	used for master browser elections. Registered by any browser or potential browser
computername	<1f>	U	NetDDE	*computername's IP number*	
computername	<20>	U	Server	*computername's IP number*	
computername	<21>	U	RAS client	*computername's IP number*	
computername	<be>	U	Netmon agent	*computername's IP number*	
computername	<bf>	U	Netmon master	*computername's IP number*	
MSBROWSE	—	G	Browser	*not normally resolved*	The full name is <01><02>__ **MSBROWSE**__ <02><01>. It is registered by any segMBs on this segment. Used by segMBs in different domains to learn of each other's presence and communicate with one another

In the Type column, U indicates a unique name, G a group name.

Notes and further reading

❏ **MS-KB-Q163409** *NetBIOS Suffixes (16th Character of the NetBIOS Name)*

Older sources containing similar information are:

❏ **MS-KB-Q119495** *List of Names Registered with WINS Service*

❏ **NT 4.0 Resource Kit** *Appendix G – NetBIOS Names*

but they are not as complete or as accurate (e.g. some older docs say *domainname* **<1D>** is a group name; in fact it is unique, as you can confirm if you run **nbtstat -n** on your PDC).

For details of normal versus Internet group types see:

❏ **MS-KB-Q140064** *WINS Static Entry Descriptions*

❏ **WINS Manager Help,** search for **Using Type Options,** and view the link **Internet Group Type**

The name **JSPNRMPTGSBSSDIR** is how the Microsoft Remote Access Service (RAS) announces itself. For details, and how to avoid having these packets broadcast every few minutes, see:

❏ **MS-KB-Q150820** *RAS Service Broadcasts Name Query Every Two Minutes*

(In **ethereal** this is displayed as **JSPNRMPTGSBSSDI<52>** because the ASCII character **R** has value 82 decimal, which is 52 hex, i.e. <52>.)

Appendix 22 DNS and NetBIOS name resolution order in Windows

Microsoft differentiates between "hostname" resolution and "NetBIOS name" resolution. (A "hostname" is what we refer to as a "DNS name" in Chapter 19.) Windows handles the two types of names differently, although few documents make this clear.

At first glance, a name like **bob.sales.example.com** is obviously a DNS name, and **carolnt** in the command "**net use \\carolnt\datadirs D:**" is obviously a NetBIOS name. However, whether a simple name (e.g. "**alice**") is a DNS name or a NetBIOS name depends on the context in which it is used and which program is using it.

To understand why Windows treats DNS names and NetBIOS names differently, we have to look at the history of NetBIOS. Before NetBIOS was modified to run over TCP/IP, all its names were of course NetBIOS names. When NetBIOS over TCP/IP (NBT) was introduced, NetBIOS applications, including all the native Windows Networking tools (file sharing, printing, etc.), still used NetBIOS names and nothing else. However, the UNIX-like TCP/IP tools such as **ping, telnet, ftp, arp, nslookup**, etc. that were ported to Windows used only DNS names and didn't use NetBIOS names at all. This meant you had two separate "namespaces" on the same network, and you had to maintain two separate but parallel infrastructures (WINS servers and DNS servers) to manage them.

With Windows-NT 4.0 the two systems were unified to some extent: you can now use DNS names, and even explicit IP numbers, in place of NetBIOS names and vice versa. For example, you can **ping** a machine by NetBIOS name (**ALICENT**) or DNS name (**alice.example.com**), and to map a share (network drive) in Windows Explorer you can use:

- the NetBIOS name **ALICENT** (Figure A22.1a), or
- Alice's IP number (Figure A22.1b), or
- her FQDN DNS name (Figure A22.1c), assuming of course that the DNS is set up correctly.

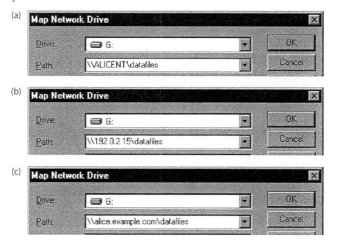

Figure A22.1 Different ways to map a share in Windows Explorer

Name resolution takes account of that as follows:

- NetBIOS programs will use the TCP/IP resolution methods (hosts file and DNS) if:
  a. the name obviously can't be a NetBIOS name, e.g. if it has more than 16 characters. Or if
  b. NetBIOS fails to resolve the name using the NetBIOS methods (cache, broadcast, WINS, **LMHOSTS**)
- Microsoft's own TCP/IP programs use the NetBIOS methods if a name can't be resolved using **hosts** or DNS. (C.f. Module 18.3, NetBIOS programs, "real" TCP/IP programs, and hybrid programs.)

The resolution order for different configurations and name types is shown in Figure A22.2. e.g. if you **telnet bob**, because this is a TCP/IP program "**bob**" could be a DNS name, so **hosts** is checked before anything else. However, if you **net view bob**, "**bob**" is now treated as a NetBIOS name, and **hosts** is tried only *after* the NetBIOS resolution methods have failed, and then only if **Enable DNS for Windows Resolution** = YES.

Figure A22.2
Resolution order for different configurations and name types

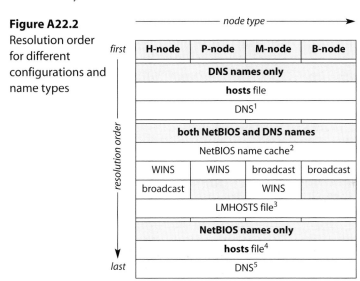

Notes:

1. only if name being resolved is not a simple name
2. note that pre-loaded **LHMOSTS** entries (#PRE) are resolved from the cache
3. only if **Enable LMHOSTS lookup** = YES
4. only if **Enable DNS for Windows Resolution** = YES
5. only if **Enable DNS for Windows Resolution** = YES and name is not a simple name

From Figure A22.2 you can see that in the resolution process taken as a whole, both types of names can use all the methods; what's different is the order in which the different methods are attempted. Note also that for DNS names, the TCP/IP methods are always tried, but for NetBIOS names, the TCP/IP methods are only used if **Enable DNS for Windows Resolution** is set to YES.

Example 1

```
ping    name
```

ping is a TCP/IP program and expects DNS names, and therefore will initially try to resolve *name* using **hosts** or DNS. If these fail, **ping** will fall back and try to resolve *name* using the NetBIOS resolution methods.

Example 2

```
net use x: \\name\datafiles
```

net use is very definitely a NetBIOS program, and assumes *name* is a NetBIOS name if at all possible:

- if *name* is 15 characters long or less, it's taken as a NetBIOS name, even if it contains dots (e.g. **b2.example.com**)
- if *name* is 16 characters long, it's still taken as a NetBIOS name, but NetBIOS resolution will almost inevitably fail because the last character of the name will be interpreted incorrectly as a NetBIOS type suffix.
  In both these cases (names less than or equal to 16 characters long), if the NetBIOS resolution fails, the system will then go on and try the TCP/IP resolution methods, but only if they are enabled; if they are not enabled, the resolution fails completely
- only if *name* is 17 characters long or more is it definitely not a NetBIOS name – it must be a DNS name instead. Accordingly, the system tries the TCP/IP resolution methods first, and if these fail it falls back to the NetBIOS methods. Note that in this case the resolution order is different to the above: here, the TCP/IP methods are tried first.

These examples illustrate that it is difficult to predict from first principles how a particular program is going to treat names for resolution. However, by observing what happens on the wire you can at least make sense of what actually occurs.

Notes and further reading

❑ **MS-KB-Q161431** *Connecting to NetBIOS Resources Using DNS Names or IP Addresses* explains the special computer name *SMBSERVER used when a client connects to a server using an IP number rather than a FQDN DNS-name or a NetBIOS name

❑ **MS-KB-Q172218** *Microsoft TCP/IP Host Name Resolution Order* describes the difference between "hostname resolution" (i.e. DNS name resolution) and NetBIOS name resolution

❑ **MS-KB-137565** *System Error 53 When Connecting to a Fully Qualified Domain Name (FQDN)*

❑ **MS-KB-Q139270** *How to Change Name Resolution Order on Windows 95 and Windows NT*

❑ **MS-KB-Q142309** *NetBIOS Name Resolution Using DNS and the HOSTS File*

❑ **MS-KB-Q230744** *Windows NT 4.0 SP4 DNR Client Does Not Send Unqualified DNS Queries* ("DNR" stands for "domain name resolver")

❑ **MS-KB-Q198550** *SP4 Changes DNS Name Resolution*

Appendix 23 Windows name resolution worksheet

a. collect the details of the PC that is resolving the name, and enter them in Worksheet 1

b. Figure A23.1 shows the expected name resolution order for the different node types and configurations. Copy the order for your node type into Worksheet 2

c. from your **ethereal** or Network Monitor trace, enter the observed order in Worksheet 2.

Worksheet 1

Control Panel > Network > Identification	
1. Computer Name	
Control Panel > Network > Protocols > TCP/IP > Properties	
2. DNS > hostname	
3. DNS > Domain	
4. DNS > DNS Service Search Order (list of DNS servers)	..............•..............•..............•.............. ....•..............•..............•.............. ....•..............•..............•..............
5. DNS > Domain Suffix Search Order	....
6. WINS Address > Enable LMHOSTS Lookup	yes / no
Run **ipconfig/all** at the command prompt	
7. hostname	
8. Node Type	
9. IP Address	..............•..............•..............•..............
10. Netmask (Sub-net Mask)	..............•..............•..............•..............
11. NetBIOS Scope ID	
12. NetBIOS Resolution Uses DNS	
13. Primary WINS Server	..............•..............•..............•..............
14. Secondary WINS Server	..............•..............•..............•..............
15. NetBIOS Resolution uses DNS	yes / no

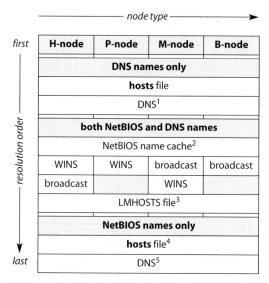

Figure A23.1 Resolution order for different configurations and name types

Notes:

1. only if name being resolved is not a simple name
2. note that pre-loaded **LHMOSTS** entries (**#PRE**) are resolved from the cache
3. only if **Enable LMHOSTS lookup** = YES
4. only if **Enable DNS for Windows Resolution** = YES
5. only if **Enable DNS for Windows Resolution** = YES and name is not a simple name

Worksheet 2 – Name resolution order for this PC

Name to be resolved:

	Expected order *(copied from Figure A23.1)*	**Observed order**
1.		
2.		
3.		
4.		
5.		
6.		
7.		
8.		

Appendix 24 The BROWSTAT command

browstat.exe is included in the NT 4.0 Server Resource Kit. Browstat's documentation in the Resource Kit lists only a few of the available commands. The following is a complete list for version "created 01 March 1996", 42,256 bytes.

Many of the commands take a *transport* argument. This is needed because if you're running more than one networking system (e.g. NetBIOS over TCP/IP as well as NetBEUI), you can have different browse lists for each. The easiest way to find the value for transport is to run **browstat status**, which shows the default *transport*. In most commands you must explicitly specify *transport*, even if there is only one.

Instead of the full command name, you can use the abbreviation shown on the right after each command.

For most commands, if you give an invalid transport or an invalid domain name, no error message is printed but the command fails. For some domain-related operations you must be logged in as a user of that domain or the command fails.

ADDALTCOMP *transport   nbname*   **AAC**

> Register *nbname* as an alternate NetBIOS computer name (**<00>**) for this machine, in addition to its existing name. Uses WINS or NetBIOS broadcasts as usual, depending on this PC's configuration

GETNETBIOS *transport*   **GN**

> Get NetBIOS names for a transport

GETDOMAIN *IPaddr*   **GWD**

> Retrieve the domain list from the WINS server on the specified IP address

GETWINS *transport*   **GW**

> Retrieve the primary and backup WINS server

OTHERDOMAIN *pdc-addr*   **OTH**

> Retrieve list of other domains that the PDC *pdc-addr* listens to

POPDOMAIN *transport domain numberOfDomains* [*AnnouncementFrequency*]   **PD**

> Issue browser **announce** requests for the specified number of randomly generated domain names

POPSERVER *transport domain numberOfMachines* [*AnnouncementFrequency*]   **PS**

> Populate a workgroup with random PC names, by issuing browser **Announce** requests. The *AnnouncementFrequency* is in milliseconds but appears to be ignored. You will then see these names if you use **net view /domain:***domain* or Windows Explorer

SD ...

> Set debug info in the browser. Options are:

> **browstat bowdebug truncate**
>
> **browstat bowdebug close**
>
> **browstat bowdebug open** *FileName*
>
> **browstat bowdebug debug** *Flags*

TRUNCLOG   **TLG**

Truncate the browser log

RPCCMP *transport* [*domain* | *server*] [*serverFlags*] [**GoForever**]   **RC**

Compare the browse list obtained using RPC with that obtained using the normal browser **NetServerEnum** request

ANNOUNCE *transport domain* [**AsMaster**]   **ANN**

Announce this machine as a potential browse server for domain.. The optional **AsMaster** argument causes this machine to be announced as a master browser instead of a potential browser

LOCALLIST *transport* [*serverFlags*]   **LL**

Retrieve the browse list from the browse server on this machine (if there is one)

FORCEANNOUNCE *transport domain*   **FA**

Issue a browser **RequestAnnouncement** browser request, i.e. force all browsers for *domain* to announce themselves

ILLEGAL *transport computer*   **ILL**

Send an illegal datagram to *computer*

MASTERANNOUNCE *transport nbname*   **MA**

Send a master announcement, specifying your machine's name as master browser, to the machine called *nbname*. (*nbname* must be a NetBIOS name, not an IP number or DNS name.)

FINDMASTER *transport*   **FM**

Find the segment master browser for this machine's domain, by forcing a **RequestAnnouncement** and listening to the replies. (The command fails if this machine is itself the master.)

DEBUG ...   **DBG**

Change browser service debug options. Usage is
browstat debug [[+-]*DebugFlag|Value*] [*computer*]
where *DebugFlag* is one of the following:

SERVER_ENUM	UTIL	CONFIG
MAIN	LOGON	BACKUP

MASTER	DOMAIN	TIMER
QUEUE	LOCKS	ALL

ENABLE   EN

Enable the browser service

DUMPNET   DN

Dump the list of networks. Appears not to work

WKSTADOM *transport domain* [**PAUSE**]   WD

"Add *domain* name". Registers *domain*<00> and then unregisters it. (If you specify **PAUSE**, it waits for you to press a key before unregistering.)

MASTERNAME *transport domain* [**PAUSE**]   MN

Registers *domain*<00> as master browser and then unregisters it. (If you specify **PAUSE**, it waits for you to press a key before unregistering.)

RPCLIST *transport* [*domain* | *server*] [*serverFlags*] [**GoForever**]   RPC

Retrieve the browse list using RPC. (This command has always failed for us if we specify *server.*)

BREAK   BRK

Break into debugger in browser service

VIEW *transport*   VW

VIEW *transport* [*domain*|*server*] /**DOMAIN**   VW

VIEW *transport* *server* /**DOMAIN** [*domainToQuery*]   VW

Remote NetServerEnum to *server* or *domain* on *transport*

TICKLE *transport* [*domain* | *server*]   TIC

Force remote master to stop and restart

STATUS [**-V**] [*domain*]   STA

Display status about the specified domain, or this domain if none specified. -V gives a more verbose listing

STATS [*computer* [**RESET**]]   STS

Dump browser statistics

LISTWFW *domain*   WFW

List WFW servers in *domain* that are running a browse server

GETPDC *transport domain*   GP

Get PDC name (<1b>) for *domain*, using NetBIOS name resolution. (If you specify a non-existent domain, you may get the unhelpful message "access is denied".)

GETMASTER *transport domain*   **GM**

    Get name of Segment Master Browser (**<1d>**) for *domain,* using
    NetBIOS name resolution

GETBLIST *transport* [[*domain*] **REFRESH**]   **GB**

    Get backup list for *domain* by issuing a browser **GetBackupListRequest**

ELECT *transport domain*   **EL**

    Force a browser election for *domain*

The table below explains the flags shown in **browstat**'s **LOCALLIST** output:

AFP	AFP Server
BBR	Backup Browser
BDC	Backup Domain Controller
DFS	Distributed File System
DL	Dial-in Server
DMB	Domain Master Browser
MBC	Member Server
MBR	Master Browser
MFPN	MS Netware
NT	Windows-NT
NV	Novell
OSF	OSF Server
PBR	Potential Browser
PDC	Primary Domain Controller
PQ	Print Server
S	Server
SQL	SQL Server
SS	Standard Server
TS	Time Source
VMS	VMS Server
W	Workstation
W95	Windows95
WFW	Windows For Workgroups
XN	Xenix

Appendix 25 Worksheet for testing a new Internet connection

When you've installed your network connection, Internet router, and firewall, you'll want to check that everything is working. Table A25.1 shows the matrix of tests that we use to test a new connection. The tests indicate quickly whether everything is working as expected. The matrix also forms a useful permanent record: if something fails later on, we can check from the matrix whether it was working previously. Figure A25.1 shows a typical network to be tested.

Notes:

1. we mark the relevant IP address beside each "from" and "to" heading box on the matrix

2. as we perform each test, we record the result in the appropriate cell

3. some combinations ought to fail, e.g. "from remote site to LAN PCs" should almost certainly be blocked by your firewall

4. testing from a remote site can be difficult unless you have branch offices or friends who help you out with a guest account. We often use a dial-up laptop (shown as "other" in the matrix) to test from outside to inside

5. testing to/from the untrusted segment (in between router and firewall) isn't essential but we do it for completeness

6. remember that the IP addresses of the firewall and internal servers may differ depending on where you're trying to connect from, because (a) the firewall has internal, external, and DMZ interfaces, and (b) you may be using NAT.

Figure A25.1
Typical network to
be tested

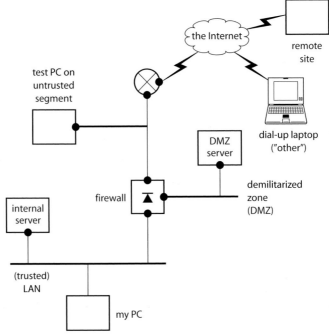

Site: Date:	to **LAN PCs**	to **internal servers**	to **DMZ**	to **untrusted segment**	to **router**	to **remote site**	to other
from **LAN PCs**							
from **internal servers**							
from **DMZ**							
from **untrusted segment**							
from **router**							
from **remote site**							
from **other**							

Table A25.1 Matrix for testing a new connection

Appendix 26 Organizing your software downloads

This method of archiving downloaded software has worked well for us for years.

- we keep a dedicated disk for archiving downloads. This is on our main file server, mounted as **/r** for "aRchives"
- all Linux machines NFS-mount the archive as local directory **/r** (so it has the same name on every machine – local or remote)
- we run Samba on the main file server, and share the **/r** directory as share name **rchives**. All Windows machines map this as local drive **R:**. (We can't use drive letter **A:** as that's the name of the floppy drive, which is why we can't mount the archive as **/a** or call it **archives**.)
- on each Windows machine we keep a local directory called **rchive-duplicate**. We use this as a cache of a few important items from the main archive that we might need when this machine's networking is broken, e.g. Windows service packs and network card drivers
- the archive has grown over the years, and it's too big and awkward to keep in a single directory, so we break it into subdirectories. Whenever we download from a site, we save the download in a directory named after the site (ignoring the initial www, etc.). To avoid having a huge list of sites, we group the site names further by initial letter, e.g. if we download a file from **www.debian.org**, we save it in **/r/d/debian.org/***filename*
- in each directory we maintain a "readme" file, saying what each file is, and giving its URL. (We use the filename **read-uit.txt** for this, in case we download a file called **readme** or **readme.txt**.)
- if we need to unpack a Zip or a **tar** file, we do it into a subdirectory called **junk**, and we often build and install software from **junk**. However, we never make any changes (or at least, any changes that we'll need again) to anything in a **junk** directory. That way we know we can always delete it if we need some extra disk space, because we can always unpack again from the original Zip or **tar** archive whenever we want.

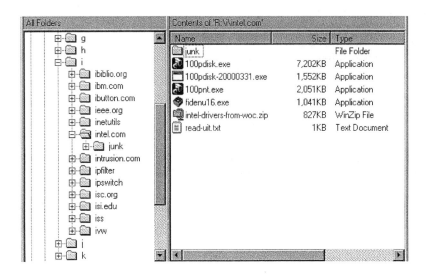

Web appendices

available at http://www.uit.co.uk/practical-tcp

Index

acknowledgements 276
connections and ports 264–8
establishing a connection 274–5
and HTTP 358
life-cycle of a connection 274–5
listening on multiple addresses 279
reliable connection provided by 262–3
sockets 281–2
special features 281
supporting NetBIOS connections 475
termination of a connection 277
and UDP 452
unique identifier for connections 266
used for long queries 400
used for zone transfer 400
TCP client, **netcat** as 432
TCP server, **netcat** as 432–3
TCP Wrappers 659, 812
tcpd 660, 812
tcpdump 4–7, 16–19, 41, 56, 216, 225, 278
alias for quick typing 24
command summary 736–40
compared with Network Monitor 487
display options 19
DNS packet display format 196–7
and **ethereal** 343
exchanging capture files 487
filter options 20
manpage 741–65
-N and -f options 358
and NetBIOS 475
NFS packet display format 456
"operation not permitted" message 23
options 22, 137, 157
output format 18
problems with 22–5, 42, 734
S and F flags in output 371
tracing packets across a router 74–5
-X option 57, 275, 280, 294
see also Appendix 4
telcos 10–11
telnet (telecommunications network protocol) 81, 270–1, 282, 614
applications 470
connection 390
as POP client 302–3
security 293
servers 271
as STMP client 294–5
terminal emulators 270
title-bar in window 272
URL type 354
used as universal TCP client 272–3, 293
terminators, Ethernet 731
text strings, specification of (**ethereal**) 801
TFTP (Trivial File Transfer Protocol) 401

Thick Ethernet 17, 160, 731
"thin client" architecture 437
Thin-net 17, 160, 731
third-party transfers, FTP 429
3Com 470
3+Open 470
three-way handshakes 632, 274–5, 588–9, 632–3
throughput of firewalls 639
TICKLE (Browstat) 826
time exceeded (ICMP) 76
time-to-live *see* TTL
timestamps (SMTP) 300
tlist (task list) 814
To: (e-mail header) 298
tombstoning 520
top-level domains (TLDs) 208
top-level media type (MIME) 322
traceroute 76–8, 203
and firewalls 148
mapping 83
problems with 147–8
showing varying paths 138–9
tracing of election 570–1
tracing of packets 4–5, 74–5, 214–15
Transmission Control Protocol *see* TCP
transport layer 405, 724
transport protocols 260, 398
see also TCP, UDP
traps (SNMP) 444, 462
tree structure, LDAP 445
tree structure, DNS 206-207
triple-DES encryption 694
"Trojan horse" programs 526, 626
Troubleshooting
basic network configuration 52–53
DNS – 246–7
Dial-up networking 678–87
e-mail send/receive, 308
firewalls 642
general techniques 51–3
HTTP 390–1
IP addresses 138–9
name resolution, NetBIOS 516–7
netmasks 140–1
network browsing, Windows 578–9
routing 140–1
Windows Networking 588–9
VPN 708–9
TRUNCLOG (Browstat) 825
trust relationships (WN) 541, 551
trusted domains (WN) 537, 551
TTL (time-to-live) 76, 198, 247, 624
caching and DNS 225
values 147
TURN command (SMTP) 292, 316
two-factor authentication (VPN) 706

Web site for this book

Register your book: receive updates, notifications about author appearances, and announcements about new editions. *www.uit.co.uk/register*

News: forthcoming titles, events, reviews, interviews, podcasts, etc. *www.uit.co.uk/news*

Join our mailing lists: get email newsletters on topics of interest. *www.uit.co.uk/subscribe*

How to order: get details of stockists and online bookstores. If you are a bookstore, find out about our distributors or contact us to discuss your particular requirements. *www.uit.co.uk/order*

Send us a book proposal: if you want to write – even if you have just the kernel of an idea at present – we'd love to hear from you. We pride ourselves on supporting our authors and making the process of book-writing as satisfying and as easy as possible. *www.uit.co.uk/for-authors*

UIT Cambridge Ltd.
PO Box 145
Cambridge
CB4 1GQ
England

Email: *inquiries@uit.co.uk*
Phone: **+44 1223 302 041**

OpenStreetMap

Using and enhancing the free map of the world

Frederik Ramm and Jochen Topf
with Steve Chilton

Second edition

OpenStreetMap is a map of the whole world that can be used and edited freely by everyone. In a Wikipedia-like open community process, thousands of contributors world-wide survey the planet and upload their results to the OpenStreetMap database. Unlike some other mapping systems on the Web, the tools and the data are free and open. You can use them and modify them as you require; you can even download all the map data and run your own private map server if you need to.

This book introduces you to the OpenStreetMap community, its data model, and the software used in the project. It shows you how to use the constantly-growing OSM data set and maps in your own projects.

The book also explains in detail how you can contribute to the project, collecting and processing data for OpenStreetMap. If you want to become an OpenStreetMap "mapper" then this is the book for you.

About the author... Frederik Ramm and Jochen Topf both joined the Open-
...2006, when they were freelance developers. Since then
...hobby their profession – by founding Geofabrik, a com-
...ervices relating to OpenStreetMap and open geodata.

...st (German) Edition

...SM newcomers. The basics are presented well and are easy
...jou do not need to be an IT specialist to contribute your first
...short time."

...well written. It is obvious that the authors have a lot of
...rience ..."

...introduction. Getting up to speed with OpenStreetMap is
...iave read this book."

ISBN: 9781906860110

Decimal, binary, and hex conversions

Decimal	Hex	Octal	Binary	ASCII	Decimal	Hex	Octal	Binary	A
0	00	000	00000000	NUL	64	40	100	01000000	
1	01	001	00000001	ctrl-A	65	41	101	01000001	
2	02	002	00000010	ctrl-B	66	42	102	01000010	
3	03	003	00000011	ctrl-C	67	43	103	01000011	
4	04	004	00000100	ctrl-D	68	44	104	01000100	
5	05	005	00000101	ctrl-E	69	45	105	01000101	
6	06	006	00000110	ctrl-F	70	46	106	01000110	
7	07	007	00000111	ctrl-G	71	47	107	01000111	
8	08	010	00001000	(backspace)	72	48	110	01001000	
9	09	011	00001001	(tab)	73	49	111	01001001	
10	0A	012	00001010	(linefeed)	74	4A	112	01001010	
11	0B	013	00001011	ctrl-K	75	4B	113	01001011	
12	0C	014	00001100	ctrl-L	76	4C	114	01001100	
13	0D	015	00001101	(carriage return)	77	4D	115	01001101	
14	0E	016	00001110	ctrl-N	78	4E	116	01001110	
15	0F	017	00001111	ctrl-O	79	4F	117	01001111	
16	10	020	00010000	ctrl-P	80	50	120	01010000	
17	11	021	00010001	ctrl-Q	81	51	121	01010001	
18	12	022	00010010	ctrl-R	82	52	122	01010010	
19	13	023	00010011	ctrl-S	83	53	123	01010011	
20	14	024	00010100	ctrl-T	84	54	124	01010100	
21	15	025	00010101	ctrl-U	85	55	125	01010101	
22	16	026	00010110	ctrl-V	86	56	126	01010110	
23	17	027	00010111	ctrl-W	87	57	127	01010111	
24	18	030	00011000	ctrl-X	88	58	130	01011000	
25	19	031	00011001	ctrl-Y	89	59	131	01011001	
26	1A	032	00011010	ctrl-Z	90	5A	132	01011010	
27	1B	033	00011011	(escape)	91	5B	133	01011011	
28	1C	034	00011100	ctrl-	92	5C	134	01011100	
29	1D	035	00011101	ctrl-	93	5D	135	01011101	
30	1E	036	00011110	ctrl-	94	5E	136	01011110	
31	1F	037	00011111	ctrl-	95	5F	137	01011111	
32	20	040	00100000	(space)	96	60	140	01100000	
33	21	041	00100001	!	97	61	141	01100001	
34	22	042	00100010	"	98	62	142	01100010	
35	23	043	00100011	#	99	63	143	01100011	
36	24	044	00100100	$	100	64	144	0110010(	
37	25	045	00100101	%	101	65	145	011001	
38	26	046	00100110	&	102	66	146	0	
39	27	047	00100111	'	103	67	147	0 1	
40	28	050	00101000	(	104	68	150	0 0	
41	29	051	00101001	)	105	69	151	0 01	
42	2A	052	00101010	*	106	6A	152	0 10	
43	2B	053	00101011	+	107	6B	153	0 11	
44	2C	054	00101100	,	108	6C	154	.00	
45	2D	055	00101101	–	109	6D	155	101	
46	2E	056	00101110	.	110	6E	156	110	
47	2F	057	00101111	/	111	6F	157	111	
48	30	060	00110000	0	112	70	160	0000	
49	31	061	00110001	1	113	71	161	0001	
50	32	062	00110010	2	114	72	162	10010	
51	33	063	00110011	3	115	73	163	110011	
52	34	064	00110100	4	116	74	164	110100	
53	35	065	00110101	5	117	75	165	110101	
54	36	066	00110110	6	118	76	166	1110110	
55	37	067	00110111	7	119	77	167	01110111	
56	38	070	00111000	8	120	78	170	01111000	
57	39	071	00111001	9	121	79	171	01111001	
58	3A	072	00111010	:	122	7A	17	01111010	
59	3B	073	00111011	;	123	7B	1	01111011	
60	3C	074	00111100	<	124	7C		01111100	
61	3D	075	00111101	=	125	7D		01111101	
62	3E	076	00111110	>	126	7E		01111110	
63	3F	077	00111111	?	127	7F	7	01111111	(d